Lecture Notes in Computer Science 11098

Commenced Publication in 1973
Founding and Former Series Editors:
Gerhard Goos, Juris Hartmanis, and Jan van Leeuwen

Editorial Board

More information about this series at http://www.springer.com/series/7410

Javier Lopez · Jianying Zhou
Miguel Soriano (Eds.)

Computer Security

23rd European Symposium
on Research in Computer Security, ESORICS 2018
Barcelona, Spain, September 3–7, 2018
Proceedings, Part I

 Springer

Editors
Javier Lopez
Department of Computer Science
University of Malaga
Málaga, Málaga
Spain

Miguel Soriano
Universitat Politècnica de Catalunya
Barcelona
Spain

Jianying Zhou
Singapore University of Technology
  and Design
Singapore
Singapore

ISSN 0302-9743   ISSN 1611-3349 (electronic)
Lecture Notes in Computer Science
ISBN 978-3-319-99072-9   ISBN 978-3-319-99073-6 (eBook)
https://doi.org/10.1007/978-3-319-99073-6

Library of Congress Control Number: 2018951097

LNCS Sublibrary: SL4 – Security and Cryptology

This Springer imprint is published by the registered company Springer Nature Switzerland AG
The registered company address is: Gewerbestrasse 11, 6330 Cham, Switzerland

Preface

This book contains the papers that were selected for presentation and publication at the 23rd European Symposium on Research in Computer Security — ESORICS 2018 – which was held in Barcelona, Spain, September 3–7, 2018. The aim of ESORICS is to further the progress of research in computer, information, and cyber security and in privacy, by establishing a European forum for bringing together researchers in these areas, by promoting the exchange of ideas with system developers, and by encouraging links with researchers in related fields.

In response to the call for papers, 283 papers were submitted to the conference. These papers were evaluated on the basis of their significance, novelty, and technical quality. Each paper was reviewed by at least three members of the Program Committee. The Program Committee meeting was held electronically, with intensive discussion over a period of two weeks. Finally, 56 papers were selected for presentation at the conference, giving an acceptance rate of 20%.

ESORICS 2018 would not have been possible without the contributions of the many volunteers who freely gave their time and expertise. We would like to thank the members of the Program Committee and the external reviewers for their substantial work in evaluating the papers. We would also like to thank the general chair, Miguel Soriano, the organization chair, Josep Pegueroles, the workshop chair, Joaquin Garcia-Alfaro, and all workshop co-chairs, the publicity chairs, Giovanni Livraga and Rodrigo Roman, and the ESORICS Steering Committee and its chair, Sokratis Katsikas.

Finally, we would like to express our thanks to the authors who submitted papers to ESORICS. They, more than anyone else, are what makes this conference possible.

We hope that you will find the program stimulating and a source of inspiration for future research.

June 2018

Javier Lopez
Jianying Zhou

ESORICS 2018

23rd European Symposium on Research in Computer Security
Barcelona, Spain
September 3–7, 2018

Organized by Universitat Politecnica de Catalunya - BarcelonaTech, Spain

General Chair

Miguel Soriano   Universitat Politecnica de Catalunya, Spain

Program Chairs

Javier Lopez   University of Malaga, Spain
Jianying Zhou   SUTD, Singapore

Workshop Chair

Joaquin Garcia-Alfaro   Telecom SudParis, France

Organizing Chair

Josep Pegueroles   Universitat Politecnica de Catalunya, Spain

Publicity Chairs

Giovanni Livraga   Università degli studi di Milano, Italy
Rodrigo Roman   University of Malaga, Spain

Program Committee

Gail-Joon Ahn   Arizona State University, USA
Cristina Alcaraz   University of Malaga, Spain
Elli Androulaki   IBM Research - Zurich, Switzerland
Vijay Atluri   Rutgers University, USA
Michael Backes   Saarland University, Germany
Carlo Blundo   Università degli Studi di Salerno, Italy
Levente Buttyan   BME, Hungary
Jan Camenisch   IBM Research - Zurich, Switzerland
Alvaro Cardenas   University of Texas at Dallas, USA
Aldar C-F. Chan   University of Hong Kong, SAR China
Liqun Chen   University of Surrey, UK

Sherman S. M. Chow	Chinese University of Hong Kong, SAR China
Mauro Conti	University of Padua, Italy
Jorge Cuellar	Siemens AG, Germany
Frédéric Cuppens	TELECOM Bretagne, France
Nora Cuppens-Boulahia	TELECOM Bretagne, France
Marc Dacier	EURECOM, France
Sabrina De Capitani di Vimercati	Università degli studi di Milano, Italy
Hervé Debar	Télécom SudParis, France
Roberto Di-Pietro	HBKU, Qatar
Josep Domingo-Ferrer	University Rovira-Virgili, Spain
Haixin Duan	Tsinghua University, China
José M. Fernandez	Polytechnique Montreal, Canada
Jose-Luis Ferrer-Gomila	University of the Balearic Islands, Spain
Simone Fischer-Hübner	Karlstad University, Sweden
Simon Foley	IMT Atlantique, France
Sara Foresti	Università degli studi di Milano, Italy
David Galindo	University of Birmingham, UK
Debin Gao	Singapore Management University, Singapore
Dieter Gollmann	Hamburg University of Technology, Germany
Dimitris Gritzalis	Athens University of Economics and Business, Greece
Stefanos Gritzalis	University of the Aegean, Greece
Guofei Gu	Texas A&M University, USA
Juan Hernández	Universitat Politècnica de Catalunya, Spain
Amir Herzberg	Bar-Ilan University, Israel
Xinyi Huang	Fujian Normal University, China
Sushil Jajodia	George Mason University, USA
Vasilios Katos	Bournemouth University, UK
Sokratis Katsikas	NTNU, Norway
Kwangjo Kim	KAIST, Korea
Steve Kremer	Inria, France
Marina Krotofil	FireEye, USA
Costas Lambrinoudakis	University of Piraeus, Greece
Loukas Lazos	University of Arizona, USA
Ninghui Li	Purdue University, USA
Yingjiu Li	Singapore Management University, Singapore
Hoon-Wei Lim	SingTel, Singapore
Joseph Liu	Monash University, Australia
Peng Liu	Pennsylvania State University, USA
Xiapu Luo	Hong Kong Polytechnic University, SAR China
Mark Manulis	University of Surrey, UK
Konstantinos Markantonakis	RHUL, UK
Olivier Markowitch	Université Libre de Bruxelles, Belgium
Fabio Martinelli	IIT-CNR, Italy
Gregorio Martinez Perez	University of Murcia, Spain

Ivan Martinovic	University of Oxford, UK
Sjouke Mauw	University of Luxembourg, Luxembourg
Catherine Meadows	Naval Research Laboratory, USA
Weizhi Meng	Technical University of Denmark, Denmark
Chris Mitchell	RHUL, UK
Haralambos Mouratidis	University of Brighton, UK
David Naccache	Ecole Normale Superieure, France
Martín Ochoa	Universidad del Rosario, Colombia
Eiji Okamoto	University of Tsukuba, Japan
Rolf Oppliger	eSECURITY Technologies, Switzerland
Günther Pernul	Universität Regensburg, Germany
Joachim Posegga	University of Passau, Germany
Christina Pöpper	NYU Abu Dhabi, UAE
Indrajit Ray	Colorado State University, USA
Giovanni Russello	University of Auckland, New Zealand
Mark Ryan	University of Birmingham, UK
Peter Y. A. Ryan	University of Luxembourg, Luxembourg
Rei Safavi-Naini	University of Calgary, Canada
Pierangela Samarati	Universitá degli studi di Milano, Italy
Damien Sauveron	XLIM, France
Steve Schneider	University of Surrey, UK
Einar Snekkenes	Gjovik University College, Norway
Willy Susilo	University of Wollongong, Australia
Pawel Szalachowski	SUTD, Singapore
Qiang Tang	LIST, Luxembourg
Juan Tapiador	University Carlos III, Spain
Nils Ole Tippenhauer	SUTD, Singapore
Aggeliki Tsohou	Ionian University, Greece
Jaideep Vaidya	Rutgers University, USA
Serge Vaudenay	EPFL, Switzerland
Luca Viganò	King's College London, UK
Michael Waidner	Fraunhofer SIT, Germany
Cong Wang	City University of Hong Kong, SAR China
Lingyu Wang	Concordia University, Canada
Edgar Weippl	SBA Research, Austria
Christos Xenakis	University of Piraeus, Greece
Kehuan Zhang	Chinese University of Hong Kong, SAR China
Sencun Zhu	Pennsylvania State University, USA

Organizing Committee

Oscar Esparza
Marcel Fernandez
Juan Hernandez
Olga Leon

Isabel Martin
Jose L. Munoz
Josep Pegueroles

Additional Reviewers

Akand, Mamun
Al Maqbali, Fatma
Albanese, Massimiliano
Amerini, Irene
Ammari, Nader
Avizheh, Sepideh
Balli, Fatih
Bamiloshin, Michael
Bana, Gergei
Banik, Subhadeep
Becerra, Jose
Belguith, Sana
Ben Adar-Bessos, Mai
Berners-Lee, Ela
Berthier, Paul
Bezawada, Bruhadeshwar
Biondo, Andrea
Blanco-Justicia, Alberto
Blazy, Olivier
Boschini, Cecilia
Brandt, Markus
Bursuc, Sergiu
Böhm, Fabian
Cao, Chen
Caprolu, Maurantonio
Catuogno, Luigi
Cetinkaya, Orhan
Chang, Bing
Charlie, Jacomme
Chau, Sze Yiu
Chen, Rongmao
Cheval, Vincent
Cho, Haehyun
Choi, Gwangbae
Chow, Yang-Wai
Ciampi, Michele
Costantino, Gianpiero
Dai, Tianxiang
Dashevskyi, Stanislav
Del Vasto, Luis
Diamantopoulou, Vasiliki
Dietz, Marietheres
Divakaran, Dinil

Dong, Shuaike
Dupressoir, François
Durak, Betül
Eckhart, Matthias
El Kassem, Nada
Elkhiyaoui, Kaoutar
Englbrecht, Ludwig
Epiphaniou, Gregory
Fernández-Gago, Carmen
Fojtik, Roman
Freeman, Kevin
Fritsch, Lothar
Fuchsbauer, Georg
Fuller, Ben
Gabriele, Lenzini
Gadyatskaya, Olga
Galdi, Clemente
Gassais, Robin
Genc, Ziya A.
Georgiopoulou, Zafeiroula
Groll, Sebastian
Groszschaedl, Johann
Guan, Le
Han, Jinguang
Hassan, Fadi
Hill, Allister
Hong, Kevin
Horváth, Máté
Hu, Hongxin
Huh, Jun Ho
Iakovakis, George
Iovino, Vincenzo
Jadla, Marwen
Jansen, Kai
Jonker, Hugo
Judmayer, Aljosha
Kalloniatis, Christos
Kambourakis, Georgios
Kannwischer, Matthias Julius
Kar, Diptendu
Karamchandani, Neeraj
Karati, Sabyasach
Karati, Sabyasachi

Karegar, Farzaneh
Karopoulos, Georgios
Karyda, Maria
Kasra, Shabnam
Kohls, Katharina
Kokolakis, Spyros
Kordy, Barbara
Krenn, Stephan
Kilinç, Handan
Labrèche, François
Lai, Jianchang
Lain, Daniele
Lee, Jehyun
Leontiadis, Iraklis
Lerman, Liran
León, Olga
Li, Shujun
Li, Yan
Liang, Kaitai
Lin, Yan
Liu, Shengli
Losiouk, Eleonora
Lykou, Georgia
Lyvas, Christos
Ma, Jack P. K.
Magkos, Emmanouil
Majumdar, Suryadipta
Malliaros, Stefanos
Manjón, Jesús A.
Marktscheffel, Tobias
Martinez, Sergio
Martucci, Leonardo
Mayer, Wilfried
Mcmahon-Stone, Christopher
Menges, Florian
Mentzeliotou, Despoina
Mercaldo, Francesco
Mohamady, Meisam
Mohanty, Manoranjan
Moreira, Jose
Mulamba, Dieudonne
Murmann, Patrick
Muñoz, Jose L.
Mykoniati, Maria
Mylonas, Alexios
Nabi, Mahmoodon

Nasim, Tariq
Neven, Gregory
Ngamboe, Mikaela
Nieto, Ana
Ntantogian, Christoforos
Nuñez, David
Oest, Adam
Ohtake, Go
Oqaily, Momen
Ordean, Mihai
P., Vinod
Panaousis, Emmanouil
Papaioannou, Thanos
Paraboschi, Stefano
Park, Jinbum
Parra Rodriguez, Juan D.
Parra-Arnau, Javier
Pasa, Luca
Paspatis, Ioannis
Perillo, Angelo Massimo
Pillai, Prashant
Pindado, Zaira
Pitropakis, Nikolaos
Poh, Geong Sen
Puchta, Alexander
Pöhls, Henrich C.
Radomirovic, Sasa
Ramírez-Cruz, Yunior
Raponi, Simone
Rial, Alfredo
Ribes-González, Jordi
Rios, Ruben
Roenne, Peter
Roman, Rodrigo
Rubio Medrano, Carlos
Rupprecht, David
Salazar, Luis
Saracino, Andrea
Schindler, Philipp
Schnitzler, Theodor
Scotti, Fabio
Sempreboni, Diego
Senf, Daniel
Sengupta, Binanda
Sentanoe, Stewart
Sheikhalishahi, Mina

Shirani, Paria
Shrishak, Kris
Siniscalchi, Luisa
Smith, Zach
Smyth, Ben
Soria-Comas, Jordi
Soumelidou, Katerina
Spooner, Nick
Stergiopoulos, George
Stifter, Nicholas
Stojkovski, Borce
Sun, Menghan
Sun, Zhibo
Syta, Ewa
Tai, Raymond K. H.
Tang, Xiaoxiao
Taubmann, Benjamin
Tian, Yangguang
Toffalini, Flavio
Tolomei, Gabriele
Towa, Patrick
Tsalis, Nikolaos
Tsiatsikas, Zisis
Tsoumas, Bill
Urdaneta, Marielba
Valente, Junia
Venkatesan, Sridhar
Veroni, Eleni
Vielberth, Manfred
Virvilis, Nick
Vizár, Damian

Vukolic, Marko
Wang, Daibin
Wang, Ding
Wang, Haining
Wang, Jiafan
Wang, Jianfeng
Wang, Juan
Wang, Jun
Wang, Tianhao
Wang, Xiaolei
Wang, Xiuhua
Whitefield, Jorden
Wong, Harry W. H.
Wu, Huangting
Xu, Jia
Xu, Jun
Xu, Lei
Yang, Guangliang
Yautsiukhin, Artsiom
Yu, Yong
Yuan, Lunpin
Zamyatin, Alexei
Zhang, Lei
Zhang, Liang Feng
Zhang, Yangyong
Zhang, Yuexin
Zhao, Liang
Zhao, Yongjun
Zhao, Ziming
Zuo, Cong

Contents – Part I

Privacy (I)

CPS and IoT Security

Contents – Part II

Multi-party Computation

SDN Security

Applied Crypto (II)

Software Security

CastSan: Efficient Detection of Polymorphic C++ Object Type Confusions with LLVM

Paul Muntean[⊠], Sebastian Wuerl, Jens Grossklags, and Claudia Eckert

Technical University of Munich, Munich, Germany
{paul.muntean,sebastian.wuerl,claudia.eckert}@sec.in.tum.de,
jens.grossklags@in.tum.de

Abstract. C++ object type confusion vulnerabilities as the result of illegal object casting have been threatening systems' security for decades.
While there exist several solutions to address this type of vulnerability,
none of them are sufficiently practical for adoption in production scenarios. Most competitive and recent solutions require object type tracking
for checking polymorphic object casts, and all have prohibitively high
runtime overhead. The main source of overhead is the need to track the
object type during runtime for both polymorphic and non-polymorphic
object casts. In this paper, we present CastSan, a C++ object type
confusion detection tool for polymorphic objects only, which scales efficiently to large and complex code bases as well as to many concurrent
threads. To considerably reduce the object type cast checking overhead,
we employ a new technique based on constructing the whole virtual table
hierarchy during program compile time. Since CastSan does not rely on
keeping track of the object type during runtime, the overhead is drastically reduced. Our evaluation results show that complex applications
run insignificantly slower when our technique is deployed, thus making
CastSan a real-world usage candidate. Finally, we envisage that based
on our object type confusion detection technique, which relies on ordered
virtual tables (vtables), even non-polymorphic object casts could be precisely handled by constructing *auxiliary* non-polymorphic function table
hierarchies for static classes as well.

Keywords: Static cast · Type confusion · Bad casting · Type safety
Type casting

1 Introduction

Real-world security-critical applications (*e.g.,* Google's Chrome, Mozilla's Firefox, Apple's Safari, etc.) rely on the C++ language as main implementation language, due to the balance it offers between runtime efficiency, precise handling of
low-level memory, and the object-oriented abstractions it provides. Thus, among
the object-oriented concepts offered by C++, the ability to use object typecasting in order to increase, or decrease, the object scope of accessible class fields

ⓒ Springer Nature Switzerland AG 2018
J. Lopez et al. (Eds.): ESORICS 2018, LNCS 11098, pp. 3–25, 2018.
https://doi.org/10.1007/978-3-319-99073-6_1

inside the program class hierarchy is a great benefit for programmers. However, as C++ is not a managed programing language, and does not offer object type or memory safety, this can potentially lead to exploits.

C++ object type confusions are the result of misinterpreting the runtime type of an object to be of a different type than the actual type due to unsafe type-casting. This misinterpretation leads to inconsistent reinterpretation of memory in different usage contexts. A typical scenario, where type confusion manifests itself, occurs when an object of a parent class is cast into a descendant class type. This is typically unsafe, if the parent class lacks fields expected by the descendant type object. Thus, the program may interpret the non-existent field or function in the descendant class constructor as data, or as a virtual function pointer in another context. Object type confusion leads to undefined behavior according to the C++ language draft [1]. Further, undefined behavior can lead to memory corruption, which in turn leads to exploits such as code reuse attacks (CRAs) [6] or even to advanced versions of CRAs including the COOP attack [30]. These attacks violate the control flow integrity (CFI) [2,3] of the program, by bypassing currently available OS-deployed security mechanisms such as DEP [26] and ASLR [28]. In summary, the lack of object type safety and, more broadly, memory safety can lead to object type confusion vulnerabilities (*i.e.*, CVE-2017-3106 [12]). The number of these vulnerabilities has increased considerably in the last years, making exploit based attacks against a large number of deployed systems an everyday possibility.

Table 1 depicts the currently available solutions, which can be used for C++ object type confusion detection during runtime. The tools come with the following limitations: (1) high

Table 1. High-level feature overview of existing C++ object type confusion checkers.

Checker	Year	Poly	Non-poly	No blacklist	Obj. Tracking	Threads
UBSan [15]	2014	✓				✓
CaVer [22]	2015	✓	✓	✓	✓	limited
Clang CFI [8]	2016	✓		✓		✓
TypeSan [18]	2016	✓	✓	✓	✓	✓
HexType [19]	2017	✓	✓	✓	✓	✓
CASTSAN	2018	✓	future work	✓	not required	✓

runtime overhead (mostly due to the usage of a compiler runtime library), (2) limited type checking coverage, (3) lack of support for non-polymorphic classes, (4) absence of threads support, and (5) high maintenance overhead, as some tools require a manually maintained blacklist.

We consider runtime efficiency and coverage to be most impactful for the usage of such tools. While coverage can be incrementally increased by supporting more object allocators (*e.g.*, child *obj=dynamic_cast<*child>(parent), ClassA *obj=new (buffer) ClassA();, char *str=(char) malloc(sizeof (S)); S *obj=reinterpret_cast<*S>(str);, see TypeSan, HexType, for more details) and instrumenting them for later object type runtime tracking, increasing performance is more difficult to achieve due to the required runtime of type tracking support on which most tools rely. Reducing runtime overhead is regarded to be far more difficult to achieve, since object type data has to be tracked at runtime and updating data structures at runtime (*i.e.,* red-black trees, etc.) has to be performed during a type check. As such, due to their perceived high runtime overhead, most of the currently available tools do not qualify as production-ready tools. Furthermore, the per-object metadata tracking mechanisms generally represent an overhead bottleneck in case the to-be hardened program contains: (1) a high volume of object allocations, (2) a large number of memory freeing operations, (3) frequent use of object casts, (4) *exotic* object memory allocators (*i.e.,* Chrom's `tcmalloc()`, object pool allocators, etc.) for which the detection tool implementation has to be constantly maintained.

We present CastSan, a Clang/LLVM compiler-based solution, usable as an always-on sanitizer for detecting all types of polymorphic-only object type confusions during run-time, with comparable cov-

Table 2. Object type confusion detection overhead for SPEC CPU2006 benchmark.

Checker	Programs		
	soplex (C++)	xalancbmk (C++)	astar (C++)
Clang-CFI [8]	5.03%	4.49%	0.9%
CastSan	2.07%	1.78%	0.3%
Speed-Up	2.42 times	2.52 times	3 times

erage to Clang-CFI [8]. CastSan has significantly lower runtime performance overhead than existing tools (see Table 2). Its technique is based on the observation, that virtual tables (vtables) of polymorphic classes can be used as a successful replacement for costly metadata storage and update operations, which similar tools heavily rely on. Our main insight is that: (1) program class hierarchies can be used more effectively to store object type relationships than Clang-CFI's bitsets, and (2) the Clang-CFI bitset checks can be successfully replaced with more efficient virtual pointer based range checks. Based on these observations, the metadata that has to be stored and checked for each object during object casting is reduced to zero. Next, the checks only require constant checking time due to the fact that no additional data structures (*i.e.,* TypeSan and HexType use both red-black trees for storing relationships between object types) have to be consulted during runtime. Finally, this facilitates efficient and scalable runtime vptr-based range checks.

CastSan performs the following steps for preparing the required metadata during compile time. First, the value of an object vptr is modified through internal compiler intrinsics such that it provides object type information at runtime. Second, these modified values are used by CastSan to compute range checks that can validate C++ object casts during runtime. Third, the computed range checks are inserted into the compiled program. The main observation, which makes the concept of vptr based range checks work, is that range checks are based on the fact, that any sub-tree of a class inheritance tree is contained in a continuous chunk of memory, which was previously re-ordered by a pre-order program virtual table hierarchy traversal.

CastSan is implemented on top of the LLVM 3.7 compiler framework [24] and relies on support from LLVM's Gold Plug-in [23]. CastSan is intended to address the problem of high runtime overhead of existing solutions by implementing an explicit type checking mechanism based on LLVM's compiler instrumentation. CASTSAN's goal is to enforce object type confusion checks during runtime in previously compiled programs. CASTSAN's object type confusion detection mechanism relies on collecting and storing type information used for performing object type checking during compile time. CASTSAN achieves this without storing new metadata in memory and by solely relying on virtual pointers (vptrs), that are stored with each polymorphic object.

We evaluated CASTSAN with the Google Chrome [16] web browser, the open source benchmark suite of TypeSan [18], the open source benchmark programs of IVT [5], and all C++ programs contained in the SPEC CPU2006 [31] benchmark. The evaluation results show that, in contrast to previous work, CASTSAN has considerably lower runtime overhead while maintaining comparable feature coverage (see Table 1 for more details). The evaluation results confirm that CASTSAN is precise and can help a programmer find real object type confusions.

In summary, we make the following contributions:

– We develop a novel technique for detection of C++ object type confusions during runtime, which is based on the linear projection of virtual table hierarchies.
– We implement our technique in a prototype, called CASTSAN, which is based on the Clang/LLVM compiler framework [24] and the Gold plug-in [23].
– We evaluate CASTSAN thoroughly and demonstrate that CASTSAN is more efficient than other state-of-the-art tools.

2   Background

Before presenting the technical details of our approach, we review necessary background information.

2.1   C++ Type Casting

Object type casting in C++ allows an object to be cast to another object, such that the program can use different features of the class hierarchy. Seen from a different angle, object typecasting is a C++ language feature, which augments object-oriented concepts such as inheritance and polymorphism. Inheritance facilitates that one class contained inside the program class hierarchy inherits (gets access) to the functionality of another class that is located above in the class hierarchy. Object casting is different, as it allows for objects to be used in a more general way (*i.e.,* using objects and their siblings, as if they were located higher in the class hierarchy). C++ provides static, dynamic, reinterpret and const casts. Note that reinterpret_cast can lead to bad casting, when misused and is unchecked "by design", as it allows the programmer to freely handle memory. In this paper, we focus on static_cast and dynamic_cast (see N4618 [1] working draft), because the misuse of these can result in bad object casting, which can further lead to undefined behavior. This can potentially be exploited to perform, for example, local or remote code reuse attacks on the software.

The terminology of this paper is aligned to the one used by colleagues [18], in order to provide terminology traceability as follows. First, *runtime type* refers to the type of the constructor used to create the object. Second, *source type* is the type of the pointer that is converted. Finally, *target type* is the type of the pointer after the type conversion.

An *upcast* is always permitted if the target type is an ancestor of the source type. These types of casts can be statically verified as safe, as the object source type is always known. Thus, if the source type is a descendant of the target type, the runtime type also has to be a descendant and the cast is legal. On the other hand, a *downcast* cannot be verified during compile time. This verification is hard to achieve, since the compiler cannot know the runtime type of an object, due to intricate data flows (for example, inter-procedural data flows). While it can be assumed that the runtime type is a descendant of the source type, the order of descendancy is not known. As only casts from a lower to a higher (or same) order are allowed, a runtime check is required to check this.

2.2   C/C++ Legal and Illegal Object Type Casts

A type cast in C/C++ is legal only when the destination type is an ancestor of the runtime type of the cast object. This is always true if the destination type is an ancestor of the source type (upcast). In contrast, if the destination type is a descendant of the source type (downcast), the cast could only be legal if the object has been upcast beforehand.

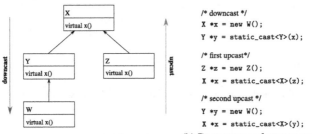

(a) Class hierarchy with four classes.   (b) Downcast and upcast cast in C++.

Fig. 1. C++ based object type down-casting and up-casting examples.

Figure 1 depicts upcast and downcast in an example hierarchy. The graph of Fig. 1(a) is a simple class hierarchy. The boxes are classes, and the arrows depict inheritance. The code of Fig. 1(b) shows how upcast and downcast look in C++. The upcast and downcast arrows besides the graph visualize the same casts that are coded in C++ in Fig. 1(a). To verify the cast, the runtime type of the object is needed. Unfortunately, the exact runtime type of an object is not necessarily known to the compiler for each cast, as explained in the previous section. While the source type is known to the compiler for each cast, it can only be used to detect very specific cases of illegal casts (*e.g.*, casts between types that are not related in any way, which means they are not in a descendant-ancestor relationship). All upcasts can be statically verified as safe because the destination type is an ancestor of the runtime type. If the destination type is not an ancestor of the runtime type, then the compiler should throw an error.

2.3 Ordered vs. Unordered Virtual Tables

In this section, we briefly describe the differences between in-memory ordered and unordered vtables and how these can be used to detect object type confusions during runtime.

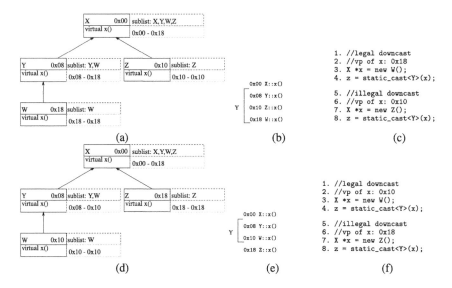

Fig. 2. Illegal and legal object casts vs. ordered and unordered virtual tables. (Color figure online)

Figure 2(a), (b), and (c) highlight the case in which an illegal object cast would not be detected if the vtables are not ordered (see blue shaded code in line number eight), while Fig. 2(d), (e), and (f) show how a legal (see green shaded code in line number four) and an illegal (see red shaded code in line number eight) object cast can be correctly identified by using the object vptr in case the vtables are ordered in memory.

On the one hand, Fig. 2(c) shows the vptr value as it would be present in the unordered case of Fig. 2(b) and (a). The object x, that is constructed at line number seven with the constructor of Z (runtime type) has a vptr of value 0x18 in the unordered case. x is referenced by a pointer of type X (source type) and at line number eight it is cast to Y (destination type). This is an illegal object cast, as Z does not inherit from Y. The vptr of x is in the range of Y built from the unordered vtable layout of Fig. 2(b). A range check would, therefore, falsely conclude that the cast is legal.

On the other hand, Fig. 2(f) depicts the same objects as constructed after ordering according to Fig. 2(e) and (d). At line number three, the object x is instantiated having (runtime) type W. The object, therefore, has a vptr with value 0x10 according to Fig. 2(d). The object is referenced by a pointer of type X (source type) and at line number four, the object x is cast to Y (destination type). This cast is a legal object cast, as the vptr 0x10 has a value between the vtable address of Y 0x08 and the address value of the last member of the sub-list of Y 0x10. Note that this memory range is depicted in Fig. 2(e). Further, at line number seven, the object x is newly allocated with the constructor of Z. Next, the object is cast to Y at line number eight. As x's vptr is 0x18, which is the vtable address of Z, it can be observed that the cast is illegal. The reason is that the vptr value 0x18 is larger than the largest value of the sub-list of Y, which is the vtable address of W, 0x10. Thus, in this way the object type confusion located at line number eight can be correctly detected.

Finally, note that the range checks, which we will use in our implementation, are precise, when the vtables of all program hierarchies are ordered with no gaps in memory according to, for example, their pre-order traversal. In case this is not guaranteed, then the range checks could generate false positives as well as false negatives (see the blue shaded code in Fig. 2(c)).

3 Threat Model

The threat model used by CASTSAN resembles HexType's threat model. Specifically, we assume a skilled attacker who can exploit any type of object type confusion vulnerability, but who does not have the capability to make arbitrary memory writes. CASTSAN's instrumentation is part of the executable program code and thus assumed to be write-protected through data execution protection (DEP) or another mechanism. Further, CASTSAN does not rely on information hiding; as such the attacker is assumed to be able to perform arbitrary reads. This is not a limitation, as CASTSAN does not rely on randomization or code shuffling as other CFI schemes [10,33]. As CASTSAN focuses exclusively on C++ object down-cast type confusions, we assume that other types of memory corruptions (i.e., buffer overflows, etc.) are combated with other types of protection mechanisms and that CASTSAN can work along these complementary defense mechanisms. Finally, we assume that for any large existing source code base, which is affected by object type confusions (e.g., [11]), this cannot currently be fixed solely by inspecting the source code statically or manually and that the attacker has access to the source code of this vulnerable application.

4   Design and Implementation

In Sect. 4.1, we present the architecture of CASTSAN, and in Sect. 4.2, we explain how virtual table inheritance tree projections are used by CASTSAN, while in Sect. 4.3, we describe our object type confusion detection checks. Finally, in Sect. 4.4, we outline CASTSAN's implementation.

4.1   Architecture Overview

CASTSAN's Main Analysis Steps. CASTSAN instruments object casts as follows: (1) source code files are fed into the Clang compiler, which adds several intrinsics needed to mark all possible cast locations in the code, (2) CASTSAN uses the vtable metadata and the virtual table hierarchies, which were embedded in each object file in the Clang front-end, (3) placeholder intrinsic-based instructions are used for recuperating the vptr and the mangled name of the object type which will be later cast, and (4) placeholder intrinsic-based instructions for the final pre-cast checks are inserted, containing the per object cast range. The intrinsics will be removed before runtime and will be converted to concrete instruction sequences used to perform the object type cast check. The placeholder intrinsics are used by CASTSAN since part of the information needed for the checking of illegal casts is not available during compile time (the vptr value is computed during runtime). Finally, during link time optimization (LTO) [25], the following operations are performed: (1) the virtual table hierarchy is constructed and decomposed into primitive vtable trees, and (2) the placeholder intrinsics used to check for down-cast violations are inserted based on the analysis of the previous primitive vtable trees.

Figure 3 depicts the placement of CASTSAN's components within the Clang/LLVM compiler framework and the analysis flow indicated by circled numbers.

Building Virtual Pointer Based Range Checks. First, the LValue (LLVM data type) ❶ and RValue (LLVM data type) ❷ casts are instrumented inside the Clang compiler with additional C++ code. Second, only the polymorphic casts are selected from these casts ❸. Third, the polymorphic casts are flagged for instrumentation using an LLVM intrinsic ❹ during LTO. Fourth, the intrinsics inserted by CASTSAN with the help of Clang are detected ❺ for later usage during LTO. Fifth, the metadata of the intrinsics is read out ❻ to acquire all necessary information about an object cast-site. Sixth, the ranges necessary for checking object type confusions are built in ❼. Note that an object range is computed by using the virtual address of the object destination type and the count of all nodes (vtables) inheriting from the destination type. Finally, the object cast-sites are instrumented with a range check ❽.

4.2   Virtual Table Inheritance Tree Projection

CASTSAN computes virtual table inheritance trees for each class hierarchy contained in the analyzed program. Next, CASTSAN uses these vtable inheritance

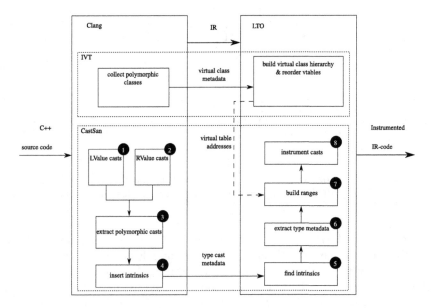

Fig. 3. CASTSAN system architecture.

trees to determine if the ancestor-descendant relation between the types of the cast objects holds. The ancestor-descendant relations between object types rely on several properties of these ordered vtable inheritance trees, which we will explain next. The root of such a virtual table inheritance tree is a polymorphic class that does not inherit from other polymorphic classes (root type). Note that a class has only one vtable associated to it. Further, each such vtable is broken into multiple primitive vtables. Also note that these vtables can occupy different places in this ordering. The children of any node in the vtable tree are all types that directly inherit from the ancestor class and are located underneath this class in the program class hierarchy. If a class inherits from multiple vtables, it has a node in any tree that the ancestor types are a part of. The leaves of a vtable tree are vtables, which have no descendants. CASTSAN will put the vtables that are in any type of a descendant-ancestor relation to each other in a single virtual inheritance tree. Next, we show how a virtual table projection list is computed.

Figure 4(a) depicts the memory layout of the vtables of the class represented by the primitive hierarchy in Fig. 4(b). The vtables contain their addresses as these are laid out in memory (*i.e.,* consider address 0x08) along with the pointers to the virtual functions (*i.e.,* Y::x()). Note that in the unordered table located on the left side of Fig. 4(a), there is no relationship between the addresses of the vtables and the class hierarchy. For simplicity reasons, we opted in Fig. 4(a) to depict each box of the vtable hierarchy to contain a single entry. In general, when there are multiple entries in each vtable contained in the vtable hierarchy, the vtables will be interleaved to ensure that their base pointers are consecutive addresses in memory. After ordering the values of the addresses of the vtables

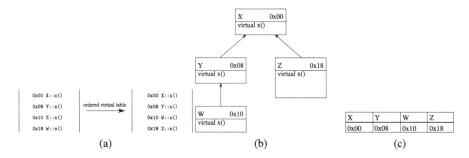

Fig. 4. Unordered and ordered (a) vtables of the tree rooted in X. The tree (b) contains the vptr of each type after ordering. (c) depicts the projected list corresponding to (b).

(right table in Fig. 4(a)) the addresses are in ascending order (*e.g.*, W inherits from Y directly, thus it comes directly after Y in the vtable). Further, after interleaving the addresses of the vtables, their values are in ascending order corresponding to the depth-first traversal, as shown in the projected list depicted in Fig. 4(c). Next, CASTSAN uses a pre-order traversal of each vtable inheritance tree in order to construct a list of vtables, which represents a projection of a tree hierarchy onto a list. For example, if the type of a vtable (first row in a box, see Fig. 4(b)) is the descendant of another type, it is inserted after the other type in the list. Further, any sub-tree of each tree is represented as a continuous sub-list of virtual tables by CASTSAN. This means that the types that inherit from the root type of the sub-tree will be inserted into the list in direct succession to the sub-tree root. Finally, the projected list will be used to compute object cast ranges which will subsequently be used to determine legal and illegal relations between the object types during a cast operation.

4.3   Object Type Confusion Detection

Virtual Pointer Usage as Runtime Object Type Identifier. CASTSAN uses the virtual pointer (vptr) of an object to identify its type at runtime. Note that any polymorphic type contains a set of virtual methods that are reachable from any object using its vptr. The vptr of a type is saved in any polymorphic object that is created using the type's constructor. By type constructor, we mean the function which is called when an object of a certain type is allocated. Furthermore, note that each legally cast instance of a polymorphic object can be uniquely identified by its vptr since the vptr of an object is always the first field of that object. CASTSAN therefore reads the vptr of any object at runtime to uniquely identify its runtime type. CASTSAN does this by loading the first 64-bit of the object into a register using an intermediate representation (IR) load instruction. This load instruction is inserted by CASTSAN during LTO for runtime usage.

Determine Object Type Inheritance at Runtime. As previously mentioned, CastSan checks object casts by using the projected virtual table hierarchy list (see Fig. 4(c) for more details). A projected class hierarchy consists of ordered vtable addresses. The runtime type of an object must inherit from the destination type of the cast in order for the cast to be legal. This happens if the vtable of the runtime type is a child in the sub-tree of the vtable of the destination type. Further, if this is the case, the runtime type comes after the destination type in the depth-first list of the tree. Since all nodes of a sub-tree are placed successively in the projected list, this means that these nodes are located before the last element of the sub-tree in the list. Therefore, CastSan does not need to traverse the whole sub-list representing the sub-tree of the destination type to check if the runtime type is part of it. It is enough to check whether it is anywhere between the first and the last element in the list. This holds because the type of the object holding the vptr has to have a vtable in the sub-tree of the destination type, which means it inherits from the destination type. Otherwise, if the vptr is not in the range, it has no vtable inheriting from the vtable of the destination type and therefore its type does not inherit from the destination type. Therefore, the object cast is illegal in this situation. CastSan implements this mechanism at runtime using range checks on the vtable pointer of an object and additionally by using the values of the vtable addresses of the destination type sub-tree. CastSan checks during runtime if the value of the vptr is larger than the vtable address of the destination type and smaller than the address value of the last vtable entry located in the sub-list corresponding to the destination type. If this holds, then the runtime type must inherit from the destination type; therefore, the cast is legal. Otherwise, if the vptr value is not contained between the above mentioned boundaries, then the runtime type does not inherit from the destination type, thus the object cast is not legal.

Virtual Table Based Range Checks. CastSan uses vtable based range checks in order to check if the vptr of an object resides between two allowed values. CastSan's range check is based on the observation that the addresses of the ordered vtables are re-arranged by interleaving them through a pre-order traversal of the inheritance trees in which these vtables are contained. Therefore, the addresses of any sub-tree lay continuously and gapless in memory. By continuously and gapless we mean that there is no starting address of another vtable not belonging to the sub-tree in between the addresses of a sub-tree, and the starting addresses of the vtable lie consecutively in memory, respectively. Further, if the vptr points to any address between the first and the last address of the sub-tree, then it has to be in the list of all addresses located in the sub-tree and therefore the cast is legal. In this way, CastSan can simplify the type check to a range check. CastSan builds a range check by using the vtable address V of the destination type X and the count c of all classes that inherit from X. V and c can be statically determined at compile time for each object cast performed in the program. To perform the check at runtime, the vptr value P is extracted from the object before the cast. Next, the following expression is evaluated by

CASTSAN during runtime. *If $V + c \geq P \geq V$ holds, then the cast is legal, oth-erwise the cast is illegal and program execution will be terminated or an error log output can be produced depending on the employed* CASTSAN usage mode flag. Note that CASTSAN offers the possibility to include in the *else*-branch of the inserted cast check the option to log back-trace information instead of ter-minating the program which is obviously not always desired (see Fig. 5 for more details).

The generated object cast range check has the following advantages com-pared to other state-of-the-art techniques. First, in terms of memory overhead, CASTSAN does not require any additional metadata at runtime to be recorded, deleted or updated in order to determine class hierarchy relationships. Second, the range check needed for the sub-typing check has $O(1)$ runtime cost com-pared to $O(n)$ runtime cost of other tools due to traversals of additional data structures (*e.g.*, red-black tree).

Instrumenting a C++ Object Cast. CASTSAN replaces the cast check intrin-sics inserted into the code within the Clang compiler with a range based cast check (see ❸ depicted in Fig. 3 for more details) during LTO. The check is sub-stituted with an equality check if the count of vtables in the range is one. The equality check matches the vtable address of the range with the vptr of the object. If the addresses are equal, then the cast is legal, otherwise it is illegal. In case the range has more elements than one, then a range check will be inserted. The steps for building and inserting the final range check are as follows. First, the value of the start address of the range is subtracted from the vptr value by CASTSAN. Further, if the pointer value was lower than the start address of the vtable, then the result is negative and the cast is illegal. Second, the result of the subtraction is next rotated by three bits to the right to remove the empty bits that define the pointer length. If the result of the subtraction was negative, this rotation shifts the sign of the result to the right, making it the most sig-nificant bit. Therefore, if the cast is illegal, then the result of the bit rotation is a large number. More specifically, the number is then larger than any result of a valid cast. This holds because the most significant bit, where the sign was shifted due to the rotation, would have been shifted to the right. This would make the number smaller than the illegal case. The result is either the distance of the destination type from the runtime type within the vtable hierarchy or an invalid large number. Finally, the value is compared to the number of vtables in the range. If the value is less than or equal to the count, then the cast is legal and program execution can continue, otherwise an illegal cast is reported. By using these instructions, the range check can ensure three preconditions for a legal cast using only one branch. If any of the following preconditions do not hold, CASTSAN will report an illegal cast. This is the case if the value of the vptr is: (1) higher than the last address in the range (*i.e.*, the type of the object is not directly related to the destination type), (2) lower than the first value of the vtable address range (*i.e.*, the runtime type of the object is an ancestor of the destination type), resulting in the negative bit being shifted to a significant bit of the subtraction result, or (3) not aligned to the pointer length (*i.e.*, the pointer is corrupted). Note that in (3) the unaligned bit is rotated to one of the significant bits or to the signing bit. Since the comparison is unsigned, the number would then again be larger than the last address in the vtable range.

Further, note that the vptr of an object can always be used to perform the check in the primary inheritance tree of the object source type. Finally, the primary inheritance tree, represents the tree which contains the virtual table of the object types as primary parent.

```
1X *x=new W();
2Y *y=static_cast<Y>(x);
3y->x();
```

(a)

```
1 0x400fe0 mov    %r15,%rdi
2 0x400fe3 callq *(%rax)
```

(b)

```
1 0x400fc0 ud2
2 0x400fcb mov    $0x401080,%ecx
3 0x400fcf mov    %rax,%rdx
4 0x400fd1 sub    %rcx,%rdx
5 0x400fd6 rol    $0x3d,%rdx
6 0x400fda cmp    $0x2
7 0x400fda ja     0x400fc0
8 0x400fe0 mov    %r15,%rdi
9 0x400fe3 callq *(%rax)
```

(c)

Fig. 5. Instrumented polymorphic C++ object type cast.

Figure 5 depicts a C++ object type cast at line number two in Fig. 5(a), the un-instrumented assembly code in Fig. 5(b), and the assembly code instrumentation added by CastSan in Fig. 5(c) (the range check is highlighted in gray shaded color). In Fig. 5(a), without line number three the compiler generates does not generate code since the Clang/LLVM compiler is designed to not generate specific code for object casts. Only for the object dispatch (see line number three), assembly code is generated. The assembly code in Fig. 5(b) corresponds to the object dispatch depicted in Fig. 5(a) at line number 3. Finally, we assume that the OS provides an $W \oplus X$ protection mechanism (*e.g.*, data execution prevention (DEP)) and thus the assembly code depicted in Fig. 5(c) cannot be modified (rewritten) by an attacker.

Next, we present the operations performed by the instructions contained in the range check (gray shaded code in Fig. 5) in order to better understand how the check operates. First, the vtable address of type X (corresponding to line number one in Fig. 5(a)) 0x401080 is loaded. In line number two, in Fig. 5(c), the fixed value of the address is moved to the register %rcx. This is done in order to load the first value of the range. Second, the vptr of the object x is moved to register %rdx depicted in line number three. This is done in order to provide the second value of the subtraction of the range check. Note that the object pointer itself was already loaded in register %rax. This is not depicted in Fig. 5 for reasons of brevity. Third, the **sub** instruction performs the subtraction of the vtable address (stored in %rcx) from the vptr (stored in %rdx). At line number five, depicted in Fig. 5(c), the pointer alignment is removed from the result by using a rotation (*i.e.*, **rol**) instruction. This is done to obtain the distance of the vptr from the vtable address of the destination type located in the vtable hierarchy. Note that if the number of all types inheriting from the destination type is higher or equal to the distance, the cast is legal. Finally, the result is compared to the constant $0x2, which is the number of all types inheriting from the destination type Y, specifically these are Y and W. Then, the program execution either jumps to the address of the instruction ud2 located at line number one in Fig. 5(c) (address 0x400fc0), which terminates the program; otherwise, the object dispatch (line number three in Fig. 5(c)) will be performed similar as in Fig. 5(b) and the program continues its execution.

4.4 Implementation

Components. CASTSAN is implemented as two module passes for the Clang/L-LVM compiler [24] infrastructure by extending LLVM (v.3.7) and relies on the Gold plug-in [23]. CASTSAN is based on the virtual table interleaving algorithm presented by Bounov *et al.* [5] from which it reuses its interleaved vtable metadata, by transporting it from the Clang compiler front-end to the LTO phase via new metadata nodes inserted into LLVM's IR code. More specifically, CASTSAN's implementation is split between the Clang compiler front-end, and a new link-time pass used for analysis and generating the final intrinsic based compiler cast checks. CASTSAN's transformations operate on LLVM's intermediate representation (IR), which retains sufficient programming language semantic information at link time to perform whole program analysis and identify all possible types of polymorphic C++ casts in order to instrument them.

Usage Modes. CASTSAN's implementation provides three operation modes with corresponding compiler flags. First, *attack prevention mode* can be used in shipped program binaries to customers. This mode can be used, if desired, to terminate program execution when an illegal cast is detected, thus providing an effective mechanism for avoiding undefined behavior which may lead to vulnerability based CRAs. Second, *software testing mode* can be used during program testing in order to detect type confusion errors and to help fix them before the software is shipped by subjecting the analyzed program to a test suite with different possible goals (*i.e.,* program path coverage, etc.). Finally, *relaxed mode* can be used to detect and log illegal casts detected during development or deployment. This last mode is mainly intended as a replacement for the situation that it is not safe to stop program execution which is mainly the case for real-world programs.

5   Evaluation

We evaluated CASTSAN by instrumenting various open source programs and conducting a thorough analysis with the goal to show its effectiveness and practicality. The experiments were performed using the open source benchmarks Type-San [18], IVT [5], Google's Chrome (v.33.0.1750.112) web browser, and SPEC CPU2006 benchmark (only for the C++ based programs), which were also used by HexType [19]. If not otherwise stated, we used the Clang -O2 compiler flag for all our experiments. In our evaluation, we addressed the following research questions (RQs).

RQ1: What is the **runtime overhead** of CastSan (Sect. 5.1)
RQ2: How **precise** is CastSan? (Sect. 5.2)
RQ3: How **effective** is CastSan? (Sect. 5.3)
RQ4: How can CastSan **assist a programmer** during a bug bounty? (Sect. 5.4)

Comparison Method. In addition to the runtime overhead and binary blow-up, the coverage and precision of HexType is compared to that of CastSan. For benchmarking SPEC CPU2006, the benchmark script of TypeSan, and the micro-benchmark of ShrinkWrap [17] was used.

Preliminaries. The script of TypeSan (approx. 606 Bash LOC) sets up a full environment consisting of: Binutils, Bash, Coreutils, CMake, Pearl. These are used for instrumenting the SPEC CPU2006, and UBench (consisting of 10 intricate C++ testcases). After the benchmark is set up, the script compiles the programs and checks each program by starting it and checking it to see if it executed successfully.

The script of IVT (approx. 200 Python LOC) is used to compile up to 50 C++ programs. Some of the programs contain object type confusions. After each instrumented program execution, the script checks if the program executed successfully or not.

Experimental Setup. We evaluated CastSan on an AMD Ryzen R7 1800x CPU using 8 cores with 16 GB of RAM running the Debian 8 Jessie OS. All benchmarks were executed 10 times to obtain reliable mean values.

Table 3. Benchmark results of running various C++ programs contained in the SPEC CPU2006 benchmark with CastSan enabled and disabled (vanilla). The values represent the mean time needed to finish running the benchmark program over 10 runs.

Benchmark	Vanilla	CastSan	Overhead
soplex	207.14	211.43	2.07%
povray	123.34	125.28	1.57%
omnetpp	269.14	270.06	0.34%
astar	334.96	335.96	0.30%
dealII	186.71	188.47	0.94%
xalanckbmk	413.67	421.03	1.78%
namd	266.42	266.43	0.00%
average			1.0%
geomean			0.92%

5.1 Performance Overhead (RQ1)

Table 3 depicts the overall runtime overhead on only the relevant C++ programs contained in the SPEC CPU2006 benchmark. The geomean value of the overhead in these benchmarks is under 1% (0.92%). As an outlier, `soplex` showed an overhead of 2.07%. For most benchmarks, the overhead is lower than 1.0%. Some SPEC CPU2006 benchmarks like `astar` do not contain static casts and thus no check is performed. These results show that the overhead is within the margin of error. This is to be expected as CASTSAN does not need to execute additional code on execution when no checkable casts are present in the code.

Table 4. Runtime overhead on Chrome with CASTSAN enabled and disabled (vanilla).

Benchmark	High/Low	Vanilla	CastSan	Overhead
gc-sunspider [32]	<	123.4	124.1	0.57%
gc-octane [27]	>	29885	29889	-0.01%
gc-drom-js [14]	>	1987.21	1991.58	-2.18%
gc-balls [4]	>	216	215	0.47%
gc-kraken [21]	<	933.1	941.2	0.87%
gc-jetstream [20]	<	184.06	184.44	0.21%
average				-0.01%
geomean				0.31%

Table 4 depicts the average and geomean runtime overheads of CASTSAN in seven of the most popular JavaScript benchmarks. The greater/less symbols (in High/Low) next to the name describe if higher (>) or lower (<) values are better in the benchmark. More precisely, higher is better for jetstream, octane, balls and dromaeo benchmarks; lower is better in sunspider and kraken. The numbers in columns Vanilla and CASTSAN represent aggregate benchmark scores and have no particular intrinsic meaning. The average value of the overhead of CASTSAN in these benchmarks is −0.01%, which is in the margin of error. The low overhead obtained when running JavaScript benchmarks in the instrumented Chrome demonstrates that CASTSAN can efficiently scale to large code bases with complex class hierarchies.

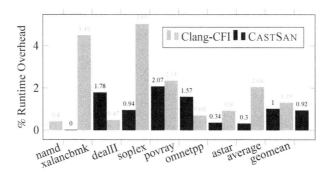

Fig. 6. Clang-CFI (gray) vs. CASTSAN (black) SPEC CPU2006 benchmark overhead.

Figure 6 depicts the average and geomean runtime overheads of CastSan in comparison with the Clang-CFI cast checker when ran on several C++ programs contained in the SPEC CPU2006 benchmark with the following compiler flags: -fsanitize=cfi-cast-strict, -fsanitize=cfi-derived-cast, and -fsanitize=cfi-unrela-ted-cast. Note that the Clang-CFI cast checker instruments the same set of static object casts as CastSan. We compared the Clang-CFI and CastSan runtime overhead w.r.t. the baseline LLVM 3.7 compilations. Note that for the baseline compilation no additional compiler flags and no LTO support (we compiled without the Clang's -flto compiler flag) was used. Finally, it can be observed that the overhead of CastSan is about two times lower on average than the overhead of Clang-CFI when running on the SPEC CPU2006 programs.

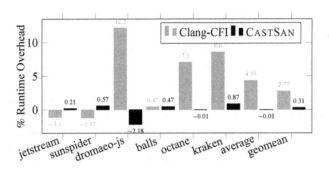

Fig. 7. Clang-CFI (gray) vs. CastSan (black) Chrome runtime overhead.

Figure 7 depicts the runtime overhead of Chrome when ran on several JavaScript benchmarks. First, we compiled with Clang-CFI, and second, with CastSan enabled and with the following compiler flags enabled: -fsanitize=cfi-cast-strict, and -fsanitize=cfi-derived-cast. We did not use the -fsanitize=cfi-unrelated-cast compiler flag, since Chrome was not able to start (crashed during start) after applying this flag. In total, the same amount of object casts where instrumented by each of the tools. However, we can observe that compared to Clang-CFI, the geomean and average overheads of CastSan are better on large code bases such as the Chrome browser. The lowest runtime overhead value, -2.18%, was obtained with CastSan when running the Dromaeo-js benchmark, while the lowest overhead, -1.17%, was obtained by Clang-CFI when running the Sunspider JavaScript benchmark. Overall, we observed a 54 times speed-up on average and 8.9 times speed-up in geomean for CastSan when compared to Clang-CFI cast checker.

5.2   Precision (RQ2)

We evaluated the precision of CastSan by using complex class hierarchies of programs contained in the open-source micro-benchmark of TypeSan [18] and the benchmark programs (in total more than 50 programs) provided by the IVT tool. This benchmark includes: (1) casts to secondary parents, (2) casts within a diamond inheritance, and (3) casts from unrelated trees.

The results indicate that each cast that is covered by CASTSAN can be precisely checked and the implementation leaves no room for unmitigated corner cases. Moreover, CASTSAN did not show the imprecisions described in the ShrinkWrap paper. There, the authors show specific cases of class inheritances (*e.g.*, diamond inheritance) where vtable based function call sanitizers allow calls to illegitimate functions of sibling classes. Finally, CASTSAN was able to cope with all complex class hierarchies contained in these benchmarks and no false negatives or false positives were reported. Thus, we conclude that CASTSAN is precise and leaves no space for untreated corner cases.

5.3   Effectiveness (RQ3)

We evaluated the effectiveness of CASTSAN by selecting the last ten type confusions reported in Google Chrome which had common weakness enumeration (CVE) reports associated. All these type confusions have been reported and partially fixed in the current Chrome browser version. The goal of this experiment is to show that CASTSAN can find object type confusions in real-world software.

We recompiled the Chrome web browser with the CASTSAN checks in place and ran all JavaScript benchmarks, which we also used to check the performance of Chrome (see Fig. 7 for more details). In total, out of the ten object type confusions, CASTSAN was able to report three type confusions at the correct location. We further investigated the other undetected type confusions and found out that these were not detected since the used JS benchmarks do not interact with the code of Chrome which contains these bugs. As such, this is an issue which can be addressed with more extensive test suites which reach the other bugs not previously detected. Finally, we conclude that CASTSAN is effective in detecting real-world type confusions.

5.4   Programmer Assistance (RQ4)

We evaluated how useful CASTSAN is in helping a programmer to find and fix a type confusion bug. For this reason, we used a well-known type confusion bug and depict the error log in order to show how the programmer is guided when fixing a type confusion bug. The goal of this experiment is to

```
1 ./Illegal Cast Detected. Printing Backtrace:
2 ./Xalan_base[0x5a3de8]
3 ./Xalan_base(_ZNK11xercesc_2_511DOMTextImpl13getParentNodeEv+0x6)[0x5cb1c6]
4 ./Xalan_base(_ZN11xercesc_2_513DOMParentNode12insertBeforeEPNS_7DOMNodeES2_+0x25a)[0x5bae2a]
5 ./Xalan_base(_ZN11xercesc_2_511DOMAttrImpl8setValueEPKt+0xb0)[0x59e6a0]
6 ./Xalan_base(_ZN11xercesc_2_512XSDDOMParser12startElementERKNS_14XMLElementDeclEjPKtRKNS_
7     11RefVectorOfINS_7XMLAttrEEEjbb+0x520)[0x6e15e0]
8 ./Xalan_base(_ZN11xercesc_2_512IGXMLScanner14scanStartTagNSERb+0x1a0f)[0x61134f]
9 ./Xalan_base(_ZN11xercesc_2_512IGXMLScanner11scanContentEv+0x171)[0x60e451]
10 ./Xalan_base(_ZN11xercesc_2_512IGXMLScanner12scanDocumentERKNS_11InputSourceE+0x67)[0x60e0c7]
11 ./Xalan_base(_ZN11xercesc_2_517AbstractDOMParser5parseERKNS_11InputSourceE+0x22)[0x5779e2]
12 ./Xalan_base(_ZN11xercesc_2_512IGXMLScanner20resolveSchemaGrammarEPKtS2_+0x685)[0x61b8c5]
13 ./Xalan_base(_ZN11xercesc_2_512IGXMLScanner19parseSchemaLocationEPKt+0xe0)[0x61b1a0]
14 ./Xalan_base(_ZN11xercesc_2_512IGXMLScanner28scanRawAttrListforNameSpacesEi+0x4b7)[0x61ad47]
15 ./Xalan_base(_ZN11xercesc_2_512IGXMLScanner14scanStartTagNSERb+0x3b2)[0x60fcf2]
16 ./Xalan_base(_ZN11xercesc_2_512IGXMLScanner11scanContentEv+0x171)[0x60e451]
17 ./Xalan_base(_ZN11xercesc_2_512IGXMLScanner12scanDocumentERKNS_11InputSourceE+0x67)[0x60e0c7]
18 ./Xalan_base(_ZN11xercesc_2_517SAX2XMLReaderImpl5parseERKNS_11InputSourceE+0x25)[0x6537f5]
19 ./Xalan_base(_ZN10XalanSourceTreeParserLiaison14parseXMLStreamERKN11xercesc_2_
20     511InputSourceERKNS_14XalanDOMStringE+0x120)[0x7c8070]
21 ./Xalan_base(_ZN10xalanc_1_824XalanDefaultParsedSourceC1ERKN11xercesc_2_511InputSourceEbPNS1_
22     12ErrorHandlerEPNS1_14EntityResolverEPKtS8_+0x1da)[0x7cb8ea]
23 ./Xalan_base(_ZN10xalanc_1_816XalanTransformer11parseSourceERKNS_15XSLTInputSourceERPKNS_
24     17XalanParsedSourceEb+0x303)[0x7cc983]
25 ./Xalan_base(_ZN10xalanc_1_816XalanTransformer9transformERKNS_15XSLTInputSourceES3_RKNS_
26     16XSLTResultTargetE+0x2a)[0x7ccaea]
27 ./Illegal instruction
```

Fig. 8. Type confusion back-trace for the `xalancbmk` program.

show that CASTSAN can effectively help a programmer to pinpoint the exact bug location. Figure 8 depicts the backtrace that CASTSAN prints out when running the xalancbmk program contained in the SPEC CPU2006 benchmark. The SPEC CPU2006 xalancbmk has a known type confusion vulnerability, as mentioned in [5], which CASTSAN is able to detect. Thus, on execution, it prints the back-trace leading to the illegal cast. Line numbers 1 to 27 are the verbose output of CASTSAN, notifying the user that an illegal cast happened during execution. In lines 25, 26 and 27 the mangled name of the exact function containing the illegal object cast is printed. Using the offset printed in the square brackets at the end of the line, a developer can find the line in the code where the illegal object cast was defined. The error log depicted in Fig. 8 demonstrates that CASTSAN is able to detect real type confusion bugs in applications by running a program in backtrace-mode. Finally, we conclude that CASTSAN can help developers during bug bounties [34], and can protect against exploitable type confusions.

6   Discussion

In this section, we present CASTSAN's limitations and discuss how to address these.

Non-polymorphic Classes. CASTSAN provides type safety for objects stemming from polymorphic classes and low runtime overhead. Further, CASTSAN cannot check casts between non-polymorphic objects. This is because only polymorphic objects have a virtual pointer (vptr). The vptr is an integral requirement for checking object type casts using CASTSAN. This means CASTSAN cannot mitigate all types of object type confusion vulnerabilities. A possible way to address this limitation is to construct for static classes an artificial virtual-table-like metadata on which CASTSAN's technique can be based such that our technique becomes usable for non-polymorphic object type casts.

Reinterpret-Cast. In C++, not only static_cast can lead to object type confusion. The misusage of reinterpret_cast can also pose threats. HexType addresses this threat by extending its type cast checking to reinterpret_cast in addition to static_cast. While this can effectively hinder a type confusion vulnerability from occurring, it is debatable if checking reinterpret_cast is viable. This question arises, as reinterpret_cast can be used as a legitimate way of breaking class hierarchy boundaries, if the memory layout of the cast types match. In this case, a type cast check based on class hierarchy information cannot be made. Therefore, if reinterpret_cast is checked for type safety, its purpose can potentially be circumvented. Similarly, as other object type confusion detection tools handle reinterpret_cast, we could use compiler runtime checking support for checking for this type of confusions.

Increasing Tool Coverage. The incremental research work between TypeSan and HexType shows that the main path for increasing object type confusion detection coverage is to support more types of memory allocators (*i.e.,* jmalloc, tcmalloc, etc.) or other more exotic ones. Further, the coverage of CASTSAN can be increased by supporting all types of C++ program locations (*i.e.,* statement types) where such vulnerabilities could manifest. Thus, CASTSAN's coverage can be consistently increased by instrumenting all these source code locations with the needed checks in place in order to check during runtime for object type confusions.

Finding New Vulnerabilities. Finding new object type confusion vulnerabilities is directly linked to increasing the tool coverage and is mainly driven by three lines of research. These are: (1) check new program locations which were previously not possible to be instrumented, (2) support new memory allocators (*e.g.,* object pool allocators, etc.), and (3) reduce the runtime overhead of an object type detection technique such that the technique becomes applicable in real-world deployment. Thus, in future work we want to increase the coverage of CASTSAN by addressing the above mentioned points.

7   Related Work

Virtual Table Pointer-Based Tools. Clang-CFI [7,9] (cast checker) is similar to CASTSAN in that it uses no runtime library and all cast check detection metadata is computed during compile time. However, there are no publicly available evaluation results of Clang-CFI, and therefore we evaluated Clang-CFI in Sect. 5 independently. Clang-CFI relies on bitsets in order to model the class hierarchy of a program. Clang-CFI uses these bitsets to encode the valid virtual table start addresses for each class. Compared to CASTSAN, Clang-CFI has a higher runtime overhead, as the bit-set checking technique on which it relies apparently is less efficient than our virtual table based technique.

C++ Object Type Runtime Tracking. All currently available polymorphic and non-polymorphic object type confusion detection tools (except Clang-CFI) rely on dynamic checks (*i.e.,* LLVM's Compiler-RT is mostly used) for several key reasons, as follows. First, the object type has to be tracked during runtime. Second, this is due to the limited precision of static analysis techniques, which cannot recuperate the object type or a set of possible types before program runtime, Third, the object type confusions manifest only during runtime. Finally, object type confusions are hard to replicate statically (*i.e.,* compile time or through symbolic execution, without running the program).

However, the most significant reason is the fact that the types of casted objects, referenced by pointers, may be program input dependent and thus only precisely obtainable during runtime. On the one hand, in the best case the allocation of the object being cast can be tracked during compile time (*e.g.,* if the runtime path from allocation to cast is linear). On the other hand, in the worst case the object type cannot be approximated (*e.g.,* the object was given via a void-pointer from an external function previously).

Compiler-Based Tools. UBsan [15], CaVer [22], TypeSan [18], and Hex-Type [19] are compiler based tools that perform object type confusion detection at runtime for C++ based programs. Since HexType is the successor of TypeSan, the tools are very similar to each other from a technical perspective. These two tools and CaVer rely on a runtime metadata service and can reach a high coverage while imposing a considerable performance overhead. CASTSAN, on the other hand, uses metadata that is statically created at compile-time and can therefore apply very performant checks at runtime. CASTSAN can protect against polymorphic casts by using vtable hierarchy based ranges and without using a black list. Compared to TypeSan, CASTSAN partially shares the instrumentation layer, which is unavoidable, but it uses completely different metadata without storing data at runtime. More precisely, CASTSAN uses the vtables of polymorphic classes. These tables, that need to be in memory at runtime anyways, already provide a view on the class hierarchy. That is enough for CASTSAN to perform runtime checks without relying on further metadata as maintained by HexType. HexType, on the other hand, reaches a higher coverage, as it can check non-polymorphic objects as well. CASTSAN is more runtime-efficient than CaVer and HexType, which both require a red-black tree to be traversed (only for the slow path) during each check.

Binary-Based Tools. Dewey *et al.* [13] were able to recuperate vtables from program binaries and detect object type confusions indirectly by checking the bounds of a virtual function call. This was achieved by enforcing a policy to check if the vptr lies inside some legitimate bounds. As suggested by the authors, their analysis is imprecise because for example—as also demonstrated by Prakash *et al.* [29]—determining the end of a vtable in binaries without RTTI information is not trivial. Thus, false positives and false negatives are raised, and as such this type of tool is in the best case usable before system deployment.

8   Conclusion and Future Work

C++ object type casting confusions have an important role in modern exploits as demonstrated by recent attacks against Mozilla's Firefox and Google's Chrome web browsers.

In this paper, we presented CASTSAN, a new polymorphic only object type confusion detection tool. CASTSAN's novel technique is based on an efficient and time constant virtual pointer range check which is possible by extracting virtual table inheritance trees out of a previously constructed virtual table inheritance hierarchy. CASTSAN constructs linear projections out of virtual table inheritance trees, which are subsequently used do build runtime object cast checks. Our evaluation results show that CASTSAN is more efficient than state-of-the-art tools (*i.e.,* Clang-CFI cast checker), and has comparable checking coverage with other state-of-the-art tools, which—in contrast—rely on runtime intensive type tracking for checking type confusions for both polymorphic and non-polymorphic objects.

In future work, we want to use our static meta-data based technique to extended existing purely runtime based object type confusion detection tools such as TypeSan and HexType. These tools use for both polymorphic and non-polymorphic object type checking a runtime library which adds considerable runtime overhead due to updates, search, and deletion of object type meta-data. We think that our approach can be used to avoid the tracking of meta-data for polymorphic objects. Further, a complementary artificial virtual table like meta-data class hierarchy can be built for non-polymorphic objects as well. Finally, in this way our technique becomes usable also in this context, thus avoiding or considerable reducing the overhead introduced by the runtime compiler checking support.

Acknowledgements. We thank Mathias Payer from EPFL, CH; for insights which helped to improve paper quality. We thank Dimitar Bounov from the University of California, San Diego, USA; and Benjamin Johnson from the Technical University of Munich, Germany for reviewing an early version of this paper. Jens Grossklags' research is supported by the German Institute for Trust and Safety on the Internet (DIVSI). Further, we thank the anonymous reviewers for their rich feedback.

References

1. 2016 Working Draft, Standard for Programming Language C++ N4618. https://goo.gl/PPJ5QC
2. Abadi, M., Budiu, M., Erlingsson, Ú., Ligatti, J.: Control flow integrity. In: CCS (2005)
3. Abadi, M., Budiu, M., Erlingsson, Ú., Ligatti, J.: Control flow integrity principles, implementations, and applications. In: TISSEC (2009)
4. Balls Browser Benchmark (2017). http://bubblemark.com/
5. Bounov, D., Kici, R.G., Lerner, S.: Protecting C++ dynamic dispatch through VTable interleaving. In: NDSS (2016)
6. Buchanan, E., Roemer, R., Shacham, H., Savage, S.: When good instructions go bad: generalizing return-oriented programming to RISC. In: CCS (2008)
7. Clang. Clang 3.9 Documentation - Control Flow Integrity. https://goo.gl/gnmoHU
8. Clang. Clang 5 Documentation - Control Flow Integrity (2017). https://goo.gl/bW4DyS
9. Clang-CFI Cast Checker Metadata. https://goo.gl/JkGDjL
10. Crane, S., et al.: It's a TRaP: table randomization and protection against function-reuse attacks. In: CCS (2015)
11. CVE-2016-1612: Bug Description and reward (2016). https://goo.gl/9SxjEA
12. CVE-2017-3106: Object Type Confusion in Adobe F. Player v. 26.0.0.137 (2017). https://goo.gl/gakD25
13. Dewey, D., Giffin, J.: Static detection of C++ VTable escape vulnerabilities in binary code. In: NDSS (2012)
14. Dromaeo Browser Benchmark (2017). http://dromaeo.com/?v8
15. Google. Undefined Behavior Sanitizer (2017). https://goo.gl/ELrNKj
16. Google. The Chromium Projects, Chromium (2017). https://goo.gl/uE486n
17. Haller, I., Goktas, E., Athanasopoulos, E., Portokalidis, G., Bos, H.: ShrinkWrap: VTable protection without loose ends. In: ACSAC (2015)
18. Haller, I., Jeon, Y., Peng, H., Payer, M., Giuffrida, C.: TypeSan: practical type confusion detection. In: CCS (2016)

19. Jeon, Y., Biswas, P., Carr, S., Lee, B., Payer, M.: HexType: efficient detection of type confusion errors for C++. In: CCS (2017)
20. JetStream Browser Benchmark (2017). http://browserbench.org/JetStream/
21. Kraken JavaScript Benchmark (2017). https://krakenbenchmark.mozilla.org/
22. Lee, B., Song, C., Kim, T., Lee, W.: Type casting verification: stopping an emerging attack vector. In: USENIX Security (2015)
23. LLVM. The LLVM Gold Plugin (2017). https://goo.gl/UjFxih
24. LLVM. LLVM Team, The LLVM compiler infrastructure project. http://llvm.org/
25. LLVM. LLVM link time optimization: design and implementation. https://goo.gl/r3RH2U
26. Microsoft. Changes to Functionality in Microsoft Windows XP SP 2. https://goo.gl/928ihY
27. Octane Browser Benchmark (2017). https://chromium.github.io/octane/
28. PaX Team: Address Space Layout Randomization (2001). https://goo.gl/Sab9YE
29. Prakash, A., Hu, X., Yin, H.: Strict protection for virtual function calls in COTS C++ binaries. In: NDSS (2015)
30. Schuster, F., Tendyck, T., Liebchen, C., Davi, L., Sadeghi, A.-R., Holz, T.: Counterfeit object-oriented programming. In: S&P (2015)
31. Standard Performance Evaluation Corporation. SPEC CPU 2006 (2017). https://goo.gl/NtmYy8
32. SunSpider 1.0.2 JavaScript Benchmark (2017). https://goo.gl/qk9uqg
33. Zhang, C., et al.: Practical control flow integrity & randomization for binary executables. In: S&P (2013)
34. Zhao, M., Grossklags, J., Liu, P.: An empirical study of web vulnerability discovery ecosystems. In: CCS (2015)

On Leveraging Coding Habits
for Effective Binary Authorship
Attribution

Saed Alrabaee$^{(\boxtimes)}$, Paria Shirani, Lingyu Wang, Mourad Debbabi,
and Aiman Hanna

Security Research Center, Concordia University, Montreal, Canada
s_alraba@encs.concordia.ca

Abstract. We propose *BinAuthor*, a novel and the first compiler-agnostic method for identifying the authors of program binaries. Having filtered out unrelated functions (compiler and library) to detect user-related functions, it converts user-related functions into a canonical form to eliminate compiler/compilation effects. Then, it leverages a set of features based on collections of authors' choices made during coding. These features capture an author's coding habits. Our evaluation demonstrated that *BinAuthor* outperforms existing methods in several respects. First, when tested on large datasets extracted from selected open-source C/C++ projects in GitHub, Google Code Jam events, and Planet Source Code contests, it successfully attributed a larger number of authors with a significantly higher accuracy: around 90% when the number of authors is 1000. Second, when the code was subjected to refactoring techniques, code transformation, or processing using different compilers or compilation settings, there was no significant drop in accuracy, indicating that *BinAuthor* is more robust than previous methods.

1   Introduction

Binary authorship attribution refers to the process of discovering information related to the author(s) of anonymous binary code on the basis of stylometric characteristics extracted from the code. It is especially relevant to security applications, such as digital forensic analysis of malicious code [30] and copyright infringement detection [33] because the source code is seldom available in these cases. However, in practice, authorship attribution for binary code still requires considerable manual and error-prone reverse engineering analysis, which can be a daunting task given the sheer volume and complexity of today's malware. Although significant efforts have been made to develop automated approaches for authorship attribution for source code [19,25,37], such techniques typically rely on features that will likely be lost in the binary code after the compilation process, for example, variable and function naming, original control and data

© Springer Nature Switzerland AG 2018
J. Lopez et al. (Eds.): ESORICS 2018, LNCS 11098, pp. 26–47, 2018.
https://doi.org/10.1007/978-3-319-99073-6_2

flow structures, comments, and space layout. Nonetheless, at the recent Black-Hat conference, the feasibility of authorship attribution for malware binaries was confirmed [5], though the process still requires considerable human intervention.

Most existing approaches to binary authorship attribution employ machine learning methods to extract unique features for each author and subsequently match the features of a given binary to identify the authors [15,19,32]. These approaches were studied and analyzed in our previous work [16], and we uncovered several issues that affect them all. Notably, a considerable percentage of the extracted features are related to compiler functions rather than to author styles, which causes a high false positive rate. Moreover, the extracted features are not resilient to code transformation methods, refactoring techniques, changes in the compilation settings, and the use of different compilers. We implemented a system that improved the accuracy obtained by Caliskan et al. [19] in attributing 600 authors from 83% to 90%, and then we scaled the results to 86% accuracy for 1500 authors.

Key Idea: We present *BinAuthor*, a system designed to recognize author *coding habits* by extracting author's choices from binary code. *BinAuthor*[1] performs a series of steps in order to capture coding habits. First, it filters unrelated functions such as compiler-related functions by proposing a method that is discussed in Sect. 2.1. Second, it labels library-related functions and free open-source related functions using our previous works, BinShape [35], SIGMA [17], and FOSSIL [18], respectively. The results of filtering process would be a set of user-related functions. Third, to eliminate the effects of changes in the compiler or the compilation settings, code transformation, and refactoring tools, *BinAuthor* converts the code into a canonical form that is robust against heavy obfuscation [38]. However, conversion is extremely slow, so we apply it only to the set of user-related functions remaining after filtering. Then we collect a set of author choices frequently made during coding (e.g., preferring to use either memcopy or bcopy). To capture the choices, we examined a large collection of source code and the corresponding assembly instructions to determine which coding habits may be preserved in the binary. Next, we designed features based on these habits and integrated them into *BinAuthor*. To verify that the features capture coding habits, we investigated the ground truth source code in a controlled experiment (using debug information) to determine if the choices are based on functionality or habit.

Contributions: The main contributions of this study are described below.

1. To the best of our knowledge, *BinAuthor* is the first effort that leverages author *coding habits* extracted from binary code for effective binary authorship attribution. This enables *BinAuthor* to work on programs with different functionalities.
2. *BinAuthor* achieves higher accuracy and survives refactoring techniques and code transformation techniques. This shows its potential for use as a practical tool that can assist reverse engineers in many security-related tasks.

---

[1] The code is available at https://github.com/g4hsean/BinAuthor.

3. *BinAuthor* is among the first approaches that performs automated author-
   ship attribution on real-world malware binaries. When we applied it to `Zeus-Citadel`, `Stuxnet-Flame`, and `Bunny-Babar` malware binaries, it automatically generated evidence of coding habits shared by each malware pair, match-
   ing the findings of antivirus vendors [3,12] and reverse engineering teams [5].

2   BinAuthor

We propose a system encompassing different components, each of which is meant
to achieve a particular purpose, as illustrated in Fig. 1. The first component
(*Filtration*), isolates user functions from compiler functions, library functions,
and open-source software packages. For this purpose, we employ BinShape, and
FOSSIL tools developed by our team beside our proposed method to identify
compiler functions. Hence, additional outcome of this component could be considered as a choice (e.g., the preference in using specific compiler or open-source
software packages). The second component (*Canonicalization*), adapts the existing framework angr [36] for lifting function into LLVM-IR, then optimizes the
lifted LLVM-IR, and finally converts the optimized IR into a canonical form. The
third component (*Choices*), analyzes user-related functions to extract possible
features that represent stylistic choices and then converts the extracted choices
into vectors. The vector of choices are used by the attribution probability function in the last component (*Classification*). The aforementioned components are
explained in depth in the remainder of this section.

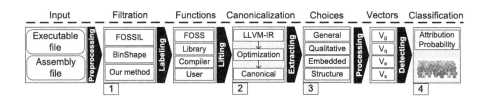

Fig. 1. *BinAuthor* architecture

2.1   Filtration Process

An important initial step in most reverse engineering tasks is to distinguish
between user functions and library/compiler functions. This step saves considerable time and helps shift the focus to more relevant functions. The filtration
process consists of three steps. First, Binshape [35] is used to label library functions. Second, FOSSIL [18] is leveraged to label the functions that are related to
specific FOSS libraries, such as `libpng`, `zlib`, and `openssl`. The last step filters
compiler-related functions, which the details are given below.

The idea is based on the hypothesis that compiler/helper functions can be identified through a collection of static signatures that are created in the training phase (e.g. opcode frequencies). We analyze a number of programs with different functionalities, ranging from a simple "Hello World!" program to programs fulfilling complex tasks. Through the intersection of these functions combined with manual analysis, we collect about 240 functions as compiler/helper functions related to two GCC and VS compilers. The opcode frequencies are extracted from these functions, after which the mean and variance of each opcode are calculated.

In other words, each disassembled program P, after passing IDA Pro, consists of n functions $\{f_1, \cdots, f_n\}$. Each function f_k is represented as m pairs of opcodes o_i, where m is the number of distinct opcodes in function f_k. Each opcode $o_i \in O$ has a pair of values (μ_i, ν_i), which represents the mean and variance values of that specific opcode. Each opcode in the target function is measured against the same opcode of all compiler functions in the training set. If the measured distance $D_{i,j}$ (i.e., i represents the training function and j represents the target function) is less than a predefined threshold value $\alpha = 0.005$, the opcode is considered as a match. A function is labeled as *compiler-related* if the matched opcodes ratio is greater than a predefined threshold value learned from experiments to be $\gamma = 0.75$; otherwise, the target function is labeled as *user-related*. Dissimilarity measurements are performed based on distance calculations as per the following equation [39]:

$$D_{i,j} = \frac{(\mu_j - \overline{\mu_j})^2}{\left(\nu_i^2 + \overline{\nu_i^2}\right)}$$

where $(\overline{\mu_j}, \overline{\nu_j})$ represents the opcode mean and variance of the target function, respectively. This dissimilarity metric detects functions, which are closer to each other in terms of types of opcodes. For instance, logical opcodes are not available in *compiler-related* functions. Finally, a score is given to every distance that is below a predefined threshold α.

2.2 Canonicalization

We use a strategy similar to that applied in the recent work by [21] when lifting the resulting user-related functions.

Lifting Binaries to Intermediate Representation (IR): We adopt the existing framework angr [36] for lifting function into LLVM-IR. We first convert the disassembled binary to the VEX-IR [29] using angr, and then implement a translator to convert the VEX-IR to LLVM-IR.

Optimizing Intermediate Representation to Optimized IR: To achieve this goal, we employ the extended version of Peggy tool [38] to optimize LLVM-IR. It performs the following tasks: dead code elimination, global value numbering, partial redundancy elimination, sparse conditional constant propagation, loop-invariant code motion, loop deletion, loop unswitching, dead store elimination, constant propagation, and basic block placement. In this way, we prevent such changes from affecting our extracted choices. For more details, we refer the reader to [38].

Canonical Form: Canonicalization offers several benefits [21]. Lifting the instructions according to LLVM may impose changes such as redundant loads, but these changes will now be reverted. Moreover, in the case of writing dependencies, canonicalization of the expression makes it possible to perform the addition with the constant first, and the result is put in the register before the subtraction is performed. Furthermore, with canonicalization, the comparison becomes simple addition with a positive constant, instead of subtraction with a negative. Note that this last step serves to reoptimize code which might not have been previously optimized [21].

2.3   Choices Categorization

Determining a set of characteristics that remain constant for a significant portion of a program written by a particular author is analogous to discovering human characteristics that can later be used to identify an individual. Accordingly, our aim is to automate the identification of program characteristics, but with a reasonable computational cost. To capture coding habits at different levels of abstraction, we consider a spectrum of habits, assuming that an author's habits can be reflected in a preference for choosing certain keywords or compilers, a reliance on the main function, or the use of an object-oriented programming paradigm. The manner in which the code is organized may also reflect the author's habits. All possible choices are stored as a template in this step. We provide a detailed description of each category of author choices in the following subsections.

2.3.1   General Choices

General choices are designed to capture an author's general programming preferences, for example, preferences in organizing the code, terminating a function, the use of particular keywords, or the use of specific resources.

(1) **Code organization:** We capture the way code is organized by measuring the reliance on the `main` function using statistical features, since it is considered a starting part for managing user functions. We define a set of ratios, shown in Table 1, that measures the actions used in the `main` function. We thus capture the percentage usage of keywords, local variables, API calls, and calling user functions, as well as the ratio of the number of basic blocks in the `main` function to the number of basic blocks in other user functions. These percentages are computed relative to the length of the `main` function, where the length signifies the number of instructions in the function. The results are represented as a vector of ratios, which is used by the detection component.

Table 1. Features extracted from the `main` function

Ratio equation	Description
#push/l	Ratio of accessing the stack to length
#push/#lea	Ratio of accessing the stack to local variables
#lea/l	Ratio of local variables to length
#calls/l	Ratio of function calls to length
#callees/l	Ratio of the calls to `main` function to length
#indirect calls/l	Ratio of API calls to length
#BBs/total # all BBs	Ratio of the number of basic blocks of the `main` function to that of other user functions
#calls/#user functions	Ratio of function calls to the number of user functions

length(l) represents number of instructions in the `main` function

(2) **Function termination:** *BinAuthor* captures the way in which an author terminates a function. This could help identify an author since programmers may favor specific ways of terminating a function. *BinAuthor* considers not just the last statement of a function as the terminating instruction; rather, it identifies the last basic block of the function with its predecessor as the terminating part. This is a realistic approach since various actions may be required before a function terminates. With this in mind, *BinAuthor* not only considers the usual terminating instructions, such as `return` and `exit`, but also captures related actions that are taken prior to termination. For instance, a function may be terminated with a display of messages, a call to another function, the release of some resources, or communication over networks. Table 2 shows examples of what is captured in relation to the termination of a function. Such features could be captured by extracting the strings and opcodes. Each feature is set to *1* if it is used to terminate a function; otherwise, it is set to *0*. The output of this component is a binary vector that is used by the detection component.

Table 2. Examples of actions taken in terminating a function

Features	
Printing results to memory	Printing results to file
Using system ("pause")	User action such as `cin`
Calling user functions	Calling API functions
Closing files	Closing resources
Freeing memory	Flushing buffer
Using network communication	Printing clock time
Releasing semaphores or locks	Printing errors

(3) **Keyword and resource preferences:** *BinAuthor* captures an author's preferences in the use of keywords or resources. We consider only groups of

preferences with equivalent or similar functionality to avoid functionality-dependent features. These include keyword type preferences for inputs (e.g., using `cin`, `scanf`), preferences for particular resources or a specific compiler (we identify the compiler by using PEiD[2]), operation system (e.g., Linux), CPU architecture (e.g., ARM), and the manner in which certain keywords are used, which can serve as further indications of an author's habits. Some of these features are identified through binary string matching, which tracks the strings annotated to `call` and `mov` instructions. For instance, excessive use of `fflush` will cause the string ''fflush'' to appear frequently in the resulting binary.

2.3.2   Quality-Related Choices

We investigate code quality in terms of compliance with C/C++ coding standards and security concerns. The literature has established that code quality can be measured using different indicators, such as testability, flexibility, and adaptability [31]. *BinAuthor* defines rules for capturing code that exhibits either relatively low or high quality. For any code that cannot be matched using such rules, the code is labelled as having regular quality, which indicates that the code quality feature is not applicable. Such rules are extracted by defining a set of signatures (sequence of instructions) for each choice. An example is introduced in Appendix A.

Examples of low-quality coding styles are reopening already opened files, leaving files open when they are no longer in use, attempting to modify constants through pointers, using float variables as loop counters, and declaring variables inside a switch statement. Such declarations, which can be captured through the structure matching of code, could be considered a structural choice, possibly resulting in unexpected/undefined behavior due to jumped-over instructions. It is for this reason that we put them in the low-quality category. Examples of high-quality coding styles are handling errors generated by library calls (i.e., examining the value returned by `fclose()`); avoiding reliance on side effects (e.g., the `++` operator) within calls such as `sizeof` or `_Alignof`; avoiding particular calls to some environments or using them with protective measures (since invoking the `system()` in Linux may lead to shell command injection or privilege escalation, using `execve()` instead is indicative of high-quality coding); and the implementation of locks and semaphores around critical sections.

2.3.3   Embedded Choices

We define embedded choices as actions that are related to coding habits present in the source code, which are not easily captured at the binary level by traditional features such as strings or graphs. Examples are initializing member variables in constructors and dynamically deleting allocated resources in destructors. Since it is not feasible to list all possible features, *BinAuthor* relies on the fact that opcodes reveal actions, expertise, habits, knowledge, and other author's

---

[2] https://www.aldeid.com/wiki/PEiD.

characteristics, and then analyzes the distribution of opcode frequencies. Our experiments showed that this distribution can effectively capture the manner in which an author manages code. Since every action in source code can affect the frequency of opcodes, *BinAuthor* targets embedded choices by capturing the distribution of opcode frequencies.

2.3.4 Structural Choices

Programmers usually develop their own structural design habits. They may prefer to use a fully object-oriented design, or they may be more accustomed to procedural programming. Structural choices can serve as features for author identification. To avoid functionality, we consider the common subgraphs for each user function and then intersect them among different user functions to identify those subgraphs that are unique and those that are common. These types of subgraphs are defined as k-graphs, where k is the number of nodes. The common k-graphs form author's signatures since they always appear, regardless of the program functionality. In addition, we consider the longest path in each user function because it reflects the way in which an author tends to use deep or nested loops. An author may organize classes either ad hoc or hierarchically by designing a driver class to contain several manager classes, where each manager is responsible for different processes (collections of threads running in parallel). Both ad hoc and hierarchical systems of organization can create a common structure in an author's programs.

2.4 Feature Vectors

General Choice Computation: To consider the reliance on the `main` function, a vector v_{g1}, representing related features, is constructed according to the equations shown in Table 1. These equations indicate the author's reliance on the `main` function as well as the actions performed by the author. *Function termination* is represented as a binary vector, (v_{g2}), which is determined by the absence or existence of a set of features for function termination. *Keyword and resource preferences* are identified through binary string matching. We extract a collection of strings from all user functions of a particular author, then intersect these strings in order to derive a persistent vector (v_{g3}) for that author. Consequently, for each author, a set of vectors representing the author's signature is stored in our repository. Given a target binary, *BinAuthor* constructs the vectors from the target and measures the distance/similarity between these vectors and those in our repository. The v_{g1} vector is compared using Euclidean distance, whereas v_{g2} vector is compared using the Jaccard similarity. For v_{g3}, the similarity is computed through string matching. Finally, the three derived similarity values are averaged in order to obtain λ_g, which is later used in Sect. 4.6 for author classification.

Quality-Related Choice Computation: We build a set of idiom templates to describe high or low quality habits. Idioms are sequences of instructions with wild-card possibility [24]. We employ the idioms templates in [24] according to our qualitative-related choice. In addition, such templates carry a meaningful connection to the quality-related choices. Our experiments demonstrate that such idiom templates may effectively capture quality-related habits. *BinAuthor* uses the Levenshtein distance [40] for this computation due to it's efficiency. The similarity is represented by λ_q as follow:

$$\lambda_q = 1 - \frac{L(C_i, C_j)}{max(|C_i|, |C_j|)}$$

where $L(C_i, C_j)$ is the Levenshtein distance between the qualitative-related choices C_i (sequence of instructions) and C_j, $max(|C_i|, |C_j|)$ returns the maximum length between two choices C_i and C_j in terms of characters.

Embedded Choice Computation: The Mahalanobis distance [26] is used to measure the dissimilarity of opcode distributions among different user functions, which is represented by λ_e. The Mahalanobis distance is chosen because it can capture the correlation between opcode frequency distributions.

Structural Choice Computation: *BinAuthor* uses subgraphs of size k in order to capture structural choices ($k = 4$, 5, and 6 through our experiments). Given a k-graph, the graph is transformed into strings using Bliss open-source toolkit [23]. Then, a similarity measurement is performed over these strings using the normalized compression distance (NCD) [20]. The reason of our choice for NCD is threefold: (i) it enhances the search performance; (ii) it allows to concatenate all the common subgraphs that appear in author's programs; and (iii) it allows to perform inexact matching between the target subgraphs and the training subgraphs. *BinAuthor* forms a signature based on these strings. The similarity obtained from this choice is represented by λ_s.

2.5   Classification

As previously described, *BinAuthor* extracts different types of choices to characterize different aspects of author coding habits. Such choices do not equally contribute to the attribution process, since the significance of these indicators are not identical. Consequently, a weight is assigned to each choice by applying logistic regression to them in order to predict class probabilities (e.g., the probability of identifying an author). For this purpose, we use the introduced dataset in Sect. 3.2; to prevent the overfitting, we test each dataset separately and then compute the average of weights. The weights are calculated as follows:

$$w_i = rnd\left((p_i/p_s)/\sum_{i=1}^{4}(p_i/p_s)\right)$$

where p_s is the smallest probability value (e.g. 0.39 in Table 3), p_i is the probability outcome from logistic regression of each choice, and the *rnd* function rounds the final value. The probability outcomes of logistic regression prediction is illustrated in Table 3.

Table 3. Logistic regression weights for choices

Choice	Probability (P_i)	$P_i/(P_s = 0.39)$	Weight $w_i = rnd\Big((p_i/p_s)/\sum_{i=1}^{4}(p_i/p_s)\Big)$
General	0.83	2.128205	0.35
Qualitative	0.63	1.615385	0.27
Structural	0.52	1.333333	0.22
Embedded	0.39	1	0.16
		$\sum_{i=1}^{4}(p_i/p_s) =$ 6.076923	

After extracting features, we define a probability value P based on obtained weights. The attribution probability is defined as follows:

$$P(A) = \sum_{i=1}^{4} w_i * \lambda_i$$

where w_i represents the weight assigned to each choice, as shown in Table 3, and λ_i is the distance metric value obtained from each choice ($\lambda_g, \lambda_q, \lambda_e$, and λ_s) as described in Sect. 2.4. We normalize the probabilities of all authors, and if $P \geq \zeta$, where ζ represents predefined threshold values, then the author is labeled as a matched author. Through our experiments, we find that the best value of ζ is 0.87. If more than one author has probability larger than the threshold value, then *BinAuthor* returns the set of those authors.

3 Evaluation

3.1 Implementation Setup

The described stylistic choices are implemented using separate Python scripts for modularity purposes, which altogether form our analytical system. A subset of the python scripts in the *BinAuthor* system is used in tandem with IDA Pro disassembler. The final set of the framework scripts perform the bulk of the choice analysis functions that compute and display critical information about an author's coding style. With the analysis framework completed, a graph database is utilized to perform complex graph operations such as k-graph extraction. The graph database chosen for this task is Neo4j. Gephi [8] is employed for all graph analysis functions, which are not provided by Neo4j. MongoDB database is used to store our features for efficiency and scalability purposes.

3.2 Dataset

Our dataset is consisted of several C/C++ applications from different sources, as described below: (i) GitHub [2]; (ii) Google Code Jam [1], an international programming competition; (iii) Planet Source Code [9]; (iv) Graduate Student Projects at our institution. Statistics about the dataset are provided in Table 4. In total, we test 800 authors from different sets in which each author has two to five software applications, resulting in a total of 3150 programs. To compile these datasets, we use GNU Compiler Collection (version 4.8.5) with different optimization levels, as well as Microsoft Visual Studio (VS) 2010.

3.3   Experimental Setup

In our experimental setup, we split the collected program binaries into ten sets, reserving one as a testing set and using the remaining nine sets as the training set. We repeat this process 100 times. In order to evaluate *BinAuthor* and to compare it with existing methods, the precision (P) and recall (R) metrics are applied as $Precision = \frac{TP}{TP+FP}, Recall = \frac{TP}{TP+FN}$, where the true positive (TP) indicates number of relevant authors that are correctly retrieved; true negative (TN) returns the number of irrelevant authors that are not detected; false positive (FP) indicates the number of irrelevant authors that are incorrectly detected; and false negative (FN) presents the number of relevant authors that are not detected.

3.4   Accuracy

The main purpose of this experiment is to evaluate the accuracy of author identification in binaries. The evaluation of *BinAuthor* is conducted using the datasets described in Sect. 3.2.

Results Comparison. We compare *BinAuthor* with the existing authorship attribution methods [15,19,32]. The source code and dataset of our previous work, OBA2 [15], is available which performs authorship attribution on a small scale of 5 authors with 10 programs for each. The source code of the two other approaches presented by Caliskan-Islam et al. [19] and Rosenblum et al. [32] are available at [7] and [4], respectively. Both Caliskan-Islam et al. and Rosenblum et al. present a largest-scale evaluation of binary authorship attribution, which contains 600 authors with 8 training programs per author, and 190 authors with at least 8 training programs, respectively. However, since the corresponding

Table 4. Statistics about the dataset used in the evaluation of *BinAuthor*

Source	# of authors	# of programs	# of functions
GitHub	150	600	110000
Google Code Jam	500	2000	23650
Planet Source Code	100	300	12080
Graduate Student Projects	50	250	9823

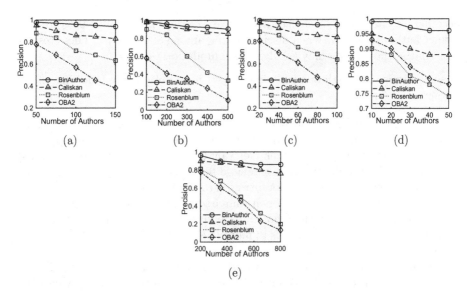

Fig. 2. Precision results of authorship attribution obtained by *BinAuthor*, Caliskan-Islam et al., Rosenblum et al., and OBA2, on (a) Github, (b) Google Code Jam, (c) Planet Source Code, (d) Graduate Student Projects, and (e) All datasets

datasets are not available, we compare *BinAuthor* with these methods by using the datasets mentioned in Table 4.

Figure 2 details the results of comparing the precision between *BinAuthor* and the aforementioned methods. It shows the relationship between the precision and the number of authors present in all datasets, where the precision decreases as the size of author population increases. The results show that *BinAuthor* achieves better precision in determining the author of binaries. Taking all four approaches into consideration, the highest precision of authorship attribution is close to 99% on the Google Code Jam with less than 150 authors, while the lowest precision is 17% when 800 authors are involved on all dataset together. We believe the reason behind Caliskan-Islam et al. approach that achieves high precision on Google Jam Code is that this dataset is simple and can be easily decompiled to source code. *BinAuthor* also identifies the authors of Github dataset with an average precision of 92%. The main reason for this is due to the fact that the authors of projects in Github have no restrictions when developing projects. In addition, the advanced programmers of such projects usually design their own class or template to be used in the projects. The lowest precision obtained by *BinAuthor* is approximately 86% on all datasets together. We have observed that *BinAuthor* achieves lower precision when it is applied on Graduate student projects. When the number of authors is 400 on the mixed dataset, the precision of Rosenblum et al. and OBA2 approaches drop rapidly to 40% on all datasets, whereas our system's precision remains greater than 86% while Caliskan-Islam et al. approach remains greater than 73%. This provides evidence for the stability of using coding habits in identifying authors. In total, the different categories of choices achieve an average precision of 98% for ten distinct authors and 86% when discriminating among 800 authors. These results show that author habits may survive the compilation process.

Observations. Through our experiments, we have noticed the following observations:

(1) *Feature Pre-processing.* We have encountered that in the existing methods, the top-ranked features are related to the compiler (e.g., stack frame setup operation). It is thus necessary to filter irrelevant functions (e.g., compiler functions) in order to better identify author-related portions of code. To this end, we utilize a more elaborate method for filtration to eliminate the compiler effects and to label library, compiler, and open-source software related functions. Successful distinction between these functions leads to considerable time savings and helps shift the focus of analysis to more relevant functions.

(2) *Source of Features.* Existing methods use disassembler and decompilers to extract features from binaries. Caliskan-Islam et al. use a decompiler to translate the program into C-like pseudo code via Hex-Ray [6]. They pass the code to a fuzzy parser for C, thus obtain an abstract syntax tree from which features can be extracted. In addition to Hex-Ray limitations [6], the C-like pseudo code is different from the original code to the extent that the variables, branches, and keywords are different. For instance, we find that a function in the source code consists of the following keywords: (`1-do`, `1-switch`, `3-case`, `3-break`, `2-while`, `1-if`) and the number of variables is 2. Once we check the same function after decompiling its binary, we find that the function consists of the following keywords: (`1-do`, `1-else/if`, `2-goto`, `2-while`, `4-if`) and the number of variables is 4. This will evidently lead to misleading features, thus increasing the rate of false positives.

3.5   Scalability

Security analysts or reverse engineers may be interested in performing large-scale author identification, and in the case of malware, an analyst may deal with an extremely large number of new samples on a daily basis. With this in mind, we evaluate how well *BinAuthor* scales. To prepare the large dataset required for large-scale authorship attribution, we obtain programs from three sources: Google

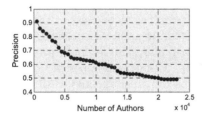

Fig. 3. Large-scale author attribution precision

Code Jam, GitHub, and Planet Source Code. We eliminate from the experiment programs that could not be compiled because they contain bugs and those written by authors who contributed only one or two programs. The resulting dataset comprised 103,800 programs by 23,000 authors: 60% from Google Code Jam, 25% from Planet source code, and 15% from GitHub. We modified the script[3] used in [19] to download all the code submitted to the Google Code Jam competition. The programs from the other two sources were downloaded manually. All the programs were compiled with the Visual Studio and GCC compilers, using the same settings as those in our previous investigations (Sect. 3). The experiment evaluate how well the top-weighted choices represent author habits.

The large-scale author identification results are shown in Fig. 3. Figure 3 shows the precision with which *BinAuthor* identifies the author, and its scaling behavior as the number of authors increases is satisfactory. Among almost 4000 authors, an author is identified with 72% precision. When the number of authors is doubled to 8000, the precision is close to 65%, and it remains nearly constant (49%) after the number of authors reaches 19,000. Additionally, we test *BinAuthor* on the programs obtained from each of the sources. The precision was high for samples from the GitHub dataset (88%) and also for samples from the Planet dataset (82%), however it was low for samples from Google Code Jam (51%). The results suggest that it is easier to perform attribution for authors who wrote code for difficult tasks than for those addressing easier tasks.

We have also investigated the impact of false positives (Appendix B), and impact of code transformation techniques (Appendix C).

3.6   Applying *BinAuthor* to Real Malware Binaries

The malware binary authorship attribution is very challenging due to the following main reason: the lack of ground truth concerning the attribution of authorship due to the nature of malware. Such limitation explains the fact that few research efforts have been seen on manual malware authorship attribution. In fact, to the best of our knowledge, *BinAuthor* is the first attempt to apply automated authorship attribution to real malware. We describe the application of *BinAuthor* to some well-known malware binaries. Details of malware dataset are shown in Table 5. Given a set of functions, *BinAuthor* clusters them based on the number of common choices.

A. Applying *BinAuthor* to Bunny and Babar: We apply *BinAuthor* to Bunny and Babar malware samples and cluster the functions based on the choices. *BinAuthor* is able to find the following coding habits automatically: the preference for using Visual Studio 2008 and the use of a common approach to managing functions (general choices); the use of one variable over a long chain (structural choice); the choice of methods for accessing freed memory, dynamically deallocating allocated resources, and reopening resources more than once in the same function (quality choices). As shown in Table 6, *BinAuthor* found functions common to Bunny and Babar that share the aforementioned coding habits:

---

[3] https://github.com/calaylin/CodeStylometry/tree/master.

Table 5. Characteristics of malware dataset

Malware	Packed	Obfuscated	Source code	Binary code	Type	# binary function	Source of sample
Zeus	✗	✗	✓	✓	PE	557	Our security lab
Citadel	✗	✗	✓	✓	PE	794	Our security lab
Flame	✗	✓	✗	✓	ELF	1434	Contagio [13]
Stuxnet	✗	✓	✗	✓	ELF	2154	Contagio [13]
Bunny	✓	✗	✗	✓	PE	854	VirusSign [14]
Babar	✓	✗	✗	✓	PE	1025	VirusSign [14]

494 functions share qualitative choices; 450 functions share embedded choices; 372 functions share general choices; and 127 functions share structural choices. Among these, *BinAuthor* found 340 functions that share 4 choices, 478 functions that share 3 choices, 150 functions that share 2 choices, and 290 functions that share 1 choice. Considering the 854 and 1025 functions in Bunny and Babar, respectively, *BinAuthor* found that 44% $((340 + 478)/(854 + 1025))$ are likely to have been written by a single author (same common choices), and 23% are likely to have been written by multiple authors (contradictive different choices inside the same function). No common choices were identified in the remaining 33%, likely because different segments or code lines within the same function were written by different authors, a common practice in writing complex software.

Table 6. Statistics of applying *BinAuthor* to malware binaries

Malware	Number of functions with common choices				Number of common functions with			
	General	Qualitative	Structural	Embedded	1 choice	2 choices	3 choices	4 choices
Bunny and Babar	372	494	127	450	290	150	478	340
Stuxnet and Flame	725	528	189	300	689	515	294	180
Zeus and Citadel	655	452	289	370	600	588	194	258

B. Applying *BinAuthor* to Stuxnet and Flame: *BinAuthor* found the following coding habits automatically: the use of global variables, Lua scripting language, a specific open-source package SQLite, and heap sort rather than other sorting methods (general choices); the choice of opening and terminating processes (qualitative choices); the presence of recursion patterns and the use of POSIX socket API rather than BSD socket API (structural choices); and the use of functions that are close in terms of the Mahalanobis distance, with distance close to 0.1. As shown in Table 6, *BinAuthor* identified functions common to Stuxnet and Flame that share the aforementioned coding habits. *BinAuthor* clustered the functions and found that 13% $((180 + 294)/(1434 + 2154))$ were written by one author, while 34% ((515 + 689)/(1434 + 2154)) were written by multiple authors. No common choices were found in the remaining 53% of the functions. The fact that these malware packages follow the same rules and set the same targets suggests that Stuxnet and Flame are written by an organization.

C. Applying *BinAuthor* to Zeus and Citadel: *BinAuthor* identified the following coding habits: the use of network resources rather than file resources, creating configurations using mostly config files, the use of specific packages such as webph and ultraVNC (general choices); the use of switch statements rather than if statements (structural choices); the use of semaphores and locks (qualitative choices); and the presence of functions that are close in terms of the Mahalanobis distance, with distance = 0.0004 (embedded choices). As listed in Table 6, *BinAuthor* found functions common to Zeus and Citadel that share the aforementioned coding habits. After *BinAuthor* clustered the functions, it appears that 33% were written by a single author, while 53% were written by the same team of multiple authors. No common choices were found for the remaining 14% of the functions. Our findings clearly support the common belief that Zeus and Citadel were written by the same team of authors.

D. Comparison with Technical Reports: We compare *BinAuthor*'s findings with those made by human experts in technical reports.

- For Bunny and Babar, our results match the technical report published by the Citizen Lab [5], which demonstrates that both malware packages were written by a set of authors according to common implementation traits (general and qualitative choices) and infrastructure usage (general choices). The correspondence between the *BinAuthor* findings and those in the technical report is the following: 60% of the choices matched those mentioned in the report, and 40% did not; 10% of the choices found in the technical report were not flagged by *BinAuthor* as they require dynamic extraction of features, while *BinAuthor* uses a static process.
- For Stuxnet and Flame, our results corroborate the technical report published by Kaspersky [12], which shows that both malware packages use similar infrastructure (e.g., Lua) and are associated with an organization. In addition, *BinAuthor*'s findings suggest that both malware packages originated from the same organization. The frequent use of particular qualitative choices, such as the way the code is secured, indicates the use of certain programming standards and strict adherence to the same rules. Moreover, *BinAuthor*'s findings provide much more information concerning the authorship of these malware packages. The correspondence between *BinAuthor*'s findings and those in the technical report is as follows: all the choices found in the report [12] were found by *BinAuthor*, but they represent only 10% of our findings. The remaining 90% of *BinAuthor*'s findings were not flagged by the report.
- For Zeus and Citadel, our results match the findings of the technical report published by McAfee [3], indicating that Zeus and Citadel were written by the same team of authors. The correspondence between the findings of *BinAuthor* and those of McAfee are as follows: 45% of the choices matched

those in the report, while 55% did not, and 8% of the technical report findings were not flagged by *BinAuthor*.

4   Related Work

Binary Authorship Attribution: Binary code has drawn significantly less attention with respect to authorship attribution. This is mainly due to the fact that many salient features that may identify an author's style are lost during the compilation process. In [15,19,32], the authors show that certain stylistic features can indeed survive the compilation process and remain intact in binary code, thus showing that authorship attribution for binary code should be feasible. The methodology developed by Rosenblum et al. [32] is the first attempt to automatically identify authors of software binaries. The main concept employed by this method is to extract syntax-based features using predefined templates such as idioms, n-grams, and graphlets. A subsequent approach (OBA2) to automatically identify the authorship of software binaries is proposed by Alrabaee et al. [15]. The main concept employed by this method is to extract a sequence of instructions with specific semantics and to construct a graph based on register manipulation. A more recent approach to automatically identify the authorship of software binaries is proposed by Caliskan-Islam et al. [19]. The authors extract syntactical features present in source code from decompiled executable binaries. Most recently, Meng et al. [27] introduce new fine-grained techniques to address the problem of identifying the multiple authors of binary code by determining the author of each basic block. The authors extract syntactic and semantic features at a basic level, such as constant values in instructions, backward slices of variables, and width and depth of a function control flow graph (CFG). Table 7 compares our approach with the aforesaid approaches. Please note that the results of code transformation (CT) section are based on conducted experiment. When we found the accuracy is dropped by 1–3%, we considered as "Not affected", while 4–14% gives "Partially affected", and finally if it was above 15%, we considered as "Affected".

Malware Authorship Attribution: Most existing work on malware authorship attribution relies on manual analysis. In 2013, a technical report published by FireEye [28] discovered that malware binaries share the same digital infrastructure and code, such as the use of certificates, executable resources, and development tools. More recently, the team at Citizen Lab attributed malware authors according to the manual analysis exploit type found in binaries and the manner by which actions are performed, such as connecting to a command and control server. The authors in [5] presented a novel approach to creating credible links between binaries originating from the same group of authors. Their goal aimed to add transparency in attribution and to supply analysts with a tool that emphasizes or denies vendor statements. The technique is based on features derived from different domains, such as implementation details, applied evasion techniques, classical malware traits, or infrastructure attributes, which are leveraged to compare the handwriting among binaries.

Table 7. Comparing different existing solutions with *BinAuthor*.

Effort	Features				Compiler				CT				Binaries	
	Syntax	Semantic	Structural	Statistical	VS	GCC	Clang	ICC	DCI	IR	IRO	RT	ELF	PE
OBA2	✗	✓	✗	✗	✓	✗	✗	✗	◑	◑	○	●	✗	✓
Caliskan	✗	✓	✓	✓	✗	✓	✗	✗	○	○	○	●	✓	✗
Rosenblum	✓	✓	✓	✗	✗	✓	✗	✗	●	●	●	○	✓	✗
Meng	✗	✓	✓	✓	✗	✓	✗	✗	◑	◑	◑	○	✓	✓
BinAuthor	✓	✓	✓	✓	✓	✓	✓	✓	○	○	○	○	✓	✓

Note: The (✓) symbol indicates that the proposal solution offers the corresponding feature. (CT) stands for code transformation. (DCI) stands for dead code insertion. (IR) stands for instruction replacement. (IRO) stands for instruction reordering. (RT) stands for refactoring techniques. (○): Not affected by the code transformation method. (●): Affected by the code transformation method. (◑): Partially affected by the code transformation method.

5 Limitations

Our work has a few important limitations.

Advanced Obfuscation: Our tool fails to handle most of the advanced obfuscation techniques, such as virtualization and jitting, since our system does not deal with bytecode.

IR: Through our experiments, we notice that optimizing IR would remove some author styles, e.g., loop deletion. We left this issue for future work by leveraging some existing work [34].

Functionality: There are some choices appear when an author implements a specific functionality. For instance, if the functionality does not have a multiple-branch logic, there is no choice between `if` and `switch`.

6 Conclusion

To conclude, we have presented the first known effort on decoupling coding habits from functionality. Previous research has applied machine learning techniques to extract stylometry styles and can distinguish between 5–50 authors, whereas we can handle up to 150 authors. In addition, existing works have only employed artificial datasets, whereas we included more realistic datasets. Our findings indicated that the precision of these techniques drops dramatically to approximately 45% at a scale of more than 50 authors. We also applied our system to known malware samples (e.g., `Zeus and Citadel`) as a case study. We realized that authors with advanced expertise are easier to attribute than authors who have less expertise. Authors of realistic datasets are easier to attribute than authors of artificial datasets. Specifically, in the GitHub dataset, the authors of a sample can be identified with greater than 90% precision. In summary, our system demonstrates superior results on more realistic datasets.

Acknowledgements. The authors thank the anonymous reviewers for their valuable comments. We also appreciate the help we received from Perry Jones in implementing *BinAuthor*. This research is the result of a fruitful collaboration between the Security Research Center (SRC) of Concordia University, Defence Research and Development Canada (DRDC) and Google under a National Defence/NSERC Research Program.

Appendix

A   Example of Qualitative Choices

Consider a template of dynamic memory allocation presented in Listing 1.1. As shown in, we have a call to `malloc`, followed by checking whether or not it is Null.

Listing 1.1. A fragment of assembly instruction that captures a bad habit of dynamic memory allocation

```
...
call ds:malloc
...
or eax, 0FFFFFFFF  // -1 if text_buffer is Null
...
xor eax, eax // 0 if text_buffer is not Null
```

The Listing 1.2 shows how the bad habit in Listing 1.1 could be considered as a good habit at the assembly level.

Listing 1.2. A fragment of assembly instruction that captures a good habit of dynamic memory allocation

```
...
call ds:malloc
...
or eax, 0FFFFFFFF  // -1 if text_buffer is Null
...
push eax      // memory address of text_buffer
call ds:free
...
xor eax, eax // 0 if text_buffer is not Null
```

B   False Positives

We investigate the false positives in order to understand the situations where *BinAuthor* is likely to make incorrect attribution decisions. For this experiment, we consider 5 programs for each author. For instance, when we have 500 authors ($5 * 500 = 2500$ programs), *BinAuthor* misclassifies 49 programs. Also, when the number of authors is 2000 ($2000 * 4 = 8000$ programs), the number of false positives is 336. We have 2000 authors from dataset used in Sect. 3.2. After investigation, we have found that the false positives rate for student dataset is the highest rate and we believe the reason behind this is that the students should follow the standard coding instructions which restrict them to have their own habits.

C   Impact of Code Transformation Techniques

Refactoring Techniques. We consider a random set of 50 files from our dataset which we use for the C++ refactoring process [10, 11]. We ignore the variable renaming since it will have no effect in binary code, we consider the following techniques of, (i) moving a method from a superclass to its subclasses, and (ii) extracting a few statements and placing them into a new method. We obtain a Precision of 91.5% in correctly classifying authors, which is only a mild drop in comparison to the 95% precision observed without applying refactoring techniques.

Impact of Obfuscation. We are interested in determining how *BinAuthor* handles simple binary obfuscation techniques intended for evading detection, as implemented by tools such as Obfuscator-LLVM [22]. These obfuscators replace instructions by other semantically equivalent instructions, introduce spurious control flow, and can even completely flatten control flow graphs. Obfuscation techniques implemented by Obfuscator-LLVM are applied to the samples prior to classifying the authors. We proceed to extract features from obfuscated samples. We obtain a precision of 92.9% in correctly classifying authors, which is only a slight drop in comparison to the 95% precision observed without obfuscation.

Impact of Compilers and Compilation Settings. We are further interested to study the impact of different compilers and compilation settings on the precision of our proposed system. We perform the following tasks: (i) testing the ability of *BinAuthor* when identifying the author from binaries compiled with the same compiler, but different compiler optimization levels. Specifically, we use binaries that were compiled with GCC/VS on x86 architecture using optimization levels O2 and O3. In this test, the precision remains same (95%). (ii) We use a different configuration to identify the author of program compiled with both a different compiler and different compiler optimization levels. Specifically, we use programs compiled for x86 with VS -O2 and GCC -O3. In this test, the precision slightly drops to 93.9%. We also redo the test for the same binaries compiled with ICC and Clang compilers. The precision remains almost the same 93.8%. This stability in the accuracy is due to the canonicalization process.

References

1. The Google Code Jam (2008–2015). http://code.google.com/codejam/
2. GitHub-Build software better (2011). https://github.com/trending?l=cpp
3. Technical report: McAfee (2011). www.mcafee.com/ca/resources/wp-citadel-trojan-summary.pdf

4. The materials supplement for the paper. Who Wrote This Code? Identifying the Authors of Program Binaries (2011). http://pages.cs.wisc.edu/~nater/esorics-supp/
5. Big Game Hunting: Nation-state malware research, BlackHat (2015). https://www.blackhat.com/docs/us-15/materials/us-15-MarquisBoire-Big-Game-Hunting-The-Peculiarities-Of-Nation-State-Malware-Research.pdf
6. Hex-Ray decompiler (2015). https://www.hex-rays.com/products/decompiler/
7. Programmer De-anonymization from Binary Executables (2015). https://github.com/calaylin/bda
8. The Gephi plugin for neo4j (2015). https://marketplace.gephi.org/plugin/neo4j-graph-database-support/
9. The planet source code (2015). http://www.planet-source-code.com/vb/default.asp?lngWId=3#ContentWinners
10. C++ refactoring tools for visual studio (2016). http://www.wholetomato.com/
11. Refactoring tool (2016). https://www.devexpress.com/Products/CodeRush/
12. Technical report, Resource 207: Kaspersky Lab Research proves that Stuxnet and Flame developers are connected, May 2012. http://www.kaspersky.com/about/news/virus/2012/
13. Contagio: malware dump, May 2016. http://contagiodump.blogspot.ca
14. VirusSign: Malware Research & Data Center, Virus Free, May 2016. http://www.virussign.com/
15. Alrabaee, S., Saleem, N., Preda, S., Wang, L., Debbabi, M.: OBA2: an onion approach to binary code authorship attribution. Digit. Investig. **11**, S94–S103 (2014)
16. Alrabaee, S., Shirani, P., Debbabi, M., Wang, L.: On the feasibility of malware authorship attribution. In: Cuppens, F., Wang, L., Cuppens-Boulahia, N., Tawbi, N., Garcia-Alfaro, J. (eds.) FPS 2016. LNCS, vol. 10128, pp. 256–272. Springer, Cham (2017). https://doi.org/10.1007/978-3-319-51966-1_17
17. Alrabaee, S., Shirani, P., Wang, L., Debbabi, M.: SIGMA: a semantic integrated graph matching approach for identifying reused functions in binary code. Digit. Investig. **12**, S61–S71 (2015)
18. Alrabaee, S., Shirani, P., Wang, L., Debbabi, M.: FOSSIL: a resilient and efficient system for identifying FOSS functions in malware binaries. ACM Trans. Priv. Secur. (TOPS) **21**(2), 8 (2018)
19. Caliskan-Islam, A., et al.: When coding style survives compilation: de-anonymizing programmers from executable binaries. Netw. Distrib. Syst. Secur. Symp. (NDSS) (2018)
20. Cilibrasi, R., Vitanyi, P.: Clustering by compression. IEEE Trans. Inf. Theory **51**(4), 1523–1545 (2005)
21. David, Y., Partush, N., Yahav, E.: Similarity of binaries through re-optimization. In: Proceedings of the 38th ACM SIGPLAN Conference on Programming Language Design and Implementation, pp. 79–94. ACM (2017)
22. Junod, P., Rinaldini, J., Wehrli, J., Michielin, J.: Obfuscator-LLVM: software protection for the masses. In: Proceedings of the 1st International Workshop on Software Protection, pp. 3–9. IEEE Press (2015)
23. Junttila, T.A., Kaski, P.: Engineering an efficient canonical labeling tool for large and sparse graphs. In: ALENEX, vol. 7, pp. 135–149. SIAM (2007)
24. Knuth, D.E.: Backus normal form vs. Backus Naur form. Commun. ACM **7**(12), 735–736 (1964)
25. Krsul, I., Spafford, E.H.: Authorship analysis: identifying the author of a program. Comput. Secur. **16**(3), 233–257 (1997)

26. Mahalanobis, P.C.: On the generalized distance in statistics. Proc. Natl. Inst. Sci. (Calcutta) **2**, 49–55 (1936)
27. Meng, X., Miller, B.P., Jun, K.-S.: Identifying multiple authors in a binary program. In: Foley, S.N., Gollmann, D., Snekkenes, E. (eds.) ESORICS 2017. LNCS, vol. 10493, pp. 286–304. Springer, Cham (2017). https://doi.org/10.1007/978-3-319-66399-9_16
28. Moran, N., Bennett, J.: Supply Chain Analysis: From Quartermaster to Sunshop, vol. 11. FireEye Labs, Milpitas (2013)
29. Nethercote, N., Seward, J.: Valgrind: a framework for heavyweight dynamic binary instrumentation. In: ACM SIGPLAN Notices, vol. 42, pp. 89–100. ACM (2007)
30. Palmer, G., et al.: A road map for digital forensic research. In: First Digital Forensic Research Workshop, Utica, New York, pp. 27–30 (2001)
31. Rajlich, V.: Software evolution and maintenance. In: Proceedings of the Future of Software Engineering, pp. 133–144. ACM (2014)
32. Rosenblum, N., Zhu, X., Miller, B.P.: Who wrote this code? Identifying the authors of program binaries. In: Atluri, V., Diaz, C. (eds.) ESORICS 2011. LNCS, vol. 6879, pp. 172–189. Springer, Heidelberg (2011). https://doi.org/10.1007/978-3-642-23822-2_10
33. Schleimer, S., Wilkerson, D.S., Aiken, A.: Winnowing: local algorithms for document fingerprinting. In: Proceedings of the 2003 ACM SIGMOD International Conference on Management of Data, pp. 76–85. ACM (2003)
34. Shirani, P., et al.: **BINARM**: scalable and efficient detection of vulnerabilities in firmware images of intelligent electronic devices. In: Giuffrida, C., Bardin, S., Blanc, G. (eds.) DIMVA 2018. LNCS, vol. 10885, pp. 114–138. Springer, Cham (2018). https://doi.org/10.1007/978-3-319-93411-2_6
35. Shirani, P., Wang, L., Debbabi, M.: BinShape: scalable and robust binary library function identification using function shape. In: Polychronakis, M., Meier, M. (eds.) DIMVA 2017. LNCS, vol. 10327, pp. 301–324. Springer, Cham (2017). https://doi.org/10.1007/978-3-319-60876-1_14
36. Shoshitaishvili, Y., et al.: SOK: (state of) the art of war: offensive techniques in binary analysis. In: 2016 IEEE Symposium on Security and Privacy, SP, pp. 138–157. IEEE (2016)
37. Spafford, E.H., Weeber, S.A.: Software forensics: can we track code to its authors? Comput. Secur. **12**(6), 585–595 (1993)
38. Tristan, J.-B., Govereau, P., Morrisett, G.: Evaluating value-graph translation validation for LLVM. ACM SIGPLAN Not. **46**(6), 295–305 (2011)
39. Wang, J.T.-L., Ma, Q., Shasha, D., Wu, C.H.: New techniques for extracting features from protein sequences. IBM Syst. J. **40**(2), 426–441 (2001)
40. Yujian, L., Bo, L.: A normalized Levenshtein distance metric. IEEE Trans. Pattern Anal. Mach. Intell. **29**(6), 1091–1095 (2007)

Synthesis of a Permissive Security Monitor

Narges Khakpour$^{(\boxtimes)}$ and Charilaos Skandylas

Linnaeus University, Växjö, Sweden
narges.khakpour@lnu.se

Abstract. In this paper, we propose a new sound method to synthesize a permissive monitor using boolean supervisory controller synthesis that observes a Java program at certain checkpoints, predicts information flow violations and applies suitable countermeasures to prevent violations. To improve the permissiveness, we train the monitor and remove false positives by executing the program along with its executable model. If a security violation is detected, the user can define sound countermeasures, including declassification to apply in the checkpoints. We implement a tool that automates the whole process and generates a monitor. We evaluate our method by applying it on the Droidbench benchmark and one real-life Android application.

1 Introduction

Confidentiality of secret information manipulated by a program is usually formalized as a noninterference baseline policy [13], which demands that low-sensitive outputs should not be influenced by high-sensitive inputs. Several methods and tools (e.g., JFlow JIF [19], Caml-based FlowCaml [25]) have been developed in the last decades to analyze or enforce confidentiality. Information flow monitors are a technique to enforce noninterference dynamically [4,7,11,14,15,22]. The idea is to monitor the executions of a program at runtime and control its compliance to security policies. As dynamic monitors only decide about the current execution, for which more information is available at runtime, they enable us to do a more precise analysis, and are usually more permissive compared to static methods [18], e.g. [21] proved that dynamic monitors are more permissive in the flow-insensitive case, where variables are assigned the security levels at the beginning of the execution and the security levels don't change during the execution. Hybrid monitors [14,20,24] are a class of dynamic monitors that combine static and dynamic analysis.

Consider the following program where h is secret and the rest of variables and objects are public:

```
obj1.x=h;
if(a>0)
   while(b>0){obj1.x=0;b=b-1;}
else  obj1.x=1;
 f(1); l=obj1.x; obj2.att=l; print(obj2);
```

© Springer Nature Switzerland AG 2018
J. Lopez et al. (Eds.): ESORICS 2018, LNCS 11098, pp. 48–65, 2018.
https://doi.org/10.1007/978-3-319-99073-6_3

If $a > 0 \land b \leq 0$ holds, then the value of h will flow to l through obj1.x and the program is insecure, otherwise the program is secure. Security type systems, one of the main techniques for static analysis, reject this program completely, while dynamic monitors allow the secure executions, i.e., if $a > 0 \land b \leq 0$ does not hold, the program is secure and executes normally, otherwise, the program is permitted to run and a certain strategy is designed to protect the system. The existing strategies either (a) manipulate the attacker's observation as soon as a violation is detected, i.e. at the observation point (e.g. print(obj2) in the above example) [14,20], (b) run several instances of the program simultaneously with various inputs to ensure that the program does not reach an insecure state [5,11], or (c) control assignment of low sensitive data in high contexts (i.e. a branch on high sensitive data) [4,26]. The approaches in category (b) are expensive and have a huge overhead, due to running several instances of the program simultaneously [12]. The methods in the categories (a) and (c) detect security violations one-step before their occurrence [20], and as a result, it becomes complicated and expensive, if possible at all, to apply a proper countermeasure to avoid information leakage.

In the above example, if executing f(1) results in modifying the database or sending data over a network and we detect the violation immediately before print(obj2), then a suitable countermeasure to fix the violation might require us to recover the system to a state where a proper countermeasure can be applied, which is difficult, if possible at all. On the other hand if we know that the condition $a > 0 \land b \leq 0$ leads to a violation before executing the program, then we are able to apply a countermeasure before f(1).

Although, dynamic monitors are usually more permissive than static methods, they still can produce false positives and are not always the most permissive monitor. Hence, it is crucial to construct sound dynamic and hybrid monitors that allow as many paths as possible. *In addition, to the best of our knowledge, there is no dynamic monitor that can predict confidentiality violations at runtime before the violation points and allows applying user-defined countermeasures, in particular declassification, to avoid security violations.*

To tackle the above challenges, we propose a new approach based on boolean supervisory controller synthesis [6] to synthesize a hybrid monitor that monitors a program written in a subset of Java at certain checkpoints, predicts security violations and applies suitable countermeasures in checkpoints to avoid future leakages. Given a program, a set of checkpoints from where the program can be observed by the monitor, a set of observation points where the attacker can observe the application in (See Fig. 2), we use the controller synthesis method proposed in [6] to synthesize a set of security guards for the checkpoints that guarantee no information leakage in future, up to the next checkpoint.

To improve the permissiveness of the monitor, we construct an executable model of the monitored program that contains only observation points and checkpoints. In the training phase, we run the program along with its executable model to train the monitor and improve its permissiveness; if a violation is predicted at runtime in a checkpoint, we execute the program model to check whether the security guard of the current checkpoint is restrictive or not. If it is restrictive, we learn and relax the security guard to allow the current (symbolic) execution path in future. After the monitor training, we construct a more lightweight monitor that controls and predicts information flow using the learnt security guards in the checkpoints to protect the program.

Furthermore, we design a set of secure countermeasures to be applied in the checkpoints in case of security violations that prevent the program from reaching an insecure state. A user-defined countermeasure can be applied at runtime, provided that it satisfies certain conditions. One of the main countermeasures that can be applied is to declassify information, i.e. degrade the security level of variables. In [16], we proved that the method is sound and enforces localized delimited release [2]. If the monitor does not perform any declassification, it enforces termination-insensitive noninterference. Furthermore, we implement a tool-set to support our method and conduct some experiments to evaluate the method. Our contributions are the following:

- *Permissive Sound Monitor.* We propose a new approach using boolean controller synthesis to efficiently construct a hybrid flow-sensitive security monitor that predicts *future* information flow at a few *predefined checkpoints* in a Java program. To improve the monitor permissiveness, we train the monitor in a testing environment and eliminate false positives as far as possible.
- *Supporting User-Defined Countermeasures.* In contrast to the existing dynamic monitors that apply a few fixed countermeasures, detecting a violation multiple steps ahead of its occurrence enables the user to design and apply various countermeasures in the checkpoints, provided that they introduce no information leakage. Our method is the first method that allows dynamic correct-by-construction information disclosure, even though the declassification policies are simple. While existing approaches enforce a variation of noninterference, our method guarantees localized delimited release, and enforces termination-insensitive noninterference in case of no information release.
- *Tool Support.* Our method is supported by a tool-set to control information flow in programs written in a sub-language of Java. We also conducted experiments to evaluate the effectiveness of the method.

This paper is organized as follows. We briefly introduce the controller synthesis problem in Sect. 2, and give an overview of the approach in Sect. 3. Section 4 presents the program syntax, the security control flow model and the program executable model. We introduce our monitor construction approach in Sect. 5. In Sect. 6, we present the toolset and evaluate the approach. In Sect. 7, we discuss related work and Sect. 8 concludes the paper.

2   Preliminaries

In this section, we briefly review the symbolic supervisory controller synthesis method proposed in [6], the goal of which is to construct a controller to control a system behavior, so that the bad states are avoided. In this method, the system behavior is represented by a symbolic control flow graph. Let $V = \langle v_1, \ldots, v_n \rangle$ be a tuple of variables, $\mathcal{D}_{v_i}$ be the (infinite) domain of a variable v_i, and $\mathcal{D}_V = \prod_{i \in [1,n]} \mathcal{D}_{v_i}$. A *valuation* $\boldsymbol{\nu}$ of V is a tuple $\langle \boldsymbol{\nu}_1, \ldots, \boldsymbol{\nu}_n \rangle \in \mathcal{D}_V$, and we show the value of v_i in $\boldsymbol{\nu}$ by $\boldsymbol{\nu}(v_i)$, $1 \leq i \leq n$. A *predicate* P over a tuple V is defined as a subset $P \subseteq \mathcal{D}_V$ (a state set for which the predicate holds). We show the union of two vectors V_1 and V_2 by $V_1 \uplus V_2$.

Definition 1 (Symbolic Control Flow Graphs). *A symbolic control flow graph (SCFG) is a tuple* $\mathcal{G} = \langle L, V, I, l_0, v_0, \Delta \rangle$ *where* L *is a finite non-empty set of locations,* $V = \langle v_1, \ldots, v_n \rangle$ *is a tuple of variables,* I *is a vector of inputs,* l_0 *is the initial location,* $v_0 \in \mathcal{D}_V$ *shows the initial valuation of the variables, and* Δ *is a finite set of symbolic transitions* $\delta = \langle G_\delta, A_\delta \rangle$ *where* $G_\delta \subseteq \mathcal{D}_{V \uplus I}$ *is a predicate on* $V \uplus I$, *which guards the transition, and* $A_\delta : \mathcal{D}_V \mapsto \mathcal{D}_{V \uplus I}$ *is the update function of* δ, *defined as a set of assignments.*

Initially, $\mathcal{G}$ is in its initial state. A transition can only be fired if its guard is satisfied and when fired, the variables are updated according to its update function. Let l and l' be two locations. We use the notation $l \xrightarrow{\langle G_\delta, A_\delta \rangle} l'$ to represent a symbolic transition $\langle G_\delta, A_\delta \rangle$ with the source l and target l'. The semantics of a SCFG $\mathcal{G}$ is defined in terms of a deterministic finite state machine.

In this method, the inputs are partitioned into two sets of *controllable* and *uncontrollable* inputs: an input is uncontrollable if it can not be prevented from occurring in a system, while controllable inputs are issued by the controller to control the system behaviour. Let $\psi : L \to \mathcal{D}_V$ be the invariants defined for the locations (i.e. an invariant $\psi(l)$ is a condition on the valuation of variables that must always hold when the system enters the location l), and $I_c \subseteq I$ be the set of controllable inputs. Given an invariant ψ and a SCFG $\mathcal{G}$, a controller $\mathcal{C} : L \to \mathcal{D}_{V \uplus I_c}$ is synthesized to observe the system and allow or prohibit the controllable inputs, so that the system $\mathcal{G}$ avoids entering a bad state, i.e. a state that does not satisfy its invariant.

3   The Method Overview

Figure 1 shows an overview of our method. The Java program is annotated with checkpoints, observations points (can be avoided), initial security labels and entry points (See Fig. 2 and Sect. 4). A checkpoint is essentially a method call in which we monitor the program, and can apply a countermeasure if needed. The checkpoints are not permitted to exist under branch statements. An observation point is a point that leads to an observation by the attacker, that is either a method call or the exit point of a branch of a conditional/loop whose other branch contains a method call observation point. We construct a boolean symbolic control flow graph that describes the program control flow enriched with security typing information (See Sect. 4) which is fed to the Reax controller synthesis tool [6]. For each checkpoint, the tool generates the abstract security guards in terms of program paths and security types that in principle show the

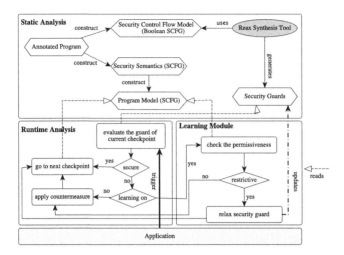

Fig. 1. The method overview

paths that do not lead to insecure states (See Sect. 5). We also express the (security) semantics of the program in terms of a symbolic control flow graph that includes both the program behaviour and the security typing information. Given the security semantics, we construct a model called program model that includes only observation points in addition to checkpoints (See Sect. 4). We propose a framework to construct a secure monitor in Sect. 5 that applies the countermeasures either in the checkpoints and/or in the observation points, depending on the user preferences.

The program is observed by the monitor in the checkpoints (e.g. the `run` method in Fig. 2) at runtime. The monitor checks the security guards of the current checkpoint to determine whether the program will reach an insecure state (e.g. in the `println` method in Fig. 2) or not. If not, the program will continue its execution. Otherwise, if the learning feature is enabled (e.g. in the training phase), the monitor executes its program model using a model execution engine to ensure that the generated security guard is not restrictive. If the generated security guard of the current checkpoint is restrictive, it is relaxed to allow this secure path henceforth, i.e. the security guards are learned and improved over time. Afterwards, the program continues its execution by applying a countermeasure. This monitor will be the most permissive monitor, if we train it sufficiently, as it will never block a secure path.

4 Security Control Flow Model

We consider a sub-language of Java whose simplified syntax of statements is shown in Fig. 3, that includes loop statements, conditional statements, assignments, a return command, constructors and method calls. In this figure, v is a variable of primitive type, e is an expression, stm is a statement, o is an

```
/* @EntryPoint */
/* @CheckPoint */
public void run(/*@SecurityInit(securityLevel="H", policyType="IC")*/
        int ah, int ad){ int ares = 0; Class1 object1 = new Class1(ad);
    int aw = object1.attr + 3;
    while (0 < aw) {
        ares = object1.attr + 10;
        object1.attr = ah + 1;
        ah = ares - 1;
        aw = aw - 3;}
    object1.attr = object1.attr * ad;
    /* @ObservationPoint (default="System.out.println(3000)")*/
    System.out.println(/* @SecurityPolicy(securityLevel="L", policyType="IC")
    */object1.attr);
}
```

Fig. 2. Java code snippet

object, $stms$ is a sequence of statements, $o.m(\overrightarrow{e})$ is a method call with arguments $\overrightarrow{e} = e_1 \dots e_m$, and $\sqrt{}$ shows an empty sequence of statements. The statements in a bracket are optional and ϵ shows no argument.

We follow a type-based flow-sensitive method and assign a security type to each variable, i.e. the security type of a variable may change during the program execution. A variable is either a primitive variable or an instance variable of a user-defined type. We consider a two-level security lattice $\langle \mathcal{L}, \sqsubseteq, \sqcup \rangle$ where $\mathcal{L} = \{H, L\}$ is the set of security types, $\sqsubseteq$ is a partial order defined over $\mathcal{L}$ and $\sqcup$ is an operator that gives the least upper bound of two elements in $\mathcal{L}$ (i.e. disjunction). The function $var(e)$ returns the variables that appear in the expression e, and if e is an object, it returns the object itself along with all its accessible attributes (i.e. its own attributes, the attributes of its attributes, etc). The notation $\bar{e}$ represents the security type of an expression e, defined as $\underset{v \in var(e)}{\sqcup} \bar{v}$, i.e. the security type of an instance variable is defined based on the security types of all its attributes.

We define an abstract security semantics for our language in terms of boolean symbolic control flow graphs partially shown in Fig. 4. We abstract away the program variables in this semantics and only consider the program control flow in addition to the variables' security types. We assign a unique abstract boolean variable called *a branch variable* to each branch that denotes if that branch is enabled or not. A loop body might change the loop guard, and subsequently, the value of its branch variable might change in each iteration. Since, we don't model the program variables and consequently the loop body behaviour, we consider an uncontrollable boolean input called *uncontrollable loop guard* for each loop and each of its internal branches that non-deterministically takes a boolean value in each state and is assigned to the corresponding branch variable after execution of the loop body.

Let $\mathcal{G} = \langle L, V, I, l_o, v_0, \Delta \rangle$ represent a SCFG that shows the security semantics of a program where Δ is defined using the rules in Fig. 4. The locations L are the set of configurations where a configuration is defined as a stack $\sigma_0 : \dots : \sigma_n$ of currently active contexts. A context σ_k, $0 \le k \le n$ shows the statements of a method body that remain to be executed or a block of instructions (e.g. loop body), and pc_{σ_k} shows the security type of the context σ_k. The state variables V include the branch variables, the security types assigned to the program variables

$$c \quad ::= o \mid \mathbf{new} \ m(\overrightarrow{e}) \mid o.m(\overrightarrow{e})$$
$$stm ::= v = e \mid o = c \mid o.m(\overrightarrow{e}) \mid \mathbf{if} \ (e) \ stms \ [\mathbf{else} \ stms \ ] \mid \mathbf{while} \ (e) \ stms \mid \mathbf{return} \ [e] \mid \surd$$
$$stms ::= stm; \ stms \mid stm;$$

Fig. 3. The statements syntax

and the set of variables representing whether two instance variables point to the same object or not. The uncontrollable inputs of I include the uncontrollable loop guards and τ that is a boolean variable associated with the non-checkpoint transitions, and its controllable inputs are boolean inputs associated with each checkpoint transition.

The rule ASSIGNL defines the semantics of a variable of primitive type where e is a method call free expression. The security type of v is modified to the upper bound of e's security level $(\bar{e})$ and the security level of current context pc_{σ_n}. To handle object aliasing in our pure boolean SCFG, for each two arbitrary object instance variables of the same type, we consider a boolean variable called *points-to variable* to indicate whether they point to the same object or not. The function alias returns a boolean variable to show if two instance variables are in aliasing relation or not, where for all o, o', $\mathsf{alias}(o, o') = \mathsf{alias}(o', o)$. When an instance variable is updated, the points-to variables in addition to the security types of the associated instance variables are updated. The rule ASSIGNO defines the semantics of an assignment where the assignee is not an attribute instance variable. This rule relates the assignee to the assigner and all the instance variables related to the assigner (i.e. UpdatePointsToVars sets their corresponding points-to variables), and changes the type of assignee to the upper bound of the assigner's type and pc_{σ_n}. It will update the security types of the attributes of instance variables newly related to the assigner (UpdateAttributesLabels) (more details in [16]).

The rule COND defines the semantics of conditional statements, and the rule WHILE1 defines the semantics of loops. In these rules, the function $mc(stms)$ shows the variables that might be modified by $stms$ and basically returns all left-hand side variables of the assignments in $stms$, and $[stms]$ indicates that the code $stms$ is executing under a branch. When the program enters a branch, a new context σ_{n+1} is created whose security type is defined as the upper bound of the current context security label (pc_{σ_n}) and the security label of e. In addition, the security labels of all variables of the unexecuted branch in the new context are updated in order to detect indirect implicit flows. The function $\chi(\sigma_0 : \ldots : \sigma_n)$ returns two unique branch variables, assigned to each branch from a configuration $\sigma_0 : \ldots : \sigma_n$. When a program exits a branch or finishes the execution of the loop body, the latest context is removed (the rule EXIT and the rule WHILE2). In addition, the branch variables of a loop body $(bv(c))$ are updated to their corresponding uncontrollable loop guard variables (LoopGuard the rule WHILE2).

$$\text{ASSIGNL}\frac{U = \{\bar{v} = \bar{e} \sqcup \text{pc}_{\sigma_n}\}}{\langle \sigma_0 : \ldots : \sigma_n = \{v = e;\}\rangle \xrightarrow{\mathsf{T},U} \langle \sigma_0 : \ldots : \sigma_n = \{\sqrt{}\}\rangle}$$

$$\text{ASSIGNO}\frac{\neg\text{Attribute}(o),\ U = \{\bar{o} = \bar{o}' \sqcup \text{pc}_{\sigma_n}, \text{alias}(o, o') = \mathsf{T}\} \cup \text{UpdatePointsToVars}(o, o') \cup \text{UpdateAttributesLabels}(o, o')}{\langle \sigma_0 : \ldots : \sigma_n = \{o = o';\}\rangle \xrightarrow{\mathsf{T},U} \langle \sigma_0 : \ldots : \sigma_n = \{\sqrt{}\}\rangle}$$

$$\text{COND}\frac{\begin{array}{l} U_1 := \{\text{pc}_{\{[c_1]\}} = \bar{e} \sqcup \text{pc}_{\sigma_n}\} \cup \bigcup_{x \in mc(c_2)} \bar{x} = \bar{x} \sqcup \text{pc}_{\sigma_n}, \\ U_2 := \{\text{pc}_{\{[c_2]\}} = \bar{e} \sqcup \text{pc}_{\sigma_n}\} \cup \bigcup_{x \in mc(c_1)} \bar{x} = \bar{x} \sqcup \text{pc}_{\sigma_n},\ (\phi_1, \phi_2) = \chi(\sigma_0 : \ldots : \sigma_n) \end{array}}{\begin{array}{l} \langle \sigma_0 : \ldots : \sigma_n = \{\mathbf{if}\ (e)\ c_1\ \mathbf{else}\ c_2\}\rangle \xrightarrow{\phi_1, U_1} \langle \sigma_0 : \ldots : \{\sqrt{}\} : \{[c_1]\}\rangle \\ \langle \sigma_0 : \ldots : \sigma_n = \{\mathbf{if}\ (e)\ c_1\ \mathbf{else}\ c_2\}\rangle \xrightarrow{\phi_2, U_2} \langle \sigma_0 : \ldots : \{\sqrt{}\} : \{[c_2]\}\rangle \end{array}}$$

$$\text{WHILE1}\frac{U_1 := \{\text{pc}_{\sigma_{n+1}} = \bar{e} \sqcup \text{pc}_{\sigma_n}\},\ U_2 := \bigcup_{x \in mc(c)} \bar{x} = \bar{x} \sqcup \text{pc}_{\sigma_n},\ (\phi_1, \phi_2) = \chi(\sigma_0 : \ldots : \sigma_n)}{\begin{array}{l} \langle \sigma_0 : \ldots : \sigma_n = \{\mathbf{while}\ (e)\ c;\}\rangle \xrightarrow{\phi_1, U_1} \langle \sigma_0 : \ldots : \{\sqrt{}\} : \sigma_{n+1} = \{[c; \mathbf{while}\ (e)\ c]\}\rangle \\ \langle \sigma_0 : \ldots : \sigma_n = \{\mathbf{while}\ (e)\ c;\}\rangle \xrightarrow{\phi_2, U_2} \langle \sigma_0 : \ldots : \{\sqrt{}\}\rangle \end{array}}$$

$$\text{WHILE2}\frac{U := \bigcup_{\phi_i \in bv(c)} \phi_i = \text{LoopGuard}(\phi_i)}{\langle \sigma_0 : \ldots : \{stms\} : \{[\mathbf{while}\ (e)\ c]\}\rangle \xrightarrow{\mathsf{T}, \emptyset} \langle \sigma_0 : \ldots : \{\mathbf{while}\ (e)\ c;\}\rangle}$$

$$\text{EXIT}\frac{}{\langle \sigma_0 : \ldots : \{stms\} : \{[\sqrt{}]\}\rangle \xrightarrow{\mathsf{T}, U} \langle \sigma_0 : \ldots : \{stms\}\rangle}$$

$$\text{CALLNT}\frac{\text{NonThirdParty}(m), U := \{\text{pc}_{\sigma_{n+1}} = \text{pc}_{\sigma_n}\},}{\langle \sigma_0 : \ldots : \sigma_n = \{v = o.m(\vec{e})\}\rangle \xrightarrow{\mathsf{T}, U} \langle \sigma_0 : \ldots : \{\mathbf{return}\ v\} : \sigma_{n+1} = \{body[\vec{e}/pr(m)]\}\rangle}$$

$$\text{RETURN}\frac{}{\langle \sigma_0 : \ldots : \{\mathbf{return}\ v;\} : \{\mathbf{return}\ x;\}\rangle \xrightarrow{\mathsf{T}, \emptyset} \langle \sigma_0 : \ldots \{v = x;\}\rangle}$$

$$\text{CALLT}\frac{\text{ThirdParty}(m),\ l = \bar{e}_1 \sqcup \ldots \sqcup \bar{e}_m \sqcup \bar{o} \sqcup \text{pc}_{\sigma_n},\ U_1 = \{\bar{v} = l\} \cup \bigcup_{0 \leq i \leq m} \bar{e}_i = l}{\begin{array}{l} \langle \sigma_0 : \ldots : \sigma_n = \{v = o.m(\vec{e})\}\rangle \xrightarrow{\vec{e}, U_1} \langle \sigma_0 : \ldots : \sigma_n = \{\sqrt{}\}\rangle \\ \langle \sigma_0 : \ldots : \sigma_n = \{v = o.m(\vec{e})\}\rangle \xrightarrow{\neg\vec{e}, \emptyset} \langle \sigma_0 : \ldots : \sigma_n = \{\sqrt{}\}\rangle \end{array}}$$

Fig. 4. The security control flow semantics

The rule CALLNT describes the security semantics of a non-third party public method invocation defined for a class of type t that creates a new context with the statements $body[\vec{e}/pr(m)]$ that is obtained by substituting the method parameters $pr(m)$ in the method body with the arguments $\vec{e}$. The return statement pops the context and populates the variable v with the return value x (the rule RETURN) where x is a variable. For third-party methods, we set the security labels of all pass-by-reference arguments and the caller to high, if the method is invoked with a high-sensitive argument or the caller is high-sensitive (rule CALLT). We assume that the caller has no static attribute.

Example 1. Figure 5(a) shows the simplified security control flow model of the while loop in Fig. 2 generated by our tool. In this figure, the conditions WA41 and NA41 are branch variables and EWA41 and ENA41 are uncontrollable loop guards.

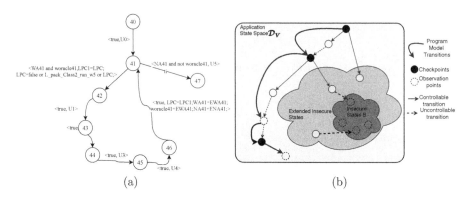

Fig. 5. (a) Security control flow model example; (b) Insecure state avoidance

Program Model. From the program semantics that is obtained by adding program variables to the security control flow semantics, we construct a program model that contains only the checkpoints and the observation points by merging the transitions (See Fig. 5(b)). We remove an unmonitorable transition t (i.e. its source is not a checkpoint or an observation point) by first propagating the transitions' guard and updates backwards to its incoming transitions, and then eliminating it. If there is no other transition from the source location of t, we remove the source location as well. The propagation continues until there is no further unmonitorable transition to process. We proved the soundness of the propagation algorithm [16].

5   Monitor Synthesis

The monitor synthesis process consists of two steps discussed in this section.

Step 1 - Generating Checkpoint Security Guards

A program is in an insecure state if it is in an observation point whose security policies have been violated, i.e. leaks information. An observation point is either a third-party method call, or the exit point of the unexecuted branch of a branch statement where the executed branch contains an observation point that is a method call. We consider the latter to be able to detect indirect information flows. For example, consider the following program where `print` is an observation point:

```
if(h>0) print(10) else h=1;
```

If `h>0`, then the attacker observes `10` in output and will know that `h` was greater than 0. If the else branch executes, since nothing is printed out, the attacker will know that `h<=0` holds. It is obvious that executing either of the branches causes information leakage. To prevent any leakage, we consider two points in this program that must be avoided: `print(1)` that should always be called with low-sensitive data, and the outgoing transition of the else branch that should be in a low-sensitive context. Insecure states are formally specified as boolean expressions defined over security labels for the locations, e.g. $\neg\ \overline{10}$ in the configuration `print(10)` in the above example.

Given the (boolean) security control flow semantics described in Sect. 4 and the specification of insecure states, we use the boolean controller synthesis method described in Sect. 2 to obtain the abstract security guards (See Fig. 5(b)). An abstract security guard describes the execution paths and security types that lead to an insecure state. The guard of a checkpoint's transition is restricted to allow only execution paths that do not cause a security violation, and the insecure paths are controlled by applying countermeasures to avoid a violation. Observe that in the security control flow model, all the transitions from the checkpoints are considered controllable and the rest of the transitions are uncontrollable (Fig. 5(b)).

To obtain the security guards in terms of program variables, we propagate each branch guard along its path to its controlling checkpoint. For instance, in our example, the simplified generated guard for the checkpoint `run` is $\neg\ \overline{ad}\ \wedge$ $\neg$WA41. To be able to evaluate this condition in the checkpoint, we propagate WA41 to the checkpoint `run` that results in `0<(d+3)`.

If there is a conditional statement after the loop in our example, we cannot propagate its conditions to the checkpoint `run`, as we need to propagate the conditions through the loop which is not always possible. To solve this problem, we assume a dummy checkpoint after the loop body, called *loop checkpoint* that is used to propagate the conditions to, instead of the controlling checkpoint (e.g. the transition from 46 to 41 in Fig. 5(a)).

Step 2 - Monitor Construction

In the second step, we design a monitor to observe a program in the checkpoints and control the information flow. In the checkpoints, if the security guard of the current checkpoint, produced in the first step, allows the execution, the program will continue its execution and the monitor state will also be updated and evolved to the next checkpoint. Otherwise, a countermeasure will be applied to protect the program. One of the main countermeasures that the user can apply is to declassify the high-sensitive information to prevent reaching insecure states. Declassifying a variable leads to downgrading its security label.

We represent a program state by $\langle c, \nu \rangle$ where c is the configuration and ν indicates the program variables valuation. A monitor state is represented by $\langle \rho, mode, I, pc, \Gamma \rangle$ where ρ is the current checkpoint of the monitor, *mode* is a variable that shows the monitoring mode (will be discussed later), I is the set of variables declassified so far, pc is the stack of security contexts, and the function Γ shows the valuation of security type variables. We represent the state of the monitored program by $\langle c, \nu \rangle \parallel \langle \rho, mode, I, pc, \Gamma \rangle$.

Let $\mathbb{C}$ be the set of checkpoint configurations, $\mathbb{L}$ be the set of observation point configurations, $\mathbb{P}$ be the set of security policies and $\rho \xrightarrow{G,A} \rho'$ represent

$$\text{NCP-SEC} \frac{\langle c, \boldsymbol{\nu}\rangle \to \langle c', \boldsymbol{\nu}'\rangle \ , \ c \notin \mathbb{C} \ , \ c \notin \mathbb{L}}{\langle c, \boldsymbol{\nu}\rangle \parallel \langle \rho, mode, I, \mathrm{pc}, \Gamma\rangle \to \langle c', \boldsymbol{\nu}'\rangle \parallel \langle \rho, mode, I, \mathrm{pc}, \Gamma\rangle}$$

$$\text{CP-INSEC1} \frac{\begin{array}{c}\langle c, \boldsymbol{\nu}\rangle \to \langle c', \boldsymbol{\nu}'\rangle, c \xrightarrow{G,A} \rho \ , \ \boldsymbol{\nu} \models G \ , \ (\boldsymbol{\nu}, \Gamma) \not\models \text{Guard}(c) \ , \ \neg\text{Restrictive}(c, \boldsymbol{\nu}, \Gamma, \mathbb{C}, \mathbb{P}) \ , \\ \text{cmeasure}(\boldsymbol{\nu}, I) = \langle \boldsymbol{\nu}'', I'\rangle \ , \ \Gamma' = \Gamma \downarrow (I'\backslash I) \ , \ \text{secure}(\text{cmeasure})\end{array}}{\langle c, \boldsymbol{\nu}\rangle \parallel \langle c, mode, I, \mathrm{pc}, \Gamma\rangle \to \langle c, \boldsymbol{\nu}''\rangle \parallel \langle c, mode, I', \mathrm{pc}, \Gamma'\rangle}$$

$$\text{CP-INSEC2} \frac{\langle c, \boldsymbol{\nu}\rangle \to \langle c', \boldsymbol{\nu}'\rangle, c \xrightarrow{G,A} \rho \ , \ \boldsymbol{\nu} \models G \ , \ (\boldsymbol{\nu}, \Gamma) \not\models \text{Guard}(c) \ , \ \neg\text{Restrictive}(c, \boldsymbol{\nu}, \Gamma, \mathbb{C}, \mathbb{P}) \ , \ \mathrm{pc}' = A(\mathrm{pc}) \ , \ \Gamma' = A(\Gamma)}{\langle c, \boldsymbol{\nu}\rangle \parallel \langle c, mode, I, \mathrm{pc}, \Gamma\rangle \to \langle c', \boldsymbol{\nu}'\rangle \parallel \langle \rho, \top, I, \mathrm{pc}', \Gamma'\rangle}$$

$$\text{CP-INSEC3} \frac{\begin{array}{c}\langle c, \boldsymbol{\nu}\rangle \to \langle c', \boldsymbol{\nu}'\rangle, c \xrightarrow{G.A} \rho \ , \ \boldsymbol{\nu} \models G \ , \ (\boldsymbol{\nu}, \Gamma) \not\models \text{Guard}(c) \ , \ \text{Restrictive}(c, \boldsymbol{\nu}, \Gamma, \mathbb{C}, \mathbb{P}) \ , \ \mathrm{pc}' = A(\mathrm{pc}) \ , \ \Gamma' = A(\Gamma)\end{array}}{\langle c, \boldsymbol{\nu}\rangle \parallel \langle c, mode, I, \mathrm{pc}, \Gamma\rangle \to \langle c', \boldsymbol{\nu}'\rangle \parallel \langle \rho, mode, I', \mathrm{pc}', \Gamma'\rangle}$$
$$\text{Guard}(c) = \text{Guard}(c) \wedge \neg path(c, \rho, \boldsymbol{\nu})$$

$$\text{OP-LINSEC} \frac{\langle c, \boldsymbol{\nu}\rangle \to \langle c', \boldsymbol{\nu}\rangle \ , \ \mathrm{pc} = \mathrm{pc}_1 : \ldots : \mathrm{pc}_{\sigma_n} \ , \ \mathrm{pc}_{\sigma_n} = L \ , \ c \neq \rho \ , \ c \notin \mathbb{C} \ , \ c \in \mathbb{L}}{\langle c, \boldsymbol{\nu}\rangle \parallel \langle \rho, \top, I, \mathrm{pc}, \Gamma\rangle \to \langle c'', \boldsymbol{\nu}\rangle \parallel \langle \rho, \top, I, \mathrm{pc}, \Gamma\rangle}$$

$$\text{OP-HINSEC} \frac{\mathrm{pc} = \mathrm{pc}_1 : \ldots : \mathrm{pc}_{\sigma_n} \ , \ \mathrm{pc}_{\sigma_n} = H \ , \ c \neq \rho \ , \ c \notin \mathbb{C} \ , \ c \in \mathbb{L}}{\langle c, \boldsymbol{\nu}\rangle \parallel \langle \rho, \top, I, \mathrm{pc}, \Gamma\rangle \to \langle \sqrt{}, \boldsymbol{\nu}\rangle \parallel \langle \rho, \top, I, \mathrm{pc}, \Gamma\rangle}$$

$$\text{CP-SEC} \frac{\langle c, \boldsymbol{\nu}\rangle \to \langle c', \boldsymbol{\nu}'\rangle \ , \ c \xrightarrow{G.A} \rho' \ , \ \boldsymbol{\nu} \models G \ , \ (\boldsymbol{\nu}, \Gamma) \models \text{Guard}(c) \ , \ \mathrm{pc}' = A(\mathrm{pc}) \ , \ \Gamma' = A(\Gamma)}{\langle c, \boldsymbol{\nu}\rangle \parallel \langle c, mode, I, \mathrm{pc}, \Gamma\rangle \to \langle c', \boldsymbol{\nu}'\rangle \parallel \langle \rho', \bot, I, \mathrm{pc}', \Gamma'\rangle}$$

Fig. 6. The behaviour of a monitored program

a symbolic transition from a checkpoint ρ to ρ' of the program model. The behavior of the monitored program is described by the rules in Fig. 6. The first rule states that if c is neither a checkpoint nor an observation point, then the program continues its normal execution. When a security violation is predicted in a checkpoint, we propose three general strategies for protection and the system administrator should apply the proper one to react to a security violation. We say a security violation is predicted in a checkpoint c in a state, if the propagated security guard generated for that checkpoint ($\text{Guard}(c)$) is not satisfied in that state.

The guards generated in the first step can sometimes be restrictive. To check if a violation prediction is restrictive or not, we execute the program model up to the next checkpoint and check if the security policies have been violated along the path or not. If there is a violated security policy along the path, it means that the prediction is correct, otherwise, the security guard is restrictive for this specific path and must be relaxed. The predicate $\text{Restrictive}(c, \boldsymbol{\nu}, \Gamma, \mathbb{C}, \mathbb{P})$ states that no security policy of $\mathbb{P}$ is violated in the states along the path from the program state $\langle c, \boldsymbol{\nu}\rangle$ to the next checkpoint.

When a violation is predicted, the monitor can apply a user-defined countermeasure cmeasure provided that this countermeasure is *secure* and the prediction is not restrictive (the rule cp-insec1 in Fig. 6). Let $\Gamma \downarrow V$ be a typing environment that degrades the security level of the variables of V in Γ. The countermeasure cmeasure should not change the value of the low-variables. In addition, it can only declassify variables that have not been modified by the program so far, i.e. $I'\backslash I \cap \boldsymbol{\nu}(mv) = \emptyset$ where $I'\backslash I$ is the set of declassified variables and mv is the set of variables modified so far. For instance, consider the following program:

```
h1=h2; f(); if (l1<10) {l2=h1;} else l2=l1; print(l2);
```

where l1 and l2 are low-sensitive, and h1 and h2 are high-sensitive. Let f() be the checkpoint and initially Γ(h1) $=$ Γ(h2) $=$ H. If we declassify h1 in the checkpoint, it also reveals h2. The reason is that the value of h1 is set to h2 before the checkpoint and if the **if** branch executes, h1 (and h2) will be copied to l2 that will be printed and revealed. Hence, we only allow declassification of variables that have not been modified. In addition, the variables declassified by applying a countermeasure shouldn't depend on the program state except for the program location. For instance, consider the following program

```
if(h3)  { h1=5;} else   h2=l1; f(); l=h1; print(l1);
```

If h3 is true, h1 becomes modified and we cannot declassify it. If h3 is false, even though h1 does not change, we do not allow it to be declassified, as it leads to the disclosure of h3 as well. Furthermore, the countermeasure should not lead the program into an insecure state again. Consider the program

```
f(); if(l1<10) {l2=h;} else l2=l1; print(l2);
```

If l1<10 $\wedge$ Γ(h) $=$ H holds in the checkpoint, the program is insecure, otherwise it's secure. As mentioned above, cmeasure cannot change any low-sensitive variable such as l1. Hence, a countermeasure that prevents the program from reaching an insecure state should include declassification of h, otherwise, l1<10 $\wedge$ Γ(h) $=$ H holds infinitely and this leads to a live lock situation where the program makes no progress and keeps constantly applying the same countermeasure. To avoid this situation, applying a countermeasure should lead to triggering a permissible transition, i.e. after applying the countermeasure, there should be a transition in the monitor that can be triggered.

Based on the above issues, a countermeasure cmeasure is secure, if for all ν that cmeasure$(\nu, I) = \langle \nu', I' \rangle$, (i) applying cmeasure does not lead the program into an insecure state, i.e. a transition from the location c in the monitor with a guard G' exists such that $\nu' \models G'$, (ii) the condition $\nu =_\Gamma \nu' \wedge I' \cap \nu'(mv) = \emptyset$ holds, and (iii) for all ν_1 and ν_2, if cmeasure$(\nu_1, I) = \langle \nu_1', I_1' \rangle$ and cmeasure$(\nu_2, I) = \langle \nu_2', I_2' \rangle$, then $I_1' = I_2'$. We say two memories ν and ν' are low-equal w.r.t. Γ, denoted by $\nu =_\Gamma \nu'$, if their low variables according to the security typing function Γ are identical, i.e. $\nu(v) = \nu'(v)$ where $\Gamma(v) = L$, $\forall v \in V$ and V is the set of program variables.

If a prediction about a violation is incorrect in a checkpoint c, the program will be allowed to execute and the security guard of the checkpoint (Guard(c)) will be weakened (the rule cp-insec3). The function $path(c, \rho, \nu)$ returns the conditions in the state ν that enable the path from c to ρ.

If the violation is predicted correctly but there is no countermeasure to apply in that checkpoint and all the future observation points up to the next checkpoints are side-effect free (i.e. return **void**), the execution mode is changed to secure ($mode = \top$) and a countermeasure is applied in the observation points, as done in [20] (the rule cp-insec2). The rule cp-sec states that if the program is in a checkpoint, and the monitor allows its transition ($\nu \models G$), then the monitor and the program evolve into their new states, and the monitoring mode changes to normal ($\bot$). In the secure mode execution, if the context is low and executing a statement in an observation point leads to a security policy violation, a default side-effect-free action c'' is performed, e.g. sending default data (the rule op-linsec), otherwise nothing happens (the rule op-hinsec). We assume that the observation points are side-effect free so that the countermeasures do not change the program semantics. The rules for the case that the learning feature is inactive are defined similarly.

In [16], we proved that a monitored program satisfies localized delimited release property [2], which states that, for any initial memory states s and s' whose secret parts may only differ, if the value of all declassified variables is the same in both s and s', then the observation sequence of the program running in state s and s' will be the same, or one is a prefix of the other. The reason for the latter case is that our method guarantees a termination-insensitive property. This notion disallows data release before it is declassified but allows release after declassification. In the case of no information release, it satisfies termination-insensitive non-interference.

6   Implementation and Evaluation

The Tool Set. We have implemented a tool to demonstrate the proposed method targeting Java applications. The tool consists of two main components: the static analysis component and the model execution engine. The static analysis requires the annotated Java application as input and (i) generates security guards for the checkpoints by employing the Reax [6] synthesis tool, (ii) automatically constructs the program model, and (iii) instruments the code for the monitoring purpose. The model execution engine executes symbolic control flow graphs and is used to run the program models.

Two versions of the monitor have been implemented. In the first version, we use the aforementioned engine to run the program model and train the monitor to eliminate false positives. In the entry point, the monitor initiates its state and loads the required information for it to function. On each of the checkpoints, the engine executes the program model until the next checkpoint, and checks if a violation has been predicted correctly. If the security guards of the current checkpoint are restrictive, it then relaxes the security guards.

In the second version, called model-execution free monitor, the program model is not executed and subsequently the monitor cannot learn new security guards. In this monitor, the security guards are checked at the checkpoints and the proper follow-up is executed if needed. If there is no violation, the security labels are updated to their values in the next checkpoint.

To assess the permissiveness of our method and the performance of tool, we applied it to a real world android application as well as multiple test cases of the Droidbench test suite. The application used is pedometer [1] with 1483 lines of code. The static experiments were performed on a Intel i7-6700 at 3.4 GHz and

32 GB of DDR4 Ram running a 64bit version of Ubuntu Linux. The dynamic experiments were performed on a Galaxy Tab S3 running android version 7.0.

We used 70 test cases from the Droidbench benchmark to evaluate the permissiveness of our method. We have achieved a precision of 100% and had 4(5%) false positives. The static analysis performance depends on the size of code, number of variables, the number of checkpoints and the average distance between them. The more checkpoints the program contains, the shorter the distance between the checkpoints and the more performant the static analysis usually should be. Figure 7(a) shows the performance results for static analysis of pedometer. That is mainly due to the guards being propagated along shorter paths when constructing the program model. The analysis of test cases in the Droidbench benchmark takes a fraction of second, as they are very small programs. Due to the small size of test cases in the Droidbench benchmark, it was not possible to have more than one checkpoint in a test case to evaluate the affect of number of checkpoints on the performance. In general, since we use *boolean* controller synthesis and state space partitioning to tackle complexity, we believe that static analysis should not be expensive, as confirmed by our current experiments so far.

The performance of the runtime monitor with learning feature is dependent on the number of the lines of code of the original program (See Fig. 7(b) for pedometer). For each instruction in the original program the monitor has to execute that instruction and update the security labels. Additionally the checkpoint guards have to be checked. As a result, we expect the runtime monitor to incur a significant performance overhead compared to the program with no monitor.

The monitor-execution free instance only checks the guards at each checkpoint and usually outperforms the runtime monitor. Its performance depends on the number of checkpoints; it sounds that the more the checkpoints the program has, the fewer checks have to be run at each one which improves performance. Note that the guards are propagated and simplified statically. An outside factor that seems to impact the monitor's performance is the JVM's optimization; when the checkpoints run many times, we noticed that the performance increases by at least an order of magnitude, e.g. from a 30% monitor running time to <1%.

Discussion. We believe that the results of static analysis are promising, mainly because the method uses boolean analysis and state partitioning. However, the performance overhead of dynamic monitor for our current test cases is scattered in quite a wide interval, e.g. from less than 1% to 40% for the model-execution free monitoring. We believe that we need to conduct many more experiments on different programs with various sizes, number of checkpoints, number of branches, number of variables etc, to be able to make a valid conclusion about the performance of the dynamic monitor. To this end, we should extend the method and tool to support exceptions, to be able to apply it on more real-life case studies. Furthermore, we are working on a new solution to run the monitor concurrently with the original program that is expected to improve the performance.

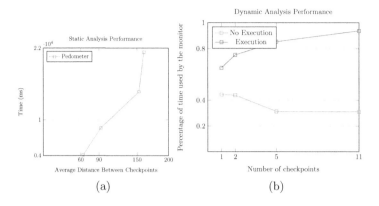

Fig. 7. Performance results

7   Related Work

There is a large body of work on verification and enforcement of noninterference as a policy to enforce confidentiality [13]. We have compared our approach with the related work in [16]. In this section, we discuss some related work.

The authors in [8] present a taxonomy of existing dynamic and hybrid monitors: no-sensitive-upgrade (NSU), permissive-upgrade (PU), hybrid monitor (HM), secure multi-execution (SME), and multiple facets (MF). The NSU [3,26] approach generates a purely dynamic monitor, that controls only one execution and disallows any upgrade of a low sensitive variable in a high context. This approach is improved in [4] by using a less-restrictive strategy in upgrading low variables in a high context, called permissive upgrade. In SME [11,17] and MF [5], multiple versions of a program are executed simultaneously, one for each security level, and the variable updates are controlled in a way that there will be no information leakage. These two categories of approaches introduce no information flow, however, they suffer from high performance overhead at runtime [5,12] that increases with the number of used security levels. Moreover, some repairable executions get blocked and the only applicable countermeasure is replacing the value of violating variables with some low-secure and safe constants.

In [9,14], the authors apply a flow-sensitive type system to instrument semantics of a program and consider unexecuted paths to detect indirect flows. Then, they statically construct a monitoring automaton that is traversed at runtime to detect security violations and apply countermeasures. In [20], the authors proposed a framework for hybrid monitors that is proven to be sound and guarantees termination insensitive noninterference for a simple language with output. It uses the countermeasures stop, suppress, or rewrite to react to a violation in output points. We extended their flow-sensitive type system with objects and method calls to instrument the program semantics. We predict violations at certain checkpoints which allows us to enforce a wider range of countermeasures at runtime to handle and resolve a security violation. Our "monitor mode" is inspired from this work as well. Taint checking is another dynamic mechanism to control information flow, by tracking data dependencies as data is propagated in the system, that is well-surveyed in [23]. However, as it only tracks explicit flows [10] and ignores implicit flows, it enforces a weaker property than noninterference.

In contrast to the existing hybrid and dynamic monitors (e.g. [3,9,11,12,14, 14,17,20,24,26]), (i) our framework provides a learning feature that enables us to train the monitor and improve its permissiveness, (ii) it supports declassification and enforces localized delimited declassification while the existing monitors usually enforce a noninterference property, and (iii) we detect a violation in the checkpoints, in several steps before its occurrence, that allows us to enforce a wider range of countermeasures at runtime to protect against leakages. The main drawback of our method is its performance overhead that we are currently trying to improve by providing concurrent versions and optimizing the security guards.

8   Concluding Remarks

In this paper, we proposed an approach and its supporting tool for generating a hybrid security monitor for a subset of Java programs. This method synthesizes a sound symbolic monitor to predict undesired information flows and apply secure (user-defined) countermeasures to prevent information leakage and enforce localized delimited declassification. Given an annotated Java program, we implemented a tool-set to automatically generate a monitor. We also carried out some preliminary experiments to assess the method.

The results of our static analysis technique are promising in terms of both performance and the number of false positives. Hence, it can be used by the users to re-design their programs to fix information leakage problems at design time. In general, dynamic and hybrid monitors suffer from performance overhead [5,12], and so does our method. To improve its performance overhead, we are working on extending the method to support concurrent execution of monitors with the program, as well as simplifying the generated guards. We will also extend the supported sub-language of Java and conduct more experiments to evaluate the effectiveness of the tool properly.

References

1. Pedometer. https://f-droid.org/packages/name.bagi.levente.pedometer/
2. Askarov, A., Sabelfeld, A.: Localized delimited release: combining the what and where dimensions of information release. In: Proceedings of the 2007 Workshop on Programming Languages and Analysis for Security, PLAS 2007, San Diego, California, USA, 14 June 2007, pp. 53–60 (2007)
3. Austin, T.H., Flanagan, C.: Efficient purely-dynamic information flow analysis. In: Proceedings of the ACM SIGPLAN Fourth Workshop on Programming Languages and Analysis for Security, PLAS 2009, New York, NY, USA, pp. 113–124 (2009)

4. Austin, T.H., Flanagan, C.: Permissive dynamic information flow analysis. In: Proceedings of the 5th ACM SIGPLAN Workshop on Programming Languages and Analysis for Security, PLAS 2010, New York, NY, USA, pp. 3:1–3:12. ACM, New York (2010)
5. Austin, T.H., Flanagan, C.: Multiple facets for dynamic information flow. In: Proceedings of the 39th Annual ACM SIGPLAN-SIGACT Symposium on Principles of Programming Languages, POPL 2012, New York, NY, USA, pp. 165–178. ACM, New York (2012)
6. Berthier, N., Marchand, H.: Discrete controller synthesis for infinite state systems with ReaX. In: 12th International Workshop on Discrete Event Systems, WODES 2014, Cachan, France, 14–16 May 2014, pp. 46–53 (2014)
7. Besson, F., Bielova, N., Jensen, T.P.: Hybrid information flow monitoring against web tracking. In: 2013 IEEE 26th Computer Security Foundations Symposium, New Orleans, LA, USA, 26–28 June 2013, pp. 240–254 (2013)
8. Bielova, N., Rezk, T.: A taxonomy of information flow monitors. In: Piessens, F., Viganò, L. (eds.) POST 2016. LNCS, vol. 9635, pp. 46–67. Springer, Heidelberg (2016). https://doi.org/10.1007/978-3-662-49635-0_3
9. Dam, M., Le Guernic, G., Lundblad, A.: TreeDroid: a tree automaton based approach to enforcing data processing policies. In: Proceedings of the 2012 ACM Conference on Computer and Communications Security, CCS 2012, New York, NY, USA, pp. 894–905. ACM, New York (2012)
10. Denning, D.E., Denning, P.J.: Certification of programs for secure information flow. Commun. ACM **20**(7), 504–513 (1977)
11. Devriese, D., Piessens, F.: Noninterference through secure multi-execution. In: 31st IEEE Symposium on Security and Privacy, S&P 2010, Berleley/Oakland, California, USA, 16–19 May 2010, pp. 109–124 (2010)
12. Desharnais, J., Kozyri, E., Tawbi, N.: Block-safe information flow control. Technical report, Cornell University (2016)
13. Goguen, J.A., Meseguer, J.: Security policies and security models. In: 1982 IEEE Symposium on Security and Privacy, Oakland, CA, USA, 26–28 April 1982, pp. 11–20 (1982)
14. Le Guernic, G., Banerjee, A., Jensen, T., Schmidt, D.A.: Automata-based confidentiality monitoring. In: Okada, M., Satoh, I. (eds.) ASIAN 2006. LNCS, vol. 4435, pp. 75–89. Springer, Heidelberg (2007). https://doi.org/10.1007/978-3-540-77505-8_7
15. Hedin, D., Sabelfeld, A.: Information-flow security for a core of JavaScript. In: 25th IEEE Computer Security Foundations Symposium, CSF 2012, Cambridge, MA, USA, 25–27 June 2012, pp. 3–18 (2012)
16. Khakpour, N., Skandylas, C.: Symbolic synthesis of a permissive security monitor: the extended version. Technical report, Linnaeus University (2018)
17. Kwon, Y., et al.: LDX: causality inference by lightweight dual execution. In: Proceedings of the Twenty-First International Conference on Architectural Support for Programming Languages and Operating Systems, ASPLOS 2016, New York, NY, USA, pp. 503–515. ACM, New York (2016)
18. Le Guernic, G.: Confidentiality enforcement using dynamic information flow analyses. Ph.D. thesis, Manhattan, KS, USA (2007)
19. Pullicino, K.: Jif: language-based information-flow security in Java. CoRR, abs/1412.8639 (2014)
20. Russo, A., Sabelfeld, A.: Dynamic vs. static flow-sensitive security analysis. In: Proceedings of the 23rd IEEE Computer Security Foundations Symposium, CSF 2010, Edinburgh, United Kingdom, 17–19 July 2010, pp. 186–199 (2010)

21. Sabelfeld, A., Russo, A.: From dynamic to static and back: riding the roller coaster of information-flow control research. In: Pnueli, A., Virbitskaite, I., Voronkov, A. (eds.) PSI 2009. LNCS, vol. 5947, pp. 352–365. Springer, Heidelberg (2010). https://doi.org/10.1007/978-3-642-11486-1_30
22. Santos, J.F., Rezk, T.: An information flow monitor-inlining compiler for securing a core of JavaScript. In: Proceedings of the ICT Systems Security and Privacy Protection - 29th IFIP TC 11 International Conference, SEC 2014, Marrakech, Morocco, 2–4 June 2014, pp. 278–292 (2014)
23. Schoepe, D., Balliu, M., Pierce, B.C., Sabelfeld, A.: Explicit secrecy: a policy for taint tracking. In: IEEE European Symposium on Security and Privacy, Euro S&P 2016, Saarbrücken, Germany, 21–24 March 2016, pp. 15–30 (2016)
24. Shroff, P., Smith, S., Thober, M.: Dynamic dependency monitoring to secure information flow. In: 20th IEEE Computer Security Foundations Symposium (CSF 2007), Venice, Italy, 6–8 July 2007, pp. 203–217, July 2007
25. Simonet, V.: The flow caml system. Software release, vol. 116, pp. 119–156 (2003). http://cristal.inria.fr/~simonet/soft/flowcaml
26. Zdancewic, S.A.: Programming languages for information security. Ph.D. thesis, Ithaca, NY, USA (2002)

MobileFindr: Function Similarity Identification for Reversing Mobile Binaries

Yibin Liao$^{(\boxtimes)}$, Ruoyan Cai$^{(\boxtimes)}$, Guodong Zhu$^{(\boxtimes)}$, Yue Yin$^{(\boxtimes)}$, and Kang Li$^{(\boxtimes)}$

University of Georgia, Athens, GA, USA
{liao,ruoyan,guodong,yin,kangli}@cs.uga.edu

Abstract. Identifying binary code at function level has been applied to a broad range of software security applications and reverse engineering tasks, including patch analysis, vulnerability assessment, code plagiarism detection, malware analysis, etc. However, various anti-reverse engineering techniques (e.g., obfuscation, anti-emulator, etc.) employed by the mobile apps make existing approaches ineffective when performing function identification. In this paper, we propose MobileFindr, an on-device trace-based function similarity identification framework on the mobile platform. MobileFindr runs on real mobile devices and mitigates many prevalent anti-reversing techniques by extracting function execution behaviors via dynamic instrumentation, then characterizing functions with collected behaviors and performing function matching via distance calculation. We have evaluated MobileFindr using real-world top-ranked mobile frameworks and applications. The experimental results showed that MobileFindr outperforms existing state-of-the-art tools in terms of better obfuscation resilience and accuracy.

Keywords: Reverse engineering · Similarity identification
Dynamic instrumentation

1 Introduction

With the general availability of closed-source applications, there is a need to identify function similarity among binary executables. For instance, in the automatic patch-based exploit generation, detecting the function similarity/difference between a pre-patch binary and post-patch binary reveals the patched vulnerability [22–24,41], and such information can be explored automatically within a few minutes [19], and generate 1-day exploits [39]. Performing function similarity measurement between intellectual property protected software binaries and suspicious binaries indicate potential cases of software plagiarism [26,32,34,43,44]. Detecting similar malicious functionality between different binary malware samples is another appealing application emerged in malware analysis, since the majority of malware samples are not brand new program but rather repacks or evolutions of previous known malicious function code [31,35].

© Springer Nature Switzerland AG 2018
J. Lopez et al. (Eds.): ESORICS 2018, LNCS 11098, pp. 66–83, 2018.
https://doi.org/10.1007/978-3-319-99073-6_4

An inherent challenge shared by the above applications is the absence of source code. Binary executable becomes the only available resource to be analyzed. A number of semantics-aware binary differencing or function similarity detecting methods have been proposed. One category is to use static analysis, which is usually based on control-flow graph (CFG) comparison [22–24,46]. At a high level, the CFG based approach extracts various robust features for a node in the control flow graph [22,24], or learns higher-level numeric feature representations from the control flow graph [23], or converts the control flow graph into embeddings [46], then perform similarity searching for the target functions. Although these studies have demonstrated that CFG based methods can be effective and scalable, all of these methods exclude obfuscated binaries, which appeared in a large number of mobile apps. Basic block semantics modeling is another approach for similarity measurement [25,34,41]. It represents the input-output relations of a basic block as a set of formulas, and then use theorem prover to perform the equivalence checking. However, the theorem prover is computationally expensive and impractical for large code bases of many real world mobile apps [22].

Another category relies on dynamic analysis, which is usually based on runtime execution behavior comparison. For example, previous work by Ming et al. achieves this by collecting system or API calls to slice out corresponding code segments and then check their equivalence with symbolic execution and constraint solving [35]. However, their trace logging component is an emulator based system, which cannot handle the environment-sensitive mobile apps that can detect sandbox environment. Egele et al. built a system called BLEX to capture the side effects of functions during execution [21]. Xu et al. built a tool called CryptoHunt to capture the specific features of cryptography functions with boolean formula [45]. All of their implementation are based on Intel's Pin framework [33], which is not work on mobile platforms generally with ARM instruction set architecture.

In this paper, we aim at improving the state of the art by proposing *trace-based function similarity mapping*, a hybrid method to efficiently search for similar functions in mobile binaries. Regardless of the optimization and obfuscation difference, similar code must still have semantically similar execution behavior, whereas different code must behave differently [21]. Our key idea is to capture the dynamic behavior features during the execution of a function along a runtime trace. More precisely, we propose to record a variety of dynamic runtime information as dynamic behavior features via dynamic instrumentation, and use stack backtrace information to locate corresponding functions that can be represented with these features. Then we calculate the similarity distance based on such features and return a list of similar functions ranked by the score of distance.

We have designed and implemented a system called *MobileFindr*, and evaluated it with a set of mobile examples under different obfuscation scheme combinations. Our experimental results show that our system can successfully identify fine-grained function similarities between mobile binaries, and outperform existing state-of-the-art approaches in terms of better obfuscation resilience and accuracy. Our evaluation with top-ranked real-world mobile apps also demonstrated the effectiveness of our system.

Correspondingly, our contributions in this paper are:

- We have proposed a novel approach, *trace-based function similarity mapping*, to perform function similarity measurement on mobile platforms. Our key solution is to capture observable dynamic behaviors along an execution trace via dynamic instrumentation, and characterize functions with such behaviors. Our approach exhibits stronger resilience to various anti-reverse engineering techniques for mobile apps. To best of our knowledge, this is the first work having such ability on mobile platforms.
- We have proposed a variety of dynamic features to record during the function execution, which allow us to approximate the semantics of a function without relying on the source code access.
- We have implemented a system called *MobileFindr* and source code is publicly available at GitHub: https://github.com/tigerlyb/MobileFindr.
- We have demonstrated the viability of our approach for top-ranked real-world mobile frameworks and apps.

The rest of this paper is organized as following. Section 2 introduces background and challenges. Section 3 presents the details of our system design and implementation. Section 4 presents our evaluation and results. Discussion and limitations are presented in Sect. 5. Then we present related work in Sect. 6, and conclude the paper in Sect. 7.

2   Background

This section introduces the background of reverse engineering, presents the popular tools that help for reverse engineering mobile apps, including various debuggers, disassemblers, decompilers, etc. Then we demonstrate motivating examples and describe possible reverse engineering challenges that can affect the state of the art function identification methods.

2.1   Reverse Engineering Mobile Apps

Reverse engineering is the process of taking a program's binary code and recreating it so as to trace it back to the original source code. It is being widely used in computer software security to enhance product features without knowing the source: find security flaws, test code compatibility, add new features or redesign the product, understand the design of malicious code, etc. In this section, we present popular reverse engineering tools for mobile apps as follows:

- **Debugger:** helps developer to understand how the program behaves at runtime without modifying the code, and allows the user to view and change the running state of a program. With the release of Xcode 5, the LLDB debugger [12], which is part of the LLVM compiler development suite, becomes the foundation for the debugging experience on Apple platforms. LLDB is fully integrated with Xcode and provides deep capabilities in a user-friendly environment. For Android platform, both LLDB and JDB (Java debugger) are integrated in the Android Studio debugger [1]. By default, Android Studio automatically choose the best option for the code you are debugging. For example, if you have any C or C++ code in the project, Android studio debugger select LLDB to debug your code. Otherwise, Android Studio uses the Java debug type.

- **Disassembler:** a software tool which transforms binary code into a human readable mnemonic representation called assembly language. Many disassemblers are available on the market, both free and commercial. Apktools [2] and baksmali [15] are free tools that can disassemble the dex format used by Dalvik, Android's Java VM implementation. The most powerful commercial disassembler is IDA Pro [9], published by Hex-Rays. It can handle binary code for a huge number of processors and has open architecture that allows developers to write add-on analytic modules.

- **Decompiler:** a software tool used to revert the process of compilation. Decompilers are different from disassemblers in one very important aspect. While both generate human readable text, decompilers generate much higher level text, which is more concise and much easier to read. For example, Android developer can use Dex2jar [5] to convert dex file to class file, and then open it in JD-GUI [10] to display Java source code. Hex-Rays Decompiler [8] is a IDA Pro extension that converts native processor code into human readable C-like pseudocode text.

2.2 Challenges

The software security community relies on such reverse engineering tools to analyze and validate programs. However, various anti-reverse engineering techniques employed by the latest mobile apps make existing reverse engineering tools ineffective. For instance, the anti-debugging and anti-emulator techniques employed by mobile apps limit the usage of many dynamic analysis tools [28,30,40]. Code obfuscation scheme provide strong protection against automated static reverse engineering tools. Moreover, different mobile apps tend to use different obfuscation techniques and even same app changes obfuscation options when updating its version. In this paper, we focus on analyzing iOS apps. Nowadays iOS developers heavily rely on code obfuscation to evade detection since iOS is a close-source platform. Therefore, in this section, we introduce different code obfuscation features as well as motivating examples for understanding each features.

Code Obfuscation. Obfuscation aims at creating obfuscated code that is difficult for humans to understand. Obfuscation techniques include modifying names of classes, fields, and methods, reordering control flow graphs, encrypting constant strings, inserting junk code, etc. To obfuscate mobile apps, we rely on a state-of-the-art open-source obfuscation tool, Obfuscator-LLVM 4.0 [29], which supports popular obfuscation transformations as follows.

– **Control Flow Flattening:** The purpose of this pass is to completely flatten the control flow graph of a program. The flag option *-split* activates basic block splitting, which improve the flattening when applied together.
– **Instructions Substitution:** The goal of this obfuscation technique simply consists in replacing standard binary operators (like addition, subtraction or boolean operators) by functionally equivalent, but more complicated sequences of instructions.
– **Bogus Control Flow:** This method modifies a function call graph by adding a basic block before the current basic block. This new basic block contains an opaque predicate and then makes a conditional jump to the original basic block. The original basic block is also cloned and filled up with junk instructions chosen at random.

```
1.   - (NSString *)encrypt1:(NSString *)message {
2.       if ([message length] == 0) {
3.           return @"NULL";
4.       }
5.
6.       NSString *key = [self makeKey1];
7.       NSString *encryptedMsg = [self xorWithString:key
     withMessage:message];
8.
9.       NSLog(@"encrypt1: %@", encryptedMsg);
10.      return encryptedMsg;
11.  }
```

Fig. 1. A motivating example: Code

Obfuscation Example. We use the example in Fig. 2 to illustrate code obfuscation on iOS platform. Figure 1 shows the Objective-C source code of a function called *encrypt1*. It takes a string message as input and xor the message with a key, then return the encrypted message. Figure 2a shows the original control flow graph without any obfuscation, which only contains 4 basic blocks. While Fig. 2b is the obfuscated version (combined all three obfuscation options above) of that function. As mentioned in Sect. 1, existing static approaches that rely on control flow graph similarity and basic block level comparison will likely not be able to make a meaningful distinction in this scenario. Alternative approaches, such as dynamic approaches, either rely on Pin tool or emulator-based system to capture execution behavior. Pin tool is not able to work on analyzing most mobile apps, since ARM processors dominate mobile platforms. The anti-emulator techniques

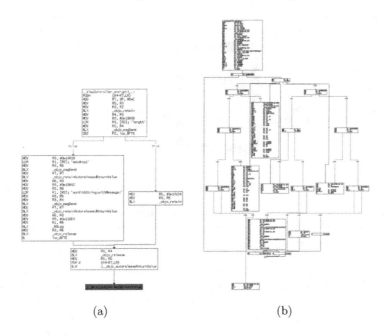

(a)   (b)

Fig. 2. A motivating example: CFG

employed by mobile apps also limit the usage of such emulator-based analysis system. To address the above mentioned challenges in the scope of matching function for mobile binaries, we design a novel on-device dynamic instrumentation system.

3   Design and Implementation

In this section, we first illustrate the design of our approach, and then detail the implementation of our system.

3.1   Overview

We present *trace-based function similarity mapping*, a hybrid method to efficiently search for similar functions in mobile binaries. More precisely, we propose to record a variety of dynamic behavior features during the execution of a function along an execution trace. We define the concept of "dynamic behavior features" broadly to include any information that can be derived from observations made during execution. Our approach works as the following: given two mobile apps A, B and a function of interest F from A. Both F and any executed functions from B are characterized with dynamic behavior features. Then we compute similarity scores between F and each function f from B, to identify which functions in B are similar to F. The novelty of our approach lies in the follows.

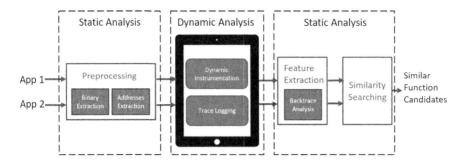

Fig. 3. Schematic overview of trace-based function similarity mapping system

– What features are useful for semantic similarity comparisons?
– How these features are captured on mobile platforms?
– How to characterize a function with such features?

Figure 3 illustrates the architecture of our system, which comprises four stages: preprocessing, on-device dynamic analysis, feature extraction and similarity searching. The preprocessing stage, as shown in the left side of Fig. 3, involves two parts: binary extraction and address extraction. It dumps the mobiles binaries from the app and extract addresses for all functions and imported libraries and frameworks. All the extracted addresses are passed to the on-device dynamic analysis stage for instrumentation and trace logging usage. The recorded traces will be analyzed by the feature extraction stage. Then we perform the similarity searching based on the function features obtained from feature extraction stage. Next, we will present each step of our system in the following sections.

3.2 Preprocessing

Binary Extraction. When you download an iOS app from the App Store, Apple injects a special 4196 byte long header into the signed binary encrypted with the public key associated with your iTunes account. For this step we choose Clutch [4], to decrypt and dump app binary. Then we disable the ASLR (Address Space Layout Randomization) to get the correct function addresses. ASLR makes the remote exploitation of memory corruption vulnerabilities significantly more difficult by randomizing the application objects location in the memory. By default iOS apps are compiled with *-pie* flag (Generate Position-Dependent Code). This flag is automatically checked in the latest version of *Xcode* in order to use ASLR. We leverage the tool *removePIE* [6] to disable the ASLR by flipping the PIE flag. After that, we put the binary back to the app and re-sign it with *ldid* [11].

Address Extraction. We utilize IDA Pro [9] to disassemble the binary obtained from previous step, extract function addresses as well as imported library addresses and framework addresses through IDAPython API. This component is implemented with 155 lines of Python code. Listing 1.1 shows an

example of a function address table extracted from the iOS app binary. Each
line consists of starting address (e.g., 0x11834), ending address (e.g., 0x11980)
and function name (e.g., *prepareToRecord* from the class *MovieRecorder*). Listing 1.2 shows an example of library addresses, which only consist the starting
addresses and library names.

Listing 1.1. Function addresses

```
...
0xb7ea,0xb964,-[VideoSnakeViewController
    toggleRecording:]
0xe2cc,0xe51c,-[VideoSnakeSessionManager
    startRecording]
0x111d8,0x1128c,-[MovieRecorder  initWithURL:]
0x1161c,0x116a8,-[MovieRecorder  delegate]
0x11834,0x11980,-[MovieRecorder  prepareToRecord]
0x11d48,0x11ebc,-[MovieRecorder  finishRecording]
...
```

Listing 1.2. Library addresses

```
...
0x1606c,__Block_copy
0x1607c,__Block_object_assign
0x1608c,__Block_object_dispose
0x1609c,__Unwind_SjLj_Register
0x160ac,__Unwind_SjLj_Resume
0x160bc,__Unwind_SjLj_Unregister
...
```

3.3   On-Device Dynamic Analysis

The on-device dynamic analysis stage performs dynamic instrumentation and
trace logging in order to record the needed information.

Dynamic Instrumentation. We utilize Frida [7], a dynamic instrumentation
toolkit, to inject scripts in app process that monitor the dynamic behavior during
execution. Frida lets you inject snippets of JavaScript or your own library into
native apps. Frida's core is written in C and injects Google's V8 engine into the
target processes, where the JavaScript gets executed with full access to memory,
hooking functions and even calling native functions inside the process.

Trace Logging. In our implementation we chose features that capture a variety
of system level information (e.g., system calls), as well as higher level attributes,
such as libc calls, objc calls, framework API invocations as follows.

- **System Calls:** e.g., *read, write, open,* etc. defined in *libsystem_kernel.dylib*
- **Library Calls:** e.g., *memset, memcpy, free,* etc. defined in *libSystem.B.dylib,* *_objc_getClass, _objc_getProtocol,* etc. defined in *libobjc.A.dylib*
- **Framework APIs:** e.g., *OpenGLES, CoreMedia, UIKit,* etc.

We leverage the Frida API to inject JavaScript at the library addresses and framework addresses to record the invocations of such features above, and generate a backtrace for the current thread, returned as an array of native pointer addresses for the subsequent steps.

3.4 Feature Extraction

Listing 1.3 illustrates the logged trace data, which consists of arrays of addresses. Each line indicates an invocation of library call or framework API call, followed by its stack backtrace information. First, we transform the addresses to function names according to the address table obtained from the preprocessing stage. For instance, 0x1609c is the starting address of *__Unwind_SjLj_Register*, 0x11892 is in the range of 0x11834 and 0x11980, which indicate the library *__Unwind_SjLj_Register* is called by function *prepareToRecord*. The rest can be done in the same manner. Listing 1.4 illustrates a full translated results from Listing 1.3.

Listing 1.3. Stack backtrace: address

```
    . . .
    0x1609c ,0x11892 ,0xe498 ,0xb92e ,0xb15a
    0x1621c ,0x118c0 ,0xe498 ,0xb92e ,0xb15a
    0x1620c ,0x118fc ,0xe498 ,0xb15a
    . . .
```

Listing 1.4. Stack backtrace: name

```
    . . .
    __Unwind_SjLj_Register ,-[MovieRecorder
       prepareToRecord] ,-[VideoSnakeSessionManager
       startRecording] ,-[VideoSnakeViewController
       toggleRecording:] ,sub_B120
    _dispatch_get_global_queue ,-[MovieRecorder
       prepareToRecord] ,-[VideoSnakeSessionManager
       startRecording] ,-[VideoSnakeViewController
       toggleRecording:] ,sub_B120
    _dispatch_async ,-[MovieRecorder prepareToRecord] ,-[
       VideoSnakeSessionManager startRecording] ,-[
       VideoSnakeViewController toggleRecording:] ,
       sub_B120
    . . .
```

Next, we match these library calls or framework API calls to its corresponding caller functions as features. Listing 1.5 represents features of function *prepare-*

ToRecord, in JSON format. The feature extraction component is implemented with 280 lines of Python code.

3.5 Similarity Searching

The function feature representation is a length-N feature list. We chose Jaccard index to measure the similarity between lists. We define sim(f, g) to be the similarity score between function f and g. We perform similarity searching as the following: starting with a known reference function in a trace, we are searching for mobile binaries containing similar functions by calculating similarity score and listing top K similar function candidates.

Listing 1.5. Function features

```
{
        "name" : "-[MovieRecorder prepareToRecord]",
        "features" : [
                [
                        "__Unwind_SjLj_Register",
                        "_dispatch_get_global_queue",
                        "_dispatch_async",
                        "__Block_object_assign",
                        "__Unwind_SjLj_Unregister"
                ]
        ]
}
```

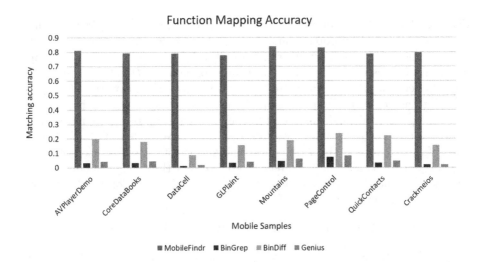

Fig. 4. Function mapping between obfuscated version and non-obfuscated version

4   Evaluation

In this section, we evaluate our system from several objectives. Particularly, we conduct our experiments to evaluate whether our system outperforms existing binary similarity detection tools in terms of better obfuscation resilience and accuracy. We designed two controlled datasets so that we have a ground truth to assess comparison results accurately. We also evaluate the effectiveness of our system in analyzing real world top-ranked iOS apps from Apple App Store.

4.1   Experiment Setup

Our on-device dynamic analysis is performed on a 32 GB Apple Jailbroken iPad (4th Generation) running iOS 8.3. The configuration of our testbed machine for feature extraction and similarity searching is shown as follows.

- CPU: Intel Core i7-6700K Processor (Eight-core with 4.00 GHz)
- Memory: 64 GB
- OS: Ubuntu Linux 14.04 LTS
- Python Version: 2.7.12
- IDA Pro Version: 6.6.

4.2   Ground Truth Dataset

Data 1. First, we collect 8 sample codes with different functionalities from official Apple developer website. For each sample we build both non-obfuscated version and obfuscated version. The obfuscated version combines all three settings in Table 1.

Data 2. Then we test our system with third-party frameworks or libraries that are commonly used by popular mobile apps. In practice, programmers usually take advantage of existing frameworks or libraries to speed up their developments. In our evaluation, we choose *AFNetworking* and *SDWebImage*, top-two ranked open source frameworks [16] as the reference implementation. Our purpose is to detect such frameworks or libraries that commonly used in different mobile apps. To this end, we collect 8 open source projects from GitHub, and reuse the provided APIs from two libraries above. We built sample apps with non-obfuscated version and 7 different combinations of the obfuscation settings, which results in 64 apps in 8 different types. We kept the debug symbols as they provide a ground truth and enable us to verify the correctness of matching using the functions symbolic names.

Table 1. Different obfuscation types and flag settings

	Type	Flag setting
1	Control flow flattening	-fla, -split, -split_num=3
2	Instruction substitution	-sub, -sub_loop=3
3	Bogus control flow	-bcf, -bcf_loop=3, -bcf_prob=40

4.3   Obfuscation Options

As mentioned in Sect. 2, we use Obfuscator-LLVM to obfuscate our ground truth mobile samples. Table 1 lists specific obfuscation settings that we use to build our ground truth iOS samples. We integrate Obfuscator-LLVM into Xcode, and enable the three obfuscation features described in Sect. 2, and apply different settings as shown in Table 1.

4.4   Peer Tools

We compare our tools with other state-of-the-art similarity detection or diffing tools that open to public: BinDiff, BinGrap, Genies. BinDiff [17] is a comparison tool for binary files, that assists vulnerability researchers and engineers to quickly find differences and similarities in disassembled code. BinGrap [3] is also a static analysis tool that perform function similarity searching, but it can output a list of functions in order of similarity. Genius is a bug search engine that performs function similarity detection based on mapping raw features of a function into a higher-level numeric vector where each dimension of the vector is the similarity distance to a categorization in the codebook. However, only partial code is available, including raw feature extraction and search. Therefore, we re-implement Genius' two core steps, codebook generation and feature encoding in python. We utilized Hungarian algorithm for calculating bipartite graph matching cost and normalized spectral clustering [38] for ACFGs (Attributed Control Flow Graph) clustering. In evaluation phrase, we adopt Nearpy [14] for LSH (Locality Sensitive Hashing) [18] and search. We used SQLite to store function information and encoded vectors. As mentioned in Sect. 1, BLEX [21], BinSim [35] and CryptoHunt [45] are not able to work on iOS platforms. To the best of our knowledge, we are the first to propose a dynamic strategy for comparing mobile binary code. This is the reason why we did not compare our evaluation to these dynamic approaches.

4.5   Evaluation Results

The first evaluation for data 1 is shown in Fig. 4. For each sample, We randomly select functions from non-obfuscated version as reference functions, then perform our *trace-based function similarity mapping* to see if we can locate the same function in obfuscated version. The second evaluation for data 2 is shown in Fig. 5. We randomly select one app from each type of apps as reference known app, and select commonly used APIs in *AFNetworking* and *SDWebImage* from that app as query functions. Then we perform *trace-based function similarity mapping* for searching the given functions in the rest apps, and list top K candidates for each app based on the similarity score. We only compare with Genius and BinGrep since BinDiff is a one-to-one mapping tool, which cannot list more than 1 candidate.

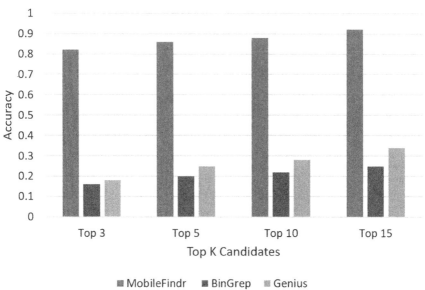

Fig. 5. Function mapping evaluation for popular third-party frameworks

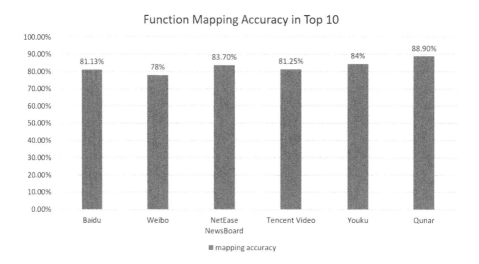

Fig. 6. Function mapping evaluation in real-world apps

Our evaluation results show that MobileFindr can achieve more than 80% accuracy in average from top 3 to top 15 similar functions, which outperforms other tools in terms of much more better accuracy and obfuscation resilience.

4.6   Real-World App Case Study

We tested MobileFindr using real-world apps to evaluate its efficiency. We evaluated 6 top-ranked iOS apps in different types, such as search engine, social networking, etc. For instance, Baidu is the world's largest Chinese search engine. We downloaded two different versions of Baidu app, version 930 and version 935. We chose version 930 as reference app and performed a simple web searching with key words: "security" for trace logging. We collected 430 functions in this trace, and then perform *trace-based function similarity mapping* to search similarity functions in the new version 935, and listed top 10 similar function candidates. MobileFindr achieve 81.13% accuracy with less than 10 min. While matching the same 430 functions in Genius, it only achieved 59.7% accuracy, but spent around 2 h in training, more than 40 h when handling function graph embeddings. Figure 6 shows the function mapping results for the 6 real-world apps.

5   Discussion

In this section, we discuss the limitations of our system and potential solutions to be investigated in future work.

First, a challenge that we already touched upon in Sect. 4 is the fact that our approach needs manual verification efforts for real world iOS apps, since we don't have access to their source code. The candidate similarity ranking produced by our system gives an ordered list of matched functions that have to be manually inspected by an analyst to verify if those functions are actually similar. Some of the existing dynamic approaches [35, 45] rely on symbolic execution to generate a set of symbolic formula, and then use theorem prover to perform the equivalence checking. However, the theorem prover is computationally expensive and impractical for large code bases of many real world mobile apps. Such an automatic verification would be ideal, but surely is a research topic in itself and is outside the scope of this work.

Second, the incomplete path coverage is a concern for all dynamic analysis system, including ours. The possible solutions are to explore more paths by automatic input generation [27, 36]. To trigger as many dynamic behaviors as possible for trace logging, we can leverage the idea of Malton [47], which proposed an efficient path exploration technique that employs in-memory concolic execution with an offloading mechanism and direct execution engine. We leave it as future work.

Third, the functions considered by us need to have a certain amount of complexity for the approach to work effectively. Otherwise, the relatively low combination number of library calls leads to a high probability for collision. Hence, we only considered functions with at lease five basic blocks, as noted in Sect. 4. For instance, the potential for bugs in small functions, however, is significantly lower than in large functions, as shown in [13]. Hence, in a real-world scenario this should be no factual limitation.

6 Related Work

There has been a substantial research on detecting binary code similarity. Existing semantics aware binary matching techniques can be classified into two categories. One is based on static information including numeric features and structural features [20,22,23,34]. Many numeric features (e.g. the number of basic blocks, the number of edges, logic instructions,local variables, etc.) and control flow graph has been demonstrated to be robust across compilers and different compile options in previous work [24,25]. The other one executes target code and collect runtime behavior [21,35,42,45]. Common execution behaviors includes stack and heap memory access, system call sequences and library calls, registers values, execution path, etc.

The combination of collected features represent as a signature of target code for matching step. It is vital to identify robust features and correctly characterize target code with the features. Bindiff [17] as an efficient binary diffing tool using a graph theoretic approach to find similarities and differences. The graph isomorphism detection on pairs of function works well when two semantically equivalent binaries have similar control flow. But CFG changes across architectures and compilers. In [23], Genius maps raw features of a function into a higher-level numeric vector where each dimension of the vector is the similarity distance to a categorization in the codebook. However, one common limitation of static approaches is incapable of handling obfuscated code. BLEX [21] collects execution side effects during function execution and uses a multidimensional vector as function signature for similarity assessment. It relies on Pin framework and can not apply to mobile binaries.

The techniques of binary matching have been driven towards to solve security problems. One common case in vulnerability assessment is that secure analysts would want to use a sample of vulnerable binary without source code to search for the similar bug across all the softwares installed in the company devices [22,37]. It is challenging for vulnerability assessment in a large code base for the following reasons: first, most commercial software projects are closed-source and only available in the binary form without debug information. Second, different versions of software may be compiled on different optimization levels and different compile tool-chain, which would radically changes both the number of nodes and structure of edges in both the control flow graph and the call graph. Third, pervasive code protection schemes, such as class and method rename, encryption of strings, control flow obfuscation and virtualization of code, render code analysis time consuming. Our evaluation have considered above situations and demonstrate that our approach can handle it.

With rapid development of open-source projects, the similarity between an licensed protected binary and a suspicious binary indicates a potential case of software plagiarism [34,43]. Existing code similarity measurement methods have been proved to be useful but remain far from perfect. Some software plagiarism detection approaches based on dynamic system call sequences have also been proposed [32,43], but they incur false negatives when the number of system calls are insufficient or when system call replacement is applied. Most of the existing methods are not effective in the presence of obfuscation techniques. Another obfuscation resilient method [34] based on symbolic execution and theorem proving bears high computational overhead.

7 Conclusion

We proposed MobileFindr, an on-device trace-based function similarity mapping system for reverse engineering mobile apps. It records a variety of dynamic runtime information as dynamic behavior features via dynamic instrumentation, and use stack backtrace information to locate corresponding functions that can be represented with these features. We evaluated it with a set of examples under different obfuscation scheme combinations. Our experimental results show that our system can successfully identify fine-grained function similarities between mobile binaries, and outperform existing state-of-the-art approaches in terms of better obfuscation resilience and accuracy. Our evaluation with top-ranked real-world frameworks and apps also demonstrated the effectiveness of our system. To the best of our knowledge, we are the first to propose a dynamic strategy for function similarity identification on the mobile platform, which is capable of mitigating many anti-reverse engineering techniques.

References

1. Android studio - debug your app. https://developer.android.com/studio/debug/index.html. Accessed 30 Jan 2018
2. Apktool - a tool for reverse engineering android apk files. https://ibotpeaches.github.io/Apktool/. Accessed 30 Jan 2018
3. Bingrep. https://github.com/hada2/bingrep. Accessed 30 Jan 2018
4. Clutch 2.0.4. https://github.com/KJCracks/Clutch/releases/tag/2.0.4. Accessed 30 Jan 2018
5. dex2jar. https://github.com/pxb1988/dex2jar. Accessed 30 Jan 2018
6. Disable aslr on ios applications. http://www.securitylearn.net/2013/05/23/disable-aslr-on-ios-applications/. Accessed 30 Jan 2018
7. Frida. https://www.frida.re/. Accessed 30 Jan 2018
8. Hex-rays decompiler. https://www.hex-rays.com/products/decompiler/index.shtml. Accessed 30 Jan 2018
9. Ida. https://www.hex-rays.com/products/ida/index.shtml. Accessed 30 Jan 2018
10. Jd-gui. http://jd.benow.ca/. Accessed 30 Jan 2018
11. ldid. http://iphonedevwiki.net/index.php/Ldid. Accessed 30 Jan 2018
12. The lldb debugger. https://lldb.llvm.org/. Accessed 30 Jan 2018
13. More complex = less secure: Miss a test path and you could get hacked. http://www.mccabe.com/pdf/MoreComplexEqualsLessSecure-McCabe.pdf. Accessed 30 Jan 2018
14. Nearpy. https://github.com/pixelogik/NearPy. Accessed 30 Jan 2018
15. smali/baksmali wiki. https://github.com/JesusFreke/smali/wiki. Accessed 30 Jan 2018
16. Top 10 libraries for ios developers. https://www.raywenderlich.com/177482/top-10-ios-developer-libraries. Accessed 30 Jan 2018

17. Zynamics bindiff. https://www.zynamics.com/bindiff.html. Accessed 30 Jan 2018
18. Andoni, A., Indyk, P.: Near-optimal hashing algorithms for approximate nearest neighbor in high dimensions. In: 47th Annual IEEE Symposium on Foundations of Computer Science, 2006. FOCS 2006, pp. 459–468. IEEE (2006)
19. Brumley, D., Poosankam, P., Song, D., Zheng, J.: Automatic patch-based exploit generation is possible: techniques and implications. In: IEEE Symposium on Security and Privacy 2008. SP 2008, pp. 143–157. IEEE (2008)
20. David, Y., Partush, N., Yahav, E.: Similarity of binaries through re-optimization. In: Proceedings of the 38th ACM SIGPLAN Conference on Programming Language Design and Implementation, pp. 79–94. ACM (2017)
21. Egele, M., Woo, M., Chapman, P., Brumley, D.: Blanket execution: dynamic similarity testing for program binaries and components. USENIX (2014)
22. Eschweiler, S., Yakdan, K., Gerhards-Padilla, E.: discovRE: efficient cross-architecture identification of bugs in binary code. In: NDSS (2016)
23. Feng, Q., Zhou, R., Xu, C., Cheng, Y., Testa, B., Yin, H.: Scalable graph-based bug search for firmware images. In: Proceedings of the 2016 ACM SIGSAC Conference on Computer and Communications Security, pp. 480–491. ACM (2016)
24. Flake, H.: Structural comparison of executable objects. In: Proceedings of the International GI Workshop on Detection of Intrusions and Malware & Vulnerability Assessment, number P-46 in Lecture Notes in Informatics, pp. 161–174. Citeseer (2004)
25. Gao, D., Reiter, M.K., Song, D.: BinHunt: automatically finding semantic differences in binary programs. In: Chen, L., Ryan, M.D., Wang, G. (eds.) ICICS 2008. LNCS, vol. 5308, pp. 238–255. Springer, Heidelberg (2008). https://doi.org/10.1007/978-3-540-88625-9_16
26. Gibler, C., Stevens, R., Crussell, J., Chen, H., Zang, H., Choi, H.: Adrob: examining the landscape and impact of android application plagiarism. In: Proceeding of the 11th Annual International Conference on Mobile Systems, Applications, and Services, pp. 431–444. ACM (2013)
27. Godefroid, P., Levin, M.Y., Molnar, D.A., et al.: Automated whitebox fuzz testing. In: NDSS, vol. 8, pp. 151–166 (2008)
28. Herremans, D.: MorpheuS: automatic music generation with recurrent pattern constraints and tension profiles (2016)
29. Junod, P., Rinaldini, J., Wehrli, J., Michielin, J.: Obfuscator-LLVM - software protection for the masses. In: Wyseur, B. (ed.) Proceedings of the IEEE/ACM 1st International Workshop on Software Protection, SPRO 2015, Firenze, Italy, 19th May 2015, pp. 3–9. IEEE (2015). https://doi.org/10.1109/SPRO.2015.10
30. Kirat, D., Vigna, G.: Malgene: automatic extraction of malware analysis evasion signature. In: Proceedings of the 22nd ACM SIGSAC Conference on Computer and Communications Security, pp. 769–780. ACM (2015)
31. Lindorfer, M., Di Federico, A., Maggi, F., Comparetti, P.M., Zanero, S.: Lines of malicious code: insights into the malicious software industry. In: Proceedings of the 28th Annual Computer Security Applications Conference, pp. 349–358. ACM (2012)
32. Liu, C., Chen, C., Han, J., Yu, P.S.: GPLAG: detection of software plagiarism by program dependence graph analysis. In: Proceedings of the 12th ACM SIGKDD International Conference on Knowledge Discovery and Data Mining, pp. 872–881. ACM (2006)
33. Luk, C.K., et al.: Pin: building customized program analysis tools with dynamic instrumentation. In: ACM SIGPLAN notices, vol. 40, pp. 190–200. ACM (2005)

34. Luo, L., Ming, J., Wu, D., Liu, P., Zhu, S.: Semantics-based obfuscation-resilient binary code similarity comparison with applications to software plagiarism detection. In: Proceedings of the 22nd ACM SIGSOFT International Symposium on Foundations of Software Engineering, pp. 389–400. ACM (2014)
35. Ming, J., Xu, D., Jiang, Y., Wu, D.: BinSim: trace-based semantic binary diffing via system call sliced segment equivalence checking. In: Proceedings of the 26th USENIX Security Symposium, pp. 253–270. USENIX Association (2017)
36. Moser, A., Kruegel, C., Kirda, E.: Exploring multiple execution paths for malware analysis. In: IEEE Symposium on Security and Privacy 2007. SP 2007, pp. 231–245. IEEE (2007)
37. Moser, A., Kruegel, C., Kirda, E.: Limits of static analysis for malware detection. In: Twenty-Third Annual Computer Security Applications Conference 2007. ACSAC 2007, pp. 421–430. IEEE (2007)
38. Ng, A.Y., Jordan, M.I., Weiss, Y.: On spectral clustering: analysis and an algorithm. In: Advances in Neural Information Processing Systems, pp. 849–856 (2002)
39. Oh, J.: Fight against 1-day exploits: diffing binaries vs anti-diffing binaries. Black Hat (2009)
40. Petsas, T., Voyatzis, G., Athanasopoulos, E., Polychronakis, M., Ioannidis, S.: Rage against the virtual machine: hindering dynamic analysis of android malware. In: Proceedings of the Seventh European Workshop on System Security, p. 5. ACM (2014)
41. Pewny, J., Garmany, B., Gawlik, R., Rossow, C., Holz, T.: Cross-architecture bug search in binary executables. In: 2015 IEEE Symposium on Security and Privacy (SP), pp. 709–724. IEEE (2015)
42. Sharma, R., Schkufza, E., Churchill, B., Aiken, A.: Data-driven equivalence checking. In: ACM SIGPLAN Notices, vol. 48, pp. 391–406. ACM (2013)
43. Wang, X., Jhi, Y.C., Zhu, S., Liu, P.: Behavior based software theft detection. In: Proceedings of the 16th ACM Conference on Computer and Communications Security, pp. 280–290. ACM (2009)
44. Wang, X., Jhi, Y.C., Zhu, S., Liu, P.: Detecting software theft via system call based birthmarks. In: Annual Computer Security Applications Conference 2009. ACSAC 2009, pp. 149–158. IEEE (2009)
45. Xu, D., Ming, J., Wu, D.: Cryptographic function detection in obfuscated binaries via bit-precise symbolic loop mapping. In: 2017 IEEE Symposium on Security and Privacy (SP), pp. 921–937. IEEE (2017)
46. Xu, X., Liu, C., Feng, Q., Yin, H., Song, L., Song, D.: Neural network-based graph embedding for cross-platform binary code similarity detection. In: Proceedings of the 2017 ACM SIGSAC Conference on Computer and Communications Security, pp. 363–376. ACM (2017)
47. Xue, L., Zhou, Y., Chen, T., Luo, X., Gu, G.: Malton: towards on-device non-invasive mobile malware analysis for art. In: 26th USENIX Security Symposium (USENIX Security 17). ACM (2017)

Blockchain and Machine Learning

Strain: A Secure Auction for Blockchains

Erik-Oliver Blass[1($\boxtimes$)] and Florian Kerschbaum[2]

[1] Airbus, Munich, Germany
erik-oliver.blass@airbus.com
[2] University of Waterloo, Waterloo, Canada
florian.kerschbaum@uwaterloo.ca

Abstract. We present Strain, a new auction protocol running on top of blockchains and guaranteeing bid confidentiality against fully-malicious parties. As our goal is efficiency and low blockchain latency, we abstain from using traditional, highly interactive MPC primitives such as secret shares. We focus on a slightly weaker adversary model than MPC which allows Strain to achieve constant latency in both the number of parties and the bid length. The main idea behind Strain is a new maliciously-secure two-party comparison mechanism executed between any pair of bids in parallel. Using zero-knowledge proofs, Strain broadcasts the outcome of comparisons on the blockchain in a way that all parties can verify each outcome. Strain's latency is not only asymptotically optimal, but also efficient in practice, requiring a total of just 4 blocks of the underlying blockchain. Strain provides typical auction security requirements such as non-retractable bids against fully-malicious adversaries.

1 Introduction

Today's blockchains offer transparency and integrity features which could make them ideal for hosting auctions. Once a bid has been submitted to a smart contract managing the auction on the blockchain, the bid cannot be retracted anymore. After a deadline has passed, everybody can verify the winning bid. Due to its attractive features, blockchain auctions are already considered in the real-world. As a prominent example to fight nepotism and corruption, Ukraine will host blockchain auctions to sell previously seized goods [33].

However, today's blockchain transparency features disqualify them in scenarios where input data must remain confidential. For example, in a procurement auction, another prime application example for blockchains [1], an *auctioneer* requests offers for some good ("Need 1M grade V2X steel screws") as part of a smart contract. A set of *suppliers* submits bids for the good, and the lowest bid wins the procurement auction. Realizing a decentralized auction as a smart contract has the above transparency features, mitigates corruption, and avoids a possibly corrupt, centralized auctioneer. Yet, bids are confidential. Suppliers have mutual distrust, and leaking the value of a bid to a competitor must be avoided. In some situations, one supplier should not even learn whether or not another supplier is participating in an auction. To make matters worse, multiple

© Springer Nature Switzerland AG 2018
J. Lopez et al. (Eds.): ESORICS 2018, LNCS 11098, pp. 87–110, 2018.
https://doi.org/10.1007/978-3-319-99073-6_5

suppliers might collude, be fully-malicious, behave randomly (not rationally), and abort participation in the auction to disturb its outcome. Still, the auction should run as expected.

Kosba et al. [26] already mention that one could revert to implementing the auction with Secure Multi-Party Computation (MPC) on the blockchain. While there has been a flurry of research on MPC, and generic frameworks are readily available [38], a main MPC drawback is its high interactivity. Yet, interactivity is extremely expensive on a blockchain in terms of latency. Broadcasting a message, changing the state of a smart contract (code execution), and any kind of party interactivity requires a valid transaction. As transactions are attached to blocks, any interactivity requires (at least) one block interval for completion. Block interval times are large, e.g., roughly 15 s for Ethereum [19]. Thus, high interactivity, a large number of MPC rounds, automatically rules out short-term, short living auctions.

This Paper. We present Strain ("Secure aucTions foR blockchAINs"), a new protocol for secure auctions on blockchains. At the heart, we improve Fischlin [21]'s comparison protocol in several key aspects tailored for adoption in blockchains. First, Strain features a distributed key generation for Goldwasser-Micali encryption based on a new mechanism to verifiably share each supplier's private key. Suppliers initially commit to their bids by encrypting them with their public key. A honest majority of suppliers can then open a commitment in case a supplier aborts the protocol.

Strain's second main feature is an efficient zero-knowledge (ZK) proof that two Goldwasser-Micali ciphertexts, encrypted under different keys, contain the same plaintext. For this proof, we require existence of a semi-honest *judge* party which must not collude with either of the comparing parties. In the context of auctions, the judge can be implemented by, e.g., the auctioneer. Using ZK proofs, the judge verifies (and publishes on the blockchain) whether both parties use previously committed values as input to the comparison. Again using a ZK proof, the comparing party then publishes the outcome of the comparison on the blockchain. Together, the two ZK proofs allow everybody to verify correctness of the comparison's result in only 3 blocks (totaling 4 blocks for the entire Strain protocol). We achieve such low latency by providing slightly weaker security guarantees than MPC would have. Specifically, the semi-honest judge would not be required in MPC. Strain also leaks the order of bids, but not their value.

Strain optionally supports anonymous auctions by using a combination of Dining Cryptographer networks and blind signatures. Suppliers can be anonymized, such that no supplier knows which other suppliers are participating in an auction. Note that we specifically avoid payment channels [37], and all communication will run through the blockchain. The advantage is no or only little data stored at parties, crucial information stored at the central ledger, and no direct network connectivity required between parties.

We benchmarked main cryptographic operations, and our analysis shows that Strain supports auctions of up to dozens of concurrent suppliers within 3 Ethereum blocks.

In summary, the *technical highlights* of this paper are:

- A new blockchain auction protocol, Strain, protecting confidentiality of bids. Strain provides provable security against fully-malicious suppliers and semi-honest auctioneers. It is efficient and completes an auction in a constant (four) number of interactions, i.e., blockchain blocks. Its round complexity is independent from the bit length of the bids (multiplicative depth of a comparison circuit) and the number of suppliers.
- After bidding, no supplier can retract or modify a bid. However, in case of dispute, commitments can be opened by an honest majority. Strain will complete, even if malicious parties fail to respond and abort the auction without any supplier being able to change their bid. Computation of the winning bid is performed solely by the suppliers and entirely on the blockchain. The contribution of the auctioneer to the auction is only to verify correctness of computations in zero-knowledge.

We stress that the lack of smart contract data confidentiality is independent from privacy-preserving coin transactions, see, e.g., ZeroCash [3] for an overview. To reach consensus, blockchain miners generally require access to all contract input data. Also, permissioned blockchains such as Hyperledger (Fabric) lack confidentiality, even if contract execution can be restricted to only those parties participating in a contract.

2   Background

Let $\mathcal{S} = \{S_1, \ldots, S_s\}$ be the set of s suppliers in the system with public-private key pairs (pk_i, sk_i). The procurement auction is run by auctioneer A having public-private key pair (pk_A, sk_A). Assume that all suppliers and A know each other's public keys, so A can run an auction accepting bids from valid suppliers only.

2.1   Preliminaries

Let λ be the security parameter. For an integer n, let QR_n be the set of quadratic residues of group $\mathbb{Z}_n$, and QNR_n is the set of quadratic non-residues of $\mathbb{Z}_n$. Function $J_n(x)$ computes the Jacobi symbol $\left(\frac{x}{n}\right)$, and we define set $\mathbb{J}_n = \{x \in \mathbb{Z}_n | J_n(x) = 1\}$. Finally, $QNR_n^1 = \{x \in QNR_n | J_n(x) = 1\}$ (set of "pseudo-squares").

Quadratic Residues Modulo Blum Integers. An integer n is a Blum integer, if $n = p \cdot q$ for two distinct primes p, q and $p = q = 3 \mod 4$. If n is a Blum integer, testing whether some $x \in \mathbb{Z}_n$ with $J_n(x) = 1$ is in QR_n can be implemented by checking whether $x^{\frac{(p-1) \cdot (q-1)}{4}} = 1 \mod n$ [25]. Moreover, observe that the DDH assumption holds in group $(\mathbb{J}_n, \cdot)$. For $r \xleftarrow{\$} \mathbb{Z}_n^*$, $g = -r^2 \mod n$ is a generator of group $(\mathbb{J}_n, \cdot)$, see Sect. A.1 of Couteau et al. [13]. In particular $z = -1 = -(1^2) \mod n$ is a generator of $\mathbb{J}_n$.

GM Encryption. A Goldwasser-Micali (GM) [23] key pair comprises private key sk^{GM} and public key pk^{GM}. For p and q being distinct, strong random primes of length λ, the private key is $sk^{\mathsf{GM}} = \frac{(p-1)\cdot(q-1)}{4}$. We require $p = q = 3 \bmod 4$, and therefore $n = p \cdot q$ is a Blum integer. We set $z = n - 1 = -1 \bmod n$. The public key is $pk^{\mathsf{GM}} = (n, z)$. With n being a Blum integer, $z \in QNR_n^1$.

With randomly chosen $r_i \xleftarrow{\$} \mathbb{Z}_n^*$, GM encryption of bit string $M \in \{0,1\}^\eta$ is $C = \mathsf{Enc}_{pk^{\mathsf{GM}}}^{\mathsf{GM}}(M_1 \ldots M_\eta) = (r_1^2 \cdot z^{M_1} \bmod n, \ldots, r_\eta^2 \cdot z^{M_\eta} \bmod n)$. All parties automatically dismiss a ciphertext C if $C \notin \mathbb{J}_n$.

Decryption of ciphertext C simply checks whether each component of $C = (c_1, \ldots, c_\eta)$ is in QR_n. As n is a Blum integer, raising c_i to secret key sk^{GM} is sufficient, i.e., you compute $M = \mathsf{Dec}_{sk^{\mathsf{GM}}}^{\mathsf{GM}}(c_1, \ldots, c_\eta) = (1 - c_1^{sk^{\mathsf{GM}}} \bmod n, \ldots, 1 - c_\eta^{sk^{\mathsf{GM}}} \bmod n)$.

Recall GM's homomorphic properties for encryptions of two bits b_1, b_2 (when obvious, we omit public-/private keys in this paper for better readability):

- $\mathsf{Dec}^{\mathsf{GM}}(\mathsf{Enc}^{\mathsf{GM}}(b_1) \cdot \mathsf{Enc}^{\mathsf{GM}}(b_2)) = b_1 \oplus b_2$ (plaintext XOR)
- $\mathsf{Dec}^{\mathsf{GM}}(\mathsf{Enc}^{\mathsf{GM}}(b_1) \cdot z) = 1 - b_1$ (flip plaintext bit b_1)
- For a GM ciphertext c, re-encryption is $\mathsf{ReEnc}^{\mathsf{GM}}(c) \leftarrow c \cdot \mathsf{Enc}^{\mathsf{GM}}(0)$.

AND-Homomorphic GM Encryption. GM encryption can be modified to support AND-homomorphism [21,34]. Specifically, let λ' be the soundness parameter of the Sander et al. [34] technique that works as follows.

A *single* bit $b = 1$ is encrypted to λ'-many random quadratic residues $\bmod n$, i.e., λ' separate GM encryptions of 0. A bit $b = 0$ is encrypted to a sequence of random elements x with $J_n(x) = 1$, i.e., λ' encryptions of randomly chosen bits $a_1, \ldots, a_{\lambda'}$. More formally, $\mathsf{Enc}^{\mathsf{AND}}(1) = (\mathsf{Enc}^{\mathsf{GM}}(0), \ldots, \mathsf{Enc}^{\mathsf{GM}}(0))$ and $\mathsf{Enc}^{\mathsf{AND}}(0) = (\mathsf{Enc}^{\mathsf{GM}}(a_1), \ldots, \mathsf{Enc}^{\mathsf{GM}}(a_{\lambda'}))$.

Decryption of a sequence of a λ'-element ciphertext checks whether all elements are in QR_n. That is, $\mathsf{Dec}^{\mathsf{AND}}(c_1, \ldots, c_{\lambda'}) = 1$, if $\forall c_i : c_i \in QR_n$, and 0 otherwise.

As an AND-encryption of 0 can result in λ' elements of QR_n, decryption is correct with probability $1 - 2^{-\lambda'}$.

$\mathsf{Enc}^{\mathsf{AND}}$ is homomorphic with respect to Boolean AND. For two ciphertexts $\mathsf{Enc}^{\mathsf{AND}}(b) = (c_1, \ldots, c_{\lambda'})$ and $\mathsf{Enc}^{\mathsf{AND}}(b') = (c_1', \ldots, c_{\lambda'}')$, $\mathsf{Dec}^{\mathsf{AND}}(c_1 \cdot c_1', \ldots, c_{\lambda'} \cdot c_{\lambda'}') = b \wedge b'$. If the c_i and c_i' are all in QR_n, so is their product. If one is in QR_n and the other in QNR_n^1, their product is in QNR_n^1. Yet, if both c_i and c_i' are in QNR_n^1, their product is in QR_n. For example, if all c_i and c_i' are in QNR_n^1, $b = b' = 0$, but $\mathsf{Dec}^{\mathsf{AND}}$ after their homomorphic combination will output 1. So, $\mathsf{Dec}^{\mathsf{AND}}$ is correct with probability $1 - 2^{-\lambda'}$. Re-encryption for AND-encryption is simply defined as $\mathsf{ReEnc}^{\mathsf{AND}}(c_1, \ldots, c_{\lambda'}) \leftarrow (\mathsf{ReEnc}^{\mathsf{GM}}(c_1), \ldots, \mathsf{ReEnc}^{\mathsf{GM}}(c_{\lambda'}))$.

Finally, we can embed an existing GM ciphertext $\gamma = \mathsf{Enc}^{\mathsf{GM}}(b)$ of bit b into an a ciphertext $\mathsf{Enc}^{\mathsf{AND}}(b) = (c_1, \ldots, c_{\lambda'})$ without decryption. First, we choose λ' random bits $a_1, \ldots, a_{\lambda'}$. Now, if $a_i = 1$, then set $c_i = \mathsf{Enc}^{\mathsf{GM}}(0)$. Otherwise, set $c_i = \mathsf{Enc}^{\mathsf{GM}}(0) \cdot \gamma \cdot z \bmod n$. In the first case, c_i is a quadratic residue independently of b ($c_i = \mathsf{Enc}^{\mathsf{GM}}(0)$). In the second case, we flip bit b

by multiplying with z (and re-encrypt the result). So, a quadratic residue c_i becomes a non-residue and the other way around. If $b = 1$, all λ' elements c_i will be quadratic residues. If $b = 0$, all λ' elements c_i will be quadratic residues only with probability $2^{-\lambda'}$, such that the embedding is correct with probability $1 - 2^{-\lambda'}$.

2.2   Blockchain

There exist several detailed introductions to blockchain and smart contract technology such as Ethereum [18]. Here, we only briefly and informally summarize properties relevant for Strain.

A blockchain is a distributed network implementing a ledger functionality. Parties can append transactions to the ledger, if the network validates transactions in a distributed fashion. Surprisingly, such a ledger is sufficient to realize distributed execution of programs called smart contracts. Using transactions, one party uploads code and state into the blockchain, and other parties modify state by stipulating code execution. For a procurement auction, auctioneer A would upload a new smart contract and allow other parties to bid. That is, the smart contract could just implement a simple, initially empty mailbox as state, and suppliers could only append data (bids and anything else) to that mailbox by transactions. All blockchain transactions are automatically signed by their generating party, and so would be the data they carry. Such a simple mailbox smart contract provides the following properties that we will need.

First, the blockchain guarantees *reliable broadcast*. Each signed transaction appending a message to the mailbox is public. Based on the blockchain's consensus, everybody in the network observes the same message appended (if valid). Being the blockchain's core feature, reliable broadcast takes one block latency. Along the same lines, we can introduce *personal messages* between parties over the blockchain. A broadcast to supplier S_i encrypted with S_i's public key realizes a secure, reliable channel to S_i.

Moreover, a blockchain automatically allows for *deadlines*. Parties participating in the blockchain receive new blocks and therefore have (weakly) synchronized clocks. Based on the current block, an auction smart contract can specify a deadline as a function of the number of future blocks.

Note that with, e.g., Ethereum, there is essentially no limit for the number of transactions per block. Miners have an incentive to include as many transactions as possible in their block to receive transaction fees. Thus, large messages can therefore be split into multiple transactions and still sent as "one message". Consequently in this paper, we silently assume that the blockchain accepts any number of messages of arbitrary length per block. In practice with Ethereum, the GasLimit upper bounds transactions and their size, but one could imagine that a long messages m is stored in a Public Bulletin Board (PBB) system, and the blockchain only stores hash of m.

To ease exposition, we also assume the blockchain consensus to be fork-free. As today's Proof-of-Work-based blockchains accept longer forks at any time, they cannot be fork-free. However in practice, a honest majority of miners guarantees

1 **forall** S_i **do**
2   └ **if** Pseudonymity **then** $S_i \rightarrow TTP$: $\mathcal{F}_{\mathsf{Pseu}}(v_i)$; **else** $S_i \rightarrow TTP$: $\mathcal{F}_{\mathsf{Auth}}(v_i)$;
3 **for** $i = 1$ **to** s **do**
4   │ **forall** $j \neq i$ **do**
5   └ └ TTP: Let $cmp_{i,j} = 1$, if $v_i > v_j$ and $cmp_{i,j} = 0$ otherwise;
6 $TTP \rightarrow \{A, S_1, \ldots, S_s\}$: $\mathcal{F}_{\mathsf{BC}}(\{cmp_{i,j} | \forall i, j \in \{1, \ldots, s\}\})$;
7 $TTP \rightarrow A$: $\{v_w | v_w = \min(v_1, \ldots, v_s)\}$;

Algorithm 1. Ideal functionality $\mathcal{F}_{\mathsf{Bid}}$ of the bidding algorithm

probability p of a future fork of length $k = O(\lambda)$ to become exponentially small, i.e., $p = e^{-\Omega(\lambda)}$ [22]. Parameter k is small in practice, e.g., $k = 6$ in Bitcoin and $k = 30$ in Ethereum. Blockchains based on Byzantine fault tolerance typically have consensus finality (and are fork-free) [39].

3   Security Definition

We define security following the standard ideal vs. real world paradigm. First, we specify an ideal functionality $\mathcal{F}_{\mathsf{Bid}}$ of our bidding protocol, see Algorithm 1.

Ideal Functionality. Our protocol emulates a trusted third party TTP that, first, receives all bids from all suppliers. If supplier pseudonymity is required, all participating suppliers S_i send their bids v_i via a pseudonymous channel, or else they send it via an authenticated channel. The trusted third party then computes result $cmp_{i,j}$ of the comparison between each bid. Finally, the trusted third party announces (broadcasts) the results of all comparisons to auctioneer A, each Supplier S_i, and all other participants of the blockchain. Similar to order preserving encryption, this reveals the total order of bids and hence the winner of the auction, but does not reveal the bids themselves.

Adversary Model. We consider two adversaries $\mathcal{A}_1$ and $\mathcal{A}_2$. These adversaries have different capabilities, are non-colluding, and control different parties. The following Theorem 1 summarizes our main contribution, and we will prove it later in the paper.

Theorem 1. *If adversary $\mathcal{A}_1$ is a static, active adversary which may control up to a threshold[1] τ of suppliers S_i, and if Adversary $\mathcal{A}_2$ is a passive adversary which may control auctioneer A, and if $\mathcal{A}_1$ and $\mathcal{A}_2$ do not collude, then protocol* Strain *implements functionality* $\mathcal{F}_{\mathsf{Bid}}$.

The order of bids is revealed to the adversary, and the auctioneer, but not the suppliers, must be only semi-honest. While this results in slightly weaker security than offered by MPC, it allows for optimally low latency. Moreover, we conjecture that this adversary model is practical in a variety of real-world scenarios.

---

[1] Threshold τ will later be used to open commitments using Shamir's secret sharing of the key, cf. Sect. 5.1.

4   Maliciously-Secure Comparisons

The first ingredient to our main contribution of secure auctions is a generic comparison construction. It allows two parties S_i and S_j (the suppliers in our application) with inputs v_i and v_j to obliviously evaluate whether or not $v_i > v_j$ without disclosing anything else to the other party. In contrast to related work, the novelty of our construction is its efficiency in the face of fully malicious adversaries. We do not rely on general MPC primitives and have asymptotically optimal complexity (3 blocks and $O(\eta)$ computation and communication cost per comparison). This allows us to easily integrate our comparison into the auction framework of Sect. 5 and, e.g., tolerate parties aborting the auction without restarting comparisons.

To realize maliciously-secure comparisons, we rely on the existence of a *judge* A (the auctioneer in our application). S_i and S_j can be fully malicious, but A must be semi-honest and moreover not collude with S_i, S_j, see Sect. 3. As long as A does not collude with S_i, S_j, neither A nor a malicious supplier learn bids of honest suppliers. An important property of our solution is that knowledge of S_i's, S_j's, and A's public keys is sufficient to verify whether $v_i > v_j$, again without learning anything else about v_i and v_j.

4.1   Secure Comparisons Against Semi-honest Adversaries

We begin by presenting Fischlin [21]'s technique for comparisons, secure against semi-honest adversaries. Subsequently, we extend comparisons to be secure against fully malicious adversaries.

Given bit representations $v_i = v_{i,1} \ldots v_{i,\eta}$ and $v_j = v_{j,1} \ldots v_{j,\eta}$, we can compute $v_i > v_j$ by evaluating Boolean circuit $F = \bigvee_{\ell=1}^{\eta}(v_{i,\ell} \wedge \neg v_{j,\ell} \wedge \bigwedge_{u=\ell+1}^{\eta}(v_{i,u} = v_{j,u}))$. We have $F = 1$ *iff* $v_i > v_j$. Observe that the main $\bigvee_{t=1}^{\eta}$ is actually an XOR: if $v_i > v_j$, exactly one term will be 1, and all other terms are 0. If $v_i \leq v_j$, all terms will be 0. Moreover, $(v_{i,u} = v_{j,u})$ equals $\neg(v_{i,u} \oplus v_{j,u})$. That can be exploited to homomorphically evaluate F using GM encryption.

1. S_i sends its GM public key $pk_i^{\mathsf{GM}} = (z_i, n_i)$ and encrypted value $C_i = \mathsf{Enc}_{pk_i^{\mathsf{GM}}}^{\mathsf{GM}}(v_i)$, a sequence of GM ciphertexts, to S_j.
2. S_j encrypts its own value v_j with S_i's public key, $C_{i,j} = \mathsf{Enc}_{pk_i^{\mathsf{GM}}}^{\mathsf{GM}}(v_j)$. S_j then homomorphically computes all $\neg(v_{i,u} \oplus v_{j,u})$ and $\neg v_{j,\ell}$ from F.
3. S_j embeds C_i and its own sequence of ciphertexts $C_{i,j}$ into AND-homomorphic GM ciphertexts as described in Sect. 2.1. Using AND-homomorphism, S_j computes a sequence $\ell = \{1, \ldots, \eta\}$ of ciphertexts $c_\ell = (v_{i,\ell} \wedge \neg v_{j,\ell} \wedge \bigwedge_{u=\ell+1}^{\eta}(v_{i,u} = v_{j_u}))$.
    Finally, S_j randomly shuffles the order of ciphertexts c_ℓ and sends resulting permutation $res_{i,j} = \pi(c_1, \ldots, c_\eta)$ back to S_i.
4. S_i can decrypt the c_ℓ in $res_{i,j}$ and learns whether $v_i \leq v_j$, if all c_ℓ decrypt to 0, or $v_i > v_j$, if exactly one ciphertext decrypts to 1 and all other to 0.

The purpose of S_j shuffling ciphertexts is to hide the position of the potential 1 decryption, thereby not leaking the position of the lowest bit differing between v_i and v_j.

Steps 2 and 3 implement a functionality which we call $\mathsf{Eval}(C_i, v_j)$ from now on.

4.2   Secure Comparisons Between Two Malicious Adversaries

Fischlin's protocol is only secure against semi-honest adversaries. However, one or *even both* parties may have behaved maliciously during comparison. Both suppliers S_i and S_j may submit different bids to distinct comparisons and supplier S_j could just encrypt any result of their choice using S_i's public key. That is, Fischlin's protocol does not ensure that $res_{i,j}$ has been computed according to the protocol specification and the fixed inputs of the suppliers.

We tackle this problem by, first, requiring both S_i and S_j to commit to their own input, simply by publishing GM encryptions C_i, C_j of v_i, v_j with their public key including a proof of knowledge of the plaintext. During comparison, S_j will prove to a judge A in zero-knowledge that S_j used the same value v_j in $C_{i,j}$ as in commitment C_j, and that S_j has performed homomorphic computation of $res_{i,j}$ according to Fischlin's algorithm. Therewith, S_i is sure that $res_{i,j}$ contains the result of comparing inputs behind ciphertexts C_i and C_j.

In the following description, we allow parties to either *publish* data or to send data from one to another. In reality, one could use the blockchain's broadcast feature to efficiently and reliably publish data to all parties or to just send a private (automatically signed) message, see Sect. 2.2.

Details. First, party S_i commits to v_i by publishing $\{pk_i^{\mathsf{GM}}, C_i = \mathsf{Enc}_{pk_i^{\mathsf{GM}}}^{\mathsf{GM}}(v_i)\}$, and party S_j commits to v_j by publishing $\{pk_j^{\mathsf{GM}}, C_j = \mathsf{Enc}_{pk_j^{\mathsf{GM}}}^{\mathsf{GM}}(v_j)\}$. Then, S_i and S_j compare their v_i, v_j following Fischlin [21]'s homomorphic circuit evaluation above. After S_j has computed $res_{i,j}$, S_j additionally computes a ZK proof $P_{i,j}^{\mathsf{eval}}$ as follows.

1. S_j adds $C_{i,j}$ and random coins for both the shuffle of $res_{i,j}$ and the AND-homomorphic embeddings to initially empty proof $P_{i,j}^{\mathsf{eval}}$.
   Let $v_{j,\ell}$ be the ℓth bit of v_j. Let $(C_j)_\ell$ be the ℓth ciphertext of GM commitment C_j, i.e., the encryption of $v_{j,\ell}$ (the ℓth bit of v_j). Let $(C_{i,j})_\ell$ be the ℓth ciphertext of $C_{i,j}$.
2. Let λ'' be the soundness parameter of our ZK proof. S_j flips $\eta \cdot \lambda''$ coins $\delta_{\ell,m}, 1 \le \ell \le \eta, 1 \le m \le \lambda''$.
3. S_j computes $\eta \cdot \lambda''$ encryptions $\gamma_{\ell,m} \leftarrow \mathsf{Enc}_{pk_j^{\mathsf{GM}}}^{\mathsf{GM}}(\delta_{\ell,m})$ and $\gamma'_{\ell,m} \leftarrow \mathsf{Enc}_{pk_i^{\mathsf{GM}}}^{\mathsf{GM}}(\delta_{\ell,m})$ and appends them to proof $P_{i,j}^{\mathsf{eval}}$.
4. S_j also computes $\eta \cdot \lambda''$ products $\Gamma_{\ell,m} = (C_j)_\ell \cdot \gamma_{\ell,m} \bmod n_j$ and $\Gamma'_{\ell,m} = (C_{i,j})_\ell \cdot \gamma'_{\ell,m} \bmod n_i$ and appends them to proof $P_{i,j}^{\mathsf{eval}}$. A product $\Gamma_{\ell,m}$ is an encryption of $\delta_{\ell,m} \oplus v_{j,\ell}$ under key pk_j^{GM}, and $\Gamma'_{\ell,m}$ is an encryption of $\delta_{\ell,m} \oplus v_{j,\ell}$ under key pk_i^{GM}.

5. S_j sends $P_{i,j}^{\text{eval}}$ to judge A.
6. Our ZK proof can either be interactive or non-interactive. We first consider the interactive version of our proof. Here, A sends back the challenge h, a sequence of $\eta \cdot \lambda''$ bits $b_{\ell,m}$, to S_j.
7. If $b_{\ell,m} = 0$, S_j sends plaintext and random coins of $\gamma_{\ell,m}$ and $\gamma'_{\ell,m}$ to A. If $b_{\ell,m} = 1$, S_j sends plaintext and random coins of $\Gamma_{\ell,m}$ and $\Gamma'_{\ell,m}$ to A.

The non-interactive version of our proof is a standard application of Fiat-Shamir's heuristic [20] to Σ-protocols and imposes slight changes to steps 5 to 7. So, let $h = H((\gamma_{1,1}, \gamma'_{1,1}, \Gamma_{1,1}\Gamma'_{1,1}), \ldots, (\gamma_{\eta,\lambda''}, \gamma'_{\eta,\lambda''}, \Gamma_{\eta,\lambda''}, \Gamma'_{\eta,\lambda''}), C_i, C_j, C_{i,j})$ for random oracle $H : \{0,1\}^* \rightarrow \{0,1\}^{\eta \cdot \lambda''}$. Instead of sending $P_{i,j}^{\text{eval}}$ to A, receiving the challenge, and replying to the challenge, S_j parses h as a series of $\eta \cdot \lambda''$ bits $b_{\ell,m}$. S_j does not send plaintexts and random coins of either $(\gamma_{\ell,m}, \gamma'_{\ell,m})$ or $(\Gamma_{\ell,m}, \Gamma'_{\ell,m})$ as above to A, but simply appends them to $P_{i,j}^{\text{eval}}$ and then sends $P_{i,j}^{\text{eval}}$ to A. In practice, we implement H by a cryptographic hash function.

So in conclusion, S_j sends proof $P_{i,j}^{\text{eval}}$ to judge A who has to verify it. Note that $P_{i,j}^{\text{eval}}$ contains ciphertext $C_{i,j}$ of S_j's input v_j under S_i's public key. The proof is zero-knowledge for judge A and very efficient, but must not be shared with party S_i. A's verification steps are as follows:

8. Judge A verifies that homomorphic computations for $res_{i,j}$ have been computed correctly, according to $C_{i,j}, C_j$, and random coins of $res_{i,j}$'s shuffle, simply by re-performing the computation.
9. For $\ell = \{1, \ldots, \eta\}$ and $m = \{1, \ldots, \}$, A verifies that homomorphic relations between $(C_i)_\ell, \gamma_{\ell,m}, \Gamma_{\ell,m}$ as well as for $(C_{i,j})_\ell, \gamma'_{\ell,m}, \Gamma'_{\ell,m}$ hold.
10. For each triple of plaintext, random coins, and ciphertexts of *either* $\gamma_{\ell,m}$ and $\gamma'_{\ell,m}$ *or* $\Gamma_{\ell,m}$ and $\Gamma'_{\ell,m}$, A checks that ciphertext results from the plaintext and random coins and that the plaintexts are the same.
11. If all checks pass, the judge A outputs $\top$, else $\bot$.

If A outputs $\top$, S_i decrypts $res_{i,j}$ and learns the outcome of the comparison, i.e., whether $v_i > v_j$.

Steps 1 to 7 implement a functionality that we call $\mathsf{ProofEval}(C_i, C_j, C_{i,j}, res_{i,j}, v_j)$ from now on. $\mathsf{ProofEval}$ is executed by S_j and uses commitments C_i and C_j and S_j's input v_j and outputs $\{C_{i,j}, res_{i,j}\}$ of $\mathsf{Eval}(C_i, v_j)$. Similarly, steps 8 to 11 realize functionality $\mathsf{VerifyEval}(P_{i,j}^{\text{eval}}, res_{i,j}, C_i, C_j)$. Executed by judge A, it outputs either $\top$ or $\bot$.

Lemma 1. *The above scheme of computing and verifying proof $P_{i,j}^{\text{eval}}$ with $\mathsf{ProofEval}$ and $\mathsf{VerifyEval}$ is a ZK proof of knowledge of v_j, such that $C_j = \mathsf{Enc}_{PK_j}^{\mathsf{GM}}(v_j)$, $\{C_{i,j}, res_{i,j}\} = \mathsf{Eval}(C_i, v_j)$, and if it is performed in λ'' rounds, the probability that S_j has cheated, but A outputs $\top$, is $2^{-\lambda''}$.*

Proof. As completeness follows directly from our description, we focus on soundness (extractability) and zero-knowledge.

(1) Knowledge Soundness. Judge A can extract v_j from S_j with rewinding access. Let $tr1(C_{i,j}, res_{i,j}, \gamma_{\ell,m}, \gamma'_{\ell,m}, \Gamma_{\ell,m}, \Gamma'_{\ell,m}, b_{\ell,m}, \ldots)$ be the trace of the first execution of $P^{\mathsf{eval}}_{i,j}$. Then judge A rewinds S_j to Step 5 and continues the protocol. Let $tr2(C_{i,j}, res_{i,j}, \gamma_{\ell,m}, \gamma'_{\ell,m}, \Gamma_{\ell,m}, \Gamma'_{\ell,m}, b_{\ell,m}, \ldots)$ be the trace of the second execution of $P^{\mathsf{eval}}_{i,j}$. If $tr1(b_{\ell,m}) = 0$ and $tr2(b_{\ell,m}) = 1$, then A learns $tr1(\delta_{\ell,m})$ and $tr2(\delta_{\ell,m} \oplus v_{j,\ell})$. Therewith, A computes $v_{j,\ell}$. As $v_{j,\ell}$ can be extracted, our Σ-protocol achieves special soundness. With challenge length λ'' for each bit of v_j, it is moreover a proof of knowledge with knowledge error $2^{-\lambda''}$ [14].

(2) Zero-Knowledge. Intuitively, the auctioneer learns nothing from the opening of either $\gamma_{\ell,m}$ and $\gamma'_{\ell,m}$ or $\Gamma_{\ell,m}$ and $\Gamma'_{\ell,m}$, since the plaintext value is always chosen uniformly random due to the uniform distribution of $\delta_{\ell,m}$. More formally, in the interactive case, we can construct a simulator $\mathsf{Sim}^{A(\{C_i,C_j\})}_{P^{\mathsf{eval}}_{i,j}}(res_{i,j})$ with rewinding access to judge $A(\{C_i, C_j\})$ following a standard simulation paradigm [27]. This ensures that we can construct a simulation of the ZK proof in the malicious model of secure computation even if bid v_j does not correspond to ciphertext $C_{i,j}$ and commitments C_i, C_j, since the simulator generates an accepting, indistinguishable output even if v_j is unknown. In the non-interactive case with Fiat-Shamir's heuristic, our ZK proof is secure in the random oracle model.   □

Note: Our proof here shows something stronger than required by the general auction protocol. We show our ZK proof to be secure even against malicious verifiers. However, auctioneer A, serving as the judge in the main protocol, is supposed to be semi-honest.

5   Blockchain Auction Protocol

After having presented our core technique for secure comparisons, we now turn to our main auction protocol Strain. Imagine that, at some point, A announces a new auction and uploads a smart contract to the blockchain. The smart contract is very simple and allows parties to comfortably exchange messages as mentioned before. The contract is signed by sk_A, so everybody understands that this is a valid procurement auction.

Overview. With the smart contract posted, the actual auction starts. In Strain, each supplier must first publicly commit to their bid. For this, we use a new verifiable commitment scheme which allows a majority of honest suppliers to open other suppliers' commitments. Therewith, we can at any time open commitments of malicious suppliers blocking or aborting the auction's progress.

After suppliers have committed to their bids (or after a deadline has passed), the protocol to determine the winning bid starts. Strain uses the new comparison technique from Sect. 4.2 to compare bids of any two parties. Auctioneer A serves as the judge. However, using our new comparison in the auctions turns out to be a challenge. Recall that, when S_i and S_j compare their bids, only S_i knows the outcome of the comparison, but nobody else. We therefore augment our comparison such that S_i can publish the outcome of the comparison, together with a (zero knowledge) proof of correctness.

To improve readability, we present Strain without optional pseudonymity and postpone pseudonymity to Sect. 5.4. For now, assume that a subset $\mathcal{S}' \subset \mathcal{S}$, $|\mathcal{S}'| = s' \leq s$ participates in the auction. Either a pseudonymous subset or all suppliers participate.

5.1 Verifiable Key Distribution for Commitments

To be able to commit to their bids, suppliers in Strain initially distribute their keying material. In the following, we devise a new key distribution technique for our specific setting. It permits supplier S_i to publish a GM public key and verifiably secret share the corresponding secret key. The crucial property of our key distribution is that a majority of honest suppliers can decrypt ciphertexts encrypted with S_i's public key. To then later commit to a value v_i, S_i encrypts v_i with their public key. For ease of exposition, we describe our key distribution with s-*out-of-s* threshold secret sharing. However, we stress that many different schemes exist for s'-*out-of-s* sharing modulo an RSA integer. For example, one could adopt and employ the schemes by Frankel [16] or Katz and Yung [25]. See also Shoup [35] for an overview.

Key Distribution. Each supplier S_i generates a GM key pair $(pk_i^{\mathsf{GM}} = (n_i = p_i \cdot q_i, z_i = n_i - 1), sk_i^{\mathsf{GM}} = \frac{(p_i-1)\cdot(q_i-1)}{4})$. To allow other suppliers S_j to open commitments from supplier S_i, S_i first computes a non-interactive ZK proof P_i^{Blum} that n_i is a Blum integer, see Blum [5] for details. Moreover, S_i computes secret shares of $\frac{(p_i-1)\cdot(q_i-1)}{4}$ for all suppliers as follows: S_i computes $s' - 1$ random shares $r_{i,1}, \ldots, r_{i,s'-1} \xleftarrow{\$} \{0, (p_i - 1) \cdot (q_i - 1)\}$ such that $\sum_{j=1}^{s'-1} r_{i,j} = \frac{(p_i-1)\cdot(q_i-1)}{4} \bmod (p_i - 1) \cdot (q_i - 1)$. This can easily be converted into a threshold scheme using Shamir's secret shares where τ is the threshold for reconstructing a secret. Supplier S_i computes signature $\mathsf{sig}_{sk_i}(r_{i,j})$ and encrypts share $r_{i,j}$ and signature $\mathsf{sig}_{sk_i}(r_{i,j})$ for supplier S_j using S_j's public key pk_j. Finally, S_i broadcasts resulting $s' - 1$ ciphertexts of share and signature pairs as well as pk_i^{GM} and P_i^{Blum} on the blockchain.

All suppliers can send their broadcasts in parallel, requiring only one block latency.

Key Verification. All s' participating suppliers start a sub-protocol to verify all s' public keys pk_i^{GM}. For each pk_i^{GM}:

1. All suppliers check proof P_i^{Blum}. If supplier S_j fails to verify the proof, S_j publishes $(i, \bot)$ on the blockchain.

2. Each supplier S_j selects a random $\rho_{i,j} \xleftarrow{\$} \mathbb{Z}_{n_i}^*$ and employs a traditional commitment scheme commit to commit to $\rho_{i,j}$. That is, each supplier S_j publishes $\mathsf{commit}(\rho_{i,j})$ on the blockchain.

3. After a deadline has passed, all suppliers open their commitments, by publishing $\rho_{i,j}$ and the random nonce used for the commitment.
All suppliers compute $x_i = \sum_{j \neq i} \rho_{i,j} \bmod n_i$ and $y_i = x_i^2$.

4. Each supplier S_j raises y_i to their share $r_{i,j}$ of $\frac{(p_i-1)\cdot(q_i-1)}{4}$ and publishes $\gamma_{i,j} = y_i^{r_{i,j}}$ on the blockchain. S_j also raises z_i to their $r_{i,j}$, i.e., $\zeta_{i,j} = z_i^{r_{i,j}}$. S_j then prepares a non-interactive ZK proof $P_{i,j}^{\mathsf{DLOG}}$ of statement $\log_{y_i} \gamma_{i,j} = \log_{z_i} \zeta_{i,j}$, see Appendix A for details. Supplier S_j publishes $\{\gamma_{i,j}, \zeta_{i,j}, P_{i,j}^{\mathsf{DLOG}}\}$ on the blockchain.

5. Finally, all $s' - 1$ suppliers verify soundness of pk_i^{GM}. Each supplier S_j computes $b_i = \prod_{j \neq i} \gamma_{i,j} = y_i^{\sum_{j=1}^{s'-1} r_{i,j}} = y_i^{\frac{(p_i-1)\cdot(q_i-1)}{4}} \bmod n_i$ and $b_i' = \prod_{j \neq i} \zeta_i = z_i^{\sum_{j=1}^{s'-1} r_{i,j}} = z_i^{\frac{(p_i-1)\cdot(q_i-1)}{4}} \bmod n_i$. If S_j detects that $b_i \neq 1$ or $b_i' \neq -1 \bmod n_i$, S_j publishes $(i, \bot)$ on the blockchain. Supplier S_j also checks $s' - 1$ proofs $P_{i,k}^{\mathsf{DLOG}}$. If one of the κ rounds outputs $\bot$ during verification, S_j publishes $(k, \bot)$ on the blockchain.

Lemma 2. *Let n_i be a Blum integer and α the sum of shares distributed by S_i. If no honest supplier publishes $(i, \bot)$, then $Pr[\alpha \neq \frac{(p_i-1)\cdot(q_i-1)}{4}] \in O(2^{-\lambda})$.*

Proof. Let y_i have no roots in $\mathbb{Z}_{n_i}$ dividing $\frac{(p_i-1)(q_i-1)}{4}$. For uniformly chosen y_i, this happens with overwhelming probability $\in O(1 - 2^{-\lambda})$. As $y_i \in QR_{n_i}$, it has order $\frac{(p_i-1)(q_i-1)}{4}$. So, $b_i = 1$ implies (I) $\alpha \bmod \frac{(p_i-1)(q_i-1)}{4} = 0$; further, since $z_i = -1 \bmod n_i$, we have $z_i^{\frac{(p_i-1)(q_i-1)}{4}} \in \{-1, 1\}$, and so (II) $z_i^{\frac{(p_i-1)(q_i-1)}{2}} = 1$. Hence $b_i' = -1$ implies $\alpha \bmod \frac{(p_i-1)(q_i-1)}{2} \neq 0$. From (I) and (II), we conclude $(\alpha \bmod \frac{(p_i-1)(q_i-1)}{4}) \bmod 2 = 1$. However, all those values will serve as private keys in GM encryption. $\square$

In conclusion, supplier S_i can verify whether their shares for supplier S_j's secret key sk_j^{GM} matches public key pk_j^{GM}. Therewith, an honest majority of suppliers will later be able to open commitments of malicious suppliers trying to block the smart contract or cheat.

Excluding Malicious Suppliers. Strain's key verification easily allows detection and exclusion of malicious suppliers. First, as all suppliers can verify proofs P_i^{Blum} and $P_{i,j}^{\mathsf{DLOG}}$ of a supplier S_i, honest suppliers can exclude S_i or S_j from further participating in the protocol in case of a bad proof.

Moreover, following our assumption of up to τ malicious suppliers, Strain allows to systematically detect and exclude malicious suppliers. Supplier S_j will reconstruct $b_i = 1$ and $b_i' = -1$ from the set of secret shares $(\gamma_{i,j}, \zeta_{i,j})$. If no subset reconstructs the correct plaintexts, S_j deduces that distributor S_i is malicious and excludes S_i. Otherwise, S_j checks that each supplier S_k's share

```
1  for i = 1 to s' do
2  |   S_i : publish {C_i ← Enc^GM_PK_i(v_i), P^enc_i ← ProofEnc(C_i, v_i)} on blockchain;
3  for i = 1 to s' do
4  |   forall j ≠ i do
5  |   |   S_j : {C_i,j, res_i,j} ← Eval(C_i, v_j);
6  |   |   S_j : P^eval_i,j ← ProofEval(C_j, C_i, C_i,j, res_i,j, v_j);
7  |   |   S_j : publish {Enc_pk_A(P^eval_i,j), res_i,j} on blockchain;
8  |   |   A : publish VerifyEval(P^eval_i,j, res_i,j, C_i, C_j) on blockchain;
9  |   |   S_i : bitset_i,j = Dec^AND_pk^GM_j(res_i,j);
10 |   |   S_i : shuffle_i,j ← Shuffle(res_i,j);
11 |   |   S_i : P^shuffle_i,j ← ProofShuffle(shuffle_i,j, res_i,j);
12 |   |   S_i : let γ_ℓ,m ← Enc^GM_PK_i(β_ℓ,m) ∈ shuffle_i,j be the shuffled ciphertexts
13 |   |_  with their random coins r_ℓ,m. Publish {P^shuffle_i,j, shuffle_i,j, β_ℓ,m, r_ℓ,m};
```

Algorithm 2. Blockchain auction protocol Π_{Strain}

reconstructs the correct plaintext. If any does not, S_j asks S_k publicly on the blockchain to reveal their exponent $r_{i,k}$ and signature $\text{sig}_{sk_i}(r_{i,k})$. If at least $\tau + 1$ suppliers ask S_k to reveal, S_k will reveal, and honest suppliers can detect whether S_k should be excluded (signature does not verify or exponent does not match secret shares) or S_i (signature verifies and exponent matches secret shares).

5.2 Determining the Winning Bid

Strain's main protocol Π_{Strain} to determine the winning bid is depicted in Algorithm 2. Within Algorithm 2, we use three ZK proofs as sub-protocols.

- $\text{ProofEnc}(C_i, v_i)$ proves in zero-knowledge the knowledge of v_i, such that $C_i = \text{Enc}^{\text{GM}}_{PK_i}(v_i)$. For an exemplary implementation we refer to Katz [24].
- $\text{ProofEval}(C_j, C_i, C_{i,j}, res_{i,j}, v_j)$ has been introduced in Sect. 4.2.
- $\text{ProofShuffle}(shuffle_{i,j}, res_{i,j})$ proves in zero-knowledge the knowledge of a permutation Shuffle with $shuffle_{i,j} = \text{Shuffle}(res_{i,j})$. There exist a large number of implementations of shuffle proofs. For one that is straightforward to adapt to GM encryption, see Ogata et al. [31]. Using this technique, one can even create shuffles with a restricted structure [32]. That is, the shuffle is only chosen from a pre-defined subset of all possible shuffles. In our case this is necessary, since we do not randomly shuffle all GM ciphertexts, but only AND-homomorphic blocks of GM ciphertexts.

ZK proofs ProofEnc and ProofShuffle are verified by all suppliers active in the auction, and, hence, verification is not explicitly shown. ZK proof ProofEval, however, is verified only by the semi-honest judge and auctioneer A.

Let $\eta \ll \lambda$ be a public system parameter determining the bit length of each bid. That is, any bid $v_i = v_{i,1} \ldots v_{i,\eta}$ can take values from $\{0, \ldots, 2^\eta - 1\}$.

Π_{Strain} starts with each supplier S_i committing to their bid v_i by publishing GM-encryption $C_i = (\text{Enc}^{\text{GM}}_{pk^{\text{GM}}_i}(v_{i,1}), \ldots, \text{Enc}^{\text{GM}}_{pk^{\text{GM}}_i}(v_{i,\eta}))$ on the blockchain. Recall that all messages on the blockchain are automatically signed by their generating party.

After a deadline has passed, suppliers determine index w of winning bid v_w by running our maliciously-secure comparison mechanism of Sect. 4.2. Any pair (S_i, S_j) of suppliers computes the comparison and publishes the result on the blockchain.

Specifically, after judge/auctioneer A has published whether S_j's computation of $C_{i,j}$ corresponds to S_j's commitment C_j, supplier S_i can decrypt $res_{i,j}$ and learn whether $v_i > v_j$. To publish whether $v_i > v_j$, S_i shuffles $res_{i,j}$ to $shuffle_{i,j}$, publishes a ZK proof of shuffle, and publicly decrypts $shuffle_{i,j}$. Therewith, everybody can verify $v_i > v_j$. If A has output $\top$, if the proof of shuffle is correct, and if $shuffle_{i,j}$ contains exactly a single 1, then $v_i > v_j$. If A has output $\top$, the shuffle proof is correct, and if $shuffle_{i,j}$ contains only 0s, then $v_i > v_j$.

A supplier S_i is the winner of the auction, if all their shuffles prove that their bid is the lowest among all suppliers. S_i can prove this by opening the plaintext and random coins of $shuffle_{i,j}$. If $v_i \leq v_j$, at least one plaintext in each consecutive sequence of λ' plaintexts is 0. If $v_i > v_j$, a consecutive sequence of λ' plaintexts is 1. Strain concludes with auction winner S_w revealing bid v_w and a plaintext equality ZK proof that commitment C_w is for v_w to auctioneer A.

5.3   Latency Evaluation

The performance of any interactive protocol or application running on top of a blockchain is dominated by block interval times. With today's block interval times in the order of several seconds, protocols requiring a lot of party interaction significantly increase the protocol's total latency, i.e., its total run time. A secure auction protocol with high latency is useless in many scenarios with automated, short-living auctions.

As a crucial performance metric, we therefore investigate Strain's latency. As key distribution is a setup-like initial process, necessary only once, and independent of actual auctions, we focus on Π_{Strain}'s latency.

Asymptotic Analysis. In Algorithm 2, Π_{Strain} starts in Line 2 by all suppliers sending a commitment to their bid together with P^{enc}. There is no interactivity between by suppliers, so all suppliers can send in parallel, requiring one block latency. After that first block has been mined, all suppliers send their P^{eval} for each other supplier to A, lines 5 to 7. Each supplier can send all P^{eval} for all other suppliers at once ($s' \cdot (s' - 1)$ hash values of the PBB). Again, there is no interactivity between suppliers, so all suppliers send in parallel in one block. Then, auctioneer A sends all VerifyEval for all comparisons at once (1 hash), Line 8, in another block. In a final block, all suppliers disclose in parallel (s' hashes) their shuffles, random coins, and corresponding P^{shuffle} (Line 13).

In conclusion, one run of Π_{Strain} requires a total of 4 blocks latency: 1 block for suppliers to commit, and then 3 blocks for core comparisons and computation of the winning bid. This number is constant in both bit length η of each bid and the number of suppliers s. In contrast, practical MPC protocols require at least

$\Omega(\eta)$ rounds. Although Fischlin's protocol only evaluates a circuit of constant multiplicative depth, it is capable of evaluating a comparison due to the shuffle of the ciphertexts before decryption.

Table 1. Execution time for Strain's main cryptographic operations

Enc^{GM}	Dec^{GM}	Enc^{AND}	Dec^{AND}	ProofEnc	VerifyEnc	Eval	ProofEval	VerifyEval
0.08 ms	46 ms	60 ms	980 ms	10 ms	9 ms	390 ms	107 ms	15 ms

ProofDLOG	VerifyDLOG	ProofShuffle	VerifyShuffle
154 ms	339 ms	633 ms	198 ms

Prototypical Implementation. To indicate its real-world practicality, we have prototypically implemented and benchmarked Π_{Strain}'s core cryptographic operations in Python. The source code is available for download [36].

In our measurements, we have set bid length η to 32 bit, allowing for either large bids or very fine-grained bids. For good security, we set the bit length of primes for Blum integers n to $|p| = |q| = 768$ bit. To achieve a small probability for soundness errors of 2^{-40}, we choose $\lambda' = \lambda'' = \kappa = 40$. We have implemented the non-interactive versions of our ZK proofs and used SHA256 as hash function. All experiments were performed on a mostly idle Linux laptop with Intel i7-6560U CPU, clocked at 2.20 GHz. Our prototypical implementation uses only one core of the CPU's four virtual cores available, but we emphasize that our cryptographic operations can run independently in parallel, e.g., for each supplier. They scale linearly in the number of (virtual) cores.

Table 1 summarizes timings for cryptographic operations. All values are the average of ten runs. Relative standard deviation for each average was low with less than 9%.

Eval. Inside the main for-loop in Π_{Strain}, operation Eval and computation of ZK proof ProofEval for A take roughly 0.5 s. Taking Ethereum's 15 s blockchain interval, a supplier could compute proofs for up to 30 other suppliers using a single core. Again, with the availability of x many cores, this number multiplies by x.

Auctioneer A executes VerifyEval for which we have implemented verification of homomorphic relations between Cs, γs, and Γs and (expensive) verification of encryptions for given random coins. Yet, verification is just (re-)computing GM encryptions with fixed coins which are included in P^{Eval}. As you can see, VerifyEval is very fast (15 ms), allowing roughly thousand comparisons in one Ethereum block interval.

ProofShuffle. As a supplier needs to compute ProofShuffle, we have modified Ogata et al. [31]'s standard shuffle to our setting. Very briefly, the idea of proving $shuffle$ to be a re-encrypted shuffle of res in zero-knowledge is to generate κ re-encrypted intermediate shuffles $shuffle'_i$ of res. For each intermediate shuffle $shuffle_i'$, the verifier ask *either* to show the permutation between res and $shuffle_i'$ and all random coins used during re-encryption *or* to show the permutation between $shuffle_i'$ and $shuffle$ and random coins used during re-encryption. Recall that re-encryption in our setting is simply multiplication with a random quadratic residue. Computing ProofShuffle is an expensive operation, taking 600 ms. Thus, in our non-optimized implementation, a supplier could prepare ≈ 25 proofs of shuffle per CPU core in one block interval. We stress that our modification to Ogata et al. [31]'s shuffle is straightforward and leave the design of more performance optimized shuffles for future work.

Note that Enc_{pk_A} is not GM encryption, but a regular hybrid encryption for auctioneer A, e.g., AES-ECC. As hybrid encryption is extremely fast compared to computation of our ZK proofs, we ignore it in our latency analysis.

ProofEnc. For the initial commitment of each supplier, we have adopted Katz [24]'s standard technique for proving plaintext knowledge to GM encryption. Again, we only summarize the main idea of our (straightforward) adoption. To prove knowledge of a single plaintext bit m, encrypted to GM ciphertext $C = r^2 \cdot z^m$, prover and verifier engage in a κ-round Σ-protocol. In each round i, the prover randomly chooses r_i and sends $A_i = r_i^4$ to the verifier. The verifier replies by sending random bit q_i, and the prover concludes the proof by sending $R_i = r^{q_i} \cdot r_i$. The verifier accepts the round, if $R_i^4 = A_i \cdot C^{2 \cdot q_i}$. For our evaluation, we have implemented a non-interactive version of this Σ-protocol. Both, computation of the ZK proof (VerifyEnc) as well as its verification (VerifyEnc) are extremely fast, taking only 10 ms for all rounds and all encrypted bits together. Note that computation of this proof is independent of the number of suppliers and has to be performed only once per auction.

ProofDLOG. Albeit part of only the initial key distribution phase, we also include computation times for computation and verification of proof P^{DLOG}. In Table 1, ProofDLOG denotes the algorithm computing proof P^{DLOG}, and VerifyDLOG is the algorithm verifying P^{DLOG}, see Appendix A for details. These computations are efficient: within one block interval, a supplier can generate ≈ 100 shares for other suppliers and verify ≈ 45.

Having in mind that our Python implementation is prototypical and not optimized for speed, we conclude that Π_{Strain}'s cryptographic operations are very efficient, allowing Strain's deployment in many short-term auction scenarios with dozens of suppliers.

5.4   Optional: Preparation of Pseudonyms

To pseudonymously place a bid in Strain, suppliers must decouple their blockchain transactions from their regular key pair (pk_i, sk_i). Ideally for each auction, supplier S_i generates a fresh random key pair (rpk_i, rsk_i) for bidding. In practice, e.g., with Ethereum, this turns out to be a challenge. To interact with a smart contract, S_i must send a transaction. Yet, to mitigate DoS attacks in Ethereum, transactions cost money of the blockchain's virtual currency. If a fresh key pair wants to send a transaction, someone must send funds to it. S_i cannot send funds to their fresh key, as this would create a visible link between S_i and (rpk_i, rsk_i).

Our idea is that A sends funds to keys that have previously been registered. To do so, S_i will register their fresh key pair (rpk_i, rsk_i) using a blind RSA signature. As a result, S_i has received a valid signature sig'_i of its random key rpk_i. Besides s, the adversary learns nothing about the rpk_is.

All suppliers send their blinded rpk_i in parallel, and A then replies with blind signatures in parallel, too. Communication latency is constant in the number of suppliers s. Note that all suppliers must request a blind signature for a random rpk_i, regardless of whether a supplier is interested in an auction or not. If a supplier does not request a blind signature, the adversary knows that they will not participate in the auction.

After a supplier has recovered their key pair (rpk_i, rsk_i), they broadcast it to the blockchain. All suppliers run a Dining Cryptographer network in parallel, see Appendix C. A supplier S_i interested in participating in the auction will broadcast (rpk_i, sig'_i), and a supplier not interested will broadcast 0s.

As a result of the DC network, everybody knows fresh, random public keys of a list of suppliers participating in the auction. Due to A's signature, everybody knows that these suppliers are valid suppliers, but nobody can link a key rpk_i to supplier S_i. Starting from now, only suppliers interested in the auction will continue by submitting a bid and determining the winning bid. Running a DC network is communication efficient. That is, all suppliers submit their s powers of rpk_i in parallel in $O(1)$ blocks.

Finally, A transfers money to each public key rpk_i, just enough such that suppliers can use their (rpk_i, rsk_i) keys to interact with the smart contract. Supplier S_i will use their new key pair (rpk_i, rsk_i) to pseudonymously participate in the rest of the protocol.

Security Analysis. For space reasons, we move the security analysis to Appendix B.

6   Related Work

MPC. Current maliciously-secure protocols of practical performance for *more than two* parties are based on secret shares [2]. They require at least as many rounds of interaction as the multiplicative depth of the circuit evaluated [28]. For comparisons this is the bit length η of the bids. Even for tiny auctions this will exceed Strain's total of four blocks. Constant-round MPC protocols, e.g. [28,29], exceed four blocks already in their pre-computation phase before any comparison has taken place. Benhamouda et al. [4] present an MPC auction protocol running on Hyperledger Fabric. The underlying primitive is Yao's MPC requiring $\Omega(\eta)$ rounds of interactivity, and it does not provide security against malicious bidders (Strain does).

Dedicated Auction Protocols. There exists a large number of specialized secure auctions protocols; for a survey see Brandt [9]. Among them, the one that compares closely to Strain is Brandt's very own auction protocol [8]. There, suppliers compute the winner of the auction, as with Strain, and the protocol requires a constant number of party interactions – as does Strain. However, Brandt encodes bids in unary notation making the protocol impractical for all but the simplest auctions. Instead, Strain encodes bids in binary notation, thus enabling efficient auctions for realistic bid values. Brandt cannot guarantee output delivery which Strain does and which we consider crucially important in practice. Brandt claims full privacy in the malicious model, but formal verification has shown that this does not necessarily hold, cf. Dreier et al. [17].

Fischlin [21] also presents a variant of his main protocol which is secure against a malicious adversary. However, that variant requires an oblivious third party A providing a public/private key pair. All homomorphic computations in Fischlin's protocol are then performed under A's public key. Simulating A on the blockchain requires distributing the private key over multiple parties. As a result, one would need a secure, distributed computation of a Goldwasser-Micali key pair. Even for the case of RSA, this is complex and requires many rounds of interactions [6], rendering it impractical on a blockchain. Instead in Strain, each party creates its own key pair and only proves correct key sharing. Furthermore, even in case A's key has been set up, Fischlin's protocol still requires six rounds for each core comparison, whereas Strain requires only three (plus one for commitments) – a noticeable difference on the blockchain. We also stress that Fischlin's protocol targets a setup with 2 parties and cannot trivially be extended to multiple parties: 2 colluding malicious parties can convince oblivious party A of any outcome of the comparison they desire. In a multi-party setting, this allows an adversary to undermine the result of an auction, even after bids have been placed. Instead in this paper, we prove that Strain is secure against a collusion of up to τ suppliers.

Cachin [10] presents a protocol for secure auctions based on the Φ-hiding assumption. A variant secure against *one* malicious party (Sect. 3.3 in [10]) requires at least 7 blocks per comparison. Instead, Strain compares in only three blocks and supports both parties to be malicious during comparisons. Moreover similar to Fischlin [21]'s protocol, it is not trivial to extend [10] to support more than one fully malicious party. The auction protocol by Naor et al. [30] requires another trusted party (the auction issuer), is based on garbled circuits, therefore communication and computation inefficient, and secure only in the semi-honest model. Damgård et al. [15]'s auction considers the very different scenario of comparing a secret value m with a public integer m. The fully malicious version of their auction (Sect. 5.3 in [15]) only copes with up to one fully malicious party. Another version (Sect. 5.1 in [15]) addresses comparing secret inputs m and x, but only with semi-honest security.

7   Conclusion

Strain is a new protocol for secure auctions on blockchains. Strain allows, for the first time, to execute a sealed bid auction on a blockchain, secure against malicious bidders, with optional bidder anonymity, and guaranteed output delivery. Strain is efficient, and its main auction part runs in a constant number of blocks. Such low latency is crucial for practical adoption and a basis for a new implementation of sealed-bid auctions over blockchains where auction results can be observed by all participants.

A   Proofs of DLOG Equivalence

As the DDH assumption holds in group $(\mathbb{J}_n, \cdot)$ for Blum integers n [13], we adopt standard ZK proofs of DLOG equivalence to our setting.

Let $y, z \in \mathbb{J}_n$ and z be a generator of group $(\mathbb{J}_n, \cdot)$. A prover knows an integer σ such that $y^\sigma = \gamma \bmod n$ and $z^\sigma = \zeta \bmod n$. For public values $\{y, z, \gamma, \zeta\}$, the prover wants to compute the statement $\log_y \gamma = \log_z \zeta$ to a verifier in zero-knowledge, i.e., without revealing any additional information about σ. This boils down to Chaum and Pedersen's ZK proof that $(y, z, Y = y^\sigma, Z = z^\sigma)$ is a DDH tuple [12]. The protocol runs in κ rounds.

In each round, (1) The prover computes $r \xleftarrow{\$} \mathbb{J}_n$ and sends $(t_1 = y^r, t_2 = z^r)$ to the verifier. (2) The verifier sends challenge $c \xleftarrow{\$} \mathbb{J}_n$ to the prover. (3) The prover sends $s = r + c \cdot \sigma$ to the verifier. (4) The verifier checks $y^s \overset{?}{=} t_1 \cdot Y^c \wedge z^s \overset{?}{=} t_2 \cdot Z^c$. If the check fails, the verifier outputs $\bot$.

We target non-interactive ZK proofs, so challenge c can be replaced in round $i \leq \kappa$ by a random oracle call $c = H(y, z, Y, Z, t_1, t_2, i)$ [20]. Let P^{DLOG} be an initially empty proof. For each round, the prover would add t_1, t_2, and s to P^{DLOG}, and then send P^{DLOG} to the verifier. Note that, if $z = -1 \bmod n$, as in our main protocol, then $z = -(1^2)$ is indeed a generator of $\mathbb{J}_n$. This ZK proof is secure in the random oracle model.

B   Security Analysis

We now prove Theorem 1. Our proof is a simulation-based proof in the hybrid model [27]. In the hybrid model, simulator $\mathcal{S}$ generates messages of honest parties interacting with malicious parties and the trusted third party TTP. Since the simulator does not use inputs of honest parties (except for forwarding to the TTP which does not leak any information), it is ensured that the protocol does not reveal any information except the result, i.e., the output of the TTP. Messages generated by the simulator must be indistinguishable from messages in the real execution of the protocol.

Proof. Let $\mathcal{S}$ be the set of all suppliers and $\overline{\mathcal{S}}$ be the suppliers controlled by adversary $\mathcal{A}_1$. We prove $IDEAL_{\mathcal{F}_{Bid}, \mathcal{S}, \overline{\mathcal{S}}}(v_1, \ldots, v_s) \equiv REAL_{\Pi_{\mathsf{Strain}}, \mathcal{A}, \overline{\mathcal{S}}}(v_1, \ldots, v_s)$.

We either establish pseudonymous (broadcast) channels over the blockchain using the protocol of Sect. 5.4 or use regular authenticated channels.

(I) In the first step of the protocol, honest suppliers $\mathcal{S}\backslash\overline{\mathcal{S}}$ commit to random bids r_i and publish corresponding ZK proofs P_i^{enc} on the blockchain. The simulator reads $P_{\overline{i}}^{\mathsf{enc}}$ of the malicious parties $\overline{\mathcal{S}}$ from the blockchain. Using the extractor for the zero-knowledge argument, the simulator extracts $v_{\overline{i}}$. The simulator sends all v_i (including those of the honest parties) to the TTP. The simulator receives from the TTP results $cmp_{i,j}$ of all comparisons and winning bid v_w for auctioneer A.

(II) For each honest party $S_i \in \mathcal{S}\backslash\overline{\mathcal{S}}$, the simulator prepares a message of random AND-homomorphic encryptions $res_{j,i}$ following Fischlin's circuit output and the result of the comparison $cmp_{j,i}$. The simulator also invokes the simulator $\mathsf{Sim}_{P_{j,i}^{\mathsf{eval}}}^{A(\{C_i,C_j\})}(res_{j,i})$ which is guaranteed to exist. Then, the simulator sends the messages to the blockchain. For each malicious party $S_{\overline{i}} \in \overline{\mathcal{S}}$ that is still active, the simulator reads $P_{j,\overline{i}}^{\mathsf{eval}}$ and $res_{j,\overline{i}}$ from the blockchain. If judge A determines that $\mathsf{VerifyEval}(P_{j,\overline{i}}^{\mathsf{eval}}, res_{j,\overline{i}}, C_j, C_{\overline{i}})$ does not check, it publishes $\perp$ on the blockchain, and supplier $S_{\overline{i}}$ is dropped from the auction. We describe later how we deal with suppliers aborting the protocol.

(III) For each honest party $S_i \in \mathcal{S}\backslash\overline{\mathcal{S}}$, the simulator prepares a message of random AND-homomorphic encryptions $shuffle_{i,j}$ following Fischlin's circuit output and the result of the comparison $cmp_{i,j}$. The simulator also invokes simulator $\mathsf{Sim}_{P^{\mathsf{shuffle}}}(shuffle_{i,j})$ for the shuffle ZK proof. It also opens the corresponding ciphertexts $\gamma_{\ell,m} \in shuffle_{i,j}$. Then the simulator sends the messages to the blockchain. For each malicious party $S_{\overline{i}} \in \overline{\mathcal{S}}$, the simulator reads $P_{\overline{i},j}^{\mathsf{shuffle}}$, $shuffle_{\overline{i},j}$, $\beta_{\ell,m}$, and $r_{\ell,m}$ from the blockchain. In case $\mathsf{VerifyShuffle}(P_{\overline{i},j}^{\mathsf{shuffle}}, shuffle_{\overline{i},j}, res_{\overline{i},j})$ does not check, the supplier $S_{\overline{i}}$ is dropped from the auction. If encrypting plaintexts $\beta_{\ell,m}$ and random coins $r_{\ell,m}$ do not result in $shuffle_{\overline{i},j}$, supplier $S_{\overline{i}}$ is dropped from the auction.

(IV) If the winner S_w of the auction is honest, i.e., $S_w \in \mathcal{S}\backslash\overline{\mathcal{S}}$, then the simulator invokes the simulator for the ZK proof and sends it and v_w (received from the TTP) to auctioneer A. In case the ZK proof does not check, S_w is removed from the auction. If the winner S_w of the auction is malicious, i.e., $S_w \in \overline{\mathcal{S}}$, then the simulator receives the winning bid value v_w and the ZK proof that it corresponds to commitment C_w. If the ZK proof does not check, S_w is removed from the auction.

It remains to show that there exists is a simulator for the view of $\mathcal{A}_2$ (the semi-honest auctioneer/judge A): in the first step of the protocol, $\mathcal{A}_2$ receives IND-CPA secure ciphertexts and zero-knowledge proofs P^{enc}. In the second step $\mathcal{A}_2$ receives further IND-CPA secure ciphertexts and zero-knowledge proofs P^{eval}. We have shown in Sect. 4.2 that P^{eval} is zero-knowledge for the auctioneer. In the third step $\mathcal{A}_2$ receives IND-CPA secure ciphertexts, ZK proofs P^{shuffle} and the opened plaintext and randomness of some ciphertexts. The plaintexts are either all 1 or all 0 depending on $cmp_{i,j}$, and the randomness can be chosen consistently for each ciphertext. Finally, $\mathcal{A}_2$ receives v_w and the ZK proof of plaintext equality to C_w. Hence the view of $\mathcal{A}_2$ is simulatable from the TTP's output, i.e., the set of results of comparisons $\{cmp_{i,j}\}$ and winning bid v_w. $\quad\square$

Dealing with Early Aborts. Strain is particularly suitable for the blockchain, as it can handle any early abort after bids have been committed. Assume supplier $S_{\bar{i}}$ has aborted the protocol or has been caught cheating. Then, all others suppliers S_i can recover its bid $v_{\bar{i}}$ using the shares of its private key $sk_{\bar{i}}^{\mathsf{GM}}$ from commitment $C_{\bar{i}} = \mathsf{Enc}_{PK_{\bar{i}}}^{\mathsf{GM}}(v_{\bar{i}})$. We emphasize that our bid opening is secure against malicious suppliers due to ZK-proof P^{DLOG}. Suppliers publish $v_{\bar{i}}$ on the blockchain, and, after the bidding protocol, winning supplier S_w reveals bid v_w to semi-honest auctioneer A (proving plaintext equality to commitment C_w in zero-knowledge). The auctioneer compares v_w to all opened bids $v_{\bar{i}}$ and, in case, chooses a different winner w'. Hence, after commitments have been sent to the blockchain, no supplier can abort the auction. Even worse, aborting the auction reveals one's bid to all other suppliers.

C   Dining Cryptographer Networks

A standard technique we use as an ingredient in Strain is a Dining Cryptographer (DC) network [11]. If out of a set of s parties (suppliers) $\{S_1, \ldots, S_s\}$ exactly *one* party S_i wants to broadcast their message m_i to all other parties, a DC network guarantees delivery of m_i to all other parties without revealing i, i.e., who has sent m_i.

Assume that all parties have exchanged pairwise secret keys $k_{i,j}$ with each other. In one round of a DC network, parties communicate in a daisy chain where party S_i sends a sum sum_i to party S_{i+1}. Upon receipt, S_{i+1} superposes sum_i with their own data and sends sum_{i+1} to S_{i+2}. Again, S_{i+2} superposes sum_{i+1} with their own data and sends sum_{i+2} to S_3 and so on. *Superposing* is simple: each party S_i XORs all pairwise keys $k_{i,j}$ of all other parties S_j to whatever previous party S_{i-1} has broadcast. Only one party S_* that wants to publish message m_* additionally XORs m_* to the previous sum. The last XOR of all data sent cancels out keys $k_{i,j}$ and m_* remains. So, a one round DC network allows one party dissemination of one message, protected by the DC network. Message m_* is public, but the sender's identity is protected. Thus, one supplier anonymously disseminates their public key, and everybody knows that this is a new valid key from one of the suppliers. Daisy chain communication can trivially be replaced by per party broadcasts, e.g., publishing to the blockchain. The advantage of the blockchain is efficiency: all parties broadcast their sums at the same time.

Multiple Messages. To disseminate multiple parties' messages, several different strategies exist to resolve *collisions* in DC networks [11]. In Strain, we employ the approach by Bos and den Boer [7]. Assume that each party S_i has exchanged $s-1$ different pairwise keys $k_{i,j,u}, 1 \leq u \leq s-1$ with each other party S_j. Now, party S_i broadcasts all s powers $< m_i^1, \ldots, m_i^n >$ of their message m_i protected by the DC network. Instead of XORing messages broadcast with keys for protection, we now operate over $GF(2^q), q \geq |m|$, and use the following trick to cancel out keys. To protect the uth power m_i^u of m_i, S_i adds all keys $k_{i,j,u}$ for $j > i$ to

$K_{i,u}$ and subtracts keys $k_{i,j,u}$ for $j < i$ from $K_{i,u}$. S_i broadcasts $m_i^u + K_{i,u}$. All parties compute power sums $p_u(m_1, \ldots, m_s) = \sum_{i=1}^{s} m_i^u, 1 \le u \le s$. Each party uses Newton identities to compute m_i from power sums. All parties publish their output at the same time in parallel which is very efficient on a blockchain.

For space reasons, we do not discuss standard approaches realizing fully-malicious security for DC networks. These approaches use "traps" to identify and blame other parties, see, e.g., [7,40,41] for an overview.

References

1. Accenture: How blockchain can bring greater value to procure-to-pay processes (2017). https://www.accenture.com
2. Archer, D.W., Bogdanov, D., Pinkas, B., Pullonen, P.: Maturity and performance of programmable secure computation. IEEE Secur. Priv. **14**(5), 48–56 (2016)
3. Ben-Sasson, E., et al.: Zerocash: decentralized anonymous payments from Bitcoin. In: Symposium on Security and Privacy, Berkeley, CA, USA, pp. 459–474 (2014)
4. Benhamouda, F., Halevi, S., Halevi, T.: Supporting private data on Hyperledger Fabric with secure multiparty computation. In: International Conference on Cloud Engineering, pp. 357–363 (2018)
5. Blum, M.: Coin flipping by telephone. In: Advances in Cryptology: A Report on CRYPTO 1981, Santa Barbara, California, USA, 24–26 August, pp. 11–15 (1981)
6. Boneh, D., Franklin, M.: Efficient generation of shared RSA keys (extended abstract). In: Kaliski, B.S. (ed.) CRYPTO 1997. LNCS, vol. 1294, pp. 425–439. Springer, Heidelberg (1997). https://doi.org/10.1007/BFb0052253
7. Bos, J., den Boer, B.: Detection of disrupters in the DC protocol. In: Quisquater, J.-J., Vandewalle, J. (eds.) EUROCRYPT 1989. LNCS, vol. 434, pp. 320–327. Springer, Heidelberg (1990). https://doi.org/10.1007/3-540-46885-4_33
8. Brandt, F.: Fully private auctions in a constant number of rounds. In: Wright, R.N. (ed.) FC 2003. LNCS, vol. 2742, pp. 223–238. Springer, Heidelberg (2003). https://doi.org/10.1007/978-3-540-45126-6_16
9. Brandt, F.: Auctions. In: Rosenberg, B. (ed.) Handbook of Financial Cryptography and Security, pp. 49–58. Chapman and Hall/CRC (2010)
10. Cachin, C.: Efficient private bidding and auctions with an oblivious third party. In: Conference on Computer and Communications Security, Singapore, pp. 120–127 (1999)
11. Chaum, D.: The dining cryptographers problem: unconditional sender and recipient untraceability. J. Cryptol. **1**(1), 65–75 (1988)
12. Chaum, D., Pedersen, T.P.: Wallet databases with observers. In: Brickell, E.F. (ed.) CRYPTO 1992. LNCS, vol. 740, pp. 89–105. Springer, Heidelberg (1993). https://doi.org/10.1007/3-540-48071-4_7
13. Couteau, G., Peters, T., Pointcheval, D.: Encryption switching protocols. Cryptology ePrint Archive, Report 2015/990 (2015). http://eprint.iacr.org/2015/990
14. Damgård, I.: On Σ-protocols (2010). http://www.cs.au.dk/~ivan/Sigma.pdf
15. Damgård, I., Geisler, M., Krøigaard, M.: Efficient and secure comparison for on-line auctions. In: Pieprzyk, J., Ghodosi, H., Dawson, E. (eds.) ACISP 2007. LNCS, vol. 4586, pp. 416–430. Springer, Heidelberg (2007). https://doi.org/10.1007/978-3-540-73458-1_30

16. Desmedt, Y., Frankel, Y.: Shared generation of authenticators and signatures (extended abstract). In: Feigenbaum, J. (ed.) CRYPTO 1991. LNCS, vol. 576, pp. 457–469. Springer, Heidelberg (1992). https://doi.org/10.1007/3-540-46766-1_37

17. Dreier, J., Dumas, J.-G., Lafourcade, P.: Brandt's fully private auction protocol revisited. J. Comput. Secur. **23**(5), 587–610 (2015)

18. Ethereum. White Paper (2017). https://github.com/ethereum/wiki/wiki/

19. Etherscan. The Ethereum Block Explorer (2017). https://etherscan.io/

20. Fiat, A., Shamir, A.: How to prove yourself: practical solutions to identification and signature problems. In: Odlyzko, A.M. (ed.) CRYPTO 1986. LNCS, vol. 263, pp. 186–194. Springer, Heidelberg (1987). https://doi.org/10.1007/3-540-47721-7_12

21. Fischlin, M.: A cost-effective pay-per-multiplication comparison method for millionaires. In: Naccache, D. (ed.) CT-RSA 2001. LNCS, vol. 2020, pp. 457–471. Springer, Heidelberg (2001). https://doi.org/10.1007/3-540-45353-9_33

22. Garay, J., Kiayias, A., Leonardos, N.: The Bitcoin backbone protocol: analysis and applications. In: Oswald, E., Fischlin, M. (eds.) EUROCRYPT 2015. LNCS, vol. 9057, pp. 281–310. Springer, Heidelberg (2015). https://doi.org/10.1007/978-3-662-46803-6_10

23. Goldwasser, S., Micali, S.: Probabilistic encryption and how to play mental poker keeping secret all partial information. In: STOCS, pp. 365–377 (1982)

24. Katz, J.: Efficient and non-malleable proofs of plaintext knowledge and applications. In: Biham, E. (ed.) EUROCRYPT 2003. LNCS, vol. 2656, pp. 211–228. Springer, Heidelberg (2003). https://doi.org/10.1007/3-540-39200-9_13

25. Katz, J., Yung, M.: Threshold cryptosystems based on factoring. Cryptology ePrint Archive, Report 2001/093 (2001). http://eprint.iacr.org/2001/093

26. Kosba, A.E., Miller, A., Shi, E., Wen, Z., Papamanthou, C.: Hawk: the blockchain model of cryptography and privacy-preserving smart contracts. In: IEEE Symposium on Security and Privacy, San Jose, USA, pp. 839–858 (2016)

27. Lindell, Y.: How to simulate it – a tutorial on the simulation proof technique. Cryptology ePrint Archive, Report 2016/046 (2016). http://eprint.iacr.org/2016/046

28. Lindell, Y., Pinkas, B., Smart, N.P., Yanai, A.: Efficient constant round multiparty computation combining BMR and SPDZ. In: Gennaro, R., Robshaw, M. (eds.) CRYPTO 2015. LNCS, vol. 9216, pp. 319–338. Springer, Heidelberg (2015). https://doi.org/10.1007/978-3-662-48000-7_16

29. Lindell, Y., Smart, N.P., Soria-Vazquez, E.: More efficient constant-round multiparty computation from BMR and SHE. In: Hirt, M., Smith, A. (eds.) TCC 2016. LNCS, vol. 9985, pp. 554–581. Springer, Heidelberg (2016). https://doi.org/10.1007/978-3-662-53641-4_21

30. Naor, M., Pinkas, B., Sumner, R.: Privacy preserving auctions and mechanism design. In: ACM Conference on Electronic Commerce, pp. 129–139 (1999)

31. Ogata, W., Kurosawa, K., Sako, K., Takatani, K.: Fault tolerant anonymous channel. In: Han, Y., Okamoto, T., Qing, S. (eds.) ICICS 1997. LNCS, vol. 1334, pp. 440–444. Springer, Heidelberg (1997). https://doi.org/10.1007/BFb0028500

32. Reiter, M.K., Wang, X.: Fragile mixing. In: Proceedings of the 11th ACM Conference on Computer and Communications Security, CCS 2004, pp. 227–235 (2004)

33. Reuters. Ukrainian ministry carries out first blockchain transactions (2017). https://www.reuters.com

34. Sander, T., Young, A.L., Yung, M.: Non-interactive CryptoComputing For NC^1. In: FOCS, pp. 554–567 (1999)

35. Shoup, V.: Practical threshold signatures. In: Preneel, B. (ed.) EUROCRYPT 2000. LNCS, vol. 1807, pp. 207–220. Springer, Heidelberg (2000). https://doi.org/10. 1007/3-540-45539-6_15
36. Strain. Source Code (2017). https://github.com/strainprotocol/
37. Tual, S.: What are State Channels? (2017). https://www.stephantual.com
38. University of Bristol. Multiparty computation with SPDZ online phase and MAS-COT offline phase (2017). https://github.com/bristolcrypto/SPDZ-2
39. Vukolić, M.: The quest for scalable blockchain fabric: proof-of-work vs. BFT replication. In: Camenisch, J., Kesdoğan, D. (eds.) iNetSec 2015. LNCS, vol. 9591, pp. 112–125. Springer, Cham (2016). https://doi.org/10.1007/978-3-319-39028-4_9
40. Waidner, M.: Unconditional sender and recipient untraceability in spite of active attacks. In: Quisquater, J.-J., Vandewalle, J. (eds.) EUROCRYPT 1989. LNCS, vol. 434, pp. 302–319. Springer, Heidelberg (1990). https://doi.org/10.1007/3-540-46885-4_32
41. Waidner, M., Pfitzmann, B.: The dining cryptographers in the disco: unconditional sender and recipient untraceability with computationally secure serviceability. In: Quisquater, J.-J., Vandewalle, J. (eds.) EUROCRYPT 1989. LNCS, vol. 434, p. 690. Springer, Heidelberg (1990). https://doi.org/10.1007/3-540-46885-4_69

Channels: Horizontal Scaling and Confidentiality on Permissioned Blockchains

Elli Androulaki[1], Christian Cachin[1], Angelo De Caro[1],
and Eleftherios Kokoris-Kogias[2(✉)]

[1] IBM Research - Zurich, Rüschlikon, Switzerland
{lli,cca,adc}@zurich.ibm.com
[2] EPFL, Lausanne, Switzerland
eleftherios.kokoriskogias@epfl.ch

Abstract. Sharding, or partitioning the system's state so that different subsets of participants handle it, is a proven approach to building distributed systems whose total capacity scales horizontally with the number of participants. Many distributed ledgers have adopted this approach to increase their performance, however, they focus on the permissionless setting that assumes the existence of a strong adversary. In this paper, we deploy channels for permissioned blockchains. Our first contribution is to adapt sharding on asset-management applications for the permissioned setting, while preserving liveness and safety even on transactions spanning across-channels. Our second contribution is to leverage channels as a confidentiality boundary, enabling different organizations and consortia to preserve their privacy within their channels and still be part of a bigger collaborative ecosystem. To make our system concrete we map it on top of Hyperledger Fabric.

1 Introduction

Blockchain technology is making headlines due to its promise of a transparent, verifiable, and tamper-resistant history of transactions that is resilient to faults or influences of any single party [3]. Many organizations [2,4,15,22] either explore the potential of distributed-ledger technology or already embrace it. This, however, is a young technology facing multiple challenges [3,6]. In this paper we look into the challenges of enabling horizontal scaling and providing privacy in the permissioned setting.

First, the scalability of distributed ledgers hinders their mainstream adoption. One class of solutions proposed is sharding [6]. Sharding [20] has been used in order to build *scale-out* systems whose capacity scales horizontally with the number of participants by using the key idea of partitioning the state. Each such state partition can handle transactions parallel to other shards. Recently, several blockchain systems [7,12] proposed sharding mostly in the context of

---

E. Kokoris-Kogias—Work done at IBM Research - Zurich.

J. Lopez et al. (Eds.): ESORICS 2018, LNCS 11098, pp. 111–131, 2018.
https://doi.org/10.1007/978-3-319-99073-6_6

permissionless blockchains, where some fraction of participating parties might be Byzantine.

A second challenge for distributed ledgers is privacy. A distributed ledger is (by design) a transparent log visible to all the participants. This, however, is a disadvantage when it comes to deploying distributed ledgers among private companies, as they want to keep their data confidential and only selectively disclose them to vetted collaborators. One solution to privacy is to hide the state from all participants by using zero-knowledge proofs [10,13,16]. However, this can pose a problem in a permissioned setting both in terms of performance (especially if the system supports smart contracts) and in terms of business logic (*e.g.*, banks need to see the transactions to balance their books).

In this paper, we look into enabling sharding in the permissioned setting, where the adversarial power can be relaxed. First we deploy channels for horizontal scaling drawing inspiration from the state of the art [7,12], but at the same time navigating the functionality and trust spectrum to create simplified protocols with less complexity and need for coordination. Then, we introduce the idea that, in a permissioned setting, we can leverage the state partition that a channels introduces as a confidentiality boundary. In the second part of the paper, we show how we enable confidential channels while preserving the ability for cross-shard transactions.

Our main contributions are (a) the support for horizontal scaling on permissioned blockchains whith cross-channel transaction semantics, (b) the use of channels as a confidentiality boundary and (c) the formalization of an asset management application on top of blockchain systems.

2   Preliminaries

Blockchain Definitions. In the context of this work, a blockchain is an append-only tamper-evident log maintained by a distributed group of collectively trusted nodes. When these nodes are part of a defined set [1], we call the blockchain *permissioned*. Inside every block there are transactions that may modify the state of the blockchain (they might be invalid [1]). A distributed ledger [23] is a generalization of a blockchain as it can include multiple blockchains that interact with each other, given that sufficient trust between blockchains exists.

We define the following roles for nodes in a blockchain:

1. **Peers** execute and validate transactions. Peers store the blockchain and need to agree on the state.
2. **Orderers** collectively form the ordering service. The ordering service establishes the total order of transactions. Orderers are unaware of the application state, and do not participate in the execution or validation of transactions. Orderers reach consensus [1,5,11,17] on the blocks in order to provide a deterministic input for the blockchain peers to validate transactions.
3. **Oracles** are special nodes that provide information about a specific blockchain to nodes not being peers of that blockchain. Oracles come with

a *validation policy* of the blockchain defining when the announcement of an oracle is trustworthy[1].

4. **(Light) Clients** submit transactions that either read or write the state of a distributed ledger. Clients do not directly subscribe to state updates, but trust some oracles to provide the necessary proofs that a request is valid.

Nodes can implement multiple roles or collapse roles (*e.g.,* miners in Bitcoin [17] are concurrently peers and orderers). In a distributed ledger that supports multiple blockchains that interoperate the peers of one blockchain necessarily implement a client for every other blockchain and trust the oracles to provide proofs of validity for cross-channel transaction. A specific oracle instantiation can be for example that a quorum (*e.g.,* $\frac{2}{3}$) of the peers need to sign any announcement for it to be valid.

Channels: In this paper we extend channels (first introduced in Hyperledger Fabric [1]), an abstraction similar to shards. In prior work [1], a channel is defined as an autonomous blockchain agnostic to the rest of the state of the system. In this work, we redefine a channel as a state partition of the full system that (a) is autonomously managed by a (logically) separate set of peers (but is still aware of the bigger system it belongs) and (b) optionally hides the internal state from the rest of the system.

A channel might communicate with multiple other channels; and there needs to be some level of trust for two channels to transact. Hence, we permit each channel to decide on what comprises an authoritative proof of its own state. This is what we call **validation policy**: clients need to verify this policy in order to believe that something happened in a channel they are transacting with. When channel A wants to transact with channel B, then the peers of A effectively implement a client of channel B (as they do not know the state of B directly). Thus, the peers of A verify that the validation policy of B is satisfied when receiving authoritative statements from channel B.

For channels to interact, they need to be aware of each other and to be able to communicate. Oracles are responsible for this functionality, as they can gossip authoritative statements (statements supported by the validation policy) to the oracles of the other channels. This functionality needs a bootstrap step where channels and validation policies are discovered, which we do not address in this paper. A global consortium of organizations could publicly announce such information; or consortia represented by channels could communicate off-band. Once a channel is established further evolution can be done without a centralized intermediary, by using skipchains [18].

Threat Model: The peers that have the right to access one channel's state are trusted for confidentiality, meaning that they will not leak the state of the channel on purpose. We relax this assumption later providing forward and backward

---

[1] *e.g.,* in Bitcoin the oracles will give proofs that have 6 Proofs-of-Work build on top of them.

secrecy in case of compromise. We assume that the ordering service is secure, produces a unique blockchain without forks and the blocks produced are available to the peers of the channels. We further assume that the adversary is computationally bounded and that cryptographic primitives (*e.g.,* hash functions and digital signatures) are secure.

System Goals: We have the following primary goals.

1. **Secure transactions.** Transactions are committed atomically or eventually aborted, both within and across channels.
2. **Scale-out.** The system supports state partitions that can work in parallel, if no dependencies exist.
3. **Confidentiality.** The state of a channel remains internal to the channel peers. The only (if any) state revealed for cross-channel transactions should be necessary to verify that a transaction is valid (e.g. does not create new assets).

3   Asset Management in a Single Channel

3.1   Unspent Transaction-Output Model

In this section, we describe a simple asset-management system on top of the *Unspent Transaction-Output* model (henceforth referred to as UTXO) that utilizes a single, non- confidential channel. In particular, we focus on the UTXO-based data model [17], as it is the most adopted data model in cryptocurrencies, for its simplicity and parallelizability.

Assets in Transactions. In a UTXO system, transactions are the means through which one or more *virtual* assets are managed. More specifically, *mint* transactions signify the introduction of new assets in the system and *spend* transactions signify the change of ownership of an asset that already exists in the system. If an asset is *divisible*, i.e., can be split into two or more assets of measurable value, then a *spend* transaction can signify such a split, indicating the owners of each resulting component of the original asset.

Assets are represented in the transactions by transaction *inputs* and *outputs*. More specifically, in the typical UTXO model, an *input* represents the asset that is to be spent and an *output* represents the new asset that is created in response of the input assets' consumption. We can think of inputs and outputs representing different phases of the state of the same asset, where state includes its ownership (shares). Clearly, an input can be used only once, as after being spent, the original asset is substituted by the output assets, and stops being considered in the system. To ensure the single-spending of any given input, transactions are equipped with information authenticating the transaction creators as the owners of the (parts of the) assets that are referenced by the transaction inputs.

In more technical terms in the standard UTXO model, *input* fields implicitly or explicitly reference *output* fields of other transactions that have not yet been spent. At validation time, verifiers would need to ensure that the outputs referenced by the inputs of the transaction have not been spent; and upon transaction-commitment deem them as spent. To efficiently look up the status of each output at validation time UTXO model is equipped with a pool of *unspent transaction outputs* (UTXO pool).

UTXO Pool. The UTXO pool is the list of transaction outputs that have not yet been *spent*. We say that an output is *spent* if a transaction that references it in its inputs is included in the list of ledger's valid transactions.

To validate a transaction, peers check if (1) the transaction inputs refer to outputs that appear in the UTXO pool as well as (2) that the transaction's creators own these outputs. Other checks take place during the transaction validation, *i.e.*, input-output consistency checks. After these checks are successfully completed, the peers mark the outputs matching the transaction's inputs as spent and add to the pool the freshly created outputs. Hence, the pool consistently includes "unspent" outputs.

Asset or Output Definition. An **asset** is a logical entity that sits behind transaction outputs, implicitly referenced by transaction outputs. As such the terms output and asset can be used interchangeably. An output (the corresponding asset) is described by the following fields:

– *namespace*, the namespace the output belongs to (e.g., a channel);
– *owner*, the owner of the output
– *value*, the value of the asset the output represents (if divisible);
– *type*, the type of the asset the output represents (if multiple types exist).

Depending on the privacy requirements and properties of the ledger they reside, outputs provide this information in the clear (e.g., Bitcoin [17] outputs) or in a concealed form (e.g., ZeroCoin [16], ZeroCash [21]). Privacy-preserving outputs are required to be cryptographically bound to the value of each of the fields describing them, whereas its plaintext information should be available to the owner of the output.

UTXO Operations. We elaborate on the UTXO system functions where we adopt the following notation. For a sequence of values $x_1, \ldots, x_i$, we use the notation $[x_i] = (x_1, \ldots, x_i)$. By slight abuse of notation, we write $x_1 = [x_1]$. We denote algorithms by sans-serif fonts. Executing an algorithm algo on input y is denoted as $y \leftarrow \mathsf{algo}(x)$, where y can take on the special value $\bot$ to indicate an error.

A UTXO system exposes the following functions:

– $\langle \mathcal{U}, pool \rangle \leftarrow \mathsf{Setup}(\kappa)$ that enables each user to issue one or more identities by using security parameter κ. Henceforth, we denote by sec_{user} the secret information associated to a user with identity *user*. Setup also generates privileged identities, i.e., identities allowed to mint assets to the system, denoted as *adm*. Finally Setup initialises the pool *pool* to $\emptyset$ and returns the set of users in the system $\mathcal{U}$ and *pool*.

– $\langle out, sec_{out} \rangle \leftarrow$ ComputeOutput($nspace, owner, value, type$), to obtain an output representing the asset state as reflected in the function's parameters. That is, the algorithm would produce an output that is bound to namespace *nspace*, owned by *owner*, and represents an asset of type *type*, and value *value*. As mentioned before, depending on the nature of the system the result of the function could output two output components, one that is to be posted on the ledger as part of a transaction (*out*) and a private part to be maintained at its owner side (sec_{out}).

– $ain \leftarrow$ ComputeInput($out, sec_{out}, pool$), where, on input an asset pool *pool*, an output *out*, and its respective secrets, the algorithm returns a representation of the asset that can be used as transaction input *ain*. In Bitcoin, an input of an output is a direct reference to the latter, i.e., it is constructed to be the hash of the transaction where the output appeared in the ledger, together with the index of the output. In ZeroCash, an input is constructed as a combination of a serial number and a zero-knowledge proof that the serial corresponds to an unspent output of the ledger.

– $tx \leftarrow$ CreateTx($[sec_{owner_i}], [ain_i], [out_j]$), that creates a transaction *tx* to request the consummation of inputs $\{ain_k\}_{k=1}^i$ into outputs $\{out_k\}_{k=1}^j$. The function takes also as input the secrets of the owners of the outputs referenced by the inputs and returns *tx*. Notice that the same function can be used to construct *mint* transactions, where the input gives its place to the freshly introduced assets description.

– $pool' \leftarrow$ ValidateTx($nspace, tx, pool$), that validates transaction inputs w.r.t. pool *pool*, and their consistency with transaction outputs and namespace *nspace*. It subsequently updates the pool with the new outputs and spent inputs and returns its new version *pool'*. Input owner of mint transactions is the admin *adm*.

Properties: Regardless of its implementation, an asset management system should satisfy the properties defined below:

– *Validity.* Let *tx* be a transaction generated from a valid input *ain* according to some pool *pool*, i.e., generated via a successful call to $tx \leftarrow$ CreateTx(sec_{owner}, ain, out'), where $ain \leftarrow$ ComputeInput($out, sec_{out}, pool$), *owner* is the owner of *out'*, and $out' \notin pool$. Validity requires that a call to $pool' \leftarrow$ ValidateTx($tx, pool$) succeeds, i.e. $pool' \neq \bot$, and that $pool' = (pool \setminus \{out\}) \cup \{out'\}$.

– *Termination.* Any call to the functions exposed by the system eventually return the expected return value or $\bot$.

– *Unforgeability.* Let an output $out \in pool$ with corresponding secret sec_{out} and owner secret sec_{owner} that is part of the UTXO pool *pool*; unforgeability requires that it is computationally hard for an attacker without sec_{out} and

sec_{owner} to create a transaction tx such that $\mathsf{ValidateTx}(nspace, tx, pool)$ will not return $\perp$, and that would mark out as spent.

- *Namespace consistency.* Let an output corresponding to a namespace $nspace$ of a user *owner*. Namespace consistency requires that the adversary cannot compute any transaction tx referencing this output, and succeed in $\mathsf{ValidateTx}(nspace', tx, pool)$, where $nspace' \neq nspace$.
- *Balance.* Let a user *owner* owning a set of unspent outputs $[out_i] \in pool$. Let the collected value of these outputs for each asset type τ be $value_\tau$. Balance property requires that *owner* cannot spend outputs of value more than $value_\tau$ for any asset type τ, assuming that it is not the recipient of outputs in the meantime, or colludes with other users owning more outputs. Essentially, it cannot construct a set of transactions $[tx_i]$ that are all accepted when sequentially[2] invoking $\mathsf{ValidateTx}(tx, pool)$ with the most recent versions of the pool *pool*, such that *owner* does not appear as the recipient of assets after the acquisition of $[out_i]$, and the overall spent value of its after that point exceeds for some asset type τ $value_\tau$.

3.2 Protocol

We defined an asset output as, $out = \langle nm, o, t, v \rangle$, where nm is a namespace of the asset, o is the identity of its owner, t the type of the asset, and v its value. In its simplest implementation the UTXO pool would be implemented as the list of available outputs, and inputs would directly reference the outputs in the pool, e.g., using its hash[3]. Clearly a valid transaction for out's spending would require a signature with sec_o.

Asset Management in a Single Channel. We assume two users Alice and Bob, with respective identities $\langle A, sec_A \rangle$ and $\langle B, sec_B \rangle$. There is only one channel ch in the system with a namespace ns_{ch} associated with ch, where both users have permission to access. We also assume that there are system administrators with secrets sec_{adm} allowed to mint assets in the system, and that these administrators are known to everyone.

Asset Management Initialization. This requires the setup of the identities of the system administrators[4]. For simplicity, we assume there is one asset management administrator, $\langle adm, sec_{adm} \rangle$. The pool is initialized to include no assets, i.e., $pool_{ch} \leftarrow \emptyset$.

Asset Import. The administrator creates a transaction tx_{imp}, as:

$$tx_{imp} \leftarrow \langle \emptyset, [out_n], \sigma \rangle,$$

---

[2] This is a reasonable assumption, given we are referring to transactions appearing on a ledger.

[3] Different approaches would need to be adopted in cases where unlinkabiltiy between outputs and respective inputs is required.

[4] Can be a list of identities, or policies, or mapping between either of the two and types of assets.

where $out_k \leftarrow$ ComputeOutput(ns_{ch}, u_k, t_k, v_k), (t_i, v_i) the type and value of the output asset out_k, u_k its owner and σ a signature on transaction data using sk_{adm}. Validation of tx_{imp} would result into $pool_{ch} \leftarrow \{pool_{ch} \cup \{[out_n]\}\}$.

Transfer of Asset Ownership. Let $out_A \in pool_{ch}$ be an output owned by Alice, corresponding a description $\langle ns_{ch}, A, t, v \rangle$. For Alice to move ownership of this asset to Bob, it would create a transaction

$$tx_{move} \leftarrow \text{CreateTx}(sec_A; ain_A, out_B),$$

where ain_A is a reference of out_A in $pool_{ch}$, and $out_B \leftarrow$ ComputeOutput (ns_{ch}, B, t, v), the updated version of the asset, owned by Bob. tx_{move} has the form of $\langle ain_A, out_B, \sigma_A \rangle$ is a signature matching A. At validation of tx_{move}, $pool_{ch}$ is updated to no longer consider out_A as unspent, and include the freshly created output out_B:

$$pool_{ch} \leftarrow (pool_{ch} \setminus \{out_A\}) \cup \{out_B\} .$$

Discussion: The protocol introduced above does provide a "secure" (under the security properties described above) asset management application within a single channel. More specifically, the *Validity* property follows directly from correctness of the application where a transaction generated by using a valid input representation will be successfully validated by the peers after it is included in an ordered block. The *Unforgeability* is guaranteed from the requirement of a valid signature corresponding to the owner of the consumed input when calling the ValidateTx function, and *Namespace consistency* is guaranteed as there is only one namespace in this setting. *Termination* follows from the liveness guarantees of the validating peers and the consensus run by orderers. Finally, *Balance* also follows from the serial execution of transactions that will spend the *out* the first time and return $\bot$ for all subsequent calls (there is no *out* in the pool).

The protocol can be extended to naively scale-out. We can create more than one channel (each with its own namespace), where each one has a separate set of peers and each channel is unaware of the existence of other channels. Although each channel can have its own ordering service, it has been shown in l [1], that the ordering service does not constitute a bottleneck. Hence, we assume that channels share the ordering service.

The naive approach has two shortcomings. First, assets cannot be transferred between channels, meaning that value is "locked" within a channel and is not free to flow wherever its owner wants. Second, the state of each channel is public as all transactions are communicated in plaintext to the orderers who act as a global passive adversary.

We deal with these problems by introducing (i) a step-wise approach on enabling cross-channel transactions depending on the functionality required and the underlying trust model (See, Sect. 4), and (ii) the notion of confidential channels (see Sect. 5). Further, for confidential channels to work we adapt our algorithms to provide confidentiality while multiple confidential channels transact atomically.

4 Atomic Cross-Channel Transactions

In this section, we describe how we implement cross-channel transactions in permissioned blockchains (that enable the scale-out property as shown in prior work [12]). We introduce multiple protocols based on the functionality required and on the trust assumptions (that can be relaxed in a permissioned setting). First, in Sect. 4.1, we introduce a narrow functionality of 1-input-1-output transactions where Alice simply transfers an asset to Bob. Second, in Sect. 4.2, we extend this functionality to arbitrary transactions but assume the existence of a trusted channel among the participants. Finally, in Sect. 4.3, we lift this assumption and describe a protocol inspired by two-phase commit [24]. These protocols do not make timing assumptions but assume the correctness of the channels to guarantee fairness, unlike work in atomic cross-chain swaps [8].

Preliminaries. We assume two users Alice (u_a), and Bob (u_b). We further assume that each channel has a validation policy and a set of oracles (as defined in Sect. 2). We assume that each channel is aware of the policies and the oracles that are authoritative over the asset-management systems in each of the rest of the channels.

Communication of Pools Content Across Channels. On a regular basis, each channel advertises its pool content to the rest of the channels. More specifically, the oracles of the asset management system in each channel are responsible to regularly advertise a commitment of the content of the channel's pool to the rest of the channels. Such commitments can be the full list of assets in the pool or, for efficiency reasons, the Merkle root of deterministically ordered list of asset outputs created on that channel.

For the purpose of this simplistic example, we assume that for each channel ch_i, a commitment (*e.g.*, Merkle root) of its pool content is advertised to all the other channels. That is, each channel ch_i maintains a table with the following type of entries: $\langle ch_j, cmt_j \rangle, j \neq i$, where cmt_j the commitment corresponding to the pool of channel with identifier ch_j. We will refer to this pool by $pool_j$.

4.1 Asset Transfer Across Channels

Let out_A be an output included in the unspent output pool of ch_1, $pool_1$, corresponding to

$$out_A \leftarrow \mathsf{ComputeOutput}(ch_1, u_a, t, v)$$

i.e., an asset owned by Alice, active on ch_1. For Alice to move ownership of this asset to Bob and in channel with identifier ch_2, she would first create a new asset for Bob in ch_2 as

$$out_B \leftarrow \mathsf{ComputeOutput}(ch_2, u_b, t, v)$$

she would then create a transaction

$$tx_{move} \leftarrow \mathsf{CreateTx}(sec_A; ain_A, out_B),$$

where ain_A is a reference of out_A in $pool_1$. Finally, sec_A is a signature matching pk_A, and ownership transfer data.

At validation of tx_{move}, it is first ensured that $out_A \in pool_1$, and that $out_A.namespace = ch_1$. out_A is then removed from $pool_1$ and out_B is added to it, i.e.,

$$pool_1 \leftarrow (pool_1 \setminus \{out_A\}) \cup \{out_B\}.$$

Bob waits till the commitment of the current content of $pool_1$ is announced. Let us call the latter $view_1$. Then Bob can generate a transaction "virtually" spending the asset from $pool_1$ and generating an asset in $pool_2$. The full transaction will happen in ch_2 as the spend asset's namespace is ch_2. More specifically, Bob creates an input representation

$$\{ain_B\} \leftarrow \mathsf{ComputeInput}(out_B; sec_B, \pi_B)$$

of the asset out_B that Alice generated for him. Notice that instead of the pool, Bob needs to provide π_B, we explain below why this is needed to guarantee the balance property. Finally, Bob generates a transaction using ain_B.

To be ensured that the out_B is a valid asset, Bob needs to be provided with a proof, say π_B, that an output matching its public key and ch_2 has entered $pool_1$, matching $view_1$. For example, if $view_1$ is the root of the Merkle tree of outputs in $pool_1$, π_B could be the sibling path of out_B in that tree with out_B. This proof can be communicated from the oracles of ch_1 to the oracles of ch_2 or be directly pulled by Bob and introduced to ch_2. Finally, in order to prevent Bob from using the same proof twice (i.e., perform a replay attack) $pool_2$ need to be enhanced with a set of spent cross-transaction outputs (ScTXOs) that keep track of all the output representations out_X that have been already redeemed in another tx_{cross}. The out_B is extracted from π_B.

Validity property holds by extending the asset-management protocol of every channel to only accept transactions that spend assets that are part of channel's name-space. *Unforgeability* holds as before, due to the requirement for Alice and Bob to sign their respective transactions. *Namespace Consistency* holds as before, as validators of each channel only validate consistent transactions; and *Termination* holds because of the liveness guarantees of ch_1 and ch_2 and the assumption that the gossiped commitments will eventually arrive at all the channels. Finally, the *Balance* property holds as Alice can only spent her asset once in ch_1, which will generate a new asset not controlled by Alice anymore. Similarly, Bob can only use his proof once as out_B will be added in the ScTXO list of $pool_2$ afterwards.

4.2   Cross-Channel Trade with a Trusted Channel

The approach described above works for cases where Alice is altruistic and wants to transfer an asset to Bob. However, more complicated protocols (e.g fair exchange) are not supported, as they need atomicity and abort procedures in place. For example, if Alice and Bob want to exchange an asset, Alice should be able to abort the protocol if Bob decides to not cooperate. With the current protocol this is not possible as Alice assumes that Bob wants the protocol to finish and has nothing to win by misbehaving.

A simple approach to circumvent this problem is to assume a commonly trusted channel ch_t from all actors. This channel can either be an agreed upon "fair" channel or any of the channels of the participants, as long as all participants are able to access the channel and create/spend assets on/from it. The protocol uses the functionality of the asset transfer protocol described above (Sect. 4.1) to implement the Deposit and Withdraw subprotocols. In total, it exposes three functions and enables a cross-channel transaction with multiple inputs and outputs:

1. **Deposit:** All parties that contribute inputs transfer the assets to ch_t but maintain control over them by assigning the new asset in ch_t on their respective public keys.
2. **Transact:** When all input assets are created in ch_t, a tx_{cross} is generated and signed by all ain owners. This tx_{cross} has the full logic of the trade. For example, in the fair exchange it will have two inputs and two outputs. This tx_{cross} is validated as an atomic state update in ch_t.
3. **Withdraw:** Once the transaction is validated, each party that manages an output transfers their newly minted assets from ch_t to their respective channels ch_{o_i}.

Any input party can decide to abort the protocol by transferring back the input asset to their channel, as they always remain in control of the asset.

The protocol builds on top of the asset-transfer protocol and inherits its security properties to the extent of the Deposit and Withdraw sub-protocols. Furthermore, the trusted channel is only trusted to provide the necessary liveness for assets to be moved across channels, but it cannot double-spent any asset as they still remain under the control of their rightful owners (bound to the owner's public key). As a result, the asset-trade protocol satisfies the asset-management security requirements because it can be implemented by combining the protocol of Sect. 4.1 for the "Transact" function inside ch_t and the asset-transfer protocol of Sect. 4.2 for "Withdraw" and "Deposit" (Fig. 1).

4.3   Cross-Channel Trade Without a Trusted Channel

A mutually trusted channel (as assumed above), where every party is permitted to generate and spend assets, might not always exist; in this section, we describe a protocol that lifts this assumption. The protocol is inspired by the Atomix protocol [12], but addresses implementation details that are ignored in Atomix, such as how to represent and communicate proofs, and it is more specialized to our asset management model.

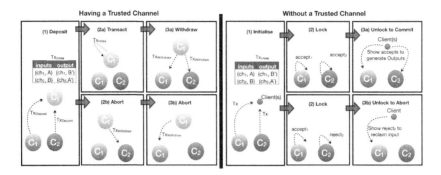

Fig. 1. Cross-channel transaction architecture overview with (4.2) and without (4.3) a trusted channel

1. **Initialize.** The transacting parties create a tx_{cross} whose inputs spend assets of some input channels (ICs) and whose outputs create new assets in some output channels (OCs). More concretely.
   If Alice wants to exchange out_A from ch_1 with Bob's out_B from ch_2. Alice and Bob work together to generate the tx_{cross} as

   $$tx_{cross} \leftarrow \mathsf{CreateTx}([sec_A, sec_B]; [ain_A, ain_B]; [out_A, out_B])$$

   where ain_A, ain_B are the input representations that show the assets to exist in the respective pools.
2. **Lock.** All input channels internally spend the assets they manage and generate a new asset bound to the transaction (we call it the "locked" asset), by using a collision resistant Hash function to derive the name-space of the new asset, as $H(tx_{cross})^5$. The locked asset's value is either equal to the sum of the assets previously spent for that channel or 0, depending on whether the tx_{cross} is valid according to the current state. In both cases there is a new asset added in $pool_i$. Or in our example:
   Alice submits tx_{cross} to ch_2, which generates the "locked" asset for tx_{cross}. Alice then receives π_B, which shows that out_B is locked for tx_{cross} and is represented by $out_{B'}$, which is the locked asset that is generated specifically for tx_{cross} and is locked for Alice but not spendable by Alice. Specifically,

   $$asset_{2'} = \langle H(tx_{cross}), t, v \rangle,$$

   where v is either equal to the value of $asset_2$ or 0, depending on whether $asset_2$ was already spent. Same process happens for Bob. Notice that the namespace of the asset change to $H(tx_{cross})$ indicates that this asset can only be used as proof of existence and not spent again in ch_2.
3. **Unlock.** Depending on the outcome of the lock phase, the clients are able to either commit or abort their transaction.

---

[5] The transaction's hash is an identifier for a virtual channel created only for this transaction.

(a) **Unlock to Commit.** If all ICs accepted the transaction (generated locked assets with non-zero values), then the respective transaction can be committed.

Each holder of an output creates an unlock-to-commit transaction for his channel; it consists of the lock transaction and an oracle-generated proof for each input asset (e.g. against the gossiped MTR). Or in our example: Alice (and Bob respectively) collects $\pi_{A'}$ and $\pi_{B'}$ which correspond to the proofs of existence of $out_{A'}$, $out_{B'}$ and submits in ch_1 an unlock-to-commit transaction:

$$tx_{uc} \leftarrow \mathsf{CreateTx}([\pi_{A'}, \pi_{B'}]; [ain_{1'}, ain_{2'}]; [out_{A''}];)$$

The transaction is validated in ch_1 creating a new asset ($out_{A''}$), similar to the one Bob spent at ch_2, as indicated by tx_{cross}.

(b) **Unlock to Abort.** If, however, at least one IC rejects the transaction (due to a double-spent), then the transaction cannot be committed and has to abort. In order to reclaim the funds locked in the previous phase, the client must request the involved ICs that already spent their inputs, to re-issue these inputs. Alice can initiate this procedure by providing the proof that the transaction has failed in ch_2. Or in our case if Bob's asset validation failed, then there is an asset $out_{B'}$ with zero value and Alice received from ch_2 the respective proof $\pi'_{B'}$. Alice will then generate an unlock-to-abort transaction:

$$tx_{ua} \leftarrow \mathsf{CreateTx}([\pi_{B'}], [ain_{2'}]; [out_{A''}])$$

which will generate a new asset $out_{A''}$ that is identical to out_A and remains under the control of Alice.

Security Arguments: Under our assumptions, channels are collectively honest and do not fail hence propagate correct commitments of their pool (commitments valid against the validation policy).

Validity and *Namespace Consistency* hold because every channel manages its own namespace and faithfully executes transactions. *Unforgeability* holds as before, due to the requirement for Alice and Bob to sign their respective transactions and the tx_{cross}.

Termination holds if every tx_{cross} eventually commits or aborts, meaning that either a transaction will be fully committed or the locked funds can be reclaimed. Based on the fact that all channels always process all transactions, each IC eventually generates either a commit-asset or an abort-asset. Consequently, if a client has the required number of proofs (one per input), then the client either holds all commit-assets (allowing the transaction to be committed) or at least one abort-asset (forcing the transaction to abort), but as channels do not fail, the client will eventually hold enough proof. Termination is bound to the assumption that some client will be willing to initiate the unlock step, otherwise his assets will remain unspendable. We argue that failure to do such only results in harm of the asset-holder and does not interfere with the correctness of the asset-management application.

Finally, *Balance* holds as cross-channel transactions are atomic and are assigned to specific channels who are solely responsible for the assets they control (as described by validity) and generate exactly one asset. Specifically, if all input channels issue an asset with value, then every output channel unlocks to commit; if even one input channel issues an asset with zero value, then all input channels unlock to abort; and if even one input shard issues an asset with zero value, then no output channel unlocks to commit. As a result, the assigned channels do not process a transaction twice and no channel attempts to unlock without a valid proof.

5   Using Channels for Confidentiality

So far we have focused on enabling transactions between channels that guarantee fairness among participants. This means that no honest participant will be worse off by participating in one of the protocols. Here, we focus on providing confidentiality among the peers of a channel, assuming that the orderers upon which the channel relies for maintaining the blockchain are not fully trusted hence might leak data.

Strawman Solution. We start with a simple solution that can be implemented with vanilla channels [1]. We define a random key k and a symmetric encryption algorithm that is sent in a private message to every participating peer. All transactions and endorsements are encrypted under k then sent for ordering, hence the confidentiality of the channel is protected by the unpredictability of the symmetric encryption algorithm.

This strawman protocol provides the confidentiality we expect from a channel, but its security is static. Even though peers are trusted for confidentiality, all it takes for an adversary to compromise the full past and future confidential transactions of the system is to compromise a single peer and recover k. Afterwards the adversary can collude with a Byzantine order to use the channels blockchain as a log of the past and decrypt every transactions, as well as keep receiving future transactions from the colluding orderer.

5.1   Deploying Group Key Agreement

To work around the attack, we first need to minimize the attack surface. To achieve this we need to think of the peers of a channel, as participants of a confidential communication channel and provide similar guarantees. Specifically, we guarantee the following properties.

1. **Forward Secrecy:** A passive adversary that knows one or more old encryption keys k_i, cannot discover any future encryption key k_j where $i < j$
2. **Backward Secrecy:** A passive adversary that knows one or more encryption keys k_i, cannot discover any previous encryption key k_j where $j < i$

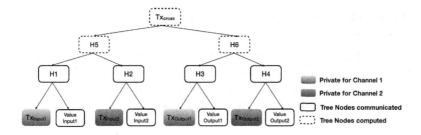

Fig. 2. Privacy preserving cross-channel transaction structure

3. **Group Key Secrecy:** It is computationally infeasible for an adversary to guess any group key k_i
4. **Key Agreement:** For an epoch i all group members agree on the epoch key k_i.

There are two types of group key agreement we look into:

Centralized Group-Key Distribution: In these systems, there is a dedicated server that sends the symmetric key to all the participants. The centralized nature of the key creation is scalable, but might not be acceptable even in a permissioned setting where different organizations participating in a channel are mutually suspicious.

Contributory Group-Key Management: In these systems, each group member contributes a share to the common group key, which is then computed by each member autonomously. These protocols are a natural fit to decentralized systems such as distributed ledgers, but they scale poorly.

We use the existence of the validation policy as an indication of the trusted entities of the channel (*i.e.,* the oracles) and create a more suitable protocol to the permissioned setting. Another approach could be to introduce a key-management policy that defines the key-generation and update rules but, for simplicity, we merge it with the validation policy that the peers trust anyway. We start with a scalable contributory group-key agreement protocol [9], namely the Tree-Based Group Diffie-Hellman system. However, instead of deploying it among the peers as contributors (which would require running view-synchronization protocols among them), we deploy it among the smaller set of oracles of the channel. The oracles generate symmetric keys in a decentralized way, and the peers simply contact their favorite oracle to receive the latest key. If an oracle replies to a peer with an invalid key, the peer can detect it because he can no longer decrypt the data, hence he can (a) provably blame the oracle and (b) request the key from another oracle.

More specifically we only deploy the group-join and group-leave protocols of [9], because we do not want to allow for splitting of the network, which might cause forks on the blockchain. We also deploy a group-key refresh protocol that is similar to group-leave, but no oracle is actually leaving.

5.2 Enabling Cross-Shard Transactions Among Confidential Channels

In the protocols we mentioned in Sect. 4, every party has full visibility on the inputs and outputs and is able to link the transfer of coins. However, this might not be desirable. In this section, we describe a way to preserve privacy during cross-channel transactions within each asset's channel.

For example, we can assume the existence of two banks, each with its own channel. It would be desirable to not expose intra-channel transactions or account information when two banks perform an interbank asset-transfer. More concretely, we assume that Alice and Bob want to perform a fair exchange. They have already exchanged the type of assets and the values they expect to receive. The protocol can be extended to store any kind of ZK-Proofs the underlying system supports, as long as the transaction can be publicly verified based on the proofs.

To provide the obfuscation functionality, we use Merkle trees. More specifically, we represent a cross-shard transaction as a Merkle tree (see Fig. 2), where the left branch has all the inputs lexicographically ordered and the right branch has all the outputs. Each input/output is represented as a tree node with two leaves: a private leaf with all the information available for the channel and a public leaf with the necessary information for third party verification of the transaction's validity.

The protocol for Alice works as follows:

Transaction Generation:

1. Input Merkle-Node Generation: Alice generates an input as before and a separate Merkle leaf that only has the type of the asset and the value. These two leaves are then hashed together to generate their input Merkle node.
2. Output Merkle-Node Generation: Similarly, Alice generates an Output Merkle node, that consists of the actual output (including the output address) on the private leaf and only the type and value of the asset expected to be credited on the public.
3. Transaction Generation: Alice and Bob exchange their public Input and Output Merkle-tree nodes and autonomously generate the full Merkle tree of the transaction.

Transaction Validation:

1. Signature Creation: Alice signs the MTR of the tx_{cross}, together with a bitmap of which leaves she has seen and accepts. Then she receives a similar signature from Bob and verifies it. Then Alice hashes both signatures and attaches them to the full transaction. This is the tx_{cross} that she submits in her channel for validation. Furthermore, she provides her full signature, which is logged in the channel's confidential chain but does not appear in the pool; in the pool the generated asset is $H(tx_{cross})$.
2. Validation: Each channel validates the signed transaction (from all inputs inside the channel's state) making sure that the transaction is semantically

correct (*e.g.,* does not create new assets). They also check that the publicly exposed leaf of every input is well generated (e.g. value and type much). Then they generate the new asset ($H(tx_{cross})$ as before) that is used to provide proof-of-commitment/abortion. The rest of the protocol (e.g. Unlock phase) is the same as Sect. 4.3.

Security and Privacy Arguments. The atomicity of the protocol is already detailed above. Privacy is achieved, because the source and destination addresses (accounts) are never exposed outside the shard and the signatures that authenticate the inputs inside the channel are only exposed within the channel. We also describe the security of the system outside the atomic commit protocol. More specifically,

1. Every tx_{cross} is publicly verifiable to make sure that the net-flow is zero, either by exposing the input and output values or by correctly generating ZK-proofs.
2. The correspondence of the public and private leaf of a transaction is fully validated by the input and/or output channel, making sure that its state remains correct.
3. The hash of the tx_{cross} is added in the pool to represent the asset. Given the collision resistance of a hash function, this signals to all other channels that the private leaves correspond to the transaction have been seen, validated and accepted.

The scheme can be further enhanced to hide the values using Pedersen commitments [19] and range-proofs similar to confidential transactions [14]. In such an implementation the Pedersen commitments should also be opened on the private leaf for the consistency checks to be correctly done.

6   Case Study: Cross-Shard Transactions on Hyperledger Fabric

In order to implement the cross-channel support on Fabric v1.1, we start with the current implementation of FabCoin [1] that implements an asset-management protocol similar to the one introduced in Sect. 3.2.

Channel-Based Implementation. As described by Androulaki et al. [1], a Fabric network can support multiple blockchains connected to the same ordering service. Each such blockchain is called a *channel*. Each channel has its own configuration that includes all the functioning metadata, such as defining the membership service providers that authenticate the peers, how to reach the ordering service, and the rules to update the configuration itself. The genesis block of a channel contains the initial configuration. The configuration can be updated by submitting a *reconfiguration transaction*. If this transaction is valid with the respect to the rules described by the current configuration, then it gets committed in a block containing only the reconfiguration transaction, and the chances are applied.

In this work, we extend the channel configuration to include the metadata to support cross-channel transactions. Specifically, the configuration lists the channels with which interaction is allowed; we call them *friend channels*. Each entry also has a *state-update validation policy*, to validate the channel's state-updates, the identities of the oracles of that channel, that will advertise state-update transactions, and the current commitment to the state of that channel. The configuration block is also used as a *lock-step* that signals the view-synchrony needed for the oracles to produce the symmetric-key of the channel. If an oracle misbehaves, then a new configuration block will be issued to ban it.

Finally, we introduce a new entity called *timestamper* (inspired by recent work in software updates [18]) to defend against freeze attacks where the adversary presents a stale configuration block that has an obsolete validation policy, making the network accepting an incorrect state update. The last valid configuration is signed by the timestampers every *interval*, defined in the configuration, and (assuming loosely synchronised clocks) guarantees the freshness of state updates[6].

Extending FabCoin to Scale-out. In FabCoin [1] each asset is represented by its current output state that is a tuple of the form $(txid.j, (value, owner, type))$. This representation denotes the asset created as the j-th output of a transaction with identifier $txid$ that has $value$ units of asset $type$. The output is owned by the public key denoted as $owner$.

To support cross-channel transactions, we extend FabCoin transactions by adding one more field, called *namespace*, that defines the channel that manages the asset (*i.e.*, $(txid.j, (namespace, value, owner, type))$).

Periodically, every channel generates a *state commitment* to its state, this can be done by one or more channel's oracles. This state commitment consists of two components: (i) the root of the Merkle tree built on top of the UTXO pool, (ii) the hash of the current configuration block with the latest timestamp, which is necessary to avoid freeze attacks.

Table 1. Atomic commit protocol on fabric channels

Protocol	Atomicity	Trust assumption	Generality of transactions	Privacy
Asset transfer (Sect. 4.1)	Yes	Nothing extra	1-input-1-ouptut	No
Trusted channel (Sect. 4.2)	Yes	Trusted intermediary channel	N-input-M-output	No
Atomic commit (Sect. 4.3)	Yes	Nothing extra	N-input-M-output	No
Obfuscated transaction AC (Sect. 5.2)	Yes	Nothing extra	N-input-M-output	Yes

---

[6] unless both the timestamp role and the validation policy are compromised.

Then, the oracles of that channel announce the new state commitment to the friend channels by submitting specific transactions targeting each of these friend channels. The transaction is committed if (i) the hashed configuration block is equal to the last seen configuration block, (ii) the timestamp is not "too" stale (for some time value that is defined per channel) and (iii) the transaction verifies against the state-updates validation policy. If those conditions hold, then the channel's configuration is updated with the new state commitment. If the first condition does not hold, then the channel is stale regarding the external channel it transacts with and needs to update its view.

Using the above state update mechanism, Alice and Bob can now produce verifiable proofs that certain outputs belong to the UTXO pool of a certain channel; these proofs are communicated to the interested parties differently, depending on the protocol. On the simple asset-transfer case (Sect. 4.1), we assume that Alice is altruistic (as she donates an asset to Bob) and request the proofs from her channel that is then communicated off-band to Bob. On the asset trade with trusted channels (Sect. 4.2) Alice and Bob can independently produce the proofs from their channels or the trusted channel as they have visibility and access rights. Finally on the asset trade of Sect. 4.3, Alice and Bob use the signed cross-channel transaction as proof-of-access right to the channels of the input assets in order to obtain the proofs. This is permitted because the tx_{cross} is signed by some party that has access rights to the channel and the channels peers can directly retrieve the proofs as the asset's ID is derived from $H(tx_{cross})$.

7   Conclusion

In this paper, we have redefined channels, provided an implementation guideline on Fabric [1] and formalized an asset management system. A channel is the same as a shard that has been already defined in previous work [7,12]. Our first contribution is to explore the design space of sharding on permissioned blockchains where different trust assumptions can be made. We have introduced three different protocols that achieve different properties as described in Table 1. Afterwards we have introduced the idea that a channel in a permissioned distributed ledger can be used as a confidentiality boundary and describe how to achieve this. Finally, we have merged the contributions to achieve a confidentiality preserving, scale-out asset management system, by introducing obfuscated transaction trees.

Acknowledgments. We thank Marko Vukolić and Björn Tackmann for their valuable suggestions and discussions on earlier versions of this work. This work has been supported in part by the European Union's Horizon 2020 research and innovation programme under grant agreement No. 780477 PRIViLEDGE.

References

1. Androulaki, E., et al.: Hyperledger fabric: a distributed operating system for permissioned blockchains. In: Proceedings of the Thirteenth European conference on Computer systems, EuroSys 2018. ACM, New York (2018). https://arxiv.org/abs/1801.10228
2. Bishop, G.: Illinois begins pilot project to put birth certificates on digital ledger technology, September 2017. https://www.ilnews.org/news/statewide/illinois-begins-pilot-project-to-put-birth-certificates-on-digital/article_1005eca0-98c7-11e7-b466-170ecac25737.html
3. Bonneau, J., Miller, A., Clark, J., Narayanan, A., Kroll, J.A., Felten, E.W.: SoK: research perspectives and challenges for bitcoin and cryptocurrencies. In: 2015 IEEE Symposium on Security and Privacy (SP), pp. 104–121. IEEE (2015). http://ieeexplore.ieee.org/abstract/document/7163021/
4. Browne, R.: IBM partners with nestle, unilever and other food giants to trace food contamination with blockchain, September 2017. https://www.cnbc.com/2017/08/22/ibm-nestle-unilever-walmart-blockchain-food-contamination.html
5. Cachin, C., Vukolic, M.: Blockchain consensus protocols in the wild. CoRR, abs/1707.01873 (2017). https://arxiv.org/abs/1707.01873
6. Croman, K., et al.: On scaling decentralized blockchains (a position paper). In: Clark, J., Meiklejohn, S., Ryan, P.Y.A., Wallach, D., Brenner, M., Rohloff, K. (eds.) FC 2016. LNCS, vol. 9604, pp. 106–125. Springer, Heidelberg (2016). https://doi.org/10.1007/978-3-662-53357-4_8. http://fc16.ifca.ai/bitcoin/papers/CDE+16.pdf
7. Danezis, G., Meiklejohn, S.: Centrally banked cryptocurrencies. In: 23rd Annual Network and Distributed System Security Symposium (NDSS), February 2016. https://eprint.iacr.org/2015/502.pdf
8. Herlihy, M.: Atomic cross-chain swaps. arXiv preprint arXiv:1801.09515 (2018)
9. Kim, Y., Perrig, A., Tsudik, G.: Tree-based group key agreement. ACM Trans. Inf. Syst. Secur. (TISSEC) **7**(1), 60–96 (2004)
10. Kokoris-Kogias, E., et al.: Hidden in plain sight: storing and managing secrets on a public ledger. Cryptology ePrint Archive, Report 2018/209 (2018). https://eprint.iacr.org/2018/209
11. Kokoris-Kogias, E., Jovanovic, P., Gailly, N., Khoffi, I., Gasser, L., Ford, B.: Enhancing bitcoin security and performance with strong consistency via collective signing. In: Proceedings of the 25th USENIX Conference on Security Symposium (2016). http://arxiv.org/abs/1602.06997
12. Kokoris-Kogias, E., Jovanovic, P., Gasser, L., Gailly, N., Syta, E., Ford, B.: OmniLedger: a secure, scale-out, decentralized ledger via sharding. In: 2018 IEEE Symposium on Security and Privacy (SP), pp. 19–34. IEEE (2018)
13. Kosba, A., Miller, A., Shi, E., Wen, Z., Papamanthou, C.: Hawk: the blockchain model of cryptography and privacy-preserving smart contracts. Technical report, Cryptology ePrint Archive, Report 2015/675 (2015). http://eprint.iacr.org
14. Maxwell, G.: Confidential transactions (2015). http://people.xiph.org/~greg/confidentialvalues.txt
15. Melendez, S.: Fast, Secure Blockchain Tech from an Unexpected Source Microsoft, September 2017. https://www.fastcompany.com/40461634/
16. Miers, I., Garman, C., Green, M., Rubin, A.D.: Zerocoin: anonymous distributed e-cash from bitcoin. In: 34th IEEE Symposium on Security and Privacy (S&P), May 2013

17. Nakamoto, S.: Bitcoin: a peer-to-peer electronic cash system (2008). https://bitcoin.org/bitcoin.pdf
18. Nikitin, K., et al.: CHAINIAC: proactive software-update transparency via collectively signed skipchains and verified builds. In: 26th USENIX Security Symposium (USENIX Security 17), pp. 1271–1287 (2017)
19. Pedersen, T.P.: Non-interactive and information-theoretic secure verifiable secret sharing. In: Feigenbaum, J. (ed.) CRYPTO 1991. LNCS, vol. 576, pp. 129–140. Springer, Heidelberg (1992). https://doi.org/10.1007/3-540-46766-1_9
20. Roy, R.: Shard âĂŞ a database design, July 2008. http://technoroy.blogspot.ch/2008/07/shard-database-design.html
21. Sasson, E., et al.: Zerocash: decentralized anonymous payments from bitcoin. In: 2014 IEEE Symposium on Security and Privacy (SP), pp. 459–474. IEEE (2014)
22. Simonsen, S.: 5 Reasons the UN is jumping on the blockchain bandwagon, September 2017. https://singularityhub.com/2017/09/03/the-united-nations-and-the-ethereum-blockchain/
23. Swanson, T.: Consensus-as-a-service: a brief report on the emergence of permissioned, distributed ledger systems. Report, April 2015
24. Wikipedia: Atomic commit, February 2018. https://en.wikipedia.org/wiki/Atomic_commit

Stay On-Topic: Generating Context-Specific Fake Restaurant Reviews

Mika Juuti[1(✉)], Bo Sun[2,3], Tatsuya Mori[3,4], and N. Asokan[1]

[1] Aalto University, Espoo, Finland
mika.juuti@aalto.fi, asokan@acm.org
[2] Cybersecurity Research Institute, National Institute of Information
and Communications Technology, Tokyo, Japan
bo_sun@nict.go.jp
[3] Department of Computer Science and Communication Engineering,
Waseda University, Tokyo, Japan
mori@nsl.cs.waseda.ac.jp
[4] Center for Advanced Intelligence Project, RIKEN, Tokyo, Japan

Abstract. Automatically generated fake restaurant reviews are a threat to online review systems. Recent research has shown that users have difficulties in detecting machine-generated fake reviews hiding among real restaurant reviews. The method used in this work (*char-LSTM*) has one drawback: it has difficulties staying in *context*, i.e. when it generates a review for specific target entity, the resulting review may contain phrases that are unrelated to the target, thus increasing its detectability. In this work, we present and evaluate a more sophisticated technique based on neural machine translation (NMT) with which we can generate reviews that *stay on-topic*. We test multiple variants of our technique using native English speakers on Amazon Mechanical Turk. We demonstrate that reviews generated by the best variant have almost optimal undetectability (class-averaged F-score 47%). We conduct a user study with experienced users and show that our method evades detection more frequently compared to the state-of-the-art (average evasion 3.2/4 vs 1.5/4) with statistical significance, at level $\alpha = 1\%$ (Sect. 4.3). We develop very effective detection tools and reach average F-score of 97% in classifying these. Although fake reviews are very effective in fooling people, effective automatic detection is still feasible.

1 Introduction

Automatically generated fake reviews have only recently become natural enough to fool human readers. Yao et al. [1] use a deep neural network (a so-called 2-layer LSTM [2]) to generate fake reviews, and concluded that these fake reviews look sufficiently genuine to fool native English speakers. They train their model

---

B. Sun—Partially completed during his Ph.D. course at Waseda University.

J. Lopez et al. (Eds.): ESORICS 2018, LNCS 11098, pp. 132–151, 2018.
https://doi.org/10.1007/978-3-319-99073-6_7

using real restaurant reviews from yelp.com [3]. Once trained, the model is used to generate reviews character-by-character. Due to the generation methodology, it cannot be easily targeted for a specific *context* (meaningful side information). Consequently, the review generation process may stray *off-topic*. For instance, when generating a review for a Japanese restaurant in Las Vegas, the review generation process may include references to an Italian restaurant in Baltimore. The authors of [1] apply a post-processing step (*customization*), which replaces food-related words with more suitable ones (sampled from the targeted restaurant). The word replacement strategy has drawbacks: it can miss certain words and replace others independent of their surrounding words, which may alert savvy readers. As an example: when we applied the customization technique described in [1] to a review for a Japanese restaurant it changed the snippet *garlic knots for breakfast with garlic knots for sushi*).

We propose a methodology based on neural machine translation (NMT) that improves the generation process by defining a context for the each generated fake review. Our context is a clear-text sequence of: the review rating, restaurant name, city, state and food tags (e.g. Japanese, Italian). We show that our technique generates review that *stay on topic*. We can instantiate our basic technique into several variants. We vet them on Amazon Mechanical Turk and find that native English speakers are very poor at recognizing our fake generated reviews. For one variant, the participants' performance is close to random: the class-averaged F-score of detection is 47% (whereas random would be 42% given the 1:6 imbalance in the test). Via a user study with experienced, highly educated participants, we compare this variant (which we will henceforth refer to as *NMT-Fake* reviews*) with fake reviews generated using the char-LSTM-based technique from [1].

We demonstrate that NMT-Fake* reviews constitute a new category of fake reviews that *cannot be detected* by classifiers trained only using previously known categories of fake reviews [1,4,5]. Therefore, NMT-Fake* reviews may go undetected in existing online review sites. To meet this challenge, we develop an effective classifier that detects NMT-Fake* reviews effectively (97% F-score). Our main contributions are:

- We present a novel method for creating machine-generated fake user reviews that **generates content based on specific context**: venue name, user rating, city etc. (Sects. 3.2 to 3.3). We demonstrate that our model can be trained faster (90% reduction in training time compared to [1], Sect. 3.3) and resulting NMT-Fake* reviews are **highly effective in fooling native English speakers** (class-averaged F-score 47%, Sect. 3.4).
- We **reproduce** a previously proposed **fake review generation method** [1] (Sect. 4.1) and show that NMT-Fake* reviews are **statistically different** from previous fake reviews, and that classifiers trained on previous fake review types do **not detect** NMT-Fake* reviews (Sect. 4.2).
- We compare NMT-Fake* reviews with char-LSTM reviews in a user study. We show that our reviews are **significantly better at evading detection** with statistical significance ($\alpha = 1\%$) (Sect. 4.3).

– We develop **highly efficient statistical detection tools** to recognize NMT-Fake* reviews with 97% F-score (Sect. 5). We plan to share the implementation of our detector and generative model with other researchers to facilitate transparency and reproducibility.

2   Background

Fake Reviews. User-generated content [6] is an integral part of the contemporary user experience on the web. Sites like tripadvisor.com, yelp.com and *Google Play* use user-written reviews to provide rich information that helps other users choose where to spend money and time. User reviews are used for rating services or products, and for providing qualitative opinions. User reviews and ratings may be used to rank services in recommendations. Ratings have an affect on the outwards appearance. Already 8 years ago, researchers estimated that a one-star rating increase affects the business revenue by 5–9% on yelp.com [7].

Due to monetary impact of user-generated content, some businesses have relied on so-called crowd-turfing *agents* [8] that promise to deliver positive ratings written by *workers* to a *customer* in exchange for a monetary compensation. Crowd-turfing ethics are complicated. For example, Amazon community guidelines prohibit buying content relating to promotions, but the act of writing fabricated content is not considered illegal, nor is matching workers to customers [9]. Year 2015, approximately 20% of online reviews on yelp.com were suspected of being fake [10].

Nowadays, user-generated review sites like yelp.com use filters and fraudulent review detection techniques. These factors have resulted in an increase in the requirements of crowd-turfed reviews provided to review sites, which in turn has led to an increase in the cost of high-quality review. Due to the cost increase, researchers hypothesize the existence of neural network-generated fake reviews. These neural-network-based fake reviews are statistically different from human-written fake reviews, and are not caught by classifiers trained on these [1].

Detecting fake reviews can either be done on an individual level or as a system-wide detection tool (i.e. regulation). Detecting fake online content on a personal level requires knowledge and skills in critical reading. In 2017, the National Literacy Trust assessed that young people in the UK do not have the skillset to differentiate fake news from real news [11]. For example, 20% of children that use online news sites in age group 12–15 believe that all information on news sites are true.

Neural Networks. Neural networks are function compositions that map input data through k subsequent layers:

$$F(x) = f_k \circ f_{k-1} \circ \cdots \circ f_2 \circ f_1 \circ x, \tag{1}$$

where the functions f_k are typically non-linear and chosen by experts partly for known good performance on datasets and partly for simplicity of computational evaluation. Language models (LMs) [12] are generative probability distributions that assign probabilities to sequences of tokens (t_i):

$$p(t_k|t_{<k}) = p(t_k|t_{k-1}, t_{k-2}, \ldots, t_2, t_1), \tag{2}$$

such that the language model can be used to predict how likely a specific token at time step k is, based on the $k-1$ previous tokens. Tokens are typically either words or characters.

For decades, deep neural networks were thought to be computationally too difficult to train. However, advances in optimization, hardware and the availability of frameworks have shown otherwise [2,13]. Neural language models (NLMs) have been one of the promising application areas. NLMs are typically various forms of recurrent neural networks (RNNs), which pass through the data sequentially and maintain a memory representation of the past tokens with a hidden context vector. There are many RNN architectures that focus on different ways of updating and maintaining context vectors: Long Short-Term Memory units (LSTM) and Gated Recurrent Units (GRUs) are perhaps most popular. Neural LMs have been used for free-form text generation. In certain application areas, the quality has been high enough to sometimes fool human readers [1].

Encoder-decoder (seq2seq) models [14] are architectures of stacked RNNs, which have the ability to generate output sequences based on input sequences. The encoder network reads in a sequence of tokens, and passes it to a decoder network (a LM). In contrast to simpler NLMs, encoder-decoder networks have the ability to use additional context for generating text, which enables more accurate generation of text. Encoder-decoder models are integral in *Neural Machine Translation (NMT)* [15], where the task is to translate a source text from one language to another language. NMT models additionally use beam search strategies to heuristically search the set of possible translations. Training datasets are parallel corpora; large sets of paired sentences in the source and target languages. The application of NMT techniques for online machine translation has significantly improved the quality of translations, bringing it closer to human performance [16].

Neural machine translation models are efficient at mapping one expression to another (one-to-one mapping). Researchers have evaluated these models for conversation generation [17], with mixed results. Some researchers attribute poor performance to the use of the negative log likelihood cost function during training, which emphasizes generation of high-confidence phrases rather than diverse phrases [18]. The results are often generic text, which lacks variation. Li et al. have suggested various augmentations to this, among others suppressing typical responses in the decoder language model to promote response diversity [18].

3   System Model

We discuss the attack model, our generative machine learning method and controlling the generative process in this section.

3.1   Attack Model

Wang et al. [8] described a model of crowd-turfing attacks consisting of three entities: **customers** who desire to have fake reviews for a particular target (e.g. their restaurant) on a particular platform (e.g. Yelp), **agents** who offer fake review services to customers, and **workers** who are orchestrated by the agent to compose and post fake reviews.

Automated crowd-turfing attacks (ACA) replace workers by a **generative model**. This has several benefits including better economy and scalability (human workers are more expensive and slower) and reduced detectability (agent can better control the rate at which fake reviews are generated and posted).

We assume that the agent has access to public reviews on the review platform, by which it can train its generative model. We also assume that it is easy for the agent to create a large number of accounts on the review platform so that account-based detection or rate-limiting techniques are ineffective against fake reviews.

The quality of the generative model plays a crucial role in the attack. Yao et al. [1] propose the use of a character-based LSTM as base for generative model. LSTMs are not conditioned to generate reviews for a specific target [2], and may mix-up concepts from different *contexts* during free-form generation. Mixing contextually separate words is one of the key criteria that humans use to identify fake reviews. These may result in violations of known indicators for fake content [19]. For example, the review content may not match prior expectations nor the information need that the reader has. We improve the attack model by considering a more capable generative model that produces more appropriate reviews: a neural machine translation (NMT) model.

3.2   Generative Model

Architecture. We propose the use of NMT models for fake review generation. The method has several benefits: (1) the ability to *learn* how to associate context (keywords) to reviews, (2) *fast* training time, and (3) a high-degree of *customization* during production time, e.g. introduction of specific waiter or food items names into reviews.

NMT models are constructions of stacked recurrent neural networks (RNNs). They include an *encoder* network and a *decoder* network, which are jointly optimized to produce a *translation* of one sequence to another. The encoder rolls over the input data in sequence and produces *one* n-dimensional context vector representation for the sentence. The decoder then generates output sequences based on the embedding vector and an *attention module*, which is taught to associate output words with certain input words. The generation typically continues until a specific *EOS* (end of sentence) token is encountered. The review length can be controlled in many ways, e.g. by setting the probability of generating the EOS token to zero until the required length is reached.

NMT models often also include a beam search [15], which generates several hypotheses and chooses the best ones amongst them. In our work, we use the greedy beam search technique. We forgo the use of additional beam searches as we found that the quality of the output was already adequate and the translation phase time consumption increases linearly for each beam used.

Dataset. We use the Yelp Challenge dataset [3] for our fake review generation. The dataset (Aug 2017) contains 2.9 million 1–5 star restaurant reviews. We treat all reviews as genuine human-written reviews for the purpose of this work, since wide-scale deployment of machine-generated review attacks are not yet reported (Sep 2017) [20]. As preprocessing, we remove non-printable (non-ASCII) characters and excessive white-space. We separate punctuation from words. We reserve 15,000 reviews for validation and 3,000 for testing, and the rest we use for training. NMT models require a parallel corpus of source and target sentences, i.e. a large set of (source, target)-pairs. We set up a parallel corpus by constructing (context, review)-pairs from the dataset. Next, we describe how we created our input context.

Context. The Yelp Challenge dataset includes metadata about restaurants, including their names, food tags, cities and states these restaurants are located in. For each restaurant review, we fetch this metadata and use it as our input context in the NMT model. The corresponding restaurant review is similarly set as the target sentence. This method produced 2.9 million pairs of sentences in our parallel corpus. We show one example of the parallel training corpus in Example 1 below:

Example 1.
5 Public House Las Vegas NV Gastropubs Restaurants > Excellent
food and service . Pricey , but well worth it . I would recommend
the bone marrow and sampler platter for appetizers .

The order [**rating name city state tags**] is kept constant. Training the model conditions it to associate certain sequences of words in the input sentence with others in the output.

Training Settings. We train our NMT model on a commodity PC with a i7-4790k CPU (4.00 GHz), with 32 GB RAM and one NVidia GeForce GTX 980 GPU. Our system can process approximately 1,300–1,500 source tokens/s and approximately 5,730–5,830 output tokens/s. Training one epoch takes in average 72 min. The model is trained for 8 epochs, i.e. over night. We call fake review generated by this model *NMT-Fake reviews*. We only need to train one model to produce reviews of different ratings. We use the training settings: adam optimizer [13] with the suggested learning rate 0.001 [15]. For most parts, parameters are at their default values. Notably, the maximum sentence length of input and output is 50 tokens by default. We leverage the framework openNMT-py [15] to teach the our NMT model. We list used openNMT-py commands in Appendix Table 4.

> Example 2. Greedy NMT
> Great food, <u>great</u> service, <u>great</u> *beer selection*. I had the *Gastropubs burger* and it was delicious. The *beer selection* was also <u>great</u>.
>
> Example 3. NMT-Fake*
> I love this restaurant. Great food, great service. It's *a little pricy* but worth it for the *quality* of the *beer* and atmosphere you can see in *Vegas*

Fig. 1. Naïve text generation with NMT vs. generation using our NTM model. Repetitive patterns are <u>underlined</u>. Contextual words are *italicized*. Both examples here are generated based on the context given in Example 1.

3.3   Controlling Generation of Fake Reviews

Greedy NMT beam searches are practical in many NMT cases. However, the results are simply repetitive, when naively applied to fake review generation (See Example 2 in Fig. 1). The NMT model produces many *high-confidence* word predictions, which are repetitive and obviously fake. We calculated that in fact, 43% of the generated sentences started with the phrase "Great food". The lack of diversity in greedy use of NMTs for text generation is clear.

In this work, we describe how we succeeded in creating more diverse and less repetitive generated reviews, such as Example 3 in Fig. 1. We outline pseudocode for our methodology of generating fake reviews in Algorithm 1. There are several parameters in our algorithm. The details of the algorithm will be shown later. We modify the openNMT-py translation phase by changing log-probabilities before passing them to the beam search. We notice that reviews generated with openNMT-py contain almost no language errors. As an optional post-processing step, we obfuscate reviews by introducing natural typos/misspellings randomly. In the next sections, we describe how we succeeded in generating more natural

---

Algorithm 1. Generation of NMT-Fake* reviews.

Data: Desired review context C_{input} (given as cleartext), NMT model
Result: Generated review *out* for input context C_{input}
set $b = 0.3$, $\lambda = -5$, $\alpha = \frac{2}{3}$, p_{typo}, p_{spell}
$\log p \leftarrow \text{NMT.decode(NMT.encode}(C_{\text{input}}))$
out $\leftarrow [\ ]$
$i \leftarrow 0$
$\log p \leftarrow \text{Augment}(\log p, b, \lambda, 1, [\ ], 0)$ — random penalty
while $i = 0$ *or* o_i *not EOS* **do**
   $\log \tilde{p} \leftarrow \text{Augment}(\log p, b, \lambda, \alpha, o_i, i)$ — start & memory penalty
   $o_i \leftarrow \text{NMT.beam}(\log \tilde{p}, \text{out})$
   out.append(o_i)
   $i \leftarrow i + 1$
end
return Obfuscate(out, p_{typo}, p_{spell})

---

sentences from our NMT model, i.e. generating reviews like Example 3 instead of reviews like Example 2.

Variation in Word Content. Example 2 in Fig. 1 repeats commonly occurring words given for a specific context (e.g. *great, food, service, beer, selection, burger* for Example 1). Generic review generation can be avoided by decreasing probabilities (log-likelihoods [2]) of the generators LM, the decoder. We constrain the generation of sentences by randomly *imposing penalties to words*. We tried several forms of added randomness, and found that adding constant penalties to a *random subset* of the target words resulted in the most natural sentence flow. We call these penalties *Bernoulli penalties*, since the random variables are chosen as either 1 or 0 (on or off).

Bernoulli Penalties to Language Model. To avoid generic sentences components, we augment the default language model $p(\cdot)$ of the decoder by

$$\log \tilde{p}(t_k) = \log p(t_k|t_i, \ldots, t_1) + \lambda q, \qquad (3)$$

where $q \in R^V$ is a vector of Bernoulli-distributed random values that obtain values 1 with probability b and value 0 with probability $1 - b_i$, and $\lambda < 0$. Parameter b controls how much of the vocabulary is forgotten and λ is a soft penalty of including "forgotten" words in a review. λq_k emphasizes sentence forming with non-penalized words. The randomness is reset at the start of generating a new review. Using Bernoulli penalties in the language model, we can "forget" a certain proportion of words and essentially "force" the creation of less typical sentences. We will test the effect of these two parameters, the Bernoulli probability b and log-likelihood penalty of including "forgotten" words λ, with a user study in Sect. 3.4.

Start Penalty. We introduce start penalties to avoid generic sentence starts (e.g. "Great food, great service"). Inspired by [18], we add a random start penalty λs^i, to our language model, which decreases monotonically for each generated token. We set $\alpha \leftarrow 0.66$ as it's effect decreases by 90% every 5 words generated.

Penalty for Reusing Words. Bernoulli penalties do not prevent excessive use of certain words in a sentence (such as *great* in Example 2). To avoid excessive reuse of words, we included a memory penalty for previously used words in each translation. Concretely, we add the penalty λ to each word that has been generated by the greedy search.

Improving Sentence Coherence. We visually analyzed reviews after applying these penalties to our NMT model. While the models were clearly diverse, they were *incoherent*: the introduction of random penalties had degraded the grammaticality of the sentences. Amongst others, the use of punctuation was erratic, and pronouns were used semantically wrongly (e.g. *he, she* might be

Algorithm 2. Pseudocode for augmenting language model.

Data: Initial log LM $\log p$, Bernoulli probability b, soft-penalty λ, monotonic factor α,
     last generated token o_i, grammar rules set G
Result: Augmented log LM $\log \tilde{p}$
 1: **procedure** AUGMENT($\log p$, b, λ, α, o_i, i)
 2:   generate $P_{1:N} \leftarrow Bernoulli(b)$ — One value $\in \{0,1\}$ per token
 3:   $I \leftarrow P > 0$ — Select positive indices
 4:   $\log \tilde{p} \leftarrow$ Discount($\log p$, I, $\lambda \cdot \alpha^i$,G)   — start penalty
 5:   $\log \tilde{p} \leftarrow$ Discount($\log \tilde{p}$, $[o_i]$, λ,G)   — memory penalty
 6:   **return** $\log \tilde{p}$
 7: **end procedure**
 8:
 9: **procedure** DISCOUNT($\log p$, I, λ, G)
10:    **for** $i \in I$ **do**
       if $o_i \in G$ **then**
       | $\log p_i \leftarrow \log p_i + \lambda/2$
       else
       | $\log p_i \leftarrow \log p_i + \lambda$
       end
       end
       return $\log p$
11: **end procedure**

---

replaced, as could "and"/"but"). To improve the authenticity of our reviews, we added several *grammar-based rules*.

English language has several classes of words which are important for the natural flow of sentences. We built a list of common pronouns (e.g. I, them, our), conjunctions (e.g. and, thus, if), punctuation (e.g.,/.,..), and apply only half memory penalties for these words. We found that this change made the reviews more coherent. The pseudocode for this and the previous step is shown in Algorithm 2. The combined effect of grammar-based rules and LM augmentation is visible in Example 3, Fig. 1.

Human-Like Errors. We notice that our NMT model produces reviews without grammar mistakes. This is unlike real human writers, whose sentences contain two types of language mistakes (1) *typos* that are caused by mistakes in the human motoric input, and (2) *common spelling mistakes*. We scraped a list of common English language spelling mistakes from Oxford dictionary[1] and created 80 rules for randomly *re-introducing spelling mistakes*. Similarly, typos are randomly reintroduced based on the weighted edit distance[2], such that typos resulting in real English words with small perturbations are emphasized. We use autocorrection tools[3] for finding these words. We call these augmentations

---

[1] https://en.oxforddictionaries.com/spelling/common-misspellings.
[2] https://pypi.python.org/pypi/weighted-levenshtein/0.1.
[3] https://pypi.python.org/pypi/autocorrect/0.1.0.

obfuscations, since they aim to confound the reader to think a human has written them. We omit the pseudocode description for brevity.

3.4   Experiment: Varying Generation Parameters in Our NMT Model

Parameters b and λ control different aspects in fake reviews. We show six different examples of generated fake reviews in Table 1. Here, the largest differences occur with increasing values of b: visibly, the restaurant reviews become more extreme. This occurs because a large portion of vocabulary is "forgotten". Reviews with $b \geq 0.7$ contain more rare word combinations, e.g. "!!!!!" as punctuation, and they occasionally break grammaticality ("experience was awesome"). Reviews with lower b are more generic: they contain safe word combinations like "Great place, good service" that occur in many reviews. Parameter λ's is more subtle: it affects how random review starts are and to a degree, the discontinuation between statements within the review. We conducted an Amazon Mechanical Turk (MTurk) survey in order to determine what kind of NMT-Fake reviews are convincing to native English speakers. We describe the survey and results in the next section.

MTurk Study. We created 20 jobs, each with 100 questions, and requested master workers in MTurk to complete the jobs. We randomly generated each survey for the participants. Each review had a 50% chance to be real or fake. The fake ones further were chosen among six (6) categories of fake reviews (Table 1). The restaurant and the city was given as contextual information to the participants. Our aim was to use this survey to understand how well English-speakers react to different parametrizations of NMT-Fake reviews. Table 3 in Appendix

Table 1. Six different parametrizations of our NMT reviews and one example for each. The context is "5 P . F . Chang's Scottsdale AZ" in all examples.

(b, λ)	Example review for context
$(0.3, -3)$	I love this location! Great service, great food and the best drinks in Scottsdale. The staff is very friendly and always remembers u when we come in
$(0.3, -5)$	Love love the food here! I always go for lunch. They have a great menu and they make it fresh to order. Great place, good service and nice staff
$(0.5, -4)$	I love their chicken lettuce wraps and fried rice!! The service is good, they are always so polite. They have great happy hour specials and they have a lot of options
$(0.7, -3)$	Great place to go with friends! They always make sure your dining experience was awesome
$(0.7, -5)$	Still haven't ordered an entree before but today we tried them once.. both of us love this restaurant...
$(0.9, -4)$	AMAZING!!!!! Food was awesome with excellent service. Loved the lettuce wraps. Great drinks and wine! Can't wait to go back so soon!!

Table 2. Effectiveness of mechanical Turkers in distinguishing human-written reviews from fake reviews generated by our NMT model (all variants).

Classification report				
Review type	Precision	Recall	F-score	Support
Human	55%	63%	59%	994
NMT-Fake	57%	50%	53%	1006

summarizes the statistics for respondents in the survey. All participants were native English speakers from America. The base rate (50%) was revealed to the participants prior to the study.

We first investigated overall detection of any NMT-Fake reviews (1,006 fake reviews and 994 real reviews). We found that the participants had big difficulties in detecting our fake reviews. In average, the reviews were detected with class-averaged *F-score of only 56%*, with 53% F-score for fake review detection and 59% F-score for real review detection. The results are very close to *random detection*, where precision, recall and F-score would each be 50%. Results are recorded in Table 2. Overall, the fake review generation is very successful, since human detection rate across categories is close to random.

We noticed some variation in the detection of different fake review categories. The respondents in our MTurk survey had most difficulties recognizing reviews of category $(b = 0.3, \lambda = -5)$, where true positive rate was 40.4%, while the true negative rate of the real class was 62.7%. The precision were 16% and 86%, respectively. The class-averaged F-score is 47.6%, which is close to random. Detailed classification reports are shown in Table 5 in Appendix. Our MTurk-study shows that *our NMT-Fake reviews pose a significant threat to review systems*, since *ordinary native English-speakers have very big difficulties in separating real reviews from fake reviews*. We use the review category $(b = 0.3, \lambda = -5)$ for future user tests in this paper, since MTurk participants had most difficulties detecting these reviews. We refer to this category as NMT-Fake* in this paper.

4   Evaluation

We evaluate our fake reviews by first comparing them statistically to previously proposed types of fake reviews, and proceed with a user study with experienced participants. We demonstrate the statistical difference to existing fake review types [1,4,5] by training classifiers to detect previous types and investigate classification performance.

4.1   Replication of State-of-the-Art Model: LSTM

Yao et al. [1] presented the current state-of-the-art generative model for fake reviews. The model is trained over the Yelp Challenge dataset using a two-layer character-based LSTM model. We requested the authors of [1] for access to their LSTM model or a fake review dataset generated by their model. Unfortunately they were not able to share either of these with us. We therefore replicated their model as closely as we could, based on their paper and e-mail correspondence[4].

We used the same graphics card (GeForce GTX) and trained using the same framework (torch-RNN in lua). We downloaded the reviews from Yelp Challenge and preprocessed the data to only contain printable ASCII characters, and filtered out non-restaurant reviews. We trained the model for approximately 72 h. We post-processed the reviews using the customization methodology described in [1] and email correspondence. We call fake reviews generated by this model LSTM-Fake reviews.

4.2 Similarity to Existing Fake Reviews

We now want to understand how NMT-Fake* reviews compare to (a) LSTM fake reviews and (b) human-generated fake reviews. We do this by comparing the statistical similarity between these classes.

For 'a' (Fig. 2a), we use the Yelp Challenge dataset. We trained a classifier using 5,000 random reviews from the Yelp Challenge dataset ("human") and 5,000 fake reviews generated by LSTM-Fake. Yao et al. [1] found that character features are essential in identifying LSTM-Fake reviews. Consequently, we use character features (n-grams up to 3).

For 'b' (Fig. 2b), we the "Yelp Shills" dataset (combination of YelpZip [4], YelpNYC [4], YelpChi [5]). This dataset labels entries that are identified as fraudulent by Yelp's filtering mechanism ("shill reviews")[5]. The rest are treated as genuine reviews from human users ("genuine"). We use 100,000 reviews from each category to train a classifier. We use features from the commercial psychometric tool LIWC2015 [21] to generated features.

In both cases, we use AdaBoost (with 200 shallow decision trees) for training. For testing each classifier, we use a held out test set of 1,000 reviews from both classes in each case. In addition, we test 1,000 NMT-Fake* reviews. Figures 2a and b show the results. The classification threshold of 50% is marked with a dashed line.

We can see that our new generated reviews do not share strong attributes with previous known categories of fake reviews. If anything, our fake reviews are more similar to genuine reviews than previous fake reviews. We thus conjecture that our NMT-Fake* fake reviews present a category of fake reviews that may go undetected on online review sites.

4.3 Comparative User Study

We wanted to evaluate the effectiveness of fake reviews againsttech-savvy users who understand and know to expect machine-generated fake reviews. We con-

---

[4] We are committed to sharing our code with bonafide researchers for the sake of reproducibility.

[5] Note that shill reviews are probably generated by human shills [20].

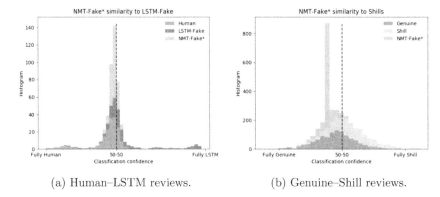

(a) Human–LSTM reviews.   (b) Genuine–Shill reviews.

Fig. 2. Histogram comparison of NMT-Fake* reviews with LSTM-Fake reviews and human-generated (*genuine* and *shill*) reviews. (a) Shows that a classifier trained to distinguish "human" vs. LSTM-Fake cannot distinguish "human" vs NMT-Fake* reviews. (b) Shows NMT-Fake* reviews are more similar to *genuine* reviews than *shill* reviews.

ducted a user study with 20 participants, all with computer science education and at least one university degree. Participant demographics are shown in Table 3 in the Appendix. Each participant first attended a training session where they were asked to label reviews (fake and genuine) and could later compare them to the correct answers – we call these participants *experienced participants*. No personal data was collected during the user study.

Each person was given two randomly selected sets of 30 of reviews (a total of 60 reviews per person) with reviews containing 10–50 words each. Each set contained 26 (87%) real reviews from Yelp and 4 (13%) machine-generated reviews, numbers chosen based on suspicious review prevalence on Yelp [4,5]. One set contained machine-generated reviews from one of the two models (NMT ($b = 0.3, \lambda = -5$) or LSTM), and the other set reviews from the other in randomized order. The number of fake reviews was revealed to each participant in the study description. Each participant was requested to mark four (4) reviews as fake.

Each review targeted a real restaurant. A screenshot of that restaurant's Yelp page was shown to each participant prior to the study. Each participant evaluated reviews for one specific, randomly selected, restaurant. An example of the first page of the user study is shown in Fig. 5 in Appendix.

Figure 3 shows the distribution of detected reviews of both types. A hypothetical random detector is shown for comparison. NMT-Fake* reviews are significantly more difficult to detect for our experienced participants. In average, detection rate (recall) is 20% for NMT-Fake* reviews, compared to 61% for LSTM-based reviews. The precision (and F-score) is the same as the recall in our study, since participants labeled 4 fakes in each set of 30 reviews [2]. The distribution of the detection across participants is shown in Fig. 3. *The difference is statistically significant with confidence level* 99% (Welch's t-test). We compared

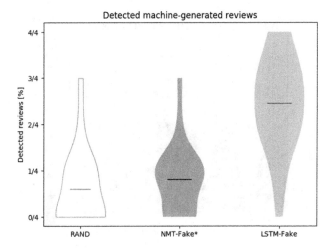

Fig. 3. Violin plots of detection rate in comparative study. Mean and standard deviations for number of detected fakes are 0.8 ± 0.7 for NMT-Fake* and 2.5 ± 1.0 for LSTM-Fake $n = 20$. A sample of random detection is shown as comparison.

the detection rate of NMT-Fake* reviews to a random detector, and find that *our participants detection rate of NMT-Fake* reviews is not statistically different from random predictions with 95% confidence level* (Welch's t-test).

5   Defenses

We developed an AdaBoost-based classifier to detect our new fake reviews, consisting of 200 shallow decision trees (depth 2). The features we used are recorded in Table 6 (Appendix). We used word-level features based on spaCy-tokenization [22] and constructed n-gram representation of POS-tags and dependency tree tags. We added readability features from NLTK [23].

Figure 4 shows our AdaBoost classifier's class-averaged F-score at detecting different kind of fake reviews. The classifier is very effective in detecting reviews that humans have difficulties detecting. For example, the fake reviews MTurk users had most difficulty detecting ($b = 0.3, \lambda = -5$) are detected with an excellent 97% F-score. The most important features for the classification were counts for frequently occurring words in fake reviews (such as punctuation, pronouns, articles) as well as the readability feature "Automated Readability Index". We thus conclude that while NMT-Fake reviews are difficult to detect for humans, they can be well detected with the right tools.

6   Related Work

Kumar and Shah [24] survey and categorize false information research. Automatically generated fake reviews are a form of *opinion-based false information*,

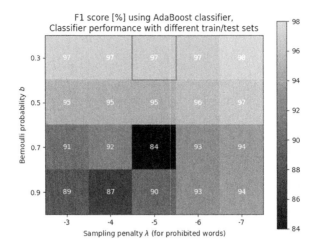

Fig. 4. Adaboost-based classification of NMT-Fake and human-written reviews. Effect of varying b and λ in fake review generation. The variant native speakers had most difficulties detecting is well detectable by AdaBoost (97%).

where the creator of the review may influence reader's opinions or decisions. Yao et al. [1] presented their study on machine-generated fake reviews. Contrary to us, they investigated character-level language models, without specifying a specific context before generation. We leverage existing NMT tools to encode a specific context to the restaurant before generating reviews. Supporting our study, Everett et al. [25] found that security researchers were less likely to be fooled by Markov chain-generated Reddit comments compared to ordinary Internet users.

Diversification of NMT model outputs has been studied in [18]. The authors proposed the use of a penalty to commonly occurring sentences (*n-grams*) in order to emphasize maximum mutual information-based generation. The authors investigated the use of NMT models in chatbot systems. We found that unigram penalties to random tokens (Algorithm 2) was easy to implement and produced sufficiently diverse responses.

7   Discussion and Future Work

What makes NMT-Fake* reviews difficult to detect? First, NMT models allow the encoding of a relevant context for each review, which narrows down the possible choices of words that the model has to choose from. Our NMT model had a perplexity of approximately 25, while the model of [1] had a perplexity of approximately 90[6]. Second, the beam search in NMT models narrows down choices to natural-looking sentences. Third, we observed that the NMT model produced *better structure* in the generated sentences (i.e. a more coherent story).

---

[6] Personal communication with the authors.

Cost of Generating Reviews. With our setup, generating one review took less than one second. The cost of generation stems mainly from the overnight training. Assuming an electricity cost of 16 cents/kWh (California) and 8 h of training, training the NMT model requires approximately 1.30 USD. This is a 90% reduction in time compared to the state-of-the-art [1]. Furthermore, it is possible to generate both positive and negative reviews with the same model.

Ease of Customization. We experimented with inserting specific words into the text by increasing their log likelihoods in the beam search. We noticed that the success depended on the prevalence of the word in the training set. For example, adding a +5 to *Mike* in the log-likelihood resulted in approximately 10% prevalence of this word in the reviews. An attacker can therefore easily insert specific keywords to reviews, which can increase evasion probability.

Ease of Testing. Our diversification scheme is applicable during *generation phase*, and does not affect the training setup of the network in any way. Once the NMT model is obtained, it is easy to obtain several different variants of NMT-Fake reviews by varying parameters b and λ.

Languages. The generation methodology is not per-se language-dependent. The requirement for successful generation is that sufficiently much data exists in the targeted language. However, our language model modifications require some knowledge of that target language's grammar to produce high-quality reviews.

Generalizability of Detection Techniques. Currently, fake reviews are not universally detectable. Our results highlight that it is difficult to claim detection performance on unseen types of fake reviews (Sect. 4.2). We see this an open problem that deserves more attention in fake reviews research.

Generalizability to Other Types of Datasets. Our technique can be applied to any dataset, as long as there is sufficient training data for the NMT model. We used approximately 2.9 million reviews for this work.

8   Conclusion

In this paper, we showed that neural machine translation models can be used to generate fake reviews that are very effective in deceiving even experienced, tech-savvy users. This supports anecdotal evidence [11]. Our technique is more effective than state-of-the-art [1]. We conclude that machine-aided fake review detection is necessary since human users are ineffective in identifying fake reviews. We also showed that detectors trained using one type of fake reviews are not effective in identifying other types of fake reviews. Robust detection of fake reviews is thus still an open problem.

Appendix

We present basic demographics of our MTurk study and the comparative study with experienced users in Table 3.

Table 3. User study statistics.

Quality	Mechanical turk users	Experienced users
Native English speaker	Yes (20)	Yes (1) No (19)
Fluent in English	Yes (20)	Yes (20)
Age	21–40 (17) 41–60 (3)	21–25 (8) 26–30 (7) 31–35 (4) 41–45 (1)
Gender	Male (14) Female (6)	Male (17) Female (3)
Highest education	High School (10) Bachelor (10)	Bachelor (9) Master (6) Ph.D. (5)

Table 4 shows a listing of the openNMT-py commands we used to create our NMT model and to generate fake reviews.

Table 5 shows the classification performance of Amazon Mechanical Turkers, separated across different categories of NMT-Fake reviews. The category with best performance ($b = 0.3, \lambda = -5$) is denoted as NMT-Fake*.

Figure 5 shows screenshots of the first two pages of our user study with experienced participants.

Table 6 shows the features used to detect NMT-Fake reviews using the AdaBoost classifier.

Table 4. Listing of used openNMT-py commands.

Phase	Bash command
Preprocessing	```python preprocess.py −train_src context−train.txt −train_tgt reviews−train.txt −valid_src context−val.txt −valid_tgt reviews−val.txt −save_data model −lower −tgt_words_min_frequency 10```
Training	```python train.py −data model −save_model model −epochs 8 −gpuid 0 −learning_rate_decay 0.5 −optim adam −learning_rate 0.001 −start_decay_at 3```
Generation	```python translate.py −model model_acc_35.54_ppl_25.68_e8.pt −src context−tst.txt −output pred−e8.txt −replace_unk −verbose −max_length 50 −gpu 0```

Table 5. MTurk study subclass classification reports. Classes are imbalanced in ratio 1:6. Random predictions are $p_{\text{human}} = 86\%$ and $p_{\text{machine}} = 14\%$, with $r_{\text{human}} = r_{\text{machine}} = 50\%$. Class-averaged F-scores for random predictions are 42%.

	Precision	Recall	F-score	Support
$(b = 0.3, \lambda = -3)$				
Human	89%	63%	73%	994
NMT-Fake	15%	45%	22%	146
$(b = 0.3, \lambda = -5)$				
Human	86%	63%	73%	994
NMT-Fake*	16%	40%	23%	171
$(b = 0.5, \lambda = -4)$				
Human	88%	63%	73%	994
NMT-Fake	21%	55%	30%	181
$(b = 0.7, \lambda = -3)$				
Human	88%	63%	73%	994
NMT-Fake	19%	50%	27%	170
$(b = 0.7, \lambda = -5)$				
Human	89%	63%	74%	994
NMT-Fake	21%	57%	31%	174
$(b = 0.9, \lambda = -4)$				
Human	88%	63%	73%	994
NMT-Fake	18%	50%	27%	164

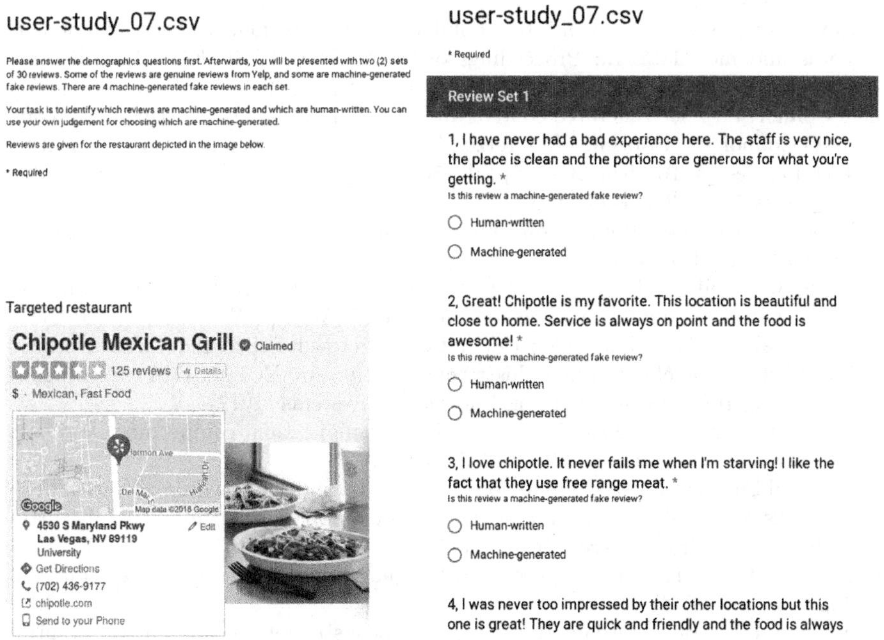

user-study_07.csv

Please answer the demographics questions first. Afterwards, you will be presented with two (2) sets of 30 reviews. Some of the reviews are genuine reviews from Yelp, and some are machine-generated fake reviews. There are 4 machine-generated fake reviews in each set.

Your task is to identify which reviews are machine-generated and which are human-written. You can use your own judgement for choosing which are machine-generated.

Reviews are given for the restaurant depicted in the image below.

* Required

Targeted restaurant

Chipotle Mexican Grill ⊘ Claimed

⬛⬛⬛⬛⬛ 125 reviews ⚖ Details

$ · Mexican, Fast Food

⌖ 4530 S Maryland Pkwy ✏ Edit
   Las Vegas, NV 89119
   University
◆ Get Directions
✆ (702) 436-9177
⮺ chipotle.com
▯ Send to your Phone

user-study_07.csv

* Required

Review Set 1

1, I have never had a bad experiance here. The staff is very nice, the place is clean and the portions are generous for what you're getting. *
Is this review a machine-generated fake review?

○ Human-written

○ Machine-generated

2, Great! Chipotle is my favorite. This location is beautiful and close to home. Service is always on point and the food is awesome! *
Is this review a machine-generated fake review?

○ Human-written

○ Machine-generated

3, I love chipotle. It never fails me when I'm starving! I like the fact that they use free range meat. *
Is this review a machine-generated fake review?

○ Human-written

○ Machine-generated

4, I was never too impressed by their other locations but this one is great! They are quick and friendly and the food is always

Fig. 5. Screenshots of the first two pages in the user study. Example 1 is a NMT-Fake* review, the rest are human-written.

Table 6. Features used in NMT-Fake review detector.

Feature type	Number of features
Readability features	13
Unique POS tags	20
Word unigrams	22,831
1/2/3/4-grams of simple part-of-speech tags	54,240
1/2/3-grams of detailed part-of-speech tags	112,944
1/2/3-grams of syntactic dependency tags	93,195

References

1. Yao, Y., Viswanath, B., Cryan, J., Zheng, H., Zhao, B.Y.: Automated crowdturfing attacks and defenses in online review systems. In: Proceedings of the 2017 ACM SIGSAC Conference on Computer and Communications Security. ACM (2017)
2. Murphy, K.: Machine Learning: A Probabilistic Approach. Massachusetts Institute of Technology, Cambridge (2012)
3. Yelp: Yelp Challenge Dataset (2013)
4. Mukherjee, A., Venkataraman, V., Liu, B., Glance, N.: What yelp fake review filter might be doing? In: Seventh International AAAI Conference on Weblogs and Social Media (ICWSM) (2013)
5. Rayana, S., Akoglu, L.: Collective opinion spam detection: bridging review networks and metadata. In: Proceedings of the 21th ACM SIGKDD International Conference on Knowledge Discovery and Data Mining (2015)
6. O'Connor, P.: User-generated content and travel: a case study on Tripadvisor.com. In: O'Connor, P., Höpken, W., Gretzel, U. (eds.) Information and Communication Technologies in Tourism 2008, pp. 47–58. Springer, Vienna (2008). https://doi.org/10.1007/978-3-211-77280-5_5
7. Luca, M.: Reviews, Reputation, and Revenue: The Case of Yelp.com. Harvard Business School, Boston (2010)
8. Wang, G., et al.: Serf and turf: crowdturfing for fun and profit. In: Proceedings of the 21st International Conference on World Wide Web (WWW). ACM (2012)
9. Rinta-Kahila, T., Soliman, W.: Understanding crowdturfing: the different ethical logics behind the clandestine industry of deception. In: ECIS 2017: Proceedings of the 25th European Conference on Information Systems (2017)
10. Luca, M., Zervas, G.: Fake it till you make it: reputation, competition, and yelp review fraud. Manage. Sci. **62**, 3412–3427 (2016)
11. National Literacy Trust: Commission on fake news and the teaching of critical literacy skills in schools. https://literacytrust.org.uk/policy-and-campaigns/all-party-parliamentary-group-literacy/fakenews/
12. Jurafsky, D., Martin, J.H.: Speech and Language Processing, vol. 3. Pearson London, London (2014)
13. Kingma, D.P., Ba, J.: Adam: a method for stochastic optimization. arXiv preprint arXiv:1412.6980 (2014)
14. Cho, K., et al.: Learning phrase representations using rnn encoder-decoder for statistical machine translation. In: Proceedings of the 2014 Conference on Empirical Methods in Natural Language Processing (EMNLP) (2014)

15. Klein, G., Kim, Y., Deng, Y., Senellart, J., Rush, A.: OpenNMT: open-source toolkit for neural machine translation. In: Proceedings of ACL, System Demonstrations (2017)
16. Wu, Y., et al.: Google's neural machine translation system: bridging the gap between human and machine translation. arXiv preprint arXiv:1609.08144 (2016)
17. Mei, H., Bansal, M., Walter, M.R.: Coherent dialogue with attention-based language models. In: AAAI, pp. 3252–3258 (2017)
18. Li, J., Galley, M., Brockett, C., Gao, J., Dolan, B.: A diversity-promoting objective function for neural conversation models. In: Proceedings of NAACL-HLT (2016)
19. Rubin, V.L., Liddy, E.D.: Assessing credibility of weblogs. In: AAAI Spring Symposium: Computational Approaches to Analyzing Weblogs (2006)
20. news.com.au: The potential of AI generated 'crowdturfing' could undermine online reviews and dramatically erode public trust. http://www.news.com.au/technology/online/security/the-potential-of-ai-generated-crowdturfing-could-undermine-online-reviews-and-dramatically-erode-public-trust/news-story/e1c84ad909b586f8a08238d5f80b6982
21. Pennebaker, J.W., Boyd, R.L., Jordan, K., Blackburn, K.: The development and psychometric properties of LIWC2015. Technical report (2015)
22. Honnibal, M., Johnson, M.: An improved non-monotonic transition system for dependency parsing. In: Proceedings of the 2015 Conference on Empirical Methods in Natural Language Processing (EMNLP). ACM (2015)
23. Bird, S., Loper, E.: NLTK: the natural language toolkit. In: Proceedings of the ACL 2004 on Interactive Poster and Demonstration Sessions. Association for Computational Linguistics (2004)
24. Kumar, S., Shah, N.: False information on web and social media: a survey. arXiv preprint arXiv:1804.08559 (2018)
25. Everett, R.M., Nurse, J.R.C., Erola, A.: The anatomy of online deception: what makes automated text convincing? In: Proceedings of the 31st Annual ACM Symposium on Applied Computing, SAC 2016. ACM (2016)

Efficient Proof Composition for Verifiable Computation

Julien Keuffer[1,2(✉)], Refik Molva[2], and Hervé Chabanne[1,3]

[1] Idemia, Issy-les-Moulineaux, France
{julien.keuffer,herve.chabanne}@idemia.com
[2] Eurecom, Biot, France
refik.molva@eurecom.fr
[3] Telecom ParisTech, Paris, France

Abstract. Outsourcing machine learning algorithms helps users to deal with large amounts of data without the need to develop the expertise required by these algorithms. Outsourcing however raises severe security issues due to potentially untrusted service providers. Verifiable computing (VC) tackles some of these issues by assuring computational integrity for an outsourced computation. In this paper, we design a VC protocol tailored to verify a sequence of operations for which no existing VC scheme is suitable to achieve realistic performance objective for the entire sequence. We thus suggest a technique to compose several specialized and efficient VC schemes with a general purpose VC protocol, like Parno et al.'s Pinocchio, by integrating the verification of the proofs generated by these specialized schemes as a function that is part of the sequence of operations verified using the general purpose scheme. The resulting scheme achieves the objectives of the general purpose scheme with increased efficiency for the prover. The scheme relies on the underlying cryptographic assumptions of the composed protocols for correctness and soundness.

Keywords: Verifiable computation · Proof composition
Neural networks

1 Introduction

While achieving excellent results in diverse areas, machine learning algorithms require expertise and a large training material to be fine-tuned. Therefore, cloud providers such as Amazon or Microsoft have started offering Machine Learning as a Service (MLaaS) to perform complex machine learning tasks on behalf of users. Despite these advantages, outsourcing raises a new requirement: in the face of potentially malicious service providers the users need additional guarantees to gain confidence in the results of outsourced computations. As an answer to this problem, verifiable computing (VC) provides proofs of computational integrity without any assumptions on hardware or on potential failures. Existing VC systems can theoretically prove and verify all **NP** computations [8].

© Springer Nature Switzerland AG 2018
J. Lopez et al. (Eds.): ESORICS 2018, LNCS 11098, pp. 152–171, 2018.
https://doi.org/10.1007/978-3-319-99073-6_8

Nevertheless, despite the variety of existing solutions, existing VC schemes have to make trade-offs between expressiveness and functionality [20] and therefore cannot efficiently handle the verifiability of a sequence of operations with a high variance in nature and complexity, like the ones involved in machine learning techniques. Even if expressive VC schemes such as Pinocchio [16] can ensure the verifiability of a machine learning algorithm, the cryptographic work required to produce the proof prevents from dealing with large but simple computations such as matrix multiplications. On the other hand, some schemes like Cormode et al.'s CMT [6] are very efficient and can deal with large computations, e.g. large matrix multiplications, but cannot handle the variety of even very simple operations such as number comparisons. Hence there is a need for a VC scheme that achieves both efficiency by handling complex operations and expressiveness through the variety of types of operations it can support. In this paper, we propose a scheme that combines a general purpose VC scheme like Pinocchio [16] or Groth's scheme [13] and various specialized VC schemes that achieve efficient verification of complex operations like large matrix multiplications.

Thanks to our proof composition scheme, the resulting VC scheme:

1. efficiently addresses the verifiability of a sequence of operations,
2. inherits the properties of the outer scheme, notably a short and single proof for a complex computation and privacy for inputs supplied by the prover.

In order to highlight the relevance of our proposal, we sketch the application of the resulting scheme on a neural network, which is a popular machine learning technique achieving state of the art performance in various classification tasks such as handwritten digit recognition, object or face recognition. Furthermore we propose a concrete instance of our scheme, using a Pinocchio-like scheme [13] and the Sum-Check protocol [15]. Thanks to our composition techniques, we are able to achieve unprecedented performance gains in the verifiability of computations involving large matrix multiplication and non-linear operations.

1.1   Problem Statement

Most applications involve several sequences of function evaluations combined through control structures. Assuring the verifiability of these applications has to face the challenge that the functions evaluated as part of these applications may feature computational characteristics that are too variant to be efficiently addressed by a unique VC scheme. For instance, in the case of an application that involves a combination of computationally intensive linear operations with simple non-linear ones, none of the existing VC techniques would be suitable since there is no single VC approach that can efficiently handle both. This question is perfectly illustrated by the sample scenario described in the previous section, namely dealing with the verifiability of Neural Network Algorithms, which can be viewed as a repeated sequence of a matrix product and a non-linear activation function. For instance, a two layer neural network, denoted by g, on an input x can be written as:

$$g(x) = W_2 \cdot f(W_1 \cdot x) \tag{1}$$

Here W_1 and W_2 are matrices and f is a non-linear function like the frequently chosen Rectified Linear Unit (ReLU) function: $x \mapsto max(0, x)$. For efficiency, the inputs are often batched and the linear operations involved in the Neural Network are matrix products instead of products between a vector and a matrix. Denoting X a batch of inputs to classify, the batched version of (1) therefore is:

$$g(X) = W_2 \cdot f(W_1 \cdot X) \tag{2}$$

In an attempt to assure the verifiability of this neural network, two alternative VC schemes seem potentially suited: the CMT protocol [6] based on interactive proofs and schemes deriving from Pinocchio [16]. CMT can efficiently deal with the matrix products but problems arise when it comes to the non-linear part of the operations since, using CMT, each function to be verified has to be represented as a layered arithmetic circuit (i.e. as an acyclic graph of computation over a finite field with an addition or a multiplication at each node, and where the circuit can be decomposed into layers, each gate of one layer being only connected to an adjacent layer). Nevertheless the second component of the neural network algorithm, that is, the ReLU activation function, does not lend itself to a simple representation as a layered circuit. [6,11] have proposed solutions to deal with non-layered circuits at the cost of very complex pre-processing, resulting in a substantial increase in the prover's work and the overall circuit size. Conversely, Pinocchio-like schemes eliminate the latter problem by allowing for efficient verification of a non-linear ReLU activation function while suffering from excessive complexity in the generation of proofs for the products of large matrices (benchmarks on matrix multiplication proofs can be found in [20]).

This sample scenario points to the basic limitation of existing VC schemes in efficiently addressing the requirements of common scenarios involving several components with divergent characteristics such as the mix of linear and non-linear operations as part of the same application. The objective of our work therefore is to come up with a new VC scheme that can efficiently handle these divergent characteristics in the sub-components as part of a single VC protocol.

1.2 Idea of the Solution: Embedded Proofs

Our solution is based on a method that enables the composition of a general purpose VC scheme suited to handle sequences of functions with one or several specialized VC schemes that can achieve efficiency in case of a component function with excessive requirements like very large linear operations. We apply this generic method to a pair of VC schemes, assuming that one is a general purpose VC scheme, called GVC, like Pinocchio [16], which can efficiently assure the verifiability of an application consisting of a sequence of functions, whereas the other VC scheme, which we call EVC, assures the verifiability of a single function in a very efficient way, like, for instance, a VC scheme that can handle large matrix products efficiently. The main idea underlying the VC composition method is that the verifiability of the complex operation (for which the GVC is not efficient) is *outsourced* to the EVC whereas the remaining non-complex functions are all

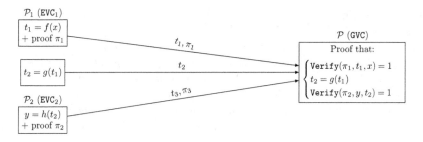

Fig. 1. High level view of the embedded proofs

handled by the GVC. In order to get the verifiability of the entire application by the GVC, instead of including the complex operation as part of the sequence of functions handled by the GVC, this operation is separately handled by the EVC that generates a standalone verifiability proof for that operation and the verification of that proof is viewed as an additional function embedded in the sequence of functions handled by the GVC. Even though the verifiability of the complex operation by the GVC is not feasible due to its complexity, the verifiability of the proof on this operation is feasible by the basic principle of VC, that is, because the proof is much less complex than the operation itself.

We illustrate the VC composition method using as a running example the Neural Network defined with formula (2) in Sect. 1.1. Here, the application consists of the sequential execution of three functions f, g and h (see Fig. 1), where f and h are not suitable to be efficiently proved using GVC while g is. Note that we consider that g cannot be proved correct by any EVC systems or at least not as efficiently as with the GVC system. The ultimate goal therefore is to verify $y = h(g(f(x)))$. In our example, $f : X \mapsto W_1 \cdot X$, $h : X \mapsto W_2 \cdot X$ and $g : X \mapsto \max(0, X)$, where X, W_1 and W_2 are matrices and g applies the max function element-wise to the input matrix X.

In order to cope with the increased complexity of f and h, we have recourse to EVC_1 and EVC_2 that are specialized schemes yielding efficient proofs with such functions. π_{EVC_1} denotes the proof generated by EVC_1 on f, π_{EVC_2} denotes the proof generated by EVC_2 on h and Π_{GVC} denotes the proof generated by GVC. For the sequential execution of functions f, g and h, denoting $t_1 = f(x)$ and $t_2 = g(t_1)$, the final proof then is:

$$\Pi_{GVC}\Big(\big(\mathtt{Verif}_{EVC_1}(\pi_{EVC_1}, x, t_1) \overset{?}{=} 1\big) \wedge \big(g(t_1) \overset{?}{=} t_2\big) \wedge \big(\mathtt{Verif}_{EVC_2}(\pi_{EVC_2}, t_2, y) \overset{?}{=} 1\big) \Big).$$
$$(3)$$

Here the GVC system verifies the computation of g and the verification algorithms of the EVC_1 and EVC_2 systems, which output 1 if the proof is accepted and 0 otherwise. We note that this method can easily be extended to applications involving more than three functions, Sect. 3 describes the embedded proof protocol for an arbitrary number of functions. Interestingly, various specialized VC techniques can be selected as EVC based on their suitability to the special functions requirements provided that:

1. The verification algorithm of each EVC proof is compatible with the GVC scheme.
2. The verification algorithm of each EVC proof should have much lower complexity than the outsourced computations (by the basic VC advantage).
3. The EVC schemes should not be VC's with a designated verifier but instead publicly verifiable [8]. Indeed, since the prover of the whole computation is the verifier of the EVC, no secret value should be shared between the prover of the EVC and the prover of the GVC. Otherwise, a malicious prover can easily forge a proof for EVC and break the security of the scheme.

In the sequel of this paper we present a concrete instance of our VC composition method using any Pinocchio-like scheme as the GVC and an efficient interactive proof protocol, namely the Sum-Check protocol [15] as the EVC. We further develop this instance with a Neural Network verification example.

1.3   Related Work

Verifying computation made by an untrusted party has been studied for a long time, but protocols leading to practical implementations are recent, see [20] and the references therein for details. Most of these proof systems build on quadratic arithmetic programs [8] and we focus on zero-knowledge succinct non-interactive arguments of knowledge (zk-SNARKs) schemes [3]. Proof composition for SNARKs have been proposed by Bitansky et al. [5] and the implementation of SNARKs recursive composition has later been proposed by Ben-Sasson et al. in [4]. The high level idea of the latter proof system is to prove or verify the satisfiability of an arithmetic circuit that checks the validity of the previous proofs. Thus, the verifier should be implemented as an arithmetic circuit and used as a sub-circuit of the next prover. However, SNARKs verifiers perform the verification checks using an elliptic curve pairing and it is mathematically impossible for the base field to have the same size as the elliptic curve group order. Ben-Sasson et al. therefore propose a cycle of elliptic curves to enable proof composition. When two such elliptic curves form a cycle, the finite field defined by the prime divisor in the group order of the first curve is equal to the base field (or field of definition) of the second curve and vice versa. Although proofs can theoretically be composed as many times as desired, this method has severe overhead. Our method has a more limited spectrum than Ben-Sasson et al.'s but our resulting system is still general purpose and enjoys the property of the GVC system, such as succinctness or efficiency for the prover. Furthermore, our proposal improves the prover time, replacing a part of a computation by sub-circuit verifying the sub-computation that can then be executed outside the prover.

In SafetyNets [9], Ghodsi et al. build an interactive proof protocol to verify the execution of a deep neural network on an untrusted cloud. This approach, albeit efficient, has several disadvantages over ours. The first is that expressivity of the interactive proof protocol used in SafetyNets prevents using state of the art activation functions such as ReLU. Indeed, Ghodsi et al. replace ReLU functions by a quadratic activation function, namely $x \mapsto x^2$, which squares the input values element-wise. This solution unfortunately causes instability during the training phase of the network compared to ReLU functions. A second disadvantage is the impossibility for the prover to prove a non-deterministic computation, i.e. to prove the correctness of a computation while hiding some inputs. As a consequence, the verifier and the prover of SafetyNets have to share the model of the neural network, namely the values of the matrices (e.g. W_1 and W_2 in formula (1)). This situation is quite unusual in machine learning: since the training of neural networks is expensive and requires a large amount of data, powerful hardware and technical skills to obtain a classifier with good accuracy, it is unlikely that cloud providers share their models with users. In contrast, with our proposed method the prover could keep the model private and nonetheless be able to produce a proof of correct execution.

1.4 Paper Organization

The rest of the paper is organized as follows: we first introduce the building blocks required to instantiate our method in Sect. 2. Following our embedded proof protocol, we first describe a VC scheme involving composition in Sect. 3 and then present a specialized instance of the GVC and EVC schemes to fit the Neural Network use-case in Sect. 4. We report experimental results on the implementation of the latter scheme in Sect. 5 and conclude in Sect. 6. A security proof of our scheme is given in Appendix A and prover's input privacy are considered in Appendix B.

2 Building Blocks

2.1 GVC: Verifiable Computation Based on QAPs

Quadratic Arithmetic Programs. In [8], Gennaro et al. defined Quadratic Arithmetic Programs (QAP) as an efficient object for circuit satisfiability. The computation to verify has first to be represented as an arithmetic circuit, from which a QAP is computed. Using the representation based on QAPs, the correctness of the computation can be tested by a divisibility check between polynomials. A cryptographic protocol enables to check the divisibility in only one point of the polynomial and to prevent a cheating prover to build a proof of a false statement that will be accepted.

Definition 1 (from [16]). *A QAP $\mathcal{Q}$ over field $\mathbb{F}$ contains three sets of $m+1$ polynomials $\mathcal{V} = \{(v_k(x))\}$, $\mathcal{W} = \{(w_k(x))\}$, $\mathcal{Y} = \{(y_k(x))\}$ for $k \in \{0, \dots, m\}$ and a target polynomial $t(x)$. Let F be a function that takes as input n elements of $\mathbb{F}$ and outputs n' elements and let us define N as the sum of n and n'. A N-tuple $(c_1, \dots, c_N) \in \mathbb{F}^N$ is a valid assignment for function F if and only if there exists coefficients $(c_{N+1}, \dots, c_m)$ such that $t(x)$ divides $p(x)$, as follows:*

$$p(x) = \left(v_0(x) + \sum_{k=1}^{m} c_k \cdot v_k(x)\right) \cdot \left(w_0(x) + \sum_{k=1}^{m} c_k \cdot w_k(x)\right) - \left(y_0(x) + \sum_{k=1}^{m} c_k \cdot y_k(x)\right).$$

$$(4)$$

A QAP $\mathcal{Q}$ that satisfies this definition computes F. It has size m and its degree is the degree of $t(x)$.

In the above definition, $t(x) = \prod_{g \in G}(x - r_g)$, where G is the set of multiplicative gates of the arithmetic circuit and each r_g is an arbitrary value labeling a multiplicative gate of the circuit. The polynomials in $\mathcal{V}$, $\mathcal{W}$ and $\mathcal{Y}$ encode the left inputs, the right inputs and the outputs for each gate respectively. By definition, if the polynomial $p(x)$ vanishes at a value r_g, $p(r_g)$ expresses the relation between the inputs and outputs of the corresponding multiplicative gate g. An example of a QAP construction from an arithmetic circuit is given in [16]. It is important to note that the size of the QAP is the number of multiplicative gates in the arithmetic circuit to verify, which also is the metric used to evaluate the efficiency of the VC protocol.

VC Protocol. Once a QAP has been built from an arithmetic circuit, a cryptographic protocol embeds it in an elliptic curve. In the verification phase, the divisibility check along with checks to ensure the QAP has been computed with the same coefficients c_k for the $\mathcal{V}$, $\mathcal{W}$ and $\mathcal{Y}$ polynomials during p's computation are performed with a pairing. This results in a publicly verifiable computation scheme, as defined below.

Definition 2. *Let F be a function, expressed as an arithmetic circuit over a finite field $\mathbb{F}$ and λ be a security parameter.*

- *$(EK_F, VK_F) \leftarrow \text{KeyGen}(1^\lambda, F)$: the randomized algorithm KeyGen takes as input a security parameter and an arithmetic circuit and produces two public keys, an evaluation key EK_F and a verification key VK_F.*
- *$(y, \pi) \leftarrow \text{Prove}(EK_F, x)$: the deterministic Prove algorithm, takes as inputs x and the evaluation key EK_F and computes $y = F(x)$ and a proof π that y has been correctly computed.*
- *$\{0, 1\} \leftarrow \text{Verify}(VK_F, x, y, \pi)$: the deterministic algorithm Verify takes the input/output (x, y) of the computation F, the proof π and the verification key VK_F and outputs 1 if $y = F(x)$ and 0 otherwise.*

Security. The desired security properties for a publicly verifiable VC scheme, namely *correctness*, *soundness* and *efficiency* have been formally defined in [8].
Costs. In QAP-based protocols, the proof consists of few elliptic curve elements, e.g. 8 group elements in Pinocchio [16] or 3 group elements in Groth's state of the art VC system [13]. It has constant size no matter the computation to be verified, thus the verification is fast. In the set-up phase, the KeyGen algorithm outputs evaluation and verification keys that depend on the function F, but not on its inputs. The resulting model is often called pre-processing verifiable computation. This setup phase has to be run once, the keys are reusable for later inputs and the cost of the pre-processing is amortized over all further computations. The bottleneck of the scheme is the prover computations: for an arithmetic circuit of N multiplication gates, the prover has to compute $O(N)$ cryptographic operations and $O(N \log^2 N)$ non-cryptographic operations.

Zero-Knowledge. QAPs also achieve the zero-knowledge property with little overhead: the prover can randomize the proof by adding multiples of the target polynomial $t(x)$ to hide inputs he supplied in the computation. The proof obtained using Parno et al.'s protocol [16] or Groth's scheme [13] is thus a zero-knowledge Succinct Non-Interactive Argument (zk-SNARK). In the zk-SNARKs setting, results are meaningful even if the efficiency requirement is not satisfied since the computation could not have been performed by the verifier. Indeed, some of the inputs are supplied by the prover and remain private, making the computation impossible to perform by the sole verifier.

2.2 EVC: Sum-Check Protocol

The Sum-Check protocol [15] enables to prove the correctness of the sum of a multilinear polynomial over a subcube, the protocol is a public coin interactive proof with n rounds of interaction. Suppose that P is a polynomial with n variables defined over $\mathbb{F}^n$. Using the Sum-Check protocol, a prover $\mathcal{P}$ can convince a verifier $\mathcal{V}$ that he knows the evaluation of P over $\{0,1\}^n$, namely:

$$H = \sum_{t_1 \in \{0,1\}} \sum_{t_2 \in \{0,1\}} \cdots \sum_{t_n \in \{0,1\}} P(t_1, \ldots, t_n) \tag{5}$$

While a direct computation performed by the verifier would require at least 2^n evaluations, the Sum-Check protocol only requires $O(n)$ evaluations for the verifier. $\mathcal{P}$ first computes $P_1(x) = \sum_{t_2 \in \{0,1\}} \cdots \sum_{t_n \in \{0,1\}} P(x, t_2, \ldots, t_n)$ and sends it to $\mathcal{V}$, who checks if $H = P_1(0) + P_1(1)$. If so, $\mathcal{P}$'s claim on P_1 holds, otherwise $\mathcal{V}$ rejects and the protocol stops. $\mathcal{V}$ picks a random value $r_1 \in \mathbb{F}$ and sends it to $\mathcal{P}$, who computes $P_2 = \sum_{t_3 \in \{0,1\}} \cdots \sum_{t_n \in \{0,1\}} P(r_1, x, t_3, \ldots, t_n)$. Upon receiving P_2, $\mathcal{V}$ checks if: $P_1(r_1) = P_2(0) + P_2(1)$. The protocol goes on until the nth round where $\mathcal{V}$ receives the value $P_n(x) = P(r_1, r_2, \ldots, r_{n-1}, x)$. $\mathcal{V}$ can now pick a last random field value r_n and check that: $P_n(r_n) = P(r_1, \ldots, r_n)$. If so, $\mathcal{V}$ is convinced that H has been evaluated as in (5), otherwise $\mathcal{V}$ rejects H. The Sum-Check protocol has the following properties:

1. The protocol is *correct*: if $\mathcal{P}$'s claim about H is true, then $\mathcal{V}$ accepts with probability 1.
2. The protocol is *sound*: if the claim on H is false, the probability that $\mathcal{P}$ can make $\mathcal{V}$ accept H is bounded by $nd/|\mathbb{F}|$, where n is the number of variables and d the degree of the polynomial P.

Note that the soundness is here information theoretic: no assumption is made on the prover power. To be able to implement the Sum-Check protocol verification algorithm into an arithmetic circuit we need a non-interactive version of the protocol. Indeed, QAP-based VC schemes require the complete specification of each computation as input to the QAP generation process (see Sect. 2.1). Due to the interactive nature of the Sum-Check protocol, the proof cannot be generated before the actual execution of the protocol. We therefore use the Fiat-Shamir transformation [7] to obtain a non-interactive version of the Sum-Check protocol that can be used as an input to GVC. In the Fiat-Shamir transformation, the prover replaces the uniformly random challenges sent by the verifier by challenges he computes applying a public hash function to the transcript of the protocol so far. The prover then sends the whole protocol transcript, which can be verified recomputing the challenges with the same hash function. This method has been proved secure in the random oracle model [17].

2.3   Multilinear Extensions

Multilinear extensions allow to apply the Sum-Check protocol to polynomials defined over some finite set included in the finite field where all the operations of the protocol are performed. Thaler [18] showed how multilinear extensions and the Sum-Check protocol can be combined to give a time-optimal proof for matrix multiplication.

Let $\mathbb{F}$ be a finite field, a *multilinear extension* (MLE) of a function $f :$ $\{0,1\}^d \to \mathbb{F}$ is a polynomial that agrees with f on $\{0,1\}^d$ and has degree at most 1 in each variable. Any function $f : \{0,1\}^d \to \mathbb{F}$ has a unique multilinear extension over $\mathbb{F}$, which we will denote hereafter by $\tilde{f}$. Using Lagrange interpolation, an explicit expression of MLE can be obtained:

Lemma 1. *Let $f : \{0,1\}^d \to \{0,1\}$. Then $\tilde{f}$ has the following expression:*

$$\forall (x_1, \ldots, x_d) \in \mathbb{F}^d, \; \tilde{f}(x_1, \ldots, x_d) = \sum_{w \in \{0,1\}^d} f(w) \chi_w(x_1, \ldots, x_d) \tag{6}$$

$$where : \quad w = (w_1, \ldots, w_d) \quad and \quad \chi_w(x_1, \ldots, x_d) = \prod_{i=1}^{d} \big(x_i w_i + (1-x_i)(1-w_i) \big) \tag{7}$$

2.4   Ajtai Hash Function

As mentioned in Sect. 1.1, our goal is to compute a proof of an expensive sub-computation with the Sum-Check protocol and to verify that proof using the Pinocchio protocol. The non-interactive nature of Pinocchio prevents from proving the sub-computation with an interactive protocol. As explained in Sect. 2.2, we turn the Sum-Check protocol into a non-interactive argument using the Fiat-Shamir transform [7]. This transformation needs a hash function to simulate the challenges that would have been provided by the verifier. The choice of the hash function to compute challenges in the Fiat-Shamir transformation here is crucial because we want to verify the proof transcript inside the GVC system, which will be instantiated with the Pinocchio protocol. This means that the computations of the hash function have to be verified by the GVC system and that the verification should not be more complex than the execution of the original algorithm inside the GVC system. For instance the costs using a standard hash function such as SHA256 would be too high: [2] reports about 27,000 multiplicative gates to implement the compression function of SHA256. Instead, we choose a function better suited for arithmetic circuits, namely the Ajtai hash function [1] that is based on the subset sum problem as defined below:

Definition 3. *Let m, n be positive integers and q a prime number. For a randomly picked matrix $A \in \mathbb{Z}_q^{n \times m}$, the Ajtai hash $H_{n,m,q} : \{0,1\}^m \to \mathbb{Z}_q^n$ is defined as:*

$$\forall x \in \{0,1\}^m, \quad H_{n,m,q} = A \times x \mod q \tag{8}$$

As proved by Goldreich et al. [10], the collision resistance of the hash function relies on the hardness of the Short Integer Solution (SIS) problem. The function is also *regular*: it maps an uniform input to an uniform output. Ben-Sasson et al. [4] noticed that the translation in arithmetic circuit is better if the parameters are chosen to fit with the underlying field of the computations. A concrete hardness evaluation is studied by Kosba et al. in [14]. Choosing $\mathbb{F}_p$, with $p \approx 2^{254}$ to be the field where the computations of the arithmetic circuit take place leads to the following parameters for approximately 100 bit of security: $n = 3, m = 1524, q = p \approx 2^{254}$. Few gates are needed to implement an arithmetic circuit for this hash function since it involves multiplications by constants (the matrix A is public): to hash m bits, m multiplicative gates are needed to ensure that the input vector is binary and 3 more gates are needed to ensure that the output is the linear combination of the input and the matrix. With the parameters selected in [14], this means that 1527 gates are needed to hash 1524 bits.

3 Embedded Proofs

3.1 High Level Description of the Generic Protocol

Let us consider two sets of functions $(f_i)_{1 \le i \le n}$ and $(g_i)_{1 \le i \le n}$ such that the f_i do not lend themselves to an efficient verification with the GVC system whereas the g_i can be handled by the GVC system efficiently. For an input x, we denote by y the evaluation of x by the function $g_n \circ f_n \circ \ldots g_1 \circ f_1$. In our embedded proof protocol, each function f_i is handled by a sub-prover $\mathcal{P}_i$ while the g_i functions are handled by the prover $\mathcal{P}$. The sub-prover $\mathcal{P}_i$ is in charge of the efficient VC algorithm EVC_i and the prover $\mathcal{P}$ runs the GVC algorithm. The steps of the proof generation are depicted in Fig. 2. Basically, each sub-prover $\mathcal{P}_i$ will evaluate the function f_i on a given input, produce a proof of correct evaluation using the EVC_i system and pass the output of f_i and the related proof π_i to $\mathcal{P}$, who will compute the next g_i evaluation and pass the result to the next sub-prover $\mathcal{P}_{i+1}$.

In the **Setup** phase, the verifier and the prover agree on an arithmetic circuit which describes the computation of the functions g_i along with the verification algorithms of the proof that the functions f_i were correctly computed. The preprocessing phase of the GVC system takes the resulting circuit and outputs the corresponding evaluation and verification keys.

In the **query** phase, the verifier sends the prover an input x for the computation along with a random value that will be an input for the efficient sub-provers $\mathcal{P}_i$.

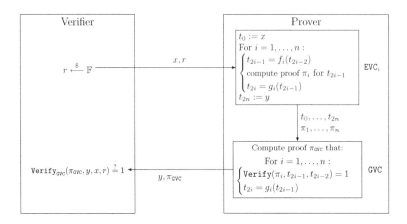

Fig. 2. Embedded proof protocol

In the **proving** phase, $\mathcal{P}_1$ first computes $t_1 = f(x)$ and produces a proof π_1 of the correctness of the computation, using the efficient proving algorithm EVC_1. The prover $\mathcal{P}$ then computes the value $t_2 = g_1(t_1)$ and passes the value t_2 to $\mathcal{P}_2$, who computes $t_3 = f_2(t_2)$ along with the proof of correctness π_2, using the EVC_2 proving system. The protocol proceeds until $y = t_{2n}$ is computed. Finally, $\mathcal{P}$ provides the inputs/outputs of the computations and the intermediate proofs π_i to the GVC system and, using the evaluation key computed in the setup phase, builds a proof π_{GVC} that for $i = 1, \ldots, n$:

1. the proof π_i computed with the EVC_i system is correct,
2. the computation $t_{2i} = g_i(t_{2i-1})$ is correct.

In the **verification** phase, the verifier checks that y was correctly computed using the GVC's verification algorithm, the couple (y, π_{GVC}) received from the prover, and (x, r).

Recall that our goal is to gain efficiency compared with the proof generation of the whole computation inside the GVC system. Therefore, we need proof algorithms with a verification algorithm that can be implemented efficiently as an arithmetic circuit and for which the running time of the verification algorithm is lower than the one of the computation. Since the Sum-Check protocol involves algebraic computations over a finite field, it can easily be implemented as an arithmetic circuit and fits into our scheme.

3.2   A Protocol Instance

In this section, we specify the embedded proofs protocol in the case where f_i are matrix products $f_i : X \mapsto W_i \times X$ and where the functions g_i cannot be efficiently verified by a VC system except by GVC. We use the Sum-Check protocol to prove correctness of the matrix multiplications, as in [18] and any QAP-based VC scheme as the global proof mechanism. We assume that the matrices involved in the f_i functions do not have the same sizes so there will be several instances of the Sum-Check protocol. It thus makes sense to define different efficient proving algorithms EVC_i since the GVC scheme requires that the verification algorithms are expressed as arithmetic circuits in order to generate evaluation and verification keys for the system. As the parameters of the verification algorithms are different, the Sum-Check verification protocols are distinct as arithmetic circuits. For the sake of simplicity, the W_i matrices are assumed to be square matrices of size n_i. We denote $d_i = \log n_i$ and assume that $n_i \geq n_{i+1}$. We denote by H the Ajtai hash function (see Sect. 2). The protocol between the verifier $\mathcal{V}$ and the prover $\mathcal{P}$, which has n sub-provers $\mathcal{P}_i$ is the following:

Setup:
- $\mathcal{V}$ and $\mathcal{P}$ agree on an arithmetic circuit $\mathcal{C}$ description for the computation. $\mathcal{C}$ implements both the evaluations of the functions g_i and the verification algorithms of the Sum-Check protocols for the n matrix multiplications.
- $(EK_\mathcal{C}, VK_\mathcal{C}) \leftarrow \mathsf{KeyGen}(1^\lambda, \mathcal{C})$

Query
- $\mathcal{V}$ generates a random challenge (r_L, r_R) such that: $(r_L, r_R) \in \mathbb{F}^{d_1} \times \mathbb{F}^{d_1}$
- $\mathcal{V}$ sends $\mathcal{P}$ the tuple (X, r_L, r_R), where X is the input matrix.

Proof: for $i = 1, \ldots, n$, on input (T_{2i-2}, r_L, r_R),

   Sub-prover $\mathcal{P}_i$:
   - computes the product $T_{2i-1} = W_i \times T_{2i-2}$, (denoting $T_0 := X$)
   - computes r_{L_i} and r_{R_i} (the d_i first component of r_L and r_R),
   - computes the multilinear extension evaluation $\widetilde{T}_{2i-1}(r_{L_i}, r_{R_i})$
   - computes with serialized Sum-Check, the proof π_i of P_i evaluation:

$$P_i(x) = \widetilde{W}_i(r_{L_i}, x) \cdot \widetilde{T}_{2i-2}(x, r_{R_i}) \text{ where } x = (x_1, \ldots, x_{d_i}) \in \mathbb{F}^{d_i}. \quad (9)$$

   - sends the tuple $(T_{2i-2}, T_{2i-1}, W_i, \pi_i, r_{L_i}, r_{R_i})$ to prover $\mathcal{P}$.

   Prover $\mathcal{P}$:
   - computes $T_{2i} = g_i(T_{2i-1})$ and sends (T_{2i}, r_L, r_R) to sub-prover $\mathcal{P}_{i+1}$
   - receiving the inputs $\{(T_{2i-2}, T_{2i-1}, W_i, \pi_i, r_{L_i}, r_{R_i})\}_{i=1,\ldots,n}$ from sub-provers:
     • Computes $\widetilde{T}_{2i-1}(r_{L_i}, r_{R_i})$.
     • Parses π_i as $(P_{i,1}, r_{i,1}, P_{i,2}, r_{i,2}, \ldots, P_{i,d_i}, r_{i,d_i})$, where the proof contains the coefficient of the degree two polynomials $P_{i,j}$ that we denote by $(a_{i,j}, b_{i,j}, c_{i,j})$ if: $P_{i,j}(x) = a_{i,j}x^2 + b_{i,j}x + c_{i,j}$
     • Verifies π_i:

       * Checks: $P_{i,1}(0) + P_{i,1}(1) \overset{?}{=} \widetilde{T}_{2i-1}(r_{L_i}, r_{R_i})$
       * Computes: $r_{i,1} = \left(\sum_j r_{L_i}[j]\right) \cdot \left(\sum_j r_{R_i}[j]\right)$
       * For $j = 2, \ldots, d_i$:
         · Check: $P_{i,j}(0) + P_{i,j}(1) \overset{?}{=} P_{i,j-1}(r_{i,j-1})$
         · Computes: $r_{i,j}$ as the product of components of the Ajtai hash function output, i.e. $r_{i,j} = \prod_{k=1}^{3} H(a_{i,j}, b_{i,j}, c_{i,j}, r_{i,j})[k]$
       * From T_{2i-2} and W_i, computes the evaluated multilinear extensions $\widetilde{W}_i(r_{L_i}, r_{i,1}, \ldots, r_{i,d_1})$ and $\widetilde{T}_{2i-2}(r_{i,1}, \ldots, r_{i,d_1}, r_{R_i})$

* Checks that $P_{d_i}(r_{i,d_i})$ is the product of the multilinear extensions $\widetilde{W}_i(r_{L_i}, r_{i,1}, \ldots, r_{i,d_i})$ and $\widetilde{T}_{2i-2}(r_{i,1}, \ldots, r_{i,d_i}, r_{R_i})$.
- Aborts if one of the previous checks fails. Otherwise, accepts T_{2i-1} as the product of W_i and T_{2i-2}.
- Repeat the above instructions until the proof π_n has been verified.
- Using the GVC scheme, computes the final proof π_{GVC} that all the EVC_i proofs π_i have been verified and all the T_{2i} values have been correctly computed from T_{2i-1}.
- Sends (Y, π_{GVC}) to the Verifier.

Verification
- $\mathcal{V}$ computes $\mathtt{Verify}(X, r_R, r_L, Y, \pi_{\mathsf{GVC}})$
- If $\mathtt{Verify}$ fails, verifier rejects the value Y. Otherwise the value Y is accepted as the result of: $Y = g_n(\ldots (g_2(W_2(g_1(W_1 \cdot X)))) \ldots)$

4 Embedded Proofs for Neural Networks

4.1 Motivation

In order to show the relevance of the proposed embedded proof scheme, we apply the resulting scheme to Neural Networks (NN), which are machine learning techniques achieving state of the art performance in various classification tasks such as handwritten digit recognition, object or face recognition. As stated in Sect. 1.1, a NN can be viewed as a sequence of operations, the main ones being linear operations followed by so-called activation functions. The linear operations are modeled as matrix multiplications while the activation functions are non-linear functions. A common activation function choice is the ReLU function defined by: $x \mapsto \max(0, x)$. Due to the sequential nature of NNs, a simple solution to obtain a verifiable NN would consist of computing proofs for each part of the NN sequence. However, this solution would degrade the verifier's performance, increase the communication costs and force the prover to send all the intermediate results, revealing sensitive data such as the parameters of the prover's NN. On the other hand, even if it is feasible in principle to implement the NN inside a GVC system like Pinocchio, the size of the matrices involved in the linear operations would be an obstacle. The upper bound for the total number of multiplications QAP-based VC schemes can support as part of one application is estimated at 10^7 [19]. This threshold would be reached with a single multiplication between two 220×220 matrices. In contrast, our embedded proof protocol enables to reach much larger matrix sizes or, for a given matrix size, to perform faster verifications of matrix multiplications.

4.2 A Verifiable Neural Network Architecture

We here describe how our proposal can provide benefits in the verification of a neural network (NN) [12]: in the sequel, we compare the execution of a GVC protocol on a two-layer NN with the execution of the embedded proof protocol on the same NN. Since NN involve several matrix multiplications, embedded proofs enable substantial gains, see Sect. 5.2 for implementation report. We stress that we consider neural networks in the *classification* phase, which means we consider that all the values have been set during the *training* phase, using an appropriate set of labeled inputs.

The NN we verify starts with a fully connected layer combined with a ReLU activation layer. We then apply a max pooling layer to decrease the dimensions and finally apply another fully connected layer. The execution of the NN can be described as: $\boxed{\text{INPUT}} \rightarrow \boxed{\text{FC}} \rightarrow \boxed{\text{RELU}} \rightarrow \boxed{\text{MAX POOLING}} \rightarrow \boxed{\text{FC}}$.

The *fully connected layer* takes as input a value and performs a dot product between this value and a parameter that can be learned. Gathering all the fully connected layer parameters in a matrix, the operation performed on the whole inputs is a matrix multiplication. The *ReLU* layer takes as input a matrix and performs the operation $x \mapsto \max(0, x)$ element-wise. The *max pooling* layer takes as input a matrix and return a matrix with smaller dimensions. This layer applies a max function on sub-matrices of the input matrix, which can be considered as sliding a window over the input matrix and taking the max of all the values belonging to the window. The size of the window and the number of inputs skipped between two mapping of the max function are parameters of the layer but do not change during the training phase nor on the classification phase. Usually a 2×2 window slides over the input matrix, with no overlapping over the inputs. Therefore, the MaxPool function takes as input a matrix and outputs a matrix which row and column size have been divided by 2. Denoting by W_1 and W_2 the matrices holding the parameters of the fully connected layers, X the input matrix, and Y the output of the NN computation, the whole computation can be described as a sequence of operations:

$$X \rightarrow T_1 = W_1 \cdot X \rightarrow T_2 = \text{ReLU}(T_1) \rightarrow T_3 = \text{MaxPool}(T_2) \rightarrow Y = W_2 \cdot T_3 \quad (10)$$

5   Implementation and Performance Evaluation

We ran two sets of experiments to compare the cost of execution between our embedded proof scheme and a baseline scheme using the GVC scheme. The first set focuses only on the cost of a matrix multiplication since these are a relevant representative of complex operations whereby the embedded proof scheme is likely to achieve major performance gains. The second set takes into account an entire application involving several operations including matrix multiplications, namely a small neural network architecture.

5.1   Matrix Multiplication Benchmark

We implemented our embedded proof protocol on a 8-core machine running at 2.9 GHz with 16 GB of RAM. The GVC system is Groth's state of the art zk-SNARK [13] and is implemented using the `libsnark` library[1] while the EVC

---

[1] Libsnark, a C++ library for zkSNARK proofs, available at https://github.com/scipr-lab/libsnark.

Table 1. Matrix multiplication benchmark

(a) Matrix multiplication proving time

n	16	32	64	128	256	512
Baseline (GVC only)	0.23 s	1.34 s	9.15 s	71.10 s	697.72	–
Embedded proofs	0.281 s	0.924 s	3.138 s	11.718 s	43.014 s	168.347 s
Time division	0.28|0.001	0.92|0.004	3.12|0.018	11.65|0.068	42.71|0.304	166.88|1.467

(b) Matrix multiplication key generation time

n	16	32	64	128	256	512
Baseline (GVC only)	0.28 s	1.56 s	10.50 s	76.62 s	585.21 s	–
Embedded proofs	0.37 s	1.03 s	3.54 s	12.95 s	47.52 s	176.41 s

(c) Matrix multiplication key generation size

n	16	32	64	128	256	512
Baseline (GVC only) PK	508 KB	5.60 MB	26.9 MB	208 MB	1.63 GB	–
Embedded proofs PK	757 kB	2.24 MB	7.87 MB	30.1 MB	118.7 MB	472 MB
Baseline (GVC only) VK	31 kB	123 kB	490 kB	1.96 MB	7.84 MB	–
Embedded proofs VK	32 KB	123 KB	491 KB	1.96 MB	7.84 MB	31.36 MB

system is our own implementation of Thaler's special purpose matrix multiplication verification protocol [18] using the NTL library[2].

The proving time reported in Table 1a measures the time to produce the proof using the EVC system and to verify the result inside the GVC system. The last row of the table breaks down the proving time into the sumcheck proof time and the embedded proof time. We note that the sumcheck proving time brings a very small contribution to the final proving time. For the value $n = 512$, the proof using the GVC is not feasible whereas the embedded proof approach still achieves realistic performance. Table 1b compares the key generation time using the embedded proof system with the one using the GVC. Table 1c states the sizes of the proving key (PK) and the verification key (VK) used in the previous scenarios. The embedded proof protocol provides substantial benefits: the protocol improves the proving time as soon as the matrix has a size greater than 32×32, giving a proving time 7 times better for 128×128 matrix multiplication and 16 times better for a 256×256 matrix multiplication. Embedded proofs also enable to reach higher value for matrix multiplications: we were able to perform a multiplication proof for 512×512 matrices whereas the computation was not able to terminate due to lack of RAM for the baseline system.

---

[2] V. Shoup, NTL – A Library for Doing Number Theory, available at http://www.shoup.net.

Table 2. Experiments on 2-layer networks

(a) NN-64-32

	KeyGen	PK size	VK size	Prove	Verify
Baseline (GVC only)	59 s	148 MB	490 kB	25.48 s	0.011 s
Embedded proofs	44 s	123 MB	778 kB	16.80 s	0.016 s

(b) NN-128-64

	KeyGen	PK size	VK size	Prove	Verify
Baseline (GVC only)	261.9 s	701.5 MB	1.96 MB	149.5 s	0.046 s
Embedded proofs	162.7 s	490 MB	3.1 MB	66.96 s	0.067 s

5.2   Two-Layer Verifiable Neural Network Experimentations

We implemented the verification of an example of 2-layer neural network, which can be seen as one matrix multiplication followed by the application of two non-linear functions, namely a ReLU and a max pooling function as described in Sect. 4. For our experiments, the max pooling layers have filters of size 2×2 and no data overlap. Thus, setting for instance the first weight matrix to 64×64, the second weight matrix size is 32×32; we denote by NN-64-32 such a neural network. Table 2a reports experiments on a 2-layer neural network with a first 64×64 matrix product, followed by a ReLU and a max-pooling function, and ending with a second 32×32 matrix product. Experimental times for a NN-128-64 network (with the same architecture as above) are reported in Table 2b.

Experiments show a proving time twice better than using the baseline proving system. The overall gain is lower than for the matrix product benchmark because the other operations (ReLU and max pooling) are implemented the same way for the two systems. It should be noted that the goal of the implementation was to achieve a proof of concept for our scheme on a complete composition scenario involving several functions rather than putting in evidence the performance advantages of the scheme over the baseline, hence the particularly low size of the matrices used in the 2-layer NN and an advantage as low as the one in Table 2a and b. The gap between the embedded proof scheme and the baseline using a realistic scenario with larger NN would definitely be much more significant due to the impact of larger matrices as shown in the matrix product benchmark.

6   Conclusion

We designed an efficient verifiable computing scheme that builds on the notion of proof composition and leverages an efficient VC scheme, namely the Sum-Check protocol to improve the performance of a general purpose QAP-based VC protocol, in proving matrix multiplications. As an application, our scheme can prove the correctness of a neural network algorithm. We implement our scheme and provide an evaluation of its efficiency. The security is evaluated in Appendix A. We stress that the composition technique described in the article can be extended using other efficient VC schemes and an arbitrary number of sequential function evaluations, provided that they respect the requirements defined in Sect. 1.2. Our proposal could be integrated as a sub-module in existing verifiable computing systems in order to improve their performance when verifying computations including high complexity operations such as matrix multiplications.

Acknowledgment. The authors would like to thank Gaïd Revaud for her precious programming assistance. This work was partly supported by the TREDISEC project (G.A. no 644412), funded by the European Union (EU) under the Information and Communication Technologies (ICT) theme of the Horizon 2020 (H2020) research and innovation programme.

A   Appendix: Embedded Proofs Security

Our embedded proof system has to satisfy the correctness and soundness requirements. Suppose that we have a GVC and n EVC systems to prove the correct computation of $y = g_n \circ f_n \circ \ldots \circ g_1 \circ f_1(x)$. We will denote by EVC_i, $i = 1, \ldots, n$ the EVC systems. We also keep notations defined in Sect. 3: the value t_i, $i = 0, \ldots, 2n$ represents intermediate computation results, t_{2i-1} being the output of the f_i function, t_{2i} being the output of the g_i function, $t_0 := x$ and $t_{2n} = y$. The EVC_i and GVC systems already satisfy the correctness and soundness requirements. Let denote by ϵ_{GVC} the soundness error of the GVC system and ϵ_{EVC_i} the soundness error of the EVC_i system. Note that while the EVC_i systems prove that $t_{2i-1} = f_i(t_{2i-2})$ have been correctly computed, the GVC system proves the correctness of $2n$ computations, namely that the *verification* of the EVC_i proofs has passed and that the computations $t_{2i} = g_i(t_{2i-1})$ are correct. Furthermore, the GVC system proves the correct execution of the function F that takes as input the tuple $(x, y, r, (t_i)_{i=1,\ldots,2n}, (\pi_i)_{i=1,\ldots,n})$ and outputs 1 if for all $i = 1, \ldots, n$, $\text{Verify}_{\text{EVC}_i}(\pi_i, t_{2i-1}, t_{2i-2}) = 1$ and $t_{2i} = g_i(t_{2i-1})$. F outputs 0 otherwise. For convenience, we denote by comp_n the function $g_n \circ f_n \circ \ldots \circ g_1 \circ f_1$.

A.1   Correctness

Theorem 1. *If the EVC_i and the GVC systems are correct then our embedded proof system is correct.*

Proof. Assume that the value $y = \text{comp}_n(x)$ has been correctly computed. This means that for $i = 1, \ldots, n$, the values $t_{2i-1} = f_i(t_{2i-2})$ and $t_{2i} = g_i(t_{2i-1})$ have been correctly computed. Since the GVC system is correct, it ensures that the function F will pass the GVC verification with probability 1, provided that its result is correct. Now, since the EVC_i systems are correct, with probability 1 we have that: $\text{Verify}_{\text{EVC}_i}(t_{2i-1}, t_{2i-2}, \pi_i) = 1$.

Therefore, if $y = \text{comp}_n(x)$ has been correctly computed, then the function F will also be correctly computed and the verification of the embedded proof system will pass with probability 1.

A.2   Soundness

Theorem 2. *If the* EVC$_i$ *and the* GVC *systems are sound with soundness error respectively equal to* ϵ_{EVC_i} *and* ϵ_{GVC}, *then our embedded proof system is sound with soundness error at most* $\epsilon := \sum \epsilon_{\text{EVC}_i} + \epsilon_{\text{GVC}}$.

Proof. Assume that a p.p.t. adversary $\mathcal{A}_{emb}$ returns a cheating proof π for a result y' on input x, i.e. $y' \neq \text{comp}(x)$ and π is accepted by the verifier $\mathcal{V}_{emb}$ with probability higher than ϵ. We then construct an adversary $\mathcal{B}$ that breaks the soundness property of either the GVC or of one of the EVC systems. We build $\mathcal{B}$ as follows: $\mathcal{A}_{emb}$ interacts with the verifier $\mathcal{V}_{emb}$ of the embedded system until a cheating proof is accepted. $\mathcal{A}_{emb}$ then forwards the cheating tuple $(x, y, r, (t_i)_{i=1,...,2n}, (\pi_i)_{i=1,...,n})$ for which the proof π has been accepted. Since $y' \neq \text{comp}(x)$, there exists an index $i \in \{1, ..., n\}$ such that either $t_{2i-1} \neq f_i(t_{2i-2})$ or $t_{2i} \neq g_i(t_{2i-1})$. $\mathcal{B}$ can thus submit a cheating proof to the GVC system or to one of the EVC$_i$ system, depending on the value of i.

Case $t_{2i-1} \neq f_i(t_{2i-2})$:
By definition of the proof π, this means that the proof π_i has been accepted by the verification algorithm of EVC$_i$ implemented inside the GVC system. $\mathcal{A}_{emb}$ can then forward to the adversary $\mathcal{B}$ the tuple $(t_{2i-1}, t_{2i-2}, \pi_i)$. Now if $\mathcal{B}$ presents the tuple $(t_{2i-1}, t_{2i-2}, \pi_i)$ to the EVC$_i$ system, it succeeds with probability 1. Therefore, the probability that the verifier $\mathcal{V}_{emb}$ of the embedded proof system accepts is superior to ϵ_{EVC_i}, which breaks the soundness property of EVC$_i$.

$$Pr[\mathcal{V}_{emb} \text{ accepts } \pi] = Pr[\mathcal{V}_{\text{EVC}_i} \text{ accepts } \pi_i \mid \mathcal{V}_{emb} \text{ accepts } \pi] \times Pr[\mathcal{V}_{emb} \text{ accepts } \pi]$$
$$= 1 \times \epsilon \geqslant \epsilon_{\text{EVC}_i}$$

Case $t_{2i} \neq g_i(t_{2i-1})$:
This means that the proof π computed by the GVC system is accepted by $\mathcal{V}_{emb}$ even if $t_{2i} \neq g_i(t_{2i-1})$ has not been correctly computed. We proceed as in the previous case: $\mathcal{A}_{emb}$ forwards $\mathcal{B}$ the cheating tuple and the cheating proof π. The tuple and the proof thus break the soundness of the GVC scheme because:

$$Pr[\mathcal{V}_{emb} \text{ accepts } \pi] = \epsilon \geq \epsilon_{\text{GVC}}$$

B   Appendix: Prover's Input Privacy

B.1   Prover's Input Privacy

The combination of the proof of knowledge and zero knowledge properties in zk-SNARK proofs enables the prover to provide some inputs for the computation to be proved for which no information will leak. Gennaro et al. proved in [8] that their QAP-based protocol (see Sect. 2.1) is zero-knowledge for input provided by the prover: there exists a simulator that could have generated a proof without knowledge of the witness (here the input privately provided by the prover). Subsequent works on QAP-based VC schemes achieve the same goal, with differences on the cryptographic assumptions and on the flavor of zero-knowledge achieved:

for instance Groth's scheme [13] achieves perfect zero-knowledge at the expense of a proof in the generic group model while Gennaro et al.'s scheme achieves statistical zero-knowledge with a knowledge of exponent assumption.

We now sketch how the zero-knowledge property is achieved for our embedded proof protocol. We first have to assume that the QAP-based VC scheme we consider for GVC can support auxiliary inputs (as in NP statements), which is achieved for Pinocchio [16] or Groth's scheme [13]. Leveraging the zero-knowledge property, the GVC prover can hide from the verifier the intermediate results of the computation provided by the sub-provers EVC_i while still allowing the verifier to check the correctness of the final result. Therefore, the overall VC system obtained by composing the EVC systems inside the GVC achieves zero-knowledge: the simulator defined for the GVC system is still a valid one. Note that even if the simulator gains knowledge of the intermediate computations performed by sub-provers EVC_i, the goal is to protect the leakage of information from *outside*, namely from the verifier. In detail, keeping the notations of Fig. 2, the verifier only knows t_0, i.e. x and t_{2n}, i.e. y, which are the inputs and outputs of the global computation. Intermediate inputs, such as $t_i, i = 1, \ldots, 2n - 1$, are hidden from the verifier even though they are taken into account during the verification of the intermediate proofs by the GVC prover. Therefore, thanks to the zk-SNARKs, the intermediate results are verified but not disclosed to the verifier.

References

1. Ajtai, M.: Generating hard instances of lattice problems (extended abstract). In: Proceedings of the Twenty-Eighth Annual ACM Symposium on the Theory of Computing, Philadelphia, Pennsylvania, USA, 22–24 May 1996, pp. 99–108 (1996)
2. Ben-Sasson, E., et al.: Zerocash: decentralized anonymous payments from bitcoin. In: 2014 IEEE Symposium on Security and Privacy SP 2014, Berkeley, CA, USA, 18–21 May 2014, pp. 459–474 (2014)
3. Ben-Sasson, E., Chiesa, A., Genkin, D., Tromer, E., Virza, M.: SNARKs for C: verifying program executions succinctly and in zero knowledge. In: Canetti, R., Garay, J.A. (eds.) CRYPTO 2013. LNCS, vol. 8043, pp. 90–108. Springer, Heidelberg (2013). https://doi.org/10.1007/978-3-642-40084-1_6
4. Ben-Sasson, E., Chiesa, A., Tromer, E., Virza, M.: Scalable zero knowledge via cycles of elliptic curves. In: Garay, J.A., Gennaro, R. (eds.) CRYPTO 2014. LNCS, vol. 8617, pp. 276–294. Springer, Heidelberg (2014). https://doi.org/10.1007/978-3-662-44381-1_16
5. Bitansky, N., Canetti, R., Chiesa, A., Tromer, E.: Recursive composition and bootstrapping for SNARKS and proof-carrying data. In: Symposium on Theory of Computing Conference, STOC 2013, Palo Alto, CA, USA, 1–4 June 2013, pp. 111–120 (2013). http://doi.acm.org/10.1145/2488608.2488623
6. Cormode, G., Mitzenmacher, M., Thaler, J.: Practical verified computation with streaming interactive proofs. In: Innovations in Theoretical Computer Science 2012, Cambridge, MA, USA, 8–10 January 2012, pp. 90–112 (2012)
7. Fiat, A., Shamir, A.: How to prove yourself: practical solutions to identification and signature problems. In: Odlyzko, A.M. (ed.) CRYPTO 1986. LNCS, vol. 263, pp. 186–194. Springer, Heidelberg (1987). https://doi.org/10.1007/3-540-47721-7_12

8. Gennaro, R., Gentry, C., Parno, B., Raykova, M.: Quadratic span programs and succinct NIZKs without PCPs. In: Johansson, T., Nguyen, P.Q. (eds.) EUROCRYPT 2013. LNCS, vol. 7881, pp. 626–645. Springer, Heidelberg (2013). https://doi.org/10.1007/978-3-642-38348-9_37

9. Ghodsi, Z., Gu, T., Garg, S.: Safetynets: verifiable execution of deep neural networks on an untrusted cloud. CoRR abs/1706.10268 (2017). http://arxiv.org/abs/1706.10268

10. Goldreich, O., Goldwasser, S., Halevi, S.: Collision-free hashing from lattice problems. Electron. Colloq. Comput. Complex. (ECCC) **3**(42) (1996). http://eccc.hpi-web.de/eccc-reports/1996/TR96-042/index.html

11. Goldwasser, S., Kalai, Y.T., Rothblum, G.N.: Delegating computation: interactive proofs for muggles. In: Proceedings of the 40th Annual ACM Symposium on Theory of Computing, Victoria, British Columbia, Canada, 17–20 May 2008, pp. 113–122 (2008)

12. Goodfellow, I., Bengio, Y., Courville, A.: Deep Learning. MIT Press, Cambridge (2016). http://www.deeplearningbook.org

13. Groth, J.: On the size of pairing-based non-interactive arguments. In: Fischlin, M., Coron, J.-S. (eds.) EUROCRYPT 2016. LNCS, vol. 9666, pp. 305–326. Springer, Heidelberg (2016). https://doi.org/10.1007/978-3-662-49896-5_11

14. Kosba, A., et al.: C∅c∅: a framework for building composable zero-knowledge proofs. Cryptology ePrint Archive, Report 2015/1093 (2015). http://eprint.iacr.org/2015/1093

15. Lund, C., Fortnow, L., Karloff, H.J., Nisan, N.: Algebraic methods for interactive proof systems. In: 31st Annual Symposium on Foundations of Computer Science, St. Louis, Missouri, USA, 22–24 October 1990, vol. I, pp. 2–10 (1990)

16. Parno, B., Howell, J., Gentry, C., Raykova, M.: Pinocchio: nearly practical verifiable computation. In: 2013 IEEE Symposium on Security and Privacy, SP 2013, Berkeley, CA, USA, 19–22 May 2013, pp. 238–252 (2013)

17. Pointcheval, D., Stern, J.: Security arguments for digital signatures and blind signatures. J. Cryptol. **13**(3), 361–396 (2000). https://doi.org/10.1007/s001450010003

18. Thaler, J.: Time-optimal interactive proofs for circuit evaluation. In: Canetti, R., Garay, J.A. (eds.) CRYPTO 2013. LNCS, vol. 8043, pp. 71–89. Springer, Heidelberg (2013). https://doi.org/10.1007/978-3-642-40084-1_5

19. Wahby, R.S., Setty, S.T.V., Ren, Z., Blumberg, A.J., Walfish, M.: Efficient RAM and control flow in verifiable outsourced computation. In: 22nd Annual Network and Distributed System Security Symposium, NDSS 2015, San Diego, California, USA, 8–11 February 2015 (2015)

20. Walfish, M., Blumberg, A.J.: Verifying computations without reexecuting them. Commun. ACM **58**(2), 74–84 (2015). http://doi.acm.org/10.1145/2641562

Hardware Security

Navigating the Samsung TrustZone and Cache-Attacks on the Keymaster Trustlet

Ben Lapid and Avishai Wool[(⊠)]

School of Electrical Engineering, Tel Aviv University, Tel Aviv, Israel
ben.lapid@gmail.com, yash@eng.tau.ac.il

Abstract. The ARM TrustZone is a security extension helping to move the "root of trust" further away from the attacker, which is used in recent Samsung flagship smartphones. These devices use the TrustZone to create a Trusted Execution Environment (TEE) called a Secure World, which runs secure processes called Trustlets. The Samsung TEE is based on the Kinibi OS and includes cryptographic key storage and functions inside the Keymaster trustlet.

Using static and dynamic reverse engineering techniques, we present a critical review of Samsung's proprietary TrustZone architecture. We describe the major components and their interconnections, focusing on their security aspects. During this review we identified some design weaknesses, including one actual vulnerability. Next, we identify that the ARM32 assembly-language AES implementation used by the Keymaster trustlet is vulnerable to cache side-channel attacks. Finally, we demonstrate realistic cache attack artifacts on the Keymaster cryptographic functions, despite the recently discovered Autolock feature on ARM CPUs.

1 Introduction

1.1 Motivation

The ARM TrustZone [3] is a security extension helping to move the "root of trust" further away from the attacker. TrustZone is a separate environment that can run security dedicated functionality, parallel to the OS and separated from it by a hardware barrier.

Recent Samsung flagship smartphones rely on Samsung's Exynos SoC architecture cf. [28]. This architecture incorporates an ARM CPU, as well as a GPU, memory and peripherals. The ARM cores in Exynos support the TrustZone security extension to create Trusted Execution Environments (TEEs). On their Exynos-based platforms, Samsung uses Trustonic's Kinibi OS as the Secure World kernel.

These TEEs are often used in scenarios which require a higher level of security or privacy guarantees, such as application of cryptographic functions, secure payments and more. Therefore, these environments present a high value target

© Springer Nature Switzerland AG 2018
J. Lopez et al. (Eds.): ESORICS 2018, LNCS 11098, pp. 175–196, 2018.
https://doi.org/10.1007/978-3-319-99073-6_9

for attackers. However, the security practices in these environments were not thoroughly studied by the research community yet.

In order to support cryptographic modules, the Android OS includes a mechanism for handling cryptographic keys and functions called the Keystore [11]. Keystore is used for several privacy related features such as full disk encryption and password storage. The Keystore depends on a hardware abstraction layer module to implement the underlying key handling and cryptographic functions; and many OEMs, including Samsung, choose to implement this module using the TrustZone.

1.2   Related Work

Lipp et al. [16] implemented cache attack techniques to recover secret keys from Java implementation of AES-128 on ARM processors, and exfiltrate additional execution information. In addition they were able to monitor cache activity in the TrustZone.

Zhang et al. [38] demonstrated a successful cache attack on a T-Table implementation of AES-128 that runs inside the TrustZone—however, their target was a development board lacking a real Secure World OS rather than a standard device. Ryan et al. [18] demonstrated reliable cache side-channel techniques that require loading a kernel module into the Normal World—which is disabled or restricted to OEM-verified modules on modern devices. To our knowledge no previous cache attacks on ARM TrustZone have been published on standard devices using publicly available vulnerabilities.

Recently, Green et al. [14] presented AutoLock, an undocumented feature in certain ARM CPUs which prevent eviction of cross-core cache sets. This feature severely reduces the effectiveness of cache side-channel attacks. The authors listed multiple CPUs that include AutoLock, and among them are the A53 and A57 used in the device we used (Samsung Galaxy S6).

Cache side-channel attacks on AES were first demonstrated by Bernstein [5] with the target being a remote encryption server with an x86 CPU. Osvik et al. [25] demonstrated the *Prime+Probe* technique to attack a T-Table implementation of AES which resides in the Linux kernel on an x86 CPU. Xinjie et al. [37] and Neve et al. [19] presented techniques which improve the effectiveness of cache side-channel attacks. Spreitzer et al. [31] demonstrated a specialization of these attacks on misaligned T-Table implementations. Neve et al. [20] discussed the effectiveness of these attacks on AES-256 and demonstrated a successful specialized attack for AES-256.

Little is publicly known about the design and implementation of the proprietary closed-source Kinibi OS [32] used as a Secure World by Samsung.

1.3   Contributions

Our first contribution is a critical review of Samsung's TrustZone architecture on the Exynos SoC platform, including the Kinibi OS. Through a combination of firmware disassembly, open-source code review and dynamic instrumentation of system processes, we are able for the first time to provide a description of all the major subsystems, with their interconnections and communication paths, of this complex proprietary system. Our review focuses on the security aspects of the architecture, and in particular on the Keymaster trustlet, which is responsible for many critical cryptographic functions. During this review we identified some design weaknesses, including one actual vulnerability.

Our next contribution is identifying that the ARM32 assembly-language AES implementation used by the Keymaster trustlet is vulnerable to cache side-channel attacks. We also identify that the Keymaster uses AES-256 in GCM mode. In a separate paper [15] we show successful cache attacks against the implementation.

Our final contribution is demonstrating realistic cache attack artifacts on the Keymaster cryptographic functions embedded in the Secure World and protected by the ARM TrustZone architecture. Contrary to prior assumptions, we found that the cache is *not* flushed upon entry to the Secure World. On the other hand, the recently discovered "AutoLock" ARM feature is a serious limitation. Nonetheless, we are able to successfully demonstrate cache side-channel effects on "World Shared Memory" buffers, and we show compelling evidence that full-blown cache attacks against the AES implementation inside the Keymaster trustlet are plausible.

Organization: In the next section we introduce some background about the ARM TrustZone and its use in Android. Section 3 describes our discoveries about the Exynos secure boot and the Kinibi secure OS. Section 4 describes the Normal World components interfacing with the secure OS. Section 5 describes our achievements in mounting cache attacks against the Keymaster trustlet, and we conclude with Sect. 6.

2   Preliminaries

2.1   ARM TrustZone Overview

ARM TrustZone security extensions [4] enable a processor to run in two states, called Normal World and Secure World. This architecture extends the concept of "privilege rings" and adds another dimension to it. In the ARMv8 ISA, these rings are called "Exception Levels" (ELs). The most privileged mode is the "Secure Monitor" which runs in EL3 and sits "above" the Secure and Normal Worlds. In the Secure World, the Secure OS kernel runs in EL1 and the Secure userspace runs in EL0. In the Normal World, an optional hypervisor may be run in EL2, the Normal OS kernel runs in EL1 and the Normal userspace runs in EL0. On the Galaxy S6 there is no hypervisor, and the Normal World OS is Android.

The separation of Secure and Normal World means that certain RAM ranges and bus peripherals may be indicated as "secure" and only be accessed by the Secure World. This means that compromised Normal World code (in userspace, kernel or hypervisor) will not be able to access these memory ranges or devices and thus pose a threat to them as well.

To allow a controlled method of passing information between the worlds, a mechanism called "World Shared Memory" allows memory pages to be accessible by both worlds. These physical memory pages reside in the Normal World, and the Secure World maps them into its processes' virtual memory as needed.

Additionally, communication may be initiated between worlds by means of SMC calls. SMC calls are basically "system calls" made by a kernel in EL1 or EL2 (either Secure or Normal) to the EL3 "Secure Monitor". These SMCs, use the "Secure Monitor" to pass information between the worlds. In particular, a common SMC is used by one world to notify the other of pending work; such SMC is implemented in the "Secure Monitor" by triggering a software interrupt in the other world. Note that ARM CPUs also have SVC calls: regular system calls from EL0 to EL1 within the same world.

It is important to note that the world separation is completely "virtual". The same cores are used to run both Secure and Normal Worlds and they use the same RAM. Therefore, they use the same cache used by the core to improve memory access times; as we shall see in Sect. 5.3, this design decision may be used to mount cache side-channel attacks.

2.2 TrustZone Usage in Android

In the Samsung/Android ecosystem, there are two major players in field of Trust-Zone implementations. One is Qualcomm, with the QSEE operating system [27] which is compatible with the Snapdragon SoC architecture used on many Samsung devices. The other is Trustonic, with the Kinibi operating system [32] which is used by Samsung in their popular Exynos SoC architecture as a part of the KNOX security system [29].

These Trusted Execution Environments (TEEs) are used for various activities within the smart device: Secure boot (see Sect. 3), Keymaster implementation (see Sect. 4.4), secure UI, kernel protections, secure payments, digital rights management (DRM) and more. Because their usage is often linked to security of privacy-critical applications, they are a high-value target. In our research we focused on the Trusted Execution Environment present in Samsung's Exynos SoC (in particular in Samsung's Galaxy S6): Secure Boot, Trustonic's Kinibi OS, Trusted Drivers and Trustlets.

2.3 Attack Model

The fundamental reason for the existence of the TrustZone is to provide a hardware-based root of trust for a trusted execution environment (TEE)—that is designed to resist even a compromised Normal World kernel.

Since the Normal World kernel, and all the kernel modules on Samsung's smartphones are signed by Samsung and verified before being loaded, injecting code into the kernel is challenging for the attacker. Our goal in this work is to demonstrate that weaker attacks, that do not require a compromised kernel, are sufficient to exfiltrate Secure World information—in particular secret key material.

In our attack mode we assume an attacker is able to execute code on a Samsung Galaxy S6 device, under **root privileges** and relevant **SELinux permissions**. Note that these privileges are significantly less than kernel privileges, since the attack code runs in EL0.

Root privileges are needed to access the */proc/self/pagemap* to identify cache sets, as described by Lipp et al. [16]. Our attack can theoretically be mounted without access to this file, but it will be substantially more difficult. SELinux permissions are needed to connect to the *mcDriverDaemon* process (see Sect. 4.2) through the Unix domain socket, and to access the */dev/mobicore* device (see Sect. 4.1), as Samsung's Keymaster HAL module uses these interfaces to load and communicate with the trustlet (see Sect. 4.4).

To achieve root privileges and the necessary SELinux permissions in our investigation we used the publicly known vulnerability called *dirtycow*. The rooting process is based on Trident [6], which uses *dirtycow*.

3   The Exynos Secure World Components

In our research we explored the inner workings of the trusted execution environment implemented in Samsung's Exynos SoC platform [28]. This platform is present in many of its flagship phones; of which we focused on the Galaxy S6. Several security researchers have previously presented different pieces of information about the TEE in this environment, but to our knowledge there is no publication which covers the TEE in a systematic manner. This section describes our findings regarding the platform's *Secure Boot* mechanism (which includes a series of bootloaders, the trusted OS and several trustlets). In Sect. 4 we describe how the Normal World OS (Android Linux) communicates with the secure OS.

Secure Boot (sboot). We started our exploration by reverse-engineering firmware images for the Galaxy S6 smartphone. We observed that these images contain several distinct files, including the Android Linux image, the *system* partition, the *Secure Boot* partition and more. Samsung does not provide much information about the *Secure Boot* apart from one short page [29]. According to that page, the boot process consists of a chain of bootloaders, starting with a primary bootloader which resides in read only memory, and each link of the chain verifies the next bootloader. Hence the remainder of this section is based on our own discoveries.

The *Secure Boot* partition lies within the *sboot.bin* file, of size 1.6 MB. Opening the file with a disassembler reveals several distinct parts. All of the parts seem to include a code segment and data segment, some are in ARM64 and some are in ARM Thumb mode. In our research we identified them as follows:

- EL3 bootloader and Monitor Code (SMC handler) (ARM64).
- Normal World bootloader (ARM64).
- The Kinibi Secure World operating system (ARM Thumb), which contains: the OS itself, Trustlet and Driver API library and what appears to be an *init*-like first user-land process.
- Three Secure World Drivers: *SecDrv, Crypto Driver* and *STH Driver* (ARM Thumb).

The EL3 Monitor. The first part in *sboot.bin* contains instructions which are reserved for EL3 execution only, such as setting the interrupt vector base and several other ARM special registers. While reverse-engineering this part, we found many similarities with ARM's reference implementation of TrustZone boot sequence. This lead us to conclude that the responsibilities of this part are: Architectural initialization, Platform initialization, Runtime services initialization and Normal World bootloader execution (See the ARM reference documents [1]).

Based on [21], we found that the registered runtime services (*rt_svc_desc_t* array [2]) gives us insight into what functionality is made available by the monitor code which runs in EL3.

It is important to note that the EL3 monitor binary is verified by an earlier bootloader and is responsible for verifying the binaries of the parts it loads: the Normal World bootloader and the secure OS.

The Normal World Bootloader. The second part we found in *sboot.bin* is the Normal World bootloader. This part runs in Normal World EL1 and has several responsibilities: booting the Android Linux kernel (after verifying its binary), requesting secure OS initialization from the monitor code, handling firmware flash requests ("Download mode"), handling "Recovery mode" requests and presenting relevant user interfaces for these modes. This part executes only on device start-up and therefore was less interesting to us. Others [8,21] have presented their research on this part.

The Kinibi Secure Operating System. The third part we found in *sboot.bin* is the Kinibi secure operating system which includes the OS, a user-space API library and an *init*-like user-space process. For the Exynos platform, Samsung has chosen to use Trustonic's Kinibi [32] as the base of their trusted execution environment. Note that Kinibi was previously called t-base or MobiCore; much of the internal naming still uses the "mobicore" name: e.g., the device */dev/mobicore* etc. Hence when we discuss the Kinibi internals we often use the name mobicore.

Surprisingly, we found that the binary code for the operating system runs in Thumb (32bit) mode even though the platform has a 64bit processor. Furthermore, we found that while the Kinibi OS is protected by the TrustZone architecture, internally it does not protect itself very well. Lacking were defenses such as Address Space Randomization (ASLR), non-executable (NX) stack, or stack canaries, which are all present in stock Android since version 4.0. Our observations about the Kinibi OS are as follows:

- Privileges are separated to: OS code—which runs in Secure World EL1; Trusted Applications (or Trustlets)—which run in Secure World EL0 as processes and have access to a limited set of system calls; and Drivers—which run in Secure World EL0 and have access to a broader set of system calls.
- Kinibi supports processes and virtual memory isolation. In addition, Drivers may spawn additional threads.
- Kinibi uses a priority based scheduler. Time quanta are made available by having the Normal World issue specific SMCs which are transfered to the Secure World OS. Without them, the secure OS would not run at all. Two methods of entry are available after initialization: SIQ - which signals the Kinibi OS that an interrupt (or an asynchronous notification) was issued by the Normal World and needs to be handled; and Yield - which means the secure OS may continue any work it chooses.
- Processes may request memory allocation. Furthermore, Drivers may request memory mapping to physical memory for integration with platform devices.
- Kinibi supports *World Shared Memory* for communication between Normal World and the Secure World—recall Sect. 2.1. In particular, Kinibi uses World Shared Memory to define the TCI (Trustlet Connector Interface) memory, which plays an important part of our research, see Sect. 5.3.
- Kinibi supports inter (secure)-process RPC-like communication. Trustlets may send requests to Drivers and receive responses via a message queue. Requests and responses are routed by an IPCH (covered below) which receives the requests from Trustlets and routes them to Drivers and vice versa. Furthermore, a notification system is supported which allows Drivers and Trustlets to wait until the Normal World has issued them a notification.
- Kinibi supports a circular buffer logging mechanism which can be read by the Normal World.

It is important to note that Kinibi OS is bound to a specific CPU core (which can be changed at runtime), and discards interrupts issued on other cores: On our device, Kinibi boots on core 0 and is later switched by default to core 1.

Analyzing the Kinibi OS reveals several distinct segments: (i) the interrupt vector base, interrupt handlers and the OS kernel initialization code; (ii) a user-space code which appears to be a shared library that is injected into Trustlets and Drivers and presents an interface to the OS. (iii) the rest of the OS kernel code; and (iv) an *init*-like secure-world user-land process which is spawned at OS kernel initialization. We omit the details.

Kinibi Drivers. The fourth part of *sboot.bin* consists of three Secure World Drivers: *SecDrv*, *Crypto Driver* and *STH Driver*. We note that the crypto driver implements various cryptographic functions over an IPC mechanism—however the Keymaster trustlet we discuss in Sect. 4.4 includes its own cryptographic implementations. We omit the details.

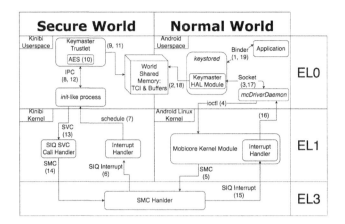

Fig. 1. Secure World/Normal World layering around the Keymaster trustlet. TCI stands for Trustlet Connector Interface, SIQ for Software Interrupt Queue. The numbers in parenthesis mark the actions illustrated in Appendix A.

4   The Exynos Normal World Components

In this section we explore the way the Normal World communicates with the Secure World and what APIs are made available to Android applications. We start by describing the MobiCore kernel module which implements the interface between the Secure World and Normal World users (other kernel modules and user-land processes). We then present our findings on the user-land process *mcDriverDaemon* and Samsung's implementation of the Keymaster HAL interface (see Fig. 1 as reference). In Appendix A we present an example of communication between the Normal World and the Secure World and trace the execution path between them.

4.1   The MobiCore Kernel Module

The MobiCore kernel module is statically linked into the Android Linux kernel image and is initialized on kernel startup. The module is licensed under "GPL V2" and therefore is open-source (source code can be found under many Android Kernel tree publications such as [9]). By reading the source code one can see that the module's responsibilities are:

– Register device files (*/dev/mobicore* and */dev/mobicore-user*) which allow user-space programs to interact with the driver (through *ioctl*, *read* and *mmap* syscalls). The *mobicore-user* device is used by user-land processes that wish to interact with the kernel module, and exposes a limited set of APIs (only mapping and registration of World Shared Memory). The *mobicore* device is used only by the *mcDriverDaemon*, is considered the *admin device* and allows for broader functionality such as: Initializing the MCI shared memory (discussed in Sect. 4.2), issuing Yield or SIQ SMC calls, locking shared memory mappings and receiving notifications of interrupts from the Secure World OS. It is important to note that only **one** process may open the *mobicore* device at any point in time: if another process tries to open it, an error will be returned. Usually, the *mcDriverDaemon* opens this device first; however, if the *mcDriverDaemon* process dies for any reason, the next process to open the *mobicore* device will receive *admin* status as far as the kernel module is concerned. This means that an attacker within our attack model (recall Sect. 2.3) can hijack the *mobicore* device and act as the *admin.*

– Register an interrupt handler which receives completion notifications from the Secure World OS. These notifications are forwarded to the active daemon.
– In order to trigger interrupts to the right core (so that Kinibi OS will not discard them), the kernel module starts a dedicated thread which is bound to the core on which the Kinibi OS is running. This thread issues SMC calls requested by other processes.
– Perform additional tasks such as initializing and periodically reading log messages from the Secure World (via a work queue and a dedicated kernel thread), migrating the Secure OS to different CPU cores if needed, managing the World Shared Memory buffers that were registered by the Normal World, handling power management notifications, and suspending/resuming the Secure OS as needed.

4.2 The mcDriverDaemon Process

The *mcDriverDaemon* binary is located within the *system* partition of the device's firmware under */system/bin/mcDriverDaemon*. A version of the daemon source code is available online [36], however we noticed some discrepancies between the online version and the binary on our device (the device probably has a newer version). The binary is executed by *init* at system startup; it immediately opens the */dev/mobicore* device and receives *admin* status. We analyzed this daemon by conducting both static analysis (reading the source code) and dynamic analysis: We killed the original daemon and quickly executed it from a root shell with a LD_PRELOAD directive. This directive injected our library (which is based on *ldpreloadhook* [26]) into the process and allowed us to hook *libc* functions which the daemon is using. These hooks gave us execution traces and raw parameters used by the running daemon, and helped us understand its inner workings. By this method, we identified the following responsibilities:

– Initialize the MobiCore Communication Interface (MCI) through the MobiCore kernel module. This maps a virtual address range in the daemon's memory to a World Shared Memory which is accessible to the Secure OS (in particular to the secure *init*-like process). As mentioned above, this allows the daemon to access the Secure OS API: Opening/Closing Trustlets, Map and Unmap World Shared Memory, Suspend and Resume the Secure OS and more.
– Periodically allow the Secure OS time quanta by calling the Yield or SIQ *ioctl* which the kernel module implements as SMC calls.

– Create and listen on *netlink* and *abstract unix domain* (*"#mcdaemon"*) sockets as servers which act as an interface for other user-land processes. This interface has a defined protocol [34] for serializing requests and responses and implements the following API: General information requests, Open/Close TrustZone device, Open/Close Trustlets (via UUID or sent data), send a Notification to trustlets and register World Shared Memory with Trustlets. A client library is available [33] for other processes to easily use.
– The *mcDriverDaemon* creates an instance of the *File System Daemon* [35] (we omit the details).

In particular, when handling *openSession* commands from Normal World clients the command receives the Trustlet UUID as an argument. The *mcDriverDaemon* then looks for the correct Trustlet to load in the Normal World file system. The daemon has two locations it looks in: */system/app/mcRegistry* (which is a read-only partition and verified at boot by *dm-verity*) and */data/app/mcRegistry* (which is a read-write partition). This request is then passed to the Secure OS which (as mentioned in Sect. 3) verifies the Trustlet's binary structure and signature before loading it into the Secure World.

The ability to load files from the read-write partition was previously exploited [7] to load old versions of trustlets which had vulnerabilities in them; thereby "bringing the attack surface to the device".

4.3   Keystore and Keymaster Hardware Abstraction Layer (HAL)

The Android Keystore system [11], which was introduced in Android 4.3, allows applications to create, store and use cryptographic keys while attempting to make the keys themselves hard to extract from the device. The documentation advertises the following security features:

– Extraction Prevention: The keys themselves are never present in the application's memory space. The applications only know of *key-blobs* which cannot be used by themselves. The *key-blobs* are usually the keys packed with extra meta-data and encrypted with a secret key by the Keymaster HAL. In the Samsung implementation we explored, the keys are bound to the secure hardware controlled by the Kinibi OS, which makes them even harder to extract: the keys themselves never leave the secure hardware unencrypted.
– Key Use Authorizations: The Keystore system allows the application to place restrictions on the generated keys to mitigate the possibility of unauthorized use. Restrictions include the choice of algorithms, padding schemes, and block modes, the temporal validity of the key, or requiring the user to be authenticated for the key to be used.

The Keystore system is implemented in the *keystored* daemon [12], which exposes a binder interface that consists of many key management and cryptographic functions. Under the hood, the *keystored* holds the following responsibilities:

– Expose the binder interface, listen and respond to requests made by applications.

– Manage the application keys. The daemon creates a directory on the filesystem for each application; the key-blobs are stored in files in the application's directory. Each key-blob file is encrypted with a key-blob encryption key (different per application) which is saved as the *masterkey* in the application's directory. The *masterkey* file itself is encrypted when the device is locked, and the encryption employs the user's password and a randomly generated salt to derive the *masterkey* encryption key.
– Relay cryptographic function calls to the Keymaster HAL device (covered below).

The Keymaster hardware abstraction layer (HAL) [10] is an interface between Android's *keystored* and the OEM implementation of a secure-hardware-backed cryptographic module. It requires the OEM to implement several cryptographic functions such as: key generation, init/update/final methods for various cryptographic primitives (public key encryption, symmetric key encryption, and HMAC), key import, public key export and general information requests. The implementation is a library that exports these functions and is implemented by relaying the request to the secure hardware runtime. The secure runtime usually encrypts generated keys with some key-encryption key (which is usually derived by a hardware-backed mechanism). Therefore, the non-secure runtime does not know the actual key that is used, but may still save it in the filesystem and subsequently use it through the Keymaster to invoke cryptographic functions with the key. In practice - this is exactly how the *keystored* daemon uses the Keymaster HAL (with the aforementioned addition of an additional encryption of the key blobs).

An example of the usage of the Keymaster HAL is the Android Full Disk Encryption feature, implemented by the userspace daemon *vold* [13], which uses the Keymaster HAL as part of the key derivation.

4.4 Samsung's Keymaster HAL and Trustlet

Samsung's Keymaster HAL library exposes the aforementioned Keymaster interface and implements its functions by making calls to the Keymaster trustlet (through *mcDriverDaemon*). The trustlet itself has UUID: *ffffffff00000000000000000000003e*, and is located in the system partition (*/system/app/mcRegistry/<UUID>.tlbin*). The Trustlet code handles the following tasks:

– Listen to various requests that are sent over the World Shared Memory and handle them.
– Key generation of RSA/EC, AES and HMAC keys. Keys are generated using random bytes from the OpenSSL FIPS DRBG module, which seeds its entropy either from *keymaster_add_rng_entropy* calls from the Normal World or from a secure PRNG made available by the Secure World Crypto Driver. Key generation requests receive a list of key characteristics (as defined by the Keymaster HAL), which describe the algorithm, padding, block mode

and other restrictions on the key. The generated keys (concatenated with their characteristics) are encrypted by a key-encryption key (**KEK**) which is unique to the Keymaster trustlet. The trustlet receives this key by making an IPC request along with a *constant* salt to a driver which uses a hardware-based cryptographic function to drive the key. The encryption used for key encryption is AES256-GCM128. The GCM IV and authentication tag are concatenated to the encrypted key before being returned to the user as a key blob. Therefore, an attacker that is able to obtain this KEK is able to decrypt all the key blobs stored in the file system—i.e., the KEK can be viewed as the "key to the kingdom", and is our target in the attacks in Sect. 5.

– Execution of cryptographic functions. The trustlet can handle begin/update/ final requests for given keys created by the trustlet. It first decrypts the key-blobs and verifies the authentication tag, then verifies that the key (and the trustlet) supports the requested operation, and then executes it. The cryptographic functions are implemented using the OpenSSL FIPS Object Module [24]. In particular, we discovered that the AES code is a pure ARMv4 assembly implementation that uses a single 1KB T-Table. In general, AES implementations based on T-Tables are vulnerable to cache attacks [25]. However, as we shall see in Sect. 5, mounting the attack in practice is not trivial.

– The trustlet handles requests for key characteristics and requests for information on supported algorithms, block modes, padding schemes, digest modes and import/export formats.

Leaking the KEK Through Vulnerabilities in Other Trustlets. One of the many trustlets created by Samsung to provide secure computations to devices is the OTP trustlet. This trustlet implements a mechanism which creates One Time Passwords on the device. Exploiting a vulnerability in the OTP trustlet discovered by Beniamini [7], we were able to recover the Keymaster KEK. The OTP vulnerability gives us the ability to read and write 4-byte words into arbitrary OTP trustlet memory and branch execution to arbitrary OTP trustlet code. We used these primitives to imitate the way the Keymaster trustlet makes a request to derive the KEK: use the write primitive to fill the request struct and the fixed Keymaster salt (which we discovered via disassembly) into the OTP trustlet memory, then used the branch primitive to call a specific trustlet API function which is available on both the OTP and Keymaster code, and finally we used the read primitive to read the result—the KEK.

We argue that another trustlet's ability to imitate the Keymaster request and receive its KEK is a vulnerability in the API design and, in particular, in the driver that implements this request. Due to the lack of even basic mitigation techniques (ASLR, stack canaries, etc.) in the Kinibi OS and userspace, we believe more vulnerabilities may well be discovered in trustlets in the future. Therefore, critical keys, such as the Keymaster KEK, should be more protected. We propose a simple countermeasure: Have the handler of the key derivation IPC request concatenate the client UUID to the salt; this will prevent different trustlets from deriving the same keys, and then a compromised trustlet will not immediately compromise the Keymaster KEK.

This vulnerability was reported to Samsung (CVE-2018-8774, SVE-2018-11792) on February 2018 and was labeled by Samsung as a "critical vulnerability." It was patched in Samsung's Android security update [30] in June 2018. In Sect. 5 we discuss an attack which aims at recovering the Keymaster key via a cache side-channel without relying on other trustlets being compromised.

5   Attacking the Keymaster Trustlet

Since Secure World computations (such as the AES implementation in the Keymaster trustlet) use the same cache as the Normal World, it is theoretically possible to mount cache attacks against the Secure World. Lipp et al. [16] suggested that the Samsung Galaxy S6 (which is built on the Exynos platform) flushes the cache when entering the TrustZone, thereby making the attack much more difficult. In contrast, we did not see any cache flushing operations when entering the TrustZone: none were present in the sources we reviewed or binaries we disassembled. Moreover, as we shall see, we were able to reliably infer execution information of Trustlets through cache side-channel artifacts. However, we encountered other hurdles. In this section we will discuss our proposed attack model, method and results.

5.1   The Target of the Attack

In our research we focused on recovery of the Keymaster KEK. Recovering this key would lead to compromise of all past, present and future Keystore keys and data encrypted by these keys on the device on which the attack was mounted on. The trustlet uses this key in several request handlers, which include: key generation, *begin* operation on keys and *get_key_characterstics*. Of these three, *get_key_characterstics* does the least amount work that's not related to key encryption; therefore we focused on this request. The request receives a buffer which should hold a key blob that consists of the encrypted key bytes and key characteristics followed by an IV and GCM authentication tag; the trustlet returns the key characteristics serialized in a buffer. Valid key blobs often include over 100 bytes of encrypted data (e.g., 32 key bytes of a stored AES-256 plus many required key characteristics), therefore the request uses the AES-256 block function at least 9 times (2 for initialization and at least 7 subsequent blocks). If we measure cache access effects only after the trustlet completes its work, the 9 block function invocations will induce too much noise and render our attacks infeasible. Therefore, instead we send *invalid* requests: having the key blob hold just one byte, a random IV, and zeros for the authentication tag. Such requests induce the two block function calls for initialization, and a single additional call to decrypt the single byte. The request then fails, therefore we do not have access to any ciphertext; but possibly, side-channel information may leak.

5.2   Challenges in Mounting the Attack

In our attempts at mounting the attack we encountered three major difficulties:
(i) finding the cache sets which correspond to the trustlet's T-Table memory,
(ii) Keymaster request execution times, (iii) facing AutoLock [14] behavior.

Searching for the T-Table. Before a cache attack can be mounted, the cache
sets which correspond to the T-Table need to be identified. Our research suggests
that the secure OS usually resides in either core 0 or 1 - both of them in the
A53 CPU. The A53 CPU in the Galaxy S6 has a 256 KB L2 cache, with 64 byte
cache lines and 16-way associativity; this means it has 256 different cache sets
(8 bits used in set addressing). The index of a cache set is determined by the
physical address of the memory which is being accessed. Because the cache lines
are 64 bytes long, the 6 least significant bits are not used in the index calculation.
Therefore the index calculation uses bits 6 through 13 of the address.

The T-Table used in the AES implementation inside the Keymaster trustlet
is 256 4-byte entries long. We also know (through analysis of the trustlet binary)
that the T-Table resides at virtual address *0x364c8*, so it is misaligned by 8
bytes, which means the T-Table spans 17 cache sets. We learn two things from
this information: (a) the entire T-Table resides in a single page of memory and
(b) that it starts at an offset of *0x4c8* inside the page. Knowing that the entire
table resides in a single page ensures that its cache set indexes are **contiguous**
(if it had spanned two pages, those pages could have been mapped to different
physical pages, resulting in a potential discontinuity).

These points allow us to narrow down the possible cache set containing the
beginning of the T-Table down to 4 options: Recall that the cache set index
calculations use bits 6 through 13 of the physical address. The in-page offset
(bits 0 through 11) of the physical address are equal to those in the virtual
address, which we have. Therefore, only bits 12 and 13 remain unknown and the
only candidates for the cache set index are: $\{19, 83, 147, 211\}$. Because we know
the T-Table cache sets are contiguous, knowing the *beginning* cache set should
give us complete information about the indexes of all the other sets.

A Synchronous Attack. Our initial attempts at discovering the T-Table location in the cache followed the *synchronous* attack model described by Osvik
et al. [25]: *prime* the cache set candidates, call the AES encryption operation
and then *probe* these cache sets and take measurements of the time it took
to access them. Unfortunately, these measurements were too noisy. We noticed
that the time it takes for the requests to complete is very long: 5–10 ms; this is
enough time for many other processes to cause cache activity which taints our
measurements.

An Asynchronous Attack. We then attempted to implement an *asynchronous*
attack model. This technique *primes* and *probes* the cache sets in a loop on a

different core than the one which runs the secure OS. However, these measurements were not helpful either: the 17 contiguous cache sets following the result of the measurements did not present activity as expected of a T-Table. We believe the AutoLock feature described by Green et al. [14], is preventing us from making correct measurements with this approach since it blocks evictions that are induced by cache activity on a different core. Therefore, both attacks we described in this section failed to detect cache access effects that reveal the true cache set index of the T-Table.

5.3   Tracing Trustlet Execution Using Flush+Reload

Lipp et al. [16] also suggested using a *Flush+Reload* attack on ARM CPUs [16], which allows cache side-channel leakage of accesses of other processes to shared memory. While this attack is less relevant to leak information on the trustlet's T-Table, it is relevant to the "TCI memory". TCI memory is World Shared Memory which is accessible by both the Secure World and the Normal World. It is, in fact, a physical memory range which is mapped to virtual addresses in both the Normal World and the Secure World. Because the same underlying physical memory is shared, the *Flush+Reload* attack is relevant in leaking information about accesses to this memory by the Secure World.

Our disassembly of the Keymaster trustlet binary code points to three distinct World Shared Memory regions which are used by the trustlet. The first is the TCI memory itself, which contains the request identifier and pointers to two additional World Shared Memory buffers; the other two are the *input* buffer (filled by the Normal World) and the *output* buffer (filled by the Secure World). Upon receiving notifications of a pending request, the trustlet accesses the TCI memory, copies the relevant information from the input buffer to private memory, executes the request, if the request was successful it fills the output buffer, and finally fills the return code in the TCI memory. Therefore, by monitoring these three addresses with the *Flush+Reload* technique, we expect to see the following hit pattern: TCI → Input → Output(if successful) → TCI. Note that this pattern leaks fairly precise timing information about when the cryptographic operations take place within the 5–10 ms the request takes to complete: AES invocations occur after the input buffer is accessed and before the output buffer is accessed (or before the second TCI access on error).

Indeed, using this method we were able to recover timestamps of these events. Figure 2 shows multiple sets of timestamps recovered through this method. In the scenario illustrated by the figure we sent malformed requests and detected three events: 1st TCI access, Input access and finally a 2nd TCI access. Figure 2 shows the 1st TCI accesses (blue asterisks) happen around 2.5 ms into the measurement. This is followed by the Input access (red dots) about 1.5 ms later—we believe the delay is caused by the IPC requests the trustlet makes before handling the incoming request. Finally, about 30 μs after the Input access, we see the 2nd TCI access (black crosses). During this 30 μs period the encryption, along with the rest of the handler logic, takes place.

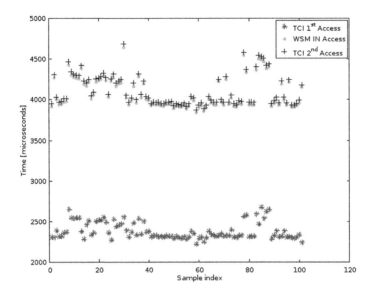

Fig. 2. Keymaster trustlet *world shared memory* (WSM) access timings (Color figure online)

These results strengthen our belief that leaking information from the Secure World is indeed possible through cache side-channel attacks.

5.4   Designing an Improved Attack

Moghimi et al. [17] demonstrated CacheZoom, an attack on Intel's secure execution environment - SGX. They use kernel mode privileges to trigger multiple clock interrupts while a secured computation is executed; these interrupts pause the secure execution and pass control to their kernel code which performs cache measurements with high temporal resolution - resulting in overall high resolution for the attack.

A similar attack is theoretically possible on ARM CPUs, since it would not be susceptible to AutoLock restrictions if it runs on the same core as the secure code. However, the attack as described requires running kernel code, which is outside our attack model (Sect. 2.3). As stated before, running kernel code is extremely difficult on modern devices since loading kernel modules is either disabled or requires OEM signatures. Therefore, we attempted to create an attack that tries to imitate CacheZoom without running kernel code.

We began by binding a single thread to the core which runs the Kinibi OS and let the thread run in a loop that measures time differences between iterations. As long as there is no work pending for the TrustZone, the Kinibi OS does not receive many execution time slices, and so our thread measures small time differences between iterations (under a microsecond). However, when requests are made to the secure OS, we notice considerably higher measurements. Usually these measurements are single gaps of hundreds of microseconds to several

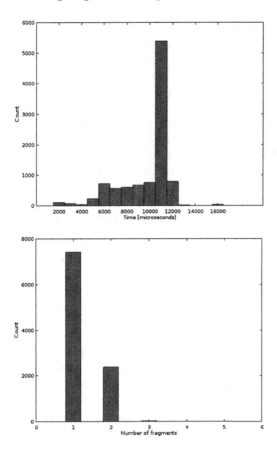

Fig. 3. Kinibi interrupted - measurements from the Normal World. Top: histogram of time difference between successive loop iterations where the difference exceeds 50 μs. Bottom: histogram of number of fragments per TrustZone call.

milliseconds—see Fig. 3 (top). This means that our thread is interrupted and the Secure World is scheduled.

Interestingly, on some occasions we observed more than one "gap fragment" per request; we believe this means that while the Secure World was running, a Normal World interrupt switched to the Linux kernel for handling that interrupt. After handling that interrupt, regular Linux scheduling took place, which first gave our iterating thread a time slice. Some time later, our thread was preempted by the kernel and execution was passed to the kernel thread which is responsible for translating Yield or SIQ requests from the *mcDriverDaemon* (which are periodically queued) to SMC calls. This kernel thread runs on the same core that the secure OS runs on (the secure OS rejects running interrupt handlers on other cores) and therefore our looping thread only resumes after the Secure World work was done or another interrupt is triggered on our core.

In Fig. 3 (bottom) we present the results mentioned above. The figure shows a histogram of the number of "gap fragments" we measured during a single call to the Keymaster. Most of the calls resulted in a single fragment, which means the Secure World was not interrupted; however, about 25% of calls resulted in two or more fragments, which implies that the Secure World was indeed interrupted. We grouped the measurements by those fragments and calculated their **sum**, as shown in the top graph. We see a clear peak around 10 ms—the total time it takes for the TrustZone to complete a request—even if the execution was interrupted and fragmented into two sessions or more. Crucially, we see that our looping thread gets control *while* the Keymaster work is paused, *on the same core*.

This evidence leads us to believe that this phenomenon can be leveraged to mount an attack on TrustZone. Our proposed attack consists of 4 Normal World user-land (EL0) threads:

1. A thread which makes Keymaster requests in a loop from one of the cores that the Kinibi OS is not bound to.
2. A looping thread running on the same core as the Secure World, which *primes* the cache sets and measures time differences between iterations. When a significant time difference is measured, it *probes* the cache sets and saves this measurement.
3. A thread running the *Flush+Reload* attack on the TCI memory, as described in Sect. 5.3 to trace the execution of the Keymaster trustlet as it handles the requests of thread #1. This allows us to select relevant measurements made by thread #2 by discarding *Prime+Probe* measurements made before the input buffer was accessed or after the output buffer (or the second TCI memory) was accessed. Thread #3 must run on a different core than thread #2.
4. A thread responsible for creating as many Normal World interrupts as possible, to increase the likelihood of interrupting the secure execution. Possible methods of doing this include creating network requests, in hope that the network card interrupts will be handled on our target core, or playing a video sequence causing graphic or sound card interrupts.

6   Conclusions

In this paper we provided, for the first time, a critical review of Samsung's proprietary TrustZone architecture. We described the major components and their interconnections, focusing on their security aspects. We discovered that the binary code for the Kinibi operating system runs in ARM32/Thumb mode even though the platform has a 64bit processor, and common OS defenses such as Address Space Randomization (ASLR), non-executable (NX) stack, or stack canaries are lacking. During this review we identified some design weaknesses, including one actual vulnerability.

We also found that the ARM32 assembly-language AES implementation used by the Keymaster trustlet is vulnerable to cache side-channel attacks. In a separate paper we demonstrated successful cache attacks on a real device, against AES-256, on the Keymaster implementation, and presented a technique for mounting side-channel attacks against AES-256 in GCM mode.

Finally, we demonstrated realistic cache attack artifacts on the Keymaster cryptographic functions, despite the recently discovered "AutoLock" ARM feature. We successfully demonstrated cache side-channel effects on "World Shared Memory" buffers, and showed compelling evidence that full-blown cache attacks against the AES implementation inside the Keymaster trustlet are plausible.

We conclude that despite the architectural protections offered by the TrustZone, cache side-channel effects are a serious threat to the current AES implementation. However, side-channel-resistant implementations, that do not use memory accesses for round calculations, do exist for the ARM platform, such as a bit-sliced implementation [23] or one using ARMv8 cryptographic extensions [22]. Using such an implementation would render most cache attacks, including ours, ineffective.

A   End-to-End Keymaster Communication Example

In the following section we describe an example of end-to-end communication between the normal and Secure World, that demonstrates how the entities mentioned above are chained together. In this section, numbers in parenthesis refer to their respective markers in Fig. 1:

1. In the Normal World user-space (NWd EL0), an application issues an encryption request to *keystored* through the *binder* interface (1). The kernel *binder* subsystem relays this request to *keystored*, which receives the request, loads the requested key file (and decrypts it with the relevant *masterkey*, recall Sect. 4.3) and calls the relevant function in the Keymaster HAL interface. Samsung's Keymaster HAL module writes a Keymaster trustlet request to TCI memory (2) and requests a trustlet notification from the *mcDriverDaemon* through the unix domain socket subsystem (3). The *mcDriverDaemon* calls the SIQ ioctl on the *mobicore* device (4).
2. In the Normal World kernel (NWd EL1), the Mobicore Kernel Module handles the ioctl by issuing a SIQ SMC (5).
3. Monitor code (EL3) is triggered to handle the SMC, it is deferred to the Mobicore SMC handler which issues an interrupt to the Kinibi OS and passes execution to it (6).
4. In the Secure World kernel (SWd EL1), the Kinibi OS interrupt handler schedules the *init*-like process and informs it of the interrupt (7).
5. In the Secure World userspace (SWd EL0), the *init*-like process handles the interrupt by sending an IPC message to the Keymaster trustlet (8). The Keymaster trustlet receives the IPC message, reads the TCI memory (9), parses and executes the request (e.g., encryption of data) (10). It then writes the output of the request to the TCI memory (11) and issues an IPC request to the *init*-like process to notify the Normal World (12). The *init*-like process then calls the SIQ SVC system call (13).

6. The Kinibi OS (SWd EL1) handles the SVC call by issuing a Normal World interrupt SMC call (14).
7. Monitor code (EL3) is triggered to handle the SMC, it is deferred to the Mobicore SMC handler which issues an interrupt to the Android Linux kernel and passes execution to it (15).
8. The Android Linux kernel (NWd EL1) interrupt handler is triggered, it calls the interrupt handler that the Mobicore kernel module registered. The Mobicore handler wakes up the *mcDriverDaemon* due to the interrupt (16).
9. Back in the Normal World userspace (NWd EL0), the *mcDriverDaemon* notifies its client of the interrupt through the unix domain socket subsystem (17). The Samsung's Keymaster HAL module receives the interrupt notification, reads and parses the response from TCI memory (18) and resumes the *keystored* function. *keystored* sends a response to the requesting application through the *binder* (19). Finally, the application execution resumes with the result.

References

1. ARM. ARM trusted firmware - firmware design documentation. https://github.com/ARM-software/arm-trusted-firmware/blob/v1.4/docs/firmware-design.rst#aarch64-bl31
2. ARM. ARM trusted firmware - runtime SVC code. https://github.com/ARM-software/arm-trusted-firmware/blob/v1.4/include/common/runtime_svc.h#L60
3. ARM. Building a secure System using TrustZone Technology. http://infocenter.arm.com/help/topic/com.arm.doc.prd29-genc-009492c/PRD29-GENC-009492C_trustzone_security_whitepaper.pdf
4. ARM. ARM trustzone (2018). https://www.arm.com/products/security-on-arm/trustzone
5. Bernstein, D.J.: Cache-timing attacks on AES (2005). https://cr.yp.to/antiforgery/cachetiming-20050414.pdf
6. freddierice. Trident - temporary root for the Galaxy S7 active. https://github.com/freddierice/trident
7. Beniamini, G.: Trust issues: exploiting TrustZone TEEs (2017). https://googleprojectzero.blogspot.co.il/2017/07/trust-issues-exploiting-trustzone-tees.html
8. Ge0n0sis. How to lock the Samsung download mode using an undocumented feature of aboot (2016). https://ge0n0sis.github.io/posts/2016/05/how-to-lock-the-samsung-download-mode-using-an-undocumented-feature-of-aboot/
9. Giesecke & Devrient. Android kernel tree - mobicore kernel module. https://android.googlesource.com/kernel/msm/+/android-msm-shamu-3.10-marshmallow-mr2/drivers/gud/MobiCoreDriver/
10. Google. Android keymaster HAL. https://source.android.com/security/keystore/implementer-ref
11. Google. Android keystore. https://developer.android.com/training/articles/keystore.html
12. Google. Android keystore - source code. http://androidxref.com/6.0.0_r1/xref/system/security/keystore/keystore.cpp

13. Google. Android vold cryptfs. http://androidxref.com/6.0.0_r1/xref/system/vold/cryptfs.c
14. Green, M., Rodrigues-Lima, L., Zankl, A., Irazoqui, G., Heyszl, J., Eisenbarth, T: Autolock: why cache attacks on ARM are harder than you think. In: 26th USENIX Security Symposium (2017)
15. Lapid, B., Wool, A.: Cache-attacks on the ARM TrustZone implementations of AES-256 and AES-256-GCM via GPU-based analysis. Cryptology ePrint Archive, Report 2018/621 (2018). http://eprint.iacr.org/2018/621
16. Lipp, M., Gruss, D., Spreitzer, R., Maurice, C., Mangard, S.: ARMageddon: cache attacks on mobile devices. In: USENIX Security Conference (2016). https://www.usenix.org/system/files/conference/usenixsecurity16/sec16_paper_lipp.pdf
17. Moghimi, A., Irazoqui, G., Eisenbarth, T.: CacheZoom: how SGX amplifies the power of cache attacks. In: Fischer, W., Homma, N. (eds.) CHES 2017. LNCS, vol. 10529, pp. 69–90. Springer, Cham (2017). https://doi.org/10.1007/978-3-319-66787-4_4
18. nccgroup. Cachegrab. https://github.com/nccgroup/cachegrab
19. Neve, M., Seifert, J.-P.: Advances on access-driven cache attacks on AES. In: Biham, E., Youssef, A.M. (eds.) SAC 2006. LNCS, vol. 4356, pp. 147–162. Springer, Heidelberg (2007). https://doi.org/10.1007/978-3-540-74462-7_11
20. Neve, M., Tiri, K.: On the complexity of side-channel attacks on AES-256 - methodology and quantitative results on cache attacks. Technical report (2007). https://eprint.iacr.org/2007/318
21. Artenstein, N., Goldman, G.: Exploiting android s-boot: getting arbitrary code exec in the Samsung bootloader (2017). http://hexdetective.blogspot.co.il/2017/02/exploiting-android-s-boot-getting.html
22. OpenSSL. ARM AES implementation using cryptographic extensions. https://github.com/openssl/openssl/blob/master/crypto/aes/asm/aesv8-armx.pl
23. OpenSSL. ARMv7 AES bit sliced implementation. https://github.com/openssl/openssl/blob/master/crypto/aes/asm/bsaes-armv7.pl
24. OpenSSL. OpenSSL FIPS. https://www.openssl.org/docs/fips.html
25. Osvik, D.A., Shamir, A., Tromer, E.: Cache attacks and countermeasures: the case of AES. In: Pointcheval, D. (ed.) CT-RSA 2006. LNCS, vol. 3860, pp. 1–20. Springer, Heidelberg (2006). https://doi.org/10.1007/11605805_1
26. Oliva, P.: ldpreloadhook. https://github.com/poliva/ldpreloadhook
27. Qualcomm. Snapdragon security (2018). https://www.qualcomm.com/solutions/mobile-computing/features/security
28. Samsung. Mobile processor: Exynos 7 Octa (7420) (2018). http://www.samsung.com/semiconductor/minisite/exynos/products/mobileprocessor/exynos-7-octa-7420/
29. Samsung. Platform security (2018). http://developer.samsung.com/tech-insights/knox/platform-security
30. Samsung. Android security updates, June 2018. https://security.samsungmobile.com/securityUpdate.smsb
31. Spreitzer, R., Plos, T.: Cache-access pattern attack on disaligned AES T-tables. In: Prouff, E. (ed.) COSADE 2013. LNCS, vol. 7864, pp. 200–214. Springer, Heidelberg (2013). https://doi.org/10.1007/978-3-642-40026-1_13
32. Trustonic. Trustonic Kinibi technology. https://developer.trustonic.com/discover/technology
33. Trustonic. Trustonic mobicore driver daemon - client library. https://github.com/Trustonic/trustonic-tee-user-space/tree/master/MobiCoreDriverLib/ClientLib

34. Trustonic. Trustonic mobicore driver daemon - command header. https://github. com/Trustonic/trustonic-tee-user-space/blob/master/MobiCoreDriverLib/ Daemon/public/MobiCoreDriverCmd.h
35. Trustonic. Trustonic mobicore driver daemon - FSD. https://github.com/ Trustonic/trustonic-tee-user-space/tree/master/MobiCoreDriverLib/Daemon/ FSD
36. Trustonic. Trustonic mobicore driver daemon - source code. https://github.com/ Trustonic/trustonic-tee-user-space/tree/master/MobiCoreDriverLib/Daemon
37. Xinjie, Z., Tao, W., Dong, M., Yuanyuan, Z., Zhaoyang, L.: Robust first two rounds access driven cache timing attack on AES. In: 2008 International Conference on Computer Science and Software Engineering, vol. 3, pp. 785–788. IEEE (2008)
38. Zhang, N., Sun, K., Shands, D., Lou, W., Thomas Hou, Y.: TruSpy: cache side-channel information leakage from the secure world on ARM devices. IACR Cryptology ePrint Archive, 2016(980) (2016)

Combination of Hardware and Software: An Efficient AES Implementation Resistant to Side-Channel Attacks on All Programmable SoC

Jingquan Ge[1,2,3], Neng Gao[2,3], Chenyang Tu[2,3(✉)], Ji Xiang[2,3], Zeyi Liu[2,3], and Jun Yuan[1,2,3]

[1] School of Cyber Security, University of Chinese Academy of Sciences, Beijing, China
[2] State Key Laboratory of Information Security, Institute of Information Engineering, CAS, Beijing, China
{gejingquan,gaoneng,tuchenyang,xiangji,liuzeyi,yuanjun}@iie.ac.cn
[3] DACAS, CAS, Beijing, China

Abstract. With the rapid development of IoT devices in the direction of multifunction and personalization, All Programmable SoC has been used more and more frequently because of its unrivaled levels of system performance, flexibility, and scalability. On the other hand, this type of SoC faces a growing range of security threats. Among these threats, cache timing attacks and power/elctromagnetic analysis attacks are two considerable ones which have been widely studied. Although many countermeasures have been proposed to resist these two types of attacks, most of them can only withstand a single type but are often incapable when facing multi-type attacks. In this paper, we utilize the special architecture of All Programmable SoC to implement a secure AES encryption scheme which can efficiently resist both cache timing and power/electromagnetic analysis attacks. The AES implementation has a beginning software stage, a middle hardware stage and a final software stage. Operations in software and start/end round of hardware are all randomized, which allow our implementation to withstand two types of attacks. To illustrate the security of the implementation, we conduct the three types of attacks on unprotected software/hardware AES, shuffled software AES and our scheme. Furthermore, we use Test Vector Leakage Assessment (TVLA) to test their security on encryption times and power/electromagnetic traces. The final result indicates that our encryption implementation achieves a high secure level with almost 0.86 times data throughput of the shuffled software AES implementation.

Keywords: All Programmable SoC · Side channel attack
AES implementation · Combination of hardware and software · TVLA

© Springer Nature Switzerland AG 2018
J. Lopez et al. (Eds.): ESORICS 2018, LNCS 11098, pp. 197–217, 2018.
https://doi.org/10.1007/978-3-319-99073-6_10

1 Introduction

In recent years, with the rapid development of Internet of Things (IoT), all kinds of IoT devices flood the market, which has greatly changed people's life style. Meanwhile, as market demand changes, the functions of IoT system are becoming more and more powerful, complex and personalized. All Programmable SoC, which combines ARM with FPGA, creates new possibilities for IoT systems, giving system architects and ARM developers a flexible platform to satisfy customer personal demands [1]. The proliferation of IoT devices brings comfort and convenience to humans, but it also allows more sensitive data to be stored on IoT devices or transmitted through the Internet. Therefore, the security of the sensitive data usage and transmission in IoT raise concerns.

Cryptography is one of the most common methods to solve security problems, and IoT devices are no exception. Modern cryptographic algorithms are considered secure from a mathematical theoretical view point. Nevertheless, weaknesses of these algorithms become easy to be exploited when they are implemented in real-world devices. These attacks, which get far more private information from the real-world implementation of cryptography, earn their well-known name as "Side Channel Attacks (SCA)". Attackers utilize characteristics such as running time [2,3], cache behavior [4], power consumption [5] and electromagnetic radiation [6] to extract secret keys from the physical executions of encryption algorithms. Among these attacks, cache timing attacks and power/electromagnetic analysis attacks are two well-developed types of attacks which have been widely studied by researchers.

Cache timing attacks utilize the difference in access times between cache and main memory to crack secret keys from the encryption time data. Kocher first proposed the concept of cache timing attacks [2]. Subsequently, Bernstein et al. performed a successful cache timing attack on the AES T-table implementation running on the PC [7]. In recent years, with the popularity of smart devices, many researchers conducted cache timing attack experiments on ARM [8–10]. Power/electromagnetic analysis attacks exploit power consumption/electromagnetic radiation to extract secret keys. In the past 20 years, a large number of researchers have devoted themselves to the research of power/electromagnetic analysis attacks. There are plenty of published results of power/electromagnetic analysis attacks on 8-bit microprocessor, FPGA, ARM, Intel/AMD processor and so on [5,6,11–14].

To thwart SCA, plenty of countermeasures have been proposed, e.g. masking [15–18], relying on the addition of random delays [19], shuffling the execution order of independent operations [20–23] and so on. Among these countermeasures, masking is the most common one. However, both the software and hardware overheads of masking are very costly. Moreover, due to the presence of glitches, the hardware masking's defense ability may be greatly reduced. Another countermeasure is adding random delays, which will increase the huge time overhead. What's more, it is easy to remove the noise of random delays with a simple preprocessing program. The third countermeasure is shuffling the execution order of independent operations. It is an appropriate countermeasure which can greatly increase power/electromagnetic noise by adding acceptable time overhead. More importantly, most of the countermeasures can only withstand a single type of side channel attacks. When facing multi-type attacks, they are usually powerless.

In addition to the above mentioned, most countermeasures use chips of widely used architectures as implementation platforms, such as 8-bit microprocessor, FPGA, ARM, Intel/AMD processor and so on. It is still a blank research field to implement schemes on the special architecture of All Programable SoC, which combines software (ARM) with hardware (FPGA). How to use it to create a more efficient and safe encryption implementation is an interesting and promising research topic.

In this paper, we introduce an AES implementation with combination of software and hardware which executed on an All Programmable SoC (Zynq-7000) and improves both the security and performance. Our main contributions are as follows:

- We propose a new encryption solution with combination of hardware and software that breaks the regularity and alignment pattern of time data and power/electromagnetic traces. By randomizing the start and end round of hardware and software stage, our scheme destroys the statistical regularity of encryption time data due to the use of cache. Meanwhile, shuffling the software execution order and randomizing hardware start round destroys the trace alignment that power/electromagnetic analysis attacks depend on. Therefore, our implementation can resist both cache timing attacks and power/electromagnetic analysis attacks. It can be used not only in AES encryption implementation, but also in many other encryption algorithms. It presents a new way to improve resistance of modern cryptographic algorithm against side channel attacks.
- To improve the data throughput of our implementation, we test the performance of the AXI-GP, AXI-HP and AXI-ACP interfaces separately on the All Programmable SoC. Finally, we choose the fastest AXI-GP interface as the data transmission channel between software and hardware for real-time and small-batch data encryption. The experimental results show that our AES implementation achieves 0.86 times data throughput of shuffled software AES implementation. The performance loss of our scheme is acceptable, especially when considering that shuffled AES implementation can only resist power/electromagnetic attacks and our scheme is equally effective against both cache timing and power/electromagnetic attacks.
- We utilize the Test Vector Leakage Assessment (TVLA) methodology to evaluate the side channel leakage of the encryption time data of three implementations. To the best of our knowledge, it is the first work to evaluate the encryption time data by the TVLA methodology. We get a clear TVLA comparison of three implementations with only 10000 samples of encryption time data each. It proves that TVLA method is very fast and effective to evaluate encryption time data.

This paper is organized as follows. Section 2 presents an overview of Zynq-7000 SoC, side channel attacks, countermeasures and TVLA. Section 3 describes our AES implementation with combination of hardware and software. Section 4 shows the results of cache timing and power/electromagnetic attacks and the TVLA leakages of encryption time data and power/electromagnetic traces. This paper ends with conclusions and discussion in Sect. 5.

2   Background and Related Work

In this section, we first elaborate the required preliminaries of Xilinx All Programmable SoC and AES, then discuss the related work of side channel attacks, countermeasures against side channel attacks and TVLA assessment method.

2.1   All Programmable SoC (Zynq-7000)

The Zynq-7000 family utilizes the Xilinx All Programmable SoC (AP SoC) architecture, which is a very creative and attractive framework. A feature-rich dual or single-core ARM Cortex-A9 MPCore based processing system (PS) and Xilinx programmable logic (PL) are grouped together into a single device. The heart of the PS is the ARM Cortex-A9 MPCore CPUs. Beyond that, PS also includes on-chip memory, external memory interfaces, and a rich set of I/O peripherals [24]. The Zynq-7000 family provide not only the performance, power, and usability of ASIC and ASSPs (Application Specific Standard Products), but also the flexibility and scalability of an FPGA. As a result, the devices of the Zynq-7000 family can be designed more freely to meet diversified and personalized applications in IoT systems.

2.2   Software and Hardware Implementations of AES

In 2001, Rijndael, which designed by J. Daemen and V. Rijmen, was specified as the Advanced Encryption Standard (AES) by the National Institute of Standards and Technology (NIST) [25]. Nowadays, it has become one of the most popular encryption algorithms and widely adopted for a variety of encryption needs. The AES algorithm is a symmetric block cipher, and several rounds of processing convert each 128-bit block. There are three different key sizes: 128 bits, 192 bits, or 256 bits, which correspond to 10 rounds, 12 rounds, or 14 rounds, respectively. For simplicity and without loss of generality, we discuss the AES implementation with a key length of 128 bits and hence 10 rounds in this paper.

AES is an iterated algorithm: Each round i takes an intermediate value series of 16 bytes $S^i = \{s^i_0, ..., s^i_{15}\}$ and a round key series of 16 bytes $RK^i = \{rk^i_0, ..., rk^i_{15}\}$ as inputs, and outputs a 16-byte intermediate value series $S^{i+1} = \{s^{i+1}_0, ..., s^{i+1}_{15}\}$. There are four algebraic operations in one round, which are called SubBytes, ShiftRows, MixColumns, and AddRoundKey. Before the first round, The input block are computed as $s^1_j = p_j \oplus rk^0_j$ where $j \in \{0, \cdots, 15\}$, with p_j representing the jth plaintext byte and rk^0_j the jth initial round key byte. And the last round omits the algebraic operation of Mix-Columns. Except the last round, all rounds have the same four steps, and each round i uses a different round key RK^i.

Software implementations of the AES usually utilize look-up tables to reduce the computational overhead. All the three operations (SubBytes, ShiftRows and MixColumns) are combined into the four look-up tables T_0, T_1, T_2, T_3, each of which consists of 256 4-byte elements and maps one byte of input to four bytes of output. The encryption round of AES software implementation using look-up tables is carried out as:

$$(s_0^{i+1}, s_1^{i+1}, s_2^{i+1}, s_3^{i+1}) = T_0[s_0^i] \oplus T_1[s_5^i] \oplus T_2[s_{10}^i] \oplus T_3[s_{15}^i] \oplus \{rk_0^i, rk_1^i, rk_2^i, rk_3^i\},$$
$$(s_4^{i+1}, s_5^{i+1}, s_6^{i+1}, s_7^{i+1}) = T_0[s_4^i] \oplus T_1[s_9^i] \oplus T_2[s_{14}^i] \oplus T_3[s_3^i] \oplus \{rk_4^i, rk_5^i, rk_6^i, rk_7^i\},$$
$$(s_8^{i+1}, s_9^{i+1}, s_{10}^{i+1}, s_{11}^{i+1}) = T_0[s_8^i] \oplus T_1[s_{13}^i] \oplus T_2[s_2^i] \oplus T_3[s_7^i] \oplus \{rk_8^i, rk_9^i, rk_{10}^i, rk_{11}^i\},$$
$$(s_{12}^{i+1}, s_{13}^{i+1}, s_{14}^{i+1}, s_{15}^{i+1}) = T_0[s_{12}^i] \oplus T_1[s_1^i] \oplus T_2[s_6^i] \oplus T_3[s_{11}^i] \oplus \{rk_{12}^i, rk_{13}^i, rk_{14}^i, rk_{15}^i\}.$$
$$\tag{1}$$

Using the method of table lookups and 16 bytes XOR, the round calculation running in software can be very fast and easy to implement. However, the large look-up tables makes the AES highly vulnerable to cache attacks, such as cache timing attack.

For hardware implementations of AES, there are three major types of schemes to meet different needs. The first type of AES designs focuses on higher data throughput with limited number of architectural optimizations, which resulted in poor resource utilization. Another part of researchers pursues better utilization of FPGA resources with suitable encryption speeds to support most of the embedded applications. The third kind of designers try their best to reduce the power consumption of AES circuits. Like AES software implementations, hardware implementations also leak side channel information, thus are vulnerable to side channel attacks.

2.3   Side Channel Attacks

Cache Timing Attacks. Between the CPU and main memory, there is a small, fast storage area which is called "cache". In order to reduce the latency of main memory accesses, CPUs employ caches to store the most frequently accessed memory locations. When CPU looks up values in main memory, CPU will store the values in the cache, where old values will be evicted from the cache. After that, lookups to the same memory address can get the data faster from the cache than main memory, which has a well-known name called "cache hit". The secret key can be recovered through the exploitation of the execution time of a cryptographic algorithm due to different access times in the memory hierarchy.

Kocher demonstrated timing attacks against a variety of software public-key systems in 1996 [2], who also proposed the concept of cache-behaviour analysis in that paper. Kelsey et al. [26] later suggested the exploitation of information leaked through cache-memory access times as a potential attack against cryptographic implementations that employ large S-boxes. With the rapid development of AES implementations, researchers pay more attention on the cache attacks against this symmetric cipher. Bernstein [7] exploited the total execution time of AES T-table implementations and showed that such an attack can be mounted remotely.

Researches mentioned above were launched successfully on Intel or AMD CPUs. On the other hand, in recent years, due to the wide-spread usage of ARM, the investigation on this type of CPU has increased. Bogdanov *et al.* proposed a type of cache-collision timing attacks on software implementations of AES running on an ARM9 board in 2010 [8]. Two years later, Weiß *et al.* demonstrated their cache timing attack on an ARM Cortex-A8 processor, who extracted sensitive keying material from an isolated trusted execution domain [9]. In 2013, Spreitzer investigated the applicability of Bernstein's timing attack and the cache-collision attack by Bogdanov *et al.* on three mobile devices, all of which employed the ARM Cortex-A CPU [10].

Power and Electromagnetic Analysis Attacks. Power analysis attacks exploit information leaked through power consumption to recover secret keys from implementations of different cryptographic algorithms. Kocher *et al.* examined Simple Power Analysis (SPA) and Differential Power Analysis (DPA) to find secret keys from cryptographic devices in 1999 [5]. Since then, power analysis attack has become a well-known and thoroughly studied threat for cryptographic implementations. In 2004, Brier *et al.* first proposed Correlation Power Analysis (CPA) attack which was more efficient than traditional DPA attack [12]. Not long after, Mangard *et al.* showed that the unmasked and masked AES hardware implementations leaked side channel information due to glitches at the output of logic gates [13].

As the name suggests, electromagnetic (EM) analysis attacks extract the secret key by exploiting data dependent EM radiations. Gandolfi *et al.* describes their electromagnetic experiments conducted on three different CMOS chips, executing three different cryptographic algorithms [6]. Agrawal *et al.* presented a systematic investigation of electromagnetic (EM) leakage from CMOS devices [11]. In 2015, Longo investigated the electromagnetic-based leakage of a complex ARM-Core SoC [14].

2.4   Countermeasures Against Side Channel Attacks

To thwart side channel attacks, researchers proposed many different countermeasures such as masking, the use of random delays and shuffling. Among the existing countermeasures, the most widely deployed one is masking [15–18]. Masking conceals all sensitive intermediate values of a computation with at least one random value. However, the cost of implementing masking increases significantly either in hardware or in software. What's more, because of the presence of glitches, masked hardware implementations can still be vulnerable to first-order DPA [13,27]. Another countermeasure is the use of random delays. Tunstall *et al.* proposed a manner of generating random delays, which reduced the time lost, while maintaining the increased desynchronization [19].

Shuffling the execution order of independent operations is a lightweight countermeasure which can amplify the power/EM noise. Herbst *et al.* described an efficient AES software implementation resistant against side channel attacks, which masked the intermediate results and shuffled the operation order at the beginning and the end of the AES execution [20]. Rivain *et al.* designed a new scalable scheme which combined high-order masking with shuffling [21]. Veyrat-Charvillon *et al.* showed a careful information theoretic and security analysis of different shuffling variants [22]. Patranabis *et al.* proposed a two-round version of the shuffling countermeasure, and tested its security using TVLA [23].

2.5   Test Vector Leakage Assessment (TVLA)

The huge threat of side channel attacks promoted NIST to organize the "Non-Invasive Attack Testing Workshop" in 2011 to establish a testing methodology which can reliably assess the physical security vulnerabilities of encryption devices. Existing assessment methods require the evaluation labs to actually check the feasibility of the state-of-the-art attacks conducted on the device under test (DUT) [28]. However, these assessment methods are very time-consuming, and the technical threshold is very high.

Goodwill et al. proposed a method (at the workshop mentioned above) that is more widely applicable and easier to implement, known as the Test Vector Leakage Assessment (TVLA) [29]. In 2015, Schneider and Moradi provided a further detail of the TVLA method [28]. TVLA uses a t-test to assess whether there is a significant difference in distribution between the groups of collected data. This method provides a robust test that can be applied to multiple types of data and intermediate values. TVLA has been first utilized to determine if the power consumption of a device relates to the data it is manipulating [29]. In fact, this method is also very effective in the assessment of the leakage of encryption time data, which will be shown in Sect. 4 of this paper.

3   AES Implementation with Combination of Hardware and Software

This section explores our AES implementation with combination of hardware and software on an Xilinx Zynq-7000 All Programmable SoC. This AES countermeasure aims to be robust against both cache timing attacks and power/electromagnetic analysis attacks, while keep performances and complexity close to unprotected AES design. We first describe the entire encryption data flow of our AES design in Sect. 3.1. In Sect. 3.2, we show the detailed description of software and hardware stages. Finally, we introduce the communication between software and hardware in Sect. 3.3.

3.1   Encryption Data Flow

The AES implementation use two random numbers R_1 and R_2 to divide the AES encryption process into three stages. Figure 1 shows the entire encryption data flow of our AES implementation with combination of hardware and software. The first and last stage run in software of PS (ARM) and the middle stage runs in

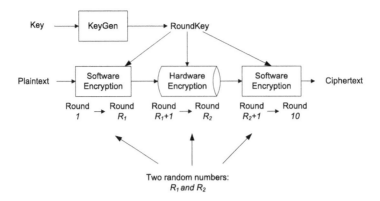

Fig. 1. Entire encryption data flow of AES implementation with combination of hardware and software.

hardware of PL (FPGA). In each round of the two software stages, the execution order of independent operations is shuffled by the two random numbers R_1 and R_2. Furthermore, the middle hardware stage has a random beginning (Round $R_1 + 1$) and a random end (Round R_2). The entire encryption process can be completed in a random time controlled by the two random numbers R_1 and R_2. All the 44 bytes round keys are pre-computed and given to the software and hardware.

3.2   Software and Hardware Stages

In each round of the beginning and final software stages, a set of sensitive operations are shuffled in terms of their execution order to amplify the noise of device power/electromagnetic leakage. As described in Eq. 1, we can divide the software AES encryption round (using look-up tables) into 4 independent operations. And which operation run first doesn't make any difference to the final result. In our AES implementation, we utilize the two random numbers R_1 and R_2 to shuffle the execution order of the 4 independent operations.

We use $s_{j,k,u,w}^i$ denotes the values of s_j^i, s_k^i, s_u^i and s_w^i. The number $R_1\%4$ decides which 4-byte intermediate value will be calculated first. If $R_1\%4 == 0$, the implementation first calculate the 4-byte values of $s_{0,1,2,3}^i$. When $R_1\%4 == 1$, $s_{4,5,6,7}^i$ will be computed first. Another number $R_2\%3$ controls the second operation and $(R_2-R_1)\%2$ corresponds to the third. For example, if $R_1\%4 == 2$, $s_{8,9,10,11}^i$ are computed first. Three 4-byte values of $s_{0,1,2,3}^i$, $s_{4,5,6,7}^i$ and $s_{12,13,14,15}^i$ are left. Then the implementation check the value of $R_2\%3$. If $R_2\%3 == 1$, the values of $s_{4,5,6,7}^i$ will be computed. Meanwhile $s_{0,1,2,3}^i$ and $s_{12,13,14,15}^i$ are left. Then the implementation check the value of $(R_2 - R_1)\%2$. If $(R_2 - R_1)\%2 == 0$, $s_{0,1,2,3}^i$ will be computed. Otherwise the implementation will calculate $s_{12,13,14,15}^i$ before $s_{0,1,2,3}^i$. The rest may be deduced by analogy. The algorithm running in the beginning software stage is described in Algorithm 1.

Algorithm 1. The beginning software stage

Input: 16-byte plaintext: $P = \{p_0, \cdots, p_{15}\}$;
11*16-byte round key: $RK^i = \{rk_0^i, \ldots, rk_{15}^i\}$, where $i \in \{0, \cdots, 10\}$;
2 random numbers: R_1 and R_2;

Output: 16-byte round R_1 output value: $Sout^{R_1} = \{sout_0^{R_1}, \cdots, sout_{15}^{R_1}\}$;

1 /* $S^i = \{s_0^i, \cdots, s_{15}^i\}$ is 16-bytes round i intermediate value.

2 $s_{j,k,u,w}^i$ denotes values of s_j^i, s_k^i, s_u^i and s_w^i. */;

3 $S^1 = P \oplus RK^0$;

4 **for** $i = 1$ to R_1 **do**

5   **if** $R_1\%4 == 0$ **then**

6   compute the values of $s_{0,1,2,3}^{i+1}$;

7   **if** $R_2\%3 == 0$ **then**

8   compute the values of $s_{4,5,6,7}^{i+1}$;

9   **if** $(R_2 - R_1)\%2 == 0$ **then**

10   compute the values of $s_{8,9,10,11}^{i+1}$;

11   compute the values of $s_{12,13,14,15}^{i+1}$;

12   **end**

13   **else**

14   compute the values of $s_{12,13,14,15}^{i+1}$;

15   compute the values of $s_{8,9,10,11}^{i+1}$;

16   **end**

17   **end**

18   **else if** $R_2\%3 == 1$ **then**

19   compute the values of $s_{8,9,10,11}^{i+1}$;

20   operations depending on $(R_2 - R_1)\%2$;

21   **end**

22   **else**

23   compute the values of $s_{12,13,14,15}^{i+1}$;

24   operations depending on $(R_2 - R_1)\%2$;

25   **end**

26   **end**

27   **else if** $R_1\%4 == 1$ **then**

28   compute the values of $s_{4,5,6,7}^{i+1}$;

29   operations depending on $R_2\%3$ and $(R_2 - R_1)\%2$;

30   **end**

31   **else if** $R_1\%4 == 2$ **then**

32   compute the values of $s_{8,9,10,11}^{i+1}$;

33   operations depending on $R_2\%3$ and $(R_2 - R_1)\%2$;

34   **end**

35   **else**

36   compute the values of $s_{12,13,14,15}^{i+1}$;

37   operations depending on $R_2\%3$ and $(R_2 - R_1)\%2$;

38   **end**

39 **end**

40 $Sout^{R_1} = S^{R_1}$;

Algorithm 2. The middle hardware stage

Input: 16-byte round R_1 intermediate value: $S^{R_1} = \{s_0^{R_1}, \cdots, s_{15}^{R_1}\}$;
11*16-byte round key: $RK^i = \{rk_0^i, \ldots, rk_{15}^i\}$, where $i \in \{0, \cdots, 10\}$;
2 random numbers: R_1 and R_2;
Output: 16-byte round R_2 output value: $Sout^{R_2} = \{sout_0^{R_2}, \cdots, sout_{15}^{R_2}\}$;
1 /* $S^i = \{s_0^i, \cdots, s_{15}^i\}$ is 16-bytes round i intermediate value. */;
2 **for** $i = (R_1 + 1)$ *to* $(R_2 - 1)$ **do**
3 | $S^{i+1} = MixColumns(ShiftRows(SubBytes(S^i))) \oplus RK^i$;
4 **end**
5   /* dummy rounds */
6 **for** $i = R_2$ *to* $(R_1 + 10)$ **do**
7 | $S^{i+1} = S^i$;
8 **end**
9 $Sout^{R_2} = S^{R_2}$;

Algorithm 3. The final software stage

Input: 16-bytes round R_2 intermediate value: $S^{R_2} = \{s_0^{R_2}, \cdots, s_{15}^{R_2}\}$;
11*16-bytes round key: $RK^i = \{rk_0^i, \ldots, rk_{15}^i\}$, where $i \in \{0, \cdots, 10\}$;
2 random numbers: R_1 and R_2;
Output: 16-bytes Ciphertext: $C = \{c_0, \cdots, c_{15}\}$;
1 /* $S^i = \{s_0^i, \cdots, s_{15}^i\}$ is 16-bytes round i intermediate value. */;
2 **for** $i = R_2$ *to* 10 **do**
        | /* Here are the same operations as Algorithm 1. */;

        | operations depending on $R_1\%4$, $R_2\%3$ and $(R_2 - R_1)\%2$;
3 **end**
4 $C = S^{10}$;

After the beginning software stage, 16-byte round R_1 intermediate value S^{R_1} will be transferred to the middle hardware stage. As Algorithm 2 shows, the middle hardware stage starts at round $R_1 + 1$ and ends at round $R_1 + 10$. It should be noted that the output value $Sout^{R_2}$ has been calculated at round $R_2 - 1$. We add round R_2 to round $R_1 + 10$ as dummy rounds. The dummy rounds are applied to make sure that attackers can't predict the number of encryption rounds in the middle hardware stage by power/electromagnetic traces. When the middle hardware stage is complete, 16-byte round R_2 intermediate value S^{R_2} will be sent to the final software stage as input. The 4 independent operations of each round are shuffled the same as the beginning software stage, see Algorithm 3.

3.3 Communication Between Software and Hardware

On the Zynq-7000 SoC, there are three types of interfaces between PS (ARM) and PL (FPGA), which are AXI-ACP, AXI-GP and AXI-HP. AXI-GP interfaces are connected directly to the ports of the master interconnect and the slave interconnect without any additional FIFO buffering. AXI-HP interfaces provide PL bus masters with high bandwidth datapaths to the DDR and OCM memories. AXI-ACP interface provides low-latency access to programmable logic masters, with optional coherency with L1 and L2 cache [24]. In order to choose the fastest interface under conditions of real-time data encryption, we tested the performance of the three types of interfaces separately.

From the perspective of the data transmission rate between hardware and software, AXI-HP and AXI-ACP are faster than AXI-GP interfaces. Therefore we first tested the AXI-HP and AXI-ACP interfaces. We apply the AXI-DMA IP core to utilize the AXI-HP and AXI-ACP interfaces. To speed up the encryption process, we enable the cache of the ARM cores. However, it will bring up two problems. First, calculated data may not be immediately sent to DDR memory, but temporarily stored in cache. Second, ARM cores can't be notified immediately that the data in DDR memory has been changed by AXI-DMA IP core. To solve this two problems, we apply the function $Xil\_DCacheFlushRange$ to flush the Dcache before AXI-DMA transferring data from software to hardware. Furthermore we run the function $Xil\_DCacheInvalidateRange$ to invalidate the Dcache after AXI-DMA moving data from hardware to software.

We then tested the performance of AXI-GP interface and got an unexpected result. Since the structure and timing of AXI-GP interface are simple, it is possible to increase the transmission rate by increasing the clock frequency. Moreover, because the data of software is directly from cache of ARM cores, it can save a lot of time to operate the cache ($Xil\_DCacheFlushRange$ and $Xil\_DCacheInvalidateRange$).

In the experiment, we found that for non-real-time bulk data encryption, using AXI-HP and AXI-ACP interfaces to transfer data is much faster than AXI-GP interface. However, for real-time and small-batch data encryption (128 bits at a time), AXI-GP is faster than AXI-HP and AXI-ACP. Table 1 shows the experimental results of the three interfaces for real-time and small-batch data encryption. Considering that our AES encryption implementation is mainly

Table 1. Performance of three interfaces for real-time and small-batch data encryption

AES implementation	PL clock frequency (MHz)	Average encryption time (clock)
AES implementation with combination of hardware and software (AXI-GP)	175	1653
AES implementation with combination of hardware and software (AXI-HP)	125	1853
AES implementation with combination of hardware and software (AXI-ACP)	125	1865

applied to real-time and small-batch data encryption scenarios, we choose the AXI-GP interface to transfer data between hardware and software.

4   Experimental Evaluation

To validate the security of our proposed AES countermeasure, we have implemented our AES design on the ZedBoard and applied cache timing and power/electromagnetic analysis attacks on it. Furthermore, the Test Vector Leakage Assessment (TVLA) tests [28] have been executed on encryption times and power/electromagnetic traces.

4.1   Cache Timing Attacks

In general, there are three types of cache attacks: trace driven, access driven and time driven attacks. Attacks presented in this paper belong to the class of the time driven attacks, so called cache timing attacks. An enormous amount of encryption samples are needed compared to the other two types of cache attacks. However, because time driven attack is the easiest option to launch, it is a huge threat to numerous real-world applications, especially to embedded and IoT systems.

In our cache timing attack experiments, we first obtain the total encryption time data of each 128-bits plaintext which is influenced by cache hits and cache misses. Then we apply two statistical methodologies (first round and final round) to extract key-related information. Finally, we give the TVLA result on encryption time data.

First Round Attacks. Modern CPUs do not store individual bytes in cache but groups of bytes from consecutive "lines" of main memory. Different CPUs have different cache line sizes. The target of our attacks is the ARM Cortex-A9 MPCore of Zynq-7000 AP SoC, which have a fixed cache line length of 32 bytes [30]. The element size of AES tables (T_0, T_1, T_2, and T_3) is 4 bytes. We use δ to denote the number of table elements in one cache line. So groups of δ ($32/4 = 8$) table elements share a line in the cache on a ARM Cortex-A9 MPCore.

For any bytes s and s' which are equal ignoring the lower $\log_2 \delta$ bits, looking up address s will take both address s and s' into cache. We represent this as $\langle s \rangle = \langle s' \rangle$. When two separate lookups s and s' satisfy $\langle s \rangle = \langle s' \rangle$, a "cache collision" occurs. On the contrary, if $\langle s \rangle \neq \langle s' \rangle$, the access to s' may result in a cache miss. On the average, the second situation will take more time because it will require a second cache lookup.

The first round attack utilized cache collisions evoked in the first round of encryption. As can be seen in Eq. 1, table T_0 uses the bytes s_0^1, s_4^1, s_8^1, s_{12}^1 in the first round. They make up a 4-bytes "family" which are used to access the same table. Three other families of 4-bytes share the tables T_1, T_2, and T_3 in round one. Two bytes s_k^1, s_j^1 in the same family will cause a cache collision if

$\langle s_k^1 \rangle = \langle s_j^1 \rangle$. So we can get the equation $\langle p_k \rangle \oplus \langle rk_k^0 \rangle = \langle p_j \rangle \oplus \langle rk_j^0 \rangle$, or after rearranging, $\langle p_k \rangle \oplus \langle p_j \rangle = \langle rk_k^0 \rangle \oplus \langle rk_j^0 \rangle$.

Due to the cache collision, plaintexts satisfying $\langle p_k \rangle \oplus \langle p_j \rangle = \langle rk_k^0 \rangle \oplus \langle rk_j^0 \rangle$ should have a lower average encryption time. We use the pair of bytes p_7 and p_{15} in T_3 family to carry out attacks. Figure 2 shows the three results of first round attacks against three different AES implementations using 1 million encryption time data. We apply the unprotected software AES implementation of *OpenSSL* and show the result of first round attack in Fig. 2a. From Fig. 2a we can see that 8 red lines denoting right $p_7 \oplus p_{15}$ produce an obvious time drop compared to other gray lines. Figure 2b shows the second successful attacks against shuffled software AES implementation which randomize the execution order of each round the same as in Algorithm 1. The third picture Fig. 2c is the result of our AES implementation with combination of hardware and software. It shows that the first round attack against our implementation fails.

The four sets of equations in Eq. 1 for key bytes in the same family are the only information we can get by first round attack. We can't gain exact key information without considering other rounds. Furthermore, the lower $\log_2 \delta$ bits of each key byte can't be learned with the given information. Therefore, the attacker must still guess a total of $4 * (8 + 3 * \log_2 \delta) = 68$ bits (for $\delta = 8$) key value to recover the full key.

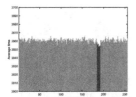 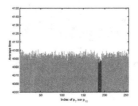 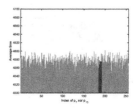

(a) The unprotected soft-ware AES implementation   (b) The shuffled software AES implementation   (c) The AES implementation with combination of hardware and software

Fig. 2. Results of first round attacks against three different AES implementations using 1 million encryption time data. X label denotes the index of $p_7 \oplus p_{15}$, while Y label presents the average encryption time. Red lines are the right indices of $\langle rk_7^0 \rangle \oplus \langle rk_{15}^0 \rangle$. Gray lines correspond to the wrong indices of $\langle rk_7^0 \rangle \oplus \langle rk_{15}^0 \rangle$. (Color figure online)

Final Round Attacks. We make final round attacks which are faster than first round attacks and can recover the full key. As mentioned in Sect. 2.2, the final encryption round of AES software implementation omits the algebraic operation of MixColumns. The final round using look-up tables in *OpenSSL0.9.7a* is carried out as:

$$(c_0, c_1, c_2, c_3) = T_4[s_0^{10}] \oplus T_4[s_5^{10}] \oplus T_4[s_{10}^{10}] \oplus T_4[s_{15}^{10}] \oplus \{rk_0^{10}, rk_1^{10}, rk_2^{10}, rk_3^{10}\},$$
$$(c_4, c_5, c_6, c_7) = T_4[s_4^{10}] \oplus T_4[s_9^{10}] \oplus T_4[s_{14}^{10}] \oplus T_4[s_3^{10}] \oplus \{rk_4^{10}, rk_5^{10}, rk_6^{10}, rk_7^{10}\},$$
$$(c_8, c_9, c_{10}, c_{11}) = T_4[s_8^{10}] \oplus T_4[s_{13}^{10}] \oplus T_4[s_2^{10}] \oplus T_4[s_7^{10}] \oplus \{rk_8^{10}, rk_9^{10}, rk_{10}^{10}, rk_{11}^{10}\},$$
$$(c_{12}, c_{13}, c_{14}, c_{15}) = T_4[s_{12}^{10}] \oplus T_4[s_1^{10}] \oplus T_4[s_6^{10}] \oplus T_4[s_{11}^{10}] \oplus \{rk_{12}^{10}, rk_{13}^{10}, rk_{14}^{10}, rk_{15}^{10}\}.$$
$$(2)$$

Moreover, the last encryption round in $OpenSSL1.1.0f$ is executed as:

$$(c_0, c_1, c_2, c_3) = T_2[s_0^{10}] \oplus T_3[s_5^{10}] \oplus T_0[s_{10}^{10}] \oplus T_1[s_{15}^{10}] \oplus \{rk_0^{10}, rk_1^{10}, rk_2^{10}, rk_3^{10}\},$$
$$(c_4, c_5, c_6, c_7) = T_2[s_4^{10}] \oplus T_3[s_9^{10}] \oplus T_0[s_{14}^{10}] \oplus T_1[s_3^{10}] \oplus \{rk_4^{10}, rk_5^{10}, rk_6^{10}, rk_7^{10}\},$$
$$(c_8, c_9, c_{10}, c_{11}) = T_2[s_8^{10}] \oplus T_3[s_{13}^{10}] \oplus T_0[s_2^{10}] \oplus T_1[s_7^{10}] \oplus \{rk_8^{10}, rk_9^{10}, rk_{10}^{10}, rk_{11}^{10}\},$$
$$(c_{12}, c_{13}, c_{14}, c_{15}) = T_2[s_{12}^{10}] \oplus T_3[s_1^{10}] \oplus T_0[s_6^{10}] \oplus T_1[s_{11}^{10}] \oplus \{rk_{12}^{10}, rk_{13}^{10}, rk_{14}^{10}, rk_{15}^{10}\}.$$
$$(3)$$

Equation 3 utilizes the T-tables $T_0, \cdots, T_3$ in a slightly adapted way while Eq. 2 use a separate T-table T_4. That's the only difference between the two implementations. Because the T-tables are typically the same, both the two implementations can't resist the final round attack. Next we take Eq. 2 as an example to describe the details of the final round attack.

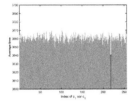 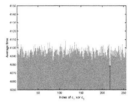 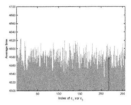

(a) The unprotected soft-   (b) The shuffled software   (c) The AES implementa-
ware AES implementation   AES implementation   tion with combination of
                                                          hardware and software

Fig. 3. Results of final round attacks against three different AES implementations using 0.3 million encryption time data. X label denotes the index of $c_1 \oplus c_5$, while Y label presents the average encryption time. Red line is the right index of $c_1 \oplus c_5$. Gray lines correspond to the wrong indices of $c_1 \oplus c_5$. (Color figure online)

For any two ciphertext bytes c_k, c_j, it holds that $c_k = rk_k^{10} \oplus T_4[s_u^{10}]$ for some u and $c_j = rk_j^{10} \oplus T_4[s_w^{10}]$ for some w. A cache collision occurs on T_4 when $s_u^{10} = s_w^{10}$. In this given condition we can get the result $T_4[s_u^{10}] = T_4[s_w^{10}]$. After variable substitution, we get the equation $c_k \oplus rk_k^{10} = c_j \oplus rk_j^{10}$, or after rearranging, $c_k \oplus c_j = rk_k^{10} \oplus rk_j^{10}$. Therefore, a cache collision occurs in T_4 when $c_k \oplus c_j = rk_k^{10} \oplus rk_j^{10}$. Otherwise, we can't ensure that s_u^{10} and s_w^{10} are in the same cache line to cause a cache collision. Because of the cache collision, ciphertexts satisfying $c_k \oplus c_j = rk_k^{10} \oplus rk_j^{10}$ should be the lowest encryption time.

We use the pair of bytes c_1 and c_5 to make the final round attacks. Figure 3 shows the three results of final round attacks against three different AES implementations using 0.3 million encryption time data. From Fig. 3a we can see that 1 red line denoting right $c_1 \oplus c_5$ is the lowest one compared to other gray lines. Figure 3b shows the second successful attack against shuffled software AES implementation. The third picture Fig. 3c is the result of our AES implementation with combination of hardware and software. It shows that the final round attack against our implementation still fails.

Timing TVLA. In order to compare the encryption time data security of our countermeasure with the unprotected and shuffled software AES implementation of *OpenSSL*, we use the Test Vector Leakage Assessment (TVLA) [28] methodology. We performed non-specific TVLA test with two sets of encryption time data. One is the set of randomly chosen plaintexts while the other is a fixed plaintext.

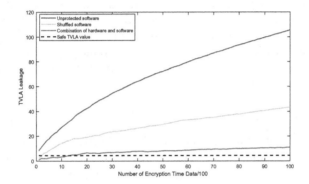

Fig. 4. Comparison of TVLA leakage from 10000 samples of encryption time data.

Figure 4 presents three comparative TVLA leakages from the three different implementations of AES, namely unprotected software AES implementation, shuffled software AES implementation and our proposed countermeasure with combination of hardware and software. Each set comprises of 10000 samples of encryption time data for both fixed and random plaintexts. It is quite clear that our countermeasure with combination of hardware and software has significantly lower side channel leakage compared to unprotected and shuffled software AES for the same number of encryption data. In power/electromagnetic side channel literature, if a TVLA leakage is less than ±4.5, it will be very difficult to break the implementation using side channel attacks. However, according to what we have learnt, there is no work to utilize TVLA methodology on encryption time data. Although the TVLA leakage of our scheme is greater than 4.5 with more than 1500 samples, we have reason to believe that it is very effective to resist cache timing attacks.

4.2 Power/Electromagnetic Analysis Attacks

Power/electromagnetic analysis attack exploits the basic concept that the side channel leakages are correlated to operations and data. At the beginning of our power/electromagnetic analysis attack experiments, we focused on both software and hardware stages as the attack target. We first tried to crack key from software stages using Longo's method [14]. However, because of our rough attack tools and poor preprocessor capability, we couldn't make our power/electromagnetic attacks successfully. In Longo's research, 46 kB data was needed to successfully attack AES decryption implementation on ARM core with GPIO-based trigger. We have reasons to believe that far more data will be needed to successfully attack our shuffled software stage.

In our following experiments, we compare power/EM traces of hardware stage with estimated power consumptions/EM radiations. An appropriate model will be required to estimate the leakages. To relate the leakages of switching activity in CMOS devices, the Hamming distance (HD) model is usually utilized. HD model assumes that the leakages are proportional to the number of both $0 \rightarrow 1$ and $1 \rightarrow 0$ transitions which produce the same amount of leakages. The jth byte HD model estimation leakage of round i w_j^i for two intermediate values s_j^i and s_j^{i+1} using the same register is given below:

$$w_j^i = HD(s_j^i, s_j^{i+1}) = HW(s_j^i \oplus s_j^{i+1}), \quad j \in \{1, \cdots, 15\}. \tag{4}$$

In Eq. 4, $HD()$ denotes the function of calculating the Hamming distance and $HW()$ represents computing the Hamming weight. W_j^i denotes the set of all w_j^i derived using Eq. 4 for all plaintexts. We assume that $l(t)$ is the t point of one power/electromagnetic trace and $L(t)$ represents the set of $l(t)$ for all power/EM traces. The correlation coefficient (Pearsons correlation coefficient) $C_j^i(t)$ between the estimation leakage set W_j^i and the t point set of all power/EM traces $L(t)$ is calculated using the equation given as:

$$C_j^i(t) = \frac{E(W_j^i L(t)) - E(W_j^i)E(L(t))}{\sqrt{Var(W_j^i)Var(L(t))}}. \tag{5}$$

In Eq. 5, $E()$ denotes the average function, while $Var()$ represents the variance function. When rk_j^i is not the correct round key, the corresponding W_j^i and $L(t)$ will have less correlation. Then the small correlation factor $C_j^i(t)$ will be obtained. On the contrary, if rk_j^i is the correct round key, the $C_j^i(t)$ corresponding W_j^i and $L(t)$ will be the highest point.

Power Analysis Attacks. Figure 5 shows the results of correlation power analysis attacks on the $HD(s_3^4, s_3^5)$ byte of two different AES implementation using 10000 power traces and the TVLA results using 5000 samples of power trace. The first implementation runs on the programmable logic (PL) of Zynq-7000 with no protection measure. The second implementation is our countermeasure with combination of hardware and software. Both the two AES implementations give

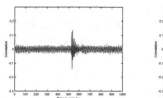 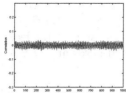 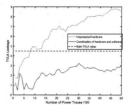

(a) Power attack on the $HD(s_3^4, s_3^5)$ byte of unprotected hardware AES implementation

(b) Power attack on the $HD(s_3^4, s_3^5)$ byte of AES implementation with combination of hardware and software

(c) Comparison of TVLA Leakage from 5000 samples of power traces.

Fig. 5. Power analysis attacks on the $HD(s_3^4, s_3^5)$ byte of two different AES implementation using 10000 power traces and TVLA result using 5000 samples. In (a) and (b), the red curve denotes the correlation coefficient of the correct round key while gray curves represents the correlation coefficient of the wrong round key. (Color figure online)

the trigger signals when hardware stage starts. For the power analysis attack on our countermeasure, we suppose the two unpredictable random numbers $R_1 = 1$ and $R_2 = 9$.

As we can see from Fig. 5a, the 532th time point has the highest correlation coefficient. It is clear that the power attack was successful on unprotect hardware AES implementation. Figure 5b shows the result of the power attack on our countermeasure. This attack failed because there are no significant higher cor-

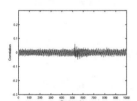 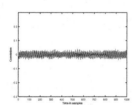 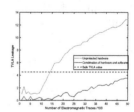

(a) Electromagnetic attack on the $HD(s_3^4, s_3^5)$ byte of unprotected hardware AES implementation

(b) Electromagnetic attack on the $HD(s_3^4, s_3^5)$ byte of AES implementation with combination of hardware and software

(c) Comparison of TVLA Leakage from 5000 samples of electromagnetic traces.

Fig. 6. Electromagnetic analysis attacks on the $HD(s_3^4, s_3^5)$ byte of two different AES implementation using 10000 electromagnetic traces and TVLA result using 5000 samples. In (a) and (b), the red curve denotes the correlation coefficient of the correct round key while gray curves represents the correlation coefficient of the wrong round key. (Color figure online)

relation coefficient at all time samples. We performed non-specific TVLA tests, which is described in Sect. 4.1, on the 532th time point of two AES implementations. Figure 5c shows that the power TVLA leakage of our countermeasure is much lower than the unprotected hardware AES implementation.

Electromagnetic Analysis Attacks. Figure 6 shows the results of correlation electromagnetic analysis attacks on the $HD(s_3^4, s_3^5)$ byte of two different AES implementation using 10000 power traces and the TVLA results using 5000 samples of power trace. The two implementations are the same as in the power attack experiments. Meanwhile we still suppose the two unpredictable random numbers $R_1 = 1$ and $R_2 = 9$ to attack our countermeasure.

From Fig. 6a we know that the electromagnetic attack on the unprotected hardware AES implementation succeed at the 523th time point. On the contrary, the attack on our countermeasure fails, as shown in Fig. 6b. Figure 6c shows that the electromagnetic TVLA leakage of our countermeasure is much lower than the unprotected hardware AES implementation at the 523th time point.

4.3   Data Throughput and FPGA Resource Requirements

We use 0.1 million encryption time data to calculate the average encryption times and data throughput of three different AES implementations. As we can see from Table 2, the AES implementation with combination of hardware and software needs average 1653 clock cycles to complete the 128-bit encryption. While unprotected and shuffled software AES implementations need 1050 and 1415 clock cycles respectively. We normalized the data throughput based on the shuffled software AES implementation because the two software stages of our countermeasure are shuffled. The data throughput of our AES implementation with combination of hardware and software is degradated by 14% compared to the shuffled software AES implementation.

Table 2. Data throughput of three different implementations

AES implementation	Average encryption time (clock)	Data throughput (normalized)
Unprotected software AES implementation	1050	1.35
Shuffled software AES implementation	1415	1
AES implementation with combination of hardware and software (AXI-GP)	1653	0.86

Table 3 shows the FPGA resource requirement of four different implementations. From Table 3 we know that the FPGA resource consumption of our AES implementation is similar to unprotected hardware AES implementation when using the AXI-GP interface for data transfer. The main reason is that we use two random numbers as the start and end signal of hardware encryption stage, which only changes few registers. Compared to the two AES implementations mentioned above, implementations using the AXI-HP and AXI-ACP interfaces take far more FPGA resource requirements due to the use of AXI-DMA IP core.

Table 3. FPGA resource requirement of four different implementations

AES implementation	Slices	LUTs	Registers
Unprotected hardware AES implementation (AXI-GP)	661(%4.97)	2052(%3.86)	1184(%1.11)
AES implementation with combination of hardware and software (AXI-GP)	634(%4.77)	2179(%4.10)	1272(%1.20)
AES implementation with combination of hardware and software (AXI-HP)	2174(%16.35)	4999(%9.40)	5618(%5.28)
AES implementation with combination of hardware and software (AXI-ACP)	2293(%17.24)	5036(%9.47)	5622(%5.28)

5 Conclusion

This paper presented a new AES implementation with combination of hardware and software based on All Programmable SoC. Compared with most of the existing countermeasures resistant to a single type of attacks, our proposed countermeasure can resist both cache timing and power/electromagnetic attacks. Our experiments illustrate that both the time and power/electromagnetic leakages from our countermeasure are significantly lower than other implementations with acceptable performance loss. The new idea "combination of hardware and software" presents a new way to improve the security of modern cryptographic implementation against side channel attacks.

Acknowledgment. This work was partially supported by National Key R&D Plan No. 2016QY03D0502, and Introducing Outstanding Young Talents Project of IIE, CAS.

References

1. Xilinx: Expanding the All Programmable SoC Portfolio. https://www.xilinx.com/products/silicon-devices/soc.html
2. Kocher, P.C.: Timing attacks on implementations of Diffie-Hellman, RSA, DSS, and other systems. In: Koblitz, N. (ed.) CRYPTO 1996. LNCS, vol. 1109, pp. 104–113. Springer, Heidelberg (1996). https://doi.org/10.1007/3-540-68697-5_9

3. Brumley, D., Boneh, D.: Remote timing attacks are practical. In: Proceedings of the 12th USENIX Security Symposium (2003)
4. Osvik, D.A., Shamir, A., Tromer, E.: Cache attacks and countermeasures: the case of AES. In: Pointcheval, D. (ed.) CT-RSA 2006. LNCS, vol. 3860, pp. 1–20. Springer, Heidelberg (2006). https://doi.org/10.1007/11605805_1
5. Kocher, P., Jaffe, J., Jun, B.: Differential power analysis. In: Wiener, M. (ed.) CRYPTO 1999. LNCS, vol. 1666, pp. 388–397. Springer, Heidelberg (1999). https://doi.org/10.1007/3-540-48405-1_25
6. Gandolfi, K., Mourtel, C., Olivier, F.: Electromagnetic analysis: concrete results. In: Koç, Ç.K., Naccache, D., Paar, C. (eds.) CHES 2001. LNCS, vol. 2162, pp. 251–261. Springer, Heidelberg (2001). https://doi.org/10.1007/3-540-44709-1_21
7. Bernstein, D.: Cache-timing attacks on AES (2005). http://cr.yp.to/antiforgery/cachetiming-20050414.pdf
8. Bogdanov, A., Eisenbarth, T., Paar, C., Wienecke, M.: Differential cache-collision timing attacks on AES with applications to embedded CPUs. In: Pieprzyk, J. (ed.) CT-RSA 2010. LNCS, vol. 5985, pp. 235–251. Springer, Heidelberg (2010). https://doi.org/10.1007/978-3-642-11925-5_17
9. Weiß, M., Heinz, B., Stumpf, F.: A cache timing attack on AES in virtualization environments. In: Keromytis, A.D. (ed.) FC 2012. LNCS, vol. 7397, pp. 314–328. Springer, Heidelberg (2012). https://doi.org/10.1007/978-3-642-32946-3_23
10. Spreitzer, R., Plos, T.: On the applicability of time-driven cache attacks on mobile devices. In: Lopez, J., Huang, X., Sandhu, R. (eds.) NSS 2013. LNCS, vol. 7873, pp. 656–662. Springer, Heidelberg (2013). https://doi.org/10.1007/978-3-642-38631-2_53
11. Agrawal, D., Archambeault, B., Rao, J.R., Rohatgi, P.: The EM side—channel(s). In: Kaliski, B.S., Koç, K., Paar, C. (eds.) CHES 2002. LNCS, vol. 2523, pp. 29–45. Springer, Heidelberg (2003). https://doi.org/10.1007/3-540-36400-5_4
12. Brier, E., Clavier, C., Olivier, F.: Correlation power analysis with a leakage model. In: Joye, M., Quisquater, J.-J. (eds.) CHES 2004. LNCS, vol. 3156, pp. 16–29. Springer, Heidelberg (2004). https://doi.org/10.1007/978-3-540-28632-5_2
13. Mangard, S., Pramstaller, N., Oswald, E.: Successfully attacking masked AES hardware implementations. In: Rao, J.R., Sunar, B. (eds.) CHES 2005. LNCS, vol. 3659, pp. 157–171. Springer, Heidelberg (2005). https://doi.org/10.1007/11545262_12
14. Longo, J., De Mulder, E., Page, D., Tunstall, M.: SoC It to EM: electromagnetic side-channel attacks on a complex system-on-chip. In: Güneysu, T., Handschuh, H. (eds.) CHES 2015. LNCS, vol. 9293, pp. 620–640. Springer, Heidelberg (2015). https://doi.org/10.1007/978-3-662-48324-4_31
15. Chari, S., Jutla, C.S., Rao, J.R., Rohatgi, P.: Towards sound approaches to counteract power-analysis attacks. In: Wiener, M. (ed.) CRYPTO 1999. LNCS, vol. 1666, pp. 398–412. Springer, Heidelberg (1999). https://doi.org/10.1007/3-540-48405-1_26
16. Ishai, Y., Sahai, A., Wagner, D.: Private circuits: securing hardware against probing attacks. In: Boneh, D. (ed.) CRYPTO 2003. LNCS, vol. 2729, pp. 463–481. Springer, Heidelberg (2003). https://doi.org/10.1007/978-3-540-45146-4_27
17. Nikova, S., Rechberger, C., Rijmen, V.: Threshold implementations against side-channel attacks and glitches. In: Ning, P., Qing, S., Li, N. (eds.) ICICS 2006. LNCS, vol. 4307, pp. 529–545. Springer, Heidelberg (2006). https://doi.org/10.1007/11935308_38
18. Nassar, M., Souissi, Y., Guilley, S., Danger, J.L.: RSM: a small and fast countermeasure for AES, secure against first- and second-order zero-offset SCAs. In: DATE, Dresden, Germany, pp. 1173–1178. IEEE Computer Society (2012)

19. Tunstall, M., Benoit, O.: Efficient use of random delays in embedded software. In: Sauveron, D., Markantonakis, K., Bilas, A., Quisquater, J.-J. (eds.) WISTP 2007. LNCS, vol. 4462, pp. 27–38. Springer, Heidelberg (2007). https://doi.org/10.1007/978-3-540-72354-7_3

20. Herbst, C., Oswald, E., Mangard, S.: An AES smart card implementation resistant to power analysis attacks. In: Zhou, J., Yung, M., Bao, F. (eds.) ACNS 2006. LNCS, vol. 3989, pp. 239–252. Springer, Heidelberg (2006). https://doi.org/10.1007/11767480_16

21. Rivain, M., Prouff, E., Doget, J.: Higher-order masking and shuffling for software implementations of block ciphers. In: Clavier, C., Gaj, K. (eds.) CHES 2009. LNCS, vol. 5747, pp. 171–188. Springer, Heidelberg (2009). https://doi.org/10.1007/978-3-642-04138-9_13

22. Veyrat-Charvillon, N., Medwed, M., Kerckhof, S., Standaert, F.-X.: Shuffling against side-channel attacks: a comprehensive study with cautionary note. In: Wang, X., Sako, K. (eds.) ASIACRYPT 2012. LNCS, vol. 7658, pp. 740–757. Springer, Heidelberg (2012). https://doi.org/10.1007/978-3-642-34961-4_44

23. Patranabis, S., Roy, D.B., Vadnala, P.K., Mukhopadhyay, D., Ghosh, S.: Shuffling across rounds: a lightweight strategy to counter side-channel attacks. In: 2016 IEEE 34th International Conference on Computer Design (ICCD), pp. 440–443. IEEE Computer Society (2016)

24. Xilinx: Zynq-7000 All Programmable SoC Technical Reference Manual (2017). https://china.xilinx.com/support/documentation/user_guides/ug585-Zynq-7000-TRM.pdf

25. National Institute of Standards and Technology (NIST): Advanced Encryption Standard (2001). http://www.itl.nist.gov/fipspubs/

26. Kelsey, J., Schneier, B., Wagner, D., Hall, C.: Side channel cryptanalysis of product ciphers. In: Quisquater, J.-J., Deswarte, Y., Meadows, C., Gollmann, D. (eds.) ESORICS 1998. LNCS, vol. 1485, pp. 97–110. Springer, Heidelberg (1998). https://doi.org/10.1007/BFb0055858

27. Moradi, A., Mischke, O., Eisenbarth, T.: Correlation-enhanced power analysis collision attack. In: Mangard, S., Standaert, F.-X. (eds.) CHES 2010. LNCS, vol. 6225, pp. 125–139. Springer, Heidelberg (2010). https://doi.org/10.1007/978-3-642-15031-9_9

28. Schneider, T., Moradi, A.: Leakage assessment methodology. In: Güneysu, T., Handschuh, H. (eds.) CHES 2015. LNCS, vol. 9293, pp. 495–513. Springer, Heidelberg (2015). https://doi.org/10.1007/978-3-662-48324-4_25

29. Goodwill, G., Jun, B., Jaffe, J., Rohatgi, P.: A testing methodology for side channel resistance validation. In: NIST Non-Invasive Attack Testing Workshop (2011). http://csrc.nist.gov/news_events/non-invasive-attack-testing-workshop/papers/08_Goodwill.pdf

30. Arm Limited: ARM Cortex-A9 Technical Reference Manual (Revision r4p1) (2016). https://static.docs.arm.com/100511/0401/arm_cortexa9_trm_100511_0401_10_en.pdf

How Secure Is Green IT? The Case of Software-Based Energy Side Channels

Heiko Mantel$^{(\boxtimes)}$, Johannes Schickel, Alexandra Weber$^{(\boxtimes)}$,
and Friedrich Weber

Department of Computer Science, TU Darmstadt, Darmstadt, Germany
{mantel,schickel,weber,fweber}@mais.informatik.tu-darmstadt.de

Abstract. Software-based energy measurement features in contemporary CPUs allow one to track and to limit energy consumption, e.g., for realizing green IT. The security implications of software-based energy measurement, however, are not well understood. In this article, we study such security implications of green IT. More concretely, we show that side-channel attacks can be established using software-based energy measurement at the example of a popular RSA implementation. Using distinguishing experiments, we identify a side-channel vulnerability that enables attackers to distinguish RSA keys by measuring energy consumption. We demonstrate that a surprisingly low number of sample measurements suffices to succeed in an attack with high probability. In contrast to traditional power side-channel attacks, no physical access to hardware is needed. This makes the vulnerabilities particularly serious.

1 Introduction

Controlling and limiting energy consumption is crucial for datacenters, both, ecologically and economically. Minimizing energy consumption is key to achieving both, green IT and higher datacenter density [17]. To support the achievement of energy-consumption goals, software-based energy measurement features have been introduced to CPUs by various vendors, e.g., by Intel [21, Chap. 14.9].

While the potential benefits of software-based energy measurement are clear [17], its security implications are not yet well-understood. To clarify such implications is our goal. More concretely, we focus on side channels that attackers might establish using software-based energy measurement. In a side-channel attack, an attacker extracts secrets, like cryptographic keys, from execution characteristics of a program, like running time [4,11,22], cache behavior [8,32,52], or power consumption [23,24,37]. Prior work on power-consumption side channels required specialized hardware or required the device under attack to use a battery.

In this article, we investigate the danger of side channels introduced by software-based energy measurement. We also evaluate the effectiveness of two candidate countermeasures against such side channels. To make things concrete, we focus on Intel RAPL, an energy measurement feature in Intel CPUs [21].

We perform our experiments on an Intel i5-4590 desktop CPU. In our experiments, we measure the energy consumption of a victim program purely in

© Springer Nature Switzerland AG 2018
J. Lopez et al. (Eds.): ESORICS 2018, LNCS 11098, pp. 218–239, 2018.
https://doi.org/10.1007/978-3-319-99073-6_11

software, using Intel RAPL. Based on our measurements, we evaluate qualitatively whether an attacker can learn secret information and then quantify this threat using statistical methods on a concrete decision procedure. Subsequently, we evaluate the effectiveness of countermeasures based on information theory.

Our main finding is that an attacker can distinguish between RSA secret keys purely by using software-based energy measurement. More concretely, the attacker can distinguish which secret key is used in the RSA implementation from the popular cryptographic library Bouncy Castle. We show that 7 observations suffice to guess the key correctly with a probability above 99%. This number of required observations is surprisingly low and the detected weakness in Bouncy Castle RSA is, hence, a serious concern. While it is clear that CPU features for increasing performance are common sources of side channels (see, e.g., caches [43] or branch prediction [1]), CPU features for controlling energy were not in the focus of research on side channels so far. Our results show that CPU features for controlling energy do introduce side channels and that these side channels are severe. That clarifies the security implications of green IT in this domain.

We investigate two candidate countermeasures against software-based energy side channels, namely the program transformations cross-copying [2] and conditional assignment [40]. We evaluate their effectiveness by the reduction in side-channel capacity that they achieve in our experiments. While cross-copying only reduces capacity by 8%, conditional assignment reduces capacity by 99%. Thus, conditional assignment could be a suitable basis for hardening security-critical implementations against software-based energy side channels.

In summary, our main contributions are (1) a qualitative and a quantitative analysis of software-based energy side channels at the example of Bouncy Castle RSA and Intel RAPL, and (2) a quantitative evaluation of the effectiveness of two candidate countermeasures against energy side channels.

2 Preliminaries

Side Channels. In 1996, Kocher showed that a naive square-and-multiply implementation of modular exponentiation is vulnerable to timing-side-channel attacks [22]. Modular exponentiation is, for example, used in RSA decryption to compute $p = c^d \pmod{n}$, for ciphertext c and secret key d [45].

```
1: Input: (d, n), c
2: r ← 1
3: for i = 1 to i = bitLength(d) do
4:     if d % 2 == 1 then
5:         r ← (r * y) % n
6:     end if
7:     y ← (y * y) % n
8:     d ← d >> 1
9: end for
10: return r % n
```

Fig. 1. Square&Multiply

A square-and-multiply implementation of modular exponentiation is given in Fig. 1. Line 5 is only executed when the condition in Line 4 evaluates to *true*. Execution of Line 5 takes additional time. Since the condition depends on bits from the exponent, the execution time of the program encodes the Hamming weight of the exponent. An attacker can exploit this variation in execution times to extract the secret exponent d [22].

In the style of Millen [39], a side channel can be modeled as an information-theoretic channel [15] with random variables X and Y as the input alphabet and output alphabet. The input alphabet are all secrets a program can process, and the output alphabet are all possible side-channel observations. The worst-case side-channel leakage can be measured by the channel capacity $C(X; Y)$ [15].

Software-Based Energy Measurement. Energy E (measured in J for *joule*) is the aggregation of instantaneous power consumption values $p(t)$ (measured in W for *watt*) over time, i.e., $E = \int_{t_0}^{t_1} p(t)dt$ [19]. Similar to [41], we define the energy consumption of a program as the energy consumed by the CPU and main memory during program execution (e.g., for arithmetics and accesses to data).

Running Average Power Limit (Intel RAPL) is a set of energy sensors on CPUs introduced with Intel's Sandy Bridge processor architecture [20]. While Intel RAPL's primary purpose is to enforce power consumption limits [21, Chap. 14], it also exposes the energy consumption of the CPU through the model-specific register (MSR) MSR_PKG_ENERGY_STATUS, which is updated every millisecond. The measurements provided are accurate [20]. Linux exposes Intel RAPL to userspace through the msr kernel module [31] and through the Power Capping framework (powercap) [30]. Both, msr and powercap, provide energy measurements in pseudo-files. The former can be accessed with root privileges, e.g., under /dev/cpu/0/msr for the first CPU. The latter can be accessed by non-privileged users under /sys/class/powercap/intel-rapl/intel-rapl:0/energy_uj. From powercap, energy measurements in the unit $\mu J = 10^{-6} J$ can be obtained.

Distinguishing Experiments. In a *distinguishing experiment*, two distinct secret inputs are passed to a program and a side channel output is repeatedly measured for each input. For instance, Mantel and Starostin use distinguishing experiments to show that a program exhibits a timing-side-channel vulnerability [36].

Based on the empirical data from a distinguishing experiment, statistical tools can be used to quantify the side-channel leakage of the program under test. For a given attacker strategy, the success probability can be computed based on hypothesis testing. Independent of an attacker strategy, the side-channel capacity $C(X; Y)$ of the program can be estimated with a statistical procedure (e.g., [12]).

A test of hypothesis is a tool to investigate conformance of a hypothesis H_0 with experimental data [48, p. 64]. We denote the alternative hypothesis by H_1. A test has two error cases: (a) the test wrongly accepts H_0 (a false positive), or (b) the test wrongly refutes H_0 (a false negative). The probabilities for a false positive and a false negative are denoted by $P(H_0|H_1)$ and $P(H_1|H_0)$.

The binomial distribution (or Bernoulli distribution) is the probability distribution for the number of successes in n independent experiments [48, p. 112]. The probability that in n experiments, each featuring success probability p, r successes are observed is $P_{n,p}(r) = \binom{r}{n} p^r p^{n-r}$, where $\binom{r}{n} = \frac{n!}{r!(n-r)!}$ is the binomial coefficient. We write $P_{n,p}(r \leq X) = \sum_{i=0}^{X} P_{n,p}(i)$ for the probability that at most X out of n experiments exhibit a success. Conversely, the probability that more than X out of n experiments exhibit a success is $P_{n,p}(r > X) = 1 - P_{n,p}(r \leq X)$.

Chothia and Smirnov show in [13] how tests of hypothesis can be used to attack e-passports. Based on a simple selection criterion, their distinguishing attack tests the hypothesis that the passport under attack belongs to the victim. Using $P(H_0|H_1)$ and $P(H_1|H_0)$, they calculate the number of observations needed to distinguish passports with error rates below 1%.

Program Transformations Against Side Channels. Multiple source-to-source program transformations were proposed for mitigating timing side channels, including cross-copying [2], conditional assignment [40], transactional branching [6], and unification [26]. The technique *cross-copying* pads branches by adding copies of the statements in one branch to the respective other branch. In the copies, dummy statements are used, which do not affect the program's state, but require the same execution time as the respective original statements. The technique *conditional assignment* removes secret-dependent branching completely and replaces assignments from the respective branches by assignments that are masked by the branching condition. Both, cross copying and conditional assignment were evaluated analytically and experimentally [2,36,40]. For instance, they were effective against the timing side channel in an implementation of Fig. 1 [36].

RSA in Bouncy Castle. Bouncy Castle is a cryptographic library for Java [29]. A provider class allows the use of Bouncy Castle through the Java Cryptography Extension (JCE). In the form of Spongy Castle [50], Bouncy Castle is widely used on Android, e.g., in the WhatsApp messenger [32]. Side channels in Bouncy Castle are, hence, a serious security threat. Recently, it was shown that Bouncy Castle 1.5's AES implementation is vulnerable to cache side-channel attacks [32].

Bouncy Castle contains implementations of various variants of the RSA asymmetric encryption scheme. The RSA encryption and decryption functionality is implemented in the Java class RSAEngine. RSAEngine can be used either directly or as backend in cipher modes, such as *OAEP* [7] and *PKCS1* [46]. An RSA key can be generated using the class RSAKeyPairGenerator.

3   Our Approach

In a side-channel attack, an attacker collects sample execution characteristics of a victim program. Based on these samples, the attacker distinguishes between the candidate secrets (e.g., valid crypto keys). The core of many side-channel attacks is to distinguish between candidate secrets from a restricted set (e.g., varying only in one bit [22] or byte [3,8]). For instance, AlFardan and Paterson [3] distinguish between two secret plaintexts based on the time that an implementation of TLS takes to decrypt them. Using distinguishing experiments [36], one can detect weaknesses in implementations that allow one to distinguish between secret inputs, e.g., as a basic step in a side-channel attack.

We define a general procedure for such experiments and use it to assess the implementation of RSA in Bouncy Castle with respect to two attacker models.

3.1   Procedure for Distinguishing Experiments

An implementation *imp* is assessed with respect to a particular security concern, namely the leakage of a secret input *s* to an attacker under an attacker

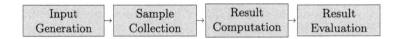

Fig. 2. Procedure for a distinguishing experiment

model a. For instance, imp could be an RSA implementation and s could be the secret RSA key. The assessment consists of four steps, visualized in Fig. 2: input generation, sample collection, result computation, and result evaluation.

In the first step, *input generation*, two input vectors to the implementation imp are generated, such that all inputs are within the spectrum of valid input data. The input vectors differ only in the secret input s. For instance, to assess the leakage of a secret RSA key, two valid secret RSA keys are generated randomly.

In the *sample collection* step, the implementation imp is run on the two input vectors that were generated in the previous step. For both runs, the observation made under the attacker model a is recorded. This step is repeated multiple times to obtain a collection of observations for each input vector.

In the *result computation* step, the arithmetic means of the two collections of observations are computed. For each collection, the frequency with which each observation occurs in the collection is computed and visualized in a histogram.

The last step is the *result evaluation*. Based on the computed results, one can detect weaknesses in implementations (if the means are clearly distinguishable and the histograms have little overlap). In addition to such qualitative results, quantitative results can be obtained through a statistical test (see Sect. 5).

3.2   Attacker Models

The sample-collection step in a distinguishing experiment depends on the attacker model. We implement this phase for two attacker models that we call *sequential* and *concurrent*. In both models, the attacker can execute an attack procedure with standard capabilities on the machine running the victim program. On Linux, attackers under both models can access powercap's pseudo-files on file system /sys. The model *sequential* captures active attackers who can trigger runs of the victim program. The model *concurrent* captures passive attackers who observe existing runs of the victim program. On Linux, unprivileged attackers can access information about running processes through file system /proc.

Implementation for Sequential. We implemented the measurement procedure for *sequential* in Python. Figure 3 shows corresponding pseudocode.

Firstly (Line 2), the attacker reads the energy-consumption counter through powercap by calling the function READCOUNTER. Secondly, the attacker waits busily for the first change to the energy-consumption counter (Lines 3–5). Once the counter has been refreshed, the attacker invokes an execution of the victim program (Line 6) using the invocation command supplied as input to the attack procedure. After executing the victim program, the attacker queries the energy-consumption counter again (Line 7). The difference between the values of the

```
1: function READCOUNTER
2:     val ← read /sys/class/powercap/intel-rapl/intel-rapl:0/energy_uj
3:     return TOINTEGER(val)
4: end function
```

```
1: Parameters: cmdLine
2: E_instant ← READCOUNTER()
3: repeat                           ▷ Align beginning of measurement with register update
4:     E_begin ← READCOUNTER()
5: until E_begin ≠ E_instant
6: INVOKE(cmdLine)                                          ▷ Execute victim program
7: E_end ← READCOUNTER()
8: if E_end < E_begin then
9:     discard measurement                                ▷ A wraparound has occurred
10: else
11:     return E_end − E_begin
12: end if
```

Fig. 3. Measurement procedure under *sequential*

```
1: Parameters: victimComm          ▷ the command name of the victim program
2: function WAITFORVICTIM
3:     while true do
4:         lastpid ← fifth field of /proc/loadavg
5:         repeat
6:             newlastpid ← fifth field of /proc/loadavg
7:         until lastpid ≠ newlastpid
8:         pid ← lastpid
9:         while pid ≤ newlastpid do
10:             comm_pid ← contents of /proc/pid/comm
11:             if comm_pid = victimComm then
12:                 return pid
13:             end if
14:             pid ← pid + 1
15:         end while
16:     end while
17: end function
18: pid ← WAITFORVICTIM()
19: E_begin ← READCOUNTER()
20: while /proc/pid/ exists do
21:     do nothing
22: end while
23: E_end ← READCOUNTER()
24: if E_end < E_begin then
25:     discard measurement                                ▷ A wraparound has occurred
26: else
27:     return E_end − E_begin
28: end if
```

Fig. 4. Measurement procedure under *concurrent*

counter before and after the victim's execution is the attacker's sample. If the sample is negative, that is, if there was a wraparound of the counter, the sample is discarded (Lines 8–9). Otherwise, the sample is returned (Lines 10–11).

Implementation for Concurrent. Since an attacker under *concurrent* cannot trigger the victim program himself, he needs to identify runs of the victim program on the system. We use Python to implement the measurement procedure under *concurrent*. Pseudocode for the procedure is shown in Fig. 4.

The attacker waits until the victim program is executed (Lines 2–17). He detects the invocation of a program by monitoring the /proc filesystem. He recognizes the victim program by the command that was used to invoke it (Line 11). Once the victim program is executed, the attacker measures the energy consumption as the difference in the energy-consumption counter (Lines 19–27).

4   Qualitative Results on **Bouncy Castle** RSA

We investigate the consequences of software-based energy measurement on software security at the example of Intel RAPL and Bouncy Castle RSA. Using a distinguishing experiment, we identify that running Bouncy Castle RSA on a system with Intel RAPL gives rise to a weakness. The energy consumption of the decryption operation allows to distinguish between secret RSA keys. In the following, we describe the setup and results of our experiment in detail.

4.1   Experimental Setup

Assessed Implementation. To assess the vulnerability of Bouncy Castle RSA, we implement a Java program, called RSA, that decrypts an RSA ciphertext using Bouncy Castle 1.53. It takes a secret key and a ciphertext as input. It decrypts the ciphertext, using the secret key, and returns the resulting plaintext.

Figure 5 lists the pseudo-code of the program. Line 4 decrypts ciphertext ct using secret key (d,n). PROCESSBLOCK is a method from Bouncy Castle's RSAEngine class, which implements the RSA decryption.

1: **Input:** $(d, n), ct$
2: $rsa \leftarrow$ NEW RSAEngine()
3: $rsa.\text{INIT}(false, (d, n))$
4: $result \leftarrow rsa.$
   PROCESSBLOCK$(ct, 0, ct.length)$
5: **return** $result$

Fig. 5. RSA decryption

Machine Configuration. We conduct our experiments on a Lenovo ThinkCentre M93p featuring one RAPL-capable Intel i5-4590 CPU @ 3.30GHz with 4GB of RAM. The machine runs Ubuntu 14.10 with a Linux kernel version 3.16.0-44-generic from Ubuntu's repository. The programs are executed using an Open-JDK 7 64-bit server Java Virtual Machine version 7u79-2.5.5-0ubuntu0.14.10.2 from Ubuntu's repository. To simulate a server machine that is shared between attacker and victim, we disable the X-server.

Parameters and Sampling. We generate two RSA keys $k1$ and $k2$ to supply as input to our RSA decryption program during our distinguishing experiment.

First, we randomly select two 1536 bit primes p and q to calculate the 3072 bit modulus $n = p * q$ shared by our keys. To select private exponents for the two keys $k1$ and $k2$, we exploit that $d * e \equiv 1 \pmod{(p-1) * (q-1)}$ must hold for valid RSA keys [45]. For $k1$, we randomly generate a public exponent e_{k1} and calculate the corresponding private exponent d_{k1}. For $k2$, we fix the public exponent to $e_{k2} = 65537$ and calculate the corresponding private exponent d_{k2}. The secret exponents that we obtain for $k1$ and $k2$ have Hamming weight 1460 and 1514, respectively. In addition to the keys, we randomly select a ciphertext $c < n$ to decrypt with both keys.

In our distinguishing experiments, we utilize our measurement procedures to collect 100000 samples per secret key under the attacker models *sequential* and *concurrent*. For the attacker model *concurrent*, under which an attacker cannot trigger executions of the victim program himself, we invoke the victim program after random delays between 100 ms and 1000 ms.

We reject outliers that lie further than six median absolute deviations from the median. For $k1$, we reject 1.24% of the samples under *sequential*, and 10.78% of the samples under *concurrent*. For $k2$, we reject 1.11% of the samples under *sequential*, and 11.01% of the samples under *concurrent*. We plot the collected samples for each key and attacker model as histograms.

4.2   Results for *Sequential*

The samples collected in our distinguishing experiment under *sequential* are depicted in Fig. 6. One histogram of energy-consumption samples is given per input. The histograms are colored based on the input: The blue (left) histogram corresponds to the samples for $k1$ with Hamming weight 1460, and the red (right) histogram corresponds to the samples for $k2$ with Hamming weight 1514.

The estimated mean energy consumption for $k1$ is $5.07J$, and for $k2$ the estimated mean energy consumption is $5.14J$. The peaks of the histograms and the mean energy consumptions for the inputs are clearly distinct.

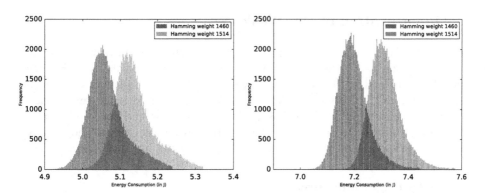

Fig. 6. Results for *sequential*   **Fig. 7.** Results for *concurrent*

Based on the histograms, an attacker under the model *sequential* can distinguish between the two secret RSA keys. Hence, there is a weakness in Bouncy Castle RSA in the presence of the Intel RAPL feature.

4.3   Results for *Concurrent*

Figure 7 shows the histograms of the samples per key under *concurrent*. Again, the blue (left) histogram corresponds to $k1$ (Hamming weight 1460) and the red (right) histogram corresponds to $k2$ (Hamming weight 1514).

The mean energy consumptions are $7.20J$ and $7.32J$ for the keys with Hamming weights 1460 and 1514, respectively. The peaks of the two histograms are clearly distinct. Interestingly, the overlap of the histograms is even a bit smaller compared to the overlap of the histograms under *sequential*. We will get back to this peculiarity in Sect. 5.

The mean energy consumptions and the histograms for the two RSA keys are clearly distinct. This means that the weakness we detected in Bouncy Castle RSA is even exposed to the weaker attacker model *concurrent*, under which an attacker only passively observes an RSA decryption.

Remark 1. Note that, the energy consumption measured under *concurrent* increased significantly by $2.13J$ and $2.18J$, respectively, compared the observations under *sequential*. This increase is due to the attacker actively monitoring the /proc filesystem to identify termination of the RSA process.

Overall, we identify a weakness in Bouncy Castle RSA that is exposed to attackers under, both, *sequential* and *concurrent*. For both attacker models, the mean energy consumption of the decryption differs significantly across the two RSA keys. Based on the histograms from our distinguishing experiments, an attacker is able to clearly distinguish between the two secret keys if he collects enough samples. In the following section, we quantify exactly how many samples an attacker needs in order to be successful.

5   Quantification of the Weakness

The results of our distinguishing experiments show that it is intuitively possible that an attacker can distinguish RSA keys by exploiting a weakness in Bouncy Castle RSA via Intel RAPL. We further investigate the likelihood of an attacker to distinguish keys. To this end, we devise a test procedure that allows an attacker to guess which of the two RSA key is used during decryption. Based on the false positive and false negative rates of the test procedure, we compute how many measurements an attacker requires to correctly guess the key in 99% of all cases.

5.1   A Distinguishing Test

Side-channel attacks, e.g., [8,13], can be mounted in two phases. In the first phase, the attacker collects a set of offline observations through the side channel as reference point, possibly on a different machine with the same software and hardware setup as the machine he shares with the victim. During the second phase, the attacker collects a set of online observations on the machine he shares with the victim. By relating his online side-channel observations with the offline observations, the attacker deduces information about the secret being processed.

For our distinguishing experiment setting, the offline observations are the collected energy-consumption characteristics of the RSA decryption operation for both, $k1$ and $k2$. The online observations would be side-channel observations collected to identify which key is used during a system run. To guess which key the system is using, the attacker compares how likely the learned energy-consumption characteristics allow him to explain the online observations. We model the guess by a statistical test to distinguish between the keys.

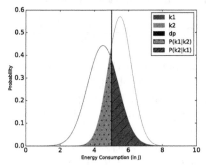

Fig. 8. Example of a distinguishing test

The attacker's distinguishing test works as follows: Given two keys, $k1$ and $k2$, with mean energy consumptions of m_{k1} and m_{k2}, where $m_{k1} < m_{k2}$, the attacker determines a *distinguishing point* $dp = \frac{m_{k1}+m_{k2}}{2}$. If the attacker observes an energy consumption less than dp, he guesses $k1$. Otherwise, he guesses $k2$. A false positive is: $k2$ was used but the attacker guesses $k1$. A false negative is: $k1$ was used but the attacker guesses $k2$.

A visualization of an example for the test is given in Fig. 8. In the example, the distributions of energy consumptions for $k1$ and $k2$ follow the normal distributions $\mathcal{N}(4.5J, 0.81)$ and $\mathcal{N}(5.5J, 0.49)$. Thus, the decision point is at $5J$. The area under the curve $k2$ to the left of dp corresponds to the false positive probability $P(k1|k2) = 23.75\%$. Conversely, the area under the curve $k1$ to the right of dp corresponds to the false negative probability $P(k2|k1) = 28.93\%$.

The attacker can use majority voting to increase his chances of guessing the correct key. For this, he observes multiple decryption operations and uses his test on each observation. Based on the individual guesses, he chooses the key on which the majority of guesses agreed. Let n be the number of observations the attacker makes. Then the false positive probability is $p^n_{P(k1|k2)} = P_{n,P(k1|k2)}(r > \lfloor \frac{n}{2} \rfloor)$ and the false negative probability is $p^n_{P(k2|k1)} = P_{n,P(k2|k1)}(r > \lfloor \frac{n}{2} \rfloor)$. Based on $P(k1|k2)$ and $P(k2|k1)$, one can determine the number n of observations needed for the attacker to distinguish $k1$ and $k2$ with 99% success rate, i.e., with $p^n_{P(k1|k2)} < 1\%$ and $p^n_{P(k2|k1)} < 1\%$. In the example from Fig. 8, $P(k1|k2) = 23.75\%$, so that 17 observations lead to a false positive rate $p^{17}_{P(k1|k2)} = 0.87\% < 1\%$. Conversely, $P(k2|k1) = 28.93\%$, so that 29 observations lead to a false negative rate below 1%, namely $p^{29}_{P(k2|k1)} = 0.81\%$. We conclude that the attacker requires 29 observations to distinguish $k1$ and $k2$ successfully in 99% of all cases.

5.2   Quantitative Results

For a quantitative evaluation of the weakness in Bouncy Castle RSA, we need to know the false positive and false negative probabilities of the distinguishing test. We estimate the probabilities based on the energy consumption characteristics collected offline by the attacker on his reference system. To estimate $P(k1|k2)$, we count the number of offline observations below dp of decryption samples with $k2$ and divide them by the total number of offline observations for $k2$. Conversely, to estimate the false negative probability we count the number of offline observations above dp of decryption samples of $k1$ and divide them by the total number of offline observations for $k1$. Formally, the probabilities can be estimated as follows. Let O_{k1} be the set of all offline observations for decryption operations with $k1$ and let O_{k2} be the set of all offline observations for $k2$.

$$P(k1|k2) = \frac{|\{x|x \in O_{k2} \wedge x < dp\}|}{|O_{k2}|} \qquad P(k2|k1) = \frac{|\{x|x \in O_{k1} \wedge x \geq dp\}|}{|O_{k1}|}$$

We evaluate the weakness for the attacker models *sequential* and *concurrent*, using our distinguishing test. For *sequential*, the distinguishing point is at $dp = 5.10J$, due to the means for $k1$ and $k2$ being $5.07J$ and $5.14J$, respectively (see Sect. 4.2). For *concurrent*, the distinguishing point is at $dp = 7.26J$, due to the means for $k1$ and $k2$ being $7.20J$ and $7.32J$, respectively (see Sect. 4.3).

The table in Fig. 9 lists the false positive and false negative probabilities $p^n_{P(k1|k2)}$ and $p^n_{P(k1|k2)}$ that result from n online observations for a given n under the two attacker models, respectively. Note that, the following equations hold: $P(k1|k2) = p^1_{P(k1|k2)}$ and $P(k2|k1) = p^1_{P(k2|k1)}$. In addition to $p^1_{P(k1|k2)}$ and $p^1_{P(k2|k1)}$, we only list the cases in which one of the probabilities falls below 1% for the first time. We highlight the first value below 1% for each of the probabilities by printing it in bold face.

The false positives for 1 observation range from 13.69% for *concurrent* to 24.75% for *sequential*. The false negatives for 1 observation range from 13.39% for *concurrent* to 19.77% for *sequential*. For 7 online observations, the false positive and false negative probabilities fall below 1% for *concurrent*. For *sequential*, the false negative probability falls below 1% at 13 observations and the false positive probability falls below 1% at 19 observations.

The distinguishing tests show that, in the worst case, only 19 observations are required to distinguish key $k1$ from key $k2$ in 99% of all cases. In this case of 19

	n	1 observation	7 observations	13 observations	19 observations
sequential	$p^n_{P(k1|k2)}$	24.75%	6.83%	2.30%	**0.83%**
	$p^n_{P(k2|k1)}$	19.77%	3.20%	**0.66%**	0.14%
concurrent	$p^n_{P(k1|k2)}$	13.69%	**0.87%**	0.07%	0.007%
	$p^n_{P(k2|k1)}$	13.39%	**0.80%**	0.06%	0.005%

Fig. 9. False-positive and false-negative rates for attackers

observations, *concurrent*'s test exhibits false negative and false positive probabilities below 0.01% each. This means that, given only 19 decryption observations, *concurrent* can distinguish both keys in 99.99% of all cases. Moreover, to distinguish both keys in 99% of all cases, *concurrent* requires only 7 observations. The finding that *concurrent*, our weakest attacker model, can distinguish both keys with high likelihood at 7 observations and, even worse, with near certainty at 19 observations, gives us reason to classify the weakness we discovered as severe.

Remark 2. A comparison across the two attacker models yields the surprising result that *concurrent* requires fewer observations than *sequential* to distinguish both keys in 99% of the cases. The 7 observations required by an attacker under *concurrent* are less than half of the 19 observations required by an attacker under *sequential*. Intuitively, an attacker under *sequential* should be able to distinguish the keys more easily than an attacker under *concurrent*, due to *sequential*'s ability to trigger victim executions and, hence, to measure more precisely.

After investigating the histograms from Sect. 4 again, our explanation is as follows. For both attacker models, *sequential* and *concurrent*, the overlap between both histograms seems to be roughly $0.25J$ wide. The estimated means differ by $0.07J$, and $0.12J$, respectively. While the width of the overlap remains similar with decreasing attacker capabilities, the means move further apart, decreasing the likelihood to observe an energy consumption value that lies in the overlap. Hence, the likelihood of an error in the distinguishing test decreases from *sequential* to *concurrent*, which is also shown by our quantitative results.

6   A Security Evaluation of Candidate Countermeasures

As we have shown in the previous sections, software-based energy side channels are a serious threat. Restricting access to software-based energy measurement features like Intel RAPL would seriously limit green IT. In contrast, software-level countermeasures would provide more flexibility, allowing energy measurement while mitigating information leakage through energy side channels.

We investigate two candidate software-level countermeasures, namely cross-copying [2] and conditional assignment [40]. Both are countermeasures against timing side channels, which ensure that equal or equivalent statements are executed across every pair of secret-dependent branches, independently of the guard. Intuitively, equal or equivalent statements should consume equivalent amounts of energy. Thus, we consider both techniques promising candidates for mitigating software-based energy side channels. In the following, we evaluate their effectiveness, using experiments and information theory.

6.1   Case Study

To investigate whether cross-copying or conditional assignment can help to mitigate leakage through software-based energy side channels, we quantify their effectiveness on a benchmark program. Motivated by the weakness that we detected

```
 1: Input: (d, n), c                      1: Input: (d, n), c
 2: r ← 1                                 2: r ← 1
 3: for i = 1 to i = bitLength(d) do      3: for i = 1 to i = bitLength(d) do
 4:     if d % 2 == 1 then                4:     mask ← ~(((d%2 − 1) >> 31) |
 5:         r ← (r ∗ y) % n                       ((1 − d%2) >> 31))
 6:     else r_dummy ← (r_dummy ∗ y) % n  5:     r ← (mask & ((r ∗ y)%n)) |
 7:     end if                                    (~mask & r)
 8:     y ← (y ∗ y) % n                   6:     y ← (y ∗ y) % n
 9:     d ← d >> 1                        7:     d ← d >> 1
10: end for                               8: end for
11: return r % n                          9: return r % n
```

Fig. 10. Cross-copied version   **Fig. 11.** Conditional-assignment version

in the Bouncy Castle RSA implementation, we use a benchmark that is relevant for RSA. More concretely, we focus on an implementation of square-and-multiply modular exponentiation (Fig. 1).

We first check that software-based energy-side-channel leakage is a concern for this benchmark implementation. To this end, we approximate the channel capacity for the implementation. In the next step, we check whether the candidate countermeasures mitigate this threat. To this end, we approximate the channel capacity of a cross-copied version of the implementation and of a conditional-assignment version of the implementation. We evaluate the effectiveness of each countermeasure by the reduction in channel capacity that it causes.

The cross-copied implementation, shown in Fig. 10, contains a dummy assignment (Line 6) in the else-branch that is equivalent to the assignment in the then-branch. The conditional-assignment version replaces the branching by assignments masked by the branching condition (Fig. 11, Line 4 and 5).

6.2   Experimental Setup

For brevity, we call the unmitigated square-and-multiply implementation *Baseline*, the cross-copied implementation *CC*, and the conditional-assignment version *CA*. For experimental evaluation, we use [36]'s Java implementation of Baseline, CC, and CA. We adapt the implementations to log the energy consumption measured through powercap. We disable the network and all but the first CPU core to reduce noise in the measurements. We disable the just-in-time (JIT) compiler of the Java VM to prevent optimizations from interfering with our results. To avoid zero energy consumption results due to execution times below 1 ms, we repeat the computation 1.31×10^5 times. This results in approximately 100 updates of the energy-consumption counter for a single execution of Baseline. We estimate the channel capacity using an iterative Blahut-Arimoto algorithm [5,10] based on the samples collected during a distinguishing experiment.

For the distinguishing experiment, we use two input vectors that share $n = 4096$ and $c = 1234567890$. One secret exponent with Hamming weight 5 ($d = 2080374784$) and one secret exponent with Hamming weight 25 ($d = 33554431$)

are used as the first and second value of the secret input, respectively. We follow [36] and collect 10000 samples per input. We reject outliers that lie further than six median absolute deviations from the median. This results in a rejection between 1.07% and 2.73% of all samples for each implementation and each input.

6.3   Experimental Results and Interpretation

The table in Fig. 12 shows the results of our experiments. The mean energy consumptions and channel capacities are given with 95% confidence intervals.

The mean energy consumption for the first input to Baseline is roughly $15373.73nJ$. The mean energy consumption for the second input to Baseline is roughly $18934.13nJ$. These means are clearly distinguishable. Hence, there is a clear security concern already in the benchmark.

To quantify the severity of the security threat, we determine the channel capacity. Since we consider a scenario in which the attacker tries to distinguish between two inputs, the secret is 1 bit, namely the choice of the input. For Baseline, $C(X;Y)$ is 0.9922 bits/symbol. That is, one attacker observation reveals almost the entire secret under the worst-case prior distribution of inputs.

Next, we investigate the results for CC. Here, the mean energy consumptions for the two inputs are roughly $20372.21nJ$ and $21040.05nJ$, respectively. The channel capacity is approximately 0.9171 bits/symbol.

Intuitively, the mean energy consumptions of CC are still clearly distinguishable. The quantification of the security concern by the channel capacity of CC confirms that the concern is still substantial. CC can still leak 91% of the secret under the worst-case prior input distribution. This shows that [36]'s cross-copying implementation does not mitigate the energy side channel significantly.

We can only speculate why cross-copying is not effective against the energy side channel in our experiments. The difference of data dependencies introduced by the branches might be responsible. In the *else* branch (Fig. 10, Line 6), the result is written to r_{dummy} instead of r. This might cause a subtle difference in energy consumption, for example, due to different patterns of pipeline stalling.

Next, we investigate the results for CA. The mean energy consumptions of CA for the two inputs are roughly $32670.41nJ$ and $32630.73nJ$, respectively. The channel capacity is approximately 0.0075 bits/symbol.

The mean energy consumptions for the two inputs to CA are almost identical and, hence, not easy to distinguish. The channel capacity is reduced almost to zero. That is, in our example, conditional assignment effectively reduces the security concern by 99%, almost eliminating the software-based energy side channel.

The successful reduction of channel capacity from Baseline to CA gives us hope that an effective countermeasure against software-based energy side channels can be designed. In particular, conditional assignment is a promising starting point in the design of such countermeasures.

	$mean(E)$ for Input 1	$mean(E)$ for Input 2	$C(X;Y)$
Baseline	$15370.07nJ \pm 3.18$	$18925.46nJ \pm 4.00$	0.9922 ± 0.00000
CC	$20372.21nJ \pm 4.48$	$21040.05nJ \pm 3.97$	0.9171 ± 0.00970
CA	$32670.41nJ \pm 5.63$	$32630.73nJ \pm 5.60$	0.0075 ± 0.00375

Fig. 12. Statistical results for modular exponentiation

7   Related Work

7.1   Power-Consumption Side Channels

Power-consumption side channels are exploited, e.g., by the techniques *Simple Power Analysis* (SPA) and *Differential Power Analysis* (DPA). These techniques were introduced by Kocher, Jaffe, and Jun in attacks on smartcards implementing the DES cryptosystem [23]. In both techniques, traces of the power consumption of a circuit are measured and analyzed. SPA is a direct interpretation of power traces and can yield information about a device's secret key during crypto computations [23,24]. DPA is a statistical method to identify correlations between data processed and power consumption [23,24]. Variations of power analysis have been used in attacks on implementations of cryptography, e.g., of DES [23,28,47], of RSA [23,24,37,42], and of AES [24,34,44]. All these attacks obtain traces of power consumption from measurements with dedicated hardware.

Recently, power-consumption side channels were exploited without dedicated hardware on mobile devices using batteries [38,51]. We briefly give an overview on Michalevsky et al.'s work on tracking Android devices through power analysis [38]. They measure the power consumption of a device using its battery monitoring unit. By their measurements, they can, e.g., track users in real-time.

Our work on software-based energy side channels differs from the previously described work on power analysis in the two following aspects.

(a) We investigate a fundamentally weaker attacker model. Our attacker is only able to measure the energy consumption, which is the aggregate of instantaneous power consumption. As a result, the observations required for an attack through software-based energy side channels are more coarse-grained.

(b) On the technical side, we use software-based measurement techniques available on machines without battery, e.g., on desktop and server machines. Software-based techniques allow an attacker to conduct his attack without dedicated hardware and without physical access to the device under attack. Thus, the observations required to exploit software-based energy side channels are easier to obtain than power traces and might be obtainable remotely in the cloud.

Overall, we think that software-based energy side channels are an interesting target for future security research because they use more coarse-grained observations that are easier to obtain.

7.2   Quantitative Side-Channel Analysis

Side channels have been the focus of many research projects since their first appearance in Kocher's work in 1996 [22]. A multitude of work focuses on exploiting side channels, e.g., [3,4,8,11,22,32,52]. In addition, analysis of side channels using information-theoretic methods has become an area of focus. Köpf and Basin propose a model to analyze adaptive side-channel attacks using information theory [25]. More concretely, they quantify the attacker's uncertainty about a secret based on the number of side-channel measurements the attacker obtained. CacheAudit [18] by Doychev, Köpf, Mauborgne, and Reineke is a tool employing program analysis and information theory to give upper bounds on information leakage through cache side channels in x86 binaries. Other work on analysis of side channels using information theory includes [9,27,33,35,49].

The mentioned works are foremost of analytic nature. On the *empirical* analysis of side channels, we are aware of only few works, e.g., [14,16,36]. Mantel and Starostin evaluate the practical effectiveness of program transformations to mitigate timing side channels [36]. For their evaluation, they consider the capacity of the timing side channel in a program. They introduce the idea of distinguishing experiments to obtain experimental results on the side-channel capacity.

We apply [36]'s concept of distinguishing experiments to show software-based energy side channels exist. Following [36]'s approach, we use channel capacity to evaluate the effectiveness of side-channel countermeasures. In summary, we build on [36]'s techniques, but apply them to a novel type of side channel.

Our distinguishing test to quantitatively evaluate the weakness in Bouncy Castle RSA is a variant of [13]'s test to distinguish e-passports. Distinguishing e-passports is done through sending a random message and a replayed message to a passport to obtain the difference in response times. Using a normal distribution as a model of response times and a manually selected distinguishing point, Chothia and Smirnov calculate the number of observations needed to distinguish passports in 98% of all cases. We transfer the test to our setting. Unlike Chothia and Smirnov, we estimate error probabilities based on offline samples alone, because our observations do not follow a normal distribution.

Like the distinguishing attack in [3] and the distinguishing experiments in [16,36] we focus on distinguishing between two secrets in our qualitative and quantitative evaluation. We take care to use two representative secrets by following standard random key generation procedures (OpenSSL's default public exponent, criteria in [45]). A notable work that distinguishes between more than two secrets is [13], which considers ten different e-passports.

8   Conclusion

Software-based energy measurement features facilitate the optimization of energy consumption, which is crucial in datacenters. We showed, at the example of Intel RAPL and Bouncy Castle RSA, that these important features also introduce a security issue. Based on only 7 energy samples measured with Intel RAPL, an attacker can distinguish between two RSA secret keys with 99% success probability. Overall, our results show that software-based energy side channels are a serious security concern.

To protect against the security issues without excluding a large fraction of programs from the optimization of energy consumption, fine-grained countermeasures are needed. We have identified conditional assignment as a promising starting point for designing such countermeasures. In our quantitative experimental evaluation of candidate countermeasures, conditional assignment was effective in the protection of our benchmark program.

Interesting directions for future work will be to derive key-recovery attacks against Bouncy Castle RSA from our results and to investigate the effect of just-in-time compilation. We hope that our approach using distinguishing experiments will also be helpful for the timely detection of side-channel vulnerabilities in other security-critical implementations.

Acknowledgements. We thank the anonymous reviewers for their helpful comments. We thank Yuri Gil Dantas, Ximeng Li, and Artem Starostin for helpful suggestions at different stages of our research project. This work has been funded by the DFG as part of the project Secure Refinement of Cryptographic Algorithms (E3) within the CRC 1119 CROSSING.

A   RSA Parameters

We list the ciphertext c, the modulus n, and, for each of $k1$ and $k2$, the private exponent d. The table in Fig. 13 lists the bit length and Hamming weight of the individual key parameters.

Variable	Bit Length	Hamming Weight
n	3071	1550
d_{k1}	2880	1460
d_{k2}	3070	1514

Fig. 13. RSA parameter information

$$c = 21\,444\,858\,737\,899\,529\,054\,620\,511\,370\,454\,507\,092\,966\,801\,560\,642\,267\,256$$
$$271\,104\,479\,565\,623\,317\,752$$

$n =$ 2 701 439 070 847 831 436 302 643 023 883 472 860 688 598 232 186 843 078 227
336 630 239 028 012 256 550 437 650 268 769 791 198 665 992 795 439 484 217
556 231 560 025 070 371 698 339 396 459 200 881 954 828 050 340 830 157 513
508 421 214 770 279 402 829 167 697 307 613 566 394 176 659 624 110 756 710
628 073 014 761 357 607 996 466 364 229 898 558 058 073 647 928 107 882 490
406 530 947 890 797 815 573 279 825 845 151 878 854 668 533 049 684 979 849
046 263 217 739 454 991 182 947 451 853 315 650 216 590 304 861 483 322 060
060 830 631 094 083 537 687 041 942 037 690 007 693 207 305 415 195 214 688
380 836 084 216 172 144 792 635 213 107 935 419 683 137 307 723 939 160 685
162 963 798 575 432 937 877 504 919 069 927 206 463 822 812 215 130 775 583
846 864 507 114 293 297 396 044 572 999 463 005 723 946 293 357 342 314 317
073 651 823 518 140 604 749 430 721 177 242 193 915 300 702 995 100 318 209
072 680 035 930 026 760 088 409 999 868 552 738 596 292 995 373 879 363 788
033 672 926 557 820 859 907 396 638 610 163 158 192 481 639 061 519 053 725
943 865 537 221 937 014 172 943 369 946 317 527 944 500 414 286 628 781 268
545 323 413 089 483 205 130 985 579 709 706 141 004 772 358 028 235 835 383
909 088 091 781

$d_{k1} =$ 834 165 241 298 999 430 572 239 556 741 255 001 409 654 369 991 231 022 229
220 766 012 080 697 463 656 309 174 093 432 158 675 603 340 216 003 665 704
131 245 121 040 967 995 188 366 594 646 886 723 499 562 164 775 785 136 008
896 297 468 405 676 356 520 936 826 945 820 428 827 348 255 217 929 032 541
402 713 897 358 199 944 878 768 362 082 394 995 264 828 906 821 922 160 081
896 178 733 905 626 880 183 545 477 730 549 240 816 967 899 639 830 638 962
585 672 589 316 902 773 646 421 798 550 172 445 107 122 780 716 202 671 225
380 537 248 843 847 787 001 886 230 297 573 272 017 826 827 441 391 799 971
383 481 609 479 693 434 609 255 364 781 237 298 674 935 211 620 000 100 041
121 931 493 922 732 461 726 369 423 008 396 966 929 501 865 211 495 345 778
306 377 790 415 705 746 828 081 157 687 854 396 051 014 887 511 709 430 472
332 036 102 915 852 198 291 900 816 398 410 487 823 293 583 922 839 328 518
348 451 707 669 403 333 993 535 972 295 702 111 655 470 282 959 323 284 437
483 178 409 938 904 891 941 353 380 152 662 307 486 605 772 459 905 400 151
595 208 101 373 686 515 401 901 692 964 058 539 933 630 431 256 790 357 003
951 566 054 871

$d_{k\cdot 2} =$ 849 669 096 348 419 204 365 570 298 477 349 071 171 614 131 865 471 357 729
223 033 692 678 706 938 741 080 172 802 999 095 258 832 447 464 674 826 253
513 078 126 047 832 149 347 969 391 019 019 909 054 959 345 128 332 576 053
617 789 744 725 266 175 298 192 375 980 008 826 221 571 989 636 873 751 134
110 143 415 982 969 381 778 707 618 076 367 532 496 926 501 132 827 071 452
381 857 918 868 318 894 249 233 517 709 784 025 494 473 083 475 794 688 338
318 669 205 292 634 477 215 223 397 852 394 761 705 823 824 009 487 094 582
053 403 448 414 519 187 059 874 506 785 829 441 820 347 012 931 983 749 032
937 029 535 204 674 669 118 349 387 871 614 945 298 028 125 580 430 251 234
668 630 080 219 358 718 245 352 291 415 465 763 013 100 923 209 592 436 665
013 250 115 828 673 733 662 998 810 262 212 481 440 283 643 807 643 936 814
117 781 430 012 258 146 460 658 672 860 115 805 136 484 154 272 106 257 859
724 501 287 380 315 081 559 737 344 179 353 409 746 394 603 117 859 928 408
887 186 955 223 875 953 551 569 984 766 380 086 437 972 232 285 448 676 372
452 773 194 118 503 147 494 678 742 399 709 855 779 414 952 984 145 813 209
160 450 714 556 753 389 051 248 506 613 925 218 229 813 615 602 923 271 485
462 745 822 621

References

1. Acıiçmez, O., Koç, Ç.K., Seifert, J.-P.: Predicting secret keys via branch prediction. In: Abe, M. (ed.) CT-RSA 2007. LNCS, vol. 4377, pp. 225–242. Springer, Heidelberg (2006). https://doi.org/10.1007/11967668_15
2. Agat, J.: Transforming out timing leaks. In: POPL, pp. 40–53 (2000)
3. AlFardan, N.J., Paterson, K.G.: Lucky thirteen: breaking the TLS and DTLS record protocols. In: S&P, pp. 526–540 (2013)
4. Andrysco, M., Kohlbrenner, D., Mowery, K., Jhala, R., Lerner, S., Shacham, H.: On subnormal floating point and abnormal timing. In: S&P, pp. 623–639 (2015)
5. Arimoto, S.: An algorithm for computing the capacity of arbitrary discrete memoryless channels. IEEE Trans. Inf. Theory **18**(1), 14–20 (1972)
6. Barthe, G., Rezk, T., Warnier, M.: Preventing timing leaks through transactional branching instructions. Electr. Notes Theor. Comput. Sci. **153**(2), 33–55 (2006)
7. Bellare, M., Rogaway, P.: Optimal asymmetric encryption. In: De Santis, A. (ed.) EUROCRYPT 1994. LNCS, vol. 950, pp. 92–111. Springer, Heidelberg (1995). https://doi.org/10.1007/BFb0053428
8. Bernstein, D.J.: Cache-Timing Attacks on AES (2005)
9. Bindel, N., Buchmann, J., Krämer, J., Mantel, H., Schickel, J., Weber, A.: Bounding the cache-side-channel leakage of lattice-based signature schemes using program semantics. In: Imine, A., Fernandez, J.M., Marion, J.-Y., Logrippo, L., Garcia-Alfaro, J. (eds.) FPS 2017. LNCS, vol. 10723, pp. 225–241. Springer, Cham (2018). https://doi.org/10.1007/978-3-319-75650-9_15
10. Blahut, R.E.: Computation of channel capacity and rate-distortion functions. IEEE Trans. Inf. Theory **18**(4), 460–473 (1972)

11. Brumley, B.B., Tuveri, N.: Remote timing attacks are still practical. In: Atluri, V., Diaz, C. (eds.) ESORICS 2011. LNCS, vol. 6879, pp. 355–371. Springer, Heidelberg (2011). https://doi.org/10.1007/978-3-642-23822-2_20
12. Chatzikokolakis, K., Chothia, T., Guha, A.: Statistical measurement of information leakage. In: Esparza, J., Majumdar, R. (eds.) TACAS 2010. LNCS, vol. 6015, pp. 390–404. Springer, Heidelberg (2010). https://doi.org/10.1007/978-3-642-12002-2_33
13. Chothia, T., Smirnov, V.: A traceability attack against e-Passports. In: Sion, R. (ed.) FC 2010. LNCS, vol. 6052, pp. 20–34. Springer, Heidelberg (2010). https://doi.org/10.1007/978-3-642-14577-3_5
14. Cock, D., Ge, Q., Murray, T.C., Heiser, G.: The last mile: an empirical study of timing channels on seL4. In: CCS, pp. 570–581 (2014)
15. Cover, T.M., Thomas, J.A.: Elements of Information Theory, 2nd edn. Wiley, Hoboken (2006)
16. Dantas, Y.G., Gay, R., Hamann, T., Mantel, H., Schickel, J.: An evaluation of bucketing in systems with non-deterministic timing behavior. In: IFIP SEC (2018, to appear)
17. David, H., Gorbatov, E., Hanebutte, U.R., Khanna, R., Le, C.: RAPL: memory power estimation and capping. In: ISLPED, pp. 189–194 (2010)
18. Doychev, G., Köpf, B., Mauborgne, L., Reineke, J.: CacheAudit: a tool for the static analysis of cache side channels. ACM Trans. Inf. Syst. Secur. 18(1), 4:1–4:32 (2015)
19. Farkas, K.I., Flinn, J., Back, G., Grunwald, D., Anderson, J.M.: Quantifying the energy consumption of a pocket computer and a Java virtual machine. In: SIG-METRICS, pp. 252–263 (2000)
20. Hähnel, M., Döbel, B., Völp, M., Härtig, H.: Measuring energy consumption for short code paths using RAPL. SIGMETRICS Perform. Eval. Rev. 40(3), 13–17 (2012)
21. Intel: Intel-64 and IA-32 Architectures Software Developer's Manual. Volume 3 (3A, 3B, & 3C): System Programming Guide (2017)
22. Kocher, P.C.: Timing attacks on implementations of Diffie-Hellman, RSA, DSS, and other systems. In: Koblitz, N. (ed.) CRYPTO 1996. LNCS, vol. 1109, pp. 104–113. Springer, Heidelberg (1996). https://doi.org/10.1007/3-540-68697-5_9
23. Kocher, P., Jaffe, J., Jun, B.: Differential power analysis. In: Wiener, M. (ed.) CRYPTO 1999. LNCS, vol. 1666, pp. 388–397. Springer, Heidelberg (1999). https://doi.org/10.1007/3-540-48405-1_25
24. Kocher, P.C., Jaffe, J., Jun, B., Rohatgi, P.: Introduction to differential power analysis. J. Cryptogr. Eng. 1(1), 5–27 (2011)
25. Köpf, B., Basin, D.A.: An information-theoretic model for adaptive side-channel attacks. In: CCS, pp. 286–296 (2007)
26. Köpf, B., Mantel, H.: Transformational typing and unification for automatically correcting insecure programs. Int. J. Inf. Sec. 6(2–3), 107–131 (2007)
27. Köpf, B., Smith, G.: Vulnerability bounds and leakage resilience of blinded cryptography under timing attacks. In: CSF, pp. 44–56 (2010)
28. Ledig, H., Muller, F., Valette, F.: Enhancing collision attacks. In: Joye, M., Quisquater, J.-J. (eds.) CHES 2004. LNCS, vol. 3156, pp. 176–190. Springer, Heidelberg (2004). https://doi.org/10.1007/978-3-540-28632-5_13
29. Legion of the Bouncy Castle Inc.: The Legion of the Bouncy Castle. https://www.bouncycastle.org/. Accessed 12 Apr 2018
30. Linux Kernel Organization Inc: Power Capping Framework. https://www.kernel.org/doc/Documentation/power/powercap/powercap.txt. Accessed 18 Apr 2018

31. Linux Programmer's Manual: MSR - x86 CPU MSR access device (2009). http://man7.org/linux/man-pages/man4/msr.4.html. Accessed 12 Apr 2018

32. Lipp, M., Gruss, D., Spreitzer, R., Maurice, C., Mangard, S.: Armageddon: cache attacks on mobile devices. In: USENIX Security, pp. 549–564 (2016)

33. Macé, F., Standaert, F.-X., Quisquater, J.-J.: Information theoretic evaluation of side-channel resistant logic styles. In: Paillier, P., Verbauwhede, I. (eds.) CHES 2007. LNCS, vol. 4727, pp. 427–442. Springer, Heidelberg (2007). https://doi.org/10.1007/978-3-540-74735-2_29

34. Mangard, S.: A simple power-analysis (SPA) attack on implementations of the AES key expansion. In: Lee, P.J., Lim, C.H. (eds.) ICISC 2002. LNCS, vol. 2587, pp. 343–358. Springer, Heidelberg (2003). https://doi.org/10.1007/3-540-36552-4_24

35. Mantel, H., Weber, A., Köpf, B.: A systematic study of cache side channels across AES implementations. In: Bodden, E., Payer, M., Athanasopoulos, E. (eds.) ESSoS 2017. LNCS, vol. 10379, pp. 213–230. Springer, Cham (2017). https://doi.org/10.1007/978-3-319-62105-0_14

36. Mantel, H., Starostin, A.: Transforming out timing leaks, more or less. In: Pernul, G., Ryan, P.Y.A., Weippl, E. (eds.) ESORICS 2015. LNCS, vol. 9326, pp. 447–467. Springer, Cham (2015). https://doi.org/10.1007/978-3-319-24174-6_23

37. Messerges, T.S., Dabbish, E.A., Sloan, R.H.: Power analysis attacks of modular exponentiation in smartcards. In: Koç, Ç.K., Paar, C. (eds.) CHES 1999. LNCS, vol. 1717, pp. 144–157. Springer, Heidelberg (1999). https://doi.org/10.1007/3-540-48059-5_14

38. Michalevsky, Y., Schulman, A., Veerapandian, G.A., Boneh, D., Nakibly, G.: Powerspy: location tracking using mobile device power analysis. In: USENIX Security, pp. 785–800 (2015)

39. Millen, J.K.: Covert channel capacity. In: S&P, pp. 60–66 (1987)

40. Molnar, D., Piotrowski, M., Schultz, D., Wagner, D.: The program counter security model: automatic detection and removal of control-flow side channel attacks. In: Won, D.H., Kim, S. (eds.) ICISC 2005. LNCS, vol. 3935, pp. 156–168. Springer, Heidelberg (2006). https://doi.org/10.1007/11734727_14

41. Noureddine, A., Rouvoy, R., Seinturier, L.: Monitoring energy hotspots in software - energy profiling of software code. Autom. Softw. Eng. **22**(3), 291–332 (2015)

42. Novak, R.: SPA-based adaptive chosen-ciphertext attack on RSA implementation. In: Naccache, D., Paillier, P. (eds.) PKC 2002. LNCS, vol. 2274, pp. 252–262. Springer, Heidelberg (2002). https://doi.org/10.1007/3-540-45664-3_18

43. Page, D.: Theoretical use of cache memory as a cryptanalytic side-channel. IACR Cryptology ePrint Archive, pp. 1–23 (2002)

44. Renauld, M., Standaert, F.-X., Veyrat-Charvillon, N.: Algebraic side-channel attacks on the AES: why time also matters in DPA. In: Clavier, C., Gaj, K. (eds.) CHES 2009. LNCS, vol. 5747, pp. 97–111. Springer, Heidelberg (2009). https://doi.org/10.1007/978-3-642-04138-9_8

45. Rivest, R.L., Shamir, A., Adleman, L.M.: A method for obtaining digital signatures and public-key cryptosystems. Commun. ACM **21**(2), 120–126 (1978)

46. RSA Laboratories: PKCS #1 v2.2: RSA Cryptography Standard (2012). https://www.emc.com/collateral/white-papers/h11300-pkcs-1v2-2-rsa-cryptography-standard-wp.pdf. Accessed 12 Apr 2018

47. Schramm, K., Wollinger, T., Paar, C.: A new class of collision attacks and its application to DES. In: Johansson, T. (ed.) FSE 2003. LNCS, vol. 2887, pp. 206–222. Springer, Heidelberg (2003). https://doi.org/10.1007/978-3-540-39887-5_16

48. Snedecor, G.W., Cochran, W.G.: Statistical Methods, 8th edn. Iowa State University Press, Ames (1989)

49. Standaert, F.-X., Malkin, T.G., Yung, M.: A unified framework for the analysis of side-channel key recovery attacks. In: Joux, A. (ed.) EUROCRYPT 2009. LNCS, vol. 5479, pp. 443–461. Springer, Heidelberg (2009). https://doi.org/10.1007/978-3-642-01001-9_26

50. Tyley, R.: Spongy Castle by rtyley. https://rtyley.github.io/spongycastle/. Accessed 12 Apr 2018

51. Yan, L., Guo, Y., Chen, X., Mei, H.: A study on power side channels on mobile devices. In: Internetware, pp. 30–38 (2015)

52. Yarom, Y., Falkner, K.: FLUSH+RELOAD: a high resolution, low noise, L3 cache side-channel attack. In: USENIX Security, pp. 719–732 (2014)

Attacks

Phishing Attacks Modifications and Evolutions

Qian Cui[1](✉), Guy-Vincent Jourdan[1], Gregor V. Bochmann[1],
Iosif-Viorel Onut[2], and Jason Flood[3]

[1] Faculty of Engineering, University of Ottawa, Ottawa, Canada
{qcui,GuyVincent.Jourdan,Bochmann}@uottawa.ca
[2] IBM Centre for Advanced Studies, Ottawa, Canada
vioonut@ca.ibm.com
[3] IBM Security Data Matrices, Dublin, Ireland
FLOODJAS@ie.ibm.com

Abstract. So-called "phishing attacks" are attacks in which phishing sites are disguised as legitimate websites in order to steal sensitive information.

Our previous research [1] showed that phishing attacks tend to be relaunched many times, after sometimes small modifications. In this paper, we look into the details of these modifications and their evolution over time. We propose a model called the *"Semi-Complete Linkage"* (*SCL*) graph to perform our evaluation, and we show that unlike usual software, phishing attacks tend to be derived from a small set of master versions, and even the most active attacks in our database only go through a couple of iterations on average over their lifespan.

We also show that phishing attacks tend to evolve independently from one another, without much cross-coordination.

Keywords: Phishing attacks · Attacks modifications
Evolution graph

1 Introduction

In 2016, the number of phishing attacks reached an all-time high, with at least 255,000 unique attack instances [2]. Unfortunately, the trend only worsened, and there are already over 580,000 unique attack instances reported up to the *3rd Quarter* of 2017 [3,4]. This growth occurred despite the public's increasing awareness and widespread tools that are used to combat these attacks. For example, browsers such as Google Chrome, FireFox, Opera and Safari all use *Google Safe Browsing*[1] to provide to their users some level of built-in protection from phishing attacks. Microsoft Internet Explorer and Edge browsers also include a similar built-in defence mechanism, called *SmartScreen*[2].

---

[1] https://safebrowsing.google.com/.

[2] https://support.microsoft.com/en-us/help/17443/windows-internet-explorer-smartscreen-filter-faq.

© Springer Nature Switzerland AG 2018
J. Lopez et al. (Eds.): ESORICS 2018, LNCS 11098, pp. 243–262, 2018.
https://doi.org/10.1007/978-3-319-99073-6_12

The majority of the literature on phishing attacks focuses on detection, e.g. by using machine learning to train a detection model, or by using the reputation of the domains hosting the attacks, or by performing visual comparisons between the phishing site and its target. However, Phishing is still very active; for instance, a FBI report estimates that there were over 25,000 victims in 2017 for a total loss of almost 30 millions US dollars in the USA alone [5]. Our inability to stop the onslaught of attacks shows that we need to go beyond merely detecting attacks. We need to better understand why phishing attacks are growing so fast and how phishers achieve this.

In our previous research [1], we showed that most phishing attacks are not created from scratch, and they are actually duplicates or small variations of previous attacks. Our experiments showed that over 90% of the phishing attacks in our database were close duplicates of other attacks in the same database. This created *clusters* of similar attacks.

In this paper, we explore the variations that are seen in these phishing attack clusters, when the attacks are not the exact replica of another attack, and some small modifications were performed over time. We try to answer the following questions: (1) What reasons push phishers to create variations instead of simply reusing exact replicas? (2) How are the attack typically modified when variations are created? (3) Can we see common trends behind these modifications across seemingly unrelated phishing attacks, or are the modifications specific to each attack cluster? Our ability to answer these questions will further enhance our understanding of the phishing ecosystem and it will help with combating the problem more effectively.

In order to answer these questions, we are using a database of over 54,000 verified phishing attack instances collected between January 2016 and October 2017. This represents a small sampling of the total number of attacks (for instance, the Anti-Phishing Working Group reports about 2 million attacks during that same period[3]). Moreover, our dataset is mostly made of attacks occurring in North America and Europe. However, the model and analysis we proposed could be applied to a larger dataset. In order to explore the evolution of phishing attacks modifications over time, we propose a new cluster structure based on what we call a *semi-complete linkage graph* (SCL). We find that most attacks are derived from a small set of master versions, with few consecutive updates and long shelf life. Moreover, we find that new variations created from a given attack usually uses patterns specific to that attack. All of the data used in this research is publicly available at http://ssrg.site.uottawa.ca/phishing_variation/.

The paper is organized as follows: In Sect. 2, we introduce various mathematical concepts that we use in our analysis. Then in Sect. 3, we present the basic results of our experiments. We discuss these results and provide a detailed analysis in Sect. 4. We provide an overview of the literature in Sect. 5 before the conclusion in Sect. 6.

---

[3] https://www.antiphishing.org/resources/apwg-reports/.

2   Phishing Attacks Clustering

In order to analyze phishing attack modifications over time, we must first group together attacks that are related and share similar features. In this section, we introduce and discuss the mathematical concepts and algorithms that we used to cluster these phishing attacks.

2.1   DOM Similarity Between Phishing Attacks

The Document Object Model (DOM) is a tree structure in which each node represents one HTML element of a web page. In previous research, a variety of techniques have been used to compare the similarity of DOMs [6]. The *Tree Edit Distance* (TED) is one of the most popular metrics for measuring the structural similarity between two DOMs. It represents the minimal number of operations (adding, removing and replacing) to convert one document into the other. However, the complexity of the best TED algorithm to date, *AP-TED* [7], is still $O(n^3)$, where n is the number of nodes in the DOM. To reduce the complexity of computing TED, some approaches based on fuzzy hash [8] or information retrieval [9,10] have been proposed. These methods are however limited and cannot be used to find out the specific differences between the trees. Therefore, they cannot be used to perform an analysis of the modifications between the trees. Our previous research [1] proposed a trade-off method, introducing *tag vectors* to compare the similarity of the DOM of phishing attacks with complexity $O(n)$. A *tag vector* is based on an ordered list of 107 possible HTML tags. The *tag vector* of a given DOM is a vector of size 107, and each element of the vector is the number of occurrences of the corresponding HTML tag in the DOM. This method does not capture the structure of the DOM, which may lead to the grouping of DOMs that have different structures but have a similar number of each type of HTML tags. However, we have looked at the trees of DOMs that have the same tag vectors in our database. We found that only 521 of these DOMs (or 0.95% of our phishing attack database) have the same tag vector but a different DOM tree. It is thus safe to use tag vectors in our case.

To compare the distance between tag vectors, in [1] we proposed to use the *Proportional Distance* (*PD*), which divides the Hamming Distance of the vectors by the number of tags that appear in at least one of the two DOMs. Formally, given two non-null tag vectors t_1 and t_2, the proportional distance between t_1 and t_2 is given as:

$$PD(t_1, t_2) = \frac{\sum_{i=1}^{n} D(t_1[i], t_2[i])}{\sum_{i=1}^{n} L(t_1[i], t_2[i])}$$

$$\text{where } D(x,y) = \begin{cases} 1 & \text{if } x \neq y \\ 0 & \text{otherwise} \end{cases} \text{ and } L(x,y) = \begin{cases} 1 & \text{if } x \neq 0 \text{ OR } y \neq 0 \\ 0 & \text{otherwise} \end{cases}$$

The proportional distance *PD* as defined in [1] does not emphasize on the "amount" of differences between each HTML tag, and simply focuses on whether the number of tags is the same. For example, the vector $t_1 = \{1, 2, 5, 6\}$ and $t_2 = \{109, 2, 5, 6\}$ both have the same distance to the vector $t_3 = \{2, 2, 5, 6\}$, that is, $PD(t_1, t_3) = PD(t_2, t_3)$. For our study, we would like to capture the fact that t_2 is more different from t_3 than t_1 is. Therefore, we define a new distance, called the *Weighted Proportional Distance* (WPD)[4] to compare the similarity of phishing attack instances. Instead of using the Hamming Distance as the numerator, we use the sum of the *Weighted Differences* (WD), defined by the following formula:

$$WD(t_1, t_2) = \sum_{i=1}^{n} \frac{|t_1[i] - t_2[i]|}{max(t_1[i], t_2[i])}$$

whereas the value of D for a given tag was boolean (0 or 1), for tags that are used in both vectors, WD will be in the range $[0, 1)$. The larger the difference between the number of tag, the larger WD.

We define S as follows:

$$S(t_1, t_2) = \sum_{i=1}^{n} EQU(t_1[i], t_2[i])$$

$$\text{where } EQU(t_1[i], t_2[i]) = \begin{cases} 1 & \text{if } t_1[i] = t_2[i] \text{ AND } t_1[i] \neq 0 \\ 0 & \text{otherwise} \end{cases}$$

Finally, the *Weighted Proportional Distance* (WPD) is defined as follows:

$$WPD(t_1, t_2) = \frac{WD(t_1, t_2)}{WD(t_1, t_2) + S(t_1, t_2)}$$

In the rest of the paper, we use WPD as the distance between our tag vectors. It should be noted that other distance metrics could be used with probably similar results. We used WPD because it is fast to compute and works well for our goal.

2.2 Optimal Threshold

In order to create clusters of similar attacks, we need to find out a good threshold for grouping vectors together. If the distance between two vectors is less than this threshold, they are considered similar and grouped into the same cluster. Otherwise, they are separated into different clusters. The *optimal* threshold is one that yields clusters that are fairly compact inside while the distance between clusters is large. Before computing this optimal threshold for our database, we first must define how vectors are connected inside each cluster.

---

[4] For consistency with the name PD, we call this value the "Weighted" PD. However, it should be noted that WPD is *not* a distance in the mathematical sense of it.

2.3   Intra-cluster Vectors Connections

There are at least two common models that are widely used when it comes to intra-cluster connections: (1) Single-linkage, where each node inside the cluster is connected to at most one parent, creating a minimal spanning tree over the elements of the cluster, or (2) Complete-linkage, where a complete graph is created between all the elements of the clusters. However, neither of these two models can accurately capture what we are trying to do here, that is, capture the evolution of the elements inside a cluster. A good model should keep a connection between the elements of a series of modifications done to a given attack (and some of these elements may end up being fairly far apart after a long series of modifications), but it should also capture the fact that some elements are at a very small distance from each other within the cluster. This idea is illustrated on Fig. 1. Vectors a, b, c and d are close to one another, meaning that there is little variation between these four vectors. On the other hand, Vector e, while still part of the same cluster, is actually relatively "far" from these first four vectors, and is only linked to them through a long series of small variations.

To capture these series of modifications done to the phishing attacks inside a cluster, we proposed to use a *Semi-Complete Linkage* (*SCL*) model. Specifically, for any pair of tag vectors t_i and t_j in the same cluster, where $i \neq j$, we have an edge $E(t_i, t_j) \in SCL$ if and only if $WPD(t_1, t_2) \leqslant OPT$, where OPT is the optimal threshold for tag vector clusters defined in Sect. 2.4. A simple way to see this model is that inside a cluster, vectors that are "similar" are linked together. This model is an intermediate model between the spanning tree and the complete graph.

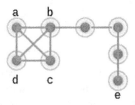

Fig. 1. An illustration of a *Semi-Complete Linkage* graph.

2.4   Quality of Clustering

We now explain how we define the *quality of clustering* and how we will compute the optimal threshold. We define $Min(C_i, C_j)$ to be the minimal distance between two clusters, which is defined as the minimum distance that can be found between two vectors, one in C_i and one in C_j. That is:

$$Min(C_i, C_j) = min(\{WPD(x, y) | \forall x \in C_i, \forall y \in C_j\})$$

As discussed in Sect. 2.3, we use the *SCL* model to capture the connections inside tag vector clusters. Thus, we define the **quality** of vector clusters with the following formula, which computes the total distance inside the clusters, and divides it by the distance between clusters. We will experimentally try different threshold to find one that minimizes this formula. The formula, which only includes the clusters that have more than one element, is as follows:

$$\frac{\frac{1}{k}\sum_{i=1}^{k}\frac{1}{|E_i|}\sum_{j=1}^{|E_i|}\{WPD(x,y)|E_j(x,y)\in SCL_i\}}{min\{Min(C_i,C_j)|i\neq j, 1\leqslant i,j\leqslant k\}}$$

where k is the number of clusters having more than one element, $E(x,y)$ is the edge between x and y in the SCL graph, C_i is the ith cluster with more than one element, SCL_i is the SCL for C_i and $|E_i|$ is the number of edges in SCL_i.

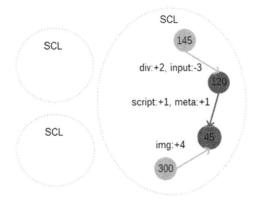

Fig. 2. Example of phishing attacks modifications graph

2.5   Phishing Attacks Modifications Graph

To analyze the evolution of phishing attacks, we computed the SCL model for each tag vector cluster, as illustrated in Fig. 2. Each node represents a unique tag vector, and the nodes label shows the number of phishing attack instances using this vector. The directed edge $E(x,y)$ captures an evolution from vector x to vector y, that is, a modification made to the corresponding attack, which transforms the original attack (which has vector x) into a slightly different attack (which has vector y). The text on the edge provides the details of the modifications. For example, an edge with the label "div:+2, input:-3" should be interpreted as meaning that two *div* tags where added to the attack and three *input* tags where removed in the creation of the new variation of the attack. The direction of the edge is determined by the reported date of the two connected vectors; the edge flows from the earlier attack to the later attack. Since several attacks will have the same vector, we consider that the "reported date" of a vector is the date at which we learned of the first attack that produced this vector.

As a consequence of this definition, a source node of the graph, that is, a node that has an in-degree of zero, is the earliest reported attack instance in our data source from this series of modifications. We color these nodes in green. Node that are variations of previously reported attacks have a positive in-degree and are shown in blue in our graph.

3   Experiments

3.1   Phishing Sites Database

We have compiled our phishing database by collecting the URLs of phishing-attack instances from the community-driven portal PhishTank[5] and the enterprise security analysis platform IBM X-Force[6]. A total of 54,575 "verified" phishing sites were collected by fetching the daily archive from PhishTank between January 1st, 2016 and October 31st, 2017 and from IBM X-Force between June 12th, 2017 and October 31st, 2017. For each phishing site, we fetched the DOM, the first URL (the reported one), the final URL (which is different from the first URL only when redirection has been used by the attacker), and a screenshot of the final page. To compare the performance of our new model with the model proposed in [1], we used a database of 24,800 legitimate sites found on Alexa[7], made of 9,737 URLs coming from the lists of "top 500" most popular sites by countries [11] and another 15,063 URLs randomly selected from the Alexa's top 100,000 to 460,697 web sites. The list of URL is available on http://ssrg.site.uottawa.ca/phishingdata/.

3.2   Vectors and Clustering Results

To compute the set of tag vectors, as was done in [1], we used the complete set of HTML elements provided by the World Wide Web Consortium [12], and removed the common tags <body>, <head> and <html>. That gave us a corpus of 107 unique tags. We then counted the number of occurrences of each tag in each DOM and used these number to create integer vectors of 107 features. We obtained 8,397 *unique* tag vectors out of the DOMs of our 54,575 phishing attack instances.

In order to compare the performance of our model to the one proposed in [1], we first trained both models with the same phishing database and computed the phishing attacks clusters and related optimal threshold. We then used our database of legitimate sites to see how many false positives each model yields.

As shown in Table 1, the SCL model has a smaller optimal threshold, but captures many more attacks than our previous models (only 3,869 undetected attacks, compared to 4,351 with the previous model). There was however a slight increase in the false positive rate, which remains very low at 0.26%. This shows that the model proposed here is more efficient than the one proposed in [1] if the aim is to detect phishing attack replicas. Similar to [1], the false negative rate is unknown since we don't know how many of the 3,869 unflagged attacks have a replica in our database.

---

[5] https://www.phishtank.com/.

[6] https://exchange.xforce.ibmcloud.com/.

[7] https://www.alexa.com/.

Table 1. Vector and clustering results for both models. "Flagged" cluster have more than one element, and the corresponding attacks are detected.

	SCL Model	Model of [1]
Optimal threshold	0.24	0.33
# of vectors	8,400	8,400
# of multiple-element clusters ("*flagged*")	941	908
# of single-element clusters	3,869	4351
# of phishing sites in flagged clusters	50,706 (92.9%)	50,224 (92.03%)
# of "similar" legitimate sites (false positive)	65 (0.26%)	58 (0.23%)

4   Analysis of the Modifications Seen in Phishing Attacks

4.1   Who Made Modifications, Phishers or Hosts?

One possible explanation for the modifications we see on different instances of the same attack is that the attack was not actually modified by the attacker, but by the hosting server, which is automatically injecting some html into the pages, e.g. some Google Analytics tracking links, some WordPress plugins or some other Javascript libraries. Since a given attack will be hosted on a range of servers, these modifications would be misinterpreted as modifications to the attack itself.

To verify this, we compared the DOM of the phishing attacks to the DOM of homepages of the server hosting these attacks. We removed all the "blanks" (including \t \r \n \f \v) from both DOMs, and we then extracted the content that was common between the two DOMs. This content could have been coming from the hosting server, and not from the attack itself. We did this for all the attack instances in our database for which the host homepage could be reached and had a different tag vector from the attack[8].

We were able to collect the DOMs of 14,584 such homepages[9]. Of these, 2,566 had some common content with the hosted attacks. A closer look at the tags involved in these common contents showed that the tag <**meta**> was involved in 2,280 of these cases, which is not surprising since <**meta**> is used for information such as encoding, page size etc., information usually set by the hosting server. The tag <**script**> was a very distant second present in only 96 cases. This shows that the tag <**meta**> is the only tag for which the hosting server can really impact our results. Therefore, we decided to remove that tag altogether from our tag vectors. Redoing the experiment of Sect. 3.2 without that tag, we find the same optimal threshold (0.24), and end up with 8,290 tag vectors distributed across 913 flagged clusters (cluster with at least 2 vectors) and 3,912 single-vector clusters. The false positive rate drops to 0.25%, as a couple of

---

[8] This excludes attacks that are located right at the homepage of the hosting server.

[9] Many hosting servers were not reachable anymore by the time we did this experiment.

legitimate sites are now correctly flagged. Out of an abundance of caution, we used that updated model in the analysis presented in the next sections.

4.2 Clusters Sample Selection

We applied the SCL model discussed in Sect. 2.3 to our 913 flagged clusters. We observed that there are several clusters with very few edges in their SCL graph, meaning that for these clusters, our database does not contain many variations of the corresponding attacks. Table 2 shows a detailed distribution of sizes of the SCL graphs. As already pointed out in [1], a small minority of the clusters cover the vast majority of the attacks. In this case, only 46.88% of the clusters have a SCL graph with two or more edges, but they contain more than 75% of the phishing attack instances. For our study, we selected the clusters having a SCL graph with 30 or more edges because they capture the majority of the phishing attack instances (52%) and they contain enough variations of the attacks to study their evolution over time.

Table 2. Number of edges and pages distribution among clusters

# of edges in the cluster	# of clusters (%-tage of total)	# of pages covered (%-tage of total)	# of edges covered
≥ 2	428 (46.88%)	41,229 (75.55%)	18,636
≥ 3	394 (43.15%)	40,579 (74.35%)	18,568
≥ 4	258 (28.26%)	38,059 (69.74%)	18,160
≥ 5	243 (26.62%)	37,321 (68.38%)	18,100
≥ 10	150 (16.43%)	34,539 (63.29%)	17,504
≥ 15	107 (11.72%)	31,638 (57.97%)	17,043
≥ 20	88 (9.64%)	30,797 (56.43%)	16,732
≥ 30	62 (6.79%)	28,801 (52.77%)	16,113
≥ 40	47 (5.15%)	26,298 (48.19%)	15,591
≥ 50	42 (4.60%)	25,306 (46.37%)	15,381

4.3 Analysis of Master Vectors

As explained in Sect. 2.5, the orientation of the edges in the SCL graphs is determined by the reported date of the DOMs creating the tag vectors, from the earlier one to the later one. We call a tag vector of in-degree zero in the SCL graph a *master vector*. Master vector represents one of the initial versions of the attack in our database. Of course, each cluster contains at least one master vector (the earliest reported vector in that cluster), but they can have several ones when the distance between the vectors is too large for them to be connected in the SCL graph. Having several master vectors in a cluster means that some attacks have been substantially modified at once, or that we are missing to intermediate steps in our database. Each non-master vector can be reached from at least one of the master vectors in the cluster. Those master vectors provide a view of the initial attacks and the non-master vectors give a view of how they evolved over time. Figure 3 shows the SCL graphs of the two largest clusters in our database (master vectors in green, non-master vectors in blue). We can see that there are far fewer master vectors than non-master ones, indicating that the majority of attacks in these clusters evolved from the original vectors.

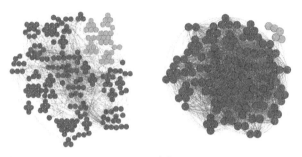

(a) SCL graph of cluster 0   (b) SCL graph of cluster 1

Fig. 3. Examples of SCL graphs

Table 3 provides an overview of the results for all 62 clusters: overall, there are 190 (10.47%) master vectors, covering around 35% of the attack instances. This shows that the master vectors are often reused to relaunch the attacks. Moreover, 34 clusters (54.84%) have two or more master vectors, suggesting several initial versions of the attack which were later merged through a series of updates.

Table 3. Overview of master/non-master vectors in the 62 largest clusters.

# of clusters	62
# of vectors	1814
# of attack instances	28,455
# of master vectors	190 (10.47%)
# of attack instances in master vectors	9,855 (34.22%)
# of clusters with two or more master vectors	34 (54.84%)
# of clusters with only one master vector	28 (45.16%)

By manually inspecting the DOMs of master vectors, we found that master vectors can be grouped into three categories: (1) Different initial versions of the attack by attackers, with enough changes to push the distance beyond the

threshold. It could be the case that the target is modified or that several new
features are released at once. Figure 4(a) shows such an example. (2) Different
steps of the same attack. Some attacks go through several steps as they attempt
to gather additional information from the victim. For example, in Fig. 4(b), a
first step is used to capture login information, and if it is provided, a second
step follows in which credit card details are requested. These different steps are
recognized as belonging to the same attack, but the difference between them
is too large for the threshold and there is no directed path between them in
the SCL graph. (3) Copies of different versions of the target site. As shown
in Fig. 4(c), sometimes the master vectors are essentially copies of the target
sites taken at different times. The target site was modified, so the corresponding
attack instances do not initially match. It is also possible that in some cases

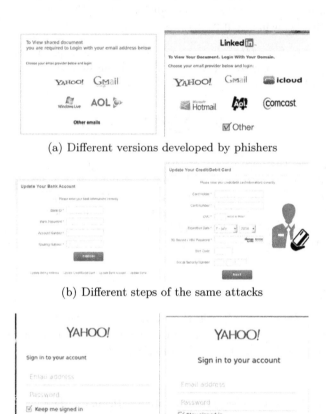

(a) Different versions developed by phishers

(b) Different steps of the same attacks

(c) Different versions copied from legitimate sites (Yahoo
login page, circa 2015 and 2016)

Fig. 4. Examples of master vectors

our database is missing an even earlier version of the attack that would yield an initial, sole master vector.

4.4   Analysis of Variation History

In order to analyze the evolution of the attacks in our database, we first introduce a few definitions. As explained before, every non-master vector v has at least one directed path in SCL from a master vector to v.

We call the *Evolution Path of* v (EP_v) the directed path from a master vector to v for which the sum of Weighted Proportional Distances of the edges along the path is minimal. In other words, EP_v is the directed path from one of the master vector to v for which the amount of transformation was the smallest.

For a non-master vector v and its evolution path $EP_v = [t_0, t_1, \ldots, t_{k-1}, t_k = v]$, we have the following definitions:

1. The *Path Distance* (PD_v) is the sum of the weighted proportional distance of the edges along the evolution path EP_v. It represents an evaluation of the "amount" of difference between v and its master vector.

$$PD_v = \sum_{i=0}^{k-1}(WPD(t_i, t_{i+1}))$$

2. The *Evolution Distance* (ED_v) is the average weighted proportional distance of edges along the evolution path EP_v. It represents the average "amount" of difference in each modification. Formally, $ED_v = PD_v/k$.
3. The *Variation Lifespan* (VL_v) is the time difference between the reported date of v and the reported date of its master vector. It represents the complete length of time during which this attack has been actively modified. If $T_{report}(t_i)$ is the reporting date of vector t_i, we have

$$VL_v = T_{report}(t_k) - T_{report}(t_0)$$

4. The *Update Interval* (UI_v), is the average of the time difference between consecutive vectors along the evolution path EP_v. It represents how often modifications are being deployed. Formally, $UI_v = VL_v/k$.

Table 4. Analysis of the evolution paths in our database.

# of evolution paths	1,230
Average *Path Distance*	0.1719
Average *Evolution Distance*	0.111
Average *Variation Lifespan*	267 days
Average *Update Interval*	186 days

Table 4 provides the average values of these attributes for all evolution paths in the selected 62 clusters. To compute these values, we have not included Evolution Paths that are included into other, longer evolution paths. The results show that in general, the attacks are only modified once every six months (186 days) and that the modifications are usually not drastic (the average WPD between these modifications is 0.111). We also see that average path distance is low, only 0.1719. Consequently, the average length of the evolution paths is only $0.1719/0.111 < 2$, less than two edges. This indicates that attackers usually do not maintain long evolution paths to create lots of variations over time. Instead, they tend to re-create new variations from the same master vectors over and over. We also find that each variation tends to stay active for a long time, around nine months (267 days).

In conclusion, we see that most phishing attack modifications are derived from a small set of master versions. Each of these modifications tend to be reused *as is* for an extended period of time. This behavior matches the "crimeware-as-a-service" model proposed by Sood et al. [13]: The underground producers build the crimewares and sell them to underground buyers who are the ones launching cyber-attacks.

4.5   Types of Modifications Seen on Phishing Attacks

In this section, we study the type of modifications that are found on our *Evolution Paths*, in order to find out if the modifications are geared toward specific attacks or if we see common trends across attacks. In the following, the analysis is done on the set of *Evolution Paths*, not on the whole *SCL* graphs. The *Evolution Paths* define a total of 1,624 edges. We will use the following two concepts:

1. The *Modified Tags* (*MT*) is the set of tags used anywhere on an edge of the set of the *Evolution Paths*. These are the tags that have been added or removed to modify attacks.
2. The *Modification Tags Subsets* (*MTS*) are all the subsets of the set of tags used on at least one edge of the set of the *Evolution Paths*. We exclude singletons from *MTS*, so we only consider subsets of at least two tags.

For example, if a *SCL* graph has only two edges, one labeled with {div:+1, a:+6} and the other one labeled with {input:+3, a:+5, h2:+1}, the set *MT* is {<div>, <a>, <input>, <h2>} and we have five subsets in *MTS*, namely {<div>, <a>}, {<input>, <a>, <h2>}, {<input>, <a>}, {<input>, <h2>}, and {<a>, <h2>}.

First, we analyzed the common modification among clusters. The top 10 most common *MT*s, and the number of clusters in which they appear, are <script> (57), <div> (53), <img> (52), <a> (51), <input> (50),
 (48), <link> (47), <span> (47), <p> (41), and <style> (40). The top 10 most common *MTS* among the selected 62 clusters are shown in Table 5. We found that beside the tags <span>, <div> and <br> that are used for spacing or containers, and the functional tags <script>, and <link> that are used for adding scripts

Table 5. The top 10 most common MTS in our database.

MTS	# of clusters	%	# of edges	%
{a, div}	45	72.58%	403	24.82%
{div, img}	44	70.97%	286	17.61%
{div, script}	44	70.97%	403	24.82%
{div, span}	40	64.52%	264	16.26%
{br, div}	39	62.90%	215	13.24%
{img, script}	39	62.90%	199	12.25%
{a, img}	37	59.68%	235	14.47%
{link, script}	37	59.68%	215	13.24%
{script, span}	35	56.45%	174	10.71%
{input, span}	35	56.45%	161	9.91%

and resources, phishers only use three tags in the top 10 MTS: <a>, <img> and <input>. Figure 5 shows two examples of substantial (visual) modifications were only one tag is actually updated. In Fig. 5(a), one <img> tag was added to change the target. In Fig. 5(b), an email credential phishing attack was converted into a tax return phishing page by changing the background images and adding 31 <input> tags.

We also note that despite the very small number of tags used to perform these modifications, none of the top MTS are used by more that 25% of the edges. In order to better understand how common or uncommon each combination of MTS is, we computed the *Jaccard Index*: for each pair of clusters, we computed the number of top 10 MTS (resp. top 10 MT) common to both clusters, divided by the number of top 10 MTS (resp. top 10 MT) included in either clusters. Figure 6 shows the distribution of the values thus obtained.

As shown in Fig. 6, the distribution of Jaccard Indexes for the pairs of top 10 MT covers a relatively wide range, from 0.1 to 0.7. This indicates that different clusters do use the same tags to create the variations, for example <div> or <input>. The distribution of Jaccard Indexes for the pairs of MTS on the other hand is very different: most indexes are less than 0.3 and the vast majority (almost 80%) are less than 0.1.

These results show that even through very few tags are actually used when the attacks are modified, the combination of tags used tends to be unique to the attack. In other words, attacks are evolving independently from one another, and the modifications are made for reasons that are specific to each attacks, and not as some sort of global update made across a range of attacks.

5   Related Work

5.1   Phishing Detection

The bulk of academic literature on phishing understandably focuses on the automatic detection of phishing sites. There are three main approaches that have been suggested.

The first one is to identify a phishing attack by comparing it with its target site to find similarities between the two. Rosiello et al. [14] propose a browser extension based on the comparison of the DOM tree, which records the mapping between sensitive information and the related information of legitimate sites (Table 6).

Several papers explore visual similarity comparison. Chen et al. [15] applied the Gestalt Theory to perform a comparison of visual similarity by using normalized compression distance (NCD) as the similarity metric. Sites logo [16] and favicon [17] comparison have also been suggested. Liu et al. [18] proposed a refined comparison method by using block level, layout and overall style similarity. A recent overview of these methods can be found in [19]. The drawback of these methods is that they require some initial knowledge of the targeted legitimate sites. Some authors have suggested to use search engines to acquire this knowledge automatically, for example Cantina [20] which attempts to find the current page on Google and warns if it is not found. Similarly, Huh et al. [21] suggested to search the site's URL in different search engines and use the number of returned pages as an indicator of phishing.

The second approach is to look for intrinsic characteristics of phishing attacks. Cantina+ [22] proposes a system using Bayesian Network mixing 15 features. Gowtham et al. [23] proposed a detection system using a Support Vector Machines (SVM) classifier and similar features to Cantina+. Their system achieved 99.65% true positive and 0.42% false positive. Daisuke et al. [24] conducted an evaluation of nine machine learning-based methods; in their study, AdaBoost provided the best performance. Some research also applies machine learning techniques for detecting phishing emails instead of the phishing site [29–31]. Danesh et al. [32] analyzed more than 380,000 phishing emails over a 15 months period. They found that some attacks keep similar messages over a long period of time, while the other attacks use different messages over time to avoid being detected by email filters.

Finally, some new approaches have been proposed recently, in which a phishing attack is compared to known ones. Our previous paper [1] found that most phishing attacks are duplicates or variations of previously reported attacks. Thus, new attack instances can be detected using these similarities. Corona et al. [25] proposed a method to detect attacks hosted on compromised servers, which compares the page of the attack with the homepage that hosts it and the pages linked by it.

Table 6. A summary of related work for phishing detection and phishing kits

Category	Work	Brief description
Comparison to target	Roiello et al. [14]	Compare the layout similarity to identify phishing attacks
	Chen et al. [15]	Applies Gestalt Theory to perform visual similarity comparison
	Chang et al. [16] and Geng et al. [17]	Identify phishing sites by comparing logos and favicons used on target sites
	Liu et al. [18]	A refined visual similarity comparison including block level, page layout and style
	Jain et al. [19]	An overview of phishing detection methods based on visual similarity comparison
Use of search engines	Cantina [20]	Query search engines with the keyword extracted from suspicious sites
	Huh et al. [21]	Feed search engines with suspicious URL, and then use the number of returned pages as the indicator of phishing
Machine learning based methods	Cantina+ [22]	Detect phishing sites using a Bayesian Network
	Gowtham et al. [23]	A SVM classifier is used to identify phishing attacks by using features similar to Cantina+
	Daisuke et al. [24]	An evaluation of nine machine learning methods
Similarity comparison to known attacks	Cui et al. [1]	Identify phishing attacks by comparing the similarity with known attacks
Similarity comparison with homepage	Corona et al. [25]	Compute the similarity score between suspicious pages and the homepage of the same site to detect inconsistencies
Analysis of phishing kits	Cova et al. [26] and Mccalley et al. [27]	Analysis of phishing kits and their obfuscation techniques
	Han et al. [28]	Analysis of phishing attacks and phishing kits collected using a honeypot

5.2   Phishing Kits

Some of the literature looks at the server side of phishing. Cova et al. [26] collected 584 "phishing kits". They analyzed the structure of the source code as

(a) One <img> tag was added between the left and the right attack

(b) Between the left and the right, 31 <img> tags are added, and the background image is changed

Fig. 5. Modification of attacks by changing one tag

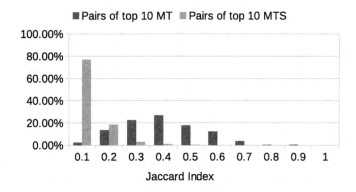

Fig. 6. Histogram of Jaccard index for top 10 MT and MTS.

well as the obfuscation techniques used. Mccalley et al. [27] did a similar and more detailed analysis of these obfuscation technique. Han et al. [28] collected phishing kits using a honeypot on which 643 unique phishing kits were uploaded. They analyzed the kits' lifespans, victims' behaviors and attackers' behaviors.

To the best of our knowledge, the only work comparable to ours is the research conducted in [32] regarding the evolution of phishing emails. This paper is the first one that gives a good picture of the evolution of phishing sites. Our study provides a detailed analysis of how attackers modify and improve their attacks, and what can motivate these modifications.

6 Conclusion and Future Work

In this paper, we have proposed a new cluster model, the *Semi-Complete Linkage* graph (*SCL*), to analyze similar phishing attack instances. This model gives us an opportunity to track the evolution of these attacks over time. We discovered that the two main reasons for attackers to update their attacks are aiming at new target and adding new features, e.g. collecting additional information or improving the interface.

Our analysis shows that most attack instances are derived from a small set of "master" attacks, with only a couple of successive versions being deployed. This shows that attackers do not tend to update and improve a baseline of their attacks, and instead keep reworking from the same base version. This suggests that the phishing ecosystem follows a producers-buyers economic model: the producers build and adapt crimewares and sell them to buyers who launch cyber-attacks but barely update them.

Finally, we have also shown that each attack tends to be modified on its own, independently from other attacks; each cluster of attacks uses its own page template and is improved without a general plan across attacks. This could be because a different attacker is beyond each attack, or more likely because attackers follow poor software engineering standards.

Our database comes from Phishtank and X-force, and it has some bias towards some brands [33] and some part of the world (in particular, it lacks data from China and Russia). Therefore, we plan to redo the experiment using a more comprehensive database in the future.

References

1. Cui, Q., Jourdan, G.V., Bochmann, G.V., Couturier, R., Onut, I.V.: Tracking phishing attacks over time. In: Proceedings of the 26th International Conference on World Wide Web, International World Wide Web Conferences Steering Committee, pp. 667–676 (2017)
2. Anti-Phishing Working Group: Global Phishing Survey: Trends and Domain Name Use in 2016 (2017). http://docs.apwg.org/reports/APWG_Global_Phishing_Report_2015-2016.pdf

3. Anti-Phishing Working Group: Phishing Activity Trends Report 1st Half 2017 (2017). http://docs.apwg.org/reports/apwg_trends_report_h1_2017.pdf
4. Anti-Phishing Working Group: Phishing Activity Trends Report 3rd Quarter 2017 (2017). http://docs.apwg.org/reports/apwg_trends_report_q3_2017.pdf
5. FBI: 2017 Internet Crime Report. https://pdf.ic3.gov/2017_IC3Report.pdf
6. Tekli, J., Chbeir, R., Yetongnon, K.: An overview on XML similarity: background, current trends and future directions. Comput. Sci. Rev. **3**(3), 151–173 (2009)
7. Pawlik, M., Augsten, N.: Tree edit distance: robust and memory-efficient. Inf. Syst. **56**, 157–173 (2016)
8. Manku, G.S., Jain, A., Das Sarma, A.: Detecting near-duplicates for web crawling. In: Proceedings of the 16th International Conference on World Wide Web, WWW 2007, New York, NY, USA, pp. 141–150 (2007)
9. Fuhr, N., Großjohann, K.: XIRQL: a query language for information retrieval in XML documents. In: Proceedings of the 24th Annual International ACM SIGIR Conference on Research and Development in Information Retrieval, pp. 172–180. ACM (2001)
10. Grabs, T.: Generating vector spaces on-thefly for flexible xml retrieval. In: [1, Citeseer] (2002)
11. Alexa: Top 500 Sites in Each Country. http://www.alexa.com/topsites/countries
12. WWW: HTML Tag Set. https://www.w3.org/TR/html-markup/elements.html
13. Sood, A.K., Enbody, R.J.: Crimeware-as-a-service-a survey of commoditized crimeware in the underground market. Int. J. Crit. Infrastruct. Prot. **6**(1), 28–38 (2013)
14. Rosiello, A.P.E., Kirda, E., Kruegel, C., Ferrandi, F.: A layout-similarity-based approach for detecting phishing pages. In: Proceedings of the 3rd International Conference on Security and Privacy in Communication Networks, SecureComm, Nice, pp. 454–463 (2007)
15. Chen, T.C., Dick, S., Miller, J.: Detecting visually similar web pages: application to phishing detection. ACM Trans. Internet Technol. **10**(2), 5:1–5:38 (2010)
16. Chang, E.H., Chiew, K.L., Sze, S.N., Tiong, W.K.: Phishing detection via identification of website identity. In: 2013 International Conference on IT Convergence and Security, ICITCS 2013, pp. 1–4. IEEE (2013)
17. Geng, G.G., Lee, X.D., Wang, W., Tseng, S.S.: Favicon - a clue to phishing sites detection. In: eCrime Researchers Summit (eCRS), pp. 1–10, September 2013
18. Liu, W., Huang, G., Xiaoyue, L., Min, Z., Deng, X.: Detection of phishing webpages based on visual similarity. In: Special Interest Tracks and Posters of the 14th International Conference on World Wide Web - WWW 2005, pp. 1060–1061 (2005)
19. Jain, A.K., Gupta, B.B.: Phishing detection: analysis of visual similarity based approaches. Secur. Commun. Netw. **2017**, 20 (2017)
20. Zhang, Y., Hong, J., Lorrie, C.: Cantina: a content-based approach to detecting phishing web sites. In: Proceedings of the 16th International Conference on World Wide Web, Banff, AB, pp. 639–648 (2007)
21. Huh, J.H., Kim, H.: Phishing detection with popular search engines: simple and effective. In: Garcia-Alfaro, J., Lafourcade, P. (eds.) FPS 2011. LNCS, vol. 6888, pp. 194–207. Springer, Heidelberg (2012). https://doi.org/10.1007/978-3-642-27901-0_15
22. Xiang, G., Hong, J., Rose, C.P., Cranor, L.: Cantina+: a feature-rich machine learning framework for detecting phishing web sites. ACM Trans. Inf. Syst. Secur. **14**(2), 21:1–21:28 (2011)
23. Gowtham, R., Krishnamurthi, I.: A comprehensive and efficacious architecture for detecting phishing webpages. Comput. Secur. **40**, 23–37 (2014)

24. Miyamoto, D., Hazeyama, H., Kadobayashi, Y.: An evaluation of machine learning-based methods for detection of phishing sites. In: Köppen, M., Kasabov, N., Coghill, G. (eds.) ICONIP 2008. LNCS, vol. 5506, pp. 539–546. Springer, Heidelberg (2009). https://doi.org/10.1007/978-3-642-02490-0_66

25. Corona, I., et al.: DeltaPhish: detecting phishing webpages in compromised websites. In: Foley, S.N., Gollmann, D., Snekkenes, E. (eds.) ESORICS 2017. LNCS, vol. 10492, pp. 370–388. Springer, Cham (2017). https://doi.org/10.1007/978-3-319-66402-6_22

26. Cova, M., Kruegel, C., Vigna, G.: There is no free phish: an analysis of "Free" and Live phishing kits. In: 2nd Conference on USENIX Workshop on Offensive Technologies (WOOT), San Jose, CA , vol. 8, pp. 1–8 (2008)

27. McCalley, H., Wardman, B., Warner, G.: Analysis of back-doored phishing kits. In: Peterson, G., Shenoi, S. (eds.) DigitalForensics 2011. IAICT, vol. 361, pp. 155–168. Springer, Heidelberg (2011). https://doi.org/10.1007/978-3-642-24212-0_12

28. Han, X., Kheir, N., Balzarotti, D.: Phisheye: live monitoring of sandboxed phishing kits. In: Proceedings of the 2016 ACM SIGSAC Conference on Computer and Communications Security, pp. 1402–1413. ACM (2016)

29. Moradpoor, N., Clavie, B., Buchanan, B.: Employing machine learning techniques for detection and classification of phishing emails. In: IEEE Computing Conference, pp. 149–156 (2017)

30. Akinyelu, A.A., Adewumi, A.O.: Classification of phishing email using random forest machine learning technique. J. Appl. Math. **2014**, 6 p. (2014)

31. Smadi, S., Aslam, N., Zhang, L., Alasem, R., Hossain, M.: Detection of phishing emails using data mining algorithms. In: 2015 9th International Conference on Software, Knowledge, Information Management and Applications (SKIMA), pp. 1–8. IEEE (2015)

32. Irani, D., Webb, S., Giffin, J., Pu, C.: Evolutionary study of phishing. In: ECrime Researchers Summit, pp. 1–10. IEEE (2008)

33. Clayton, R., Moore, T., Christin, N.: Concentrating correctly on cybercrime concentration. In: WEIS (2015)

SILK-TV: Secret Information Leakage
from Keystroke Timing Videos

Kiran S. Balagani[1], Mauro Conti[2], Paolo Gasti[1], Martin Georgiev [3,4P],
Tristan Gurtler [1,5P], Daniele Lain[2(✉),6P], Charissa Miller [1,7P], Kendall Molas[1],
Nikita Samarin [3,8P], Eugen Saraci[2], Gene Tsudik[3], and Lynn Wu [1,9P]

[1] New York Institute of Technology, New York, USA
[2] University of Padua, Padua, Italy
daniele.lain@inf.ethz.ch
[3] University of California, Irvine, USA
[4] University of Oxford, Oxford, UK
[5] University of Illinois at Urbana-Champaign, Champaign, USA
[6] ETH Zurich, Zurich, Switzerland
[7] Rochester Institute of Technology, Rochester, USA
[8] University of California, Berkeley, USA
[9] Bryn Mawr College, Philadelphia, USA

Abstract. Shoulder surfing attacks are an unfortunate consequence of
entering passwords or PINs into computers, smartphones, PoS terminals, and ATMs. Such attacks generally involve observing the victim's
input device. This paper studies leakage of user secrets (passwords and
PINs) based on observations of *output* devices (screens or projectors)
that provide "helpful" feedback to users in the form of masking characters, each corresponding to a keystroke. To this end, we developed a
new attack called *Secret Information Leakage from Keystroke Timing
Videos (SILK-TV)*. Our attack extracts inter-keystroke timing information from videos of password masking characters displayed when users
type their password on a computer, or their PIN at an ATM or PoS. We
conducted several studies in various envisaged attack scenarios. Results
indicate that, while in some cases leakage is minor, it is quite substantial in others. By leveraging inter-keystroke timings, *SILK-TV* recovers
8-character alphanumeric passwords in as little as 19 attempts. However,
when guessing PINs, *SILK-TV* yields no substantial speedup compared to
brute force. Our results strongly indicate that secure password masking
GUIs must consider the information leakage identified in this paper.

1 Introduction

Passwords and PINs are prevalent user authentication techniques primarily
because they are easy to implement, require no special hardware, and users
tend to understand them well [11]. However, one of their inherent disadvantages
is susceptibility to shoulder surfing attacks [23] of which there are two main

K. Balagani—Authors are listed in alphabetical order.

© Springer Nature Switzerland AG 2018
J. Lopez et al. (Eds.): ESORICS 2018, LNCS 11098, pp. 263–280, 2018.
https://doi.org/10.1007/978-3-319-99073-6_13

types: (1) input-based and (2) output-based. The former is more common; in it, the adversary observes an input device (keyboard or keypad) as the user enters a secret (password or PIN) and learns the key-presses. The latter involves the adversary observing an output device (screen or projector) while the user enters a secret which is displayed in cleartext. The principal distinction between the two types is adversary's proximity: observing input devices requires the adversary to be closer to the victim than observing output devices, which tend to have larger form factors, i.e., physical dimensions.

Completely disabling on-screen feedback during secret entry (as in, e.g., Unix `sudo` command) mitigates output-based shoulder-surfing attacks. Unfortunately, it also impacts usability: when deprived of visual feedback, users cannot determine whether a given key-press was registered and are thus more apt to make mistakes. In order to balance security and usability, user interfaces typically implement password masking by displaying a generic symbol (e.g., "•" or "∗") after each keystroke. This technique is commonly used on desktops, laptops and smartphones as well as on public devices, such as Automated Teller Machines (ATMs) or Point-of-Sale (PoS) terminals at shops or gas stations.

Despite the popularity of password masking, little has been done to quantify how visual keystroke feedback impacts security. In particular, masking assumes that showing generic symbols does not reveal any information about the corresponding secret. This assumption seems reasonable, since visual representation of a generic symbol is independent of the key-press. However, in this paper we show that this assumption is incorrect. By leveraging precise inter-keystroke timing information leaked by the appearance of each masking symbol, we show that the adversary can significantly narrow down the user secret's search space. Put another way, the number of attempts required to brute-force a secret decreases appreciably when the adversary has access to inter-keystroke timing information.

There are many realistic settings where visual inter-keystroke timing information (leaked via appearance of masking symbols) is readily available while the input information is not, i.e., the input device is not easily observable. For example, in a typical lecture or classroom scenario, the presenter's keyboard is usually out of sight, while the external projector display is wide-open for recording. Similarly, in a multi-person office scenario, an adversarial co-worker can surreptitiously record the victim's screen. The same holds in public scenarios, such as PoS terminals and ATMs, where displays (though smallish) tend to be easier to observe and record than entry keypads.

In this paper we consider two representative scenarios: (1) a presenter enters a password into a computer connected to an external projector; (2) a user enters a PIN at an ATM in a public location. The adversary is assumed to record keystroke feedback from the projector display or an ATM screen using a dedicated video camera or a smartphone. We note that a human adversary does not need to be present during the attack: recording might be done via an existing camera either pre-installed or pre-compromised by the adversary, possibly remotely, e.g., as in the infamous Mirai botnet [14].

Contributions. The main goal of this paper is to quantify the amount of information leaked through video recordings of on-screen keystroke feedback. To this end, we conducted extensive data collection experiments that involved 84 subjects[1]. Each subject was asked to type passwords or PINs while the screen or projector was video-recorded using either a commodity video camera and a smartphone camera. Based on this, we determined the key statistical properties of resulting data, and set up an attack, called *SILK-TV*: Secret Information Leakage from Keystroke Timing Videos. It allows us to quantify reduction in brute-force search space due to timing information. *SILK-TV* leverages multiple publicly available typing datasets to extract population timings, and applies this information to inter-keystroke timings extracted from videos.

Our results show that video recordings can be effective in extracting precise inter-keystroke timing information. Experiments show that *SILK-TV* substantially reduces the search space for each password, even when the adversary has no access to user-specific keystroke templates. When run on passwords, *SILK-TV* performed better than random guessing between 87% and 100% of the time, depending on the password and the machine learning technique used to instantiate the attack. The resulting average speedup is between 25% and 385% (depending on the password), compared to random dictionary-based guessing; some passwords were correctly guessed in as few as 68 attempts. A single password timing disclosure is enough for *SILK-TV* to successfully achieve these results. However, when the adversary observes the user entering the password three times, *SILK-TV* can crack the password in as few as 19 attempts. Clearly, *SILK-TV*'s benefits depend in part on the strength of a specific password. With very common passwords, benefits of *SILK-TV* are limited. Meanwhile, we show that *SILK-TV* substantially outperforms random guessing with less common passwords. With PINs, disclosure of timing poses only a minimal risk – *SILK-TV* reduced the number of guessing attempts by a mere 3.8%, on average.

Paper Organization. Section 2 overviews state-of-the-art in password guessing based on timing attacks. Section 3 presents *SILK-TV* and the adversary model. Section 4 discusses our data collection and experiments. We then present the results on password guessing using *SILK-TV* in Sect. 5, and on PIN guessing in Sect. 6. The paper concludes with the summary and future work directions in Sect. 7.

2   Related Work

There is a large body of prior work on timing attacks in the context of keyboard-based password entry. Song et al. [21] demonstrated a weakness that allows the adversary to extract information about passwords typed during SSH sessions. The attack relies on the fact that, to minimize latency, SSH transmits each keystroke immediately after entry, in a separate IP packet. By eavesdropping on such packets, the adversary can collect accurate inter-keystroke timing information. Authors in [21] showed that this information can be used to restrict

---

[1] Where required, IRB approvals were duly obtained prior to the experiments.

the search space of passwords. The impact of this work is significant, because it shows the power of timing attacks on cracking passwords.

There are several studies of keystroke inference from analysis of video recordings. Balzarotti et al. [4] addressed the typical shoulder-surfing scenario, where a camera tracks hand and finger movements on the keyboard. Text was automatically reconstructed from resulting videos. Similarly, Xu et al. [30] recorded user's finger movements on mobile devices to infer keystroke information. Unfortunately, neither attack applies to our sample scenarios, where the keyboard is invisible to the adversary.

Shukla et al. [20] showed that text can be inferred even from videos where the keyboard/keypad is not visible. This attack involved analyzing video recordings of the back of the user's hand holding a smartphone in order to infer which location on the screen is tapped. By observing the motion of the user's hand, the path of the finger across the screen can be reconstructed, which yields the typed text. In a similar attack, Sun et al. [22] successfully reconstructed text typed on tablets by recording and analyzing the tablet's movements, rather than movements of the user's hands.

Another line of work aimed to quantify keystroke information inadvertently leaked by motion sensors. Owusu et al. [16] studied this in the context of a smartphone's inertial sensors while the user types using the on-screen keyboard. The application used to implement this attack does not require special privileges, since modern smartphone operating systems do not require explicit authorization to access inertial sensors data. Similarly, Wang et al. [27] explored keystroke information leakage from inertial sensors on wearable devices, e.g., smartwatches and fitness trackers. By estimating the motion of a wearable device placed on the wrist of the user, movements of the user's hand over a keyboard can be inferred. This allows learning which keys were pressed during the hand's path. Compared to our work, both [16,27] require a substantially higher level of access to the user's device. To collect data from inertial sensors the adversary must have previously succeeded in deceiving the user into installing a malicious application, or otherwise compromised the user's device. In contrast, *SILK-TV* is a fully passive attack.

Acoustic emanations represent another effective side-channel for keystroke inference. This class of attacks is based on the observation that different keyboard keys emit subtly different sounds when pressed. This information can be captured (1) locally, using microphones placed near the keyboard [3,32], or (2) remotely, via Voice-over-IP [8]. Also, acoustic emanations captured using multiple microphones can be used to extract locations of keys on a keyboard. As shown by Zhou et al. [31], recordings from multiple microphones can be used to accurately quantify *time difference of arrival (TDoA)*, and thus triangulate positions of pressed keys.

3   System and Adversary Model

We now present the system and adversary model used in the rest of the paper.

We model a user logging in (authenticating) to a computer system or an ATM using a PIN or a password (*secret*) entered via keyboard or keypad (*input device*). The user receives immediate feedback about each key-press from a screen, a projector, or both (*output device*) in the form of dots or asterisks (*masking symbols*). Shape and/or location of each masking symbol does not depend on which key is pressed. The adversary can observe and record the output device(s), though not the input device or the user's hands. An example of this scenario is shown in Fig. 1. The adversary's goal is to learn the user's secret.

The envisaged attack setting is representative of many real-world scenarios that involve low-privilege adversaries, including: (1) a presenter in a lecture or conference who types a password while the screen is displayed on a projector. The entire audience can see the timing of appearance of masking symbols, and the adversary can be anyone in the audience; (2) an ATM customer typing a PIN. The adversary who stands in line behind the user might have an unobstructed view of the screen, and the timing of appearance of masking symbols (see Fig. 2); and (3) a customer enters her debit card PIN at a self-service gas-station pump. In this case, the adversary can be anyone in the surroundings with a clear view of the pump's screen.

Although these scenarios seem to imply that adversary is located near the user, proximity is not a requirement for our attack. For instance, the adversary could watch a prior recording of the lecture in scenario (1); or, could be monitoring the ATM machine using a CCTV camera in (2); or, remotely view the screen in (3) through a compromised IoT camera.

Also, we assume that, in many cases, the attack involves multiple observations. For example, in scenario (1), the adversary can observe the presenter during multiple talks, without the presenter changing passwords between talks. Similarly, in scenario (2), customers often return to the same ATM.

Fig. 1. Example attack scenario.

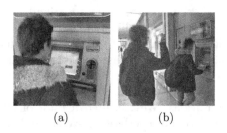

(a)   (b)

Fig. 2. Attack example – ATM setting. (a) Adversary's perspective. (b) Outsider's perspective.

4   Overview and Data Collection

Recall that *SILK-TV* confines the information about the secret that the adversary can capture to inter-keystroke timings leaked by the output device while the user types a secret. The goal is to analyze differences between the distribution of inter-keystroke timings and infer corresponding keypairs. This data is used to identify the passwords that are most likely to be correct, thus restricting the brute-force search space of the secret. To accurately extract inter-keystroke timing information, we analyze video feeds of masking symbols, and identify the frame where each masking symbol first appears. In this setting, accuracy and resolution of inter-keystroke timings depends on two key factors: refresh frequency of the output device, and frame rate of the video camera. Inter-keystroke timings are then fed to a classifier, where classes of interest are keypairs. Since we assume that the adversary has no access to user-specific keystroke information, the classifier is trained on population data, rather than on user-specific timings.

In the rest of this section, we detail the data collection process. We collected password data from two types of output devices: a VGA-based external projector, and LCD screens of several laptop computers. See Sect. 4.1 for details of these devices and corresponding procedures. For PIN data, we video-recorded the screen of a simulated ATM. Details can be found in Sect. 4.2.

4.1 Passwords

We collected data using an EPSON EMP-765 projector, and using the LCD screens of the subjects' laptops computers. In the projector setting, we asked the subjects to connect their own laptops so they would be using a familiar keyboard. The refresh rate of both laptop and projector screens were set to 60 Hz – the default setting for most systems. This setting introduces quantization errors of up to about $1/60$ s ≈ 16.7 ms. Thus, events happening within the same refresh window of 16.7 ms are indistinguishable. We recorded videos of the screen and the projector using the rear-facing camera of two smartphones: Samsung Galaxy S5 and iPhone 7 Plus. With both phones, we recorded videos at 120 frames per second, i.e., 1 frame every 8.3 ms. To ease data collection, we placed the smartphones on a tripod. When recording the projector, the tripod was placed on a table, filming from a height of about 165 cm, to be horizontally aligned with respect to the projected image. When recording laptop screens, we placed the smartphone above and to the side of the subject, in order to mimic the adversary sitting behind the subject.

All experiments took place indoors, in labs and lecture halls at the authors' institutions. We recruited a total of 62 subjects, primarily from the student population of two large universities. Most participants were males in their 20 s, with a technical background and good typing skills. We briefed each subject on the nature of the experiment, and asked them to type four alphanumerical passwords: "jillie02", "william1", "123brian", and "lamondre". We selected these passwords uniformly at random from the RockYou dataset [1] in order to simulate realistic passwords. The subjects typed each password three times, while our data collection software recorded ground-truth keystroke timings of correctly typed passwords with millisecond accuracy. Timings from passwords that were typed incorrectly were discarded, and subjects were prompted to re-type the password whenever a mistake was made. The typing procedure lasted between 1 and 2 min, depending on the subject's typing skills. All subjects typed with the "touch typing" technique, i.e., using fingers from both hands.

4.2 PINs

We recorded subjects entering 4-digit PINs on a simulated ATM, shown in Fig. 3. Our dataset was based on experiments with 22 participants; 19 subjects completed three data collection sessions, while 4 subjects completed only one session, resulting in a total of 61 sessions. At the beginning of each session, the subject was given 45 s to get accustomed with the keypad of the ATM simulator. During this time, they were free to type as they pleased. Next, a subject was shown a PIN on the screen for ten seconds (Fig. 4a), and, once it disappeared from the screen, asked to enter it four times (Fig. 4b). Subjects were advised not to read the PINs out loud. This process was repeated for 15 consecutive PINs. During each session, subjects were presented with the same 15-PIN sequence 3 times. Subjects were given a 30-s break at the end of each sequence.

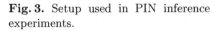

(a)   (b)

Fig. 3. Setup used in PIN inference experiments.

Fig. 4. ATM simulator during a data collection session. (a) The simulator displays the next PIN. (b) A subject types the PIN from memory.

Specific 4-digit PINs were selected to test whether: (1) inter-keypress time is proportional to Euclidean Distance between keys on the keypad; and (2) the *direction of movement* (up, down, left, or right) between consecutive keys in a keypair impacts the corresponding inter-key time. We show an example of these two situations on the ATM keypad in Fig. 5. We chose a set of PINs that allowed collection of a significant number of key combinations appropriate for testing both hypotheses. For instance, PIN 3179 tested horizontal and vertical distance two, while 1112 tested distance 0 and horizontal distance 1.

Sessions were recorded using a Sony FDR-AX53 camera, with the pixel resolution of 1,920 × 1,080 pixels, and 120 frames per second. At the same time, ATM simulation software collected millisecond-accurate inter-key distance ground truth by logging each keypress. PIN feedback was shown on a DELL 17″ LCD screen with a refresh rate of 60 Hz, which resulted to each frame being shown for 16.7 ms.

4.3   Timing Extraction from Video

We developed software that analyzes video recordings to automatically detect appearance of masking symbols and log corresponding timestamps. This software uses OpenCV [17] to infer the number of symbols present in each image. All frames are first converted to grayscale, and then processed through a bilateral filter [25] to reduce noise due to the camera's sensor. Resulting images are analyzed using Canny Edge detection [9] to capture the edges of the masking symbol. External contours are compared with the expected shape of the masking symbol. When a masking symbol is detected, software logs the corresponding frame number.

Our experiments show that this technique leads to fairly accurate inter-keystroke timing information. We observed average discrepancy of 8.7 ms (*stdev* of 26.6 ms) between the inter-keystroke timings extracted from the video and ground truth recorded by the ATM simulator. Furthermore, 75% of inter-keystroke timings extracted by the software had errors under 10 ms, and 97% had errors under 20 ms. Similar statistics hold for data recorded on keyboards for the passwords setting. Figure 6 shows the distribution of error discrepancies.

5   Password Guessing Using *SILK-TV*

SILK-TV treats identifying digraphs from keystroke timings as a multi-class classification problem, where each class represents one digraph, and input to the classifier is a set of inter-keystroke times. Without loss of generality, in this

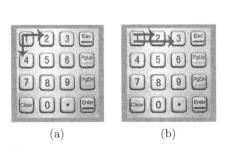

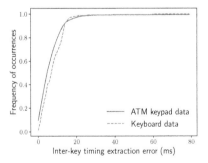

Fig. 5. ATM keypad in our experiments. (a) To type keypairs 1–2 and 1–4, the typing finger travels the same distance in different directions. (b) Keypairs 1–2 and 1–3 require the typing finger to travel different distances in the same direction.

Fig. 6. CDF showing error distribution of inter-keystroke timings extracted from videos.

section, we assume that the user's password is a sequence of lowercase alphanumeric characters typed on a keyboard with a standard layout.

To reconstruct passwords, we compared two classifiers: Random Forest (RF) [13] and Neural Networks (NN) [19]. RF is a well-known classification technique that performs well for authentication based on keystroke timings [6]. Input to RF is one inter-keystroke timing, and its output is a list of N digraphs ranked based on the probability of corresponding to input timing. NN is a more complex architecture designed to automatically determine and extract complex features from the input distribution. In our experiments, the input to NN is a list of inter-keystroke timings corresponding to a password. This enables NN to extract features, such as arbitrary n-grams, or timings corresponding to non-consecutive characters. NN's output is a guess for the entire password. We instantiated NN using the following parameters:

- number of units in the hidden layer – 128 (with ReLU activation functions);
- inclusion probability of the dropout layer – 0.2;
- number of input neurons – 25;
- number of output layers – 25 which represents one character in one-hot encoding. Output layers use softmax activation function;
- training was performed using batch sizes of 40 and 100 epochs. We used the Adam optimizer with a learning rate of 0.001.

Classifier Training. We trained *SILK-TV* on three public datasets [5,18,26] that contain keystroke timing information collected from English free-text. Using these datasets for training, we modeled an attack that relies exclusively on *population data*. Without loss of generality, we filtered the datasets to remove all timings that do not correspond to digraphs composed of alphanumeric lowercase characters. This is motivated by the datasets' limited availability of digraph samples that contain special characters. In practice, the adversary could collect these timings using, for instance, crowdsourcing tools such as Amazon Mechanical Turk. To take care of uneven frequencies of different digraphs, we underrepresented the most frequent digraphs in the dataset. Data in public datasets was often gathered from free-text typing of volunteers. Therefore, more frequent digraphs in English were represented more than rarer ones. For example, considering `lamondre`, digraph `re` appears 43,606 times in the population dataset, while `am` – only 6,481. Similarly, in `123brian`, digraph `ri` occurs 19,782 times, while `3b` – only 138. We therefore under-sampled each digraph appearing more than 1,000 times to 1,000 randomly selected occurrences. Similarly, we excluded infrequent digraphs that appeared under 100 times in the whole dataset.

Attack Process. To infer the user's secret from inter-keystroke timings, *SILK-TV* leverages a dictionary of passwords (e.g., a list of passwords leaked by online services [1,2,10,24]), possibly expanded using techniques such as probabilistic context-free grammars [29] and generative adversarial networks [12]. When evaluating *SILK-TV*, we assume that the user's secret is in the dictionary. In practice, this is often the case, as many users use the same weak passwords (e.g., only 36% of the password of RockYou is unique [15]), and reuse them across many different services [11,28]. Given that the size of a reasonable password dictionary

is on the order of billions of entries[2], the goal of *SILK-TV* is to narrow down the possible passwords to a small(er) list, e.g., to perform online attacks. This list is then ranked by the probability associated with each entry, computed from inter-keystroke timing data.
Specifically:

1. Using RF, for each inter-key time extracted from video (corresponding to a digraph), *SILK-TV* returns a list of N possible guesses, sorted by the classifier's confidence. Next, *SILK-TV* ranks the passwords in the dictionary by resulting probabilities as follows: for each password, *SILK-TV* identifies the position in the ranked list of predictions for the first digraph of the password being guessed, and assigns that position as a "penalty" to the password. By performing these steps for each digraph, *SILK-TV* obtains a total penalty score for each password, i.e., a score that indicates the probability of the password given the output of the RF.

   For example, to rank the password jillie02, *SILK-TV* first considers the digraph ji, and the list of predictions of RF for the first digraph. It notes that ji appears in such list as the X-th most probable; therefore, it assigns X as the penalty for jillie02. Then, it considers il, which appears in Y-th position in the list of predictions for the second digraph. Penalty for jillie02 is thus updated to $X + Y$. This operation is repeated for all the 7 digraphs, thus obtaining the final penalty score.

2. Using NN, *SILK-TV* computes a list of N possible guesses, sorted by the classifier's confidence of each guess. In this case, the *SILK-TV* processes the entire list of flight times at once, rather than refining its guess with each digraph.

We considered the following attack settings: *single-shot*, and *multiple recordings*. With the former, the adversary trains *SILK-TV* with inter-keystroke timings from population data, i.e., from users other than the target, e.g., from publicly available datasets, or by recruiting users and asking them to type passwords. In this scenario, the adversary has access to the video recording of a single password entry session. With multiple recordings, the adversary trains *SILK-TV* as before, and additionally, has access to videos of multiple login instances by the same user.

Training *SILK-TV* exclusively with population data leads to more realistic attack scenarios than training it with user-specific data, because usually the adversary has limited access to keystrokes samples from the target user. Further, access to user-specific data will likely improve the success rate of *SILK-TV*.

5.1   Results

In this section, we report on *SILK-TV* efficacy in reducing search time on the RockYou [1] password dataset compared to random choice, weighted by probability. We restricted experiments to the subset of 8-character passwords from

---

[2] See for example the lists maintained by https://haveibeenpwned.com/.

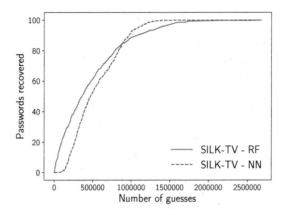

Fig. 7. CDF of the amount of passwords recovered by *SILK-TV*—*Population Data* attack scenario.

RockYou, since the adversary can always determine password length by counting the number of masking symbols shown on the screen. This resulted in 6,514,177 passwords, out of which 2,967,116 were unique.

Attack Baseline. To establish the attack baseline, we consider an adversary that outputs password guesses from a leaked dataset in descending order of frequency. (Ties are broken using random selection from the candidate passwords.) Because password probabilities are far from uniform (e.g., in RockYou, top 200 8-character passwords account for over 10% of the entire dataset), this is the best adversarial strategy given no additional information on the target user.

Passwords selected for our evaluation represent a mix of common and rare passwords. Thus, they have widely varying frequencies of occurrence in Rock-You and expected number of attempts needed to guess each password using the baseline attack varies significantly. For example, expected number of attempts for:

- `123brian` (appears 6 times) – 93,874;
- `jillie02`, (appears only once) – 1,753,571;
- `lamondre` (appears twice) – 397,213;
- `william1` (appears 1,164 times) – only 187.

Single-shot. Results in the single-shot setting are summarized in Table 1. Cumulative Distribution Function (CDF) of successfully recovered passwords is reflected in Fig. 7, and breakdown of results (by target password) is shown in Fig. 8.

Results show that, for uncommon passwords (`jillie02` and `lamondre`), *SILK-TV* consistently outperforms random guessing. In particular, for `jillie02` both RF and NN greatly exceed random guessing, since both their curves in Fig. 8 are above random guess baseline. For `lamondre`, RF shows an advantage over random guess in 76% of the instances, while NN never beats the baseline.

Table 1. *SILK-TV—Single-shot* setting. *Avg*: average number of attempts to guess a password; *Stdev*: standard deviation; *Rnd*: number of guesses for the baseline adversary; *<Rnd*: how often *SILK-TV* outperforms random guessing; *Best*: number of attempts of the best guess; *<n*: how many passwords are successfully guessed within first $n = 20,000/100,000$ attempts.

	Avg	Stdev	Med	Rnd	<Rnd	Best	<20k	<100k
Random forest								
123brian	581,743	414,761	508,332	93,874	8.7%	5,535	1.1%	9.3%
jillie02	749,718	448,319	656,754	1,753,571	97.8%	28,962	0.0%	2.7%
lamondre	301,906	334,681	199,344	397,213	75.0%	145	13.0%	33.7%
william1	246,437	264,090	145,966	187	0.5%	68	10.9%	39.9%
Neural network								
123brian	923,534	165,454	886,802	93,874	0.0%	577,739	0.0%	0.0%
jillie02	456,811	210,512	383,230	1,753,571	100.0%	164,754	0.0%	0.0%
lamondre	517,472	189,355	493,713	397,213	28.8%	148,403	0.0%	0.0%
william1	265,813	140,753	215,840	187	0.0%	45,176	0.0%	3.8%

For common passwords, sorted random guess wins over *SILK-TV*. In particular, 123brian is both popular (i.e., 93,874-th most popular password of the set, corresponding to the top 3% of the RockYou dataset) and very hard to recover with *SILK-TV*. This can be observed from Fig. 8, where the curves corresponding to 123brian are least steep. Finally, william1, being the 187-th most popular password, is always recovered early in our baseline attack, with the notable exception of one instance by RF.

In general, *SILK-TV* wins over the sorted random guess on infrequent passwords, such as jillie02 and lamondre, that appear only once or twice, respectively. Such infrequent passwords exhibit the same random guess baseline curve and average, reported in Table 1 and shown in Fig. 8. Given the similar steepness of CDF curves in Fig. 8, which hint that *SILK-TV* 's performance might be similar for many other passwords, *SILK-TV* can probably outperform the baseline for uncommon passwords. We also note that uncommon passwords represent the vast majority of user-chosen passwords: 90% of RockYou passwords appear at most twice, and 80% exactly once. We expect that a realistic adversary would first generate password guesses based on their frequency alone (as in our baseline attack), and then switch to *SILK-TV* once these frequencies drop below some threshold.

Finally, we highlight that random guess baseline is computed on the distribution of passwords in RockYou. Other datasets might have different distributions: for example, in the *10 million password list* dataset [7], jillie02, lamondre, and 123brian appear only once, while william1 appears 176 times.

We believe that the discrepancy between performance of *SILK-TV* on various passwords is due to how frequently the digraphs in each password appear in

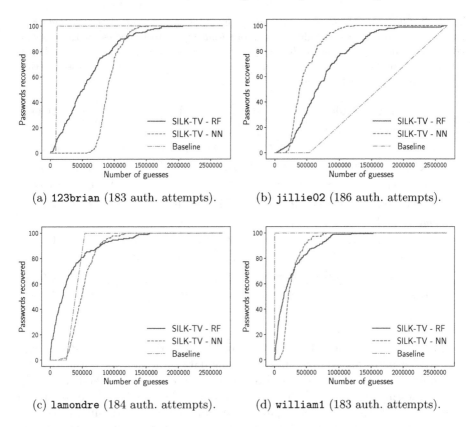

(a) `123brian` (183 auth. attempts).   (b) `jillie02` (186 auth. attempts).

(c) `lamondre` (184 auth. attempts).   (d) `william1` (183 auth. attempts).

Fig. 8. CDF for the number of passwords recovered by *SILK-TV*, for each target password. Plots also show the baseline attack for the corresponding password.

training data. Specifically, even with our under-representation, all digraphs in `william1`, with the exception of `m1`, are far more frequent in the training data than `12`, `23`, `3b`, or `02`.

Regarding specific classifiers, RF overtakes NN in most instances. For example, when guessing `123brian` (Fig. 8a), NN performs worse than random guessing for first 800,000 attempts. Afterwards, NN outperforms both random guessing and RF. Furthermore, while RF can guess a substantial percentage of passwords within 20,000, 50,000 and 100,000 attempts, NN cannot achieve the same result.

In terms of minimum number of guesses per password, RF recovered `william1` in 68, `lamondre` in 145, `123brian` in 5,535, and `jillie02` in 28,962 attempts. NN required a consistently higher minimum number of attempts for each password.

Multiple Recordings. Information from three login instances was used as follows. We averaged classifiers' predictions over three login instances for a given user, and ranked passwords accordingly.

Table 2. *SILK-TV—Multiple recordings* setting. *Avg*: average number of attempts to guess a password; *Stdev*: standard deviation; *Rnd*: number of guesses for the baseline adversary; $<Rnd$: how often *SILK-TV* outperforms random guessing; *Best*: number of attempts of the best guess; $<n$: how many passwords are successfully guessed within first $n = 20{,}000/100{,}000$ attempts.

	Avg	Stdev	Med	Rnd	$<$Rnd	Best	$<$20k	$<$100k
Random forest								
123brian	552,574	468,539	402,166	93,874	14.1%	13,931	4.7%	14.1%
jillie02	713,895	410,225	606,403	1,753,571	100.0%	67,875	0.0%	1.6%
lamondre	398,186	425,811	236,905	397,213	65.6%	404	6.2%	25.0%
william1	370,933	602,654	148,405	187	1.6%	19	17.2%	42.2%
Neural network								
123brian	922,655	129,927	889,406	93,874	0.0%	676,418	0.0%	0.0%
jillie02	439,414	155,385	402,332	1,753,571	100.0%	205,645	0.0%	0.0%
lamondre	503,248	137,276	504,493	397,213	21.3%	182,123	0.0%	0.0%
william1	248,769	103,240	216,630	187	0.0%	86,213	0.0%	1.6%

Results are summarized in Table 2, and Fig. 9. Although *SILK-TV* still consistently outperforms random guessing, using data from multiple authentication recordings leads to mostly identical results overall with both RF and NN. *SILK-TV* 's guessing success rate for 123brian and jillie02 is slightly improved compared to the previous setting and minimum number of attempts to recover each password diminished slightly. We recovered william1 in 19, lamondre in 404, 123brian in 13,931, and jillie02 in 67,875 attempts. Overall, results show that there are no substantial benefits in using timing data from three recordings from the same user.

6   PIN Guessing Using *SILK-TV*

We now discuss PIN-related results, specifically, relationships between: (1) inter-keystroke timings and Euclidean Distance between consecutive keys, and (2) inter-keystroke timings and direction of movement on the keypad.

We are not aware of any publicly-available PIN timing datasets that can be used to train *SILK-TV*. To address this issue, we divided our dataset in two parts. The first was used as training, and the second – as testing, data. To compute the attack baseline, we considered all PINs to be equally likely.

Distance. Across all subjects, we observed that distributions of inter-keystroke latencies were distinct in all cases (for p-value $< 5 \cdot 10^{-6}$), with the following exceptions: (1) latencies for distance 2 (e.g., keypair 1–3) were close to latencies for distance 3 (keypair 2–0); (2) latencies for distance 2 were close to latencies for diagonal 1×1 (e.g., keypair 4–8); latencies for distance 3 were close to

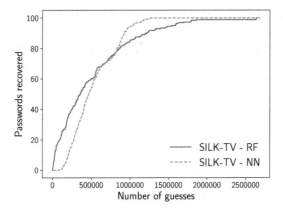

Fig. 9. CDF showing number of passwords recovered by *SILK-TV* in the *Multiple recordings* scenario.

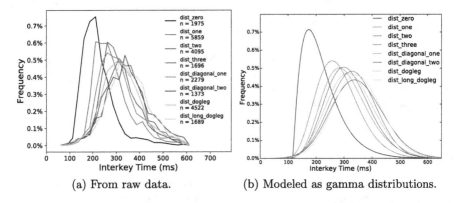

(a) From raw data.   (b) Modeled as gamma distributions.

Fig. 10. Inter-keystroke timings of all possible distances for ATM keypad typing.

latencies for 2×1 diagonal (i.e. "2" to "9", "1" to "6", etc.), and diagonal 2×2 (e.g., keypair 7–3), and diagonal 3×2 (e.g., keypair 3–0). Figure 10a shows the various probability distributions, while Fig. 10b models these different probability distribution functions as gamma distributions. In Fig. 10a, dist_zero indicates keypairs composed of the same two digits. dist_one, dist_two, and dist_three shows timings distributions for keypairs with horizontal or vertical distance one (e.g., keypair 2–5), two (e.g., 2–8), and three (2–0), respectively. dist_diagonal_one and dist_diagonal_two indicates keypairs with diagonal distance one (e.g., 2–4) and distance two (e.g., 1–9), respectively. dist_dogleg and dist_long_dogleg show timing distributions of keypairs such as 1–8 and 0–3. In Fig. 10b, dist_one_horizontal and dist_one_vertical indicate Euclidean Distance right in the left/right directions, and up/down directions, respectively, while dist_one_up, dist_one_down, dist_one_left, and dist_one_right indicate distances one in the up, down, left, and right directions.

Direction. The relative orientation of key pairs characterized by the same Euclidean distance (e.g., 2–3 vs. 2–5) has a negligible impact on the corresponding inter-key latency. We observed that the distributions of keypress latencies observed from each possible direction between keys were not significantly different (for p-value $< 10^{-4}$). Figure 11 shows different probability distributions relative to various directions for Euclidean distance 1.

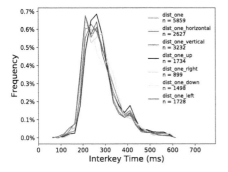
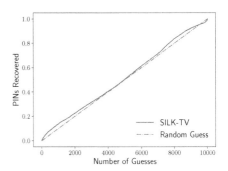

Fig. 11. Frequency of inter-keystroke timings for Euclidean Distance of one. dist_one indicates latency distribution for distance one in any direction.

Fig. 12. CDF showing the number of PINs recovered by *SILK-TV*, compared to the baseline.

6.1   Pin Inference

Using the data we collected, we mapped the distribution of inter-keypress latencies, and used the resulting probabilities to test the effectiveness of PINs prediction from inter-key latencies.

To guess PINs from our inter-key latencies, we used data from 14 users to model the inter-key latencies as gamma distributions. Then, we tested the data from the remaining users. Figure 12 shows the effectiveness of these predictions compared to brute-force guesses. Due to the lack of separation between the distribution of most distances and directions, the improvement compared to brute force is small (in the -1% to 4% range), leading to an average reduction in guessing attempts of about 3.8%.

7   Conclusion

In this paper, we have shown that inter-key timing information disclosed by showing password masking symbols can be effectively used to reduce the cost of password guessing attacks. To determine the impact of this side channel, we recorded videos from 84 subjects, typing several passwords and PINs under different conditions: in a lecture hall, while their laptop was collected to a projector; in a classroom setting; and using a simulated ATM machine. Our results show that: (1) it is possible to infer very accurate timing information from videos of LCD screens and projectors (the average error was 8.7ms, which is corresponds with the duration of a frame when the refresh rate of a display is set to 60 Hz); (2) inter-keystroke timings reduce the number of attempts to recover a password by 25% and 385%, with some passwords guessed within 19 attempts. We consider this a substantial reduction in the cost of password guessing attacks, to the point that we believe that masking symbols should not be publicly displayed when typing passwords; and (3) disclosing inter-keystroke timings have a relatively small impact on PIN guessing attacks (the average reduction in the number of attempts required to guess a 4-digit PIN was 3.8%).

Clearly, the benefits of *SILK-TV* compared to our baseline attack vary depending on how common the user's password is. For very common (and therefore very easy to guess) passwords, our results show that *SILK-TV* might not be needed. On the other hand, the speedup offered by *SILK-TV* when guessing rare passwords is substantial. Given the effectiveness of this attack on password guessing, we think that future work should consider countermeasures that strike the right balance between usability and security when displaying masking symbols. For instance, GUIs may not display masking symbols on a secondary screen (e.g., projectors), or may display new masking symbols at fixed intervals (say, every 250ms). Clearly, both countermeasures have usability implications, and we leave the quantification of this impact to future work.

Acknowledgements. Kiran Balagani and Paolo Gasti were supported but the National Science Foundation under Grant No. CNS-1619023. Tristan Gurtler, Charissa Miller, Kendall Molas, and Lynn Wu were supported by the National Science Foundation under Grant No. CNS-1559652. This work is partially supported by the EU TagItSmart! Project (agreement H2020-ICT30-2015-688061), and the EU-India REACH Project (agreement ICI+/2014/342-896).

References

1. Rockyou password leak (2010). http://downloads.skullsecurity.org/passwords/rockyou.txt.bz2
2. Linkedin password leak (2016). https://hashes.org/leaks.php
3. Asonov, D., Agrawal, R.: Keyboard acoustic emanations. In: IEEE S&P (2004)
4. Balzarotti, D., Cova, M., Vigna, G.: ClearShot: eavesdropping on keyboard input from video. In: IEEE S&P (2008)
5. Banerjee, R., Feng, S., Kang, J.S., Choi, Y.: Keystroke patterns as prosody in digital writings: a case study with deceptive reviews and essays. In: EMNLP. Association for Computational Linguistics (2014)
6. Bartlow, N., Cukic, B.: Evaluating the reliability of credential hardening through keystroke dynamics. In: IEEE ISSRE (2006)
7. Burnett, M.: Today I am releasing 10 million passwords (2015). https://xato.net/today-i-am-releasing-ten-million-passwords-b6278bbe7495
8. Compagno, A., Conti, M., Lain, D., Tsudik, G.: Don't skype & type!: Acoustic eavesdropping in Voice-Over-IP. In: ACM ASIACCS (2017)
9. Ding, L., Goshtasby, A.: On the canny edge detector. Pattern Recogn. **34**(3), 721–725 (2001)

10. Fiegerman, S.: Yahoo says 500 million accounts stolen (2017). http://money.cnn.com/2016/09/22/technology/yahoo-data-breach/index.html

11. Florencio, D., Herley, C.: A large-scale study of web password habits. In: ACM WWW (2007)

12. Hitaj, B., Gasti, P., Ateniese, G., Perez-Cruz, F.: PassGAN: a deep learning approach for password guessing. arXiv preprint arXiv:1709.00440 (2017)

13. Ho, T.K.: Random decision forests. In: IEEE Document Analysis and Recognition (1995)

14. Kolias, C., Kambourakis, G., Stavrou, A., Voas, J.: DDoS in the IoT: Mirai and other botnets. Computer 50(7), 80–84 (2017)

15. Ma, J., Yang, W., Luo, M., Li, N.: A study of probabilistic password models. In: IEEE S&P (2014)

16. Owusu, E., Han, J., Das, S., Perrig, A., Zhang, J.: ACCessory: password inference using accelerometers on smartphones. In: ACM HotMobile (2012)

17. Pulli, K., Baksheev, A., Kornyakov, K., Eruhimov, V.: Real-time computer vision with OpenCV. Commun. ACM 55(6), 61–69 (2012)

18. Roth, J., Liu, X., Metaxas, D.: On continuous user authentication via typing behavior. IEEE Trans. Image Process. 23(10), 4611–4624 (2014)

19. Schalkoff, R.J.: Artificial Neural Networks, vol. 1. McGraw-Hill, New York (1997)

20. Shukla, D., Kumar, R., Serwadda, A., Phoha, V.V.: Beware, your hands reveal your secrets! In: ACM CCS (2014)

21. Song, D.X., Wagner, D., Tian, X.: Timing analysis of keystrokes and timing attacks on SSH. In: USENIX Security Symposium (2001)

22. Sun, J., Jin, X., Chen, Y., Zhang, J., Zhang, Y., Zhang, R.: VISIBLE: video-assisted keystroke inference from tablet backside motion. In: NDSS (2016)

23. Tari, F., Ozok, A., Holden, S.H.: A comparison of perceived and real shoulder-surfing risks between alphanumeric and graphical passwords. In: ACM SOUPS (2006)

24. The Password Project (2017). http://thepasswordproject.com/leaked_password_lists_and_dictionaries

25. Tomasi, C., Manduchi, R.: Bilateral filtering for gray and color images. In: IEEE Computer Vision (1998)

26. Vural, E., Huang, J., Hou, D., Schuckers, S.: Shared research dataset to support development of keystroke authentication. In: IEEE IJCB (2014)

27. Wang, C., Guo, X., Wang, Y., Chen, Y., Liu, B.: Friend or foe? Your wearable devices reveal your personal pin. In: ACM ASIACCS (2016)

28. Wang, C., Jan, S.T., Hu, H., Bossart, D., Wang, G.: The next domino to fall: empirical analysis of user passwords across online services. In: ACM CODASPY (2018)

29. Weir, M., Aggarwal, S., De Medeiros, B., Glodek, B.: Password cracking using probabilistic context-free grammars. In: IEEE S&P (2009)

30. Xu, Y., Heinly, J., White, A.M., Monrose, F., Frahm, J.M.: Seeing double: reconstructing obscured typed input from repeated compromising reflections. In: ACM CCS (2013)

31. Zhu, T., Ma, Q., Zhang, S., Liu, Y.: Context-free attacks using keyboard acoustic emanations. In: ACM CCS (2014)

32. Zhuang, L., Zhou, F., Tygar, J.D.: Keyboard acoustic emanations revisited. ACM TISSEC 13(1), 3 (2009)

A Formal Approach to Analyzing
Cyber-Forensics Evidence

Erisa Karafili[1]([✉]), Matteo Cristani[2], and Luca Viganò[3]

[1] Department of Computing, Imperial College London, London, UK
e.karafili@imperial.ac.uk
[2] Dipartimento di Informatica, Università di Verona, Verona, Italy
matteo.cristani@univr.it
[3] Department of Informatics, King's College London, London, UK
luca.vigano@kcl.ac.uk

Abstract. The frequency and harmfulness of cyber-attacks are increasing every day, and with them also the amount of data that the cyber-forensics analysts need to collect and analyze. In this paper, we propose a formal analysis process that allows an analyst to filter the enormous amount of evidence collected and either identify crucial information about the attack (e.g., when it occurred, its culprit, its target) or, at the very least, perform a pre-analysis to reduce the complexity of the problem in order to then draw conclusions more swiftly and efficiently.

We introduce the Evidence Logic $\mathcal{EL}$ for representing simple and derived pieces of evidence from different sources. We propose a procedure, based on monotonic reasoning, that rewrites the pieces of evidence with the use of tableau rules, based on relations of trust between sources and the reasoning behind the derived evidence, and yields a consistent set of pieces of evidence. As proof of concept, we apply our analysis process to a concrete cyber-forensics case study.

1 Introduction

The frequency and harmfulness of cyber-attacks are increasing every day, and with them also the amount of data that cyber-forensics analysts need to collect and analyze. In fact, forensics investigations often produce an enormous amount of evidence. The pieces of evidence are produced/collected by various sources, which can be humans (e.g., another analyst) or forensic tools such as intrusion detection system (IDS), traceback systems, malware analysis tools, and so on.

When a forensics analyst evaluates a cyber-attack, she first collects all the relevant evidence containing information about the attack and then checks the sources of the evidence in order to evaluate their reliability and to resolve possible inconsistencies arising from them. Based on the collected information, which might be different depending on the information sources and the trust relation between the analyst and the sources, the analyst might reconstruct different, possibly faulty, courses of events. State of the art approaches don't really manage to cope well with such situations.

© Springer Nature Switzerland AG 2018
J. Lopez et al. (Eds.): ESORICS 2018, LNCS 11098, pp. 281–301, 2018.
https://doi.org/10.1007/978-3-319-99073-6_14

To reason about the collected evidence, we need to formalize the fact that the analyst trusts more some sources than others for particular pieces of evidence, e.g., a source S_1 is more trusted than another source S_2 for attack similarity as tool S_1 specializes in malware analysis whereas tool S_2 specializes in deleted data. We also need to distinguish between the evidence and its interpretation that an analyst may consider in order to perform a correct analysis and attribution of the cyber-attack.

Our main contribution in this paper is the introduction of the *Evidence Logic $\mathcal{EL}$*, which allows an analysts to represent the different pieces of evidence, together with their sources and relations of trust, and reason about them by eliminating the conflicting pieces of evidence during the analysis process.

As a concrete motivating example, consider the data breach of the Democratic National Committee (DNC) network, during the last US presidential campaign, when Wikileaks and other websites published several private emails in October and November 2016. DNC used the services of a cyber-security company, CrowdStrike, to mitigate the attacks and to conduct a forensics investigation. CrowdStrike stated that the main attack occurred between March and April 2016, and identified it as a *spear phishing* campaign that used Bitly accounts to shorten malicious URLs. The phishing campaign was successful as different IDs and passwords were collected.

However, TheForensicator, an anonymous analyst, stated that the attack actually occurred on the 5th of July 2016, not in March/April, as the metadata released by an alleged attacker were created on the 5th of July 2016, and the data-leak occurred physically as the data were transferred at the speed of around 23 MB/s, and this speed is possible only during a physical access. Another cyber-security company, FireEye, stated that it is possible to have a non-physical data-transfer speed of 23 MB/s. What should an analyst conclude from these discording statements and pieces of evidence? How can a decision be made?

$\mathcal{EL}$ is able to deal with this type of discordances, and based on relations of trust on the sources and reasonings, to arrive at a certain conclusion. $\mathcal{EL}$ is composed of three separate layers: the first layer $\mathcal{EL}_E$ deals with pieces of evidence, the second layer $\mathcal{EL}_I$ focuses on the evidence interpretations, and the third layer $\mathcal{EL}_R$ focuses on the reasoning involved in the evidence. Reasoning with $\mathcal{EL}$ amounts to applying a rewriting system that spans formulas in all three levels to reach a conclusion, ruling out discordances and inconsistencies. Applying the reasoning process of $\mathcal{EL}$ to the different pieces of evidence from the various sources, the analyst can decide the type of the attack and when it occurred. For instance, regarding the speed of transferability, if the analyst trusts FireEye more than TheForensicator, then she does not take into consideration the evidence that the data transfer was physical. Hence, she concludes that the attack occurred during March/April 2016 and not in July 2016.

We proceed as follows. In Sects. 2 and 3, we give the syntax and semantics of the Evidence Logic $\mathcal{EL}$, respectively. In Sect. 4, we introduce the rules of the rewriting system of $\mathcal{EL}$ and we give a concrete procedure that uses the rewriting rules to prove the satisfiability of a given $\mathcal{EL}$-theory (which is a finite and non-empty set of formulas of the three layers of $\mathcal{EL}$). We prove the rewriting system to be sound and the procedure to be correct (the proofs of the theorems are given in the Appendix). Section 6 concludes the paper by discussing related work and future work.

2   The Syntax of the Evidence Logic $\mathcal{EL}$

The *Evidence Logic* $\mathcal{EL}$ that we propose enables a cyber-forensics analyst to represent the various plausible pieces of evidence that she collected from different sources and reason about them. To that end, the analyst should distinguish between the evidence and its interpretation. In a nutshell:

- *evidence* represents information related to the attack, where a given (piece of) evidence usually represents an event, its occurrence and the source of the information of the occurrence of the event (which can be another analyst, a cyber-forensics tool, etc.);
- *evidence interpretation* represents what the analyst thinks[1] about the occurrence of an event e and about the occurrences of the events causing e.

$\mathcal{EL}$ contains two types of well-formed formulas: *labeled formulas*, to formalize the pieces of evidence and interpretation, and *relational formulas*, to formalize relations of *trust* between sources of evidence and their reasonings. $\mathcal{EL}$ also contains a rewriting system (composed of a set of tableau rules) to build the analyst's interpretations from forensics evidence. For the sake of readability, we omit to model explicitly the analyst who is reconstructing and attributing the cyber-attack, but we simply silently assume her existence.

$\mathcal{EL}$ is composed of three separate layers: the first layer $\mathcal{EL}_E$ shows how the well-formed formulas for pieces of evidence are built, the second layer $\mathcal{EL}_I$ focuses on the evidence interpretations, and the third layer $\mathcal{EL}_R$ focuses on the reasoning involved in the evidence. In the following, we discuss each of the layers in detail.

2.1 $\mathcal{EL}_E$: Evidence

Definition 1. *Given* $t, t_1, \ldots t_n \in T$, $a, a_1, \ldots a_n \in Ag$, $r_1, r_2 \in \mathcal{R}$, $p \in Vars_S$ *and* $\phi, \phi_1, \ldots, \phi_n \in Lit$, *the set* ρ *of formulas of* $\mathcal{EL}_E$ *is*

$$\rho ::= a : (t : \phi) \mid a : (t : \phi) \, [a_1 : (t_1 : \phi_1) \mid \ldots \mid a_n : (t_n : \phi_n)]_r \mid a_1 \lhd_p a_2 \mid r_1 \prec r_2$$

We introduce all these notions, and the four kinds of formulas, step by step. A piece of evidence asserts what a source thinks about the temporal occurrence of an event, i.e., whether an event occurred or not in a particular instance of time. To formalize this, we use two finite[2] and disjoint sets of labels,

---

[1] We deliberately use the verb "thinking" to avoid suggesting any epistemic or doxastic flavor, as in $\mathcal{EL}$ we do not consider the modalities of knowledge or belief.

[2] In principle, there is nothing in our logic that prevents us from considering countable, possibly infinite, sets of labels, but here we consider finite sets for simplicity.

- *source labels* $Ag = \{a_1, a_2, \ldots, a_n\}$ for forensic sources, which we call *agents*, regardless of whether they are human or not, and
- *temporal labels* $T = \{t_1, t_2, \ldots, t_m\}$ for instants of time,

along with

- a set of *propositional variables* $Vars = \{p_1, p_2, \ldots, p_n\}$ that represent the occurrences of *forensics events* (so that p represents the occurrence of an event and $\neg p$ represents that p does not occur),
- a set of *reasoning rules* (or simply *reasonings*) $\mathcal{R} = \{r_1, r_2, \ldots, r_l\}$ that represent the reasoning used by the agents to conclude further evidence.

The set of *literals* $Lit = \{p_1, \neg p_1, \ldots, p_n, \neg p_n\}$ consists of each propositional variable and its negation. We write ϕ, possibly subscripted, to denote a literal.

Instants of time are labels associated to elements of a single given stream. Thus, the labels that represent the instants of time cannot be processed for consistency, and no assertions regarding relations between them is allowed.

Example 1. Consider again the motivating example that we discussed in the Introduction. The set of agents is composed of the analyst (whose existence we silently assume) and the sources CrowdStrike (*CS*), TheForensicator (*TF*) and FireEye (*FE*); thus, $Ag = \{CS, TF, FE\}$. The sources make statements about events occurring in two instants of time: "March/April 2016" and "5th of July 2016" represented respectively by t_1 and t_2.   □

We formalize two different types of evidence: simple and derived one. The *simple evidence* is a labeled formula of the form

$$a : (t : \phi),$$

expressing that the agent represented by the source label a thinks that the literal ϕ is true at the instant of time represented by the temporal label t. For short, we will say that a thinks that ϕ is true at t.

Example 2. The simple evidence $FE : (t_2 : SpeedTr(23MB/s))$ expresses that *FE* states that the non-physical transferability speed, *SpeedTr*, can be *23MB/s* at t_2.   □

The *derived evidence* is a labeled formula of the form

$$a : (t : \phi) \, [a_1 : (t_1 : \phi_1) \mid a_2 : (t_2 : \phi_2) \mid \ldots \mid a_n : (t_n : \phi_n)]_r,$$

expressing that agent a thinks that ϕ is true at instant of time t *because* of reasoning r, where a_1 thinks that ϕ_1 is true at t_1, ... and a_n thinks that ϕ_n is true at t_n. In other words, based on r, a thinks that ϕ is *caused*[3] by $\phi_1, \cdots, \phi_n$

---

[3] We use the term "cause" to describe the events that an agent thinks were the preconditions for a certain derived evidence. In this work, we will not focus on the causality relationships between events.

(with their respective time instants and agents). The reasoning r of the derived evidence $a : (t : \phi)$ is composed of simple and/or derived pieces of evidence. We include a constraint in our syntax that does not permit cycles between derived pieces of evidence, so that if $a_i : (t_i : \phi_i) \; [\cdots \mid a_j : (t_j : \phi_j) \mid \ldots]_r$, then we do not accept in our language the formula $a_j : (t_j : \phi_j) \; [\cdots \mid a_i : (t_i : \phi_i) \mid \ldots]_{r'}$.

A reasoning r can be used by different agents to arrive at the same conclusion (derived evidence), using the same pieces of evidence. An agent can use different reasonings $r_i, \cdots, r_j$ to conclude the same derived evidence, where the pieces of evidence used by the reasonings are different from one reasoning to the other.

Example 3. CS says that the *Attack* occurred at time t_1, based on reasoning r_1 and CS's evidence about a spear phishing campaign *SpPhish* and its success *SucPhish* at t_1. The latter is based on r_2 and CS's pieces of evidence that in t_1: the malicious link was clicked *LinkCl*, the malicious form was filled *FFill*, and the data were stolen *DStolen*. We thus have:

$$CS : (t_1 : Attack) \; [CS : (t_1 : SpPhish) \mid CS : (t_1 : SucPhish)]_{r_1}$$
$$CS : (t_1 : SucPhish) \; [CS : (t_1 : LinkCl) \mid CS : (t_1 : FFill) \mid CS : (t_1 : DStolen)]_{r_2}$$

Instead, *TF* says that based on r_3 the *Attack* occurred at t_2 because the metadata *MetaC* were created at t_2 and the access was physical *PhysA*. The latter is true because *TF* states that it is not true that *SpeedTr* is *23MB/s*:

$$TF : (t_2 : Attack) \; [TF : (t_2 : MetaC) \mid TF : (t_2 : PhysA)]_{r_3}$$
$$TF : (t_2 : PhysA) \; [TF : (t_2 : \neg SpeedTr(23MB/s))]_{r_4} \qquad \square$$

To allow an analyst to distinguish the events that can be expressed by a simple or derived evidence, the set of propositional variables *Vars* is composed by two disjoint subsets *Vars_S* and *Vars_D* that respectively represent the events that can be part of simple and derived evidence, i.e., $Vars = Vars_S \cup Vars_D$ with $Vars_S \cap Vars_D = \emptyset$. By extension, we write $\phi \in Lit_S$ if ϕ is p or $\neg p$ with $p \in Vars_S$, and $\phi \in Lit_D$ if ϕ is p or $\neg p$ with $p \in Vars_D$.

Hence, if $\phi \in Lit_S$, then $a : (t : \phi)$ is a simple evidence, whereas if $\phi \in Lit_D$ and $\phi_i \in Lit$ for $i \in \{1, \ldots, n\}$, then $a : (t : \phi) \; [a_1 : (t_1 : \phi_1) \mid \ldots \mid a_n : (t_n : \phi_n)]_r$ is a derived evidence. For simplicity, we will assume that a variable that represents an event given by a simple evidence is part of *Vars_S* and that a variable that represents an event given by a derived evidence is part of *Vars_D*.

Example 4. The variables of the events of our example are divided in the two following disjoint subsets: $Vars_S = \{SpPhish, LinkCl, FFill, DStolen, MetaC, SpeedTr(23MB/s)\}$ and $Vars_D = \{Attack, SucPhish, PhysA\}$. $\qquad \square$

The temporal labels can have *temporal constraints* such as $t_1 \leq t$ or $t_n < t$. As we consider time to be *linear* and every instant of time is mapped to only one element of the natural numbers, our syntax doesn't need to include a precedence relation, as it represents the classical precedence relation between natural numbers.

In addition to ordering events with respect to time, the analyst can consider the *trust(worthiness)* relations that she has with the sources with respect to their assertions in the simple evidence, i.e., she might think that one source is more reliable than another one with respect to a particular event (and its negation). For instance, a_i might be more trustworthy than a_j with respect to an event p (and thus also $\neg p$), where $p \in Vars_S$. In general, if there exists a trust relation between two agents $a_i, a_j \in Ag$ for an event $p \in Vars_S$, then we have that either a_i is more trustworthy than a_j with respect to p, or a_j is more trustworthy than a_i with respect to p. We formalize this by introducing the *trust relation* $\lhd : Ag \times Ag \times Vars_S$. Then, the *relational formula* $a_i \lhd_p a_j$ expresses that a_j is more trustworthy than a_i with respect to p.

Example 5. We write $TF \lhd_{SpeedTr(23MB/s)} FE$ to formalize that the analyst trusts FE more than TF w.r.t. the simple evidence $SpeedTr(23MB/s)$.   □

The analyst can also consider the trust(worthiness) relations about the reasonings she used. In particular, given two conflicting derived pieces of evidence that use two different reasonings, the analyst can consider one reasoning to be more trustworthy than the other one. We formalize this by introducing the *trust relation* $\prec : \mathcal{R} \times \mathcal{R}$. Then, the *relational formula* $r_i \prec r_j$ expresses that reasoning r_j is more trustworthy than reasoning r_i.

2.2 $\mathcal{EL}_I$: Evidence Interpretation

An *evidence interpretation* (or simply *interpretation*) is what the cyber-forensics analyst thinks that is plausibly true. To formalize this, the second level $\mathcal{EL}_I$ of $\mathcal{EL}$ employs a simplified variant of *Linear Temporal Logic (LTL)*. $\mathcal{EL}_I$ inherits from $\mathcal{EL}_E$ the temporal labels T, the reasonings $\mathcal{R}$ and the propositional variables *Vars* (and thus also the literals *Lit*).

Definition 2. *Given* $t, t_1, \ldots t_n \in T$, $\phi, \phi_1, \ldots, \phi_n \in Lit$, $r \in \mathcal{R}$ *and* $\phi' \in Lit_D$, *the set* φ *of formulas of* $\mathcal{EL}_I$, *called* interpretations, *is*

$$\varphi ::= \ t : \phi \mid t_1 : \phi_1 \wedge t_2 : \phi_2 \wedge \ldots \wedge t_n : \phi_n \rightarrow_r t : \phi'$$

$t : \phi$ means that the analyst thinks that ϕ is true at t, whereas $t_1 : \phi_1 \wedge \ldots \wedge t_n : \phi_n \rightarrow_r t : \phi'$ means that the analyst thinks that ϕ' is true at the instant of time t, based on reasoning r, if ϕ_i is true at t_i for all $i \in \{1, \ldots, n\}$. An interpretation expresses a positive event (the occurrence of an event, e.g., $t : p$) or a negative event (the non occurrence of an event, e.g., $t : \neg p$). The interpretations of the temporalized logic $\mathcal{EL}_I$ that express positive events represent the *plausible pieces of evidence* and help the analyst to perform a correct analysis.

2.3 $\mathcal{EL}_R$: Evidence Reasoning

The third layer $\mathcal{EL}_R$ of $\mathcal{EL}$ is the *reasoning layer* and deals with the reasoning behind the derived evidence. Also $\mathcal{EL}_R$ uses LTL and inherits from $\mathcal{EL}_E$ the temporal labels T, the reasonings $\mathcal{R}$ and the propositional variables *Vars*.

Definition 3. *Given $t \in T$, $\phi \in Lit_D$ and $r, r_k, \ldots, r_l \in \mathcal{R}$, the set ψ of formulas of $\mathcal{EL}_R$ is*

$$\psi ::= (t : \phi)_r \mid (t : \phi)_{r, r_k, \ldots, r_l}.$$

The *reasoning* involves only derived pieces of evidence, which we can divide in two types. The *first type of derived evidence*, $(t : \phi)_r$, is composed of only simple pieces of evidence; in this case, the only reasoning is the one made by the agent that states the derived evidence $a : (t : \phi) [a_1 : (t_1 : \phi_1) \mid \ldots \mid a_j : (t_j : \phi_j)]_r$, where $\phi_i \in Lit_S$ for $i \in \{1, \ldots, j\}$. The *second type of derived evidence*, $(t : \phi)_{r, r_k, \ldots, r_l}$, is composed of simple and derived pieces of evidence; in this case, the reasoning involves the one of the agent stating the derived evidence, $a : (t : \phi) [a_1 : (t_1 : \phi_1) \mid \ldots \mid a_j : (t_j : \phi_j)]_r$, as well as all the reasonings involved in the derived pieces of evidence $\phi_i \in Lit$ for $i \in \{1, \ldots, j\}$ that are part of reasoning r. The first type is clearly a special case of the second one, but we keep both for the sake of understandability.

3   The Semantics of the Evidence Logic $\mathcal{EL}$

Definition 4. *The plausible pieces of evidence are a finite stream of temporal instants in which at every instant of time we may associate a finite number of occurrences or not occurrences of an event.*

The agents are associated to a given finite set of values, and the trust relationship between agents is interpreted as a partial order on the agents. The same applies to the reasonings: they are associated to a finite set of values and the trust relationship between them is interpreted as a partial order on the reasonings.

Definition 5. *A model of the evidence language $\mathcal{EL}$ is a tuple*

$$\mathfrak{M} = \{Ag^\mathfrak{I}, \mathcal{F}^\mathfrak{I}, \mathcal{PO}^\mathfrak{I}, \mathcal{TR}^\mathfrak{I}, Vars^\mathfrak{I}, \mathcal{R}^\mathfrak{I}, \mathfrak{I}\}$$

where:

- *$\mathfrak{I}$ is the interpretation function, where we interpret time as natural numbers, i.e., $t^\mathfrak{I} \in \mathbb{N}$ for every $t \in T$;*
- *$Ag^\mathfrak{I} = \{a_1{}^\mathfrak{I}, \ldots a_n{}^\mathfrak{I}\} = \{a_1, \ldots a_n\} = Ag$ is a set of agents;*
- *$\mathcal{F}^\mathfrak{I}$ is a function that maps pairs of instants of time and formulas to True or False (this mapping is used in the second layer of $\mathcal{EL}$, where we have $t : \phi$);*
- *$\mathcal{PO}^\mathfrak{I} = \{\lhd_{p_i}{}^\mathfrak{I}\}$ is a set of trust relationships between agents, where for every $p \in Vars_S$, if $\lhd_p{}^\mathfrak{I} \in \mathcal{PO}^\mathfrak{I}$, then $\lhd_p{}^\mathfrak{I} = \{(a_i{}^\mathfrak{I}, a_j{}^\mathfrak{I}) \mid a_i \lhd_p a_j\}^*$, where $*$ is the transitive closure of $\lhd$;*
- *$\mathcal{TR}^\mathfrak{I} = \{\prec^\mathfrak{I}\}$ is a set of trust relationship between reasonings, where for every $r \in \mathcal{R}$, if $\prec^\mathfrak{I} \in \mathcal{TR}^\mathfrak{I}$, then $\prec^\mathfrak{I} = \{(r_i{}^\mathfrak{I}, r_j{}^\mathfrak{I}) \mid r_i \prec r_j\}^*$, where $*$ is the transitive closure of $\prec$;*
- *$Vars^\mathfrak{I} = Vars = \{p_1, \cdots, p_n\}$ is a set of events;*
- *$\mathcal{R}^\mathfrak{I} = \mathcal{R} = \{r_1, r_2, \cdots, r_n\}$ is a set of reasoning rules.*

Slightly abusing notation, we use $Ag^{\mathcal{I}}$ to denote also a set of functions, each function $a_i^{\mathcal{I}} : \mathbb{N} \times Lit \rightarrow \{True, False\}$ associating to an instant of time t a set of formulas that are true at t, where $a_i^{\mathcal{I}}(t, p) = True$ when $a_i : (t : p)$ is asserted, $a_i^{\mathcal{I}}(t, p) = False$ when $a_i : (t : \neg p)$ is asserted, $a_i^{\mathcal{I}}(t, \neg p) = True$ when $a_i : (t : \neg p)$ is asserted, $a_i^{\mathcal{I}}(t, \neg p) = False$ when $a_i : (t : p)$ is asserted. The same applies to $\mathcal{R}^{\mathcal{I}}$, each function $r_i^{\mathcal{I}} : \mathbb{N} \times Lit \rightarrow \{True, False\}$ such that $(t, p)_{r_i^{\mathcal{I}}} = True$ when $(t : p)_{r_i}$ is asserted, $(t, p)_{r_i^{\mathcal{I}}} = False$ when $(t : \neg p)_{r_i}$ is asserted, $(t, \neg p)_{r_i^{\mathcal{I}}} = True$ when $(t : \neg p)_{r_i}$ is asserted, $(t, \neg p)_{r_i^{\mathcal{I}}} = False$ when $(t : p)_{r_i}$ is asserted. Thus, $a_i^{\mathcal{I}}$ and $\mathcal{F}^{\mathcal{I}}$ both associate to every t a set of formulas that are true at t; the difference is that we use the $a_i^{\mathcal{I}}$ in the evidence layer $\mathcal{EL}_E$ and $\mathcal{F}^{\mathcal{I}}$ in the interpretation layer $\mathcal{EL}_I$.

In order to avoid having clear contradictions in the models, we constrain the functions $Ag^{\mathcal{I}}$ and $\mathcal{R}^{\mathcal{I}}$ as follows:

$(COND_1)$: If $a^{\mathcal{I}}(t, p) = True$, then $a^{\mathcal{I}}(t', p) = False$ for all $t' \neq t$.
$(COND_2)$: If $(t, p)_{r^{\mathcal{I}}} = True$, then $(t', p)_{r^{\mathcal{I}}} = False$ for all $t' \neq t$.
$(COND_3)$: Every $\lessdot_p^{\mathcal{I}}$ is an irreflexive and antisymmetric relation.
$(COND_4)$: Every $\prec^{\mathcal{I}}$ is an irreflexive and antisymmetric relation.

A $\mathcal{EL}$-theory is built by using $\mathcal{EL}$ to express a finite and non-empty set of formulas of the three layers, including the trust relationships.

4   The Rewriting System of the Evidence Logic $\mathcal{EL}$

In this section, we introduce the *rewriting system* of $\mathcal{EL}$, which, as proved in Theorem 1, is sound. Given pieces of evidence, the rewriting system yields a consistent set of pieces of evidence by translating pieces of evidence into interpretations and reasonings, and resolving their discordances. In particular, the rewriting system uses the tableau rules in Table 1 and applies them via the procedure in Algorithm 1: given a $\mathcal{EL}$-theory $\mathcal{E}$, which is a non-empty set of formulas, the rewriting system generates a new set of formulas $\widehat{\mathcal{E}}$ that replaces $\mathcal{E}$, where the single rewritings correspond to interpretations and reasonings of the theory. More specifically, the rewriting system takes a $\mathcal{EL}$-theory of the first level and rewrites it into a $\mathcal{EL}$-theory of the second and third level, until all the formulas are interpreted, by adding formulas to the theory or eliminating formulas from the theory, with the use of *insertion* or *elimination rules*.

The rules in Table 1 have as premises (above the line) a set of formulas and a $\mathcal{EL}$-theory $\mathcal{E}$, although we don't show $\mathcal{E}$ for readability, and as conclusion (below the line) $\mathcal{E} \cup \{\phi\}$ or $\mathcal{E} \setminus \{\phi\}$, depending on whether the rule is an insertion or elimination rule that respectively inserts or eliminates ϕ. The *insertion* rule introduce formulas for resolving temporal discordances and interpreting pieces of evidence. The *elimination* rules resolve discordances of event occurrences by deleting formulas based on the trust relations among agents and reasonings. The *closure rules* are part of the elimination rules, and discover discordances in $\mathcal{E}$ that cannot be solved, eliminate all the formulas of the set $\mathcal{E}$ and give as result the empty set $\bot$.

Table 1. Rules of the rewriting system of $\mathcal{EL}$

$$\frac{a:(t:\phi)}{\mathcal{E}\cup\{t:\phi\}}\,\mathcal{L}_1 \qquad\qquad \frac{(t:\phi)_{r,\cdots,r_n}}{\mathcal{E}\cup\{t:\phi\}}\,\mathcal{L}_1'$$

$$\frac{a:(t:\phi)\;[a_1:(t_1:\phi_1)\mid\cdots\mid a_n:(t_n:\phi_n)]_r}{\mathcal{E}\cup\{a_i:(t_i:\phi_i)\}_{\forall i\in\{1,\cdots,n\}\;\phi_i\in Lit_S}\cup\{t_1:\phi_1\wedge\cdots\wedge t_n:\phi_n\rightarrow_r t:\phi\}}\,\mathcal{L}_2$$

$$\frac{t_1:\phi_1\wedge\cdots\wedge t_n:\phi_n\rightarrow_r t:\phi\quad t_1:\phi_1\quad\cdots\quad t_n:\phi_n}{\mathcal{E}\cup\{(t:\phi)_r\}}\,(\rightarrow)$$

$$\frac{t_1:\phi_1\wedge\cdots\wedge t_n:\phi_n\rightarrow_r t:\phi\quad(t_1:\phi_1)_{r_1/\emptyset}\quad\cdots\quad(t_n:\phi_n)_{r_n/\emptyset}}{\mathcal{E}\cup\{(t:\phi)_{r,r_1/\emptyset,\cdots,r_n/\emptyset}\}}\,(\rightarrow')$$

$$\frac{a_1\lhd_p a_2\quad a_2\lhd_p a_3}{\mathcal{E}\cup\{a_1\lhd_p a_3\}}\,\text{TRANS}\lhd \qquad \frac{r_1\prec r_2\quad r_2\prec r_3}{\mathcal{E}\cup\{r_1\prec r_3\}}\,\text{TRANS}\prec$$

$$\frac{a_1:(t_1:\phi)\quad a_2:(t_2:\phi)}{\mathcal{E}\cup\{a_1:(t_2:\neg\phi),a_2:(t_1:\neg\phi)\}}\,\mathcal{D}_1[*] \qquad \frac{(t_1:\phi)_{r_1}\quad(t_2:\phi)_{r_2}}{\mathcal{E}\cup\{(t_2:\neg\phi)_{r_1},(t_1:\neg\phi)_{r_2}\}}\,\mathcal{D}_1'[*]$$

$$\frac{(t_1:\phi)_{r_1,r_i,\cdots,r_j}\quad(t_2:\phi)_{r_2,r_m,\cdots,r_n}}{\mathcal{E}\cup\{(t_2:\neg\phi)_{r_1,r_i,\cdots,r_j},(t_1:\neg\phi)_{r_2,r_m,\cdots,r_n}\}}\,\mathcal{D}_1''[*]$$

$$\frac{a_2\lhd_p a_1\quad a_1:(t:\phi)\quad a_2:(t:\neg\phi)}{\mathcal{E}\setminus\{a_2:(t:\neg\phi)\}}\,\mathcal{D}_2[\diamond] \qquad \frac{r_2\prec r_1\quad(t:\phi)_{r_1}\quad(t:\neg\phi)_{r_2}}{\mathcal{E}\setminus\{(t:\neg\phi)_{r_2}\}}\,\mathcal{D}_2'$$

$$\frac{r_2\prec r_1\quad(t:\phi)_{r_1,r_i,\cdots,r_j}\quad(t:\neg\phi)_{r_2,r_m,\cdots,r_n}\quad\Delta}{\mathcal{E}\setminus\{(t:\neg\phi)_{r_2,r_m,\cdots,r_n},\Delta\}}\,\mathcal{D}_2''[\star]$$

$$\frac{a:(t_1:\phi)\quad a:(t_2:\phi)}{\bot}\,\mathcal{C}_C[*] \qquad \frac{(t_1:\phi)_{r,\cdots,r_i}\quad(t_2:\phi)_{r,\cdots,r_j}}{\bot}\,\mathcal{C}_C'[*]$$

$$\frac{a\lhd_p a}{\bot}\,\mathcal{C}_T \qquad \frac{r\prec r}{\bot}\,\mathcal{C}_T' \qquad \frac{t:\phi\quad t:\neg\phi}{\bot}\,\mathcal{C}_P$$

where $[*]=[t_1\neq t_2]$, $[\diamond]=[\phi\in Lit_S,\,\phi$ is p or $\neg p]$, and $[\star]=[\Delta=\bigcup_{(t':\psi)_\varrho\in\mathcal{E}\,s.t.\,r_2\in\varrho}(t':\psi)_\varrho]$

4.1 Rewriting Rules

We now explain the rules in more detail, starting from the transformation rules that transform the formulas into the various layer formulas.

Rule $\mathcal{L}_1$ transforms a simple evidence into a temporal formula of the interpretation layer, whereas $\mathcal{L}_1'$ transforms formulas of the reasoning layer into a temporal formula of the interpretation layer.

Example 6. An application of $\mathcal{L}_1$ in our use example is:

$$\frac{FE:(t_2:SpeedTr(23MB/s))}{\mathcal{E}\cup\{t_2:SpeedTr(23MB/s)\}}\,\mathcal{L}_1$$

$\square$

Rule $\mathcal{L}_2$ transforms a derived evidence into an interpretation formula and, if possible, also introduces new pieces of evidence. Thus, given a derived evidence $a:(t:\phi)\;[a_1:(t_1:\phi_1)\mid\cdots\mid a_n:(t_n:\phi_n)]_r$, $\mathcal{L}_2$ inserts the temporal formula

$t_1 : \phi_1 \wedge \ldots \wedge t_n : \phi_n \to_r t : \phi$ and all $a_i : (t_i : \phi_i)$ for $\phi_i \in Lit_S$ and $i \in \{1, \ldots, n\}$. Note that rule $\mathcal{L}_2$ inserts in the theory only the simple pieces of evidence that were part of the reasoning, and not the derived ones, as we expect the pieces of evidence that are part of their reasonings to be part of the theory too.

Example 7. In our example, $\mathcal{L}_2$ is applied to all derived pieces of evidence given by the sources. When it applies to CS's first evidence, it transforms only the simple evidence about the spear phishing campaign, but not the successful phishing evidence as it is a derived one. The same occurs to TF's first evidence where just $MetaC$ is introduced:

$$\frac{CS : (t_1 : Attack)\ [CS : (t_1 : SPhish)\ |\ CS : (t_1 : SucPhish)]_{r_1}}{\mathcal{E} \cup \{CS : (t_1 : SPhish)\} \cup \{t_1 : SPhish \wedge t_1 : SucPhis \to_{r_1} t_1 : Attack\}}\ \mathcal{L}_2$$

$$\frac{TF : (t_2 : Attack)\ [TF : (t_2 : MetaC)\ |\ TF : (t_2 : PhysA)]_{r_3}}{\mathcal{E} \cup \{TF : (t_2 : MetaC)\} \cup \{t_2 : MetaC \wedge t_2 : PhysA \to_{r_3} t_2 : Attack\}}\ \mathcal{L}_2$$

$$\frac{TF : (t_2 : PhysA)\ [TF : (t_2 : \neg SpeedTr(23MB/s))]_{r_4}}{\mathcal{E} \cup \{TF : (t_2 : \neg SpeedTr(23MB/s))\} \cup \{t_2 : \neg SpeedTr(23MB/s) \to_{r_4} t_2 : PhysA\}}\ \mathcal{L}_2$$

Applying $\mathcal{L}_2$ to the second evidence of CS yields $\mathcal{E} \cup \{CS : (t_1 : LinkCl), CS : (t_1 : FFill), CS : (t_1 : DStolen)\}$ and $t_1 : LinkCl \wedge t_1 : FFill \wedge t_1 : DStolen \to_{r_2} t_1 : SucPhish$. $\qquad\square$

Rules $(\to)$ and $(\to')$ transform the interpretation formulas introduced by $\mathcal{L}_2$ into reasoning formulas (derived evidence of the two types).

Example 8. Applying $(\to)$ to CS's derived pieces of evidence yields:

$$\frac{t_1 : LinkCl \wedge t_1 : FFill \wedge t_1 : DStolen \to_{r_2} t_1 : SucPhish\ \ t_1 : LinkCl\ \ t_1 : FFill\ \ t_1 : DStolen}{\mathcal{E} \cup \{(t_1 : SucPhish)_{r_2}\}}\ (\to)$$

Applying $(\to')$ to the second type of derived evidence for CS yields

$$\frac{t_1 : SPhish \wedge t_1 : SucPhish \to_{r_1} t_1 : Attack\ \ t_1 : SPhish\ \ (t_1 : SucPhish)_{r_2}}{\mathcal{E} \cup \{(t_1 : Attack)_{r_1, r_2}\}}\ (\to')$$

$\square$

The $\lhd$ and $\prec$ relations are transitive ones. TRANS$\lhd$ and TRANS $\prec$ extend the trust relations between agents and reasonings, e.g., if a_1 is less trusted than a_2 with respect to p, and a_2 is less trusted than a_3 with respect to p, then TRANS$\lhd$ inserts into the theory the conclusions that a_1 is less trusted than a_3 with respect to p (the same applies to $\prec$ with TRANS $\prec$).

The discordance resolution rules resolve temporal and factual discordances, where events are instantaneous and not recurring. A *temporal discordance* about an event occurs when two agents state that it occurred in two different instants of time, e.g., Alice states that x occurred at t_1 and Bob states that it occurred at t_2. A *factual discordance* about an event occurs when there are inconsistent statements about the occurrence of an event at an instant of time, e.g., Alice states that at t occurred p and Bob states that at t did not occur p.

Rules $\mathcal{D}_1$, $\mathcal{D}_1'$ and $\mathcal{D}_1''$ transform temporal discordances into factual ones, where $\mathcal{D}_1$ works with simple pieces of evidence, $\mathcal{D}_1'$ with derived pieces of evidence of the first type, and $\mathcal{D}_1''$ with derived pieces of evidence of the second type (note that $\mathcal{D}_1'$ is a special case of $\mathcal{D}_1''$). Thus, if the $\mathcal{EL}$-theory $\mathcal{E}$ contains the evidence belonging to two different agents about the same event p, occurring at two different instants, then the evidence of the occurrence or not of p with respect to both agents and both instants of time are inserted in the theory.

Rule $\mathcal{D}_2$, $\mathcal{D}_2'$ and $\mathcal{D}_2''$ solve the factual discordances based on the relations of trust, where $\mathcal{D}_2$ eliminates from the theory the evidence of the less trusted agent, whereas $\mathcal{D}_2'$ and $\mathcal{D}_2''$ eliminate the evidence of the less trusted reasoning. $\mathcal{D}_2''$ eliminates also every evidence that has inside its reasoning the removed evidence, as captured by the side condition where Δ is the set of all derived pieces of evidence that have r_2 in their reasonings: $\Delta = \bigcup_{(t':\psi)_\varrho \in \mathcal{E} \ s.t. \ r_2 \in \varrho} (t' : \psi)_\varrho]$, where $\varrho = \{r_k, \cdots, r_l\}$.

Example 9. $\mathcal{D}_2$ solves the discordance of the speed transfer:

$$\frac{TF \lhd_{SpeedTr(23MB/s)} FE \quad FE : (t_2 : SpeedTr(23MB/s)) \quad TF : (t_2 : \neg SpeedTr(23MB/s))}{\mathcal{E} \setminus \{TF : (t_2 : \neg SpeedTr(23MB/s))\}} \ \mathcal{D}_2$$

□

The rewriting system has five closure rules that correspond to five discordances that cannot be solved resulting in the empty theory $\perp$. $\mathcal{C}_C$ applies when an agent contradicts herself, $\mathcal{C}_C'$ when a reasoning contradicts itself. $\mathcal{C}_T$ and $\mathcal{C}_T'$ apply when an agent/reasoning is more trusted than herself/itself (we avoid these types of conflicts in the semantics thanks to $COND_1$ and $COND_2$, where $\lhd$ and $\prec$ are irreflexive). Finally, $\mathcal{C}_P$ captures contradictions of the second layer, where two temporal formulas state the occurrence and non occurrence of an event at the same instant of time. This discordance occurs when we were not able to solve it using the trust relations.

Theorem 1. *The rewriting system of $\mathcal{EL}$ is sound.*

The proof of the theorem is in the Appendix.

4.2 Rewriting Procedure

We give a procedure that uses the rewriting rules to prove the satisfiability of a given $\mathcal{EL}$-theory. This procedure defines an order of application of the rules that rewrites the $\mathcal{EL}$-theory as defined in Algorithm 1. Theorem 2 tells us that the procedure is correct (the theorem is proved in the Appendix).

Given a $\mathcal{EL}$-theory, the procedure starts by generating all the trust relations, applying (TRANS$\lhd$) and (TRANS $\prec$). Any contradiction that exists between trust relations is immediately captured by $\mathcal{C}_T$ and $\mathcal{C}_T'$. $\mathcal{L}_2$ is applied to transform any

Algorithm 1. Algorithm for the Rewriting Procedure

1: **while** We can apply Trans◁, Trans ≺ rules **do**
2:     Apply Trans◁ and Trans ≺ rules
3: **end while**
4: Apply $\mathcal{C}_T$ and $\mathcal{C}'_T$; **if** we have ⊥, **then** We do not have a model. Exit! **endif**
5: **while** We can apply $\mathcal{L}_2$ rule **do** Apply $\mathcal{L}_2$ rule **end while**
6: **while** We can apply $\mathcal{D}_1$, $\mathcal{D}_2$ rules **do** Apply $\mathcal{D}_1$, $\mathcal{D}_2$ rules **end while**
7: Apply $\mathcal{C}_C$; **if** we have ⊥, **then** We do not have a model. Exit! **endif**
8: **while** We can apply $\mathcal{L}_1$ rule **do** Apply $\mathcal{L}_1$ rule **end while**
9: **while** We can apply ($\rightarrow$) rule **do** Apply ($\rightarrow$) rule **end while**
10: **while** We can apply $\mathcal{D}'_1$, $\mathcal{D}'_2$ rules **do** Apply $\mathcal{D}'_1$, $\mathcal{D}'_2$ rules **end while**
11: **while** We can apply ($\rightarrow'$) rule **do** Apply ($\rightarrow'$) rule **end while**
12: **while** We can apply $\mathcal{D}''_1$, $\mathcal{D}''_2$ rules **do** Apply $\mathcal{D}''_1$, $\mathcal{D}''_2$ rules **end while**
13: Apply $\mathcal{C}'_C$; **if** we have ⊥, **then** We do not have a model. Exit! **endif**
14: **while** We can apply $\mathcal{L}'_1$ rule **do** Apply $\mathcal{L}'_1$ rule **end while**
15: Apply $\mathcal{C}_P$; **if** we have ⊥, **then** We do not have a model. Exit! **endif**

---

derived evidence into its interpretations. If needed, $\mathcal{D}_1$ and $\mathcal{D}_2$ are applied. At this point all possible simple pieces of evidence are generated. Any contradiction between first layer formulas is captured by $\mathcal{C}_C$. Afterwards, $\mathcal{L}_1$ transforms any simple evidence into second layer formulas that are used by ($\rightarrow$) to obtain reasoning layer formulas. $\mathcal{D}'_1$ and $\mathcal{D}'_2$ are applied to solve discordances between reasoning layer formulas based on the reasonings' trust relations. The result of the previous rules is used by ($\rightarrow'$) to generate reasoning layer formulas from derived pieces of evidence of the second type. If any discordance arises, it is solved by $\mathcal{D}''_1$ and $\mathcal{D}''_2$, where rule $\mathcal{D}''_2$ not only takes out the not preferred evidence, but also any derived evidence that uses it as a precondition. If no contradiction between reasoning rules is captured by $\mathcal{C}'_C$, then $\mathcal{L}'_1$ transforms all reasoning layer formulas into interpretation layer ones. If $\mathcal{C}_P$ applies, then there is a contradiction and we have ⊥, else no further transformation can be done, and the resulting set of formulas is the model of $\mathcal{EL}$-theory.

Example 10. By applying the procedure we find that ($\rightarrow$) can be applied only to *CS*'s pieces of evidence as the derived ones of *TF* are missing their premises, removed by $\mathcal{D}_2$. Applying $\mathcal{L}'_1$ yields t_1 : *Attack* and the analyst concludes that the attack occurred during March/April 2016.   □

Theorem 2. *The order of the rules in Algorithm 1 used by the rewriting procedure is correct.*

5   A Detailed Case Study: Attribution of a Cyber-Attack

The Evidence Logic $\mathcal{EL}$ can be used in diverse application areas where there is a need to analyze and reason about conflicting data/knowledge. In this section, as a concrete proof of concept to show how to apply $\mathcal{EL}$ during the investigations on

Fig. 1. Application of the rewriting procedure

a cyber-attack, we discuss a cyber-forensics case study in which the analyst needs to collect various pieces of evidence and analyze them to decide who performed the attack; this process is called *attribution* of the attack to a particular entity.

As we remarked above, forensics investigations typically produce an enormous amount of evidence that need to be analyzed. The pieces of evidence are produced/collected by various sources, which can be humans (e.g., another analyst) or forensic tools such as intrusion detection system (IDS), traceback systems, malware analysis tools, and so on. The analyst trusts more some sources than others for particular pieces of evidence, e.g., source S_1 is more trusted than source S_5 for attack similarity as tool S_1 specializes in malware analysis whereas tool S_5 specializes in deleted data. The collected evidence can be conflicting or bring to conflicting results. The $\mathcal{EL}$ Logic represents the evidence, together with its sources and relations of trust, and reasons about it, by eliminating the conflicting evidence and helping the analyst during the analysis process.

Suppose the analyst has collected (from analysts $A_1, \ldots, A_4$ and sources S_1, S_2, S_3) and is analyzing, using $\mathcal{EL}$, the following pieces of evidence, representing events related to the attack that occurred (for the sake of space, we give a simplified but realistic version of the evidence that can be easily extended).

$A_1 : t : Culprit(C, Attack)[S_1 : t : sIP(Attack, IP) \mid S_1 : t : Geoloc(IP, C) \mid S_2 : t : Cap(C, Attack)]_{r_1}$

$A_2 : t : Culprit(C, Attack)[S_2 : t : Motive(C, Attack) \mid S_2 : t : Cap(C, Attack)]_{r_2}$

$A_3 : t : \neg Culprit(C, Attack)[S_3 : t : \neg Cap(C, Attack) \mid S_4 : t : \neg Fin(C, Attack)]_{r_3}$

$A_4 : t : \neg Culprit(C, Attack)[S_1 : t : sIP(Attack, IP) \mid S_1 : t : Geoloc(IP, C) \mid S_7 : t : Spoofed(IP)]_{r_4}$

$S_1 : t : sIP(Attack, IP)$

$S_1 : t : Geoloc(IP, C)$

$S_2 : t : Cap(C, Attack)[S_6 : t_1 : Admit(C, Attack') \mid S_1 : t : Sim(Attack, Attack')]_{r_5}$

$S_3 : t : \neg Cap(C, Attack)[S_6 : t_1 : Admit(C, Attack') \mid S_5 : t : \neg Sim(Attack, Attack')]_{r_6}$

$S_2 : t : Motive(C, Attack)[S_5 : t : EConf(C, Victim)]_{r_7}$

$\qquad S_5 \lhd_{Sim} S_1 \qquad r_1 \prec r_4 \qquad r_4 \prec r_2 \qquad r_2 \prec r_3$

$sIP(Attack, IP)$ means that the $Attack$ came from IP; $Geoloc(IP, C)$ that IP has country C as geographical location; $Cap(C, Attack)$ that country C has the capability of conducting the $Attack$. Analyst A_1 states that (based on reasoning r_1), given country C is capable of performing the $Attack$ (stated by S_2) and it came from IP located in C (stated by S_1), then C performed (is the culprit of) the attack, i.e., $Culprit(C, Attack)$. A_2 states that C is the culprit (based on r_2), as it has the capability of and the motive $Motive(C, Attack)$ for performing it (both stated by S_2). A_3 states that C is not the culprit (based on r_3), as it is not capable of and (as stated by S_4) does not have the financial resources $Fin(C, Attack)$ for commissioning the attack. A_4 states that C is not the culprit (based on r_4), as the IP's are $Spoofed$ (stated by S_7), so their geolocation cannot be used. Source S_1 states that the IP from which the attack originated is located in C. S_2 states that C is capable (based on r_5), as C admitted to be the culprit of a previous attack, i.e., $Admit(C, Attack')$, at t_1 (stated by S_6), and the latter is similar (Sim) to $Attack$ (stated by S_1). S_3 states that C is not capable of performing $Attack$ (based on r_6), as $Attack'$ that C admitted to have performed, is not similar to $Attack$ (stated by S_5). S_2 states that C has motive for the attack (based on r_7), as C has an economical conflict $EConf$ with the attack $Victim$ (stated by S_5). Our analyst trusts more source S_1 than S_5 for the similarity between attacks, and reasoning r_3 more than r_2, r_2 more than r_4 and r_4 more than r_1.

The simple pieces of evidence of this use case are:

$Vars_S = \{sIP(Attack, IP), Geoloc(IP, C), Fin(C, Attack), Admit(C, Attack'),$
$\qquad Sim(Attack, Attack'), Spoofed(IP), EConf(C, Victim)\}.$

Let us now apply $\mathcal{EL}$'s rewriting procedure. We start with rules TRANS◁ and TRANS≺: the first cannot be applied, the second yields $r_1 \prec r_2$, $r_1 \prec r_3$ and $r_4 \prec r_3$. Neither $\mathcal{C}_T$ nor $\mathcal{C}_T'$ can be applied. We show the application of $\mathcal{L}_2$ to the pieces of evidence in (1)–(7) in Fig. 1. In (8) rule $\mathcal{D}_2$ eliminates $S_5 : t : \neg Sim(Attack, Attack')$. No contradiction is captured by $\mathcal{C}_C$, and $\mathcal{L}_1$ transforms all first layer formulas into second layer ones:

$$\mathcal{E} \cup \{t : sIP(Attack, IP), t : Geoloc(IP, C), t : \neg Fin(C, Attack), t : Spoofed(IP)$$
$$t_1 : Admit(C, Attack'), t : Sim(Attack, Attack'), t : EConf(C, Victim)\}.$$

(9)–(11) show applications of ($\rightarrow$) to any evidence that has its premises in the theory. $\mathcal{D}_1'$ and $\mathcal{D}_2'$ cannot be applied as there is no temporal/factual discordance between derived pieces of evidence of the first type. Applying ($\rightarrow'$) produces derived pieces of evidence of the second type for A_1 and A_2 as shown in (12)–(13). A_3's evidence is not derived as C is capable to perform the attack. Rule $\mathcal{D}_1''$ cannot be applied. Rule $\mathcal{D}_2''$ is applied, as shown in (14)-(15), to the conflicting pieces of evidence where the reasonings' trust relations apply. Finally, $\mathcal{L}_1'$ transforms all third layer formulas into second layer ones:

$$\mathcal{E} \cup \{t : sIP(Attack, IP), t : Geoloc(IP, C), t : \neg Fin(C, Attack), t : Spoofed(IP)$$
$$t_1 : Admit(C, Attack'), t : Sim(Attack, Attack'), t : Cap(C, Attack),$$
$$t : EconfConflict(C, Victim), t : Motive(C, Attack), t : Culprit(C, Attack)\}.$$

The analyst, given the result of the procedure, concludes that the culprit of the *Attack* is C.

The question of "who performed the attack" is, in general, not an easy one to answer, but we believe that $\mathcal{EL}$ can be successfully used to analyze and filter the large amount of cyber-forensics evidence that an analyst needs to deal with. At the very least, $\mathcal{EL}$ allows an analyst to perform a first, formal filtering of the evidence and obtain different plausible conclusions, which the analyst can then further investigate.

6   Related Work and Concluding Remarks

When we introduced $\mathcal{EL}$ and discussed how it allows analysts to reason about simple and derived evidence given by different sources, we deliberately did not use the notion of "belief". We chose to do so as the main scope of our work is not to consider modalities of knowledge or belief, but to introduce a procedure that analyzes and filters the potentially enormous amount of forensics evidence, eliminate discordances and reach conclusions. The notion of evidence (both simple and derived evidence) can be represented quite naturally as agents' beliefs and, in fact, the reasoning process in $\mathcal{EL}$ could be considered a belief revision process. However, our procedure, differently from the belief revision process, uses a monotonic reasoning, does not distinguish between beliefs and knowledge, is based on the notion of trust, and does not apply the principle of minimal change.

Belief revision is the process of integrating new information with existing beliefs or knowledge [4,7,9,10,17]. It is performed based on the knowledge and beliefs of the user and the beliefs of other agents announced, privately [1,6] or publicly [5,14], and it uses non-monotonic reasoning. In our approach, we use *monotonic reasoning* as we expect only the final set, that represents our theory, to be consistent. Our procedure deals with conflicting pieces of evidence, which are analyzed by expanding or contracting the evidence set. In case of unsolved inconsistencies, our theory is empty. The procedure does not incorporate every incoming information in the evidence set, but rather the new evidence is included or not depending on the trust relations. This is different from the classical AGM belief revision [2], where the *principle of minimal belief change* applies.

Our analysis can be seen as a revision procedure, where we do not distinguish between beliefs and knowledge. Thus, all the pieces of evidence can be treated as beliefs, and there is no space for personal or common belief/knowledge. Some works have considered belief revision that uses relation of trust between agents [3,8,12,13]. However, not much effort has been devoted to working with a relation of trust relative to the reasoning used to arrive to certain conclusions. Our trust relations do not have a grading system, like the one in [13], which is difficult to define for cyber-forensics data, but use comparable trust between the sources based on the evidence, similar to [12], where a notion of trust restricted to a domain of expertise is used. As future work, we plan to use Bayesian belief networks [8], and the Dempster-Shafer theory to quantify the level of trust for the evidence, and to enrich our framework with trust reinforcement mechanisms.

To the best of our knowledge, the only attempt at using belief revision during cyber-attacks' investigations is [15,16], where a *probabilistic structure argumentation* framework is used to analyze contradictory and uncertain data. Our procedure does not deal with probabilities, but with preferences between sources and reasoning rules. We believe this to be a more accommodating approach, especially for the main use case, investigations of cyber-attacks, where calculating and revising probabilities is resource consuming. The framework of [15,16] allows attackers to use, during the deceptive attempts, the well-known *specificity criteria*, i.e., the rule that uses more pieces of evidence is preferable. We avoid this type of deceptive attempts as the trust relations are given by the analyst.

$\mathcal{EL}$ is based on LTL. Another approach is to use *Temporal Defeasible Logic* [4], where knowledge is represented as norms with temporal scope [11]. For the sake of simplicity, our stream of time is discrete and provided initially. As future work, we plan to consider the flow of time as not provided and as non-discrete in order to have temporal relations between labels that represent the instants of time.

Another distinctive feature of our approach with respect to the rest of the literature that focuses on agents' trust relations and their reputation systems is the fact that we engage not only with the trust between agents, but also with the reasoning behind the evidence. Hence, even when a particular agent is not trusted, if the reasoning behind the evidence is sound, we might take it into account. The notion of trust, also seen as preference, is subjective to the analyst, and we assume that agents are sincere, and thus share all their information. As future work, we plan to incorporate both a reputation revision process, where the trustworthiness and reliability of the sources is analyzed and revised based on past experience, and private/public announcements. Finally, on the theoretical side, we plan to investigate the completeness of the rewriting system and algorithm, whereas on the practical side, we plan to fully automate our analysis process and to perform an evaluation analysis on real evidence of cyber-attacks.

Acknowledgments. Erisa Karafili was supported by the European Union's H2020 research and innovation programme under the Marie Skłodowska-Curie grant agreement No. 746667.

A   Appendix: Soundness of the Rewriting System and Correctness of the Algorithm

In this appendix, we prove the soundness of the rewriting system of $\mathcal{EL}$ and the correctness of Algorithm 1. Given a theory $\mathcal{E}$ and $\mathcal{EL}$'s rewriting system, the application of at least one of its closure rules generates an empty set. In fact, every theory that contains $\perp$ is equivalent to the empty theory. When the input theory is not empty and has *no contradiction*, then the theory rewritten by $\mathcal{EL}$ should give as result a non empty theory.

As usual in *tableau rewriting systems*, we define three fundamental notions: open, closed, and exhausted theories. A theory is *closed* when it contains a contradiction and it is *open* when it does not. A theory is *exhausted* when it is a fixpoint with respect to the rewriting process, i.e., by applying the rewriting system to an exhausted theory $\mathcal{E}$, we always obtain $\mathcal{E}$. Under the grounded semantics introduced in Sect. 3, we prove the soundness of the rewriting system by showing that open theories have models under the semantics, and closed ones have not. Thus, when we find an open and exhausted theory, we can prove the existence of a model.

We show now that the rules that rewrite a theory $\mathcal{E}$ into $\widehat{\mathcal{E}}$ without introducing $\perp$ constitute by themselves a sound system. The proofs of Lemmas 1 and 2 are straightforward and are omitted for the sake of space.

Lemma 1. *If a satisfiable $\mathcal{EL}$-theory $\mathcal{E}$ is rewritten into an exhausted theory $\widehat{\mathcal{E}}$, without using the closure rules, then $\widehat{\mathcal{E}}$ entails consequence C only when C is a consequence of $\mathcal{E}$.*

Lemma 2. *If an unsatisfiable $\mathcal{EL}$-theory $\mathcal{E}$ is rewritten into an exhausted theory $\widehat{\mathcal{E}}$, then $\widehat{\mathcal{E}}$ is empty.*

Lemma 3. *Given a satisfiable theory $\mathcal{E}$, the rewriting system $\mathcal{EL}$ rewrites the theory in an open and exhausted one.*

Proof. This lemma is proved by contradiction. Assume that $\mathcal{E}$ is non empty and satisfiable, and is rewritten by $\mathcal{EL}$ into an exhausted closed theory $\widehat{\mathcal{E}}$. Starting from a satisfiable theory $\mathcal{E}$ there are five cases of rewriting it in a contradictory theory that gives as result $\perp$. In the definition of model in Sect. 3, we introduced four conditions that constrain the behavior of interpretations. Below we provide the complete analysis only for the first case (that is provided as a consequence of $COND_1$). The other cases are a natural extension of this one and are omitted for the sake of space. The first case occurs when applying the $\mathcal{C}_C$ rule. We have that: $a^{\mathfrak{I}}(t_1, p) = True$, and $a^{\mathfrak{I}}(t_2, p) = True$. $COND_1$ implies that a propositional variable referred to an agent a can be true in only one instant of time, thus, $\mathcal{E}$ is not satisfiable.   ■

Lemma 3 introduces a result for $\mathcal{EL}$-soundness as it guarantees that irregardless of the order in which we apply the rules, we catch a contradiction at a given point. Thus, as a direct consequence of the grounded semantics, of Lemmas 2 and 3 we obtain Theorem 1.

When a sound rewriting system exists in a logical reasoning system we always have a method to deliver satisfiability check of a theory. In this case, we apply the rules to a theory until we reach a fixpoint. If we aim at developing an effective method, however, we need to provide a proof of termination for such a method. For the rewriting system of $\mathcal{EL}$ we can prove that a simple approach, based on the execution of the rules in a given order, is sufficient to provide an effective method for satisfiability checking. This is the result of correctness of Algorithm 1. Firstly, in Lemma 4, we prove that the existence of $\perp$ in a theory, if not introduced by default, is the consequence of the application of the rules in a specific order.

Lemma 4. *If a satisfiable $\mathcal{EL}$-theory $\mathcal{E}$ is rewritten into a contradictory $\widehat{\mathcal{E}}$, then we have:*

1. *rewritten the theory by using $\mathcal{L}_1$ before $\mathcal{D}_1$ and $\mathcal{D}_2$, or*
2. *rewritten the theory by using $\mathcal{L}'_1$ before $\mathcal{D}'_1$, $\mathcal{D}''_1$, $\mathcal{D}'_2$ and $\mathcal{D}''_2$, or*
3. *rewritten the theory by using $(\rightarrow)$ before $\mathcal{D}_1$ and $\mathcal{D}_2$, or*
4. *rewritten the theory by using $(\rightarrow')$ before $\mathcal{D}'_1$ and $\mathcal{D}'_2$, or*
5. *applied (TRANS◁) after $\mathcal{D}_1$ and $\mathcal{D}_2$, and*
6. *applied (TRANS ≺) after $\mathcal{D}'_1$, $\mathcal{D}''_1$, $\mathcal{D}'_2$ and $\mathcal{D}''_2$.*

Proof. There are two cases when $\widehat{\mathcal{E}}$ is empty: either (1) the theory $\mathcal{E}$ is empty or (2) a closure rule was used. The first case is not possible by definition of the theory, as we assume that $\mathcal{E}$ is not empty. The second case occurs if at least one of the five closure rules applied. Suppose by contradiction that rule $\mathcal{C}_T$ or $\mathcal{C}'_T$ is used to compute the contradictory $\widehat{\mathcal{E}}$. The application of this rule leads to a contradiction as $\mathcal{E}$ is satisfiable, whilst $\mathcal{C}_T$ or $\mathcal{C}'_T$ are applied when there is a contradiction in the theory. The same applies for rules $\mathcal{C}_C$ and $\mathcal{C}'_C$.

Suppose, ad absurdum, that $\mathcal{C}_P$ leads to a contradictory $\widehat{\mathcal{E}}$. The premises of $\mathcal{C}_P$ are obtained using rules $\mathcal{L}_1$, $\mathcal{L}'_1$, $\mathcal{L}_2$, $(\rightarrow)$ and $(\rightarrow')$. The first case for having a contradiction captured by $\mathcal{C}_P$ is when $\mathcal{L}_1$ is applied before $\mathcal{D}_1$ and $\mathcal{D}_2$. This happens because a contradiction is found that in fact was solved by $\mathcal{D}_1$ and $\mathcal{D}_2$, as $\mathcal{E}$ is satisfiable. The second case for having a contradiction captured by $\mathcal{C}_P$ is when $\mathcal{L}'_1$ is applied before $\mathcal{D}'_1$, $\mathcal{D}''_1$, $\mathcal{D}'_2$ and $\mathcal{D}''_2$. This happens because a contradiction is found that in fact was solved by $\mathcal{D}'_1$, $\mathcal{D}''_1$, $\mathcal{D}'_2$ and $\mathcal{D}''_2$, as $\mathcal{E}$ is satisfiable. The third case for having a contradiction captured by C_P is when $(\rightarrow)$ is applied before $\mathcal{D}_1$ and $\mathcal{D}_2$. This happens because the formulas that were introduced produce the contradictions that in fact were solved by $\mathcal{D}_1$ and $\mathcal{D}_2$, as $\mathcal{E}$ is satisfiable. The fourth case is similar to the third and occurs when $(\rightarrow')$ is applied before $\mathcal{D}_1'$ and $\mathcal{D}_2'$. The fifth case for having a contradiction captured by C_P is when TRANS◁ is applied after $\mathcal{D}_1$ and $\mathcal{D}_2$. This happens because the contradictions found could be solved by $\mathcal{D}_1$ and $\mathcal{D}_2$ if the TRANS◁ rule was applied before, as $\mathcal{E}$ is satisfiable. The sixth case for having a contradiction captured by C_P is when TRANS $\prec$ is applied after $\mathcal{D}_1'$, $\mathcal{D}_1''$, $\mathcal{D}_2'$ and $\mathcal{D}_2''$. This happens because the contradictions found could be solved by $\mathcal{D}_1'$, $\mathcal{D}_1''$, $\mathcal{D}_2'$ and $\mathcal{D}_2''$ if the TRANS $\prec$ rule was applied before, as $\mathcal{E}$ is satisfiable. ∎

We are now able to prove that the rewriting procedure introduced in Sect. 4.2 establishes satisfiability as defined in Definition 5. We prove that the provided *specific* order of application of the rewriting rules determines the existence of a model. Given Theorem 1, we prove that the rewriting given by Algorithm 1 is exhausted. Theorem 2 follows by applying Lemmas 3 and 4.

Proof (Theorem 2). Based on the semantics introduced in Sect. 3 and given that Algorithm 1 applies the rules in the order specified in Lemma 4, we show that every theory that is unsatisfiable is rewritten by Algorithm 1 in a closed one, and consequently, every open theory resulting by the rewriting procedure, is also exhausted. We prove this by induction on the theory construction.

The base cases occur for a relational formula, a simple evidence, or a derived one. For lack of space, we omit the proofs as they follow quite straightforwardly by the definitions of relational formula, simple evidence, derived evidence, and the ◁ and $\prec$ relations.

For the inductive step, we assume that $\mathcal{E}$ is formed by either n relational formulas, or a blend of n formulas, and that we know that the claim is true for $n - 1$ formulas, and we show that the claim then holds also for n formulas.

Assume that $\mathcal{E}$ is formed by n different relational formulas. The only rules that can be applied are TRANS◁ and TRANS $\prec$, and the algorithm applies them. If $\mathcal{E}$ is unsatisfiable, then $\widehat{\mathcal{E}}$ is empty as rule C_T or rule C_T' capture any existing contradictions between relational formulas. If $\mathcal{E}$ is satisfiable, then $\widehat{\mathcal{E}}$ is open and exhausted as the algorithm has applied all possible rules.

Assume that $\mathcal{E}$ is formed by n different simple pieces of evidence. The algorithm first tries to apply $\mathcal{D}_1$. If $\mathcal{E}$ is unsatisfiable and there are discordances, then $\widehat{\mathcal{E}}$ is empty, because the algorithm applies C_C. If there are no discordances in $\mathcal{E}$, then the algorithm translates all the rules into second layer formulas, by applying rule $\mathcal{L}_1$. Since $\mathcal{E}$ is unsatisfiable, the algorithm applies the closing rule C_P to capture the discordances between second layer formulas, and $\widehat{\mathcal{E}}$ is empty. If $\mathcal{E}$ is satisfiable, then the algorithm applies $\mathcal{L}_1$, and $\widehat{\mathcal{E}}$ is open and exhausted as the algorithm has applied all possible rules.

Assume that $\mathcal{E}$ is formed of n different derived pieces of evidence. The algorithm tries to apply the rules in the following order: $\mathcal{L}_2$, $\mathcal{D}_1$, $\mathcal{L}_1$, $(\rightarrow)$, $\mathcal{D}_1'$, $(\rightarrow')$, $\mathcal{D}_1''$ and $\mathcal{L}_1'$. If $\mathcal{E}$ is unsatisfiable, then the algorithm applies one of the closing rules $\mathcal{C}_C$, $\mathcal{C}'_C$ and $\mathcal{C}_P$ to capture the discordances between formulas of the different layers, and $\widehat{\mathcal{E}}$ is empty. If $\mathcal{E}$ is satisfiable, then the algorithm yields a $\widehat{\mathcal{E}}$ that is open and exhausted as it has applied all possible rules.

Assume that $\mathcal{E}$ is formed of n different formulas (pieces of evidence and relational formulas). The algorithm tries to apply all of its rules. If $\mathcal{E}$ is unsatisfiable, then the algorithm applies one of the closing rules to capture the discordances between formulas of the different layers, and $\widehat{\mathcal{E}}$ is empty. We know that our algorithm is able to capture all the contradictions, because the algorithm first applies all the rules that can surface all the possible contradictions and then it applies the appropriate closing rule. If $\mathcal{E}$ is satisfiable, then the algorithm yields a $\widehat{\mathcal{E}}$ that is open and exhausted as it has applied all possible rules.   ■

References

1. Ågotnes, T., Balbiani, P., van Ditmarsch, H., Seban, P.: Group announcement logic. J. Appl. Logic **8**(1), 62–81 (2010)
2. Alchourròn, C.E., Gärdenfors, P., Makinson, D.: On the logic of theory change: partial meet contraction and revision functions. J. Symbolic Logic **50**, 510–530 (1985)
3. Alechina, N., Jago, M., Logan, B.: Preference-based belief revision for rule-based agents. Synthese **165**(2), 159–177 (2008)
4. Augusto, J.C., Simari, G.R.: Temporal defeasible reasoning. Knowl. Inf. Syst. **3**(3), 287–318 (2001)
5. Balbiani, P., van Ditmarsch, H., Herzig, A., de Lima, T.: A tableau method for public announcement logics. In: Olivetti, N. (ed.) TABLEAUX 2007. LNCS (LNAI), vol. 4548, pp. 43–59. Springer, Heidelberg (2007). https://doi.org/10.1007/978-3-540-73099-6_6
6. Balbiani, P., Guiraud, N., Herzig, A., Lorini, E.: Agents that speak: modelling communicative plans and information sources in a logic of announcements. In: AAMAS 2011, vol. 1–3. pp. 1207–1208 (2011)
7. Baltag, A., Smets, S.: Conditional doxastic models: a qualitative approach to dynamic belief revision. Electr. Notes Theor. Comput. Sci. **165**, 5–21 (2006)
8. Barber, K.S., Kim, J.: Belief revision process based on trust: agents evaluating reputation of information sources. In: AGENTS 2000, pp. 73–82 (2000)
9. van Benthem, J.: Dynamic logic for belief revision. J. Appl. Non-class. Logics **17**(2), 129–155 (2007)
10. Dix, J., Hansson, S.O., Kern-Isberner, G., Simari, G.R.: Belief change and argumentation in multi-agent scenarios. Ann. Math. Artif. Intell. **78**(3), 177–179 (2016)
11. Governatori, G., Terenziani, P.: Temporal extensions to defeasible logic. In: Orgun, M.A., Thornton, J. (eds.) AI 2007. LNCS (LNAI), vol. 4830, pp. 476–485. Springer, Heidelberg (2007). https://doi.org/10.1007/978-3-540-76928-6_49
12. Hunter, A., Booth, R.: Trust-sensitive belief revision. In: IJCAI 2015, pp. 3062–3068 (2015)
13. Lorini, E., Jiang, G., Perrussel, L.: Trust-based belief change. In: ECAI 2014 - Including PAIS 2014, pp. 549–554 (2014)
14. Plaza, J.: Logics of public communications. Synthese **158**(2), 165–179 (2007)

15. Shakarian, P., Simari, G.I., Moores, G., Parsons, S.: Cyber attribution: an argumentation-based approach. In: Cyber Warfare - Building the Scientific Foundation, pp. 151–171 (2015)
16. Shakarian, P., et al.: Belief revision in structured probabilistic argumentation - model and application to cyber security. Ann. Math. Artif. Intell. **78**(3–4), 259–301 (2016)
17. Van Ditmarsch, H., van Der Hoek, W., Kooi, B.: Dynamic Epistemic Logic, vol. 337. Springer, Heidelberg (2007). https://doi.org/10.1007/978-1-4020-5839-4

Malware and Vulnerabilities

Beneath the Bonnet: A Breakdown of Diagnostic Security

Jan Van den Herrewegen$^{(\boxtimes)}$ and Flavio D. Garcia

University of Birmingham, Birmingham, UK
{jxv572,f.garcia}@cs.bham.ac.uk

Abstract. An Electronic Control Unit (ECU) is an automotive computer essential to the operation of a modern car. Diagnostic protocols running on these ECUs are often too powerful, giving an adversary full access to the ECU if they can bypass the diagnostic authentication mechanism. Firstly, we present three ciphers used in the diagnostic access control, which we reverse engineered from the ECU firmware of four major automotive manufacturers. Next, we identify practical security vulnerabilities in all three ciphers, which use proprietary cryptographic primitives and a small internal state. Subsequently, we propose a generic method to remotely execute code on an ECU over CAN exclusively through diagnostic functions, which we have tested on units of three major automotive manufacturers. Once authenticated, an adversary with access to the CAN network can download binary code to the RAM of the microcontroller and execute it, giving them full access to the ECU and its peripherals, including the ability to read/write firmware at will. Finally, we conclude with recommendations to improve the diagnostic security of ECUs.

1 Introduction

The functionality of a modern road vehicle is determined by a few dozen Electronic Control Units (ECUs). These ECUs are interconnected via one or several Controller Area Network (CAN) [10] buses. Powerful diagnostic protocols are put in place by the manufacturer to update or patch the vehicle in case of malfunction. The most prevalent diagnostic standards are Unified Diagnostic Services (UDS) [11] and its predecessor, Keyword Protocol 2000 (KWP2000) [12], which provide manufacturers and service technicians with advanced diagnostic features such as upload and download functionality. The main diagnostic access control mechanism is the so called 'seed-key protocol', a challenge-response protocol used to authenticate diagnostic devices. Even more sophisticated diagnostic protocols such as the Universal Measurement and Calibration Protocol (XCP) [1] enable service technicians to fully fine-tune ECUs. The functionality provided by XCP goes beyond that of traditional diagnostic protocols found in ECUs, which a knowledgeable attacker could abuse to take control of an ECU over CAN.

This work was partly funded by EPSRC Fellowship EP/R008000/1.

J. Lopez et al. (Eds.): ESORICS 2018, LNCS 11098, pp. 305–324, 2018.
https://doi.org/10.1007/978-3-319-99073-6_15

In many cars, diagnostic communication occurs on the CAN bus available on the OBD-II [13] port, which every vehicle commissioned in the European Union since 2004 [5] must be equipped with. However, the automotive network was never designed with an adversary in mind: the CAN bus is an unencrypted and unauthenticated network. Thus, ECUs cannot distinguish diagnostic messages originating from a diagnostic client from messages sent by an adversary. Previous research has indicated that individual ECUs connected to the internal network of a modern car can be compromised [17,18]. This becomes even more worrying when combined with a remote exploit, as demonstrated in [24]. After having gained access to the Telematics Unit, Valasek and Miller managed to remotely control crucial functionality of the car. With advanced features such as in-vehicle connectivity becoming the norm in modern cars, the automotive industry needs to shift towards better diagnostic security in ECUs.

Our Contribution. The contribution of this paper is three-fold:

- Through reverse-engineering the ECU firmware of three different manufacturers, we recovered the ciphers used in the diagnostic authentication protocol, which we present here in full detail.
- We propose a practical cryptanalysis of each of these ciphers, showing that the diagnostic authentication protocols can be easily bypassed with neglibible computational complexity.
- We propose a generic method to remotely execute code on an ECU by exploiting UDS and XCP features, giving us read/write access to the internal memory of the ECU and its peripherals.

Related Work. With its transformation towards more complex vehicular systems, the automotive industry is no stranger to cryptographic attacks against several security mechanisms it has put in place. Bogdanov first attacked the KeeLoq block cipher, which is used in various automotive anti-theft mechanisms, in [2], while further attacks on this cipher appear in [2,9,14]. Furthermore, an immobiliser system is in place to prevent an attacker from starting the car without a valid key fob. Ciphers used in the immobiliser system in various cars include the DST40 cipher, Megamos Crypto and the Hitag2 cipher, attacked respectively by Bono et al. in [3], Verdult et al. in [26,28] and in [27].

Several papers in the literature assess diagnostic security in ECUs, beginning with the work of Koscher et al. [17], which experimentally tests the security and capabilities of ECUs. The authors tamper with several safety-critical ECUs by sending diagnostic messages, while they reprogram the telematics unit to act as a bridge between the high-speed and low-speed CAN bus in the vehicle. The reprogramming of the unit consists of downloading code to its RAM memory and executing it. No access control mechanism was implemented on the studied ECU's.

Additionally, Miller and Valasek reverse engineered the complete reprogramming procedure on two Ford ECUs by analysing a diagnostic tool [18]. The tool reprograms the units by downloading a piece of code to the RAM memory of the microcontroller, which subsequently handles the reflashing of the unit. The authors abuse this mechanism to execute their own code on the ECU. After authenticating to the ECU, the authors use several diagnostic primitives to download the code to the unit. Once certain prerequisites have been met, a different diagnostic service makes the ECU jump to the downloaded code and thus execute it. No access restrictions are in place on the microcontroller, giving the code full access to peripherals such as the CAN bus.

Finally, Khan [15] raises several issues on security in the UDS protocol, the access control mechanism in particular. The paper states multiple security flaws in the security access service provided by UDS, more specifically on challenge generation and the complexity of the employed cipher. Furthermore, Khan notes that an attacker can recover the cipher and secret keys from the firmware.

Overview. The rest of this paper is organised as follows. Section 2 gives an overview of the most prevalent diagnostic protocols we have encountered in ECUs. In Sect. 3 we follow up with a description of the ciphers used in the diagnostic access control mechanism in several ECUs and propose ways to bypass these. In Sect. 4 we propose a method to remotely execute code on an ECU when having access to the CAN bus, of which we demonstrate the capabilities in Sect. 5. We discuss our findings in Sect. 7, while we suggest countermeasures and mitigations in Sect. 6. Finally, we conclude in Sect. 8.

2   Background

This section summarizes the most prevalent diagnostic protocol in ECUs, namely the Unified Diagnostic Services. We have encountered its predecessor, the Keyword Protocol 2000 in older ECUs, but since both protocols are very similar, we will only outline the main features of UDS. Note that we use the concepts *tester* and *client* interchangeably, both denoting the diagnostic device querying the ECU. Moreover, we briefly introduce diagnostic communication channels and summarize the main features of the XCP protocol.

2.1   Unified Diagnostic Services

The UDS standard defines several diagnostic sessions: in the default session an ECU executes its normal function in the internal vehicular network. A diagnostic client can change the active session with the *DiagnosticSessionControl* service to either a programming session or an extended diagnostic session, however the available functionality in these sessions is left up to the manufacturer's discretion.

The main access control mechanism is a challenge-response (also known as *seed-key* in automotive terminology) protocol specified by the *SecurityAccess* service, as depicted in Fig. 1. In order to authenticate to the ECU, a diagnostic client must send a *challenge request* to the ECU, which subsequently replies with a randomly generated challenge (also called the *seed* in automotive terminology).

Both the client and ECU calculate a *response* (also called the *key* in automotive terminology) from this challenge according to a manufacturer-specific cipher, based on a shared secret. The client is authenticated if it supplies the ECU with a valid response. Multiple security levels are defined in UDS, which the manufacturer is free to use for different levels of access. UDS only specifies the challenge-response protocol, leaving the choice of the cipher up to the manufacturer.

A tester can use the *RoutineControl* service to execute preprogrammed functions in the ECU, with each routine uniquely defined by a two byte identifier. The client can pass arguments in a routine control call if needed. The standard specifies some routines and their respective identifiers, such as the *EraseMemory* routine with identifier 0xFF00, while the identifier range 0x200-0xC000 is reserved for manufacturer specific use.

Finally, the *RequestDownload* service provides a diagnostic client with functionality to download data to the ECU. Before sending the data with the *TransferData* service, the tester must specify an address where the data will be downloaded to along with the size of the data. The tester should invoke the *RequestTransferExit* service on completion of the transfer.

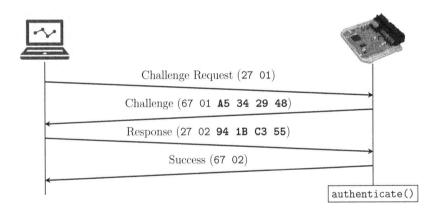

Fig. 1. The challenge-response protocol specified by UDS

2.2 Diagnostic Communication Channels

Neither UDS nor KWP 2000 specify the exact nature of the diagnostic communication channel (namely on which CAN ID each ECU listens for diagnostic messages). This is manufacturer specific, although there are some similarities across manufacturers. Since CAN frames with a lower identifier have priority over those with a higher identifier on the bus, diagnostic CAN identifiers are usually within the range 0x700-0x7FF. Additionally, there is generally a clear relation between the CAN ID on which an ECU receives diagnostic messages, and on which ID it replies (e.g. $\text{ID}_{send} = \text{ID}_{recv} + 8$).

2.3 Universal Measurement and Calibration Protocol

Both XCP and its predecessor, the CAN Calibration Protocol (CCP) [16] are standardized by the Association for Standardization of Automation and Measuring Systems (ASAM). XCP is an application protocol which defines advanced features such as arbitrary read/write access to variables in ECU memory, synchronous data acquisition and flash programming of ECUs for development purposes. A diagnostic tool, also called the *master* in XCP, can analyse the connected ECUs, or *slaves*, through various XCP commands specified in the standard. The master has access to variables in memory by way of an ECU description file exclusive to each ECU, and can even download a reflashing kernel to the RAM for reprogramming purposes. Automotive software companies such as Vector Informatik support XCP solutions for ECUs of over 30 major automotive manufacturers [25], alluding to the extensive use of the XCP standard in the automotive industry.

3 Cryptanalysis of Diagnostic Protocols

In this section we analyse the ciphers used in the diagnostic challenge-response protocol, which we extracted from ECUs of three different automotive manufacturers. We recovered and analysed the firmware of 13 ECUs in total, comprising 8 different car models. We focused our efforts on ECUs with a security critical function, such as the Instrument Cluster and Body Control Module (which handle immobiliser functionality and store its secret keys), a Gateway (which separates the critical high speed CAN bus from other low speed buses), and a Telematics Unit (which provides connectivity to the outside world). Next, we revisit the cipher first described by Valasek and Miller in [18] and present new vulnerabilities, making it easy to circumvent in practise. Using the IDA Pro disassembler we have recovered challenge-response ciphers from the firmware of Ford, Volvo, Fiat and Audi ECUs. We present these ciphers and analyse their security.

3.1 Obtaining and Analysing ECU Firmware Images

On all ECUs we have studied, the firmware was located in the internal flash memory of the microcontroller. We managed to extract the firmware from these embedded devices through a debug interface, such as a Joint Test Action Group (JTAG) or a Background Debug Mode (BDM) interface, which is often exposed on a group of test points on the Printed Circuit Board (PCB). Next, we load the firmware into the IDA Pro disassembler on the correct memory address, which is specified in the datasheet of the microcontroller. For microcontrollers that incorporate a paging mechanism, such as the MC9S12XE (used on certain Ford Instrument Clusters and Body Control Modules), we first need to separate the firmware into chunks equal to the page size of the microcontroller. Once loaded, we can locate the cipher used in the diagnostic authentication protocol by searching for functions that contain constants used in UDS, more specifically frequently used diagnostic error codes and/or service identifiers. Since the manufacturer often reuses ECUs running the same or at least a very similar firmware version across different cars and models, we only need to go through this process once for every ECU type.

Notation and Variables. To avoid any ambiguity, we will use the following notation in this section. C denotes the random challenge generated by the ECU, whereas R denotes the corresponding response. v_i denotes bit i of a variable v, with v_0 being the least significant (rightmost) bit, whereas $v[i]$ denotes byte i of v, with $v[0]$ being the most significant (leftmost) byte. $v \lll i$ refers to a rotation of v by i bits to the left. Finally, (v, w) denotes a concatenation of bytes v and w, with w the least significant byte.

3.2   Analysis of the Ford Challenge-Response Cipher

In this section we perform a cryptanalysis of the Ford cipher, which we have located in the firmware of several Ford ECUs but also in some Volvo units through our reverse engineering efforts. We introduce the cipher and demonstrate how an attacker can break it by means of an attack over CAN. We have found this cipher in the ECUs shown in Table 1.

Table 1. ECUs on which we examined and identified the Ford cipher

Make	Year	Model	ECU
Ford	2010	Focus MK2	Body control module
			Instrument Cluster
	2012, 2014, 2016	Focus MK3	Body control module
			Instrument cluster
	2008	Fiesta MK6	Instrument cluster
	2013, 2014, 2015, 2017	Fiesta MK7	Instrument cluster
			Body control module
Volvo	2015	V50	Telematics unit

Cipher Details. Both the challenge and response are three bytes in Ford ECUs. The cipher uses a slightly modified version of the Galois Linear-Feedback Shift Register (Galois LFSR) with an internal state of 24 bits, which is initialised with a constant (0xC541A9) stored in the firmware of the ECU. The output bit of the LFSR is XORed with a bit from a 64-bit input register R consisting of a 40-bit *secret* S and the 24-bit challenge C. Figure 2 depicts the structure of the modified Galois LFSR, while Definition 1 details the input bit of the cipher in round i. The cipher runs for 64 rounds: in the first 24 rounds, the challenge is shifted into the internal state, after which the cipher absorbs the 40-bit secret into its internal state. In each round, the XOR of the output bit of the LFSR and the input bit of the register is fed back into the tapped bits. The final response is derived from the 24-bit LFSR-state by permuting the nibbles of the state, as shown in Definition 2.

Fig. 2. Structure of the Ford LFSR

Definition 1. Given challenge C and secret S, input bit R_i in round i is defined as follows.

$$R_i = \begin{cases} C_i, & \text{if } i < 24 \\ S_{24-i}, & \text{if } 24 \leq i < 64 \end{cases}$$

Definition 2. Let the nibble representation of the internal state Y be $n_0, \ldots, n_5 = Y[0], \ldots, Y[2]$. Then the permutation $P_1(n_0, \ldots, n_5) : \mathbb{F}_2^{24} \to \mathbb{F}_2^{24}$ is defined as follows.

$$P_1(n_0, \ldots, n_5) = \begin{pmatrix} n_0 \ n_1 \ n_2 \ n_3 \ n_4 \ n_5 \\ n_3 \ n_4 \ n_2 \ n_0 \ n_5 \ n_1 \end{pmatrix}$$

Weaknesses. The internal state of the Galois-LFSR used in the Ford algorithm contains merely 24 bits of entropy. What is even worse, we have observed the same start state and tapping sequence across *all* ECUs we have studied. With no added entropy from a varying start state or tapping sequence, only the 40-bit secret is unknown to an attacker. Through empirical tests we discovered that only the first 24 secret bits shifted into the internal state add entropy. In the subsequent 16 rounds we can set the input bit to zero, making the cipher a standard Galois-LFSR. One valid challenge-response pair enables an attacker to retrieve 24 bits of the secret, and thus recover the structure of the cipher. The attacker can obtain a valid challenge-response pair by making a diagnostic device authenticate to the ECU, which Valasek and Miller demonstrated in [18]. The cipher, however, can be broken even without knowledge of a challenge-response pair.

Attack over CAN. We demonstrate how an attacker can recover the secret used in the Ford cipher for a particular ECU without knowledge of any successful authentication pairs. Access to the diagnostic interface of the ECU is the only prerequisite for this attack.

Delay Mechanism. Unified Diagnostic Services specify an error code which indicates a delay timer is active on the ECU in case of too many failed security access attempts. The specifics of this mechanism are left up to the manufacturer. Many

ECUs implement this delay functionality and disable the security access service temporarily after a certain amount of failed attempts. An attacker can bypass this by requesting a soft reset using the *ECUReset* diagnostic service, which resets all timers and variables. Following a reset the attacker must request a new diagnostic session before they can request a new challenge.

Recovering Diagnostic Secrets on Ford and Volvo ECUs. We conducted our attack both on a 2012 Ford Body Control Module (BCM) and a 2015 Volvo Telematics Unit. These particular units do not implement the delay mechanism after a failed security access attempt. Once we request a diagnostic programming session, the units remains in programming mode until no further diagnostic messages are detected for a certain period ($\sim$5 s). Each security access attempt requires four CAN messages: a challenge request and reply followed by a response and a final message indicating whether the response was valid or not. All CAN frames are 8 bytes for the Ford diagnostic packages, making a physical CAN frame on the bus 135 bits in the worst case, with stuffing bits taken into account [20]. On the BCM, the diagnostic interface is available on the high speed CAN network, which runs at 500 kbit/s. One security access attempt takes four CAN frames or maximum 540 bits, so with a bitrate of 500 kbit/s that makes for a minimum of 1.08 ms per attempt, calculation time or other delays not taken into account. Since we reduced the complexity from 2^{40} of a brute-force attack to only 2^{24} attempts, this results in a search time of approximately 5 h in the best case scenario. Due to all other delays, the attack we implemented took approximately 15 h. We would like to emphasise that, since all ECUs use the same secret, an attacker only needs to do this once.

3.3 Analysis of the Fiat Challenge-Response Cipher

Through reverse engineering the firmwares of both a current Fiat Body System Interface (BSI) and its predecessor, used in cars before 2012, we have extracted the following cipher used for the security access service. We present the cipher used in the older Fiat BSI for security level 1 and discuss flaws in the design and key generation process.

Cipher Details. Both the challenge and response are 32-bit in the Fiat implementation of the security access service. The cipher uses two 16-bit LFSRs, both with the structure depicted in Fig. 3. Both LFSRs absorb one input bit in each round, as detailed in Definition 4. The cipher runs for 24 rounds: in the first 8 rounds different constants ($S[0]$ and $S[2]$) are shifted into each state, whereas in the remaining 16 rounds the cipher absorbs one bit of the preprocessed challenge bytes into the state. Finally, the 32-bit response is derived from the LFSRs by combining the 16-bit internal states.

Definition 3. For a given byte b, the permutation $P_2(b) : \mathbb{F}_2^8 \to \mathbb{F}_2^8$ is defined as follows.

$$P_2(b) = \begin{pmatrix} b_7 & b_6 & b_5 & b_4 & b_3 & b_2 & b_1 & b_0 \\ b_3 & b_0 & b_6 & b_1 & b_7 & b_4 & b_2 & b_5 \end{pmatrix}$$

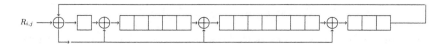

Fig. 3. Structure of the Fiat LFSR

Definition 4. With given challenge C and secret bytes $S[0], \ldots, S[3]$, input bit $R_{i,j}$ in round i for LFSR j is defined as follows.

$$R_{i,0} = (C[0] \oplus S[1], C[2] \ggg 5, S[0])_i$$
$$R_{i,1} = (C[3] \oplus S[3], P_2(C[1]), S[2])_i$$

Analysis of the Cipher. There are several issues in the design and secret generation of the cipher. The cipher uses two 16-bit LFSRs instead of one 32-bit LFSR, which reduces the entropy added by the tapped bits and start state significantly. An exhaustive search over the secret space would take 2^{48} tries, since an attacker must guess the 16-bit start state, the 16-bit tapping sequence and the 8-bit constants $S[0] \ldots S[3]$. However, Table 2 depicts the constants found in the firmware of two different Fiat ECUs. Only the tapped bits, $S[0]$ and $S[2]$ differ. The nibbles of $S[0]$ and $S[2]$ are reversed in the firmware of the ECUs. Only the tapped bits in the LFSR are significantly different across the two different ECUs, which reduces the time of an exhaustive search to only $2^{16} = 65536$ attempts.

We have implemented this attack on a Fiat Grande Punto BSI. The diagnostic interface of this unit is available on the high-speed CAN bus, which runs at 500 kbit/s. The ECU enables a delay timer after receiving two unsuccesfull security access attempts, which lasts 10 s. However, to circumvent this delay it suffices to establish a default session and immediately thereafter request a new programming session, which resets the timers on the ECU. Thus, every two security access attempts require 12 CAN frames: a programming mode request and response, four frames for obtaining and validating a challenge-response pair (which we do twice) and finally a default mode request and response. This makes for an average of 6 frames per attempt, which comes to a maximum of 810 bits (including stuffing bits) on the CAN bus. For the reduced search space of 65536 attempts this results in a minimum search time of 106 s. The attack we implemented took just over an hour, which is mostly due to the delay incurred when changing from and to a programming session. An attacker only needs to perform this attack once, since diagnostic secrets are shared across similar types of ECUs.

Table 2. Secrets found in the firmware of two different Fiat ECUs

ECU	$S[0]$	$S[1]$	$S[2]$	$S[3]$	Taps	Start state
Fiat BSI 2012+	0x12	0xDC	0x34	0x7A	0x8408	0xFFFF
Fiat BSI 2012−	0x21	0xDC	0x43	0x7A	0x3423	0xFFFF

3.4   Analysis of the Volkswagen Group Cipher

Through analysing firmwares of both Volkswagen and Audi ECUs, we reverse engineered the ciphers used in a 2009 Audi Gateway Control Unit and a 2010 VW Passat Instrument Cluster. The implementation of the cipher in these Volkswagen Group (VAG) ECUs goes as follows. Each ECU contains the same algorithm which interprets a sequence of bytes stored in the firmware as commands on the internal state. The cipher uses the randomly generated challenge as the initial internal state. Subsequently, the algorithm reads the sequence of bytes, which are parsed as opcodes for the cipher. Each opcode denotes an operation on the internal 32-bit state, with the five basic operations being: rotate the state to the left/right, add/subtract a constant to/from the state and XOR the state with a constant. Based on this information we present the cipher we extracted from the Audi Gateway Control Unit and assess its security.

Code listing 1. Audi gateway challenge-response algorithm

```
 1: function CHALLENGE-RESPONSE(C)                        ▷ With C - 32-bit challenge
 2:     S = C
 3:     for i in {0 ... 10} do
 4:         S = S ≪ 1
 5:         feedback = S ∧ 1
 6:         if i ∈ {0, 2, 6, 7} then
 7:             if feedback == 1 then                     ▷ For rounds 0, 2, 6 and 7
 8:                 S = S ∧ (∼ 1)                          ▷ Clear the feedback bit
 9:                 S = S ⊕ 0x04C11DB7                     ▷ XOR the tapped bits
10:             end if
11:         else
12:             if feedback == 1 then
13:                 S = S ⊕ 0x04C11DB7
14:             else
15:                 S = S | 1                             ▷ Set the feedback bit
16:             end if
17:         end if
18:     end for
19:     return S
20: end function
```

Cipher Details. Code Listing 1 details the cipher, which runs for 10 rounds. In each round, the cipher rotates the state to the left. The cipher is a standard Galois LFSR: if the feedback bit is set, a constant (the tapped bits, i.e. 0x04C11DB7 in the code below) is XORed into the state. Depending on the round, the feedback bit is either set or cleared.

Weaknesses. Since the internal state of the cipher is equal to the generated challenge, only the 32-bit tapping sequence adds entropy to the cipher. An attacker with access to one challenge-response pair can recover this 32-bit constant by performing an exhaustive search over the 32-bit secret space. It should be noted that the flexible nature of the structure of the cipher makes it more difficult for an attacker to recover the secrets in different ECUs. Indeed, in several VW Instrument Clusters we found that the cipher runs for a different number of rounds and XORs the state with multiple constants, making the cipher more secure.

Additionally, we identified a supplementary security issue in the firmware of this particular unit: if the diagnostic client provides an invalid response, the ECU performs an extra check, which compares the response to a hardcoded value (i.e. 0xCAFFE012). The diagnostic tool is authenticated if it provides this value as the response. Regardless of existing vulnerabilities in the cipher, a hardcoded backdoor on the ECU introduces extra security implications.

4   Remote Code Execution over CAN

The ciphers we studied in Sect. 3 are in place to protect the ECU from unauthorised access. Once a diagnostic device is authenticated, the ECU unlocks priviliged diagnostic functionality, part of which allows executing more advanced diagnostic protocols like XCP. Despite its widespread use in the automotive industry, we failed to locate the XCP protocol in the firmware of the ECUs we studied. Instead, we found that the Original Equipment Manufacturer (OEM) enables a download of the XCP stack to the RAM of an ECU through various diagnostic services. Piggybacking on this required functionality for the XCP protocol, we have identified a generic approach to execute arbitrary code on an ECU over the CAN bus. Through our own reverse engineering efforts we have encountered this mechanism in ECUs made by several manufacturers. Provided that an attacker can bypass the access control mechanism of the diagnostic protocol as we showed in Sect. 3, the only prerequisite is that they can send and receive messages on the CAN bus. An attacker with access to the OBD-II port or who has compromised an ECU on the network, such as the Telematics Unit, can abuse this functionality to control or reprogram additional ECUs.

The outline of this section is as follows. After specifying the general method to execute code on an ECU, we show how an adversary with access to the CAN bus can abuse this mechanism to gain read/write access to the firmware of ECUs of several manufacturers. From now on we will refer to the piece of binary code that is sent to the ECU as the *secondary bootloader*.

Downloading Sequence. Figure 4 shows the sequence of diagnostic messages required to execute the secondary bootloader on an ECU. Firstly, the diagnostic client must request a programming session. Until the client authenticates itself to the ECU, any necessary functionality remains unavailable. Once authenticated, the client can carry out certain checks and assertions about the ECU. These usually include reading out the software version and part number of the module as the secondary bootloader is dependent on the microcontroller. The client can transfer the secondary bootloader to the ECU through the download services provided by the running diagnostic protocol. Finally, the client requests a routine control either before or after the download (dependent on the manufacturer) in order to redirect the program flow to the secondary bootloader, which now resides in RAM.

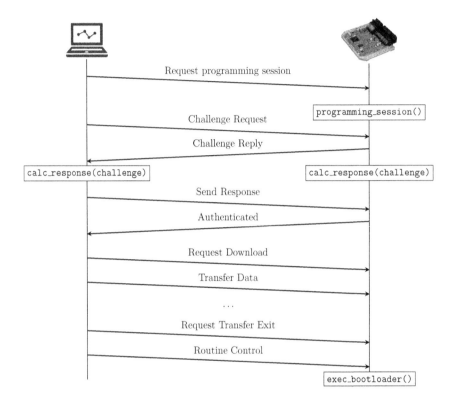

Fig. 4. Execution of the secondary bootloader

Memory Limitations. The ECU only provides a small area in RAM for the secondary bootloader, which usually suffices if the downloaded code performs a simple task (such as updating a variable in memory). Otherwise, the bootloader can download additional code into the RAM of the unit over the CAN bus.

4.1 Use Case: Changing the Odometer on a Ford Instrument Cluster

We have managed to change the odometer value on a 2016 Ford Focus Instrument Cluster (IC) through the secondary bootloader. The download of the secondary bootloader goes as follows for all Ford and Volvo ECUs we have analysed. With the ECU in a programming session and our device authenticated, we send a *requestDownload* message. The request has two arguments: the download address, which is located in RAM, and the size of the bootloader. If the microcontroller uses a paging mechanism, the address consists either of a page number and address within the page, or a physical address. Subsequently, we can transfer the secondary bootloader using the *transferData* service, after which the ECU expects a *requestTransferExit* message. Finally, to execute the downloaded code, we must send a *routineControl* message. Arguments to this message are the routine identifier, which is `0x301`, and the exact address where the microcontroller should jump to. The mileage on this Instrument Cluster is stored on an external Electrically Erasable Programmable Read-Only Memory (EEPROM) chip, namely the M95320 manufactured by ST Microelectronics. The main microcontroller, a Renesas μPD70F3425, is connected to the EEPROM chip through a Serial Peripheral Interface (SPI). Once we identified the pins used for the serial communication with the EEPROM chip, we managed to arbitrarily reduce the mileage by writing the desired value to the memory locations where the mileage is stored. Multiple ECUs store the mileage in a modern car, meaning that an attacker must repeat this process for all relevant ECUs if he wishes to successfully tamper with the mileage in a car.

It should be noted that Valasek and Miller first documented this bootloader mechanism to reprogram a Ford Smart Junction Box in [18]. There are several differences to the sequence denoted above compared to what Valasek and Miller describe. Firstly, the address the authors specify in the download request to the ECU is zero, which makes the ECU download the code to a predefined address in RAM. Subsequently, the authors call a routine control with identifier `0x304`, making the ECU jump to the same predefined address as the download. Finally, the code is only executed if the first four bytes of the secondary bootloader are equal to a value stored in the firmware of the ECU. We have only encountered this 'security' feature in one of the Ford ECUs we analysed.

4.2   Use Case: Reprogramming a Fiat Body System Interface

We have analysed the reprogramming process for both a current Delphi Fiat Body System Interface (BSI) and its predecessor, which are deployed in a range of Fiat vehicles. Execution of the secondary bootloader goes as follows for both Fiat BSIs. The ECU must be in a programming session and 'unlocked' for security level 1, following the steps from Sect. 3. In order to execute the downloaded code after the download, we must first write the identifiers with ID's `0xF184` and `0xF185` through the *writeDataByIdentifier* service. This sets a flag in memory necessary for the following routine control to complete successfully. Next, we must execute the *eraseMemory* routine control with arguments the identifier (`0xFF00`), the start address and end address of the memory area in RAM to which we will download the code. In order to make the microcontroller jump to the code, it is crucial that this range is equal to the size of the downloaded data. Otherwise, the download will terminate normally but will not result in a jump to RAM. If all prerequisites described above are met, the microcontroller will jump to a predefined address in RAM after the last *TransferData* request.

This address is set in the firmware and is dependent on the memory layout of the microcontroller as the bootloader always resides in RAM. Hence, in order to redirect the program flow to our code, this predefined address must be contained within the download range of the bootloader. Trace 1 shows the required diagnostic messages to execute the bootloader.

While the microcontroller runs on a 32-bit architecture, both addresses required as arguments in the routine control preceding the download are only 3 bytes long. The ECU translates these by prepending them with 0xFF, resulting in an address located in RAM. Before the ECU executes the downloaded code, it activates the watchdog timer in reset mode, which generates an unmaskable reset interrupt when the timer overflows, making the microcontroller reboot. The secondary bootloader can circumvent this mechanism by resetting the timer before an overflow occurs, implying that the unit will only resume its normal functionality once the bootloader performs a manual reset, for instance by jumping to the reset vector.

Trace 1. Executing the secondary bootloader on a Fiat BSI

```
0x18da40f1   2  10  2                        Programming session
0x18daf140   6  50  2  0  32  1  f4  0
0x18da40f1   2  27  1                        Security access
0x18daf140   6  67  1  81  6e  e7  f8  0
0x18da40f1   6  27  2  ac  eb  3e  3e
0x18daf140   2  67  2  78  0  0  0  0
0x18da40f1   10  10  2e  f1  85  1  a8  bc    Write data by ID
0x18daf140   30  0  0  ff  ff  ff  ff  ff
0x18da40f1   21  ad  cf  cf  ce  ce  c9  ca
0x18da40f1   22  13  6  21
0x18daf140   3  6e  f1  85  ff  ff  ff  ff
0x18da40f1   10  10  2e  f1  84  1  a8  bc    Write data by ID
0x18daf140   30  0  0  ff  ff  ff  ff  ff
0x18da40f1   21  ad  cf  cf  ce  ce  c9  ca
0x18da40f1   22  13  6  21
0x18daf140   3  6e  f1  84  ff  ff  ff  ff
0x18da40f1   10  a  31  1  ff  0  ff  ca      Routine control
0x18daf140   30  0  0  ff  ff  ff  ff  ff
0x18da40f1   21  a0  ff  cf  9f
0x18daf140   4  71  1  ff  0  0  0  0
0x18da40f1   10  b  34  0  44  0  ff  ca      Request download
0x18daf140   30  0  0  ff  ff  ff  ff  ff
0x18da40f1   21  a0  0  0  5  0
0x18daf140   4  74  20  4  2  ff  ff  ff
0x18da40f1   10  22  36  1  e0  7  60  1      Transfer Data
             . . .
```

5   Building a Firmware Modification and Extraction Framework

We demonstrate the capabilities of the secondary bootloader by developing a firmware modification and extraction framework. Using the procedure detailed in Sect. 4, we can execute arbitrary code on any ECU that implements this mechanism. The code downloaded to the ECU is binary machine code, so at the very least we must know the architecture of the ECU. Many microcontrollers used in ECUs are automotive-grade microcontrollers and thus incorporate at least

Table 3. ECUs on which we implemented the firmware extraction framework

Make	Year	Model	ECU	Microcontroller	Architecture
Ford	2012	Focus MK3	Body control module	MC9S12XEP768	HCS12X
	2012, 2014, 2016	Focus MK3	Instrument cluster	μPD70F3425	V850E
	2008	Fiesta MK6	Instrument cluster	MC9S12HZ256	HCS12
	2013, 2014, 2015, 2017	Fiesta MK7	Instrument cluster	MC9S12XEQ384	HCS12X
Volvo	2015	V50	Telematics unit	SH7267	SH2A[a]
Fiat	>2012	500	Body system interface	μPD70F3379	V850E1
	<2012	Grande Punto	Body system interface	μPD70F3237	V850E1

[a] We failed to extract the firmware from this unit because we did not have access to a CAN driver

one on-chip CAN interface. This framework aims to transmit the firmware over CAN so the code must contain a minimal microcontroller-specific CAN driver with transmitting capabilities. Table 3 lists the ECUs on which we implemented this framework, along with the incorporated microcontroller and the architecture on which it runs. We built a cross toolchain from the GNU GCC source to compile our code for each architecture we encountered.

Downloading and Executing the Code. The ECU only accepts downloads to a specific area in RAM which varies in different ECUs. Additionally, some units only accept a *RequestDownload* message with a 4 byte address and a 4 byte size, while others are more flexible. UDS provides a set of common negative response codes. If the ECU receives a request with the incorrect format, it replies with a negative response with code 0x13, which means *incorrect message length or invalid format*. Contrarily, if the format of the request is correct but the address or size is not within the correct range, the unit responds with error code 0x31, indicating *request out of range*. The ECU does not limit the amount of unsuccessful download requests, so we can find this address by covering the complete address space of the microcontroller. Provided that we know the memory layout of the microcontroller, we can limit the range significantly since the address is located in RAM. To further reduce the range, we can increment the address by 0x10 each time while the size remains constant. With a common ECU RAM size of 128 KiB, that makes for a maximum of 8192 attempts.

We can transmit the firmware of an ECU over CAN by dereferencing a pointer and transmitting it until all valid addresses are covered. It suffices to jump to the reset vector to resume normal operation of the ECU. Additionally, we can modify certain crucial parts of the firmware from within the secondary bootloader.

Gaining Access to All Diagnostic Security Levels. In order to be able to authenticate to the ECU on all security levels, an attacker must only recover one secret, namely the secret required for downloading the secondary bootloader to the ECU. In the ECUs we have analysed this was always security level 1 in programming mode. The bootloader can extract the firmware, which includes the cipher secrets for additional levels of security. This renders the multiple levels of security defined in diagnostic standards obsolete, provided that an attacker can locate the secrets in the firmware of the ECU.

6 Mitigation

The only security measure preventing an attacker from downloading code to the unit is the security access service. It is therefore crucial that the challenge-response protocol implemented by the manufacturer is cryptographically sound. Khan [15] proposes the use of the Advanced Encryption Standard for the challenge-response protocol. Given the keys are diversified per car and ECU this would enhance the seed-key security significantly. However, since AES is a symmetric key encryption scheme, the encryption key must be stored in the firmware of the ECU. Unless special hardware is used to protect against reading this encryption key, an attacker can recover the secret key and use it on other ECUs which employ the same key.

A public-key based approach would mitigate the key diversification issues and does not require additional hardware. When a diagnostic client is connected, no time constraints are in place since the car is meant to be stationary during diagnostic maintenance. To mitigate the risk of replay attacks, the challenge is 128 bits long. The diagnostic client generates the response by signing the received challenge with its private key. The ECU verifies the response under the public key, which can be stored in the firmware of the unit. With the computational limitations of ECUs in mind, often running on a 32-bit or even 16-bit architecture, the Elliptic Curve Digital Signature Algorithm (ECDSA) with curve NIST P-256 [21] would be a suitable candidate [8], resulting in a response length of 512 bits.

Moreover, to mitigate the risk of unauthorised code execution on the ECU, the manufacturer can take a similar public-key based approach. If the ECU only accepts downloaded code signed with authorised private keys, no attacker can execute code through this mechanism without knowledge of a valid private key. An attacker with access to the firmware could overwrite the public key with their own public key, which allows them to download code to the unit signed with the attacker's private key. However, we argue that an attacker with the possibility to overwrite the public key can equally overwrite any code in the ECU, making the bootloader mechanism obsolete. Even with access to the firmware, an attacker can't recover any private keys necessary to execute code on other similar ECUs.

Finally, more secure CAN communication would mitigate the risk of an attacker controlling the complete network from a previously compromised node. Radu et al. proposed LeiA [22], a light-weight authentication protocol for ECUs connected to the CAN bus. In order to transmit on a certain CAN ID, a node must have the authentication key corresponding to that identifier. A node transmits a Message Authentication Code (MAC) along with each message. Receiving nodes can check the validity of the sender simply by computing the same MAC. In this scenario, a node would be secure against attacks from the internal network if no other node has the authentication key for its diagnostic CAN ID.

7   Discussion

Security of Diagnostic Authentication Mechanisms. All the ciphers studied in Sect. 3 use some form of proprietary cryptography, with an insufficient challenge and response size of 24 or 32 bits, and an equally small internal state of the cipher. We have shown that if an attacker can obtain a challenge-response pair they can then often recover secret keys of the cipher. No time constraints exist when the ECU is connected to a testbench, as described in [19], making a successfull attack over CAN possible.

Efficiently generating and diversifying cryptographic keys for each individual car and ECU remains a difficult issue to solve for manufacturers, as shown in previous research [7,28]. Valasek and Miller raised the issue of diagnostic key diversification when extracting a set of secrets from a diagnostic device. They (re)used these secrets to authenticate to two ECUs under test. We have encountered similar issues for diagnostic secrets. From our experiments, diagnostic secrets are not diversified for ECUs in each car. An attacker who can recover the secrets for one ECU often has access to other ECUs of the same type or function, since manufacturers reuse these across different models.

Implications. There are several implications of the insecurity of the bootloader mechanism. Firstly, by dumping the firmware of security sensitive ECUs (such as the Passive Keyless Entry or immobilizer), an attacker can recover cryptographic keys necessary to unlock or start the vehicle. An attentive reader might say that an attacker with access to the internal network does not need to recover cryptographic keys. However, Checkoway et al. present an analysis of remote attack services in [4]. More remote vulnerabilities are covered in the literature [6, 23,24]. These are often generic to the model or even make of the car, implicating that if an attacker gains access to a car through one of these generic remote channels, they could read out cryptographic keys specific to that car.

Additionally, an attacker with access to the CAN bus through the OBD-II port, a compromised ECU or maybe by simply pulling a camera or parking sensor can reprogram or even disable connected ECUs. They can escalate an existing vulnerability to take control over ECUs on the same CAN bus as the compromised node, potentially magnifying the impact of a remote exploit. This would make the notion of an automotive worm possible.

Responsible Disclosure. Following standard responsible disclosure practise, we have informed the relevant car manufacturers of the vulnerabilities described in this paper in April 2018, five months ahead of publication. It should be noted that, even though the production of an ECU is outsourced to a third party (a Tier 2 or 3 supplier), the OEMs specify the required diagnostic functionality in their ECUs.

8   Conclusion

In this paper we expose several vulnerabilities in diagnostic security. Firstly, we demonstrate how an attacker can bypass the challenge-response security used in diagnostic protocols. All the studied ciphers use some sort of proprietary cryptography, namely a slighlty adapted version of the Galois-LFSR. 32- or 24-bit challenges and responses and an equally small internal state further add to the insecurity of the ciphers. We demonstrate this by conducting an attack over CAN and recovering secrets through a limited amount of challenge-response pairs. Furthermore, we document the secondary bootloader, a piece of machine code which a CAN node can download to the RAM of a connected ECU through various diagnostic functions. An attacker can abuse this mechanism to recover cryptographic keys, adjust variables in memory or simply disable the ECU. Utilising the functionality implemented for this secondary bootloader, we build a generic firmware modification and extraction framework. To conclude, the challenge-response protocol is the main (and often only) access control mechanism on the ECUs we have studied. The proprietary ciphers used in this protocol are substandard, making it possible for an attacker to bypass these and control all peripherals of the microcontroller through the secondary bootloader, which they can download to RAM. Well deployed public-key cryptographic primitives would mitigate both of these issues.

References

1. The Universal Measurement and Calibration Protocol Family. Standard, Association of Standardisation and Automation and Measuring Systems (2016)
2. Bogdanov, A.: Linear slide attacks on the KeeLoq block cipher. In: Pei, D., Yung, M., Lin, D., Wu, C. (eds.) Inscrypt 2007. LNCS, vol. 4990, pp. 66–80. Springer, Heidelberg (2008). https://doi.org/10.1007/978-3-540-79499-8_7
3. Bono, S., Green, M., Stubblefield, A., Juels, A., Rubin, A.D., Szydlo, M.: Security analysis of a cryptographically-enabled RFID device. In: Proceedings of the 14th USENIX Security Symposium (USENIX Security 2005), pp. 1–16. USENIX Association (2005)
4. Checkoway, S., et al.: Comprehensive experimental analyses of automotive attack surfaces. In: 20th USENIX Security Symposium (USENIX Security 2011). USENIX Association (2011)
5. European Directive: 98/69/EC of the European Parliament and of the Council of 13 October 1998 relating to measures to be taken against air pollution by emissions from motor vehicles and amending Council Directive 70/220/EEC. Official J. Eur. Communities L **350**(28), 12 (1998)
6. Foster, I., Prudhomme, A., Koscher, K., Savage, S.: Fast and vulnerable: a story of telematic failures. In: Proceedings of the 9th USENIX Conference on Offensive Technologies, WOOT 2015 (2015)
7. Garcia, F.D., Oswald, D., Kasper, T., Pavlidès, P.: Lock it and still lose it-on the (in) security of automotive remote keyless entry systems. In: 25th USENIX Security Symposium (USENIX Security 2016), pp. 929–944. USENIX Association (2016)

8. Gura, N., Patel, A., Wander, A., Eberle, H., Shantz, S.C.: Comparing elliptic curve cryptography and RSA on 8-bit CPUs. In: Joye, M., Quisquater, J.-J. (eds.) CHES 2004. LNCS, vol. 3156, pp. 119–132. Springer, Heidelberg (2004). https://doi.org/10.1007/978-3-540-28632-5_9

9. Indesteege, S., Keller, N., Dunkelman, O., Biham, E., Preneel, B.: A practical attack on KeeLoq. In: Smart, N. (ed.) EUROCRYPT 2008. LNCS, vol. 4965, pp. 1–18. Springer, Heidelberg (2008). https://doi.org/10.1007/978-3-540-78967-3_1

10. Road vehicles - controller area network (CAN) - part 1: data link layer and physical signalling. Standard, International Organization for Standardization, Geneva, CH (2015)

11. Road vehicles unified diagnostic services (UDS) specification and requirements. Standard, International Organization for Standardization, Geneva, CH (2006)

12. Road vehicles diagnostic systems keyword protocol 2000 part 3: application layer. Standard, International Organization for Standardization, Geneva, CH (1999)

13. Diagnostic Connector Equivalent to ISO/DIS 15031-3. Standard, SAE, International (2012)

14. Kasper, M., Kasper, T., Moradi, A., Paar, C.: Breaking KEELOQ in a flash: on extracting keys at lightning speed. In: Preneel, B. (ed.) AFRICACRYPT 2009. LNCS, vol. 5580, pp. 403–420. Springer, Heidelberg (2009). https://doi.org/10.1007/978-3-642-02384-2_25

15. Khan, J.: ADvanced Encryption STAndard (ADESTA) for diagnostics over CAN. SAE Int. J. Passeng. Cars - Electron. Electr. Syst. **8**(2), 296–305 (2015)

16. Kleinknecht, H.: Can calibration protocol version 2.1. Germany: ASAM eV, pp. 2–18 (1999)

17. Koscher, K., et al.: Experimental security analysis of a modern automobile. In: 2010 IEEE Symposium on Security and Privacy (SP), pp. 447–462. Institute of Electrical and Electronics Engineers (2010)

18. Miller, C., Valasek, C.: Adventures in automotive networks and control units. Def. Con. **21**, 260–264 (2013)

19. Miller, C., Valasek, C.: Car hacking: for poories. Technical report, IOActive Report (2015)

20. Nolte, T., Hansson, H., Norström, C., Punnekkat, S.: Using bit-stuffing distributions in can analysis. In: IEEE Real-Time Embedded Systems Workshop at the Real-Time Systems Symposium (2001)

21. Pornin, T.: Deterministic Usage of the Digital Signature Algorithm (DSA) and Elliptic Curve Digital Signature Algorithm (ECDSA). RFC 6979 (2013)

22. Radu, A.-I., Garcia, F.D.: LeiA: a lightweight authenticatiton protocol for CAN. In: Askoxylakis, I., Ioannidis, S., Katsikas, S., Meadows, C. (eds.) ESORICS 2016. LNCS, vol. 9879, pp. 283–300. Springer, Cham (2016). https://doi.org/10.1007/978-3-319-45741-3_15

23. Rouf, I., et al.: Security and privacy vulnerabilities of in-car wireless networks: a tire pressure monitoring system case study. In: 19th USENIX Security Symposium (USENIX Security 2010). USENIX Association (2010)

24. Valasek, C., Miller, C.: Remote exploitation of an unaltered passenger vehicle. Technical report, Illmatics (2015)

25. Vector Informatik: Product Catalog 5 (2010)

26. Verdult, R., Garcia, F.D.: Cryptanalysis of the megamos crypto automotive immobilizer. USENIX; login, pp. 17–22 (2015)

27. Verdult, R., Garcia, F.D., Balasch, J.: Gone in 360 s: hijacking with Hitag2. In: 21st USENIX Security Symposium (USENIX Security 2012), pp. 237–252. USENIX Association (2012)
28. Verdult, R., Garcia, F.D., Ege, B.: Dismantling megamos crypto: wirelessly lock-picking a vehicle immobilizer. In: 22nd USENIX Security Symposium (USENIX Security 2013), pp. 703–718. USENIX Association (2013)

Extending Automated Protocol State Learning for the 802.11 4-Way Handshake

Chris McMahon Stone[1(✉)], Tom Chothia[1], and Joeri de Ruiter[2]

[1] School of Computer Science, University of Birmingham, Birmingham, UK
c.mcmahon-stone@cs.bham.ac.uk
[2] Radboud University, Nijmegen, The Netherlands

Abstract. We show how state machine learning can be extended to handle time out behaviour and unreliable communication mediums. This enables us to carry out the first fully automated analysis of 802.11 4-Way Handshake implementations. We develop a tool that uses our learning method and apply this to 7 widely used Wi-Fi routers, finding 3 new security critical vulnerabilities: two distinct downgrade attacks and one router that can be made to leak some encrypted data to an attacker before authentication.

1 Introduction

Automated, systematic analysis of protocol implementations has proven to be an effective tool for security analysis, approaches taken include fuzz testing [1,2], model-based testing [3,4] and protocol state fuzzing (also known as state machine inference) [5–7]. The latter of these methods works by learning the state machine implemented by a particular device or application, in a black-box fashion, by sending different sequences of messages and observing the corresponding outputs. Analysis of these state machines can then be carried out to spot any unexpected logic flow. Such discoveries could be benign divergences from the protocol specification, or result in security vulnerabilities.

In this paper we utilise state machine inference in order to carry out a black-box analysis of implementations of the IEEE 802.11 4-Way Handshake protocol. This widely used protocol is the means by which authentication and session key establishment is carried out on IEEE 802.11 (WPA or WPA2 certified Wi-Fi) networks. In contrast to the manual, model-based testing of the 4-Way Handshake by Vanhoef et al. [4], our method has the advantage of being fully automatic. Manual analysis is a long and arduous task, and requires extensive knowledge of the protocol specification to decide whether every possible test case should fail or pass. Automated learning only requires the tester to specify a set of the possible input messages, i.e., the generation of tests is fully automatic and complete. Furthermore, state machine learning automatically adapts future and successive test cases according to the results of previous ones. For example, if one particular message sequence discovers some erroneous state or unexpected output, it does not stop testing there. The algorithm will continue to explore the

© Springer Nature Switzerland AG 2018
J. Lopez et al. (Eds.): ESORICS 2018, LNCS 11098, pp. 325–345, 2018.
https://doi.org/10.1007/978-3-319-99073-6_16

state space beyond this and therefore cover more ground than is possible with model-based testing.

A naive application of learning to the 4-Way Handshake protocol would fail to handle the implementations time-based behaviour, e.g., message retransmissions and timeouts, though, in general, time-based behaviour can be entirely arbitrary. In protocol settings, past studies have needed to artificially suppress time-based behaviour, as formal time learning algorithms are non-practical due to their high complexity (see for example [8]). This has been done in various ways, for instance, ignoring re-transmissions and manually setting timeouts for responses to ensure time behaviour is not triggered [6,9], or mapping multiple outputs within manually specified times to single state transitions [7,10]. The former technique disables time learning altogether. In the latter, timeouts are manually identified and multiple responses are merged into one, reducing the state space but potentially missing important behaviour.

The quality of the transmission medium and query interfaces can also effect the ability to learn a system. Sometimes a response might be missed and incorrectly marked as a timeout, or a query is not processed by the target and a retransmission occurs, effectively making the system non-deterministic. This poses an issue for naive model-based learning, which requires that the system under test is completely deterministic.

In this paper we propose practical methods to efficiently learn protocol time behaviour and overcome non-determinism. To learn time behaviour we reduce the complexity by making reasonable assumptions about the operation of network protocols. We separate time learning into a secondary learning step. This enables us to first learn non-time based behaviour, without incurring the costly time-complexity that timeouts induce. Throughout this process, we run an error correction method that handles query-response inconsistencies, thereby ensuring learning termination. We implement these methods and use our tool to learn models of the 4-Way Handshake on 7 access points, without which would not have been possible. Our results include the discovery of three vulnerabilities: two distinct downgrade attacks and leakage of multicast data. To summarise, our contributions are as follows:

- We adapt standard Mealy machine inference to learn common time based behaviour in protocols. This is done efficiently and without the need for complex timed automata modelling.
- We provide a practical method to overcome occasional non-deterministic behaviour in protocols.
- We implement our solution and carry out protocol state fuzzing of a range of 4-Way Handshake implementations.

Our tool, along with model diagrams and other information related to this work will be made available online[1].

---

[1] https://chrismcmstone.github.io/wifi-learner/.

2   Related Work

State Machine Learning methods, particularly those based on LearnLib library [11,12], have been successfully applied to demystify legacy software [13] and combined with fuzzing for software deobfuscation [14]. The technique has also been used in security related use cases, such as TLS [7], SSH implementations [6], the biometric passport [15] and bank cards [5].

Not in a security setting, but still relevant due to their handling of timing and retransmissions, Fiterău-Broştean et al. [9] carry out a combined model learning and model checking of TCP implementations. Due to the lack of expressivity of Mealy machines, they eliminated the timing based behaviour and retransmissions. To achieve this, they make sure the learning queries were short enough to not trigger any timed behaviour and ensured that the network adapter ignored all retransmissions. Similarly, in a study involving the application of active learning to IoT communication, Tappler et al. [10] deal with timeouts by adopting the technique used by [7], whereby a manually learned single timeout is set for the receipt of all messages to all queries. All messages received within that time are then mapped to an abstract output symbol. The problem with this approach is that it does not allow queries that are interleaved between consecutive message responses. It also assumes the timeouts are the same for all queries. Our approach on the other hand only requires an upper-bound timeouts and learns time related states such that querying is permitted providing the responses are non-retransmissions. Jonsson et al. [16] have presented some preliminary work on the theoretical side of learning Mealy machines with timers however this work has not yet lead to a practical implementation.

IEEE 802.11, also commonly referred to as Wi-Fi, has been the subject of a wide array of past research. The original Wi-Fi security mechanism, WEP, is broken [17,18]. WEP was replaced by TKIP (based on the RC4 cipher) and then CCMP (based on AES). While TKIP is insecure it is still supported by most WPA2 access points (APs). The 4-Way Handshake, which is deployed to authenticate clients and negotiate session keys, has undergone extensive formal analysis [19–22]. Denial of Service vulnerabilities were discovered [19,20], and fixes [21] integrated into the 802.11i specification. The design of the 4-Way Handshake was analysed by Vanhoef et al. [23], who focused on the transmission of the group-key, for which a downgrade attack was discovered that forces the group key to be encrypted using the vulnerable RC4 cipher.

The security of Wi-Fi implementations has also been the subject of many studies [2,24]. Vanhoef et al. apply manual, model-based testing techniques [4], which resulted in the discovery of different DoS and downgrade attacks. More recently, Vanhoef et al. discovered a series of vulnerabilities in how retransmissions of key exchange messages are handled, which lead to the reuse of keystreams [25].

3   Background

3.1   The 802.11 4-Way Handshake

The full 802.11 4-Way Handshake consists of a network discovery and a 802.11 authentication and association stage:

Network Discovery. This stage consists of the stations (clients) searching for available networks and their capabilities. This is done passively, by observing broadcasted Beacons, or actively, by sending and receiving probes. The stations learn which cipher suites are supported (TKIP and/or CCMP) and which version of WPA (1 or 2). Both the cipher suites and WPA version are encapsulated in the Robust Security Network Element (RSNE).

Authentication and Association. Before the 4-Way Handshake, the client must "authenticate" and associate with the AP. Here "authentication" is simply an exchange of messages that any client can carry out. The real authentication takes place in the 4-Way Handshake. In the association stage, the client chooses an RSNE and the AP will subsequently accept or reject the connection based on that choice. If accepted, the 4-Way Handshake will then begin.

The 4-Way Handshake provides mutual authentication for a client and authenticator (usually an access point) based on a pre-shared key (PSK). The PSK is used in combination with two nonces, a client nonce (SNonce) and authenticator nonce (ANonce), as well as the MAC addresses of both parties, to generate a session key: the Pairwise Transient Key (PTK).

The 4-Way Handshake, as shown in Fig. 1, is initiated by the AP, who communicates its nonce to the client. The client then generates its own nonce, and sends it to the AP in Message 2, along with a Message Integrity Code (MIC) that is calculated over the whole frame using the PTK. The AP can then verify the client has derived the correct PTK by generating the PTK itself, and checking

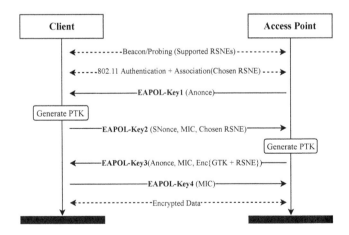

Fig. 1. The 4-Way Handshake.

that the MIC is valid. It can also detect a downgrade attack by verifying that the RSNE matches that in the earlier Association stage. If all is well, the AP responds with Message 3, which contains the encrypted Group Key and RSNE. The client can then verify the RSNE is consistent with previous messages, if so acknowledge with Message 4 and if not, abort the connection.

Messages are encapsulated within EAPOL-Key frames. These include nonces, version numbers, MICs, replay counters and so on. In our state machine learning of the 4-Way Handshake we only consider the most crucial of these (with respect to security). Our chosen fields are specified in Sect. 4.5. The reader can find complete information on EAPOL-Key frame structure and contents by referring to the 802.11 specification [26].

3.2   State Machine Learning

We use Mealy machines to formalise the state machines that are implemented for the 4-Way Handshake.

Definition 1. *A Mealy machine is a tuple* $(I, O, Q, q_0, \delta, \lambda)$, *where* I *and* O *are the sets of input and output symbols (also known as input and output alphabet respectively)*, Q *is the non-empty set of states*, $q_0 \in Q$ *is the initial state*, δ *is a transition function* $Q \times I \rightarrow Q$, *and* λ *is an output function* $Q \times I \rightarrow O$.

When a Mealy machine is in a state $q \in Q$ and receives as input $i \in I$, it transitions to the state $\delta(q, i)$ and produces an output $\lambda(q, i)$.

In the context of learning protocol implementations, we consider Mealy machines that are *complete* and *deterministic*. This means that for each state $q \in Q$, and input $i \in I$, there is exactly one mapping specified by δ and λ.

A classical procedure for learning a state machine is using the L^* algorithm by Angluin [27]. This approach was adapted by Niese to learn Mealy machines [28] and later optimized by Shabaz et al. [29]. The approach consists of two components: An *oracle* (or *teacher*), that acts as an interface to the executing SUL (System Under Learning), and a *learner*, that is only aware of the input and output symbol sets I and O, and can additionally request the oracle to reset the SUL to the start state q_0.

The algorithm works by sending *output queries* that are strings from I^+. The oracle responds with the corresponding output strings from the machine. Each *output query* is preceded by a *reset query*. Using the responses the learner builds up a hypothesis of the state machine as implemented in the SUL.

The next stage of the algorithm is to send an equivalence query to the *oracle*. In this stage, the hypothesis is checked against the actual state machine. If the *oracle* states that the hypothesis is correct, the algorithm terminates. Otherwise, the oracle will respond with the contradicting output string, i.e. a *counterexample*. In the latter case, the learner refines its hypothesis with the *counterexample* and continues the learning process until it has a new acceptable hypothesis. Note that as this is black-box testing, i.e. the oracle cannot access the internal implementation of the SUL, and only a finite number of test cases can be performed, the equivalence checking can only be approximated. The consequence of this is that in some cases it may only be possible to learn a subset of the SUL's behaviour. The most popular learning algorithms are implemented in the LearnLib [30] library, which we use in the development of our tool.

4   Adapting State Machine Learning for Wi-Fi

4.1   Learning Protocols with Errors

A requirement of existing state machine learning methods is that the SUL behaves in a totally deterministic manner, i.e., the same message sent to the device always leads to the same reply. While protocols such as the 4-Way Handshake are specified as deterministic, in practice, the unreliable medium will occasionally lead to lost and corrupting packets and so not meet this requirement. Therefore, to be able to learn these implementations, we must provide a method which stops occasional errors disrupting the learning process.

Running our algorithm on 7 routers, LearnLib reported non-determinism for between 0.5% and 8% of queries (full details are in Sect. 5). This error rate means that most attempts to learn a router will fail before the state machine can be found. The errors were mainly due to either a message not being received and the response timing out, or a message not being received and a previous message being retransmitted. In the later case, there is no way to tell from a single response alone if the message is a genuine reply to a query or if it is a retransmission due to a lost message.

To deal with non-determinism we maintain a record (or cache), separate from LearnLib, which records all input sequences, all corresponding responses, and the number of times those inputs and responses have been seen. LearnLib will throw an exception when a series of inputs gives a different output to one we have previously seen. We can then handle this exception, and execute a form of 'majority vote' error correction in order to decide on the correct response. This works as follows:

1. Whenever we execute a query (and for each subsection of the query) we record the query, and the response seen.
2. When LearnLib reports non-determinism we record the query and observed response (which could be a timeout) and we look at the total observations for all responses to the query that triggered the exception. Then:
   (a) If the response that triggered the exception is now the strictly most common response, we decide that our previous observations must have been errors. We then remove all queries which have the prefix that triggered the exception from our database of learnt queries, because we concluded they were based on learning an error.
   (b) If the response that triggered the exception is not the strictly most common response, we decide that the response seen is an error, and we retry the query (after updating our record of seen responses).

To avoid non-determinism in equivalence queries, we take a more straight-forward approach. If a counter-example is found, then it is repeatedly queried against the SUL, with varying time gaps in-between. Only if the results are consistent is the counter-example then processed by the learning algorithm.

On average, we require in the region of 1000 queries to learn a model. Our method, and optimisations, leads to queries being executed an average of 15 times. Assuming the highest error rate we saw of 8% means that the chance that we learn an error response, rather than the correct response for any query is less than 0.01% (full calculations are given in the appendix). Working backwards from the failure probability, we find that our method will have a 95% confidence of returning the correct automata for error rates of up to 10%. Higher confidence and higher acceptable error rates can be achieved by retrying queries that are not strictly needed by our method, e.g., if we repeat queries to ensure that they are tried at least 100 times we can provide 95% confidence of learning an automata correctly for error rates of up to 30%.

When an error response becomes the most common response to a particular query our method will discard useful information and so be inefficient. For the worst error rate we observed, 8% we calculate the probability of discarding a correct response to a query with 15 tests as 0.00756, more tests do not increase this probability significantly. On the other hand an error rate of 30% would lead to a 0.18 probability of discarding useful data. We note that for such high error rates we could cache the learn queries rather than discarding them so as to avoid having to relearn responses.

4.2   Learning Time-Based Behaviour

To accommodate time behaviour into our models, we first make a number of assumptions about the types of time-based behaviour we expect from protocols like the 802.11 handshake. These assumptions include the types of timers in operation and what we consider to be a change of state. This allows us to enforce restrictions on the types of queries that can be executed, thereby making the problem of learning timed models tractable.

Assumption 1. At any given state, there is only one timer in operation, which could expire and trigger output.

To achieve feasible learning times within the Mealy machine model, we limit the number of timers so that there is never more than one timer running at the same time. Indeed, for the purpose of learning the 802.11 handshake this was sufficient. We believe this also to be the case for other similar protocols.

Assumption 2. If a message is retransmitted, it is only when these retransmissions stop, that the state of the SUL will change.

What we mean by this, is that in the scenario of the SUL retransmitting a message, the only aspect of the state that has changed, is the progression of time. Conversely, if a transmitted message differs from the previous transmitted message, then we infer that the state of the SUL has changed. It is not likely that the SUL will retransmit messages indefinitely. Most protocols will implement some sort of timeout mechanism as we will see.

It follows from Assumption 2 that we can consider a retransmission state as a sub-state of its parent. That is, since it is only time that has progressed, all query-responses will remain the same, therefore:

Assumption 3. Any queries after, a observing a retransmitted message, will have the same responses as before the retransmission.

Additionally, we assume that the modeller is able to provide estimated values for a normal response time and upper-bound timeout. The normal response time should be large enough to give the SUL sufficient time to provide non-timer based responses. Essentially, as long as it takes the SUL to receive and process a message, and send a response. In Wi-Fi we set this in the region of 0.2–0.5 s. For other protocols, or testing set ups, the value should be set according to the quality of the medium on which the protocol is running. For example, one could conceive of a protocol running across further distances, and as such require a longer time allowance for single input/output queries. The second value is an upper-bound timeout. This is required to prevent the learner waiting endlessly if there has been a silent timeout. It should be sensibly set to a maximum value that you expect the SUL to maintain a connection for. E.g., we set this to 20 s, as we expect any timers to have expired and connections to be dropped if the handshake has not completed within that time.

Solution Overview

In our solution, we split the learning procedure into two stages. The first stage will discover behaviour such as the normal flow of the handshake, and states unrelated to time. I.e., we first build a *base* model, which we can later use to learn time behaviour. This way, we can carry out extensive and thorough equivalence checking of the base model, without triggering long timeouts - which causes a blow up in learning time-complexity. The latter stage then uses the base model to identify time-based states, including retransmissions, timeouts and anything else. To this end, we employ two measures. First we use the cache described in Sect. 4.1, which records all query/responses in a database. This enables us to separate each stage of the learning. Second, we adopt the I/O automata learning method presented in [31]. That is, we employ a transducer that translates the non-Mealy-machine compatible SUL behaviour, into sequences of query-responses that the Mealy machine can understand. This technique enables us to enforce learning restrictions for each corresponding stage. The transducer is implemented as a state machine itself, namely a learning purpose (LP). We construct the learning purpose such that it enforces the following restrictions on the types of permitted queries.

1. Each input symbol $i \in I$ constituting a query, maps to a single output from the set $O \cup \{TO_s \vee TO_b\}$. Where, TO represents a timeout, which is set to the normal response time for the first stage (TO_s), and to the upper-bound timeout for the second (TO_b).

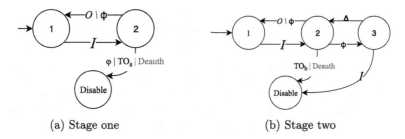

(a) Stage one   (b) Stage two

Fig. 2. Learning purposes used for each learning stage. The two timeouts are indicated by TO_s, TO_b, ϕ indicates the last accepted response (retransmission), and Δ a delay action. (Color figure online)

2. If a retransmission[2] is observed, we disable all inputs. An exception is made in the second learning stage where we allow the delay action Δ beyond this point.

The learning purpose representing the described properties for each corresponding stage is depicted in Fig. 2. We can see that the learner will begin at state 1, where any input is enabled. From there, the resulting output O from the SUL will determine the next transition and so on. As soon as the *disable* state is transitioned to, any subsequent inputs will be disabled, meaning that corresponding outputs will be the '−' symbol. We include an optimisation of this feature which is detailed in Sect. 4.4.

When testing 802.11 handshake implementations, we can make some adjustments to the learning purpose to improve efficiency further. Since we know that a Deauth indicates a reset of the protocol, we can disable any queries which trigger this output. This modification is highlighted in blue in Fig. 2.

Stage 1 Learning. Run learning with the full alphabet and the learning purpose from Fig. 2a enforced. Once a hypothesis has been produced, we run Chow's W-Method [32] for equivalence checking. This guarantees all states within the restriction of the learning purpose will be discovered (given an upper bound on the number of states). On average this stage will complete quickly, as all time based behaviour (which dramatically increases the execution time of each query) is ignored. Any counter-examples discovered in this stage will be recorded in order to reconstruct the model in the second stage.

Stage 2 Learning. Given the base model we learn in the first stage, we can then begin to learn the time related behaviour as follows:

1. Firstly, we delete all entries in the cache oracle that have resulted in the small timeout - TO_s. When learning is restarted, these deleted entries will be posed to the SUL again, this time with the new learning purpose from Fig. 2b.

---

[2] Retransmissions definitions can be customised. For the purpose of testing Wi-Fi, we define a retransmission to be an identical message as before, with the exception of the Replay Counter value.

2. Learning is restarted using the new learning purpose. Each query in this stage will first check the cache oracle to see if there is a corresponding response from the first stage. Once a hypothesis has been conjectured, we apply the same counterexamples learned in stage 1.
3. We then begin an equivalence checking stage with the intention of learning all timeouts. That is, for each state already learned, we simply pose queries consisting of many delay actions. The resulting model will represent the base model from stage one, with time based behaviour included. Any non-retransmission, timeout or disconnect states discovered in this stage will also undergo further equivalence checking.

4.3   Broadcast/Multicast Traffic

In addition to unicast traffic, 802.11 networks must facilitate the transmission of messages via broadcast or multicast distribution. The former, broadcast addressing, is where messages are sent to all nodes on the network. The latter, multicast addressing, is another form of one-to-many distribution where messages are sent to a select subset of nodes on the network. The existence of these types of messages on a network poses a problem for learning a deterministic state machine exhibited by an AP. The reason for this is that the processes producing this traffic on the network are generally independent of that running the 4-Way Handshake. Moreover, other nodes on the network can produce this traffic.

One solution to avoid this source of non-determinism would be to ignore these messages. However, this is not an option if we want to incorporate this traffic into our state machine model. Instead, we make a fundamental assumption about what exactly indicates a state change: we assume that multicast or broadcast message will never indicate a state change. In the context of Wi-Fi, this makes sense—the 4-Way Handshake is between the AP and an individual client, as such, all indications of this protocol state change will be made with unicast messages. Working under this assumption we are able to incorporate broadcast/multicast message observation into our model as follows:

1. Learn the model as defined in previous sections but ignore all broadcast/multicast messages.
2. We then transition to each of the states, and wait for a fixed period, with the intention of detecting any broadcast/multicast traffic. This information is then integrated into the model.

4.4   Additional Optimisation

Query Disabling. The constraints that we enforce with the learning purpose (see Fig. 2), such as disabling any queries beyond a deauthentication or timeout, can be exploited for further efficiency gain. Namely, if we ever observe a query response containing an 'disable output' $(-)$, then we know that any additional inputs beyond that point will also have the 'disable output'. This enables us to maintain a cache of all queries, and their corresponding responses, that result

Table 1. Parameter definitions for the 802.11 handshake input alphabet.

Parameter	Tag	Values	Description
Key Descriptor	KD	WPA1/2, WPA2, RAND	Indicates the EAPOL Key type: WPA, WPA2 or a random value
Cipher Suites	CS	MD5, SHA1	Ciphers and hash functions used for encrypting the Key Data field and calculating the MIC. Options are MD5 + RC4 or SHA1 + AES
RSN Element	RSNE	cc, tc, ct, tt	The chosen ciphersuite combination of TKIP (t) and CCMP (c) for the group and unicast traffic respectively
Key Information	KF	P, M, S, E	The combination of four flags in the Key Info field: Pairwise (P), MIC (M), Secure (S), Encrypted (E), or - when none is set
Nonce	NONC	W	The Nonce field contains a consistent (default) or inconsistent (W) nonce
MIC	MIC	F	The MIC field contains a valid (default) or invalid (F) Message Integrity Code
Replay Counter	RC	W	The Replay Counter is set to a correct (default) or an incorrect value (W)

in the learning purpose transitioning to the disable state. This cache can then be used as a lookahead oracle for further queries. For example, say the query $q = \{assoc, delay, data, data\}$ results in response $r = \{accept, E1, timeout, -\}$. The lookahead oracle can then record this query-response pair, as it ended up in a disable state (indicated by the fourth output $-$). If then, the learner poses the query $q_2 = \{assoc, delay, data, data, E4\}$, we already know what the response will be because q is a prefix of q_2, and q ended up in the disable state. Therefore, we can automatically generate the response $r_2 = \{accept, E1, timeout, -, -\}$ without actually querying the SUL.

WPA/2 Specific Optimisation. In Sect. 4.2, we show how exploiting our prior knowledge of observing the *Deauthentication* frame, to indicate a reset of the protocol, can be used to improve learning efficiency. Similarly, we also implement a check which disables queries after a successful handshake/connection has completed and verified (Table 1).

4.5   4-Way Handshake Input/Output Learning Alphabet

Inputs. Our abstract input alphabet consists of messages of the structure:
$$i \in I := \texttt{MsgType(Params)}$$
Where MsgType is one of {Association, EAPOL 2, EAPOL 4} and has associated parameters defined in the table below. Associations only permit the RSNE parameter, whereas for EAPOL-Key messages, it can be any. We also include the Delay action (Δ), (Unencrypted) Data, and Encrypted Data (TKIP and AES). We denote the Broadcast/Multicast Delay input (described in Sect. 4.3) as BRD in our models. In total our input alphabet consists of 45 unique messages. We

note that a complete set of all possible combinations of the various EAPOL fields would consist of 1000s of frames. We therefore select the most important fields and values with respect to security.

Outputs. Messages received as output from the AP are parsed into the following format:

$$o \in O := \texttt{MsgType(Params)|Timestamp}$$

Where `Timestamp` indicates the time elapsed since the last received message.

4.6   Implementation Details

Network Data. When learning the state machines of our selected APs, we ensure that there is constant traffic, including unicast, broadcast and multicast, circulating on the network at all times. This enables us to learn broadcast and multicast traffic and also detect successful handshakes as mentioned below. We achieve this by operating a node on the network which run scripts to send: traffic directly to the fuzzer's MAC address (e.g. raw data), multicast traffic (e.g. using mDNS), and broadcast traffic (e.g. ARP).

Verifying and Resetting Connections. As the last message of the 4-Way Handshake is sent to the client, and hence our learner, the corresponding response will normally be a timeout, therefore we need to distinguish between the case where a handshake has finished successfully and other kinds of time-outs. As mentioned in the previous section, we operate a node on the network that constantly sends unicast data addressed to our learner's MAC address. Therefore, once a handshake is complete we observe these messages and can decrypt them to verify the contents. If this succeeds, we then check that the fuzzer can itself send encrypted data. This is done by sending an ARP-request for the MAC address of the gateway IP and waiting for an appropriate response.

Multi-core/Interface Sniffing and Injecting. Due to the unreliability of Wi-Fi monitor mode for 802.11 frame injection and sniffing, we use two physically independent interfaces for each task—sending queries and sniffing for responses. We then have two processes running in parallel so that sniffing and injection can be carried out simultaneously. This is all implemented in Python using the Scapy[3] library.

5   Results

We used our adapted state machine learning algorithm to automatically learn 7 AP-side implementations of the 4-Way Handshake (see Table 2). In this section we will discuss the effect of our learning improvements, as well as the most notable results, including vulnerabilities, time behaviour and other interesting observations. This paper contains figures of two of the learned models, the rest are available online[4].

---

[3] http://www.secdev.org/projects/scapy/.
[4] https://chrismcmstone.github.io/wifi-learner/.

Table 2. Learning statistics for the access points we tested. Total queries excludes discards, total learning time includes time taken for error correction.

Model	Version	States	# Queries (Ex. error correction)	Error (%) rate	Learn time (hh:mm)
TP-Link WR841HP	V1_150519	6	963	5	1:32
Cisco WAP121	1.0.6.2	12	1163	4	1:42
TP-Link AC1200	140224	12	1113	8	2:35
iOS Personal Hotspot	8.1.3	6	887	2	5:46
ZxYEL AMG1302	V2	13	1684	1	1:53
D-Link DWRr600b	2.0.0EUb02	12	1113	1	1:18
Android hostapd	Oreo 8.0	12	1113	0.5	0:58

Time Behaviour. Three of the access points we tested exhibited the same timeout behaviour (3 retransmissions of message 1 and 3 with one second gaps, before ending with a deauthentication). Others had similar behaviour but over different times. One did not retransmit messages but timed out after 6 s (see Fig. 3). Most interestingly, the Cisco WAP121 started sending encrypted data after 3 re-transmissions of message 3 over a period of 4 s. We discuss this in more detail in Sect. 5.2. We note that this finding in particular could not be detected by previous methods. The iOS model stands out in that it took significantly longer to learn than the others. The reason for this is that it appears to silently timeout and hence hit the upper-bound timeouts mentioned in Sect. 4.2. Indeed, the implementation appears to be very minimalist, only responding to queries it considers to be correct, and ignoring those that are not. Nevertheless, this exemplifies the importance of the first stage of our learning method. By setting a small timeout (the 'normal response time'), when the learner carries out the equivalence checking stage, these queries will not suffer from this long timeout. Hence, thorough fuzzing was still possible, despite then having to relax this restriction for the second stage.

Non-determinism. In Table 2 we state the error rate for each of the implementations we tested. We calculated this as the proportion of total executed queries that were detected as an error. An increased error rate had a direct effect on the time taken to learn. This is demonstrated by the TP-Link AC1200 which had an almost identical model to Android Hostapd, yet took over double the time to learn. In this particular case, the high error rate was due to the AP carrying over data from previous handshake executions with a relatively high probability.

Query Reduction. We were able to significantly reduce the number of queries required by the learning algorithm vs those actually posed to the SUL. Most of this reduction is down to the restrictions we enforce (i.e. delays after retransmissions (Sect. 4.2) and Wi-Fi specific optimisations (Sect. 4.4). For example, the iOS model required over 20,000 queries in total but only 887 were actually queried, the rest predicted.

Similar Models. Our results reveal that three of the implementations appear to be very similar (TP-Link AC1200, Android Hostapd and D-Link DWRr600b). These models are somewhat different though, for example with respect to broadcast traffic, the DLink AP constantly broadcasted both Beacon frames and Probe Responses, whereas the TP-Link and hostapd only broadcasted Beacons. The implementations are also distinguished via their learning error rate, and as a result learning time. The TP-Link suffered from high error rate due to reasons stated above. Whereas, the other two APs had a very similar error rate.

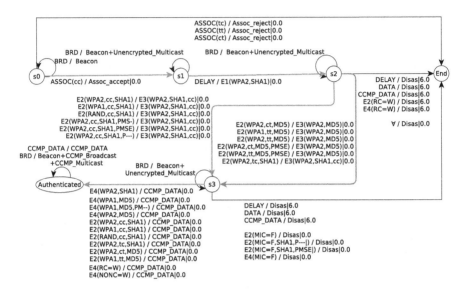

Fig. 3. State machine for the TP-Link TL-WR841HP, with normal transitions highlighted in green and those contributing to vulnerabilities in red. (In the interest of brevity we only include a selection of the most important transition labels. All queries that are 'disabled' are not included. We use the ∀ symbol to denote all input messages not specified in other transitions.) (Color figure online)

5.1   Encrypted Multicast Traffic Leakage

Using the broadcast/multicast learning feature of our framework, we discovered that the TP-Link WR841HP transmits multicast data in plaintext when put in a certain state (see states 1 and 2 in Fig. 3). More specifically, before a handshake is initiated, any multicast data will be sent encrypted with each unicast session key for all of the connected clients. However, during the execution of a 4-Way Handshake with a new client, and before the client has proven knowledge of the PSK (by sending a valid Message 2), this data will broadcast unencrypted to the client. Indeed, immediately after the 4-Way Handshake is completed, the data will only be sent encrypted. This represents a leakage of (potentially) sensitive multicast data.

5.2   Downgrade Vulnerabilities

In two access points we discovered downgrade attacks, namely for the Cisco WAP121 and the TP-Link TL-WR841HP.

Forcing Group Key Encryption with RC4. Figure 3 shows the learned state machine implemented by the TP-Link WR841HP. We can see that despite initiating the connection in the Association stage with AES-CCM for both group and unicast keys, after starting the 4-Way Handshake using AES-CCM, the AP will surprisingly still accept a TKIP-formatted Message 2. In other words, if the client switches ciphers mid-handshake, the AP will do also. This is indicated by the AP's response from state 3 to state 5, where it switches cipher suites to use TKIP's MD5 for the MIC, and encrypting the network's group key with RC4. Of particular significance is that this is in spite of the AP being set to exclusively use AES-CCM. Indeed, this is also advertised in the AP's Beacon and Probe Response messages.

To exploit this vulnerability, the adversary can set up their own AP with the same SSID as the target. This AP, however, only advertises support for TKIP in the beacons/probe response. As shown in Fig. 4, the attacker will simultaneously carry out a 4-Way Handshake with the target AP, using AES-CCMP as the selected cipher. Messages will be selectively forwarded and altered between the target AP and client. Message 1 will contain the same nonce (for generation of the session key), but will be altered such that the cipher suite flag is set to TKIP. The client will generate its own nonce, calculate the session key, then send a TKIP MICed Message 2, which will be forwarded unchanged to the AP. This is accepted by the target and induces a downgrade to TKIP, resulting in a TKIP protected Message 3 response. The attacker will then observe this message, and can extract the RC4 protected GTK. With this, the key can be recovered and used for various attacks (see [23]).

AP-Side AES-CCMP to TKIP Downgrade. Both the Cisco WAP121 and TP-Link WR841HP are vulnerable to AP-side downgrade attacks. That is, when both AES-CCMP and TKIP are supported by the AP and client, an attacker can force usage of TKIP. Normally, the client will always choose the more secure AES-CCMP.

With the Cisco WAP121, this vulnerability is indicated by the fact that Message 4, the message sent by the client to confirm the selected cipher, is not required by the AP. We can see from the state machine diagram Fig. 5 in Appendix A, after 3 re-transmissions of Message 3 over a period of 4 s, the AP will give up waiting for a response and complete the connection anyway. An illustrated exploitation of this vulnerability in depicted in Fig. 6.

The affected TP-Link AP is also vulnerable to the same attack but in a slightly different way. That is, the AP does require a response to Message 3, but will accept a Message 2 in the place of Message 4. This enables an attacker to forge Message 4 by inducing a client to retransmit Message 2 and thereby carry out an AP-side downgrade attack.

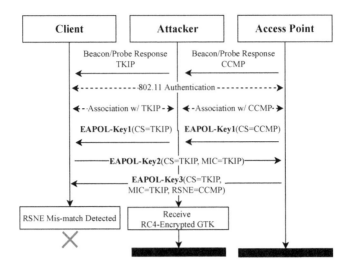

Fig. 4. Downgrade attack on the TP-Link WR841P to force encryption of the Group Key (GTK) with RC4

For both APs, this attack is limited to downgrading the AP only. Correctly implemented clients will detect this downgrade through an inconsistency of the RSNE information which is selected in the Association stage and later encrypted and encapsulated within Message 3 from the AP. The client will decrypt the contents of the message, find that in fact the AP supports AES-CCMP and should then drop the connection.

Despite this, the flaw still represents a genuine vulnerability; any clients with existing connections could be forced to carry out a new 4-Way Handshake, e.g. due to roaming/signal loss or a client side deauthentication attack. Any data in the queue from the previous connection will then be secured with TKIP.

Disclosure. TP-Link and Cisco have been fully informed of the vulnerabilities found, and in line with responsible disclosure, were given 6 months to address the vulnerabilities before publication. We also note that TP-Link no longer sell the vulnerable AP.

6   Conclusion

In this paper we introduced methods to handle the non-deterministic and timing related behaviour for lossy protocols such as Wi-Fi. These methods have been shown to be effective to infer models of numerous implementations of the 802.11 4-Way Handshake. This resulted in the discovery of several security vulnerabilities in widely used routers. The software will be made available as open source. In future work we want to extend the tool to handle the recently introduced

WPA3. This uses the same 4-Way Handshake making it possible to use our tool on implementations of WPA3 with only minor changes.

We would like to apply our time learning technique to more protocols where time is important, particularly other protocols where long timeouts are present, making standard learning difficult to use. There are many security protocols where timing plays an important role, especially those running on unreliable mediums, such as other wireless protocols (Bluetooth, Zigbee, LTE), distance-bounding protocols (MasterCard's RRP, NXP's "proximity check" [33]), and others (DTLS, QUIC). We would also like to experiment with relaxing our assumptions. For instance, considering situations where multiple clocks are in operation.

Acknowledgements. This work has been supported by the Netherlands Organisation for Scientific Research (NWO) through Veni project 639.021.750.

A   Diagrams

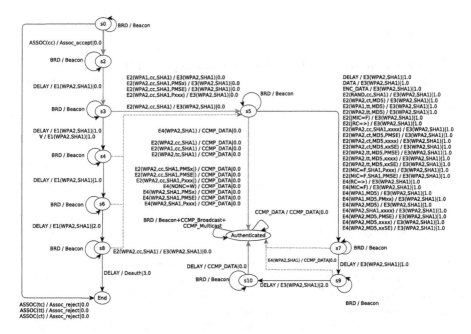

Fig. 5. Learned model for the Cisco WAP121. Note that for retransmission states, assumed transitions (as per Assumption 3) are represented by dotted blue lines. (Color figure online)

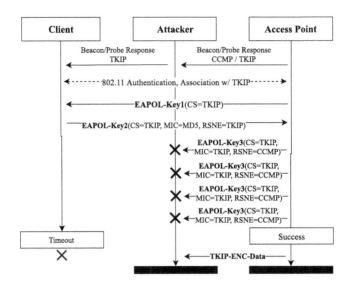

Fig. 6. Downgrade attack on the Cisco WAP121 to force usage of TKIP

B   Calculations

We assume the probability of any error response is p_e, and that, for every query we have at least n responses. Therefore, the probability that i of the observed responses are correct is the number of all possible combinations of i and $n - i$ responses times the probability of i correct responses and $n - i$ errors:

$$correct(i) = {}^nC_i p_e^i (1 - p_e)^{n-i} = \frac{n!}{i!(n-i)!} p_e^{n-i} (1 - p_e)^i$$

and the probability that the majority of observed responses are correct is: $mCorrect = \Sigma_{i=n/2\ldots n} correct(i)$. The probability that the correct output is the most commonly observed for m different queries strings is then $mCorrect^m$.

For the TP-Link AC1200, with an error rate of 8% and 1113 queries the chance of learning it correctly is 0.9925, for all other routers the probability of learning correctly was greater. Taking an average of 1000 queries and the average number of queries returned by our method (15), we see that a 10% error rate gives us a probability that the result is correct of 0.96, and with 100 tests and a 30% error rate the probability that they are all correct is 0.97.

Also important is the probability that our method will discard correct queries that has been correctly learned. We assume the worse case which is that there is only one incorrect message. In this case correctly learned queries are only discarded at the ith test if, the at the $i - 2^{th}$ test the incorrect response has been seen 1 time less than the correct message, and the incorrect response is seen for the next two messages.

It is only possible to have one less incorrect than correct message for an odd number of tests. The probably of this happening is at the $2m + 1$th step:

$$oneOff(2m + 1) = {}^{2m+1}C_m p_e^m (1 - p_e)^{m+1} = \frac{(2m + 1)!}{m!(m + 1)!} p_e^m (1 - p_e)^{m+1}$$

and the probably of correct queries being discarded at the $2m + 1$th step as: $discard(2m + 1) = oneOff(2m - 1)p_e^2$. Following the discard of a correct state, there will be one more vote for the error response, therefore to return to the correct state and discard it again, we require 2 more correct responses than error respondences followed by 2 error responses to trigger the discard:

$$nextD(2m) = {}^{2m-2}C_{m-2} p_e^{m-2} (1 - p_e)^m p_e p_e = \frac{(2m-2)!}{(m-2)!m!} p_e^m (1 - p_e)^m$$

for $m \geq 2$.

The probability that the first discard of the correct query happens at a particular step is:

$firstD(3) = (1 - p_e)p_e p_e$

$firstD(2m + 1) = discard(2m + 1) - \Sigma_{i=1...m-1}.firstD(2i + 1).nextD(2(m - i)$

So, therefore the probably of any discard of a correct response in the first n tests is:

$$AnyDiscard(x) = \Sigma_{i=1...x} firstD(x)$$

References

1. Banks, G., Cova, M., Felmetsger, V., Almeroth, K., Kemmerer, R., Vigna, G.: SNOOZE: toward a stateful NetwOrk prOtocol fuzZEr. In: Katsikas, S.K., López, J., Backes, M., Gritzalis, S., Preneel, B. (eds.) ISC 2006. LNCS, vol. 4176, pp. 343–358. Springer, Heidelberg (2006). https://doi.org/10.1007/11836810_25
2. Butti, L., Tinnes, J.: Discovering and exploiting 802.11 wireless driver vulnerabilities. J. Comput. Virol. **4**(1), 25–37 (2008)
3. Broy, M., Jonsson, B., Katoen, J.-P., Leucker, M., Pretschner, A. (eds.): Model-Based Testing of Reactive Systems. LNCS, vol. 3472. Springer, Heidelberg (2005). https://doi.org/10.1007/b137241
4. Vanhoef, M., Schepers, D., Piessens, F.: Discovering logical vulnerabilities in the Wi-Fi handshake using model-based testing. In: Asia Conference on Computer and Communications Security. ACM (2017)
5. Aarts, F., de Ruiter, J., Poll, E.: Formal models of bank cards for free. In: Sixth International Conference on Software Testing, Verification and Validation Workshops, ICSTW. IEEE (2013)
6. Fiterău-Broştean, P., Lenaerts, T., Poll, E., de Ruiter, J., Vaandrager, F., Verleg, P.: Model learning and model checking of SSH implementations. In: 24th International SPIN Symposium on Model Checking of Software, SPIN 2017 (2017)
7. de Ruiter, J., Poll, E.: Protocol state fuzzing of TLS implementations. In: USENIX Security, vol. 15 (2015)
8. Grinchtein, O., Jonsson, B., Leucker, M.: Learning of event-recording automata. In: Lakhnech, Y., Yovine, S. (eds.) FORMATS/FTRTFT 2004. LNCS, vol. 3253, pp. 379–395. Springer, Heidelberg (2004). https://doi.org/10.1007/978-3-540-30206-3_26

9. Fiterău-Broştean, P., Janssen, R., Vaandrager, F.: Combining model learning and model checking to analyze TCP implementations. In: Chaudhuri, S., Farzan, A. (eds.) CAV 2016. LNCS, vol. 9780, pp. 454–471. Springer, Cham (2016). https://doi.org/10.1007/978-3-319-41540-6_25

10. Tappler, M., Aichernig, B.K., Bloem, R.: Model-based testing IoT communication via active automata learning. In: 2017 IEEE International Conference on Software Testing, Verification and Validation, ICST 2017, pp. 276–287 (2017)

11. Raffelt, H., Steffen, B., Berg, T., Margaria, T.: LearnLib: a framework for extrapolating behavioral models. Int. J. Softw. Tools Technol. Transf. (STTT) **11**(5), 393–407 (2009)

12. Isberner, M., Howar, F., Steffen, B.: The open-source LearnLib. In: Kroening, D., Păsăreanu, C.S. (eds.) CAV 2015. LNCS, vol. 9206, pp. 487–495. Springer, Cham (2015). https://doi.org/10.1007/978-3-319-21690-4_32

13. Margaria, T., Niese, O., Raffelt, H., Steffen, B.: Efficient test-based model generation for legacy reactive systems. In: Ninth IEEE International High-Level Design Validation and Test Workshop, pp. 95–100. IEEE (2004)

14. Janssen, M.: Combining learning with fuzzing for software deobfuscation (2016)

15. Aarts, F., Schmaltz, J., Vaandrager, F.: Inference and abstraction of the biometric passport. In: Margaria, T., Steffen, B. (eds.) ISoLA 2010. LNCS, vol. 6415, pp. 673–686. Springer, Heidelberg (2010). https://doi.org/10.1007/978-3-642-16558-0_54

16. Jonsson, B., Vaandrager, F.: Learning mealy machines with timers. http://www.sws.cs.ru.nl/publications/papers/fvaan/MMT/

17. Fluhrer, S., Mantin, I., Shamir, A.: Weaknesses in the key scheduling algorithm of RC4. In: Vaudenay, S., Youssef, A.M. (eds.) SAC 2001. LNCS, vol. 2259, pp. 1–24. Springer, Heidelberg (2001). https://doi.org/10.1007/3-540-45537-X_1

18. Tews, E., Beck, M.: Practical attacks against WEP and WPA. In: Proceedings of the Second ACM Conference on Wireless Network Security, pp. 79–86. ACM (2009)

19. He, C., Mitchell, J.C.: Analysis of the 802.11 i 4-way handshake. In: Proceedings of the 3rd ACM Workshop on Wireless Security, pp. 43–50. ACM (2004)

20. Mitchell, C.: Security analysis and improvements for IEEE 802.11 i. In: 12th Annual Network and Distributed System Security Symposium, NDSS (2005)

21. He, C., Sundararajan, M., Datta, A., Derek, A., Mitchell, J.C.: A modular correctness proof of IEEE 802.11 i and TLS. In: Proceedings of the 12th ACM Conference on Computer and Communications Security, pp. 2–15. ACM (2005)

22. Wang, L., Srinivasan, B.: Analysis and improvements over DoS attacks against IEEE 802.11 i standard. In: 2nd Conference on Networks Security Wireless Communications and Trusted Computing, NSWCTC. IEEE (2010)

23. Vanhoef, M., Piessens, F.: Predicting, decrypting, and abusing WPA2/802.11 group keys. In: USENIX Security Symposium (2016)

24. Mendonça, M., Neves, N.: Fuzzing Wi-Fi drivers to locate security vulnerabilities. In: 7th Dependable Computing Conference, EDCC. IEEE (2008)

25. Vanhoef, M., Piessens, F.: Key reinstallation attacks: Forcing nonce reuse in WPA2. In: 24th ACM Conference on Computer and Communication Security (2017)

26. Group, I.W., et al.: IEEE standard for information technology–Telecommunications and information exchange between systems–Local and metropolitan area networks–Specific requirements–Part 11: Wireless LAN Medium Access Control (MAC) and Physical Layer (PHY) specifications. IEEE Std 802(11) (2010)

27. Angluin, D.: Learning regular sets from queries and counterexamples. Inf. Comput. **75**(2), 87–106 (1987)

28. Niese, O.: An integrated approach to testing complex systems. Ph.D. thesis. Universität Dortmund (2003)
29. Shahbaz, M., Groz, R.: Inferring mealy machines. In: Cavalcanti, A., Dams, D.R. (eds.) FM 2009. LNCS, vol. 5850, pp. 207–222. Springer, Heidelberg (2009). https://doi.org/10.1007/978-3-642-05089-3_14
30. Raffelt, H., Steffen, B., Berg, T.: LearnLib: a library for automata learning and experimentation. In: Proceedings of the 10th International Workshop on Formal Methods for Industrial Critical Systems. ACM (2005)
31. Aarts, F., Vaandrager, F.: Learning I/O automata. In: Gastin, P., Laroussinie, F. (eds.) CONCUR 2010. LNCS, vol. 6269, pp. 71–85. Springer, Heidelberg (2010). https://doi.org/10.1007/978-3-642-15375-4_6
32. Chow, T.S.: Testing software design modeled by finite-state machines. IEEE Trans. Softw. Eng. **3**, 178–187 (1978)
33. Chothia, T., de Ruiter, J., Smyth, B.: Modeling and analysis of a hierarchy of distance bounding attacks. In: 27th USENIX Security Symposium, USENIX Security 2018. USENIX Association, Baltimore (2018). https://www.usenix.org/conference/usenixsecurity18/presentation/chothia

Automatic Detection of Various Malicious Traffic Using Side Channel Features on TCP Packets

George Stergiopoulos, Alexander Talavari, Evangelos Bitsikas, and Dimitris Gritzalis[(⊠)]

Information Security and Critical Infrastructure Protection (INFOSEC) Laboratory, Department of Informatics, Athens University of Economics and Business, Athens, Greece
{geostergiop, dgrit}@aueb.gr, alex.talavari@gmail.com

Abstract. Modern intrusion detection systems struggle to detect advanced, custom attacks against most vectors; from web application injections to malware reverse connections with encrypted traffic. Current solutions mostly utilize complex patterns or behavioral analytics on software, user actions and services historical data together with traffic analysis, in an effort to detect specific types of attacks. Still, false positives and negatives plague such systems. Behavioral-based security solutions provides good results but need large amounts of time and data to train (often spanning months or even years of surveillance) - especially when encryption comes into play. In this paper, we present a network-traffic monitoring system that implements a detection method using machine learning over side channel characteristics of TCP/IP packets and not deep packet inspection, user analytics or binary analysis. We were able to efficiently distinguish normal from malicious traffic over a wide range of attacks with a true positive detection rate of about 94%. Few similar efforts have been made for the classification of malicious traffic but existing methods rely on complex feature selection and deep packet analysis to achieve similar (or worse) detection rates. Most focus on encrypted malware traffic. We manage to distinguish malicious from normal traffic in a wide range of different types of attacks (e.g. unencrypted and encrypted malware traffic and/or shellcode connections, website defacing attacks, ransomware downloaded cryptolocker attacks, etc.) using only few side channel packet characteristics and we achieve similar or better overall detection rates from similar detection systems. We compare seven different machine learning algorithms on multiple traffic sets to produce the best possible results. We use less features than other proposed solutions and thus require less data and achieve short times during training and classification.

Keywords: Malware traffic · Malware detection · Machine learning
Defacement · SVR · Neural networks · CART · Botnet · Reverse shells
Trojan

© Springer Nature Switzerland AG 2018
J. Lopez et al. (Eds.): ESORICS 2018, LNCS 11098, pp. 346–362, 2018.
https://doi.org/10.1007/978-3-319-99073-6_17

1   Introduction

One of the most serious open issues in securing today's IT networks is the inability of current solutions (i.e. intrusion detection and prevention systems (IDPS), antivirus etc.) to detect advanced and often meticulously custom ongoing malicious attacks. Such attacks are often tailored to specific victims and sophisticated code is used that is not currently known by the security community. Security companies need to update their security solutions constantly, only to often fail to detect "0-day" malware and custom attacks against all vectors, from injecting commands to websites to detecting encrypted malware traffic. Also, some attacks such web application defacements utilize custom string and hex coding of malicious data that cannot be efficiently detected.

Current solutions utilize either complex pattern matching or behavioral analytics on software, users and services in an effort to classify ongoing network events as suspicious. Still, false positives and negatives plague signature-based security software. On the other hand, behavioral based models have better detection rates but require large periods of time to effectively monitor users and systems and/or big datasets describing multiple scenarios to be able to accurately detect malicious traffic [22]; often unrealistically large amounts of data and time. On top of these, modern malware uses encrypted traffic or inject themselves to whitelisted apps (e.g. browsers) to communicate with C&C servers and exfiltrate data, which makes behavioral analysis and pattern matching even less successful over network traffic.

1.1   Contribution

We present a network traffic monitoring system that implements machine learning over network captures to distinguish normal from multiple types of malicious TCP/IP traffic. A few similar efforts have been made for classification of some types of malicious traffic (e.g. encrypted malware traffic), yet existing methods rely mostly on complex feature selection and/or large datasets. Overall, the main contributions of this article are summarized as follows:

1. We manage to simultaneously detect multiple types of malicious traffic (unencrypted and encrypted malware traffic and/or shellcode connections, website defacing attacks, ransomware downloaded cryptolocker attack, etc.) using a few side channel characteristics of TCP packets and not complex features or deep packet inspection.
2. We achieve the same or better overall detection rates with similar detection systems while using less features (e.g. no TLS, certification features or deep packet inspection). Consequently, our system requires less training and classification.
3. We test and compare seven (7) different machine learning algorithms over millions of network captures spanning 8 GB of network. Experiments showed that decision tree classifiers have good detection rates with side channel features but may be prone false positives with packet crafting feature values and consequently trick our classifier. Using KNN seems to greatly reduce this. However, we should avoid neural networks as preliminary tests with neural networks show that they offer

worse detection rates while requiring way larger amounts of time and data for training. Also, in some instances, neural networks seem prone to biases.

4. Our system provides faster training and classification than other detection systems during offline training and testing due to its smaller feature set. The use of side channel features greatly reduces the size of traffic data that needs to be analyzed for training or detecting of various types of malicious traffic and not only encrypted malware, which seems to dominate current research projects.

Specifically, we first select an optimal set of features from raw features extracted from TCP traffic packets. We minimize the number of features used in similar previous research by only utilizing the ones that refer to side channel characteristics; i.e. packet size ratios and timing events between packets. We provide experiments on real-world malicious traffic data from three different datasets, namely FIRST 2015 [5], Milicenso [6] and CTU13-1 [7]) to demonstrate the effectiveness and efficiency of our approach over multiple types of malicious traffic, even with fewer, selected features.

Section 2 presents related work concerning malicious network traffic and similar classification approaches and argues about the differences with our presented system. Section 3 describes the datasets utilized in the current project and presents our data sanitization process. Section 4 presents the detection methodology implemented in the proposed system. Section 5 describes our experimental results, while Sect. 6 discusses further improvements and potential future work.

2   Related Work

Most mainstream approaches to detecting malicious traffic mostly rely on heuristic analysis of packets, payloads and session trends (like packets per min) along with botnet architecture [8, 9, 10]. Others rely on statistical analysis for classifying various types of traffic [20].

Our approach is similar to [13, 27]. In [13], researchers utilize some of the same features as we do to extract information from the physical aspects of the network traffic. They too utilize machine learning but focus on OSI layer 7 features to distinguish between malicious and normal encrypted traffic. Thus, significant differences exist. The main differences of our work with [13, 27] are the following: (a) We do not restrict our machine learning and detection system only to encrypted traffic but try to achieve similar (or even better) detection rates without distinguishing between different malicious traffic, (b) we provide full payload analysis per packet and in relation to previous packets sent, whereas researchers in [13] researchers analyze tuples that check payload sizes for entire originator-responder sessions, (c) we minimize selected features by only using the ones that refer to side channel characteristics, while achieving better results, and (d) we do not aim to only understand and distinguish malicious encrypted traffic from malware but extend this to multiple types of both encrypted and unencrypted malicious traffic, ranging from defacing attacks, reverse shells, encrypted connections etc.

Cisco published a white paper concerning new advancements in detecting malicious traffic using similar side channel features [27]. Cisco utilizes similar types of data elements or telemetry that are independent of protocol details, such as the lengths and arrival times of messages within a flow. Their technology supports various Cisco routers and switches to perform detection of malicious traffic in network sessions that utilize the Transport Layer Security (TLS) protocol.

In summary, we manage similar performance and smaller datasets utilizing only five features on side channel characteristics, twenty two (22) features less than [13] and four (4) less than Cisco [27].

Authors in [21] also use malicious HTTPS traffic to train neural networks and sequence classification to build a system capable of detecting malware traffic over encrypted connections. Similarities with our work is that we use features to train a machine learning algorithm. The difference with our work is that: (a) we are able to detect multiple types of malicious traffic and not only encrypted malware traffic and (b) we utilize less data (and corresponding domain features) while achieving better and faster results, albeit not only on encrypted traffic but on a dataset consisting of 200 K traffic samples of different malicious traffic flows.

Using CART and KNN decision algorithms instead of neural networks, we can achieve faster classification once the system is trained and have a more interpretable model to detect hidden interconnections of traffic features. On the other hand, neural networks might be more accurate (although our preliminary results do not support this), provided there is enough training data, although they can be prone to over-fitting as well; this is why another reason why we tested other algorithms more suitable to unknown dataset characteristics.

Other approaches in analyzing encrypted HTTPS traffic are few [18, 19]. Most of them focus on identifying target malware/botnet servers [19] or web servers contacted [18], instead of understanding malicious traffic of various types.

The following publications are worth mentioning although they differentiate and either utilize different technologies to achieve similar goals, or aim to analyze different aspects of network traffic albeit with similar algorithms. Authors in [11, 17] utilize signal processing techniques (e.g., Principal Component Analysis (PCA)) to create aggregates of traffic and payload inspection data, in an effort to detect anomalous changes to network flows [14]. They utilize a distance metric to understand network-change patterns in traffic. Lakhina et al. [15] modelled network flows as combinations of eigen flows to distinguish between short-lived traffic bursts, trends, noise, or normal traffic. Terrell et al. [16] grouped network traces into time-series and selected features, such as the entropy of the packet and port numbers, to detect traffic anomalies. While these approaches are based on models of malware behavior (not unlike signature-based intrusion detection), our approach seeks to identify important features on the physical characteristics of malicious network sessions and utilize them to train machine learning algorithms. This way, we increase the detection rate by (a) not relying on instances of malware traffic to understand future malware and (b) by creating a trained model that predicts the value of a network TCP sessions based on network values of several input (or independent variables). Our approach is nonparametric, therefore it does not rely on data belonging to a particular type of distribution. Also, it can utilize variables multiple times in different decision analyses, thus uncovering complex interdependencies between sets of variables [12].

The selected machine learning algorithm and relevant network features enhance malicious traffic detection in both encrypted and unencrypted traffic, ranging from a series of different malicious types such as botnets, defacement attacks, reverse shells, Trojans, etc. To our knowledge, no other prototype is able to accomplish this.

3   Datasets

We utilized datasets with both malicious and normal traffic from various sources to build our database. Selecting useful and balanced datasets was vital in order to be certain that the achieved detection rates correspond to real-world capabilities. Datasets are public and contain traffic of real malware, defacing attacks, reverse shells and software exploitation attacks along with normal traffic.

To guarantee the malicious traffic data quality and validate our detection rates, we opted to use malicious traffic from datasets built from major companies and institutions. The datasets used both for training and testing our system are the following:

- FIRST 2015 [5]: Dataset created for the needs of a hands-on lab for Network Forensics. It is a collection of 4.4 GB pcap files containing normal as well malicious traffic. Traffic is composed from Reverse Shell shellcode connections, website defacing attacks, ransomware downloaded attack cryptolocker and a command and conquer exploit attack (C2) over SSL that takes over the victim machine.
- Milicenso [6]: Dataset containing normal and malware traffic for the Ponmocup Malware. It contains malicious traffic from a malware/trojan that connects the victim PC on a botnet.
- CTU13-1 [7]: Dataset containing Botnet Traffic of the Neris Botnet. All traffic is mostly encrypted botnet traffic, because the normal traffic that was captured at the same time is not public.

Dataset traffic was included in pcap and pcapng files containing captured packets. Packets from the FIRST 2015 were pcap files captured using Snort [24], whereas Milicenso and CTU13-1 datasets were raw tcpdumps of monitored connections. Traffic flows are captured using methods like WireShark [23], Snort [24], or raw TCP dumps.

3.1   Threat Model

Aforementioned datasets contain malicious traffic that covers a range of different attack scenarios.

First 2015 dataset

- **Website defacement attack** (FrogSquad defacement, First 2015). Attackers uploaded a FrogSquad image to: www.pwned.se/skyblue/fr.jpg.
- **Webshell (PHP backdoor)** on infected web server. FrogSquad sent multiple commands using cm0 backdoor. FrogSquad traffic from later come back, from the same class CIP network.
- **Spear Phising email attack.** APT4711 spear phishing email to Krusty (192.168.0.54). From First2015 [5]: "Krusty uses SSL encrypted IMAP (TCP 993)

towards imap.google.com, so we cannot inspect the contents of his email. However, we do know that Krusty opened the attachment at 10.35.36 UTC, which caused a Command-and-control (C2) software do be downloaded".

- **Malware traffic (reverse shell).**

CTU-13-1 dataset

As mentioned on the CTU-13 manual [7], "The CTU-13 is a dataset of botnet traffic that was captured in the CTU University, Czech Republic, in 2011. The goal of the dataset was to have a large capture of real botnet traffic mixed with normal traffic and background traffic". Traffic selected for our experiments contain several botnet scenarios with more than 160 different malware samples. Scenarios include:

Click Fraud attacks. The bot sent spam, connected to an HTTP CC, and use HTTP to do some ClickFraud.

IRC communication for spam and clickjacking. Neris botnet that run for 6.15 h in a University network. The botnet used an HTTP based C&C channel and not an IRC C&C channel as it was erroneously reported before. Send SPAM and perform click-fraud using some advertisement services.

Malware traffic. The machine was successfully infected with POST requests. Malware connect to command & control (CnC) server using a raw TCP connection.

Encrypted malware traffic. HTTPS and SSH traffic.

UDP and ICMP DDoS.

Trickbot banking Trojan. Trickbot (Trojan.Trickybot) C2 over HTTPS. • Uses Scheduled Tasks to re-run the main binary every few minutes and connect using SSL port. Most – but not all –communication with C&C is encrypted.

The dataset contains Background, Botnet, C&C Channels and Normal botnent traffic flows.

Milicenso dataset

This dataset contains traffic from live use of the Ponmocup malware/Trojan infection and communication traffic. Traffic contains:

Redirect domains, kritikaa.ilanes.com 178.211.33.205
Malware download, ml.buymeaslut.com 82.211.45.82
C2 /phone home, intohave.com 64.179.44.188 (DNS request only).

3.2   Data Validation

Since the dataset is mainly comprised of malicious traffic captures, the first step was to balance the amount of normal and malicious traffic. To ensure the quality of the dataset used, we opted for two things:

- Provide as much 'normal' traffic as malicious one per session analyzed. Normal traffic originates from different types of services and network communications. For each setup, referenced datasets provide more information [5, 6, 7].
- Increase the amount of encrypted malware traffic to approach data sizes of other attacks. FIRST [5] dataset encrypted malicious traffic was noticeably less than other

forms of malicious traffic. To achieve this, we utilized the Trickbot network to obtain captures from CTU-13 extended dataset pcaps [7].

Since our task is not to distinguish between specific types of malware but rather a high-level detection of any type of malicious traffic, the notion of a biased dataset in terms of having the same amount of malicious traffic for each type of attack is not as relevant as in [13]. Also, our dataset is comprised of real traffic data from multiple types of attacks, either from captured malware, capture-the-flag hacking events or similar environments. Thus, a potential imbalance of malicious traffic sub-classes within each attack) is a real world representation and needs not to be tampered with (e.g. the no of packets corresponding to malware reverse connection in comparison with the no of packets corresponding to service exploitation during the same attack. Also, the amount of data for all types of attacks is big enough to exclude unrealistic biases in data. Thus, there is no need for rebalancing the classes of malicious traffic, the only exception being the addition of extra encrypted malicious traffic from different case studies, due to the small size of network captures in comparison with the rest.

We opt to report detection results using accuracy, precision, recall and f1 score in both mixed (shuffled) and ordered dataset samples. These are popular metrics and indicators of the overall performance of the prototype [3] and are used in multiple similar research projects [13, 18].

4 Detection Methodology

4.1 Problem Definition

Given a TCP/IP network traffic flow, our system aims to sample and classify each connection as malicious (i.e. produced by malicious events such as a web attack or malware) or normal. Essentially, the system is comprised of two parts: traffic flow side channel feature selection and network traffic classification.

Side channel feature selection: The first task is to choose correct, descriptive features of TCP traffic that do not refer to the content of a packet, but rather to the physical characteristics, such as time ratio between packet sending, size of payload etc.

Traffic classification: The second task is to use the selected features to classify new traffic streams as malicious or normal. We do not aim to distinguish between types of malicious traffic. It is our belief that human interaction and digital forensics will always provide better solutions in dissecting security events. Instead, our system aims to warn against any potential malicious traffic for response teams to take action.

4.2 Feature Selection

In this subsection we discuss the features we selected to feed into our Machine-Learning algorithms and the rationale of the proposed system. We use features based on side channel characteristics of TCP traffic to analyze packet-to-packet sequences inside network sessions.

It is known that for any set of features, "there will be a fundamental limit to the kind of determinations a NIDS can develop from them" [31]. Choosing a correct set of features must always take into account the diversity of normal as well as malicious traffic. A good approach is to examine the invariance of features in diverse malicious traffic scenarios [31]. To this end, we opted to base our feature selection on previous publications [13, 26, 27] that utilized similar side-channel packet features for similar purposes. Authors in [13] and Cisco [27] made extensive tests and concluded in similar albeit quite larger feature sets than us. Authors in [26] had previously used a subset of features also found in [13, 27], albeit for different purposes (i.e. to leak sensitive information from web application content).

Our intuition was that, the intersection of these features sets could minimize the features needed for the detection of malicious traffic, while at the same time achieve the same results. Also we believed that the same feature set could expand potential malicious traffic detection beyond encrypted malicious traffic; which was the focus of [13, 27]. Thankfully, we found that these types of features are enough to identify malicious traffic. Since these features do not require complex aggregation of information, the runtime footprint is small and the system can be easily adapted to analyze traffic in real-time. Overall, we opt for five features on side channel characteristics, twenty two (22) features less than [13] and four (4) less than Cisco [27].

Packet Size (Ps): Every connection is defined by the packets exchanged between a sender and a receiver. Packet size is known to be good both for predicting the type of connection and protocols used [25]. For that reason this is a basic feature of our project.

Payload Size (PAs): It is a feature that defines a packet. The payload is the heart of any malicious traffic. In TCP, the payload is enclosed in the TCP Data Segment. Research has shown that side channel analysis of payload sizes can be used as a feature for information leakage [26].

Payload Ratio (Pr): It refers to the ratio of the payload size to the total packet size. Malicious traffic can exhibit similar patterns concerning content ratios, so we opted to include this as a basic feature. The formula is shown below, where PAs refers to the payload size and Ps refers to the packet size

$$Pr = \frac{PAs}{Ps} \tag{1}$$

Ratio to Previous Packet (Rpp): We noticed that, when malicious traffic flows inside the network, the packets are sequential and often exhibit specific trends in size. This can be used for fingerprinting malicious traffic. By comparing two packets in a row that belong in the same session, we can get the ratio to the previous packet. The value defaults to 0 for the first packet of the session. The formula is shown below.

$$Rpp = \frac{Pp}{PPs} \tag{2}$$

where Pp refers to the current packet size and PPs to the previous packet size in the same session.

Time Difference (Td): The time difference between a packet and the previous packet of a session can be used to fingerprint malicious traffic. The value defaults to 0 for the first packet of a session. The formula is:

$$Td = Pt - PPt \tag{3}$$

Pt refers to Packet time and PPt to Previous Packet time. Both times refer to how long it took for a packet to be delivered.

Flag: A simple label that classifies the packet as either 0 or 1, where 0 stands for normal traffic and 1 for malware traffic.

Fig. 1. Workflow of the system from network capture to classification (training & validation)

4.3 Traffic Classification

Our proposed system utilizes offline training to train a machine learning algorithm. The offline analysis aims to extract traffic patterns and train the classifiers with labelled traffic flows from real-world datasets. These real-world traffic flows from different apps, malware types and attacks provide the data to train and verify our system's classifier. Each traffic flow contains a sequence of packets and corresponding sessions along with packet receiving time, packet length, and packet protocol type. We opted to use the Scikit-learn library over Python to train and implement our classification system. The workflow of the entire system is depicted in Fig. 1. The above mentioned features and labelled traffic flows are used for training multiple algorithms. Deciding on a machine-learning algorithm was no trivial task. For experiments, we opted to compare results between seven algorithms (see Table 1). Algorithms were selected as follows: We gathered all machine learning categories used in similar research [16, 26, 27] and detected their predictive model (e.g. decision tree, neural networks etc.). Then we opted to use the most efficient algorithms from each model area.

The data mining module was also implemented using Python. It utilizes the Scapy [1] Python library for packet captures and feature extraction to the SQL database for easier manipulation of samples for machine-learning modules.

Using CART and KNN decision algorithms instead of neural networks, we can achi-eve faster classification once the system is trained and have a more interpretable model to detect hidden interconnections of traffic features. On the other hand, neural networks might be more accurate, provided there is enough training data, although they can be prone to over-fitting as well; another reason why we tested other algorithms mo —re suitable to unknown dataset characteristics. Preliminary tests showed that neural networks take a lot of time without having clear advantages over others neither in classification nor optimization (see Sect. 5.1).

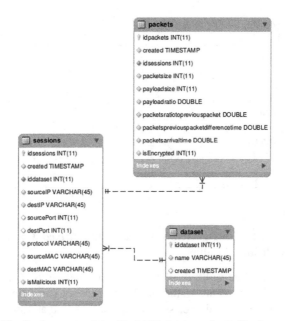

Fig. 2. Structure of the MariaDB database for traffic dataset

Table 1. Machine learning algorithms tested for malicious traffic discrimination

Logistic Regression	Linear Discriminant (LDA)	K-Neighbours (KNN)
Decision Tree (CART)	Gaussian Naïve Bayes	Support Vector (SVC)
Neural Network (Multilayer Perception)		

The machine-learning module uses Pandas [2] and Scikit-learn [3] Python libraries. Input files are CSV records exported from the database. The module performs machine-learning on the dataset using the aforementioned machine learning algorithms.

The database used is MariaDB [4]. MariaDB is a fork of the MySQL database after the acquisition of the later from Oracle. It was chosen due to its performance gains over MySQL when exporting CSV files. The database role is to reduce the footprint on the system disk while allowing us to create specialized subsets from available data for testing our Machine Learning module. Database structure is presented in Fig. 2.

5 Experimental Results

The proposed system was tested on a Dell Inspiron 15-3537 (Intel Core i7-4500U, 8 GB RAM). Parsing PCAPs to build the SQL database for later training and building the system took approximately 10 h. Classification and training took about 15 min for experiment 1 and 5 min for experiment 2 on average, for all models. All tests utilized Python and the above mentioned libraries. A sample SQL query for selecting random side channel data samples from the database is depicted at Table 2.

Table 2. Sample SQL query for exporting random malware packet characteristics from dataset

```
SELECT
p.packetsize,p.payloadsize,p.payloadratio,p.packetsratiot
opreviouspacket,p.packetspreviouspacketdifferencetime,s.i
sMalicious
INTO OUTFILE "/tmp/outmalware.csv"
FIELDS TERMINATED BY ',' OPTIONALLY ENCLOSED BY '"'
LINES TERMINATED BY "\n" FROM packets AS p INNER JOIN
sessions s ON (p.idsessions = s.idsessions) WHERE
s.isMalicious = 1 ORDER BY RAND()  LIMIT 10000000 ;
```

5.1   Experiment 1: Entire Datasets with Randomly Mixed Traffic - All Types of Malicious Traffic

In the first experiment we utilized all traffic from all datasets. Classification used random samples from the entire traffic database; malicious and normal traffic. The number of packets used for testing classification can be found at Table 3. The random selection of various types of malicious traffic was performed uniformly using MariaDB at the time of CSV export. This aims to remove any bias in data selection. The dataset was split 70/30 and all ~ 8 GB of dataset traffic was utilized. Side channel features were extracted from each packet and imported to MariaDB. This includes the FIRST 2015, Milisenco, and CTU-13 datasets, along with all packets from each network session. This is done to test non homogenous network traffic behavior with our feature extraction. All types of malicious traffic were used in this experiment.

Table 3. Traffic packets from sessions in dataset

Total malicious traffic	6669881
Total non-malicious traffic	7968518
Non malicious non encrypted	6337244
Non malicious encrypted	1631274
Malicious non encrypted	6214670
Malicious encrypted	455211
Total	**14638399**

Machine learning and classification results are depicted at Tables 4 and 5. By viewing the hit map for true positives (TP), true negatives (TN), false positives (FP) and false negatives (FN), it is obvious that CART and KNN algorithms have a clear advantage over others in detecting malicious traffic using side channel characteristics of packets. CART gets a 94.5% detection rate with 4.4% FP and 6.8% FN, while KNN achieves 94% detection with about 5% FP and 7.7% FN, on the 200 K network traffic sessions sample. We opted not include SVC because the algorithm does not seem to scale as well as the rest of the machine learning models. Overall, CART and KNN are the best performing models and they will the ones used on the following experiment.

Table 4. Detection comparison of algorithms – Experiment 1

AI	Accuracy	True Pos	False Pos	False Neg	True Neg
LR	0.61625	137214	25753	89370	47663
LDA	0.62428	145331	17636	95078	41955
KNN	**0.92987**	152077	10890	9541	127492
CART	**0.94506**	152560	10407	7256	129777
NB	0.52005	154225	8742	135241	1792
SVC	0.77211	148421	13017	82517	56045

Table 5. Performance comparison of algorithms – Experiment 1

AI	Precision		Recall		F1-score		Support	
	0	1	0	1	0	1	0	1
LR	0.61	0.65	0.84	0.35	0.70	0.45	162967	137033
LDA	0.60	0.70	0.89	0.31	0.72	0.43	162967	137033
KNN	0.95	0.91	0.92	0.94	**0.94**	**0.93**	162967	137033
CART	0.96	0.92	0.94	0.95	**0.95**	**0.94**	162967	137033
NB	0.53	0.17	0.95	0.02	0.68	0.03	162967	137033
SVC	0.78	0.75	0.74	0.79	0.76	0.77	162967	137033

An interesting finding was that, decreasing the overall size of the random network traffic sample under classification seems to increase the detection rate (i.e. detection of potential malicious traffic). To support this and remove potential biases in smaller sets of captured traffic, we tried various combinations of malicious and normal traffic, as we will show in Experiment 2.

Preliminary tests with neural networks show that these classification algorithms provide worse results that decision tree (such as CART, LDA) and instance-based algorithms like KNN. Notice here that preliminary tests with neural networks show that they offer worse detection rates to the aforementioned algorithms while requiring way larger amounts of time and data for training (see Tables 6 and 7). Also, in some instances, neural networks seem prone to biases.

Table 6. Detection comparison for neural networks (Multilayer Perception)

AI	Accuracy	True Pos	False Pos	False Neg	True Neg
NN (Multilayer Perceptron)	0.85031	152616	10351	7062	129971

Table 7. Performance of basic neural networks (Multilayer Perception)

AI	Precision		Recall		F1-score		Support	
	0	1	0	1	0	1	0	1
NN (Multilayer Perceptron)	0.86	0.84	0.86	0.83	0.86	0.83	162967	137033

5.2   Experiment 2: 20 K Limited Packet Sample for Feature Testing - All Types of Malicious Traffic

As mentioned previously, we detected that utilizing smaller network flow data over a trained classifier to detect malicious traffic seems to increase the True Positive detection rate. Thus, in this second experiment we purposely only use 20 K malicious packets (and consequently the same amount of clean, normal traffic) from the FIRST 2015 Dataset to test our classifier. This experiment provided insight of the performance of each algorithm with limited data.

Again, the random selection was performed uniformly by MariaDB at the time of CSV export to remove any bias. The number of packets is deliberately small since we want to confirm our assumptions at the feature selection stage of the project that the selected side channel features are pretty good for classifying malicious traffic even when data is scarce. Again, the sample along with equal sized normal traffic was split (70–30) for updating the classifier and testing for malicious traffic detection. All types of malicious traffic were used in this experiment.

After running the ml.py module on our dataset we get the following table of results. By viewing the hit map for true positives (TP), true negatives (TN), false positives (FP) and false negatives (FN), it is obvious that some algorithms have a clear advantage over others. Specifically, CART and KNN show good potential, with ~89% detection rate for any given mixed malicious traffic sample, with low false negatives and false positives (around 10%). Execution times for offline training only took a couple of minutes and validation took <2 min. This proves that, even with random session, limited amount of data to train a classifier, the selected features provide very good results given the situation in very small timeframes (see Tables 8 and 9).

An interesting find is that SVC performance increases noticeably when smaller datasets are used for training and classification. This shows that SVC is prone to biases since, as we increase the training sample, its detection rate falls the fastest. KNN and CART still hold the best result percentages, while their drop in detection rates is expected; albeit very small considering the difference in data.

Table 8. Detection comparison of algorithms – Experiment 2

AI	Accuracy	True Pos	False Pos	False Neg	True Neg
LR	0.539125	1276	801	1062	861
LDA	0.548375	1321	756	1070	853
KNN	**0.888312**	1878	199	264	1659
CART	**0.888625**	1904	173	283	1640
NB	0.542625	187	1890	21	1902
SVC	0.873062	2014	63	428	1495

Table 9. Performance comparison of algorithms – Experiment 2

AI	Precision		Recall		F1-score		Support	
	0	1	0	1	0	1	0	1
LR	0.55	0.52	0.61	0.45	0.58	0.48	2077	1923
LDA	0.55	0.53	0.64	0.44	0.59	0.48	2077	1923
KNN	0.88	0.89	0.90	0.86	**0.89**	**0.88**	2077	1923
CART	0.87	0.90	0.92	0.85	**0.89**	**0.88**	2077	1923
NB	0.90	0.50	0.90	0.99	0.16	0.67	2077	1923
SVC	0.82	0.96	0.97	0.78	0.89	0.86	2077	1923

5.3 Experiment 3: Detection of Encrypted Malware Traffic

Many companies (e.g. CISCO [27]) are publishing technical reports about new intrusion detection systems (IDSes) that utilize similar features, yet only detect encrypted malicious traffic. To our knowledge, no tool is able to generalize this ability to multiple types of malicious traffic, from defacement SQLi attacks to encrypted traffic, botnets and injections like ours. Still, for arguments sake, we opt to show that malicious encrypted malware traffic can be distinguished using less features than [27] while still maintaining a high detection rate. During the third and last experiment, we focus only on the selected side channel features (Sect. 4.2) and show that we are still able to adequately detect encrypted malicious traffic.

For this experiment, our trainer program selected samples from all different encrypted malicious traffic sessions from all datasets; whether botnets, reverse shells, malware data transfer etc. To remove biases, the experiment was executed three times using (i) uniformly random samples from all datasets and types of encrypted traffic (e.g. see Table 2 above), (ii) biased (more botnet traffic in terms of 80%–20%), and (iii) per dataset. The dataset was split 70–30 for training and classification.

The hit maps for true positives (TP), true negatives (TN), false positives (FP) and false negatives (FN) are depicted at Tables 10 and 11 (averages from three executions).

This experiment yielded the best results. From observations, we can conclude that these types of side channel features are effective for discriminating encrypted malware traffic; especially if we do not care to understand the type of malicious encrypted traffic or the content being transmitted. We noticed a low percentage of False Positives and False negatives ($\sim 8\%$ of the total positive malicious sample).

Table 10. Detection comparison for encrypted malicious traffic – Experiment 3

AI	Accuracy	True Pos	False Pos	False Neg	True Neg
KNN	0.996334	488685	1495	648	135118
CART	**0.99852**	488849	**440**	**484**	136173

Table 11. Performance comparison for encrypted malicious traffic – Experiment 3

AI	Precision		Recall		F1-score		Support	
	0	1	0	1	0	1	0	1
KNN	1.0	1.0	1.0	0.99	**1.0**	0.99	489333	136613
CART	1.0	1.0	1.0	1.0	**1.0**	**1.0**	489333	136613

6 Conclusions, Findings and Future Work

In this paper, we presented seven (7) machine-learning algorithms and their performance for detecting multiple types of malicious traffic, both encrypted and unencrypted, based on selected side channel features. The project currently works retroactively on already captured data. The presented experiments adequately prove that side channel characteristics of TCP packets can be effectively used together with machine learning to detect most types of malicious traffic, even if wide differences exist on the types of ongoing attacks and to their corresponding traffic.

Some of our most important conclusions are the following:

- The best detection rate achieved was about 94.2% on CART and 93.4% using KNN algorithms, on full-scale mixed types of malicious data for various datasets totaling about ~8 GB in size.
- Preliminary results show that machine learning algorithms that utilize Decision Tree classifiers may be prone to packet crafting, if an attacker has access to the prediction model, parameters and the entire sample. Although this is generally not feasible, we should state here that the possibility exists. To this end, preliminary tests may support that Instance based algorithms like KNN along with the selected side channel features greatly reduce such attacks.
- We detected specific, descriptive features describing side channel characteristics of TCP packets (such as packet size, delivery time ratios etc.) and built lightweight classification modules (less than a few megabytes) that are able to run on real time traffic and detect ongoing malicious attacks to enhance network security. We showed that we can achieve very good malicious traffic detection percentages without utilizing full-scale TLS and connection certification features, but instead focus only on typical side channel packet characteristics.
- The use of side channel features *significantly reduces the amount of analysis* and network traffic that needs to be saved for detection. Thus, the system can be used to supplement network security analysts to gain a better understanding of their network traffic and get robust alerts on security incidents without relying on error-prone IDPS pattern matching or heavy behavioral analytics. We plan to combine our system with well-known traffic monitoring systems, like Bro [28], Snort [29], or Suricata [30].

Our experiments demonstrated the applicability of the proposed system for detecting multiple types of malicious traffic *without discriminating among types of malicious attacks.*

Our future work aims to build a working prototype for large-scale enterprise networks and work along well-known network traffic sniffers and monitoring systems (Bro, Snort, Suricata). We also aim to extend the system to incorporate more features like "connection type" and "TTL" feature to further enhance the detection mechanisms against DDoS attacks and spoofed packets.

References

1. Biondi, P.: Scapy (2011)
2. McKinney, W.: PyData development team. Pandas: Powerful Python Data Analy. Toolkit 1625 (2015)
3. Pedregosa, F., et al.: Scikit-learn: machine learning in Python. J. Mach. Learn. Res. **12**, 2825–2830 (2011). http://scikit-learn.org/
4. MariaDB database server. https://mariadb.com/ Accessed 1 Jan 2018
5. First.org, Hands-on Network Forensics - Training PCAP dataset from FIRST 2015. www.first.org/_assets/conf2015/networkforensics_virtualbox.zip
6. Milicenso, Ponmocup Malware dataset (Update 2012-10-07, http://security-research.dyndns.org/pub/botnet/ponmocup/analysis_2012-10-05/analysis.txt Accessed 1 Jan 2018)
7. CTU-13 dataset, CTU University, Czech Republic, 2011, https://mcfp.felk.cvut.cz/publicDatasets/CTU-Malware-Capture-Botnet-1/
8. Livadas, C., Walsh, B., Lapsley, D., Strayer, T.: Using machine learning techniques to identify botnet traffic. In: Proceedings of the IEEE LCN Workshop on Network Security (2006)
9. Cooke, E., Jahanian, F., McPherson, D.: The zombie roundup: understanding, detecting, and disrupting botnets. In: Proceedings of the Workshop on Steps to Reducing Unwanted Traffic on the Internet (2005)
10. Binkley, J., Singh, S.: An algorithm for anomaly-based Botnet detection. In: Proceedings of the Workshop on Steps to Reducing Unwanted Traffic on the Internet (2006)
11. Gu, G., Porras, P., Yegneswaran, V., Fong, M.W., Lee, W.: BotHunter: detecting malware. Infection through IDS-Driven Dialog Correlation. In: Proceedings of the USENIX Security Symposium (2007)
12. Timofeev, R.: Classification and regression trees (cart) theory and applications. Humboldt University, Berlin (2004)
13. Střasák, F.: Detection of HTTPS malware Traffic (Detekce Malware v HTTPS komunikaci). BSC thesis. České vysoké učení technické v Praze. Vypočetní a informační centrum (2017)
14. Taylor, C., Alves-Foss, J.: NATE - network analysis of anomalous traffic events, a low-cost approach. In: Proceedings of the New Security Paradigms Workshop (2001)
15. Lakhina, A., Papagiannaki, K., Crovella, M.: Structural analysis of network traffic flows. In: Proceedings of ACM SIGMETRICS/Performance (2004)
16. Terrell, J., et al.: Multivariate SVD analyses for network anomaly detection. In: (Poster) Proceeding of ACM SIGCOMM (2005)
17. Yen, T.-F., Reiter, M.K.: Traffic aggregation for malware detection. In: Zamboni, D. (ed.) DIMVA 2008. LNCS, vol. 5137, pp. 207–227. Springer, Heidelberg (2008). https://doi.org/10.1007/978-3-540-70542-0_11
18. Kohout, J., Pevny, T.: Automatic discovery of web servers hosting similar applications. In: Proceedings of the IFIP/IEEE International Symposium on Integrated Network Management, IEEE, pp. 1310–1315 (2015)

19. Lokoč, J., Kohout, J., Čech, P., Skopal, T., Pevný, T.: k-NN classification of Malware in HTTPS traffic using the metric space approach. In: Chau, M., Wang, G.A., Chen, H. (eds.) PAISI 2016. LNCS, vol. 9650, pp. 131–145. Springer, Cham (2016). https://doi.org/10.1007/978-3-319-31863-9_10
20. Crotti, M., et al.: Traffic classification through simple statistical fingerprinting. ACM SIG-COMM Comput. Commun. Rev. **37**(1), 5–16 (2007)
21. Prasse, P., et al.: Malware Detection by HTTPS Traffic Analysis (2017)
22. Chari, S., et al.: A platform and analytics for usage and entitlement analytics. IBM J. Res. Dev. **60**(4), 7-1 (2016)
23. Combs, G.: "Wireshark." (2007). http://www.wireshark.org/lastmodified Accessed 12 Feb
24. Roesch, M.: Snort: lightweight intrusion detection for networks. In: Lisa, Vol. 99, no. 1 (1999)
25. Liu, J., et al.: Effective and real-time in-app activity analysis in encrypted internet traffic streams. In: Proceedings of the 23rd ACM SIGKDD International Conference on Knowledge Discovery and Data Mining. ACM (2017)
26. Chen, S., et al.: Side-channel leaks in web applications: a reality today, a challenge tomorrow. In: IEEE Symposium on 2010 Security and Privacy, IEEE (2010)
27. Encrypted Traffic Analytics, Cisco public, White paper (2017). www.cisco.com/c/dam/en/us/solutions/collateral/enterprise-networks/enterprise-network-security/nb-09-encrytd-traf-anlytcs-wp-cte-en.pdf Accessed Mar 2018
28. Bro, I.: http://www.bro-ids.org (2008)
29. Beale, J., Baker, A., Esler, J.: Snort: IDS and IPS toolkit. Syngress (2007)
30. Suricata, I.D.S.: open-source IDS. IPS/NSM engine (2014). (http://suricata-ids.org/)
31. Sommer, R., Paxson, V.: Outside the closed world: on using machine learning for network intrusion detection. In: IEEE Symposium on 2010 Security and Privacy (SP), IEEE (2010)

PwIN – Pwning Intel piN: Why DBI is Unsuitable for Security Applications

Julian Kirsch$^{(\boxtimes)}$, Zhechko Zhechev, Bruno Bierbaumer, and Thomas Kittel

Technical University of Munich, Munich, Germany
{kirschju,zhechev,bierbaumer,kittel}@sec.in.tum.de

Abstract. Binary instrumentation is a robust and powerful technique which facilitates binary code modification of computer programs even when no source code is available. This is achieved either statically by rewriting the binary instructions of the program and then executing the altered program or dynamically, by changing the code at run-time right before it is executed. The design of most Dynamic Binary Instrumentation (DBI) frameworks puts emphasis on ease-of-use, portability, and efficiency, offering the possibility to execute *inspecting* analysis code from an *interpositioned* perspective maintaining full access to the instrumented program. This has established DBI as a powerful tool utilized for analysis tasks such as profiling, performance evaluation, and prototyping.

The interest of employing DBI tools for binary hardening techniques (e.g. Program Shepherding) and malware analysis is constantly increasing among researchers. However, the usage of DBI for security related tasks is questionable, as in such scenarios it is important that analysis code runs *isolated* from the instrumented program in a *stealthy* way.

In this paper, we show (1) that a plethora of literature implicitly seems to assume *isolation* and *stealthiness* of DBI frameworks and strongly challenge these assumptions. We use Intel Pin running on x86-64 Linux as an example to show that assuming a program is running in context of a DBI framework (2) the presence thereof can be detected, (3) policies introduced by binary hardening mechanisms can be subverted, and (4) otherwise hard-to-exploit bugs can be escalated to full code execution.

Keywords: Dynamic Binary Instrumentation · Intel Pin
Control Flow Integrity · Program shepherding · Malware analysis
Evasive malware · Virtual machine escape · Exploitation

1 Introduction

Malware continues to be a growing cyber security threat even nowadays. In the early days of the Internet malware was developed for mainly experimental reasons [26]. However, in recent years we are witnesses of malware utilized for theft of confidential data, denial-of-service of commercial systems, or even black mailing and cyber espionage. Industry and academia are constantly striving to develop countermeasures against these threats in form of advanced malware

© Springer Nature Switzerland AG 2018
J. Lopez et al. (Eds.): ESORICS 2018, LNCS 11098, pp. 363–382, 2018.
https://doi.org/10.1007/978-3-319-99073-6_18

detection approaches. However, malware developers continue to become more creative in their attempt to hinder the analysis of malware samples. Dynamic Binary Instrumentation (DBI) can help analysts to inspect applications' characteristics or alter their functionalities even when no source code is available. Therefore, DBI is easily employed as a malware analysis tool where the existence of anti-analysis techniques and the absence of source code are very common.

Similarly, computer systems are often subject to external attacks that aim to gain control over their functionality by leveraging malicious inputs. Such attacks attempt to trigger existing programming mistakes in software such as memory corruption bugs to subvert execution. DBI frameworks provide a possibility to conveniently add new functionalities to existing binaries, thus rendering these frameworks useful to harden software. One peculiarity, illustrating this approach, is *program shepherding* [17] – a technique that involves monitoring of all control transfers to ensure that each satisfies a given security policy, such as restricted code origins and controlling return targets. According to the program shepherding's paradigms this is possible because the hardened application is executed in the context of a DBI framework. A typical example of program shepherding is the implementation of Control Flow Integrity (CFI) policies using DBI to operate on Commercial Off-The-Shelf (COTS) binaries.

In this work we challenge both scenarios painted above. We argue that the original intent driving the motivation to build DBI frameworks was the ability to execute analysis code in a way that *interposes* execution of the instrumented program, *i.e.* analysis code can subscribe to be *notified* of any occurring event taking place in context of the instrumented program. Furthermore, an important design goal of DBI was to equip analysis code with full *inspection* capabilities covering the complete architectural state of the target. In practice this is typically achieved by introducing a single address space for both, analysis code and instrumented program.

This key observation is the main motivation behind our research. We show that due to the shared memory model, DBI frameworks in their current state are inherently incapable of providing neither *stealthiness* of the analysis code nor *isolation* of the analysis code against manipulations of the instrumented target. In our opinion, this *conceptionally renders them unsuitable for malware analysis and program shepherding*.

In a nutshell, this paper makes the following contributions:

Relevance. We identify DBI to be a common instrument for security-related tasks such as malware analysis and application hardening in literature.

Detectability. We demonstrate that it is trivial for an application to detect whether it is running in context of a DBI framework, enabling malicious software to behave in different ways during analysis.

Escapability. We attest that a malicious application can break out of the instrumentation engine and execute arbitrary code outside of the DBI framework.

Increased Attack Surface. We argue that counter-intuitively instead of *increasing* security by introducing DBI based software hardening measures, DBI actually *decreases* the overall security by escalating an otherwise hard-to-exploit real world bug (CVE-2017-13089) into full code execution.

2   Background and Related Work

In this chapter we discuss background about essential characteristics of DBI in general, introduce a consistent taxonomy used throughout this work, and discuss the usage of DBI frameworks for security in academic literature.

2.1   Dynamic Binary Instrumentation

A typical DBI framework consists of three components in a single address space:

1. The compiled target program which functionality should be altered
2. The functionality that is to be added to the target program
3. The DBI platform injecting the additional code into the target binary and ensuring proper execution.

Implementers typically develop their own *analysis plugins* which the *instrumentation platform* injects into the binary code of an application (*instrumented application*) that should be analyzed. The instrumentation platform exposes an API that enables the analysis plugin to register callbacks for certain events happening during the execution of the instrumented application. For example, it might be desirable for an analysis plugin implementing a *shadow stack* to receive a callback whenever the instrumented application tries to execute a `call` or `ret` instruction (*interposition*). Once the analysis plugin is notified (synchronously) of the execution of such an instruction, it may now freely inspect or modify all register and memory contents of the instrumented application (*inspection*).

2.2   Required Security Properties of Analysis Frameworks

In context of this work, we follow the taxonomy of Garfinkel and Rosenblum [14] to outline key requirements that any dynamic analysis framework needs to fulfill. In accordance to this work, we introduce analysis plugin and the instrumentation platform to form the *analyzing system*, as opposed to the instrumented application which constitutes the *analyzed system*. Then, the Garfinkel and Rosenblum taxonomy can be rephrased to DBI tools as follows:

R1 Interposition. *The analyzing system can subscribe to and is notified of certain events within the analyzed system.* For DBI this means that the instrumentation platform stops execution of the instrumented application and transfers control to the analysis plugin once certain events occur.

R2 Inspection. *The analyzing system has access to the full state of the analyzed system. Thus, the analyzed system is unable to evade analysis.* In context of our work this implies that the analysis plugin can freely access and modify all memory and register contents of the instrumented application.

R3 Isolation. *The analyzed system is unable to tamper with the analyzing system or any other analyzed system.* This means that the instrumentation platform and analysis plugin have to defend themselves against (malicious) modifications performed by the instrumented application.

In addition, researchers realized that dynamic analysis systems suitable to handle malware also need to operate in a way *transparent to the analyzed system*. This has the simple reason that so-called split personality malware might evade dynamic analysis if it is capable of detecting the analysis environment, as pointed out by Lengyel *et al.* [20]:

R4 Stealthiness. *The analyzed system is unable to detect if it currently undergoes analysis.* This means that the instrumented application must not be able to infer the presence of the instrumentation platform.

2.3   DBI Use in Literature

There are numerous examples of DBI utilization not only by the research community but also in commercial software development.

Binary Analysis. Many researchers develop DBI tools in order to perform analysis of binaries, *e.g.* Salwan *et al.* developed *Triton* [30], a concolic execution framework. Clause *et al.* [9] implement a dynamic taint analysis tool which supports data-flow and control-flow based tainting using DBI. Other analysis tools based on Intel Pin include a debugging backend shipped by default with the Interactive Disassembler (IDA) as well as *Lighthouse*[1], a coverage measurement tool created to enrich static analysis with dynamic information.

Bug Detection. Even in 2018, vulnerabilities resulting from memory corruption bugs [25] are still problematic. Many researchers implement vulnerability detection and prevention tools using DBI to limit the potential damage. This is the case because DBI provides them the advantage so that custom security code may be directly executed within the analyzed/hardened program. The Valgrind distribution includes a lot of profiling and debugging tools, such as *Memcheck* [22] which detects memory-management problems, as well as the heap profiler *Massif* [24]. Similarly, on the Windows family of Operating Systems (OSs) *Dr. Memory* [7] is a memory monitoring tool built on the DynamoRIO framework capable of identifying memory-related programming errors.

Program Shepherding/(CFI). A lot of research is recently conducted regarding program shepherding and CFI which attempts to restrict the set of possible control flow transfers to those that are strictly required for correct program execution [3]. In order to implement this approach, Davi *et al.* [10] developed a Pintool that dynamically enforces sanitizing return address checks by employing a shadow stack at run-time. While the idea of a shadow stack is much older [8,33], the advantage of this approach was the ease of development of the dynamic security enforcement tool. A similar approach was chosen by van der Veen *et al.* who developed a Linux kernel module and a Dyninst plugin [32] which both determine and restrict the valid execution paths and thereby ensure correct

---

[1] https://github.com/gaasedelen/lighthouse.

program execution. Instead of verifying the return address's validity, Tymburibá *et al.* [31] in contrast try to utilize Return-Oriented programming (ROP) gadgets' characteristics in order to prevent the hijacking of program's execution flow. In their Pintool called *RipRop* they detect unusually high rates of successive indirect branches during the execution of unusually short basic blocks, which may be an indication of a undergoing ROP attack. Later, in the same year Follner *et al.* present *ROPocop* [13], another Code-Reuse Attack (CRA) detection framework targeted at Windows x86 binaries. It combines the idea of Tymburibá *et al.* together with a custom shadow stack and a technique which ensures no data is unintentionally executed. Yet another example of a Pintool utilized in ROP attack detection was proposed by Elsabagh *et al.* Their tool *EigenROP* attempts to detect anomalies in the execution process [11], due to execution of ROP gadgets, based on directional statistics and the program's own characteristics. Finally, Qiang *et al.* built a fully context-sensitive CFI tool [28] on top of Pin that may be used to protect COTS binaries. Among other advantages is that the tool checks the execution path instead of checking each edge in this execution path one by one which helps accelerate the process.

Malware Analysis. In addition, many security analysts employ DBI tools to study and profile malicious programs' behavior. Both to harden productive applications as well as to understand and reverse engineer potentially malicious program functionality in a sandbox environment. For instance, Gröbert *et al.* take advantage of a Pintool to generate execution traces and apply several heuristics to automate the identification of cryptographic primitives [15] in malicious samples. Kulakov developed a Pintool which performs static malware analysis in order to generate a loose timeline of the whole execution [19]. Additionally, he created an IDA plugin for better visualization of the data. Banescu *et al.* [4] proposed an empirical framework which is able to behaviorally obfuscate standard malware binaries. The program's observable behavior or path is defined by all internal computations and the sequence of accomplished system calls during its execution. In order to obfuscate malware samples, Banescu *et al.* [4] implemented a Pintool which inserts and reorders system calls into the binary without modifying its functionality but altering its known observable behavior.

Note that for the latter two of these domains, both Isolation and Stealthiness are a fundamental requirement to provide the proposed security guarantees.

2.4   Scope

To our perception, the most prominent examples of DBI frameworks nowadays are Intel Pin [21], Dyninst [5], Valgrind [23], DynamoRIO [6] and (more recently) QBDI [2] and Skorpio [29]. In the following, we focused (almost exclusively) on Intel Pin version 3.5 in Just-In-Time (JIT) mode on Linux while checking our results also against other common DBI implementations. We also utilize, as the time of writing, the latest release of Ubuntu 17.10 (64 bit) so that we can benefit

Table 1. Description of different DBI detection techniques. An asterisk (*) in the first column indicates a technique newly discovered during our research. All other techniques were adopted from their 32 bit versions targeting Windows presented in [12], except enter which is proposed by Ahmed Bougacha (See Footnote 3).

Technique	Type	Brief description
envvar	EA	Checks for Pin specific environment variables on stack
enter	CA	Checks whether enter instruction is legal and can be executed
fsbase*	CA	Checks if fsbase value is the same using rdfsbase and prctl
jitbr*	CO	Detects time overhead when a conditional branch is jitted
jitlib	CO	Detects JIT compiler overhead when a library is loaded
nx*	CA	Tries to execute code on a non-executable page
pageperm	EA	Checks for pages with rwx permissions
mapname	EA	Checks mapped files' names for known values (*pinbin*, *vgpreload*)
ripfxsave	CA	Executes fxsave instruction and checks the saved rip value
ripsiginfo*	CA	Causes an int3 and checks the saved rip value in fpregs
ripsyscall	CA	Checks whether rip value is saved in rcx after a syscall
smc*	CA	Check whether the framework detects Self-Modifying Code
vmleave	EA	Checks for known code patterns (VMLeave)

from the latest security mechanisms, such as, for example, a higher number of randomized bits by Address Space Layout Randomization (ASLR)[2].

Note that from the previously defined requirements, R1 (Interposition) and R2 (Inspection) are fundamental features of DBI. In the following sections, we will challenge the previously defined requirements R3 (Isolation) and R4 (Stealthiness) and show that subversion of any thereof consequently also annihilates R1 (Interposition) and R2 (Inspection).

3   Stealthiness

In this section we present several techniques that reliably detect the presence of different DBI frameworks. To achieve this, we not only adopted several existing DBI detection techniques [12] to Linux x86-64 but also found new, previously

---

[2] See /proc/sys/vm/mmap_rnd_bits.

Table 2. Detection mechanisms on different DBI frameworks. A ✗ indicates that the test reliably detects the presence of the indicated DBI framework, a ✗ means that a particular test does not detect the presence of the respective DBI framework.

Technique	Type	Pin	Valgrind	DynamoRIO	QBDI
jitbr	CO	✗	✗	✗	✗
jitlib	CO	✗	✗	✗	✗
pageperm	EA	✗	✗	✗	✗
vmleave	EA	✗	✗	✗	✗
mapname	EA	✗	✗	✗	✗
smc	CA	✗	✗	✗	✗
ripfxsave	CA	✗	✗	✗	✗
ripsiginfo	CA	✗	✗	✗	✗
ripsyscall	CA	✗	✗	✗	✗
nx	CA	✗	✗	✗	✗
envvar	EA	✗	✗	✗	✗
fsbase	CA	✗	–	✗	✗
enter	CA	✗	✗	✗	✗

unknown detection techniques. We group detection techniques in three categories; (1) code cache/instrumentation artifacts (CA), (2) JIT compiler overhead (CO), and (3) runtime environment artifacts (EA). In this paper we only describe techniques from categories (1) and (3) in detail. While we explain these techniques on Pin, we found them also applicable to other DBI implementations.

We have developed a tool called *jitmenot* which employs 13 different DBI detection mechanisms summarized in Table 1, 7 of which were adopted from their Windows specific 32 bit counterparts presented elsewhere [12] and one was proposed by Ahmed Bougacha[3]. In the following, we describe only the most prominent examples for space reasons. Our testing tool *jitmenot* is released under an open-source license and can be downloaded from GitHub[4]. See Table 2 for an overview of which detection technique is able to detect which of the analyzed DBI frameworks.

3.1   Code Cache/Instrumentation Artifacts

In the first category – code cache artifacts – we include anomalies introduced by the fact that the executed code is not the original one.

Abusing the syscall Instruction (ripsyscall). One less known property of the x86-64 architecture is that when executing any system call via the syscall instruction, the current instruction pointer value is copied to the rcx register [16], such that the kernel can restore execution correctly via the sysret instruction later. As operation of the OS's kernel happens transparently, user land perceives

---

[3] http://repzret.org/p/detecting-valgrind.
[4] https://github.com/zhechkoz/PwIN.

the `syscall` instruction to have the side effect of setting the `rcx` register to the instruction right behind the `syscall`. The `ripsyscall` method involves the way the DBI frameworks emulate system calls. For example, when Pin has to accomplish some task outside of the Virtual Machine (VM), such as forwarding a system call request from the instrumented application or determining the next basic block to execute, the register state of the instrumented application is saved and the VM is left.

However, this is not the case for an instrumented application executed within DBI. Since, DBI frameworks wrap all system calls performed by the instrumented application, they need to save the program's register state before switching from the context of the instrumented application to its own internal state. When re-entering the context of the instrumented application, apart from the system call's result in `rax`, no other side effects are propagated back to the program. As a result, the `rcx` register observed by the instrumented application stays constant across system calls. This discrepancy can be used as a detection mechanism.

Self-modifying Code (`smc`). Yet another code cache artifact involves the way DBI frameworks handle Self-Modifying Code (SMC) together with the fact that instrumentation is done at basic block granularity. According to Intel, the Pin framework, for example, does attempt to detect manipulations of the original code of the instrumented application by exposing the `PIN_Set-Smc-Support` configuration option and a corresponding callback function `TRACE_-AddSmc-Detected-Function`. However, the analysis plugin programmer has to manually trigger code cache invalidation upon receiving a SMC notification to re-trigger the JIT compiler for the altered code. If the analysis plugin programmer does not handle SMC, or does not invalidate the code cache, the instrumented application could detect the presence of Pin as follows: First, the instrumented application marks its own code as readable, writeable and executable prior to executing a probe instruction once, making sure it gets placed into the code cache. Then the malicious tool modifies the immediate operand of the probe `mov` instruction from I_0 to I_1 in the code cache. Since Pin does not automatically invalidate the code cache only the original code is modified, resulting in `mov` ending up with immediate operand I_0. If the same sequence is executed outside of a instrumentation platform, the code change takes effect immediately and the `mov` instruction will use I_1 as immediate operand. Only if the analysis plugin monitors all write accesses of the application to its own text segment it can reliably detect SMC. Furthermore, a code cache invalidation request after every write (incurring performance overhead) is needed to prevent the attack sketched above.

Wrong Emulation of `enter` Instruction (`enter`). Some DBI frameworks, such as Valgrind, first translate the program into a processor-neutral Intermediate Representation (IR), which is then instrumented by the analysis plugin and in the end compiled to machine code. This implies that the DBI framework is capable of emulating the whole instruction set of the processor. However, since some instructions are less frequently used than others, DBI developers choose to either partially or completely not support them. An example of such an instruction is the x86 enter instruction [16], which creates a stack frame for a procedure. This instruction executes as expected in a non-instrumented environment. However, when a program instrumented by Valgrind attempts to execute enter, a signal is raised because this particular instruction is not implemented in the IR. By catching this signal, an application can determine whether it is instrumented or not. Note that this behavior is not observed in Intel Pin since it does not rely on IR for instrumentation.

Neglecting No-eXecute Bit (nx). W⊕X is an exploitation mitigation technique enabling the OS to mark writeable pages in memory as not executable. The consistent application of W⊕X denies an attacker the ability to introduce own code into the address space of a program before transferring the execution flow to it. However, when the JIT compiler of a DBI framework fetches new instructions for instrumentation, it does not check whether the source memory is marked as executable; as long as the page is readable the JIT compiler will translate any data present and emit executable assembly instructions. Note that **all** DBI frameworks we tested were vulnerable to this problem. Clearly, this is a huge security issue, as this implies that **any program** instrumented by a **DBI** framework **effectively** has **W⊕X disabled**. We utilized this fact as a detection technique in the following way: (1) Allocate a new page on the heap without execute permissions and place valid code in it, (2) then execute it. Without instrumentation, on any modern OS, a program trying to execute code on a page without x permissions will result in a crash. Otherwise, if the program is being instrumented, the program will be allowed to continue. This difference allows us to determine whether an application is currently instrumented or not.

Therefore, if it is possible to divert execution to a user-controllable buffer, an attacker can place shellcode in it and the VM will execute it. This effectively violates the Isolation property of DBI. Later we present a real-world example of how this can be leveraged to achieve a fully working exploit. This classifies as a major vulnerability issue not only in PinDBI framework but also in all other DBI engines which we tested as can be seen in Table 2. Nevertheless, introducing proper checks for correct memory page permissions before fetching code from memory could resolve this issue. This can be accomplished either in the JIT compiler or as a temporary fix integrated in the instrumentation platforms.

Real Instruction Pointer (ripfxsave/ripsiginfo). This technique was already introduced by Falcón and Riva [12]. However, as detection of the real rip also is a building block for attacks (against the DBI Isolation property) described later in this paper, we briefly summarize the techniques nevertheless.

In a nutshell, the DBI framework VMs execute only the translated and instrumented code of the application residing in the code cache but never the original code in the original text segment of the instrumented application. To maintain compatibility with non-relocatable applications, Pin attempts to mask the VM's rip with the instrumented program's original rip value whenever necessary.

One technique for finding the real rip abuses the systems Floating Point Unit (FPU): First, any FPU instruction (*e.g.* fldz) is executed. Afterwards, the FPU state is saved using the fxsave instruction. This state includes the address of the most recently executed FPU instruction, which is not masked by any instrumentation platform. A malicious instrumented application can then compare this value to the (masked) value when directly reading the `rip` register. If the values do not match, the application is being instrumented.

The same can be achieved on Linux with the help of the OS: The `sigaction` system call allows the calling process to examine and/or specify the action to be associated with a specific signal. When configured, the OS provides information about the context at the time the signal occurred. If we execute any floating-point instruction and then initiate a signal (for instance by deliberately triggering a segmentation fault), the context argument passed to the signal handler contains the state of the FPU registers. By comparing these values with the corresponding `rip`, one can again determine whether the program is being instrumented.

3.2   Environment Artifacts

In this section we identify environmental artifacts introduced by DBI frameworks. By this we refer to anomalies in the execution environment. For example, the memory layout varies drastically with the usage of instrumentation platforms. Searching for DBI artifacts such as strings or particular code patterns in memory reveals the presence of a DBI tool inside the target process memory.

Pin Internal Environment Variables. Firstly, Pin expects certain environment variables in order to run properly (e.g. `PIN_INJECTOR64_LD_LIBRARY_PATH`). Because the framework spawns the instrumented process as its own child, these inherited environment variables can still be found in the instrumented application's memory. Querying them by means of `getenv` can therefore expose the underlying JIT engine.

Page Permissions and Code Patterns. A side effect of the JIT engine is the presence of pages that are marked simultaneously as readable, writeable, and executable. An attacker can use this knowledge to scan the address space for such pages (e.g. using `/proc/self/maps` on Linux). Knowing that `rwx` memory is not present in a particular binary this discrepancy reveals the presence of the JIT compiler' code cache.

Additionally, an attacker can scan the whole memory for mapped pages and compare names of memory mapped files with names related to the DBI framework (*e.g. pinbin* for Pin). Moreover, as the instrumented application and the analysis plugin share one address space, the full implementation of the instrumentation platform has to be present as well. For example, an attacker can search for specific code patterns such as the characteristic implementation of the transition between the instrumented application and the analysis plugin (`VMLeave`). This code sequence is distinctive because it saves the current VM context on the stack and restores the jitted application's registers, generating assembly code that can easily be recognized.

Another method revealing the JIT engine's presence relies on an egg-hunting approach: A simple loop might scan all pages for a unique 8-byte-pattern. Under normal circumstances, the pattern should be observed exactly once in the address space (the operand of the comparison). However, when executed in context of a DBI framework, the pattern emerges at least twice: Once in the original code and once in the code cache.

3.3 Summary

As one can see, an instrumented application can notice whether it is currently being executed in a DBI environment. By nature, JIT compilers cause a lot of noise which is not only hard to disguise but trying to do so introduces even more irregularities in the instrumented program execution (cf. [27]). It follows that, the requirement R4 (Stealthiness) which is essential for security applications such as malware analysis cannot be hold by DBI frameworks.

4 Isolation

After discussing detectability of DBI frameworks, the following section focuses on the methods and possibilities to escape from and consequently evade the instrumentation. In the original work describing Pin [21] in Sect. 3.3.1 the authors state that the instrumented application's code is never executed – instead it is translated (from machine instructions to the same kind of machine instructions) and executed together with the analysis plugin's procedures within a custom virtual environment (the Pin VM). All executed machine instructions reside in the VM (code cache) and the effect of any instruction cannot *escape* from the VM region. Like other VMs, the Pin framework manages the instrumented program's instruction pointer and translates each basic block of the original code lazily (*i.e.* when reached by the execution flow). Two properties make Pin subject to attacks compromising isolation: First, the VM may and will reuse already compiled code because of optimization benefits. Second, Pin does not employ any integrity checks of already translated instructions in the code cache. Therefore, we can alter already executed instructions in memory, as they (comfortably) reside on pages marked `rwx` by the instrumentation platform. Experimental evidence from Sect. 3 indicates that the code cache implemented by other DBI tools behaves in accordance with Pin's code cache. However, we target the DBI implementation of Pin on `x86-64` Linux in the following sections.

For this we distinguish two different attacker models, and describe an escaping mechanism suitable for each.

A1 Control of Code and Data. This is the most potent attacker. She can freely specify which code is executed in the instrumented application and is able to freely interact with the application while instrumented. In reality, such an attacker would craft a malicious binary in the hope that an analyst would execute the binary in a instrumentation platform.

A2 Control of only Data. This is the weaker of the two attacker models. In this case, an attacker only possesses copies of the instrumented application, instrumentation platform, analysis plugin, and all depending dynamic libraries. However, this attacker is also able to freely interact with the application containing memory corruption vulnerabilities while executed in an DBI framework. In practice this is the case when some binary hardening policy implemented using DBI gets attacked over the network.

While detectability always required an attacker of type **A1**, we show that it is possible for an attacker of type **A2** to escape from the instrumentation if the attacked program contains what is commonly referred to as a write-where-what vulnerability.

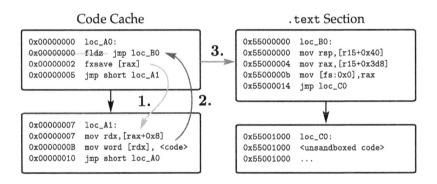

Fig. 1. A minimal program escaping from the Pin VM.

4.1   Escaping from Pin's Instrumentation Using Direct Code Cache Modification

First, we describe the escaping technique for the more potent attacker **A1** whose goal is to execute arbitrary code without Pin's instrumentation engine being able to embed callbacks notifying the analysis plugin. The existence of the just-in-time compilation allows us to first execute a basic block in order to allow the Pin VM to translate its assembly code and place its address in an internal hash table to find it later. Then the instrumented program can find the translated version of the basic block in the code cache (using the real instruction pointer detection techniques described in the previous section). It can then modify the jitted code arbitrarily. Once the execution flow reaches the modified basic block a second time, Pin will effectively execute whatever an attacker placed there. Figure 1 depicts the steps needed.

Prior to escaping from the VM, one first has to use any of the techniques to find the real `rip` value discussed in Sect. 3 (Block `loc_A0` in Fig. 1 showing the `ripfxsave` technique). As expected, Pin executes these instructions within its own code cache. As a result, at the end of block loc_A0, rax now points to the FPU context containing a pointer to the beginning of loc_A0. Then (step **1.**), execution is redirected to block loc_A1 using a jmp instruction, where an attacker places code that *patches out* the first instruction of loc_A0 and replaces it with a control flow change eventually reaching loc_B0 (step **2.**). Then, when the control flow reaches loc_A0 for the second time, the modified instructions placed there will be executed, now redirecting execution to block loc_B0 *residing in the original code* (step **3.**). As the code cache is mapped rwx, this does not trigger any page fault, hence the instrumentation engine does not get notified of the breach happening in the VM. To maintain ABI compatibility to arbitrary code embedded into the malicious executable, block loc_B0 needs to restore the rsp and fsbase registers, which, due to the code generation strategy of the JIT compiler are conveniently accessible via a structure pointed to by register r15. Now, execution can move on to any arbitrary code loc_C0 in the original executable prepared by the attacker – as all pages are mapped executable there is no mechanism allowing Pin to re-trigger the JIT compiler process to embed its instrumentation hooks. In fact, from Pin's perspective the application is still executed in the VM and awaits to regain control again, which never happens.

4.2 Escaping from Pin's Instrumentation Using an Existing Memory Corruption

As previously stated, it is also possible under certain circumstances to evade the instrumentation if only an attacker of type **A2** is present. Escaping the Pin sandbox in Linux without necessarily knowing any code cache address is also possible: We measured the relative offsets between all mapped pages in different executions of an application instrumented by Pin. As it can be seen in Fig. 3 (top right on page 18), the offset between libc and the code cache, as well as pinbin (main Pin binary) and Pin's own stack is constant. Leaking addresses from any of these code regions therefore allows us to reliably find the other mappings. Consequently, we can utilize all gadgets present in the code basis to build ROP chains, or directly write shellcode using a write-what-where vulnerability into the code cache. This is due to the fact that, as already explained, the Pin framework copies itself into the application's memory by allocating memory using mmap. As pointed out in earlier work [18], the addresses of consecutively allocated memory allocations returned by mmap are predictable (*i.e.* relative distances remain constant) in Linux. Thus, all required information can be calculated a priori based on known binaries of Pin, the analysis plugin, the instrumented application, and all dynamic link libraries (cf. Fig. 3 in the Appendix).

Since Pin does not monitor its code cache for external changes and does not restrict its execution to known memory locations, one can alter the instrumented processes memory in any suitable way. Moreover, the address of the code cache in the Linux version of Pin can be calculated by using any leaked address from other similarly created memory region. Therefore, if the binary contains a function that is executed twice and after its first invocation, a malicious user overwrites this function's instructions in the code cache, they are able to gain full control over the application. Unfortunately, such a function (`rtld_lock_default_lock`) is contained within the dynamic loader, a core component of the Linux OS.

5   Increased Attack Surface

Previously we have shown that DBI frameworks are both detectable and escapable rendering them as not suitable for binary hardening or malware analysis. In this section, we show how implementing security mechanisms enforced by executing a given COTS binary in a DBI environment even introduces more possibilities to exploit already present bugs (i.e. attack surface is *increased* instead of *decreased*). To support this claim we discuss an example where a vulnerability that is not trivial to exploit during normal execution *becomes exploitable* when executed within a DBI framework interacting with an attacker of type **A2**.

5.1   The Return of Aleph One

During the study of detectability properties of instrumentation platforms we already pointed out that they fail to check the permissions of the code that is to be processed by their JIT engines. This means *any* data in memory can (and will) be translated to executable instructions if reached by the control flow. This transfers us back to the dawn of buffer overflows and shellcode execution era. As a simple example we can run an application which jumps to shellcode on the stack. Normally, because of the set No-eXecute bit in the page tables of the stack, the program would crash as soon as the instruction pointer points to an address on the stack. However, instrumenting the same binary with Pin does not crash the application. In fact, the execution continues and opens a shell.

5.2   Turning CVE-2017-13089 to a Code Execution Bug with the Help of Intel Pin

To underline the exploitability claim, we have implemented a Proof Of Concept binary (*PwIN*) that exploits an existing CVE vulnerability (CVE-2017-13089, cf. [1]) that is not easily exploited when executed in a normal environment. CVE-2017-13089 is a bug in *wget* versions older than 1.19.2 found in `http.c:skip_short_body()`. The bug itself is described in more detail in the next section. Without Intel Pin the strongest attack (known to us) results in a $\frac{1}{16}$ probability of leaking an arbitrary file stored on the victim to the server (see below). We will discuss how the same bug can be escalated to full code execution if the victim is instrumented using Intel Pin.

Description of the Bug. The vulnerable function in *wget* is called when processing HTTP redirects together with HTTP chunked encoding. The chunk parser uses `strtol()` to parse each chunk's length into a variable of type `long`. Prior to copying a chunk's contents into a buffer on the stack, the code validates

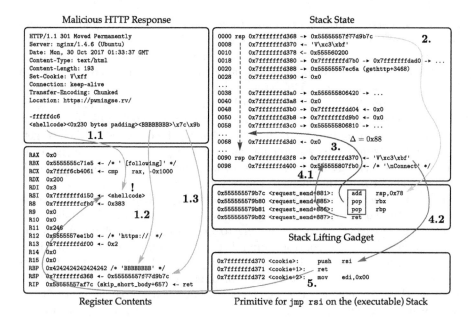

Fig. 2. Control flow and state changes of *wget* when attacked by a malicious server. The last control transfers (**4.2** in purple and **5.** in red) mark the transitions that are enabled by the usage of Pin. Under normal circumstances, the program would crash as the buffers on the stack containing the malicious shellcode would not be executable. (Color figure online)

that the chunk size specified in the HTTP request fits into the buffer, forgetting to ensure the supplied signed value is actually a *positive* number. The code then tries to skip the chunk in pieces of 512 bytes but ends passing a negative length to connect.c:fd_read(). Unfortunately, fd_read()'s length argument is of type int, thus the high 32 bits of the length variable are discarded. Therefore, values in the range 0xffffffff00000000 to 0xffffffffffffffff pass all checks while the truncation to a 32 bit value still allows an attacker to control the length of the read chunk and to overflow the dlbuf variable, a buffer of fixed size, on the stack.

Exploitation of the Bug. The bug allows for a continuous write of arbitrary data on the stack. Due to the absence of stack canaries, the saved return address on the stack can be compromised. However, without the knowledge of the current state of ASLR, there is not much an attacker can do, as she does not know any pointer pointing into valid memory (the binary is compiled as position independent executable). Consequently, the only remaining option to continue exploitation is a *partial pointer override*. With this technique, an attacker abuses the fact that ASLR operates at a page $(4096 = 2^{12}$ bytes) granularity. Therefore, the lowest 12 bits of any object within the address space are deterministic.

As a consequence, an attacker can now *trade* the number of ROP gadgets reachable by a `ret` for exploit reliability by overwriting parts of the saved return pointer on the stack. For example, a two-byte partial pointer overwrite needs to guess $2 \cdot 8 - 12 = 4$ bits of randomness, allowing to transfer control to a region sharing the same $2^{2 \cdot 8} = 65536$ bytes region with the original return address. Automatically evaluating all targets within this region using dynamic analysis does not unveil any target where an attacker could trivially obtain arbitrary code execution. The only noteworthy effect that can be observed is when targeting `body_file_send()`, as register allocation (cf. Fig. 2) matches the signature of this function with `rsi` pointing to attacker controlled data specifying a file name to transfer from the client to the server.

However, when running in context of Intel Pin we can inject and execute shellcode situated in non-executable memory regions, reducing the challenge of achieving code execution to *just* having to find a reliable mechanism to jump to a pointer to data we control. Our full exploit chain is visualized in Fig. 2: Fortunately, when reaching the end of the `skip_short_body()` function the `rsi` register (step **1.1**) contains the address of `dlbuf` (controlled by the attacker). However, there are no convenient gadgets reachable with a partial overwrite on the return address which may divert the code execution to the address contained in `rsi`. We remedy this by injecting our own `jmp rsi` gadget into a buffer that we can divert control to using the partial overwrite in step **1.3**. As expected, before reaching the return pointer on the stack, we inevitably have to load an invalid pointer to `rbp` register (step **1.2**) which fortunately, does not negatively influence our future actions. We can reach a stack lifting gadget with a partial overwrite (step **2.**) that increments the stack pointer by $\Delta = 0x88$ bytes (step **3.**). The new stack pointer location now points to a pointer to the *UTF-8* encoded value of the contents of the `Set-Cookie` header of the HTTP response. At this point the `ret` will transfer control to an attacker controlled buffer (steps **4.1** and **4.2**) but the UTF-8 encoding constrains the shellcode in an uncomfortable way. Luckily enough, the string `V\xff` is encoded to `V\xc3\xbf` which is perfectly valid UTF-8 *and* disassembles to `push rsi; ret` at the same time. As `rsi` still points to (now unconstrained) attacker controlled shellcode from the HTTP response body residing in `dlbuf`, this control transfer (step **5.**) is the last step in achieving code execution. This attack succeeds with a probability of $\frac{1}{16}$, due to the partial pointer override used in the first step.

6   Discussion

We conclude this work by inviting other researchers to reproduce our findings, discussing limitations and future improvements.

6.1   Reproducibility and Source Code Availability

In the spirit of open research and to enable others to reproduce our findings, we publish the source code of all the experiments conducted in context of this work. A Docker container is available via download at https://kirschju.re/pwin.

6.2 Limitations and Future Work

There are some known limitations associated with the proposed methodologies. First, the detect mechanism can be avoided by extending DBI frameworks. However, we already discussed that the JIT compiler introduces a lot of noise in the normal execution of the application, constantly turning up new possibilities to detect irregularities. Secondly, to escape the DBI sandbox, the application has to execute a function at least twice and simultaneously know its address in the code cache. Moreover, it needs to alter this function in the code cache before its last execution. Additionally, to escape DBI without knowing exactly the address of a function executed at least twice, requires calculation of the necessary memory locations. This is only possible, since the offset between pages created by mmap is constant [18]. However, the attacker has to possess copies of the instrumented application, instrumentation platform, analysis plugin, and all depending dynamic libraries because they all reside in the code cache and influence the fixed offsets between memory regions.

The research presented in this work discussed in detail the disadvantages of utilizing DBI engines in the security domain. The most fundamental problem is that DBI logic and application reside in the same address space, with no isolation present. The question remains how Intel Pin and other DBI frameworks can mitigate this problem in the future and how these techniques would influence our research. A possible mitigation strategy might introduce Intel Memory Protection Keys to change memory access permissions from user space without sacrificing performance.

6.3 Conclusion

In this paper, we showed that DBI frameworks are commonly used in a context of security, both as an analysis platform, as well as a hardening tool. Thus we systematically discussed the requirements for DBI frameworks to be used within such a context. We showed, that DBI is not able to hold these requirements in practice. We demonstrate, that the stealthiness requirement does not hold in practice by enumerating different inherent techniques to detect DBI. In addition, we also attested that DBI does not sufficiently isolate instrumented applications from the instrumentation framework, which provides a possibility for instrumented applications to gain arbitrary code execution on the analysis system. Finally, we argue, that instead of *increasing* security by introducing DBI based software hardening measures, DBI actually *decreases* the overall security by escalating an otherwise hard-to-exploit real world bugs into to full code execution. To support our claim, we implemented a couple of Proof Of Concepts to support our claims, which we are happy to freely share with the community.

A   Appendix

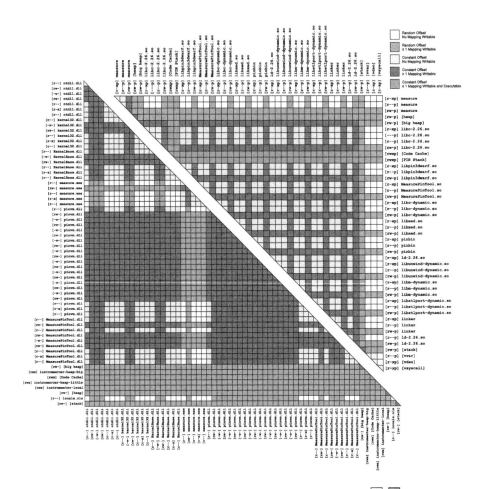

Fig. 3. Color matrices showing **memory regions** sharing random (☐/■) or constant (☐/■ /■) **distances** with each other for applications instrumented by Linux (above right) and Windows (down left) version of Pin. The region names in **red** are additional components added by the instrumentation framework while in **black** are presented the program's original mapped files. (Color figure online)

References

1. CVE-2014-0160. Available from MITRE, CVE-2017-13089. https://cve.mitre.org/cgi-bin/cvename.cgi?name=CVE-2017-13089. Accessed 24 Apr 2018
2. QuarkslaB Dynamic binary Instrumentation (QBDI). https://qbdi.quarkslab.com/. Accessed 24 Apr 2018
3. Abadi, M., Budiu, M., Erlingsson, Ú., Ligatti, J.: Control-flow integrity principles, implementations, and applications. ACM Trans. Inf. Syst. Secur. **13**, 4:1–4:40 (2009)
4. Banescu, S., Wüchner, T., Guggenmos, M., Ochoa, M., Pretschner, A.: FEEBO: an empirical evaluation framework for malware behavior obfuscation. arXiv preprint arXiv:1502.03245 (2015)
5. Bruening, D., Duesterwald, E., Amarasinghe, S.: Design and implementation of a dynamic optimization framework for windows. In: 4th ACM Workshop on Feedback-Directed and Dynamic Optimization (FDDO-4) (2001)
6. Bruening, D., Garnett, T., Amarasinghe, S.: An infrastructure for adaptive dynamic optimization. In: International Symposium on Code Generation and Optimization, CGO 2003, pp. 265–275. IEEE (2003)
7. Bruening, D., Zhao, Q.: Practical memory checking with Dr. Memory. In: Proceedings of the 9th Annual IEEE/ACM International Symposium on Code Generation and Optimization, pp. 213–223. IEEE Computer Society (2011)
8. Chiueh, T.c., Hsu, F.H.: RAD: a compile-time solution to buffer overflow attacks. In: 21st International Conference on Distributed Computing Systems, pp. 409–417. IEEE (2001)
9. Clause, J., Li, W., Orso, A.: Dytan: a generic dynamic taint analysis framework. In: Proceedings of the 2007 International Symposium on Software Testing and Analysis, pp. 196–206. ACM (2007)
10. Davi, L., Sadeghi, A.R., Winandy, M.: ROPdefender: a detection tool to defend against return-oriented programming attacks. In: ASIACCS (2011)
11. Elsabagh, M., Barbará, D., Fleck, D., Stavrou, A.: Detecting ROP with statistical learning of program characteristics. In: Proceedings of the Seventh ACM on Conference on Data and Application Security and Privacy, pp. 219–226. ACM (2017)
12. Falcón, F., Riva, N.: Dynamic binary instrumentation frameworks: i know you're there spying on me. In: RECon 2012 (2012). https://recon.cx/2012/schedule/attachments/42_FalconRiva_2012.pdf. Accessed 25 Apr 2018
13. Follner, A., Bodden, E.: ROPocop - dynamic mitigation of code-reuse attacks. J. Inf. Secur. Appl. **29**, 16–26 (2016)
14. Garfinkel, T., Rosenblum, M., et al.: A virtual machine introspection based architecture for intrusion detection. In: NDSS, vol. 3, pp. 191–206 (2003)
15. Gröbert, F., Willems, C., Holz, T.: Automated identification of cryptographic primitives in binary programs. In: Sommer, R., Balzarotti, D., Maier, G. (eds.) RAID 2011. LNCS, vol. 6961, pp. 41–60. Springer, Heidelberg (2011). https://doi.org/10.1007/978-3-642-23644-0_3
16. Intel Corporation: Intel® 64 and IA-32 Architectures Software Developer's Manual, January 2018
17. Kiriansky, V., Bruening, D., Amarasinghe, S.P.: Secure execution via program shepherding. In: Proceedings of the 11th USENIX Security Symposium, pp. 191–206. USENIX Association, Berkeley (2002)
18. Kirsch, J., Bierbaumer, B., Kittel, T., Eckert, C.: Dynamic loader oriented programming on Linux. In: ROOTS (2017)

19. Kulakov, Y.: MazeWalker - enriching static malware analysis. In: RECon 2017 (2017). https://recon.cx/2017/montreal/resources/slides/RECON-MTL-2017-MazeWalker.pdf. Accessed 25 Apr 2018
20. Lengyel, T.K., Maresca, S., Payne, B.D., Webster, G.D., Vogl, S., Kiayias, A.: Scalability, fidelity and stealth in the DRAKVUF dynamic malware analysis system. In: Proceedings of the 30th Annual Computer Security Applications Conference, pp. 386–395. ACM (2014)
21. Luk, C.K., et al.: Pin: building customized program analysis tools with dynamic instrumentation. In: ACM Sigplan Notices, vol. 40, pp. 190–200. ACM (2005)
22. Nethercote, N., Seward, J.: How to shadow every byte of memory used by a program. In: VEE (2007)
23. Nethercote, N., Seward, J.: Valgrind: a framework for heavyweight dynamic binary instrumentation. In: ACM Sigplan Notices, vol. 42, pp. 89–100. ACM (2007)
24. Nethercote, N., Walsh, R., Fitzhardinge, J.: Building workload characterization tools with Valgrind. In: IISWC (2006)
25. One, A.: Smashing the stack for fun and profit. In: Phrack 49 (1996)
26. Orman, H.: The Morris worm: a fifteen-year perspective. IEEE Secur. Priv. **99**(5), 35–43 (2003)
27. Polino, M., et al.: Measuring and defeating anti-instrumentation-equipped malware. In: Polychronakis, M., Meier, M. (eds.) DIMVA 2017. LNCS, vol. 10327, pp. 73–96. Springer, Cham (2017). https://doi.org/10.1007/978-3-319-60876-1_4
28. Qiang, W., Huang, Y., Zou, D., Jin, H., Wang, S., Sun, G.: Fully context-sensitive CFI for COTS binaries. In: Pieprzyk, J., Suriadi, S. (eds.) ACISP 2017. LNCS, vol. 10343, pp. 435–442. Springer, Cham (2017). https://doi.org/10.1007/978-3-319-59870-3_28
29. Quynh, N.A.: Skorpio: advanced binary instrumentation framework. In: OPCDE 2018, Dubai, April 2018
30. Saudel, F., Salwan, J.: Triton: a dynamic symbolic execution framework. In: Symposium sur la sécurité des technologies de l'information et des communications, SSTIC, France, Rennes, 3–5 June 2015, pp. 31–54. SSTIC (2015)
31. Tymburibá, M., Emilio, R., Pereira, F.: RipRop: a dynamic detector of ROP attacks. In: Proceedings of the 2015 Brazilian Congress on Software: Theory and Practice, p. 2 (2015)
32. van der Veen, V., et al.: Practical context-sensitive CFI. In: Proceedings of the 22nd ACM SIGSAC Conference on Computer and Communications Security, pp. 927–940. ACM (2015)
33. Vendicator, S.S.: A Stack Smashing Technique Protection Tool for Linux (2000). http://www.angelfire.com/sk/stackshield/info.html. Accessed 24 Apr 2018

Protocol Security

POR for Security Protocol Equivalences
Beyond Action-Determinism

David Baelde[1], Stéphanie Delaune[2(✉)], and Lucca Hirschi[3]

[1] LSV, ENS Paris-Saclay & CNRS, Inria, Université Paris-Saclay, Cachan, France
[2] Univ Rennes, CNRS, IRISA, Rennes, France
stephanie.delaune@irisa.fr
[3] Department of Computer Science, ETH Zurich, Zurich, Switzerland

Abstract. Formal methods have proved effective to automatically analyse protocols. Recently, much research has focused on verifying *trace equivalence* on protocols, which is notably used to model interesting *privacy* properties such as anonymity or unlinkability. Several tools for checking trace equivalence rely on a naive and expensive exploration of all interleavings of concurrent actions, which calls for partial-order reduction (POR) techniques. In this paper, we present the first POR technique for protocol equivalences that does not rely on an action-determinism assumption: we recast trace equivalence as a reachability problem, to which persistent and sleep set techniques can be applied, and we show how to effectively apply these results in the context of symbolic execution. We report on a prototype implementation, improving the tool DeepSec.

1 Introduction

Security protocols are notoriously difficult to design and their flaws can have a huge impact. Leaving aside implementation flaws and weaknesses of cryptographic primitives, there is already a long history of logical mistakes in the basic design of protocols, *e.g.*, [4,5,13,30]. At this level of detail, protocols can however be represented in the so-called symbolic model, which makes them amenable to automated formal verification. This approach has lead to mature tools and industrial successes, *e.g.*, [6,15,31].

Verification techniques have focused at first on reachability properties of protocols, used to model, *e.g.*, secrecy or authentication. More recently, equivalence properties have received a lot of attention, as they are often necessary to model privacy properties such as ballot secrecy in e-voting [25], anonymity or unlinkability [4,16]. Equivalence verification is complex, and each of the various state-of-the-art techniques has its own limitations. Tools for verifying scenarios with

This work has been partially supported by the European Research Council (ERC) under the European Union's Horizon 2020 research and innovation program (grant agreement No 714955-POPSTAR), as well as from the French National Research Agency (ANR) under the project TECAP.

© Springer Nature Switzerland AG 2018
J. Lopez et al. (Eds.): ESORICS 2018, LNCS 11098, pp. 385–405, 2018.
https://doi.org/10.1007/978-3-319-99073-6_19

an unbounded number of sessions such as Proverif [15] or Tamarin [14] are usually efficient but only support a constrained form of equivalence, namely *diff-equivalence*, which is too limiting, *e.g.*, to model unlinkability [29]. Many tools for verifying bounded scenarios rely on symbolic execution [24]. For instance, Apte [18] and its successor DeepSec [21] implement an algorithm that explores all symbolic executions, maintaining pairs of sets of symbolic states and solving at each step complex equality, deducibility and indistinguishability constraints. Akiss [17] follows a different approach, enumerating all symbolic executions to check that none yields a non-equivalence witness. The strength of these tools is that they decide *trace equivalence*, which can adequately capture *e.g.*, unlinkability. However, their algorithms are very costly and, despite recent progress, it is still only possible to analyse small scenarios in a reasonable amount of time.

All the techniques mentioned above for deciding trace equivalence of security protocols rely on an enumeration of all symbolic executions including all interleavings of concurrent actions. This is obviously a cause of major inefficiency, which has lead to a quest for *partial-order reduction* (POR) techniques. These techniques, which have a long and successful history in traditional software verification [11,28,33], generally consist in leveraging action independencies to restrict the interleavings that a model-checking algorithm explores. In the context of verifying reachability properties for security protocols, some specific POR techniques have sometimes had to be devised [22,32], but there have also been successful uses of generic POR techniques such as *sleep sets* [23] (see [9] for a detailed discussion). In the context of verifying *trace equivalence* for security protocols, the only available POR techniques are, to the best of our knowledge, the ones we proposed in [8,9]. These *ad hoc* techniques have lead to significant performance gains in Apte and DeepSec [9,21]. However, they crucially rely on an *action-determinism* assumption (*i.e.*, once the observable trace is fixed, the system is deterministic) which is in practice limiting. For instance, there is no precise modeling of unlinkability involving action-deterministic systems.

In this paper, we present the first POR technique for checking trace equivalence on security protocols, without any action-determinism assumption. Our first step towards this goal is to recast the trace equivalence problem as a reachability problem in a carefully designed labeled transition system (LTS), to which we can then apply persistent and sleep set techniques. However, this result is not directly useful in practice, for several reasons. First, this LTS is infinitely branching, due to the arbitrary choices that the attacker can make when interacting with the protocol. This is the main issue addressed in protocol equivalence checkers, typically through symbolic execution. Second, determining when two actions are independent (the first ingredient of POR techniques) is far from obvious in our LTS. Independencies are often approximated through simple static checks in practical POR algorithms [28] but, as we shall see, it does not seem feasible in our setting without losing too many independencies. Instead, we determine independencies by exploring symbolic executions. We ignore constraint solving in that process, as it would be too expensive: this trade-off allows us to detect enough independencies at a reasonable cost. More generally, we show how to compute persistent sets in the same style, to eventually obtain a symbolic form of the sleep set technique. Third, the direct symbolic approach would still be overly expensive, due to another typical state explosion problem caused by conditionals [12]. We circumvent it by showing that conditionals can be simplified, and often eliminated, in a way that does not affect persistent set computations. This approach yields a POR technique that is fast enough and allows to significantly reduce the number of symbolic traces to consider when checking trace equivalence. It is also independent of the specific verification algorithms that will be used to check equivalence along the reduced set of traces. We implemented the technique as a library to validate it experimentally.

Outline. We present a standard security protocol model in Sect. 2. After recalling persistent and sleep set techniques in Sect. 3, we design in Sect. 4 our concrete equivalence LTS to which they apply. Section 5 then defines a symbolic abstraction of this LTS, and shows how it can be used to obtain effective POR algorithms, notably through the collapse of conditionals. Finally, we present our implementations and experimental results in Sect. 6. Detailed proofs of all our results are available in [10].

2   Model for Security Protocols

We model security protocols in a variant of the applied pi-calculus [1]: processes exchange messages represented by terms quotiented by an equational theory.

2.1   Syntax

We assume a number of disjoint and infinite sets: a set Ch of channels, denoted by c or d; a set $\mathcal{N}$ of *names*, denoted by n or k; a set $\mathcal{X}$ of *variables*, denoted by x or y; and a set $\mathcal{W}$ of *handles* of the form $w_{c,i}$ with $c \in Ch$ and $i \in \mathbb{N}$, which will be used for referring to previously output terms. Next, we consider a *signature* Σ consisting of a set of function symbols together with their arity. Terms over a set of atomic data A, written $\mathcal{T}(A)$, are inductively generated from A and function symbols from Σ. When $A \subseteq \mathcal{N}$, elements of $\mathcal{T}(A)$ are called *messages* and written m. When $A \subseteq \mathcal{W}$, they are called *recipes* and written M, N. Intuitively, recipes express how a message has been derived by the environment (attacker) from the messages obtained so far. Finally, we consider an equational theory E over terms to assign a meaning to function symbols in Σ.

Protocols are then modelled through *processes* using the following grammar:

$$P, Q := 0 \mid \mathsf{in}(c,x).P \mid \mathsf{out}(c,u).P \mid \mathsf{if}\ u = v\ \mathsf{then}\ P\ \mathsf{else}\ Q \mid (P \mid Q) \mid P + Q$$

where $c \in Ch$, $u, v \in \mathcal{T}(\mathcal{N} \uplus \mathcal{X})$ and $x \in \mathcal{X}$. The process 0 does nothing. The process $\mathsf{in}(c,x).P$ expects a message m on the public channel c, and then behaves like $P\{x \mapsto m\}$, *i.e.*, P in which x has been replaced by m. The process $\mathsf{out}(c,u).P$ outputs u on the public channel c, and then behaves like P. We have constructions to perform tests (modulo E), parallel composition, and non-deterministic choice. We do not consider replication, and thus we do not need a specific "new" operation: we assume that names are implicitly freshly generated.

Example 1. We consider $\Sigma_{enc} = \{enc, dec, mac, \langle\ \rangle, proj_1, proj_2, nonce_{err}, mac_{err}\}$. The symbols enc, dec, and mac of arity 2 represent encryption, decryption and message authentication code; concatenation of messages is modelled through the symbol $\langle\ \rangle$ of arity 2, with projection functions $proj_1$ and $proj_2$ of arity 1. The function symbols $nonce_{err}$ and mac_{err} are constants (arity 0) that are used to model error messages. Then, we reflect the properties of the cryptographic primitives through the equational theory induced by the following equations:

$$dec(enc(x, y), y) = x, \quad proj_1(\langle x, y\rangle) = x,, \text{ and } proj_2(\langle x, y\rangle) = y.$$

We consider the BAC protocol used in e-passports which aims at establishing a fresh session key derived from k_P and k_R. Informally, we have:

1. $P \to R : n_P$
2. $R \to P : enc(\langle n_R, \langle n_P, k_R\rangle\rangle, k_E), mac(enc(\langle n_R, \langle n_P, k_R\rangle\rangle, k_E), k_M)$
3. $P \to R : enc(\langle n_P, \langle n_R, k_P\rangle\rangle, k_E), mac(enc(\langle n_P, \langle n_R, k_P\rangle\rangle, k_E), k_M)$

The keys k_E and k_M are long term keys shared between the passport P and the reader R. First, P sends a fresh random number n_P to the reader, and the reader answers to this challenge by generating its own nonce n_P, as well as k_R to contribute to a fresh session key. This encryption together with a mac is sent to the passport. The passport will then check the mac, decrypt the ciphertext and verify whether the nonce inside corresponds to the nonce n_P generated at the first step. In case decryption fails or the nonce inside the message is not the expected one, an error message will be sent. Otherwise, a message is sent to the reader. After checking that the message is the expected one, both entities are able to compute the fresh session key derived form k_R and k_P. In our syntax, we model the role of the passport as follows:

$$
\begin{aligned}
P(k_E, k_M) = \ &out(c, n_P).in(c, x).\\
&\text{if } mac(proj_1(x), k_M) = proj_2(x)\\
&\text{then if } proj_1(proj_2(dec(proj_1(x), k_E))) = n_P\\
&\qquad \text{then } out(c, \langle m_P, mac(m_P, k_M)\rangle).0\\
&\qquad \text{else } out(c, nonce_{err}).0\\
&\text{else } out(c, mac_{err}).0
\end{aligned}
$$

where $m_P = enc(\langle n_P, \langle proj_1(dec(proj_1(x), k_E)), k_P\rangle\rangle, k_E)$.

2.2   Semantics

A *configuration* $\mathcal{K}$ is a pair $(\mathcal{P}; \phi)$ where: $\mathcal{P}$ is either a multiset of processes with no free variable, or a special object $\perp_i$ with $i \in \mathbb{N}$; and $\phi = \{w_i \triangleright m_i\}_{1 \leq i \leq n}$ is a *frame*, i.e., a substitution of *domain* $dom(\phi) = \{w_1, \ldots, w_n\} \subseteq \mathcal{W}$ such that the m_i are messages. Configurations $(\perp_i; \phi)$ are called *ghost configurations* dead at age i, and will only become useful in Sect. 4. Other configurations are said to be *alive*.

$$(\{\texttt{in}(c,x).Q\} \uplus \mathcal{P}; \phi) \xrightarrow{\texttt{in}(c,M)} (\{Q\{x \mapsto M\phi\}\} \uplus \mathcal{P}; \phi) \qquad \text{if } M \in \mathcal{T}(\text{dom}(\phi))$$

$$(\{\texttt{out}(c,u).Q\} \uplus \mathcal{P}; \phi) \xrightarrow{\texttt{out}(c,\texttt{w}_{c,i})} (\{Q\} \uplus \mathcal{P}; \phi \cup \{\texttt{w}_{c,i} \triangleright u\}) \quad \text{with } i = \#_c(\text{dom}(\phi))$$

$$(\{\texttt{if } u = v \texttt{ then } Q_1 \texttt{ else } Q_2\} \uplus \mathcal{P}; \phi) \xrightarrow{\tau} (\{Q_1\} \uplus \mathcal{P}; \phi) \qquad \text{if } u =_{\mathsf{E}} v$$

$$(\{\texttt{if } u = v \texttt{ then } Q_1 \texttt{ else } Q_2\} \uplus \mathcal{P}; \phi) \xrightarrow{\tau} (\{Q_2\} \uplus \mathcal{P}; \phi) \qquad \text{if } u \neq_{\mathsf{E}} v$$

$$(\{Q_1 + Q_2\} \uplus \mathcal{P}; \phi) \xrightarrow{\tau} (\{Q_1\} \uplus \mathcal{P}; \phi) \qquad (\{Q_1 + Q_2\} \uplus \mathcal{P}; \phi) \xrightarrow{\tau} (\{Q_2\} \uplus \mathcal{P}; \phi)$$

$$(\{Q_1 \mid Q_2\} \uplus \mathcal{P}; \phi) \xrightarrow{\tau} (\{Q_1, Q_2\} \uplus \mathcal{P}; \phi) \qquad (\{0\} \uplus \mathcal{P}; \phi) \xrightarrow{\tau} (\mathcal{P}; \phi)$$

Fig. 1. Operational semantics of processes

The operational semantics is given as an LTS on (alive) configurations, with the relation $\xrightarrow{\alpha}$ defined in Fig. 1. There, the index of the next output to be performed on channel c is defined as

$$\#_c(\text{dom}(\phi)) = \max(\{0\} \cup \{j + 1 \mid \texttt{w}_{c,j} \in \text{dom}(\phi)\}).$$

A process may input a term that an attacker built using the knowledge available to him through the frame, where messages output by the protocol are added. The output rule slightly differs from the standard one, which would use a fresh handle variable. Our use of fixed constants $\texttt{w}_{c,i}$ makes it possible to view the transition system as a standard LTS, without any notion of freshness or α-renaming. Anticipating on the next sections where we build on top of this a different LTS encoding trace equivalence, we note that this design choice does not create spurious dependencies. We do not model internal communications, assuming instead that the attacker controls all communications (all channels are public). The last rules evaluate conditionals (modulo E), break parallel operators, remove null processes, and perform non-deterministic choices.

The relation $\mathcal{K} \xrightarrow{\alpha_1 \cdots \alpha_k} \mathcal{K}'$ between configurations, where $k \geq 0$ and each α_i is an observable or a τ action, is defined in the usual way. Given a sequence tr of actions, we denote obs(tr) the sequence of actions obtained by erasing τ actions.

Example 2. Let $\mathcal{K}_{\mathsf{same}} = (P(k_E, k_M); \phi_0)$ with $\phi_0 = \{\texttt{w}_{c',0} \triangleright \langle m'_R, \text{mac}(m'_R, k_M) \rangle\}$ and $m'_R = \text{enc}(\langle n'_R, \langle n'_P, k'_R \rangle \rangle, k_E)$. Intuitively, the configuration $\mathcal{K}_{\mathsf{same}}$ represents a situation where the attacker initially knows part of a past transcript (*i.e.*, ϕ_0) of the passport under consideration (*i.e.*, $P(k_E, k_M)$). We have that

$$\mathcal{K}_{\mathsf{same}} \xrightarrow{\texttt{out}(c,\texttt{w}_{c,0}).\texttt{in}(c,\texttt{w}_{c',0}).\tau.\tau.\texttt{out}(c,\texttt{w}_{c,1})} (0; \phi_0 \uplus \{\texttt{w}_{c,0} \triangleright n_P; \texttt{w}_{c,1} \triangleright \text{nonce}_{\mathsf{err}}\}).$$

2.3 Equivalences

Many privacy-type properties (*e.g.*, ballot privacy in e-voting, unlinkability) are modelled relying on trace equivalence. In our setting, this behavioural equivalence relies on a notion of static equivalence that captures indistinguishable sequences of messages.

Definition 1. *Two frames ϕ and ψ are in* static equivalence, *$\phi \sim_s \psi$, when* $\mathrm{dom}(\phi) = \mathrm{dom}(\psi)$*, and $M\phi =_\mathsf{E} N\phi$ iff $M\psi =_\mathsf{E} N\psi$ for any $M, N \in \mathcal{T}(\mathrm{dom}(\phi))$.*

This equivalence is then lifted from sequences of messages to configuration.

Definition 2. *Let $\mathcal{K}_P = (\mathcal{P}; \phi)$ and $\mathcal{K}_Q = (\mathcal{Q}; \psi)$ be two configurations with* $\mathrm{dom}(\phi) = \mathrm{dom}(\psi)$*. We write $\mathcal{K}_P \sqsubseteq_t \mathcal{K}_Q$ if for every execution $\mathcal{K}_P \xrightarrow{\mathsf{tr}_1} (\mathcal{P}'; \phi')$, there exists tr_2 and $(\mathcal{Q}'; \psi')$ such that $\mathcal{K}_Q \xrightarrow{\mathsf{tr}_2} (\mathcal{Q}'; \psi')$, $\mathsf{obs}(\mathsf{tr}_1) = \mathsf{obs}(\mathsf{tr}_2)$ and* $\phi' \sim_s \psi'$*. Then, $\mathcal{K}_P \approx_t \mathcal{K}_Q$, if $\mathcal{K}_P \sqsubseteq_t \mathcal{K}_Q$ and $\mathcal{K}_Q \sqsubseteq_t \mathcal{K}_P$.*

Example 3. Consider the configuration $\mathcal{K}_{\mathsf{diff}} = (P(k'_E, k'_M); \phi_0)$ which models the fact that the attacker is now in presence of an other passport that the one that produced ϕ_0. We have that $\mathcal{K}_{\mathsf{same}} \not\sqsubseteq_t \mathcal{K}_{\mathsf{diff}}$, which means that the attacker is able to detect the presence of a passport for which he has partial knowledge of a past session (*i.e.*, ϕ_0). To see this, consider the trace from Example 2. It is possible to produce the same trace starting from $\mathcal{K}_{\mathsf{diff}}$, but the resulting frame is then $\phi' = \phi_0 \uplus \{\mathsf{w}_{c,0} \triangleright n_P; \mathsf{w}_{c,1} \triangleright \mathsf{mac}_{\mathsf{err}}\}$ which does not satisfy the test $\mathsf{w}_{c,1} = \mathsf{nonce}_{\mathsf{err}}$ contrary to the frame produced starting from $\mathcal{K}_{\mathsf{same}}$. This corresponds to a well-known unlinkability attack discovered in [4] on French passports. This attack can be easily fixed by using the same error message in both cases. In such a case, the inclusion holds. This is a non trivial inclusion that can be automatically established by the DeepSec verification tool.

For illustrative purposes, we have only considered here a simple scenario for which configurations under study are actually action-deterministic, *i.e.*, where for any s and α there is at most one s' such that $s \xrightarrow{\alpha} s'$. In practice, we want to consider more complex scenarios involving several passports and readers, which results in configurations that are *not* action-deterministic: several passports can output on the same channel at the same time. In particular, unlinkability is expressed as an equivalence between processes that are not action-deterministic [4]. When considering unlinkability, we also note that using *diff-equivalence* instead of trace equivalence, as is done in Tamarin and Proverif when checking equivalences for unbounded sessions, systematically leads to false attacks [29]. For such properties, one thus has to resort to verifying trace equivalence in the bounded setting. However, the lack of POR techniques supporting non-action-deterministic processes is a major problem, since equivalence verification tools perform very poorly when the state explosion problem is left untamed.

3 Persistent and Sleep Sets in a Nutshell

We review the key concepts of persistent and sleep sets, based on [28] but slightly reformulated. These general concepts apply to an action-deterministic LTS. We thus assume, in this section, a set of states Q, a set of actions T, and a partial transition function $\delta : Q \times T \to Q$. We write $s \xrightarrow{\alpha} s'$ when $s' = \delta(s, \alpha)$. We say that α is *enabled* in state s if there exists an s' such that $s' = \delta(s, \alpha)$. The set of enabled actions in s is written $E(s)$. A state s is *final* when $E(s) = \emptyset$.

Definition 3. *Independence is the greatest relation $\leftrightarrow \subseteq T \times Q \times T$ that is symmetric, irreflexive and such that, for all $(\alpha, s, \beta) \in \leftrightarrow$ (written $\alpha \leftrightarrow_s \beta$):*

- *if $s \xrightarrow{\alpha} s'$ then $\beta \in E(s)$ iff $\beta \in E(s')$;*
- *if $s \xrightarrow{\alpha} s_1$ and $s \xrightarrow{\beta} s_2$, then $s_1 \xrightarrow{\beta} s'$ and $s_2 \xrightarrow{\alpha} s'$ for some s'.*

Persistent Sets. A set $T \subseteq E(s)$ is *persistent in s* if, for all non-empty sequences of actions $s = s_0 \xrightarrow{\alpha_0} s_1 \dots s_n \xrightarrow{\alpha_n} s_{n+1}$ such that $\alpha_i \notin T$ for all $0 \leq i \leq n$, we have that $\alpha_n \leftrightarrow_{s_n} \alpha$ for all $\alpha \in T$. We may note that $E(s)$ is persistent in s. In practice, persistent sets may be computed from *stubborn* sets (see [10]).

In the following, we assume a function $\mathsf{p_{set}} : Q \times T^* \to 2^T$ which associates to any state $s \in Q$ and any sequence w such that $s \xrightarrow{w} s'$ with $E(s') \neq \emptyset$, a non-empty set of actions $\mathsf{p_{set}}(s, w)$ which is persistent in s'.

A trace $s_0 \xrightarrow{\alpha_0} s_1 \dots \xrightarrow{\alpha_n} s_{n+1}$ is *persistent*, written $s_0 \xrightarrow{\alpha_0 \dots \alpha_n}_{\mathsf{p_{set}}} s_{n+1}$, if $\alpha_i \in \mathsf{p_{set}}(s_0, \alpha_0 \dots \alpha_{i-1})$ for all $0 \leq i \leq n$.

Proposition 1. *Let s' be a final state that is reachable from s. We have that s' is also reachable from s through a trace that is persistent.*

Sleep Sets. If a persistent set contains two independent actions, then the associated search has redundancies. This has lead to the introduction of sleep sets. This technique relies on an arbitrary ordering $<$ on actions. A sleep set execution is an execution $(s_0, \emptyset) = (s_0, z_0) \xrightarrow{\alpha_0} (s_1, z_1) \dots \xrightarrow{\alpha_n} (s_{n+1}, z_{n+1})$ with states in $Q \times 2^T$ such that $s_0 \xrightarrow{\alpha_0 \dots \alpha_n}_{\mathsf{p_{set}}} s_{n+1}$, and for any $0 \leq i \leq n$ we have $\alpha_i \notin z_i$ and $z_{i+1} = \{\beta \in z_i \mid \alpha_i \leftrightarrow_{s_i} \beta\} \cup \{\beta \in \mathsf{p_{set}}(s_0, \alpha_0 \dots \alpha_{i-1}) \mid \beta < \alpha_i, \ \alpha_i \leftrightarrow_{s_i} \beta\}$.

Proposition 2. *Let s' be a final state that is reachable from s (in the original LTS). We have that s' is also reachable from $(s, \emptyset)$ through a sleep set execution.*

4 Concrete LTS for Security Protocols

In order to apply the POR techniques of Sect. 3, we need to reformulate trace equivalence as a reachability property of final states in some LTS.

Given a set of handles $W \subseteq \mathcal{W}$, we define $\mathsf{Conf}(W)$ as the set of alive and *quiescent* configurations with a frame of domain W. An alive configuration $(\mathcal{P}; \phi)$ is quiescent if any $P \in \mathcal{P}$ is of the form $\mathsf{in}(c, x).P'$ or $\mathsf{out}(c, t).P'$ (in other words, no τ action can be triggered from it). We define the set of dead configurations over W as $\mathsf{Conf}_\perp(W) = \{(\perp_j; \phi) \mid \mathrm{dom}(\phi) \subseteq W \text{ and } j \in \mathbb{N}\}$.

We define our *trace equivalence LTS* as follows:

- States are of the form $\langle|\mathbb{A} \approx \mathbb{B}|\rangle$ where $\mathbb{A}, \mathbb{B} \subseteq \mathsf{Conf}(W) \cup \mathsf{Conf}_\perp(W)$ for some $W \subseteq \mathcal{W}$, and at least one configuration in $\mathbb{A} \cup \mathbb{B}$ is alive. The *domain* $\mathrm{dom}(s)$ of such a state is W, and its *age* is $\mathsf{age}(s) = \max(\{0\} \cup \{j+1 \mid (\perp_j, \phi) \in \mathbb{A} \cup \mathbb{B}\})$.
- Actions are of the form $\mathsf{out}(c, \mathsf{w}_{c,i})$ or $\mathsf{in}(c, M)$ with $c \in \mathcal{Ch}$, $i \in \mathbb{N}$, $M \in \mathcal{T}(\mathcal{W})$.
- The transition relation is given by

$$s = \langle|\mathbb{A} \approx \mathbb{B}|\rangle \xrightarrow{\alpha} \langle|\mathbb{A}_a \uplus \mathbb{A}_n \uplus \mathbb{A}_g \approx \mathbb{B}_a \uplus \mathbb{B}_n \uplus \mathbb{B}_g|\rangle$$

where $\mathbb{A}_g, \mathbb{A}_a, \mathbb{A}_n$ are given below (and $\mathbb{B}_g, \mathbb{B}_n$, and $\mathbb{B}_a$ are defined similarly):

- $\mathbb{A}_a = \{A' \mid \exists A \in \mathbb{A} \text{ such that } A \xmapsto{\alpha} A'' \xmapsto{\tau^*} A' \not\xmapsto{\tau}\}$,
- $\mathbb{A}_n = \{(\bot_{\mathsf{age}(s)}; \phi) \mid (\mathcal{P}; \phi) \in \mathbb{A}, (\mathcal{P}; \phi) \text{ is alive}, (\mathcal{P}; \phi) \not\xmapsto{\tau}\}$, and
- $\mathbb{A}_g = \mathbb{A} \cap \mathsf{Conf}_\bot(\mathsf{dom}(s))$.

The transitions gather all alternatives that can perform the same output (resp. input) action. Therefore, even if our protocol allows several alternatives for a given observable action, our resulting trace equivalence LTS is action-deterministic. Configurations that cannot execute such an action become ghosts. A ghost configuration $(\bot_i; \phi)$ is a configuration that cannot evolve anymore; its index i will crucially be used to know what other frames were present when it died (see Example 4).

Given a set of configurations $\mathbb{A}$, we define $\mathbb{A}^{\geq i}$ as the set of all configurations of $\mathbb{A}$ that are still alive at age i. More formally, we have that:

$$\mathbb{A}^{\geq i} = \{(\mathcal{P}, \phi) \in \mathbb{A} \mid (\mathcal{P}, \phi) \text{ is alive or } \mathcal{P} = \bot_j \text{ with } j \geq i\}$$

We write $\phi \sqsubseteq_s \psi$ when $\mathsf{dom}(\phi) \subseteq \mathsf{dom}(\psi)$ and both frames are in static equivalence on their common domain, i.e., $\phi \sim_s \psi|_{\mathsf{dom}(\phi)}$. We lift $\sqsubseteq_s$ to a set of frames (and thus configurations): $\phi \sqsubseteq_s \Psi$ when there exists $\psi \in \Psi$ such that $\phi \sqsubseteq_s \psi$.

Definition 4. *A state $s = \langle|\mathbb{A} \approx \mathbb{B}|\rangle$ is* left-bad *when there exists $(\mathcal{P}; \phi) \in \mathbb{A}$ such that:*
- *either $(\mathcal{P}; \phi)$ is a ghost, i.e., $\mathcal{P} = \bot_j$ for some j, and $\phi \not\sqsubseteq_s \mathbb{B}^{\geq j}$;*
- *or $(\mathcal{P}; \phi)$ is alive and $\phi \not\sqsubseteq_s (\mathbb{B} \cap \mathsf{Conf}(\mathsf{dom}(s)))$.*

The notion of being right-bad *is defined similarly, and we say that a state s is* bad *when it is right-bad or left-bad.*

We will see that trace inequivalence implies the existence of a bad state. Thanks to ghosts, this will directly imply the existence of a final bad state. Fundamentally, ghosts are there to avoid that partial-order reduction makes us miss a bad state by not exploring certain transitions. Of course, practical verification algorithms will never perform explorations past a state that corresponds to a inequivalence witness. Note, however, that detecting such states is only possible thanks to complex constraint solving, which we cannot afford in our symbolic POR algorithms. Hence, one important aspect in our design of ghosts is that they lift well to the "unsolved" symbolic setting.

Example 4. Ghosts are crucial to make sure that progressing in the LTS never kills a witness of inequivalence. For instance, consider the two processes:
$P_u = \mathsf{out}(c, u) + (\mathsf{out}(c, n).\mathsf{out}(d, n'))$ where $u \in \{\mathsf{a}, \mathsf{b}\}$ are two public constants. Consider $s_0 = \langle|(P_\mathsf{a}; \emptyset) \approx (P_\mathsf{b}; \emptyset)|\rangle$ and $s_0 \xrightarrow{\mathsf{out}(c, \mathsf{w}_{c,0})} s_1 \xrightarrow{\mathsf{out}(d, \mathsf{w}_{d,0})} s_2$ where:
- $s_1 = \langle|\{(0; \{\mathsf{w}_{c,0} \triangleright \mathsf{a}\}), A\} \approx \{(0; \{\mathsf{w}_{c,0} \triangleright \mathsf{b}\}), A\}|\rangle$
- $s_2 = \langle|\{(\bot_0; \{\mathsf{w}_{c,0} \triangleright \mathsf{a}\}), A'\} \approx \{(\bot_0; \{\mathsf{w}_{c,0} \triangleright \mathsf{b}\}), A'\}|\rangle$
- $A = (\mathsf{out}(d, n'); \{\mathsf{w}_{c,0} \triangleright n\})$, and $A' = (0; \{\mathsf{w}_{c,0} \triangleright n, \mathsf{w}_{d,0} \triangleright n'\})$.

Note that s_1 is bad because $\{\mathsf{w}_c^0 \triangleright \mathsf{a}\} \not\sim_s \{\mathsf{w}_c^0 \triangleright \mathsf{b}\}$ and s_2 is bad because the ghost configurations are not statically equivalent either. However, without the ghost configurations, s_2 would not be bad (neither left nor right).

Our first contribution is a result that reduces trace equivalence to reachability of a final bad state in our trace equivalence LTS, on which POR techniques can be applied.

Proposition 3. *Let A_0 and B_0 be two alive configurations of same domain, and $s_0 = \langle |A_0 \approx B_0| \rangle$ where $\mathbb{A}_0 = \{A \mid A_0 \xrightarrow{\tau}^* A \not\xrightarrow{\tau}\}$, and $\mathbb{B}_0 = \{B \mid B_0 \xrightarrow{\tau}^* B \not\xrightarrow{\tau}\}$. The following conditions are equivalent:*

1. *A_0 is trace included in B_0, i.e., $A_0 \sqsubseteq_t B_0$;*
2. *no left-bad state is reachable from s_0 in the trace-equivalence LTS;*
3. *no left-bad, final state is reachable from s_0 in the trace-equivalence LTS.*

5   POR in Symbolic Semantics

The POR techniques of Sect. 3 apply to the LTS of Sect. 4, but this is not directly usable in practice because our trace equivalence LTS is infinitely branching. Symbolic execution is typically used to circumvent such problems, both in traditional software verification [12] and security protocol analysis [19,20]. In this section, we define a symbolic abstraction of our trace equivalence LTS, and we show how it can be used to effectively apply the persistent and sleep set techniques.

5.1   Symbolic Equivalence LTS

As is common in symbolic semantics for security protocols [19,20], we rely on *second-order variables*, which will be instantiated by recipes, and *first-order variables*, which will be instantiated by messages. First-order variables are distinct from standard variables occurring in processes to represent input messages. More precisely, when an input is executed symbolically, the associated variable will be substituted by a first-order variable. As a result, standard variables will only occur bound in symbolic processes, while first-order variables will only occur free. Conversely, only first-order variables will be allowed to occur free in processes, frames, and states.

Second-order and first-order variables will respectively be of the form $X^{c,i}$ and $x_\phi^{c,i}$ where $c \in Ch$, $i \in \mathbb{N}$, and ϕ is a symbolic frame, *i.e.*, a frame whose terms may contain first-order variables. Intuitively, $X^{c,i}$ stands for the recipe used for the ith input on channel c, and $x_\phi^{c,i}$ will be instantiated by the message resulting from that recipe in the context of the frame ϕ. The use of variables with explicit c, i parameters avoids us to deal with freshness or α-renaming issues when implementing the symbolic analysis. We denote $vars^1(t)$ (resp. $vars^2(t)$) the first-order (resp. second-order) variable occurring in t. Finally, $vars(R)$ is the set of handles that occur in a recipe R. We say that a symbolic frame ϕ is *well-founded* if, whenever $\phi(\mathsf{w}_{c,i}) = t$ and $x_\psi^{d,j} \in vars^1(t)$, we have that ϕ is a strict extension of ψ meaning that $\phi|_{\mathrm{dom}(\psi)} = \psi$ (denoted $\psi \sqsubseteq \phi$), and $\psi \neq \phi$. This well-foundedness condition will obviously be preserved in symbolic executions: if t is the ith output on channel c, it may only depend on inputs received before that output, *i.e.*, at a time where the frame ψ does not contain $\mathsf{w}_{c,i}$. From now on, we impose that all frames are well-founded, which allows us to define the first-order substitution associated to a second-order substitution.

Definition 5 *(λ_θ). Let θ be a substitution mapping second-order variables to recipes. Its associated first-order substitution λ_θ is the unique substitution of (infinite) domain $\{x_\phi^{c,i} \mid vars(X^{c,i}\theta) \subseteq \mathrm{dom}(\phi)\}$ such that $\lambda_\theta(x_\phi^{c,i}) = (X^{c,i}\theta)(\phi\lambda_\theta)$, which can be defined by induction on the size of frame domains.*

We now define symbolic actions and states, and their concretisations. We take *symbolic actions* of the form $\mathsf{out}(c, \mathsf{w}_{c,i})$ and $\mathsf{in}(c, X^{c,i}, W)$, where $c \in \mathcal{C}h$, $i \in \mathbb{N}$ and $W \subseteq \mathcal{W}$. Given a substitution θ mapping second-order variables to recipes, we define the θ-concretisations of symbolic actions as follows: $\mathsf{out}(c, \mathsf{w}_{c,i})\theta = \mathsf{out}(c, \mathsf{w}_{c,i})$, and $\mathsf{in}(c, X^{c,i}, W)\theta = \mathsf{in}(c, R)$ when $X^{c,i}\theta = R \in \mathcal{T}(W)$. We will use constraints which are conjunctions of equations and disequations over (symbolic) terms, *i.e.*, terms that may contain first-order variables. The empty constraint is written $\top$, and conjunction is written $\wedge$ and considered modulo associativity-commutativity.

A *symbolic state* $S = \langle \mathbb{A} \approx \mathbb{B} \rangle_{\mathcal{C}}^I$ is formed from a mapping $I : \mathcal{C}h \to \mathbb{N}$ providing input numbers, a constraint $\mathcal{C}$, and two sets $\mathbb{A}$ and $\mathbb{B}$ of *symbolic configurations*, *i.e.*, configurations that may contain first-order variables. We further require that:

- there is at least one alive configurations in $\mathbb{A} \cup \mathbb{B}$;
- all alive configurations in $\mathbb{A} \cup \mathbb{B}$ share the same frame domain, noted $\mathrm{dom}(S)$;
- any ghost configuration in $\mathbb{A} \cup \mathbb{B}$ should have a domain $W \subseteq \mathrm{dom}(S)$;
- processes in configurations do not contain null processes, and do not feature top-level conditionals, parallel and choice operators.

With this in place, we define the solutions of $S = \langle \mathbb{A} \approx \mathbb{B} \rangle_{\mathcal{C}}^I$ as the set $\mathsf{Sol}(S)$ containing all the substitutions θ such that:

- $\mathrm{dom}(\theta) = \{X^{c,i} \mid i < I(c)\}$;
- for any $u = v$ (resp. $u \neq v$) in $\mathcal{C}$, $u\lambda_\theta =_{\mathsf{E}} v\lambda_\theta$ (resp. $u\lambda_\theta \neq_{\mathsf{E}} v\lambda_\theta$).

Given S and $\theta \in \mathsf{Sol}(S)$, we define its θ-concretisation $S\theta$ as $\langle |\mathbb{A}\lambda_\theta \approx \mathbb{B}\lambda_\theta| \rangle$.

Remark 1. Beyond the differences in formalism, our notion of solution is quite close to ones found, *e.g.*, in [19,20], with one difference: when no $x_\phi^{c,i}$ variable occurs in S, $\theta(X^{c,i})$ is completely unconstrained. This means that when an input variable is unused in the input's continuations, our solutions are incorrect wrt. the corresponding recipe. We do not need to worry about this mismatch, though, because we only need a symbolic semantics that covers all concrete executions; it does not need to be sound. In fact, our analysis will never rely on the existence of a solution for a given symbolic state. It will never check that a term is deducible, and will almost ignore (dis)equality constraints, only checking for immediate contradictions among them.

We can now define symbolic transitions, and establish their completeness.

Definition 6. *Consider a symbolic state $S = \langle \mathbb{A} \approx \mathbb{B} \rangle_{\mathcal{C}}^I$ and a symbolic action A, the possible transitions $S \xrightarrow{A} S'$ are defined by mimicking concrete transitions as follows:*

– *We first execute the action A, gathering all possible resulting configurations into a pre-state $S_A = \langle \mathbb{A}' \approx \mathbb{B}' \rangle_{\mathcal{C}}^{I'}$. To be possible, such a transition has to be of the form $A = \text{in}(c, X^{c,i}, W)$ with $i = I(c)$, or $A = \text{out}(c, w_{c,i})$ with $i = \#_c(\text{dom}(S))$. The resulting pre-state S_A is not a valid state because it may contain e.g., top-level conditionals, choice operators. This pre-state also includes ghosts $(\bot_n; \phi)$ of the configurations $(\mathcal{P}; \phi)$ of S that could not perform A, where $n = \text{age}(S)$ as defined in the concrete semantics. We define I' to coincide with I on all channels, except on c where $I'(c) = I(c) + 1$ when A is an input on c. When executing $A = \text{in}(c, X^{c,i}, W)$ in a configuration $(\mathcal{P}; \phi)$ of S that can perform an input on c, we use the term $X^{c,i}_{\phi|W}$ to substitute for the input variable.*

– *Then we declare $S \xrightarrow{A} S'$ if S' is a state that can be obtained from S_A by repeatedly performing the following operations, until none applies:*

  • *If a configuration features a top-level conditional, the conditional is replaced by one of its branches, and the constraints are enriched accordingly.*

  • *If a configuration features a top-level choice operator, it is replaced by the two configurations where the choices are made.*

  We also require that S' does not have an immediately contradicting constraint, i.e., a constraint containing an equation and its negation.

A perhaps surprising consequence of our definition is that, if $\text{in}(c, X^{c,i}, W)$ is enabled in S, then any $\text{in}(c, X^{c,i}, W')$ is also enabled. Allowing smaller domains is important for checking independencies. We also allow larger domains, possibly even larger than $\text{dom}(S)$, mainly because it simplifies the theory, at no cost in practice.

Example 5. Consider arbitrary terms t, u, and $v \neq v'$, and the symbolic state $S = \langle (\mathcal{P}; \psi) \approx (\mathcal{P}; \psi') \rangle_{\top}^{I}$ where $\mathcal{P} = \text{in}(c, x).\text{if } x = t \text{ then out}(c, \text{ok}) \text{ else } 0$,

$$\phi = \{ w_{c,0} \mapsto u \}, \quad \psi = \phi \uplus \{ w_{d,0} \mapsto v \} \text{ and } \psi' = \phi \uplus \{ w_{d,0} \mapsto v' \}.$$

We illustrate how the choice of W affects which transitions are possible from state S with action $A = \text{in}(c, X^{c,i}, W)$, where $i = I(c)$ is the only value that allows this action to execute, and I' coincides with I except on c for which $I'(c) = I(c) + 1$. If $W = \{ w_{c,0} \}$, then there are two possible transitions:

$$S \xrightarrow{A} \langle (\text{out}(c, \text{ok}); \psi) \approx (\text{out}(c, \text{ok}); \psi') \rangle_{X^{c,i}_{\phi} = t}^{I'} \qquad S \xrightarrow{A} \langle (0; \psi) \approx (0; \psi') \rangle_{X^{c,i}_{\phi} \neq t}^{I'}$$

If $W = \{ w_{c,0}, w_{d,0} \}$, four transitions are possible, notably including

$$S \xrightarrow{A} \langle (\text{out}(c, \text{ok}); \psi) \approx (0; \psi') \rangle_{X^{c,i}_{\psi} = t, \, X^{c,i}_{\psi'} \neq t}^{I'}.$$

Indeed, we are considering here an input whose recipe may exploit the different frames of our two configurations. It is a priori possible that the resulting message passes the test $x = t$ only in one configuration.

Remark 2. It may be useful to note that the following property is preserved by symbolic execution, though we do not exploit it: in a configuration $(\mathcal{P}; \phi)$ of a state $\langle \mathbb{A} \approx \mathbb{B} \rangle_{\mathcal{C}}^{I}$, the only first-order variables that appear are of the form $\mathsf{x}_{\psi}^{c,i}$ with $\psi \sqsubseteq \phi$ and $i < I(c)$.

Proposition 4. *Let $S = \langle \mathbb{A} \approx \mathbb{B} \rangle_{\mathcal{C}}^{I}$ be a symbolic state, $\theta \in \mathsf{Sol}(S)$. Let s' and α be such that $S\theta \xrightarrow{\alpha} s'$. There exists S', A and $\theta' \sqsupseteq \theta$ (i.e. $\theta'|_{\mathrm{dom}(\theta)} = \theta$) such that $S \xrightarrow{A} S'$, $\theta' \in \mathsf{Sol}(S')$, $\alpha = A\theta'$, and $s' = S'\theta'$. Moreover, if α is of the form $\mathsf{in}(c, R)$, the proposition holds with $A = \mathsf{in}(c, \mathsf{X}^{c, I(c)}, W)$ for any W such that $\mathrm{vars}(R) \subseteq W$.*

5.2   Independence Relations

We first define the *enabled symbolic independence* relation, and show that it is a sound abstraction of independence for enabled actions. For that, we assume here a notion of *incompatible* constraints. It can be anything as long as two constraints $\mathcal{C}$ and $\mathcal{C}'$ are only declared incompatible when $\mathcal{C} \wedge \mathcal{C}'$ is unsatisfiable. In practice, we only check for immediate contradictions, *i.e.*, the presence of an equation and its negation. This allows us to easily check $\Leftrightarrow^{ee}$ in the implementation.

Definition 7. *Given a symbolic state S, and two symbolic actions A and B enabled in S, we write $A \Leftrightarrow_{S}^{ee} B$ when:*

- *A and B are neither two inputs nor two outputs on the same channel;*
- *for any $S \xrightarrow{A} S_A$, $S \xrightarrow{B} S_B$, we have that $S_A \xrightarrow{B} S_{AB}$ and $S_B \xrightarrow{A} S_{BA}$ for some symbolic states S_{AB} and S_{BA};*
- *for any $S \xrightarrow{A} S_A \xrightarrow{B} S_{AB}$, and $S \xrightarrow{B} S_B \xrightarrow{A} S_{BA}$, we have that S_{AB} and S_{BA} have incompatible constraints, or $S_{AB} = S_{BA}$.*

We now turn to defining a sound abstraction of independence between a concretely disabled and enabled action. Intuitively, $A \Leftrightarrow_{S}^{de} B$ will guarantee that executing concretisations of B cannot enable new concretisations of A.

Definition 8. *Given a symbolic state S, as well as two symbolic actions A and B, we write $A \Leftrightarrow_{S}^{de} B$ when B is enabled in S, and*

- *either A is not enabled in S' for any S' such that $S \xrightarrow{B} S'$;*
- *or A is enabled in S but A/B are not of the form $\mathsf{in}(c, \mathsf{X}^{c,i}, W)/\mathsf{out}(d, \mathsf{w}_{d,j})$ with $\mathsf{w}_{d,j} \in W$.*

Proposition 5. *Let S be a symbolic state and A and B be two symbolic actions. Let $\theta \in \mathsf{Sol}(S)$, $s = S\theta$ and α (resp. β) be a concretisation of A (resp. B).*

- *If $A \Leftrightarrow_{S}^{ee} B$, and $\alpha, \beta \in E(s)$, then $\alpha \leftrightarrow_{s} \beta$.*
- *If $A \Leftrightarrow_{S}^{de} B$, $\alpha \notin E(s)$ and $\beta \in E(s)$, then $\alpha \leftrightarrow_{s} \beta$.*

Example 6. Let $\mathcal{P} = \mathsf{in}(c, x).\mathsf{out}(c, x) \mid \mathsf{out}(d, t)$, and $S = \langle\!\langle (\mathcal{P}; \emptyset) \approx (\mathcal{P}; \emptyset) \rangle\!\rangle_{\top}^{I_0}$ with $I_0(c) = 0$ for any $c \in Ch$. We have $\mathsf{in}(c, \mathsf{X}^{c,0}, \emptyset) \Leftrightarrow_{S}^{ee} \mathsf{out}(d, \mathsf{w}_{d,0})$: inputs and outputs commute, for inputs whose recipes rely on the currently available (empty) domain. We have $\mathsf{in}(c, \mathsf{X}^{c,0}, \emptyset) \Leftrightarrow_{S}^{de} \mathsf{out}(d, \mathsf{w}_{d,0})$ (the output does not enable new concretisations for the input) but *not* $\text{in}(c, X^{c,0}, \{w_{d,0}\}) \Leftrightarrow^{de}_S$ $\text{out}(d, w_{d,0})$ (the input is feasible, but performing it after the output would enable new concretisations).

5.3 Persistent Set Computation

Having defined over-approximations of transitions and dependencies, we now describe how to compute, for a state S, a set of actions $T^+(S)$ that yields a persistent set for any concretisation of S. More precisely, we shall compute stubborn sets (cf. [10]).

Our symbolic LTS is still infinitely branching, due to the absence of constraints on inputs domains W. However, when exploring the LTS, it often suffices to consider inputs with a canonical domain, *i.e.*, the domain of the current state. We formalise this by defining the *enabled cover* of a symbolic state S: $EC(S)$ is the set of all actions that are enabled in S, with the constraint that inputs are of the form $\text{in}(c, X^{c,i}, \text{dom}(S))$. Proposition 4 already ensures that any concrete action in $E(S\theta)$ can be mapped to a symbolic action in $EC(S)$.

Definition 9. *Let S be a symbolic state, A and B be two symbolic actions such that B is enabled in S. We say that $A \Leftrightarrow_S B$ when (i) $A \Leftrightarrow^{de}_S B$ and, (ii) if A is enabled in S then $A \Leftrightarrow^{ee}_S B$.*

Given a symbolic state S, we say that a set of actions X is a *symbolic stubborn set for S* when $X \cap EC(S) \neq \emptyset$ and, for any $A \in X$ and any execution

$$S = S_1 \overset{B_1}{\twoheadrightarrow} S_2 \ldots S_n \overset{B_n}{\twoheadrightarrow} S_{n+1} \text{ with } B_i \in EC(S_i) \text{ for all } 1 \leq i \leq n$$

such that $A \not\Leftrightarrow_{S_n} B_n$, there exists $1 \leq i \leq n$ such that $B_i \in X$.

We assume a computable function which associates to any symbolic state S such that $EC(S) \neq \emptyset$ a set $T^+(S)$ that is a symbolic stubborn set for S. Computing $T^+(S)$ is typically achieved as a least fixed point computation, initialising the set with an arbitrary action in $EC(S)$, exploring executions that avoid the current set and adding actions B_n when they are dependent with an action already in the set. In this process all transitions in the enabled cover of S and its successors are considered (unless they are in the current set) without caring for the existence of a solution for the visited states. The computation is carried out with each possible action of $EC(S)$ as its initial set, and a result of minimal cardinality is kept. In the worst case, it will be $EC(S)$ itself.

If done in a depth-first fashion, the computation is (a symbolic approximation of) Godefroid's stubborn set computation through first conflict relations [28]. It is however more efficient to perform the explorations in breadth, since the addition of an action along an exploration can potentially prevent the continuation of another exploration. In any case, the details of how $T^+(S)$ is computed do not matter for correctness.

Example 7. Consider the process $P = \text{in}(c, x).Q \mid \text{in}(d, x).\text{out}(d, t).Q'$ where Q, Q' and t are arbitrary. Consider computing $T^+(S)$ for $S = \langle (P; \emptyset) \approx (P; \emptyset) \rangle^{I_0}_{\top}$, initialising the set with $A_0 = \text{in}(c, \mathsf{X}^{c,0}, \emptyset)$. Since $A_0 \Leftrightarrow_S \text{in}(d, \mathsf{X}^{d,0}, \emptyset)$ we have to explore successors of S by the input on d. There is only one, call it S'. We have $A_0 \Leftrightarrow_{S'} \text{out}(d, \mathsf{w}_{d,0})$, so again we consider the successor S'' by the output action. We have $A_1 = \text{in}(c, \mathsf{X}^{c,0}, \{\mathsf{w}_{d,0}\}) \in EC(S'')$ with $A_1 \not\Leftrightarrow_{S''} A_0$, hence we add A_1 to our set. We repeat the process from S. We have that $A_1 \Leftrightarrow_S \text{in}(d, \mathsf{X}^{d,0}, \emptyset)$, then $A_1 \not\Leftrightarrow_{S'} \text{out}(d, \mathsf{w}_{d,0})$. More precisely, we have that $A_1 \not\Leftrightarrow_{S'}^{de} \text{out}(d, \mathsf{w}_{d,0})$. Hence we add $A_2 = \text{out}(d, \mathsf{w}_{d,0})$ to our set. Because $A_2 \not\Leftrightarrow_S^{de} \text{in}(d, \mathsf{X}^{d,0}, \emptyset) = A_3$, we will also add that action in the next iteration. We thus obtain $T^+(S) = \{A_0, A_1, A_2, A_3\}$, satisfying our specification of T^+. This symbolic stubborn set yields the symbolic persistent set $T^+(S) \cap EC(S) = \{\text{in}(c, \mathsf{X}^{c,0}, \emptyset), \text{in}(d, \mathsf{X}^{d,0}, \emptyset)\}$; in that case, no reduction is possible. However, starting with process $P \mid \text{out}(e, t').P'$ and initialising the set with $A_4 = \text{out}(e, \mathsf{w}_{e,0})$ will often lead to a very good reduction, i.e., a singleton.

Proposition 6. *Let S be a symbolic state such that $EC(S) \neq \emptyset$, and $T = \{A\theta \mid A \in T^+(S)\}$. For any $\theta' \in \mathsf{Sol}(S)$, the set $T \cap E(S\theta')$ is persistent in $S\theta'$.*

Having computed symbolic persistent sets, we now define a persistent set assignment $\mathsf{p}_{\mathsf{set}}$ for the concrete LTS. By completeness, we know that, for any concrete execution $s_0 \xrightarrow{\alpha_0} s_1 \ldots \xrightarrow{\alpha_{n-1}} s_n$ there exists $S_0 \xrightarrow{A_0} S_1 \ldots \xrightarrow{A_{n-1}} S_n$ and $\theta_0 \sqsubseteq \theta_1 \ldots \sqsubseteq \theta_n$ with θ_0 the empty substitution, $\theta_i \in \mathsf{Sol}(S_i)$ and $S_i \theta_i = s_i$ for all $i \in [0; n]$, and $A_i \theta_{i+1} = \alpha_i$ for all $i \in [0; n-1]$. We assume a choice function abs which, to each such concrete execution associates a symbolic abstraction: $\mathsf{abs}(s_0, \alpha_0 \ldots \alpha_{n-1}) = (S_0, S_1, \ldots, S_n)$. We can assume that the choice is compatible with prefixing:

$$\mathsf{abs}(s_0, \alpha_0 \ldots \alpha_n) = (S_i)_{0 \leq i \leq n+1} \text{ implies } \mathsf{abs}(s_0, \alpha_0 \ldots \alpha_{n-1}) = (S_i)_{0 \leq i \leq n}.$$

Building on this, we define $\mathsf{p}_{\mathsf{set}}(s_0, \alpha_0 \ldots \alpha_{n-1}) = \{A\theta \mid A \in T^+(S_n)\} \cap E(S_n \theta_n)$ where $\mathsf{abs}(s_0, \alpha_0 \ldots \alpha_{n-1}) = (S_0, \ldots, S_n)$, which, by Proposition 6, is a persistent set in s_n (uniquely defined as the state reachable from s_0 after $\alpha_0 \ldots \alpha_{n-1}$). In other words, we obtain the persistent set for a concrete state from the symbolic persistent set of one of its symbolic abstractions, but we choose this abstraction depending on the concrete execution and not only its resulting state.

With this in place, Proposition 1 guarantees that for any execution from s_0 to a final state s_f, there exists a persistent execution (wrt. $\mathsf{p}_{\mathsf{set}}$) from s_0 to s_f. Hence, the search for final bad states can be restricted to only explore concretizations of *symbolic persistent traces*, i.e., symbolic executions where the only transitions considered for a state S are those in $T^+(S) \cap EC(S)$.

5.4   Symbolic Sleep Sets

We finally describe how we implement sleep sets symbolically. We shall define a symbolic LTS with sleep sets, whose states (S, Z) compound a symbolic state S and a set of symbolic actions Z. The sleep set technique relies on a strict ordering of actions, but the order is only relevant for comparing independent actions, which do not have the same skeleton (the skeleton of an action denotes its input/output nature and its channel). Thus, we assume a strict total order $<$ on action skeletons, and lift it to symbolic and concrete actions. Then, a sleep set execution in our symbolic LTS is any execution

$$(S_0, \emptyset) = (S_0, Z_0) \xrightarrow{A_0} (S_1, Z_1) \ldots (S_n, Z_n) \xrightarrow{A_n} (S_{n+1}, Z_{n+1})$$

such that for $0 \leq i \leq n$, we have that $A_i \in T^+(S_i) \cap EC(S_i)$, $A_i \notin Z_i$, and $Z_{i+1} = \{B \in Z_i \mid B \Leftrightarrow^{ee}_{S_i} A_i\} \cup \{A' \in T^+(S_i) \cap EC(S_i) \mid A' < A_i, \ A' \Leftrightarrow^{ee}_{S_i} A_i\}$.

These symbolic sleep set executions are complete with respect to the sleep set technique applied to our concrete LTS with the $\mathsf{p_{set}}$ function defined above.

Proposition 7. *Let* $(s_0, \emptyset) \xrightarrow{\alpha_0} (s_1, z_1) \ldots \xrightarrow{\alpha_{n-1}} (s_n, z_n)$ *be a sleep set execution in our initial LTS. Then, there is* $(S_0, \emptyset) \xrightarrow{A_0} (S_1, Z_1) \ldots \xrightarrow{A_{n-1}} (S_n, Z_n)$ *a sleep set execution in our symbolic LTS, and substitutions* $\emptyset = \theta_0 \sqsubseteq \theta_1 \ldots \sqsubseteq \theta_n$ *such that* $s_i = S_i \theta_i$, $\alpha_i = A_i \theta_{i+1}$ *for* $i \in [1; n-1]$, *and* $s_n = S_n \theta_n$.

Example 8. Let S be the state from Example 7. Starting with $(S, \emptyset)$, we may perform two transitions in the sleep LTS: $A_0 = \mathtt{in}(c, \mathsf{X}^{c,0}, \emptyset)$ and $A_3 = \mathtt{in}(d, \mathsf{X}^{d,0}, \emptyset)$. Assuming that $S \xrightarrow{A_0} S_c$ and $A_0 > A_3$, we have $(S, \emptyset) \xrightarrow{A_0} (S_c, \{A_3\})$. Assuming now that Q starts with another input on c, the persistent set for S_c will contain inputs on c and d. However, executing A_3 is not allowed in $(S_c, \{A_3\})$. Intuitively, while the persistent set technique only looks forward, the sleep set technique also takes into account the past, and indicates here that exploring A_3 is not useful after A_0, since it can equivalently be performed before it.

5.5 Collapsing Conditionals

The above techniques allow us, in principle, to compute significantly reduced set of symbolic traces whose concretisations contain a witness of non-equivalence when such a witness exists. However, the algorithm for computing persistent sets is quite inefficient when applied on practical case studies: it relies on explorations of their symbolic LTS, which is highly branching and too large due to conditionals. This is a typical problem of symbolic execution, which manifests itself acutely in our setting, where the branching factor of a state is generally the product of those of its configurations. We circumvent this difficulty by observing that stubborn sets for a state (and its sleep set executions) can be computed by analysing a transformed state where conditionals are pushed down. Our transformation can often completely eliminate conditionals in our case studies, and is key to obtaining acceptable performances.

To justify an elementary step of this transformation, we consider a symbolic state S containing a conditional we would like to simplify: $S = S'[\mathtt{if}\ u = v\ \mathtt{then}\ P\ \mathtt{else}\ Q]$ ($S'[\cdot]$ denotes a state with a hole). We require that P and Q are respectively of the form $\alpha.P'$ and $\beta.Q'$ where α and β have the same skeleton. We make the observation that, independently of the execution and the evaluation of the test $u = v$, the same action will be released and, in case of outputs, the precise output term has little impact in the context of our symbolic analysis. Following this intuition, we would like to postpone the conditional by considering $S^c = S'[\gamma.\mathtt{if}\ u = v\ \mathtt{then}\ P'\ \mathtt{else}\ Q']$, where γ is either the input $\alpha = \beta$, or a well-chosen combination of the outputs α and β. The choice of γ should ensure that the transformation cannot create action independencies that did not hold before the transformation. Formally, we assume a fresh function symbol Δ of arity 4, and take $S^c = S'[T^c]$ where T^c is defined as:

$$\mathsf{in}(c,x).\mathtt{if}\ u = v\ \mathtt{then}\ P'\ \mathtt{else}\ Q'\ \text{when}\ (\alpha,\beta) = (\mathsf{in}(c,x),\mathsf{in}(c,x))$$

$$\mathsf{out}(c,\Delta(t,t',u,v)).\mathtt{if}\ u = v\ \mathtt{then}\ P'\ \mathtt{else}\ Q'\ \text{when}\ (\alpha,\beta) = (\mathsf{out}(c,t),\mathsf{out}(c,t'))$$

Proposition 8. *For any execution $S = S_0 \xrightarrow{A_1} S_1 \dots \xrightarrow{A_n} S_n$, there is an execution $S^c = T_0 \xrightarrow{A_1} T_1 \dots \xrightarrow{A_n} T_n$, such that, for any A and $i \in [1;n]$, $A \Leftrightarrow_{T_{i-1}} A_i$ (resp. $A_i \Leftrightarrow_{T_{i-1}} A$) implies $A \Leftrightarrow_{S_{i-1}} A_i$ (resp. $A_i \Leftrightarrow_{S_{i-1}} A$).*
Hence, $T^+(S^c)$ is a symbolic stubborn set for S and any sleep set execution from S is also a sleep set execution from S^c.

Repeatedly applying this result, we can eliminate most conditionals from our protocols, and compute stubborn sets and sleep set executions efficiently.

6   Implementation and Benchmarks

The results of the previous sections allow us to compute a set of symbolic actions, that can be used to restrict the search when looking for a witness of non-equivalence. By Proposition 3, $(P_1;\emptyset) \not\approx (P_2;\emptyset)$ iff a bad state can be reached from $s_0 = \langle |\mathbb{B}_1 \approx \mathbb{B}_2| \rangle$, where $\mathbb{B}_i = \{\mathcal{K}_i \mid (P_i;\emptyset) \xmapsto{\tau}^* \mathcal{K}_i \not\xrightarrow{}\}$. By Proposition 2, this implies the existence of a sleep set execution in our trace equivalence LTS from $(s_0,\emptyset)$ to a bad state. By Proposition 7, this implies the existence of a concrete execution whose underlying symbolic trace $S_0 = \langle \mathbb{B}_1 \approx \mathbb{B}_2 \rangle \xrightarrow[\top]{I_0} \xrightarrow{A_0} \dots \xrightarrow{A_n} S_{n+1}$ is a sleep set execution in our symbolic LTS. Such symbolic traces can be computed.

6.1   Implementation

To concretely realise and evaluate our techniques, we have implemented our symbolic analysis as a standalone library called Porridge [7], and have interfaced it with Apte in the first place, and then with its successor DeepSec, once this tool has been made available [21]. These tools perform an exhaustive search for non-equivalence witnesses using symbolic execution. Conceptually, this search can be seen as a naive symbolic exploration, combined with an elaborate constraint solving procedure. The two aspects being orthogonal, we can straightforwardly obtain a correct optimisation by restricting the symbolic exploration according to the set of traces computed by Porridge.

Porridge. The library is open-source, written in OCaml. The code implements exactly the techniques presented above, with only a few minor additions. It consists of ~6k LoC. Performance-wise, we heavily make use of hashconsing and memoization, but not from multicore programming yet. The design of

Table 1. Relative speed-up and reduction of explorations with Porridge vs. without Porridge. In the last column, we show the computation time without Porridge. The size refers to the total number of processes in parallel.

Test	Size	Time (ratio)	Explorations (ratio)	Time (s)
BAC (unlinkability)	4	7.6	7.23	12.23
Private Auth. (anonymity)	2	1.25	2.71	0.04
Private Auth. (anonymity)	3	1.67	4.01	0.04
Private Auth. (anonymity)	4	8.21	10.51	1.17
Private Auth. (anonymity)	5	14.89	16.61	10.57
Private Auth. (anonymity)	6	60.2	36.75	4864
Private Auth. (unlinkability)	2	2.29	9.6	0.16
Private Auth. (unlinkability)	3	14.06	29.77	79.57
Private Auth. (unlinkability)	4	46.2	46.69	7171
Feldhofer (anonymity)	2	1	4.72	0.03
Feldhofer (anonymity)	3	4.63	7.08	0.37
Feldhofer (anonymity)	4	22.47	16.3	544.93
Feldhofer (unlinkability)	4	36.27	22.58	1510.09

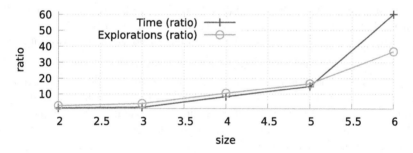

Fig. 2. Relative speed-up and reduction of explorations with Porridge vs. without Porridge on Private Authentication (ANO) of different sizes.

the library, with an independent POR functor, makes it easy to apply symbolic POR analyses to other LTS; we can already perform POR for trace inclusion, and expect to use this flexibility to consider slightly different protocol semantics.

Integration in Apte and DeepSec. As mentioned above, Apte and DeepSec are based on constraint solving procedures on top of which an exhaustive and naive symbolic executions exploration is performed. This exploration is naive in the sense that all interleavings are considered (except for the specific case of action-deterministic protocols already discussed in introduction). We have shown that restricting the exploration to symbolic sleep set traces still yields a decision procedure for trace equivalence. This restriction is easily implemented, as lightweight modifications (∼500 LoC) of Apte and DeepSec. Note that the differences between the semantics presented in Sect. 2 and the ones used by those tools can easily be ignored by slightly restricting the class of protocols. Concretely, we exploit the class of protocols with non-blocking outputs as done in [9], which is not restrictive.

6.2   Experimental Evaluation

We have carried out numerous benchmarks, focusing on DeepSec since it is both more general and more efficient than Apte, and measuring the improvements brought by Porridge in terms of computation time and number of explorations. The latter is also a good indicator of the effectiveness of the reduction achieved since it represents the number of times DeepSec explores an action and applies its costly constraint solving procedure.

Case Studies. We verify some privacy properties on several real-life protocols of various sizes by modifying the number of sessions being analysed. We model unlinkability [4,29] of the BAC protocol [4], of Private Authentication [2] and of Feldhofer [26], and anonymity as well for some of them. The results are shown in Table 1 and make use of processes that are not action-deterministic.

Setup. We run DeepSec and Porridge both compiled with OCaml 4.06.0 on a server running Ubuntu 16.04.5 (Linux 4.4.0) with $12 * 2$ Intel(R) Xeon(R) CPU E5-2650 v4 @ 2.20 GHz and 256 GB of RAM. We run each test on a single core with a time-out of 2 h (real-time) and maximal memory consumption of 10 GB.

Results. We report in Table 1 the relative speed-up of computation time and the reduction of explorations brought by Porridge. We plot the same information for numerous sizes of Private Authentication in Fig. 2. We observe that speed-ups are closely related to the reduction achieved on the number of explorations. As the size of protocols increases, Porridge quickly speeds up computations by more that one order of magnitude.

7   Conclusion

We have presented the first POR technique that is applicable to verifying trace equivalence properties of security protocols, without any action-determinism assumption. Our contributions are: an equivalence LTS that recasts trace equivalence as a reachability property; a symbolic abstraction of the equivalence LTS on which persistent and sleep set techniques can be effectively computed; a collapse of conditionals that significantly speeds up these computations. Our technique applies to a wide class of protocols, has been implemented as a library and integrated in the state-of-the-art verifier DeepSec, showing significant performance improvements on case studies.

Compared to (our) earlier work on POR for protocol equivalences [8,9], we follow a radically different approach in this paper to obtain a technique that applies without any action-determinism assumption. In the action-deterministic case, the two techniques achieve similar but incomparable reductions: sleep sets are more efficient on *improper blocks*, but the focused behavior of *compression* is unmatched with sleep sets. Finally, we note that although sleep sets allow to recover a form of *dependency constraint*, we do not know how to justify its use in practice outside of the action-deterministic case. We hope that future work will allow to unify and generalize both techniques.

A crucial aspect of our new approach is that it manages to leverage classic POR techniques, namely persistent and sleep sets, for use in our specific security setting. In fact, we view this work as a first step towards bridging the gap between standard POR and security-specific techniques. As usual in POR, many variations (*e.g.*, in how we integrate with the equivalence verifiers) and approximations (*e.g.*, in independencies or stubborn set computations) should be explored to look for performance gains. The recent work on *dynamic POR* [3,27] (DPOR), which aims to find a trade-off between performance and quality of the computed persistent sets, is of particular interest here, though it is unclear at this point to which extent generic results can be extracted from the above-mentioned works for re-use in our security setting.

References

1. Abadi, M., Fournet, C.: Mobile values, new names, and secure communication. In: Proceedings of the 28th Symposium on Principles of Programming Languages (POPL 2001), pp. 104–115. ACM Press (2001)
2. Abadi, M., Fournet, C.: Private authentication. Theor. Comput. Sci. **322**(3), 427–476 (2004)
3. Abdulla, P., Aronis, S., Jonsson, B., Sagonas, K.: Optimal dynamic partial order reduction. ACM SIGPLAN Not. **49**(1), 373–384 (2014)
4. Arapinis, M., Chothia, T., Ritter, E., Ryan, M.: Analysing unlinkability and anonymity using the applied pi calculus. In: Proceedings of 23rd Computer Security Foundations Symposium (CSF 2010), pp. 107–121. IEEE Computer Society Press (2010)
5. Armando, A., Carbone, R., Compagna, L., Cuellar, J., Abad, L.T.: Formal analysis of SAML 2.0 web browser single sign-on: breaking the SAML-based single sign-on for Google apps. In: Proceedings of the 6th ACM Workshop on Formal Methods in Security Engineering (FMSE 2008), pp. 1–10 (2008)
6. Armando, A., et al.: The AVISPA tool for the automated validation of internet security protocols and applications. In: Etessami, K., Rajamani, S.K. (eds.) CAV 2005. LNCS, vol. 3576, pp. 281–285. Springer, Heidelberg (2005). https://doi.org/10.1007/11513988_27
7. Baelde, D., Delaune, S., Hirschi, L.: Porridge, an OCaml library implementing POR techniques for checking trace equivalence of security protocols. https://hal.inria.fr/hal-01821474
8. Baelde, D., Delaune, S., Hirschi, L.: Partial order reduction for security protocols. In: Proceedings of the 26th International Conference on Concurrency Theory

(CONCUR 2015). LIPIcs, Madrid, Spain, vol. 42, pp. 497–510. Leibniz-Zentrum für Informatik (2015)

9. Baelde, D., Delaune, S., Hirschi, L.: A reduced semantics for deciding trace equivalence. Log. Methods Comput. Sci. **13**(2:8), 1–48 (2017)

10. Baelde, D., Delaune, S., Hirschi, L.: POR for security protocols equivalences: beyond action-determinism. Technical report (2018). https://arxiv.org/abs/1804.03650

11. Baier, C., Katoen, J.-P.: Principles of Model Checking (Representation and Mind Series). The MIT Press, Cambridge (2008)

12. Baldoni, R., Coppa, E., D'Elia, D.C., Demetrescu, C., Finocchi, I.: A survey of symbolic execution techniques. ACM Comput. Surv. **51**(3), 50:1–50:39 (2018). https://doi.org/10.1145/3182657. ISSN 0360-0300

13. Basin, D., Cremers, C., Meier, S.: Provably repairing the ISO/IEC 9798 standard for entity authentication. J. Comput. Secur. **21**(6), 817–846 (2013)

14. Basin, D., Dreier, J., Sasse, R.: Automated symbolic proofs of observational equivalence. In: Proceedings of the 22nd ACM Conference on Computer and Communications Security (CCS 2015), pp. 1144–1155. ACM (2015)

15. Blanchet, B.: An efficient cryptographic protocol verifier based on prolog rules. In: Proceedings of the 14th Computer Security Foundations Workshop (CSFW 2001), pp. 82–96. IEEE Computer Society Press (2001)

16. Bruso, M., Chatzikokolakis, K., den Hartog, J.: Formal verification of privacy for RFID systems. In: Proceedings of the 23rd IEEE Computer Security Foundations Symposium (CSF 2010). IEEE Computer Society Press (2010)

17. Chadha, R., Ciobâcă, Ş., Kremer, S.: Automated verification of equivalence properties of cryptographic protocols. In: Seidl, H. (ed.) ESOP 2012. LNCS, vol. 7211, pp. 108–127. Springer, Heidelberg (2012). https://doi.org/10.1007/978-3-642-28869-2_6

18. Cheval, V.: APTE: an algorithm for proving trace equivalence. In: Ábrahám, E., Havelund, K. (eds.) TACAS 2014. LNCS, vol. 8413, pp. 587–592. Springer, Heidelberg (2014). https://doi.org/10.1007/978-3-642-54862-8_50

19. Cheval, V., Comon-Lundh, H., Delaune, S.: Trace equivalence decision: negative tests and non-determinism. In: Proceedings of the 18th Conference on Computer and Communications Security (CCS 2011). ACM Press (2011)

20. Cheval, V., Cortier, V., Delaune, S.: Deciding equivalence-based properties using constraint solving. Theor. Comput. Sci. **492**, 1–39 (2013)

21. Cheval, V., Kremer, S., Rakotonirina, I.: DEEPSEC: deciding equivalence properties in security protocols - theory and practice. In: Proceedings of the 39th IEEE Symposium on Security and Privacy (S&P 2018). IEEE Computer Society Press (2018)

22. Clarke, E., Jha, S., Marrero, W.: Partial order reductions for security protocol verification. In: Graf, S., Schwartzbach, M. (eds.) TACAS 2000. LNCS, vol. 1785, pp. 503–518. Springer, Heidelberg (2000). https://doi.org/10.1007/3-540-46419-0_34

23. Cremers, C.J.F., Mauw, S.: Checking secrecy by means of partial order reduction. In: Amyot, D., Williams, A.W. (eds.) SAM 2004. LNCS, vol. 3319, pp. 171–188. Springer, Heidelberg (2005). https://doi.org/10.1007/978-3-540-31810-1_12

24. Delaune, S., Hirschi, L.: A survey of symbolic methods for establishing equivalence-based properties in cryptographic protocols. J. Log. Algebraic Methods Program. **87**, 127–144 (2017)

25. Delaune, S., Kremer, S., Ryan, M.D.: Verifying privacy-type properties of electronic voting protocols. J. Comput. Secur. **4**, 435–487 (2008)

26. Feldhofer, M., Dominikus, S., Wolkerstorfer, J.: Strong authentication for RFID systems using the AES algorithm. In: Joye, M., Quisquater, J.-J. (eds.) CHES 2004. LNCS, vol. 3156, pp. 357–370. Springer, Heidelberg (2004). https://doi.org/10.1007/978-3-540-28632-5_26
27. Flanagan, C., Godefroid, P.: Dynamic partial-order reduction for model checking software. ACM SIGPLAN Not. **40**, 110–121 (2005)
28. Godefroid, P.: Partial-order methods for the verification of concurrent systems. Ph.D. thesis, Université de Liège (1995)
29. Hirschi, L., Baelde, D., Delaune, S.: A method for verifying privacy-type properties: the unbounded case. In: Proceedings of the 37th IEEE Symposium on Security and Privacy (S&P 2016), San Jose, California, USA, pp. 564–581, May 2016
30. Lowe, G.: Breaking and fixing the needham-schroeder public-key protocol using FDR. In: Margaria, T., Steffen, B. (eds.) TACAS 1996. LNCS, vol. 1055, pp. 147–166. Springer, Heidelberg (1996). https://doi.org/10.1007/3-540-61042-1_43
31. Meier, S., Schmidt, B., Cremers, C., Basin, D.: The TAMARIN prover for the symbolic analysis of security protocols. In: Sharygina, N., Veith, H. (eds.) CAV 2013. LNCS, vol. 8044, pp. 696–701. Springer, Heidelberg (2013). https://doi.org/10.1007/978-3-642-39799-8_48
32. Mödersheim, S., Viganò, L., Basin, D.: Constraint differentiation: search-space reduction for the constraint-based analysis of security protocols. J. Comput. Secur. **18**(4), 575–618 (2010)
33. Peled, D.: Ten years of partial order reduction. In: Hu, A.J., Vardi, M.Y. (eds.) CAV 1998. LNCS, vol. 1427, pp. 17–28. Springer, Heidelberg (1998). https://doi.org/10.1007/BFb0028727

Automated Identification of Desynchronisation Attacks on Shared Secrets

Sjouke Mauw[1,2], Zach Smith[1(✉)], Jorge Toro-Pozo[1],
and Rolando Trujillo-Rasua[2,3]

[1] CSC, University of Luxembourg, Esch-sur-Alzette, Luxembourg
zach.smith@uni.lu
[2] SnT, University of Luxembourg, Esch-sur-Alzette, Luxembourg
[3] School of Information Technology, Deakin University, Geelong, Australia

Abstract. Key-updating protocols are a class of communication protocol that aim to increase security by having the participants change encryption keys between protocol executions. However, such protocols can be vulnerable to desynchronisation attacks, a denial of service attack in which the agents are tricked into updating their keys improperly, impeding future communication. In this work we introduce a method that can be used to automatically verify (or falsify) resistance to desynchronisation attacks for a range of protocols. This approach is then used to identify previously unreported vulnerabilities in two published RFID grouping protocols.

1 Introduction

Key-updating protocols form a class of communication protocols in which participants change their encryption keys between executions. Such protocols are used in several domains - the Signal protocol uses the Diffie-Hellman Double Ratchet algorithm [19], and the Gossamer protocol [18] also uses updating keys. Many grouping protocols [12,21], which aim to prove that two or more RFID tags are simultaneously present, also use such methods.

There are several formally defined security properties which demonstrate the benefits of key-updating protocols. For example, *forward privacy*, introduced by Avoine [2], prevents an attacker from learning about past sessions, even after compromising a participant. *Post-compromise security*, as defined by Cohn-Gordon et al. [5], states that if an adversary compromises an agent, their influence can be reversed if they do not continually monitor communication.

Such goals are typically realised by security protocols which update encryption keys, for example by using a one-way hash function. This way, if an adversary learns the encryption keys used in a single session, they cannot reconstruct past keys. However such methods introduce the problem of requiring the protocol participants to *synchronise* their key updates - so that their local states remain consistent.

© Springer Nature Switzerland AG 2018
J. Lopez et al. (Eds.): ESORICS 2018, LNCS 11098, pp. 406–426, 2018.
https://doi.org/10.1007/978-3-319-99073-6_20

The synchronisation requirement of key-updating protocols has created new attack vectors. If improperly designed or implemented, an attacker can cause agents to update their keys in an improper manner, preventing them from correctly interpreting communications from their partner. This kind of Denial-of-Service attack is called a *desynchronisation attack* [7]. Such attacks allow an adversary to prevent future runs of a communication protocol, stopping the protocol from achieving its intended purpose.

Security properties for communication protocols can be formally verified using symbolic analysis. This type of analysis is well-supported by a range of automated proving tools such as ProVerif [3] and Tamarin [17], which typically attempt to reduce analysis of the protocol to a bounded case. This is especially true in the case of *stateless* protocols, where information between sessions is never carried forwards to future executions. However, key-updating protocols are inherently *stateful* - information must be preserved between sessions. This can cause problems in analysis due to the explosion of the state space. Indeed, reachability queries are in general an undecidable problem [4,10].

Existing Formalisms of Desynchronisation Resistance. Desynchronisation represents a class of attacks that are not covered by traditional definitions. A protocol that is impervious to such attacks is said to be *desynchronisation resistant*, and while there is a strong intuitive understanding of what this property means, there are few attempts at formal definitions in the literature.

There exist a variety of works that either claim a form of desynchronisation resistance [13,15,22,25] or provide a desynchronisation attack on published protocols [14,16,23]. Both types of papers only provide an informal treatment of the topic, without automated tool support. Only few papers provide a formal definition of a desynchronisation attack or desynchronisation resistance. We will briefly discuss two of these approaches, namely the work of Van Deursen et al. [6] and the work of Radomirović and Dashti [20].

Van Deursen et al. [6] introduce desynchronisation in the context of RFID protocols. They say an RFID reader *owns* a tag if it knows a secret key allowing it to authenticate the tag in absence of the adversary. A protocol is then said to be desynchronisation resistant if being owned is an *invariant* property. For example, if there is a time t such that a tag T is owned by a reader R, then at time $t + 1$ there must exist some reader R' (who may be the same or different to R) which 'owns' T. The authors demonstrate how existing RFID protocols violate their definition. They do not provide, however, any means for formally verifying that it holds for an arbitrary protocol.

A second existing approach that relates to desynchronisation resistance is the work on *derailing attacks* by Radomirović and Dashti [20]. In a *derailing attack*, a protocol is led away from its intended execution by an adversary. Reachable states in the protocol are labelled as *safe*, *unsafe*, or *transitional*, describing whether a desirable 'success' condition is reachable from the current point. A protocol is said to be *susceptible to derailing attacks* if there exists a reachable state S such that in absence of the adversary, there are no safe states that are reachable from S.

Contributions. In this paper, a formal definition of desynchronisation resistance is given in terms of the traces of a security protocol. The definition we provide can be seen as an extension of the two theories above. Like Radomirović and Dashti, our definition concerns the reachability of certain states, and an examination of the transitions between them. Like Deursen et al., the knowledge of secret keys is an important factor in our definitions. However, we go further by providing a set of conditions for key-updating protocols that allows for automated verification (or falsification) of desynchronisation.

Although traditional security protocol verification tools allow for *reachability* queries, they lack inherent support for the *liveness* properties that we are verifying. As such, we provide under- and over- approximations in the form of verifiable security properties.

Organisation. In Sect. 2, a detailed introduction to multiset rewriting theory is given, presenting the language that will be used throughout the paper. In Sect. 3, a series of definitions regarding reachability are provided, and used to create a formal definition of desynchronisation resistance. In Sect. 4, the model is refined to focus on sequential key-updating protocols. A set of security properties are provided that are proved to be sufficient to ensure desynchronisation resistance in this setting. Section 5 shows the result of applying this analysis to existing secret-updating protocols by using the automated verification tool Tamarin. Novel attacks are found on a number of protocols in the literature. Finally in Sect. 6, we discuss future work, as well as related concepts.

2   Security Protocol Model

In order to model security protocols in which shared secrets are updated, a *multiset rewriting* model will be used. Multiset rewriting is a common basis for modelling stateful systems. In a stateful system, different sessions can be dependent on each other, with information that is dynamic between executions.

A protocol specification covers a set of rules that govern how a multiset describing the protocol state is allowed to proceed. This state contains information such as the messages that have been sent by different participants of the protocol, markers denoting if certain stages of the protocol have been successfully reached, and the knowledge and actions of an adversary who seeks to undermine the protocol's successful execution.

2.1   Multiset Rewriting

The multisets used in our model are built on terms constructed from an order-sorted signature, such as those described by Goguen and Meseguer [11]. An *order-sorted signature* is a triple $(\mathcal{S}, \leq, \Sigma)$, where $\leq$ is a partial ordering on a set of types $\mathcal{S}$, and Σ is a collection of functions between types. For two types s and t we define $\Sigma_{s,t}$ to be the functions in Σ which map from type s to type t.

Further, we use the standard notation for the Cartesian product of sets, so for example:

$$f \in \Sigma_{\mathbb{R}^2, \mathbb{N}} := f \colon \mathbb{R} \times \mathbb{R} \to \mathbb{N}.$$

Our model must track not only the messages that are on the network, but also auxiliary information about the state, such as an agent's encryption keys. To do this, we define two top types msg and fact, and further define subtypes public, nonce $<$ msg, and agent, const $<$ public.

The set of terms over $\mathcal{S}$ is defined iteratively, as follows. First, for each type $s \in \mathcal{S}$ we build two infinite carrier sets N_s and V_s of *names* (i.e. known values) and *variables* (i.e. unknown or uninstantiated values) of type s. We refer to these types of terms as *atoms*. We will often use the following notation for variables:

$$x, y \colon \text{nonce}, \qquad m, k \colon \text{msg}, \qquad A, B \colon \text{agent}.$$

From here, successive terms are built by the application of functions from Σ on the atoms. Given a term t, we define the set of *subterms* of t as follows. If t is an atom, then $subterms(t) = \{t\}$. Otherwise, we have $t = f(t_1, t_2, \ldots, t_n)$ for some function symbol $f \in \Sigma$. In this case, we define

$$subterms(t) = \{t\} \cup \{subterms(t_1), \ldots, subterms(t_n)\}.$$

A term t is *ground* if $subterms(t) \cap V_s = \emptyset$, and we denote the set of all (ground) terms of type s as Ter_s ($GTer_s$). A (ground) substitution σ is a partial function from variables to (ground) terms of the same type or supertype. Given a substitution σ and a term t, we write $t\sigma$ to denote the application of the substitution. Given a set $S = \{t_1, \ldots, t_n\}$, we write $S\sigma = \{t_1\sigma, \ldots, t_n\sigma\}$. We say σ is a *grounding substitution* for S if all terms in $S\sigma$ are ground.

The model is extended with an equational theory E, which describes the semantics of the functions in Σ. Pairs $lhs = rhs$ in E define an equivalence relation $\simeq_E$ on terms constructed using $(\mathcal{S}, \leq, \Sigma)$.

Example 1. We define the pair operator $\langle \_, \_ \rangle \in \Sigma_{\text{msg} \times \text{msg}, \text{msg}}$, and the corresponding projection functions $fst, snd \in \Sigma_{\text{msg}, \text{msg}}$ such that $fst(\langle x, y \rangle) = x$ and $snd(\langle x, y \rangle) = y$.

The equivalence relation E is extended to other terms in the algebra in the natural way, e.g. $fst(\langle \langle x, y \rangle, z \rangle) \simeq_E \langle x, y \rangle$.

A multiset is a set, M, counted with multiplicity - multiple copies of an element k can be contained in M. We write $|k|_M$ to denote the number of occurrences of k in M, with $|k|_M = 0$ if $k \notin M$. Given a set S, we write $\mathcal{M}(S)$ to denote the collection of all multisets that can be written using elements of S.

The multisets we will study are a restricted subset of those constructible using the order-sorted signature $(\mathcal{S}, \leq, \Sigma)$ above. In particular, we define the *universe* of states, $\mathbb{U}(\Sigma)$ as:

$$\mathbb{U}(\Sigma) = \mathcal{M}(\{f(t_1, \ldots, t_i) \mid i \geq 0 \wedge f \in \Sigma_{\mathsf{msg}^i,\mathsf{fact}} \wedge$$
$$\forall k \in \{1 \ldots i\}. \, t_k \in GTer_{msg}\}).$$

Each element $S \in \mathbb{U}(\Sigma)$ represents a single valid *state* of a protocol execution. We now look at how we can move from one state to the next.

A *rule* r is defined by a pair (lhs, rhs) of multisets. Suppose σ is a grounding substitution for lhs. A *rule application* $r\sigma$ is a mapping $\mathbb{U}(\Sigma) \rightarrow \mathbb{U}(\Sigma)$. It acts on a state $S \in \mathbb{U}(\Sigma)$ by identifying a submultiset of S equivalent to $\sigma(lhs)$, and replacing it with $\sigma(rhs)$. Note that multiset rules must respect the equational theory E, so that $S \simeq_E S' \implies r\sigma(S) \simeq_E r\sigma(S')$. We express protocol rules as labelled transitions.

Example 2. Consider the protocol rule `Combine`:

$$\frac{\mathrm{A}(x) \quad \mathrm{A}(y)}{\mathrm{B}(x,y)} \; \texttt{Combine},$$

which takes two terms of type `fact` built with symbol A, and returns a new `fact` which contains the subterms of the two previous terms. Let $S = \{\mathrm{A}(a), \mathrm{A}(b), \mathrm{A}(c)\}$. The substitution $\sigma = \{x \mapsto a, y \mapsto b\}$ maps:

$$\{\mathrm{A}(a), \mathrm{A}(b), \mathrm{A}(c)\} \xrightarrow{r\sigma} \{\mathrm{B}(a,b), \mathrm{A}(c)\}$$

Definition 2.1 (Protocol specification). *A protocol specification P is defined by a tuple $(\Sigma, E, R, S^{start})$ where:*

- *$\Sigma = (F, \mathscr{F})$ is a collection of function symbols of signature types $\Sigma_{\mathsf{msg}^*,\mathsf{msg}}$ and $\Sigma_{\mathsf{msg}^*,\mathsf{fact}}$, respectively.*
- *E is an equational theory over $\Sigma_{\mathsf{msg}^*,\mathsf{msg}}$.*
- *R is a collection of* rules.
- *$S^{start} \subseteq \mathbb{U}(\Sigma)$ is a collection of potential starting states.*

The set of starting states will usually be infinite, as they carry the details of a specific execution - the number of participating agents, their encryption keys, and so on.

A *trace*, τ, on P is a choice of starting state $S^0 \in S^{start}$ and a finite ordered list of rule applications $(r_1\sigma_1 \ldots r_n\sigma_n)$ such that each successive application $S^0 \xrightarrow{r_1\sigma_1} \ldots \xrightarrow{r_n\sigma_n} S^n$ is valid.

The intermediate states in a trace can be reconstructed from the choices of rule applications. Given a trace $\tau = (S^0, (r_1\sigma_1 \ldots r_n\sigma_n))$, a second trace τ' is an *extension* of τ, writing $\tau \sqsubseteq \tau'$, if $\tau' = (S^0, (r_1\sigma_1 \cdots r_n\sigma_n \ldots r_{n+k}\sigma_{n+k}))$. Similarly, we also say that τ is a *prefix* of τ' in this case.

Given a trace τ we write $\mathrm{firstState}(\tau)$ and $\mathrm{lastState}(\tau)$ to denote the first state and the (implicit) last state in the trace. We write $\mathrm{rules}(\tau)$ to denote the set of rules $\{r_1, \ldots, r_n\}$ in τ. We write $\mathrm{traces}(P)$ to denote the set of all possible traces on the protocol P.

We define an *event fact*, $E^\star$ to be a fact which appears only on the right-hand side of rules in R. Such facts can never be removed from the state of the protocol. Intuitively, while standard facts mark the *current* situation of a state, event facts form an indelible history of all important occurrences in a trace.

As such, we define the multiplicity of an event fact in a trace without ambiguity as $|E^\star(t_1 \ldots t_n)|_\tau := |E^\star(t_1 \ldots t_n)|_{\text{lastState}(\tau)}$,

We define a quasi-order on event facts within traces, $<_\tau$, as follows. Given two event facts $E^\star(t_1 \ldots t_n), F^\star(s_1 \ldots s_m)$, we say $E^\star(t_1 \ldots t_n) <_\tau F^\star(s_1 \ldots s_m)$ if there exists a prefix $\tau' \sqsubseteq \tau$ such that:

$$\big(|E^\star(t_1 \ldots t_n)|_{\tau'} > 0\big) \wedge \big(|F^\star(s_1 \ldots s_m)|_{\tau'} = 0\big) \wedge \big(|F^\star(s_1 \ldots s_m)|_\tau > 0\big).$$

In particular, this means that $F^\star$ was added to the state at some point after $E^\star$. In addition, we write $E^\star(t_1 \ldots t_n) \leq_\tau F^\star(s_1 \ldots s_m)$ to indicate that $E^\star(t_1 \ldots t_n) <_\tau F^\star(s_1 \ldots s_m)$ or $\{E^\star(t_1 \ldots t_n), F^\star(s_1 \ldots s_m)\} \subseteq \text{firstState}(\tau)$.

We reserve several symbols in $\mathscr{F}$ for all protocols, with the following interpretations:

- Net(msg) represents a message on the communication network.
- Fr(nonce) represents that the nonce in the argument has been freshly generated. By convention, we require that freshly generated terms are atomic.
- K(msg) represents that the adversary 'knows' the term in the argument.

Additional event facts are introduced as a consequence of the security requirements of the protocol being analysed. In Sects. 3 and 4, we will introduce several more event fact symbols used in order to analyse key-updating protocols.

2.2   The Adversary

An important concept in discussing the security of a protocol is an understanding of the adversary's capabilities. In this work, the Dolev-Yao adversary model [8] is used. The Dolev-Yao adversary is assumed to have full control over the communication network. We make the *perfect cryptography assumption*: the adversary is incapable of decrypting messages without the appropriate key.

The adversary knowledge is modelled using facts K. The initial knowledge of the adversary is defined by the starting states of the protocol specification, but at a minimum contains all terms of type public. A set of additional protocol rules describe the capabilities of the adversary. These protocol rules allow the adversary to eavesdrop, block or modify messages that are sent on the communication network. We assume that all protocols being studied contain (at least) the set of adversary rules provided in Fig. 1. The set of rules which model the actions of the adversary is denoted as Adv.

Given a state S, adversary knowledge K and a term x, we write $(S, K) \vdash x$ to indicate that some combination of (only) the rules in Fig. 1 will allow the adversary to derive x from the state S.

$$\frac{\text{Net}(x)}{\text{Net}(x) \quad \text{K}(x)} \text{ Eavesdrop} \qquad \frac{\text{Net}(x)}{\text{K}(x)} \text{ Block}$$

$$\frac{\text{K}(x)}{\text{K}(x) \quad \text{Net}(x)} \text{ Inject} \qquad \frac{\text{K}(x_1, \ldots, x_n)}{\text{K}(f(x_1, \ldots, x_n))} \text{ Function}$$

Fig. 1. The minimal set of adversary rules.

We often also grant the adversary the limited ability to *corrupt* an agent, learning the value of any secret keys they hold. This is done through either the choice of starting states, or additional adversary rules.

2.3   Security Claims

Given a protocol P, a *security claim* on P is a first-order logic statement about the existence and ordering of event facts in traces of P.

We note that the validity of security claims is dependent upon a faithful description of the protocol in question. For example, in order to make security claims about the *secrecy* of certain knowledge, we should expect the protocol specification to contain $\text{Secret}^\star(t)$ (or similar) facts denoting the terms that are believed to be secret.

3   Desynchronisation Resistance

The intuition behind desynchronisation is that the protocol reaches a state from which it can no longer proceed in a meaningful way. In order to define precisely what this means, we must start with a notion of *reachability*. We refine this definition to progressively stronger versions, before introducing our definition of *desynchronisation resistance*.

Reachability is a property describing the ability of the protocol to transition from a given state to some desirable situation. We will want to ensure that in any reasonable conditions, the adversary cannot prevent the protocol from completing, but rather only delay it.

Definition 3.1 (State Reachability). *Given a protocol* $P = (\Sigma, E, R, S^{start})$, *a set of rules* $W \subseteq R$ *and two states* $S, S' \in \mathbb{U}(\Sigma)$, *we say that* S' *is* reachable *from* S *avoiding* W, *denoted by* $S \rightsquigarrow_{\neg W} S'$, *if:*

$$\forall \tau \in \text{traces}(P). \text{lastState}(\tau) = S \implies$$
$$\exists \tau' \in \text{traces}(P). \tau \sqsubseteq \tau' \wedge \text{lastState}(\tau') = S' \wedge \text{rules}(\tau' \setminus \tau) \cap W = \emptyset.$$

Note that we pay particular attention to the idea of reachability avoiding certain rules. We wish to show that no matter which actions an adversary takes, it is possible for the execution of a protocol to continue once the adversary becomes inactive. As such, we use $\rightsquigarrow_{\neg Adv}$ to denote reachability in absence of the adversary, and $\rightsquigarrow$ for the particular case when no rules are forbidden.

Given a protocol $P = (\Sigma, E, R, S^{start})$ and a state $S \in \mathbb{U}(\Sigma)$ we define the set of states reachable from S as reachable$(S) = \{S' \in \mathbb{U}(\Sigma) \mid S \rightsquigarrow S'\}$. Overloading notation, we define the set of states reachable by P as reachable$(P) = \bigcup_{S^0 \in S^{start}}$ reachable(S^0).

Next, the notion of reachability is extended from the context of states to the context of event facts.

Definition 3.2 (Event Reachability). *Let P be a protocol, $S \in \mathbb{U}(\Sigma)$ a state, W a set of rules and $\mathrm{E}^\star$ an event fact. We say that $\mathrm{E}^\star$ is reachable from S avoiding W, denoted by $S \rightsquigarrow_{\neg W} \mathrm{E}^\star$, if:*

$$\exists S' \in \mathbb{U}(\Sigma). \ (S \rightsquigarrow_{\neg W} S') \wedge (|\mathrm{E}^\star|_S < |\mathrm{E}^\star|_{S'}).$$

Intuitively, given a trace τ that contains S, it is possible to extend τ in such a way that the event fact $\mathrm{E}^\star$ is reached. Like before, we will write $S \rightsquigarrow \mathrm{E}^\star$ to indicate $S \rightsquigarrow_{\neg \emptyset} \mathrm{E}^\star$.

Reachability captures the idea that a desired state or event can be achieved once. However, we desire that our protocol not only be able to successfully complete once, but arbitrarily many times. To do this, we need a definition stronger than standard reachability. To do so, we introduce the event facts:

- Complete*(agent, agent) indicates that the first agent believes they have successfully completed a run of the protocol with the second.
- Corrupt*(agent) represents that the named agent has performed an action that deviates from their protocol specification, or that the adversary has stolen confidential data from them.

Desynchronisation occurs when two agents who were originally able to finish a protocol execution lose this ability.

Definition 3.3 (Desynchronisation Resistance). *A protocol P is desynchronisation resistant if:*

$$\forall A, B \colon \text{agent}, S^0 \in S^{start}. \ S^0 \rightsquigarrow_{\neg Adv} \text{Complete}^\star(A, B) \implies$$
$$\left(\forall \tau \in \text{traces}(P). \ \text{firstState}(\tau) = S^0 \implies \right.$$
$$\text{lastState}(\tau) \rightsquigarrow_{\neg Adv} \text{Complete}^\star(A, B) \vee$$
$$\text{Corrupt}^\star(A) \in \tau \vee$$
$$\left. \text{Corrupt}^\star(B) \in \tau \right).$$

Intuitively, if A and B are able to complete the protocol once without any actions being performed by the adversary, then they will always be able to do this, except in the case that one of the participants been corrupted, giving secret data to the adversary.

4   Verifying Desynchronisation Resistance

In this section we look at a specific instantiation of the theory in the previous sections, and show that it can be used to verify desynchronisation resistance. We also provide 'lower' and 'upper' bounds to desynchronisation resistance, proving that violating this combination of properties results in an attack. Note that other choices of environment could be made depending on the target domain, with comparable results.

We model a synchronous key updating environment, in which a pair of agents each store a number of secret communication keys to be used with their intended partner. In an ideal execution, the keys stored by one agent will always correspond to those stored by their partner.

4.1   A Sequential Key Updating Environment

Recall that a protocol specification is defined by a tuple $(\Sigma, E, R, S^{start})$, where Σ is further divided into the collections F and $\mathscr{F}$ of functions on terms and fact symbols. We provide next a framework composed of F, E, and $\mathscr{F}$. Depending on the protocol, it may be necessary to extend the equational theory. The set of rules R is a consequence of the protocol being examined.

$$F = \{senc\colon \mathsf{msg} \times \mathsf{msg} \to \mathsf{msg},\ sdec\colon \mathsf{msg} \times \mathsf{msg} \to \mathsf{msg},$$
$$aenc\colon \mathsf{msg} \times \mathsf{msg} \to \mathsf{msg},\ adec\colon \mathsf{msg} \times \mathsf{msg} \to \mathsf{msg},$$
$$pk\colon \mathsf{msg} \to \mathsf{msg},\ h\colon \mathsf{msg} \to \mathsf{msg}\}.$$
$$E = \{sdec(senc(msg, key), key) = msg,$$
$$adec(aenc(msg, pk(ltk)), ltk) = msg\}.$$

The function symbols in F represent the standard symmetric and asymmetric encryption and decryption functions, and E defines their semantics.

$$\mathscr{F} = \{\ \mathrm{ShKeys}(\mathsf{agent}, \mathsf{agent}, \langle \mathsf{nonce}, \ldots \rangle),\ \mathrm{Session}(\mathsf{agent}, \mathsf{agent}, \langle \mathsf{msg}, \ldots \rangle),$$
$$\mathrm{AddKey}^{\star}(\mathsf{agent}, \mathsf{agent}, \mathsf{msg}),\ \mathrm{DropKey}^{\star}(\mathsf{agent}, \mathsf{agent}, \mathsf{msg}),$$
$$\mathrm{Complete}^{\star}(\mathsf{agent}, \mathsf{agent})\}.$$

The facts ShKeys and Session provide information about the knowledge of an agent. ShKeys facts represent their *long term* knowledge, in the form of communication keys for use with a named partner. Session facts are used to store session data for a single execution of the protocol. The AddKey* and DropKey* event facts mark changes to the stored keys of an agent.

Definition 4.1 (Starting States). *The set of starting states S^{start} is the set composed of all $S^0 \in \mathbb{U}(\Sigma)$ that satisfy the following conditions:*

(*i*) $\nexists x\colon \mathsf{msg}.\, \mathrm{Net}(x) \in S^0$,

(*ii*) $\nexists A, B\colon \mathsf{agent}, y\colon \mathsf{msg}.\; \mathrm{Session}(A, B, y) \in S^0$,

(*iii*) $\forall A, B\colon \mathsf{agent}, k_1, \ldots, k_n\colon \mathsf{msg}.\; \mathrm{ShKeys}(A, B, \langle k_1, \ldots, k_n \rangle) \in S^0 \implies$

$\quad \nexists l_1, \ldots, l_m\colon \mathsf{msg}, \langle k_1, \ldots, k_n \rangle \neq \langle l_1, \ldots, l_m \rangle.\; \mathrm{ShKeys}(A, B, \langle l_1, \ldots, l_m \rangle) \in S^0$,

(*iv*) $\forall A, B\colon \mathsf{agent}, k_i\colon \mathsf{msg}.$

$\quad \mathrm{ShKeys}(A, B, \langle \ldots k_i \ldots \rangle) \in S^0 \implies \mathrm{AddKey}^\star(A, B, k_i) \in S^0$,

(*v*) $\forall A, B\colon \mathsf{agent}, k\colon \mathsf{msg}.\; \mathrm{AddKey}^\star(A, B, k) \in S^0 \iff$

$\quad \exists k_1 \ldots k_n\colon \mathsf{msg}.\; \mathrm{ShKeys}(A, B, \langle \ldots k \ldots \rangle) \in S^0 \lor \mathrm{DropKey}^\star(A, B, k) \in S^0$

(*vi*) $\forall A, B\colon \mathsf{agent}, k\colon \mathsf{nonce}.\; \big(\mathrm{ShKeys}(A, B, \langle \ldots k \ldots \rangle) \in S^0 \land ((S^0, K) \vdash k)\big) \implies$

$\quad \mathrm{Corrupt}^\star(A) \in S^0 \lor \mathrm{Corrupt}^\star(B) \in S^0$.

We note the following intuitions behind the above requirements:

(*i*) A starting state may not contain messages.

(*ii*) A starting state may not contain session data.

(*iii*) An agent stores only one set of keys for use with each potential communication partner.

(*iv*) If a starting state contains an agent A who stores a secret key k_i for communicating with an agent B, then there is a corresponding AddKey* fact showing that A has added this key.

(*v*) If a starting state contains an AddKey* fact, then either the corresponding agent has that key in their knowledge, or there is also a corresponding DropKey* fact.

(*vi*) If a starting state contains an agent A who stores a secret key k_i for communicating with an agent B, and the adversary knows the value k_i, then either A or B is corrupt.

We point out that a starting state does allow for instances of the Complete* event fact. This does not interfere with any reachability claims, as these describe the ability to add *new* instances of these event facts to the trace.

In addition, we grant the adversary two capabilities. Firstly, the adversary is able to "corrupt" an agent, learning any secret keys they are holding. Second, we allow the adversary to "cancel" the session of an agent, causing them to lose any stored session data. For example, this models the ability of an adversary to block messages sent on the network until an agent assumes their partner has halted communication. We do this by requiring that the set of rules R contains the rules `Corrupt` and `Sess_Cancel`, defined below.

$$\frac{\mathrm{ShKeys}(A, B, \langle k_1 \ldots k_n \rangle)}{\mathrm{K}(\langle k_1 \ldots k_n \rangle) \quad \mathrm{Corrupt}^\star(A)}\; \texttt{Corrupt} \qquad \frac{\mathrm{Session}(A, B, y)}{}\; \texttt{Sess\_Cancel}$$

4.2   Satisfying Desynchronisation Resistance

Given a protocol constructed in the model above, we provide a set of conditions that are sufficient to satisfy desynchronisation resistance.

We start with a predicate stating whether two agents share a *common key* in a given state. Let P be a protocol and $S \in$ reachable(P). We say that two agents A and B have a common key in S, denoted CommonKey$_{A,B}(S)$, if and only if:

$$\exists k_1, \ldots, k_n, l_1, \ldots, l_m \colon \mathsf{msg}. \ \big(\{k_1, \ldots, k_n\} \cap \{l_1, \ldots, l_m\} \neq \emptyset \wedge$$
$$\text{ShKeys}(A, B, \langle k_1, \ldots, k_n \rangle) \in S \wedge \text{ShKeys}(B, A, \langle l_1, \ldots, l_m \rangle) \in S \big) .$$

Now we define *reachability conditional on a common key* as the property of a protocol that two agents are able to complete the protocol with each other in absence of the adversary if and only if they have a common key.

Property 4.2 (Reachable Conditional on Common Key). *We say that P satisfies* completion conditional on a common key *if:*

$$\forall S^0 \in S^{start}, A, B \colon \mathsf{agent},$$
$$S^0 \rightsquigarrow_{\neg Adv} \text{Complete}(A, B) \iff \text{CommonKey}_{A,B}(S^0).$$

With these in mind, we now define several other properties describing the nature in which the shared keys used by agents in a protocol are updated. Properties 4.3 and 4.4 give syntactic requirements on protocols. In particular, we require that a protocol's specification is consistent in the way that ShKeys linear facts are modified with respect to the addition of the AddKey* and DropKey* event facts. We also make the assumption that an agent always stores the same number of encryption keys for communicating with their partner.

Property 4.3 (Well-Formed Key Updates). *A protocol $P = (\Sigma, E, R, S^{start})$ satisfies* Well-Formed Key Updates *if the following two conditions hold for all rules $r \in R$:*

$$\text{AddKey}^\star(A, B, k) \in rhs(r) \iff$$
$$\big(\exists k_1 \ldots k_n, l_1 \ldots l_m. \ \text{ShKeys}(A, B, \langle k_1 \ldots k \ldots k_n \rangle) \in rhs(r) \wedge$$
$$\text{ShKeys}(A, B, \langle l_1 \ldots l_m \rangle) \in lhs(r) \wedge \forall i . l_i \neq k\big) ,$$
$$\text{DropKey}^\star(A, B, k) \in rhs(r) \iff$$
$$\big(\exists k_1 \ldots k_n, l_1 \ldots l_m. \ \text{ShKeys}(A, B, \langle k_1 \ldots k \ldots k_n \rangle) \in lhs(r) \wedge$$
$$\text{ShKeys}(A, B, \langle l_1 \ldots l_m \rangle) \in rhs(r) \wedge \forall i . l_i \neq k\big) .$$

Next we define the *Key Conservation* property. It states that every agent must keep the same number of keys during the execution of the protocol. We also require each rule to consider at most a single shared key fact.

Property 4.4 (Key Conservation). *A protocol $P = (\Sigma, E, R, S^{start})$ satisfies* Key Conservation *if for every rule $r \in R$, and every $A, B \colon \mathsf{agent}$, $k_1, \ldots, k_n \colon \mathsf{msg}$, there exists an instance of $\text{ShKeys}(A, B, \langle k_1, \ldots, k_n \rangle)$ on the left-hand side of r if and only if there is some $l_1, \ldots, l_n \colon \mathsf{msg}$ such that the right-hand side of r contains $\text{ShKeys}(A, B, \langle l_1, \ldots, l_n \rangle)$.*

Next we define *Key Uniqueness* as the notion that a given encryption key will only be generated at most once. Once discarded by an agent they will never re-use it, nor can a different pair of agents ever (intentionally or otherwise) generate the same encryption key.

Definition 4.5 (Key Uniqueness). *A protocol P satisfies* Key Uniqueness *if for every $\tau \in$ traces(P) and every A, B, A', B' : agent and every k : msg with $\{A, B\} \neq \{A', B'\}$ it holds that:*

$$\text{AddKey}^{\star}(A, B, k) \in \tau \implies$$
$$|\text{AddKey}^{\star}(A, B, k)|_{\tau} = 1 \land |\text{AddKey}^{\star}(A', B', k)|_{\tau} = 0.$$

We next describe the properties of *Key Preparedness* and *Key Resilience*. Together with Key Uniqueness, these are the main security requirements that are to be verified. Intuitively, they provide a semi-strict ordering on the key updates of paired agents.

Definition 4.6 (Key Preparedness for agents A and B). *A protocol P satisfies* Key Preparedness *for agents A and B if*

$$\forall \tau \in \text{traces}(P), \forall k \colon \text{msg},$$
$$\text{AddKey}^{\star}(A, B, k) \in \tau \implies \text{AddKey}^{\star}(B, A, k) \leq_{\tau} \text{AddKey}^{\star}(A, B, k).$$

Definition 4.7 (Key Resilience for agents A and B). *A protocol P satisfies* Key Resilience *for agents A and B if*

$$\forall \tau = (S^0, (r_i \sigma_i)) \in \text{traces}(P), \forall k \colon \text{msg},$$
$$\text{DropKey}^{\star}(A, B, k) \in \tau \implies$$
$$\text{DropKey}^{\star}(B, A, k) \leq_{\tau} \text{DropKey}^{\star}(A, B, k).$$

The second case in the Key Resilience claim accounts for the trivial case of a starting state containing DropKey* facts for which we cannot be sure of the source.

We note that the above properties are verifiable, either by examination of the protocol specification (Properties 4.2, 4.3 and 4.4), or through verification of traces in an automated prover tool (Definitions 4.5, 4.6 and 4.7). We denote the properties as WF, KC, KU, KP and KR respectively for Well Formedness, Key Conservation, Key Uniqueness, Key Preparedness and Key Resilience.

Theorem 4.8 (Sufficiency). *Let $P = (\Sigma, E, R, S^{start})$ be a protocol that satisfies Properties 4.2, 4.3, 4.4 and Definition 4.5. P satisfies desynchronisation resistance if for all $S^0 \in S^{start}$ and all agents A, B such that CommonKey$_{A,B}(S^0)$, one of the following conditions holds:*

- *Key Preparedness (Definition 4.6) for agents A and B holds, and Key Resilience (Definition 4.7) for agents B and A holds, or*
- *Key Preparedness (Definition 4.6) for agents B and A holds, and Key Resilience (Definition 4.7) for agents A and B holds.*

Before we begin the proof of Theorem 4.8, we provide some helper lemmas. We define the $strip()$ function, which allows us to transform a state into a starting state.

Definition 4.9 (Strip Function). *We define the function $strip()$, which maps from states to states. We define $strip(S)$ to be the multiset that is equal to S, but with all instances of* Session, K *and* Net *removed.*

Lemma 4.10. *Let P be a protocol which satisfies Key Conservation (Property 4.4) and Well-Formed Key Updates (Property 4.3). Suppose $S \in$ reachable(P). Then $strip(S)$ is a starting state of this protocol, as per the requirements of starting states in Definition 4.1.*

Proof. Points (i), (ii) and (vi) are immediate from the absence of corresponding facts. (iii) is a consequence of Key Conservation, (iv) and (v) from Well-Formed Key Updates.   □

Lemma 4.11. *Let P be a protocol which satisfies Key Conservation (Property 4.4) and Well-Formed Key Updates (Property 4.3), and τ a trace of P with final state S. Suppose γ is a trace of P with starting state $strip(S)$ that contains no adversary rules. Then $\gamma \cdot \tau \in$ traces(P) is a trace extension of τ.*

Proof. Suppose $\gamma = (strip(S), r_1\sigma_1 \ldots r_n\sigma_n)$. We claim that the series of rule applications $r_1\sigma_1 \ldots r_n\sigma_n$ are valid from the state S. Indeed, the rule application $r_1\sigma_1$ can be dependent only on ShKeys facts, as these are the only linear facts which can be in a starting state. These facts exist in both S and $strip(S)$. By the same logic, the rest of the series of applications are also valid.   □

Proof (Theorem 4.8). Assume that the agents A and B are not corrupt. Without loss of generality, we assume the first case holds - that we have Key Preparedness for A and B, and Key Resilience for B and A.

Our proof proceeds in two steps. First, we show that the common key predicate is sufficient to ensure completion from *any* state, not just the starting states:

$$\forall S \in \text{reachable}(P),$$
$$\text{CommonKey}_{A,B}(S) \implies S \rightsquigarrow_{\neg Adv} \text{Complete}(A, B).$$

Secondly, we show that the common key property is *invariant*:

$$\forall S \in \text{reachable}(P), r \in R,$$
$$(\text{CommonKey}_{A,B}(S) \wedge S \xrightarrow{r\sigma} S') \implies \text{CommonKey}_{A,B}(S').$$

From these two claims, the result will immediately follow. To show the first point, we use the $strip()$ function from Definition 4.9. Note that if A and B have a common key in S, then they have a common key in $strip(S)$. Then, by Lemma 4.11, the claim follows.

For the second point, we must show that for any rule application $r\sigma$ in which a DropKey* event fact is added, the common key predicate is preserved. Indeed, the well-formedness properties of Property 4.3 ensure that these are the only possible rule applications which can affect the predicate.

Suppose we have $S \in \text{reachable}(P)$ such that $\text{CommonKey}_{A,B}(S)$, and a rule application $r_n\sigma_n$. We split into the cases when DropKey$^\star(A, B, k)$ is added, or when DropKey$^\star(B, A, k)$ is added. Suppose now $r_n\sigma_n$ adds DropKey$^\star(A, B, k)$, then:

$$\overset{KC}{\Longrightarrow} \exists k': \text{msg.} \qquad r_n\sigma_n \text{adds } \text{AddKey}^\star(A, B, k')$$

$$\overset{KP}{\Longrightarrow} \exists i < n. \qquad r_i\sigma_i \text{ adds } \text{AddKey}^\star(B, A, k')$$

$$\overset{KU}{\Longrightarrow} \nexists j. \qquad r_j\sigma_j \text{ adds } \text{DropKey}^\star(A, B, k')$$

$$\overset{KDR}{\Longrightarrow} \nexists m. \qquad r_m\sigma_m \text{ adds } \text{DropKey}^\star(B, A, k')$$

$$\Longrightarrow \qquad \text{ShKeys}(B, A, \langle \ldots, k', \ldots \rangle) \in S$$

and so now k' is a common key after the rule application. Therefore the Common Key predicate is preserved.

Suppose instead $r_n\sigma_n$ adds DropKey$^\star(B, A, k)$, then:

$$\overset{KDR}{\Longrightarrow} \exists i < n. \qquad r_i\sigma_i \text{ adds } \text{DropKey}^\star(A, B, k)$$

$$\overset{WF}{\Longrightarrow} \exists j < i. \qquad r_j\sigma_j \text{ adds } \text{AddKey}^\star(A, B, k)$$

$$\overset{KU}{\Longrightarrow} \nexists l \neq i. \qquad r_l\sigma_i \text{ adds } \text{AddKey}^\star(A, B, k)$$

$$\Longrightarrow \qquad \text{ShKeys}(A, B, \langle \ldots, k, \ldots \rangle) \notin S$$

and so k was not a common key before the rule application. Therefore since S contained some key k' that was a common key, so does the state after the rule application, and so the common key predicate is preserved. $\qquad\square$

Theorem 4.8 provides a set of sufficient conditions to ensure that a protocol in our model satisfies desynchronisation resistance. We provide one example of a *necessary* condition to satisfy desynchronisation resistance: any protocol that fails to meet this condition also fails to provide resistance against desynchronisation attacks.

Theorem 4.12 (Necessity). *Let $P = (\Sigma, E, R, S^{start})$ be a protocol that satisfies Properties 4.2, 4.3, and 4.4. Let $S^0 \in S^{start}$ and $\text{ShKeys}(A, B, k) \in S^0$ (i.e. A stores exactly one key for B) and assume P does not satisfy Key Preparedness (Definition 4.6) for A and B. Then P either contains no reachable key update rule applications for A, or it does not satisfy desynchronisation resistance.*

Proof. Suppose P contains at least one key update rule for A. We will construct a trace from which the Complete$^\star(A, B)$ is no longer reachable without adversary interference.

Let $\tau = (S^0, r_1\sigma_1, \ldots, r_n\sigma_n)$ be a trace such that $r_n\sigma_n$ is a key update rule application for A that violates the Key Preparedness property. Consider the state $strip(\text{lastState}(\tau))$. Note this state is reachable from $\text{lastState}(\tau)$ through the rules SH_CANCEL and BLOCK.

By Reachability Conditional on a Common Key (Property 4.2), there exist no traces starting from $strip(\text{lastState}(\tau))$ that lead to the Complete$^\star(A, B)$ event fact without adversary interference. Thus desynchronisation resistance is violated.   □

5   Automated Verification

In this section we discuss the automated verification of the security properties from the previous section in the proving tool Tamarin. Tamarin uses multiset rewriting theory at its core, allowing for our model to be naturally implemented. We discuss the basic details of the implementation of the properties from Sect. 4 in Tamarin, before discussing two protocols that were analysed and shown to have attacks by using the Tamarin prover. In Appendix A we discuss some of the obstacles overcome in the implementation. The full implementations, along with diagrams and full descriptions of the attack traces can be found on our git repository[1], along with several other demonstrations of the security properties defined in this paper.

Definitions 4.5, 4.6, and 4.7 can be readily implemented in Tamarin. The remaining definitions used in our results can be verified syntactically from a protocol specification. With these considerations, our security properties can be analysed.

We note that the environment introduced in Sect. 4 is applicable to a large majority of key updating protocols. For example, many modern messaging applications make use of variations of the Diffie-Hellman Double Ratchet algorithm, which satisfies Common-Key Reachability (Property 4.2), Key Conservation (Property 4.4), and Key Uniqueness (Property 4.5). Note that Well-Formedness is a consequence of the specification of the protocol, not the protocol itself. The Gossamer protocol in the RFID domain also satisfies these properties. As a consequence, the verification of these protocols is limited only by the power of the analysis tools involved.

5.1   Identified Attacks

Our analysis identified novel attacks in two papers from the domain of RFID grouping protocols. In particular, these protocols were shown to violate the conditions of Theorem 4.12.

A desynchronisation attack was found on the grouping protocol of Sundaresan, Doss, and Zhou [26]. The attack consists of a modified replay message, taking advantage of the algebraic properties of the exclusive-OR function, which

---

[1] https://github.com/DesynchTamarin/desynch.

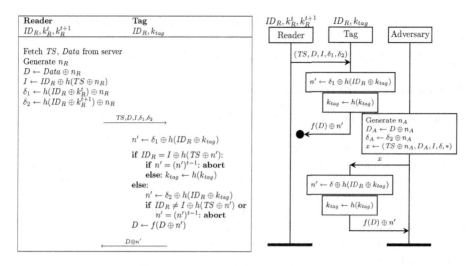

Fig. 2. The grouping protocol of Sundaresan et al. (left), and attack trace (right)

is used to mask data. This replay causes an RFID tag to incorrectly authenticate the adversary as a valid reader, updating their key past a safe threshold. The intended execution of the protocol, and a trace which leads to a desynchronisation attack, can be found in Fig. 2. A very similar attack can be found on another RFID grouping protocol, by Sundaresan, Doss, Piramuthu and Zhou [24].

An attack was also found on the 'two-round grouping proof' of Abughazalah, Markantonakis and Mayes [1]. This protocol consists of a single message-response round which allows multiple tags to authenticate to a single RFID reader. However, a modified replay attack abuses a built-in measure that allows a tag to 'reset' its group key. In this instance, the adversary can launch countless replay messages, causing a tag to update its personal encryption key arbitrarily many times. Further information about the attack can be found in Appendix B.

6 Conclusion

Denial-of-Service attacks are often not considered in the analysis of security protocols, mainly because such attacks are hard to distinguish from regular omissions in the underlying communication channel. However, some types of DoS attacks are aimed at vulnerabilities at the protocol level. A typical example is formed by the class of desynchronisation attacks, which aim to disrupt all future communications between the protocol agents by desynchronising their communication keys.

Even though such desynchronisation attacks have been known for over a decade, formal analysis tools have been lacking. In this paper we have addressed this issue by developing a formal definition of desynchronisation resistance using a protocol model based on multiset rewriting. This definition has been operationalised by defining a set of sufficient and necessary conditions that can be easily validated by current state-of-the-art verification tools, such as Tamarin. We showed the applicability of our methodology by deriving two novel desynchronisation attacks on published RFID protocols.

A   Tamarin Implementation Details

In Tamarin, executions always begin from the empty trace. The adversary knowledge is assumed to contain all public terms (such as the names of agents). To model this, we add a set of additional rules describing the establishment of shared keys between agents, as well as corruption rules where agents reveal their secret information to the adversary. Such rules are commonplace, and are comparable to those found in the Tamarin User Manual [27].

Tamarin allows for the implementation of user-defined equational theories. However, it requires that they be *subterm convergent*. We note that progress has been made on implementing more permissive equational theories, such as the work by Dreier et al., which provides an extension allowing for *AC-convergent* [9] equational theories.

Because of this, in some cases we are required to under-approximate the equational theory of a protocol. The most notable example of this is with the exclusive-or (XOR) operator. This under-approximation means that any identified attack traces are still valid, but it is possible that Tamarin will incorrectly report that a property holds. This is a limitation of the tool, not of the model itself.

Tamarin supports unbounded analysis, using induction arguments to successfully limit the search space in its backwards search approach. However, for stateful protocols, it is not uncommon for Tamarin to require assistance in finding proofs, sometimes failing to terminate. This means that at times we have aided the tool by manually identifying minor 'helper' lemmas which identify the key induction steps needed.

For ease of readability, we have assumed that the participants of a protocol can be assigned to *roles*. For example, in the RFID case, an agent may be a *tag* or a *reader*. As such, the event fact AddKey* is divided into the two event facts TagAddsKey* and ReaderAddsKey*.

B   Attack on the Two-Round Grouping Proof of Abughazalah, Markantonakis and Mayes

Abughazalah, Markantonakis and Mayes provide a two-round RFID grouping proof protocol [1], which uses updating keys. An RFID tag stores two updating keys, for authenticating itself as well as identifying the group that it is a part of.

A system is in place to allow a tag to re-synchronise its group key if it is absent for a run of the protocol, and does not receive the needed message to cause it to update its key naturally. However, this system allows for replay attacks to cause a tag to desynchronise its personal key with that stored by the verifier.

The analysis of the protocol in Tamarin revealed that it fails to satisfy the conditions of Theorem 4.12, resulting in an attack.

Protocol Description. The protocol is described in detail in the original paper. Here, we provide a simplified description of the protocol for the sake of conciseness. For example, the attack involves communication only between the reader and a single tag, so we focus on only looking at one tag. We also adopt the slightly adapted notation from Table 1. A diagram of the intended execution of the protocol is provided in Fig. 3.

Table 1. Notation used in the protocol by Abughazalah et al.

ID_G	The identity of the reader, a secret value
ID_T	The identity of the tag, a secret value
k_G	A secret key for the group being tested
k_T	A secret key for the specific tag being tested
TS^t	An encrypted timestamp, used in construction of the proof
n_R	A fresh (random) nonce generated by the reader
n_T	A fresh (random) nonce generated by the tag
$h(\cdot)$	A cryptographic hash function

Attack Trace Description. The grouping protocol has the advantage of requiring only two exchanged messages during its main execution between the reader and tag. However, this results in a vulnerability which leads to a desynchronisation attacks. The protocol was analysed in Tamarin, with the server role merged into the reader role. This is because the reader and server are assumed to have a secure communications channel.

Note that blocking the tag's message to the reader during a run of the protocol leads to a situation where the tag updates its secret, but the reader will not. The next time the protocol runs, the tag will receive the first message from the reader. Regardless of whether the reader updated the group key k_G (which it may have, because of the presence of other tags in the group completing the protocol), the tag will authenticate to this message and update its key a further time.

The authors seem aware of this problem, and suggest that it is possible for the server to calculate future values of the tag's key in order to prevent desynchronisation. However, there exists the capability to perform replay former messages, causing the tag to update its personal key arbitrarily many times.

As mentioned in the protocol paper, each tag stores previous nonces that they successfully authenticated to. However, an RFID tag has limited memory capacity - a typical EPC Generation 2 tag (such as those mentioned in the paper) has around 512 bits of storage space, meaning that there is very little space to store previously received nonces.

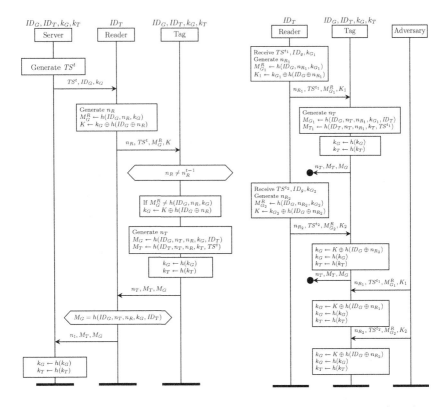

Fig. 3. Two-rounds grouping proof protocol (left) and attack trace (right).

As such, if an adversary is able to eavesdrop at least two runs of the protocol, a tag will readily accept a replay of a message from a previous execution. At this point, the tag will update its key. The adversary can then replay a different message, and repeat this cycle as long as desired.

References

1. Abughazalah, S., Markantonakis, K., Mayes, K.: Two rounds RFID grouping-proof protocol. In: 2016 IEEE International Conference on RFID, RFID 2016, Orlando, FL, USA, 3–5 May 2016, pp. 161–174 (2016)
2. Avoine, G.: Adversarial model for radio frequency identification. IACR Cryptology ePrint Archive 2005, 49 (2005)
3. Blanchet, B.: An efficient cryptographic protocol verifier based on prolog rules. In: CSF 2001, pp. 82–96 (2001)
4. Blanchet, B.: Using Horn clauses for analyzing security protocols. In: Formal Models and Techniques for Analyzing Security Protocols, vol. 5, pp. 86–111 (2011)
5. Cohn-Gordon, K., Cremers, C., Garratt, L.: On post-compromise security. In: CSF 2016, pp. 164–178. IEEE (2016)

6. van Deursen, T., Mauw, S., Radomirović, S., Vullers, P.: Secure ownership and ownership transfer in RFID systems. In: Backes, M., Ning, P. (eds.) ESORICS 2009. LNCS, vol. 5789, pp. 637–654. Springer, Heidelberg (2009). https://doi.org/ 10.1007/978-3-642-04444-1_39

7. van Deursen, T., Radomirovic, S.: Attacks on RFID protocols. IACR Cryptology ePrint Archive 2008, 310 (2008)

8. Dolev, D., Yao, A.C.: On the security of public key protocols. IEEE Trans. Inf. Theory **29**(2), 198–207 (1983)

9. Dreier, J., Duménil, C., Kremer, S., Sasse, R.: Beyond subterm-convergent equational theories in automated verification of stateful protocols. In: Maffei, M., Ryan, M. (eds.) POST 2017. LNCS, vol. 10204, pp. 117–140. Springer, Heidelberg (2017). https://doi.org/10.1007/978-3-662-54455-6_6

10. Durgin, N.A., Lincoln, P., Mitchell, J.C.: Multiset rewriting and the complexity of bounded security protocols. J. Comput. Secur. **12**(2), 247–311 (2004)

11. Goguen, J.A., Meseguer, J.: Order-sorted algebra I: equational deduction for multiple inheritance, overloading, exceptions and partial operations. Theor. Comput. Sci. **105**(2), 217–273 (1992)

12. Juels, A.: "Yoking-proofs" for RFID tags. In: 2nd IEEE Conference on Pervasive Computing and Communications Workshops (PerCom 2004 Workshops), Orlando, FL, USA, 14–17 March 2004, pp. 138–143 (2004)

13. Jung, S.W., Jung, S.: HRP: A HMAC-based RFID mutual authentication protocol using PUF. In: International Conference on Information Networking (ICOIN), pp. 578–582. IEEE (2013)

14. Kapoor, G., Piramuthu, S.: Vulnerabilities in some recently proposed RFID ownership transfer protocols. In: First International Conference on Networks and Communications, pp. 354–357. IEEE (2009)

15. Li, Q.S., Xu, X.L., Chen, Z.: PUF-based RFID ownership transfer protocol in an open environment. In: 15th International Conference on Parallel and Distributed Computing, Applications and Technologies, pp. 131–137. IEEE (2014)

16. Li, T., Wang, G.: Security analysis of two ultra-lightweight RFID authentication protocols. In: Venter, H., Eloff, M., Labuschagne, L., Eloff, J., von Solms, R. (eds.) SEC 2007. IIFIP, vol. 232, pp. 109–120. Springer, Boston, MA (2007). https://doi. org/10.1007/978-0-387-72367-9_10

17. Meier, S., Schmidt, B., Cremers, C., Basin, D.: The TAMARIN prover for the symbolic analysis of security protocols. In: Sharygina, N., Veith, H. (eds.) CAV 2013. LNCS, vol. 8044, pp. 696–701. Springer, Heidelberg (2013). https://doi.org/ 10.1007/978-3-642-39799-8_48

18. Peris-Lopez, P., Hernandez-Castro, J.C., Tapiador, J.M.E., Ribagorda, A.: Advances in ultralightweight cryptography for low-cost RFID tags: gossamer protocol. In: Chung, K.-I., Sohn, K., Yung, M. (eds.) WISA 2008. LNCS, vol. 5379, pp. 56–68. Springer, Heidelberg (2009). https://doi.org/10.1007/978-3-642-00306-6_5

19. Perrin, T., Marlinspike, M.: The double ratchet algorithm. GitHub Wiki (2016)

20. Radomirovic, S., Dashti, M.T.: Derailing attacks. In: Security Protocols XXIII - 23rd International Workshop, Cambridge, UK, 31 March- 2 April 2015, Revised Selected Papers, pp. 41–46 (2015)

21. Saito, J., Sakurai, K.: Grouping proof for RFID tags. In: 19th International Conference on Advanced Information Networking and Applications (AINA 2005), Taipei, Taiwan, 28–30 March 2005, pp. 621–624 (2005)

22. Srivastava, K., Awasthi, A.K., Kaul, S.D., Mittal, R.C.: A hash based mutual RFID tag authentication protocol in telecare medicine information system. J. Med. Syst. **39**(1), 153 (2015)
23. Sun, D., Zhong, J.: Cryptanalysis of a hash based mutual RFID tag authentication protocol. Wirel. Pers. Commun. **91**(3), 1085–1093 (2016)
24. Sundaresan, S., Doss, R., Piramuthu, S., Zhou, W.: A robust grouping proof protocol for RFID EPC C1G2 tags. IEEE Trans. Inf. Forensics Secur. **9**(6), 961–975 (2014)
25. Sundaresan, S., Doss, R., Zhou, W.: Secure ownership transfer in multi-tag/multi-owner passive RFID systems. In: Symposium on Selected Areas in Communications, Globecom 2013, pp. 2891–2896. IEEE (2013)
26. Sundaresan, S., Doss, R., Zhou, W.: Zero knowledge grouping proof protocol for RFID EPC C1G2 tags. IEEE Trans. Comput. **64**(10), 2994–3008 (2015)
27. The Tamarin Team: MS Windows NT Kernel Description (2018). https://tamarin-prover.github.io/manual/tex/tamarin-manual.pdf

Stateful Protocol Composition

Andreas V. Hess[1]([✉])[iD], Sebastian A. Mödersheim[1][iD],
and Achim D. Brucker[2][iD]

[1] DTU Compute, Technical University of Denmark, Lyngby, Denmark
{avhe,samo}@dtu.dk
[2] The University of Sheffield, Sheffield, UK
a.brucker@sheffield.ac.uk

Abstract. We prove a parallel compositionality result for protocols with a shared mutable state, i.e., stateful protocols. For protocols satisfying certain compositionality conditions our result shows that verifying the component protocols in isolation is sufficient to prove security of their composition. Our main contribution is an extension of the compositionality paradigm to stateful protocols where participants maintain shared databases. Because of the generality of our result we also cover many forms of sequential composition as a special case of stateful parallel composition. Moreover, we support declassification of shared secrets. As a final contribution we prove the core of our result in Isabelle/HOL, providing a strong correctness guarantee of our proofs.

1 Introduction

The typical use of communication networks like the Internet is to run a wide variety of security protocols in parallel, for example TLS, IPSec, DNSSEC, and many others. While the security properties of many of these protocols have been analyzed in great detail, much less research has been devoted to their parallel composition. It is far from self-evident that the parallel composition of secure protocols is still secure, in fact one can systematically construct counter-examples. One such problem is if protocols have similar message structures of different meaning, so that an attacker may be able to abuse messages, or parts thereof, that he has learned in the context of one protocol, and use them in the context of another where the same structure has a different meaning. Thus, we have to exclude that the protocols in some sense "interfere" with each other. However, it is unreasonable to require that the developers of the different protocols have to work together and synchronize with each other. Similarly, we do not want to reason about the composition of several protocols as a whole, neither in manual nor automated verification. Instead, we want a set of sufficient conditions and a composition theorem of the form: every set of protocols that satisfies the conditions yields a secure composition, provided that each protocol is secure in isolation. The conditions should be realistic so that many existing protocols like TLS (without modifications) actually satisfy them, and they should be simple,

© Springer Nature Switzerland AG 2018
J. Lopez et al. (Eds.): ESORICS 2018, LNCS 11098, pp. 427–446, 2018.
https://doi.org/10.1007/978-3-319-99073-6_21

in the sense that checking them is a static task that does not involve considering the reachable states.

The main contribution of this paper is the extension of the compositionality paradigm to *stateful* protocols, where participants may maintain a database (e.g., a list of valid public keys) independent of sessions. Such databases do not necessarily grow monotonically during protocol execution—we allow, for instance, negative membership checks and deletion of elements from databases. Moreover, we allow for such databases to be *shared* between the protocols to be composed. For instance, in the example of public keys, there could be several different protocols for registering, certifying, and revoking keys that all work on the same public-key database. Since such a shared database can potentially be exploited by the intruder to trigger harmful interferences, an important part of our result is a clear coordination of the ways in which each protocol is allowed to access the database. This coordination is based on assumptions and guarantees on the transactions that involve the database. Moreover, this also allows us to support protocols with the declassification of long-term secrets (e.g., that the private key to a revoked public key may be learned by the intruder without breaking the security goals). The result is so general that it actually also covers many forms of *sequential composition* as a special case, since one can for instance model that one protocol inserts keys into a database of fresh session keys, and another protocol "consumes" and uses them.

The proof of the main result is by a reduction to a problem finding solutions for intruder constraints: given a satisfiable constraint representing an attack on the composition, we show that the projection of the constraints to the individual protocols are satisfiable. This particular tricky part of the proof has been formalized in the interactive theorem prover Isabelle/HOL. This formalization, along with all proofs, is available at:

https://people.compute.dtu.dk/samo/composec.html

An extended version of this paper that includes the pen-and-paper proofs and short explanations of the Isabelle proofs is also available at this website [15]. Last but not least, as already indicated in [17], the formulation of the problem over intruder constraints allows us to apply our result with a variety of protocol formalisms such as applied-π calculus and multi-set rewriting.

The rest of the paper is organized as follows. Preliminaries are introduced in Sect. 2. In Sect. 3 we define stateful constraints and protocols. Afterwards we define protocol composition and introduce a keyserver protocol example in Sect. 4. We define our compositionality conditions and prove our main result in Sect. 5. Finally, we conclude in Sect. 6 and discuss related work.

2   Preliminaries

2.1   Terms and Substitutions

We model terms over a countable signature Σ of function symbols and a countably infinite set $\mathcal{V}$ of variable symbols. We do not fix here a particular set of cryptographic operators but rather parameterize our theory over arbitrary Σ. A term is either a variable $x \in \mathcal{V}$ or a composed term of the form $f(t_1, \ldots, t_n)$ where $f \in \Sigma^n$ and t_i are terms and Σ^n denotes the symbols in Σ of *arity* n. The set of *constants* $\mathcal{C}$ is defined as Σ^0. The set of variables of a term t is denoted by $fv(t)$ and if $fv(t) = \emptyset$ then t is *ground*. Both of these notions are extended to sets of terms. By $\sqsubseteq$ we denote the *subterm* relation.

Substitutions are defined as functions from variables to terms. The domain of a substitution δ is denoted by $dom(\delta)$ and is defined as the set of variables that are not mapped to themselves by δ: $dom(\delta) \equiv \{x \in \mathcal{V} \mid \delta(x) \neq x\}$. The substitution image, $img(\delta)$, is then defined as the image of $dom(\delta)$ under δ: $img(\delta) \equiv \delta(dom(\delta))$. If the image of δ is ground then δ is said to be a *ground substitution*. Additionally, we define an *interpretation* to be a substitution that assigns a ground term to every variable: $\mathcal{I}$ is an interpretation iff $dom(\mathcal{I}) = \mathcal{V}$ and $img(\mathcal{I})$ is ground. We extend substitutions to functions on terms and set of terms as expected. For substitutions δ with finite domain we will usually use the common value mapping notation: $\delta = [x_1 \mapsto t_1, \ldots, x_n \mapsto t_n]$. Finally, a substitution δ is a *unifier of* terms t and t' iff $\delta(t) = \delta(t')$.

2.2   The Intruder Model

The intruder model follows the standard of Dolev and Yao, roughly, the intruder can encrypt and decrypt terms where he has the respective keys, but he cannot break the cryptography. This is often done by a set of rules specialized to the concrete cryptographic functions, but since our model is parameterized over an arbitrary set Σ, we also need to parameterize it over (a) a predicate `public` over Σ that says for each function whether it is available to the intruder and (b) a function Ana that takes a term t and returns a pair (K, T) of sets of terms. The meaning is: from the term t the intruder can obtain the terms T, provided that he knows all the "keys" in the set K. For instance if crypt is a public function symbol to represent asymmetric encryption and inv is a private function symbol (i.e., $\neg$`public(inv)`) mapping public keys to the corresponding private key, then we may define $\mathsf{Ana}(\mathsf{crypt}(k, m)) = (\{\mathsf{inv}(k)\}, \{m\})$ for any terms k and m. Thus we can inductively define the relation $\vdash$, where $M \vdash t$ means that an intruder who knows the set of terms M can derive the message t as the least relation that includes M, is closed under composition with public functions and is closed under analysis with Ana as follows where $\Sigma_{pub}^n \equiv \{f \in \Sigma^n \mid \mathtt{public}(f)\}$:

Definition 1 (Intruder model)

$$\frac{}{M \vdash t} \; (Axiom), \; t \in M \qquad \frac{M \vdash t_1 \;\; \cdots \;\; M \vdash t_n}{M \vdash f(t_1, \ldots, t_n)} \; (Compose), \; f \in \Sigma_{pub}^n$$

$$\frac{M \vdash t \quad M \vdash k_1 \;\; \cdots \;\; M \vdash k_n}{M \vdash t_i} \; (Decompose), \mathsf{Ana}(t) = (K, T), \quad t_i \in T, K = \{k_1, \ldots, k_n\}$$

Note that [16] in contrast considers only public function symbols; one can simulate however a private function symbol of arity n by a public function symbol of arity $n+1$ where the additional argument is used with a special constant that is never given to the intruder; in this way all results can be lifted to a model with both private and public function symbols. For instance we can encode $\mathsf{inv} \in \Sigma^1$ in terms of a public symbol $\mathsf{inv}' \in \Sigma^2$ and a special secret constant $\mathsf{sec}_{\mathsf{inv}}$.

Our results will not work with an arbitrary analysis function, so we make the following requirements on Ana:

1. $\mathsf{Ana}(x) = (\emptyset, \emptyset)$ for variables $x \in \mathcal{V}$,
2. $\mathsf{Ana}(f(t_1, \ldots, t_n)) = (K, T)$ implies $T \subseteq \{t_1, \ldots, t_n\}$, finite K, and $fv(K) \subseteq fv(f(t_1, \ldots, t_n))$,
3. $\mathsf{Ana}(f(t_1, \ldots, t_n)) = (K, T)$ implies $\mathsf{Ana}(\delta(f(t_1, \ldots, t_n))) = (\delta(K), \delta(T))$.

Note that Ana must be defined for arbitrary terms, including terms with variables (while the standard Dolev-Yao deduction is typically applied to ground terms). The three conditions regulate that Ana is also meaningful on symbolic terms. The first requirement says that we cannot analyze a variable. The second requirement says that the result of the analysis are *immediate* subterms of the term being analyzed, and the keys can be any finite set of terms, but built with only variables that occur in the term being analyzed. The third requirement says that analysis does not change its behavior when instantiating a term (that is not a variable).

Example 1. We model asymmetric encryption and signatures with the following Ana theory: $\mathsf{Ana}(\mathsf{crypt}(k, m)) = (\{\mathsf{inv}(k)\}, \{m\})$, $\mathsf{Ana}(\mathsf{sign}(k, m)) = (\emptyset, \{m\})$. We will also later use some transparent functions: $\mathsf{Ana}(\mathsf{pair}(t, t')) = (\emptyset, \{t, t'\})$ and $\mathsf{Ana}(\mathsf{update}(s, t, u, v)) = (\emptyset, \{s, t, u, v\})$. For all other terms t: $\mathsf{Ana}(t) = (\emptyset, \emptyset)$.

3   Stateful Protocols

We now introduce a strand-based protocol formalism for stateful protocols adapted from [17]. This formalism is compact and reduced to the key concepts needed here, while more complex formalisms like process calculi can easily be fitted similarly. The semantics is defined by a symbolic transition system where constraints are built-up during transitions. The models of the constraints then constitute the concrete protocol runs. We will use a typing result that shows that for a large class of protocols, it is without loss of attacks to restrict the constraints to well-typed models [17].

3.1   Stateful Symbolic Constraints

We use *intruder constraints* as a key concept for reasoning about protocol executions and attacks. This is in fact applicable with a variety of protocol verification formalisms, such as process calculi or multi-set rewrite rules. The idea is to define a *symbolic* transition system where the variables of sent and received messages of the original protocol formalism are not instantiated (only renamed as necessary) and formulate symbolic constraints on these variables: the intruder needs to be able to construct each message an honest agent receives from the messages the honest agents have sent up to that point. When equipping these constraints also with equalities and inequalities, the set of all executions (and the attack predicates) of many formalisms like Applied π-calculus can be described by a set of constraints. An attack can then be defined by satisfiability of a constraint in which the intruder produces a secret. *Stateful constraints* can furthermore express queries and updates on databases. They are defined as finite sequences of *steps* and are built from the following grammar where t and t' ranges over terms and $\bar{x}$ over finite variable sequences $x_1, \ldots, x_n$:

$$\mathcal{A} ::= \mathsf{send}(t).\mathcal{A} \mid \mathsf{receive}(t).\mathcal{A} \mid t \doteq t'.\mathcal{A} \mid (\forall \bar{x}.\ t \neq t').\mathcal{A} \mid$$
$$\mathsf{insert}(t, t').\mathcal{A} \mid \mathsf{delete}(t, t').\mathcal{A} \mid t \mathrel{\dot{\in}} t'.\mathcal{A} \mid (\forall \bar{x}.\ t \mathrel{\dot{\notin}} t').\mathcal{A} \mid 0$$

Instead of $\forall \bar{x}.\ t \neq t'$ and $\forall \bar{x}.\ t \mathrel{\dot{\notin}} t'$ we may write $t \neq t'$ and $t \mathrel{\dot{\notin}} t'$ whenever $\bar{x}$ is the empty sequence. We may also write $t \mathrel{\dot{\notin}} f(\_)$ for $f \in \Sigma^n$ as an abbreviation of $\forall x_1, \ldots, x_n.\ t \mathrel{\dot{\notin}} f(x_1, \ldots, x_n)$. The *bound variables* of a constraint $\mathcal{A}$ consists of its variable sequences while the remaining variables, $fv(\mathcal{A})$, are the *free variables*. Also, by $trms(\mathcal{A})$ we denote the set of terms occurring in $\mathcal{A}$ and the *set of set operations* of $\mathcal{A}$, called $setops(\mathcal{A})$, is defined as follows where $(\cdot, \cdot) \in \Sigma^2_{pub}$:

$$setops(\mathcal{A}) \equiv \{(t, s) \mid \mathsf{insert}(t, s) \text{ or } \mathsf{delete}(t, s) \text{ or } t \mathrel{\dot{\in}} s \text{ or } \forall \bar{x}.\ t \mathrel{\dot{\notin}} s \text{ occurs in } \mathcal{A}\}$$

For the semantics of constraints we first define a predicate $[\![M, D; \mathcal{A}]\!]\ \mathcal{I}$, where M is a ground set of terms (the intruder knowledge), D is a ground set of tuples (the state of the sets), $\mathcal{A}$ is a constraint, and $\mathcal{I}$ is an interpretation as follows:

$$
\begin{aligned}
[\![M, D; 0]\!]\ \mathcal{I} \quad &\text{iff} \quad true \\
[\![M, D; \mathsf{send}(t).\mathcal{A}]\!]\ \mathcal{I} \quad &\text{iff} \quad M \vdash \mathcal{I}(t) \text{ and } [\![M, D; \mathcal{A}]\!]\ \mathcal{I} \\
[\![M, D; \mathsf{receive}(t).\mathcal{A}]\!]\ \mathcal{I} \quad &\text{iff} \quad [\![\{\mathcal{I}(t)\} \cup M, D; \mathcal{A}]\!]\ \mathcal{I} \\
[\![M, D; t \doteq t'.\mathcal{A}]\!]\ \mathcal{I} \quad &\text{iff} \quad \mathcal{I}(t) = \mathcal{I}(t') \text{ and } [\![M, D; \mathcal{A}]\!]\ \mathcal{I} \\
[\![M, D; (\forall \bar{x}.\ t \neq t').\mathcal{A}]\!]\ \mathcal{I} \quad &\text{iff} \quad [\![M, D; \mathcal{A}]\!]\ \mathcal{I} \text{ and } \mathcal{I}(\delta(t)) \neq \mathcal{I}(\delta(t')) \\
&\qquad \text{for all ground substitutions } \delta \text{ with domain } \bar{x} \\
[\![M, D; \mathsf{insert}(t, s).\mathcal{A}]\!]\ \mathcal{I} \quad &\text{iff} \quad [\![M, \{\mathcal{I}((t, s))\} \cup D; \mathcal{A}]\!]\ \mathcal{I} \\
[\![M, D; \mathsf{delete}(t, s).\mathcal{A}]\!]\ \mathcal{I} \quad &\text{iff} \quad [\![M, D \setminus \{\mathcal{I}((t, s))\}; \mathcal{A}]\!]\ \mathcal{I} \\
[\![M, D; t \mathrel{\dot{\in}} s.\mathcal{A}]\!]\ \mathcal{I} \quad &\text{iff} \quad \mathcal{I}((t, s)) \in D \text{ and } [\![M, D; \mathcal{A}]\!]\ \mathcal{I} \\
[\![M, D; (\forall \bar{x}.\ t \mathrel{\dot{\notin}} s).\mathcal{A}]\!]\ \mathcal{I} \quad &\text{iff} \quad [\![M, D; \mathcal{A}]\!]\ \mathcal{I} \text{ and } \mathcal{I}(\delta((t, s))) \notin D \\
&\qquad \text{for all ground substitutions } \delta \text{ with domain } \bar{x}
\end{aligned}
$$

We then define that $\mathcal{I}$ is a *model* of $\mathcal{A}$, written $\mathcal{I} \models \mathcal{A}$, iff $[\![\emptyset, \emptyset; \mathcal{A}]\!]\ \mathcal{I}$.

A crucial requirement on constraints is that they are well-formed in the sense that every variable first occurs in a message the intruder sends, or in a positive check like $t \doteq t'$ or $t \mathrel{\dot{\in}} s$, and that the intruder knowledge monotonically grows over time. The latter condition is already built-in in our constraint notation, the former is expressed as follows: A constraint $\mathcal{A}$ is *well-formed w.r.t.* the set of variables X (or just *well-formed* if $X = \emptyset$) iff the free variables and the bound variables of $\mathcal{A}$ are disjoint and $wf_X(\mathcal{A})$ holds where:

$$
\begin{array}{lll}
wf_X(0) & \text{iff} & true \\
wf_X(\text{receive}(t).\mathcal{A}) & \text{iff} & fv(t) \subseteq X \text{ and } wf_X(\mathcal{A}) \\
wf_X(\text{send}(t).\mathcal{A}) & \text{iff} & wf_{X \cup fv(t)}(\mathcal{A}) \\
wf_X(t \doteq t'.\mathcal{A}) & \text{iff} & fv(t') \subseteq X \text{ and } wf_{X \cup fv(t)}(\mathcal{A}) \\
wf_X(\text{insert}(t,t').\mathcal{A}) & \text{iff} & fv(t) \cup fv(t') \subseteq X \text{ and } wf_X(\mathcal{A}) \\
wf_X(\text{delete}(t,t').\mathcal{A}) & \text{iff} & fv(t) \cup fv(t') \subseteq X \text{ and } wf_X(\mathcal{A}) \\
wf_X(t \;\dot{\in}\; t'.\mathcal{A}) & \text{iff} & wf_{X \cup fv(t) \cup fv(t')}(\mathcal{A}) \\
wf_X(\mathfrak{a}.\mathcal{A}) & \text{iff} & wf_X(\mathcal{A}) \text{ otherwise}
\end{array}
$$

Note that this allows to "introduce" variables in a send step, on the left-hand side of an equation, or in a positive set-membership check (and we will work only with well-formed constraints throughout the paper).

3.2 Typed Model

Our result is based on a typed model of protocols, i.e., where the intruder by definition cannot send ill-typed messages. [17] shows that this is not a restriction for a large class of so-called *type-flaw resistant* stateful protocols, since for every ill-typed attack also exists a well-typed one. This gives a sufficient condition for protocols to satisfy a prerequisite of our compositionality result. The definition of typed model is then as follows. Type expressions are terms built over the function symbols of Σ and a finite set $\mathfrak{T}_a$ of *atomic* types like Agent and Nonce. Further, we define a typing function Γ that assigns to every variable a type, to every constant an atomic type, and that is extended to composed terms as follows: $\Gamma(f(t_1, \ldots, t_n)) = f(\Gamma(t_1), \ldots, \Gamma(t_n))$ for every $f \in \Sigma^n \setminus \mathcal{C}$ and terms t_i. We also require that $\{c \in \mathcal{C} \mid \mathtt{public}(c), \Gamma(c) = \beta\}$ is infinite for each $\beta \in \mathfrak{T}_a$, thus giving the intruder access to an infinite supply of terms of each atomic type.

The sufficient condition for a protocol to satisfy the typing result is now based on the following notions. A substitution δ is *well-typed* iff $\Gamma(x) = \Gamma(\delta(x))$ for all $x \in \mathcal{V}$. Given a set of messages that occur in a protocol we define the following set of sub-message patterns, intuitively the ones that may occur during constraint reduction:

Definition 2 (Sub-message patterns). *The* sub-message patterns $SMP(M)$ *for a set of messages M is defined as the least set satisfying the following rules:*

1. $M \subseteq SMP(M)$.
2. *If $t \in SMP(M)$ and $t' \sqsubseteq t$ then $t' \in SMP(M)$.*
3. *If $t \in SMP(M)$ and δ is a well-typed substitution then $\delta(t) \in SMP(M)$.*
4. *If $t \in SMP(M)$ and $\mathsf{Ana}(t) = (K, T)$ then $K \subseteq SMP(M)$.*

The sufficient condition for the typing result is now that non-variable sub-message patterns have no unifier unless they have the same type:

Definition 3 (Type-flaw resistance). *We say a set M of messages is type-flaw resistant iff $\forall t, t' \in SMP(M) \setminus \mathcal{V}. \; (\exists \delta. \; \delta(t) = \delta(t')) \longrightarrow \Gamma(t) = \Gamma(t')$. We may also apply the notion of type-flaw resistance to a constraint $\mathcal{A}$ to mean that:*

– $trms(\mathcal{A}) \cup setops(\mathcal{A})$ is type-flaw resistant,
– if t and t' are unifiable then $\Gamma(t) = \Gamma(t')$, for all $t \doteq t'$ occurring in $\mathcal{A}$,
– $\Gamma(fv(t) \cup fv(t')) \subseteq \mathfrak{T}_a$ for all $\mathsf{insert}(t,t')$ and $\mathsf{delete}(t,t')$ occurring in $\mathcal{A}$, and
– $\Gamma((fv(t) \cup fv(t')) \setminus \bar{x}) \subseteq \mathfrak{T}_a$ for all $\forall \bar{x}. \ t \not\doteq t'$ and $\forall \bar{x}. \ t \not\doteq t'$ occurring in $\mathcal{A}$.

We have formalized in Isabelle/HOL the following typing result theorem, which shows that for type-flaw resistant protocols it is safe to check satisfiability of constraints within the typed model [17]:

Theorem 1 ([17]). *If $\mathcal{A}$ is a well-formed, type-flaw resistant constraint, and if $\mathcal{I} \models \mathcal{A}$, then there exists a well-typed interpretation $\mathcal{I}_\tau$ such that $\mathcal{I}_\tau \models \mathcal{A}$.*

3.3   Protocol Semantics

Protocols are defined as sets $\mathcal{P} = \{R_1, \ldots\}$ of *transaction rules* of the form: $R_i = \forall x_1 \in T_1, \ldots, x_n \in T_n.$ new $y_1, \ldots, y_m. \ S$ where S is a *transaction strand*, i.e., of the form $\mathsf{receive}(t_1). \cdots .\mathsf{receive}(t_k).\phi_1 \cdots \phi_{k'}.\mathsf{send}(t'_1). \cdots .\mathsf{send}(t'_{k''})$ where

$$\phi ::= t \doteq t' \mid \forall \bar{x}. \ t \not\doteq t' \mid t \doteq t' \mid \forall \bar{x}. \ t \not\doteq t' \mid \mathsf{insert}(t,t') \mid \mathsf{delete}(t,t')$$

The prefix $\forall x_1 \in T_1, \ldots, x_n \in T_n$ denotes that the transaction strand S is applicable for instantiations σ of the x_i variables where $\sigma(x_i) \in T_i$. The construct new $y_1, \ldots, y_m$ represents that the occurrences of the variables y_i in the transaction strand S will be instantiated with fresh terms. We extend $trms(\cdot)$ and $setops(\cdot)$ to transactions strands, rules, and protocols as expected.

We define a transition relation $\Rightarrow_{\mathcal{P}}^\bullet$ for protocol $\mathcal{P}$ where states are constraints and the initial state is the empty constraint 0. First we define the *dual* of a transaction strand S, written $dual(S)$, as "swapping" the direction of the sent and received messages of S: $dual(\mathsf{send}(t).S) = \mathsf{receive}(t).dual(S)$, $dual(\mathsf{receive}(t).S) = \mathsf{send}(t).dual(S)$, and otherwise $dual(\mathsf{s}.S) = \mathsf{s}.dual(S)$. The transition $\mathcal{A} \Rightarrow_{\mathcal{P}}^\bullet \mathcal{A}.dual(\alpha(\sigma(S)))$ is then applicable if these conditions are met:

1. $(\forall x_1 \in T_1, \ldots, x_n \in T_n.$ new $y_1, \ldots, y_m. \ S) \in \mathcal{P}$,
2. $dom(\sigma) = \{x_1, \ldots, x_n, y_1, \ldots, y_m\}$,
3. $\sigma(x_i) \in T_i$ for all $i \in \{1, \ldots, n\}$,
4. $\sigma(y_i)$ is a fresh ground term of type $\Gamma(y_i)$ for all $i \in \{1, \ldots, m\}$, and
5. α is a variable-renaming of the variables of $\sigma(S)$ where α is well-typed and the variables in $img(\alpha)$ do not occur in $\sigma(S)$.

Hence transaction rules are processed atomically, and converted into constraints, during transitions. Note that each transaction rule can be executed arbitrarily often and so we support an unbounded number of "sessions". For instance, the transaction rule $\forall A \in \mathsf{Hon}.$ new $PK. \ \mathsf{insert}(PK, \mathsf{ring}(A))$ models that each honest agent $a \in \mathsf{Hon}$ can insert one fresh key into its keyring $\mathsf{ring}(a)$ during each application of the transaction rule. This rule can be executed any number of times with any agent $a \in \mathsf{Hon}$ and a fresh value for PK each time.

We say that a constraint $\mathcal{A}$ is *reachable* in protocol $\mathcal{P}$ if $0 \Rightarrow_{\mathcal{P}}^{\bullet\star} \mathcal{A}$ where $\Rightarrow_{\mathcal{P}}^{\bullet\star}$ denotes the transitive reflexive closure of $\Rightarrow_{\mathcal{P}}^{\bullet}$. We need to ensure that these constraints are well-formed and we will therefore always assume the following sufficient requirement on the protocols $\mathcal{P}$ that we work with: for any transaction strand S occurring in any rule $\forall x_1 \in T_1, \ldots, x_n \in T_n.$ new $y_1, \ldots, y_m. \ S$ of $\mathcal{P}$ the constraint $dual(S)$ is well-formed w.r.t. the variables $\{x_1, \ldots, x_n, y_1, \ldots, y_m\}$. In other words, the variables of S must first occur in either a receive step, a positive check ($\doteq, \dot{\in}$), or be part of $\{x_1, \ldots, x_n, y_1, \ldots, y_m\}$.

To model goal violations of a protocol $\mathcal{P}$ we first fix a special constant unique to $\mathcal{P}$, e.g., $\mathsf{attack}_{\mathcal{P}}$. Secondly, we add the rule $\mathsf{receive}(\mathsf{attack}_{\mathcal{P}})$ to $\mathcal{P}$ that we use as a signal for when an attack has occurred. The protocol then has a (well-typed) attack if there exists a (well-typed) satisfiable reachable constraint of the form $\mathcal{A}.\mathsf{send}(\mathsf{attack}_{\mathcal{P}})$. A protocol with no attacks is *secure*.

With sets we can model events, e.g., asserting an event e amounts to inserting e into a distinguished set of events while checking whether e has previously occurred (or not) corresponds to a positive (respectively negative) set-membership check. We therefore support all security properties expressible in the geometric fragment [1]. This covers many standard reachability goals such as authentication; it seems that any significantly richer fragment of first-order logic would be incompatible with our result. We do not currently support privacy-type properties, i.e., where goal violations occur if the observable behavior of protocols can be distinguished.

4   Composition and a Running Example

The core definition of this paper is rather simple: we define the *parallel composition* $\mathcal{P}_1 \parallel \mathcal{P}_2$ of protocols $\mathcal{P}_1$ and $\mathcal{P}_2$ as their union: $\mathcal{P}_1 \parallel \mathcal{P}_2 \equiv \mathcal{P}_1 \cup \mathcal{P}_2$. Protocols $\mathcal{P}_1$ and $\mathcal{P}_2$ are also referred to as the *component protocols* of the composition $\mathcal{P}_1 \parallel \mathcal{P}_2$. For such a composed protocol the reachable constraints in $\mathcal{P}_1 \parallel \mathcal{P}_2$ will in general contain steps originating from both component protocols. To keep track of where a step in a constraint originated we assign to each step a *label* $\ell \in \{1, 2, \star\}$. The steps that are exclusive to the first component are marked with 1 while the steps exclusive to the second are marked with 2. In addition to the protocol-specific labels we also have a special label $\star$ that we explain later.

Let $\mathcal{A}$ be a constraint with labels and $\ell \in \{1, 2, \star\}$, we define $\mathcal{A}|_{\ell}$ to be the projection of $\mathcal{A}$ to the steps labeled ℓ or $\star$ (so the $\star$-steps are kept in every a projection). We extend projections to transaction rules and protocols as expected. We may also write $\mathcal{P}^{\star}$ instead of $\mathcal{P}|_{\star}$.

4.1   A Keyserver Example

As a running example, Figs. 1 and 2 define two keyserver protocols that share the same databases of valid public keys registered at the keyserver. In a nutshell, the first protocol $\mathcal{P}_{ks,1} = \{R_1^1, \ldots, R_1^{10}\}$ allows users to register public keys out of band and to update an existing key with a new one (revoking the old key in

$\boxed{1} \equiv$	1: receive(sign(inv(PK), pair(A, NPK))). $\star$: $PK \,\dot{\in}\,$ valid(A,S). $\star$: $NPK \,\dot{\notin}\,$ valid($\_$). 1: $NPK \,\dot{\notin}\,$ revoked($\_$)
R_1^1	$\forall A \in$ Hon, $S \in$ Ser. 1: receive(inv(PK)). $\star$: $PK \,\dot{\in}\,$ valid(A,S). 1: send(attack$_1$)
R_1^2	$\forall A \in$ Hon, $S \in$ Ser. $\boxed{1}$. $\star$: $NPK \,\dot{\notin}\,$ begin$_1$(A,S). 1: send(attack$_1$)
R_1^3	$\forall A \in$ Hon, $S \in$ Ser. $\boxed{1}$. $\star$: $NPK \,\dot{\in}\,$ begin$_1$(A,S). $\star$: $NPK \,\dot{\in}\,$ end$_1$(A,S). 1: send(attack$_1$)
R_1^4	$\forall A \in$ Dis. new PK. $\star$: send(PK). $\star$: send(inv(PK))
R_1^5	$\forall A \in$ Hon, $S \in$ Ser. new PK. 1: insert(PK, ring(A)). $\star$: insert(PK, valid(A,S)). $\star$: insert(PK, begin$_1$(A,S)). $\star$: insert(PK, end$_1$(A,S)). $\star$: send(PK)
R_1^6	$\forall A \in$ Hon, $S \in$ Ser. new NPK. 1: $PK \,\dot{\in}\,$ ring(A). 1: delete(PK, ring(A)). 1: insert(NPK, ring(A)). $\star$: insert(NPK, begin$_1$(A,S)). $\star$: send(NPK). 1: send(sign(inv(PK), pair(A, NPK)))
R_1^7	$\forall A \in$ Hon, $S \in$ Ser. $\boxed{1}$. $\star$: $NPK \,\dot{\in}\,$ begin$_1$(A,S). $\star$: $NPK \,\dot{\notin}\,$ end$_1$(A,S). $\star$: delete(PK, valid(A,S)). $\star$: insert(NPK, valid(A,S)). 1: insert(PK, revoked(A,S)). $\star$: insert(NPK, end$_1$(A,S)). $\star$: send(inv(PK))
R_1^8	$\forall A \in$ Dis, $S \in$ Ser. $\boxed{1}$. $\star$: delete(PK, valid(A,S)). $\star$: insert(NPK, valid(A,S)). 1: insert(PK, revoked(A,S))
R_1^9	$\forall A \in$ Dis, $S \in$ Ser. 1: receive(PK). $\star$: $PK \,\dot{\notin}\,$ valid($\_$). $\star$: insert(PK, valid(A,S))
R_1^{10}	1: receive(attack$_1$)

Fig. 1. The transaction rules of the first keyserver protocol $\mathcal{P}_{ks,1}$.

the process), while the second protocol $\mathcal{P}_{ks,2} = \{R_2^1, \ldots, R_2^{10}\}$ uses a different mechanism to register new public keys.

We use here three atomic types: the type of agents Agent, public keys PubKey, and the type Attack of the attack$_i$ constants. We partition type Agent into the honest users Hon, the dishonest users Dis, and the keyservers Ser. There are sets for authentication goals begin$_1$, end$_1$, begin$_2$, and end$_2$, and all protocol steps related to these sets are highlighted in gray; let us first ignore these.

Protocol $\mathcal{P}_{ks,1}$. In the first protocol, rule R_1^5 models that an honest user registers a new public key PK out of band (e.g., by physically visiting a registration site); this is achieved by inserting PK (in the same transaction) both into a keyring ring(A) for user A and into a shared database valid(A,S) of the user's currently

$\boxed{2} \equiv 2\colon \mathsf{receive}(\mathsf{crypt}(PK, \mathsf{update}(A, S, NPK, \mathsf{pw}(A,S))))$.

  2: $PK \mathrel{\dot\in} \mathsf{pubkeys}(S)$. 2: $NPK \mathrel{\dot\notin} \mathsf{pubkeys}(\_)$. 2: $NPK \mathrel{\dot\notin} \mathsf{seen}(\_)$

R_2^1	$\forall A \in \mathsf{Hon}, S \in \mathsf{Ser}$. 2: $\mathsf{receive}(\mathsf{inv}(PK))$. $\star$: $PK \mathrel{\dot\in} \mathsf{valid}(A,S)$. 2: $\mathsf{send}(\mathsf{attack}_2)$
R_2^2	$\forall A \in \mathsf{Hon}, S \in \mathsf{Ser}$. $\boxed{2}$. $\star$: $NPK \mathrel{\dot\notin} \mathsf{begin}_2(A,S)$. 2: $\mathsf{send}(\mathsf{attack}_2)$
R_2^3	$\forall A \in \mathsf{Hon}, S \in \mathsf{Ser}$. $\boxed{2}$. $\star$: $NPK \mathrel{\dot\in} \mathsf{begin}_2(A,S)$. $\star$: $NPK \mathrel{\dot\in} \mathsf{end}_2(A,S)$. 2: $\mathsf{send}(\mathsf{attack}_2)$
R_2^4	$\forall A \in \mathsf{Dis}$. new PK. $\star$: $\mathsf{send}(PK)$. $\star$: $\mathsf{send}(\mathsf{inv}(PK))$
R_2^5	$\forall A \in \mathsf{Hon}, S \in \mathsf{Ser}$. new NPK. 2: $PK \mathrel{\dot\in} \mathsf{pubkeys}(S)$. $\star$: $\mathsf{insert}(NPK, \mathsf{begin}_2(A,S))$. $\star$: $\mathsf{send}(NPK)$. 2: $\mathsf{send}(\mathsf{crypt}(PK, \mathsf{update}(A,S,NPK,\mathsf{pw}(A,S))))$
R_2^6	$\forall A \in \mathsf{Hon}, S \in \mathsf{Ser}$. $\boxed{2}$. $\star$: $NPK \mathrel{\dot\in} \mathsf{begin}_2(A,S)$. $\star$: $NPK \mathrel{\dot\notin} \mathsf{end}_2(A,S)$. $\star$: $\mathsf{insert}(NPK, \mathsf{valid}(A,S))$. $\star$: $\mathsf{insert}(NPK, \mathsf{end}_2(A,S))$. 2: $\mathsf{insert}(NPK, \mathsf{seen}(A))$
R_2^7	$\forall A \in \mathsf{Dis}, S \in \mathsf{Ser}$. 2: $\mathsf{send}(\mathsf{pw}(A,S))$
R_2^8	$\forall A \in \mathsf{Dis}, S \in \mathsf{Ser}$. $\boxed{2}$. $\star$: $\mathsf{insert}(PK, \mathsf{valid}(A,S))$. 2: $\mathsf{insert}(PK, \mathsf{seen}(A))$
R_2^9	$\forall S \in \mathsf{Ser}$. new PK. 2: $\mathsf{insert}(PK, \mathsf{pubkeys}(S))$. $\star$: $\mathsf{send}(PK)$
R_2^{10}	2: $\mathsf{receive}(\mathsf{attack}_2)$

Fig. 2. The transaction rules of the second keyserver protocol $\mathcal{P}_{ks,2}$.

valid keys. There is also a corresponding rule for dishonest users: R_1^9. Dishonest users may register in their name any key they know (hence the $\mathsf{receive}(PK)$ step), so the key is not necessarily freshly created; also we do not model a keyring for them. (Rule R_i^4 gives the intruder access to arbitrarily many fresh key pairs.)

Secondly, we model a key update with revocation of old keys. To request an update of key PK with a newly generated key NPK at server S, an honest user sends NPK signed with PK as in R_1^6. (For this rule there is no equivalent for the dishonest agents, since they may produce an arbitrary update request message.)

The rule R_1^7 shows how S receives the update message from an honest agent: it checks ($\boxed{1}$) that the key PK is currently valid, and that NPK is neither registered as valid or revoked. If so, it updates its databases accordingly: it moves the old key from $\mathsf{valid}(A,S)$ to $\mathsf{revoked}(A,S)$ and registers the new key NPK by inserting it into $\mathsf{valid}(A,S)$. Also, we reveal here $\mathsf{inv}(PK)$, in order to specify that the protocol must even be secure when old private keys are leaked. This is an example of declassification of a secret shared between two protocols: after intentionally revealing $\mathsf{inv}(PK)$ it should no longer count as a secret. The rule R_1^8 is the pendant for dishonest agents. The last rule R_1^{10} acts as a signal for when an attack has occurred in $\mathcal{P}_{ks,1}$.

Protocol $\mathcal{P}_{ks,2}$. The second protocol has another mechanism to register new keys: every user has a password $\mathsf{pw}(A, S)$ with the server (the dishonest agents reveal their password to the intruder with rule R_2^7). Instead of using a (possibly weak) password for an encryption, the registration message is encrypted with the public key of the server (rule R_2^5). For uniformity, we model the server's public keys in a set $\mathsf{pubkeys}(S)$ that is initialized with rule R_2^9 (in fact, the server may thus have multiple public keys). Rule R_2^6 models how the server receives a registration request (in case of honest users): to protect against replay, the server uses a set seen of seen keys (this may in a real implementation be a buffer-timestamp mechanism). Rule R_2^8 is the pendant for the dishonest users. Finally, the rule R_2^{10} acts as a signal for when an attack has occurred in $\mathcal{P}_{ks,2}$.

Authentication. Besides the secrecy goal R_i^1 that no valid private key of an honest agent may ever be known by the intruder, the crucial authentication goal is that all insertions into $\mathsf{valid}(A, S)$ for honest A are authenticated. The classical injective agreement is modeled by the steps highlighted in gray: when an honest agent generates a fresh key for server, it inserts it into a special set begin, and whenever a server accepts a key that appears to come from an honest agent A, then it inserts it into a special set end. (Note that these sets exist only in our model to specify the goals.) It is a violation of non-injective agreement if the server accepts a key that is not in begin (rule R_i^2), and of injective agreement if the server accepts a key that is already in end (rule R_i^3).

Such a specification is more declarative when one separates the protocol rules from the attack rules, but that has one drawback: if the protocol indeed had an attack, then one would allow the server to actually insert an unauthenticated key into its database and then in the next step the attack rule fires. For the composition result, however, we want that each protocol can rely on the other protocols to never insert unauthenticated keys into the database. This is why we integrate in rules R_i^6 of each protocol the checks that we are in an authenticated case (otherwise, the rules R_i^2 or R_i^3 fire). This is similar to a "lookahead" where we prevent the execution of a transition if it leads to an attack, and directly trigger an attack. This computation of the lookahead version of goals may of course be lifted from the user by verification tools.

5   The Compositionality Results

With stateful protocols and parallel composition defined we can now formally define the concepts underlying our results and state our compositionality theorems. We first provide a result on the level of constraints and afterwards show our main theorems for stateful protocols.

5.1   Protocol Abstraction

Note that all steps containing the valid set family in our keyserver example have been labeled with $\star$. Labeling operations on the shared sets with $\star$ is actually an important part of our compositionality result and we now explain why.

Essentially, compositionality results aim to prevent that attacks can arise from the composition itself, i.e., attacks that do not similarly work on the components in isolation. Thus we want to show that attacks on the composed system can be sufficiently decomposed into attacks on the components. This however cannot directly work if the components have shared sets like valid in the example: if one protocol inserts something to a set and the other protocol reads from the set, then this trace in general does not have a counter-part in the second protocol alone. We thus need a kind of *interface* to how the two protocols can influence their shared sets. In the key server example, both protocols can insert public keys into the shared set valid, the first protocol can even remove them. The idea is now that we develop from each protocol an *abstract* version that subsumes all the modifications that the concrete protocol can perform on the shared sets. This can be regarded as a "contract" for the composition: each protocol *guarantees* that it will not make any modifications that are not covered by its abstract protocol, and it will *assume* that the other protocol only makes modifications covered by the other protocol's abstraction. We will still have to verify that each individual protocol is also secure when running together with the other abstract protocol, but this is in general much simpler than the composition of the two concrete protocols. (In the special case that the protocols share no sets, i.e. like in all previous parallel composition results, the abstractions are empty, i.e., we have to verify only the individual components.)

In general, the abstraction of a component protocol $\mathcal{P}$ is defined by restriction to those steps that are labeled $\star$, i.e., $\mathcal{P}^\star$. We require that at least the modification of shared sets are labeled $\star$. In the keyserver example we have also labeled the operations on the authentication-related sets with a $\star$ (everything highlighted in gray): we need to ensure that we insert into the set of valid keys of an honest agent only those keys that really have been created by that agent and that have not been previously inserted. So the contract between the two protocols is that they only insert keys that are properly authenticated, but the abstraction ignores how each protocol achieves the authentication (e.g. signatures vs. passwords and seen-set). There are also some outgoing messages labeled with $\star$ which we discuss a little below.[1]

Example 2. Consider the abstractions of rules R_2^5 and R_2^6:

$$\forall A \in \mathsf{Hon}, S \in \mathsf{Ser}.\ \mathsf{new}\ NPK.$$
$$\star\colon \mathsf{insert}(NPK, \mathsf{begin}_2(A, S)).$$
$$\star\colon \mathsf{send}(NPK)$$

$$\forall A \in \mathsf{Hon}, S \in \mathsf{Ser}.$$
$$\star\colon NPK \mathrel{\dot\in} \mathsf{begin}_2(A, S).$$
$$\star\colon NPK \mathrel{\ddot\notin} \mathsf{end}_2(A, S).$$
$$\star\colon \mathsf{insert}(NPK, \mathsf{valid}(A, S)).$$
$$\star\colon \mathsf{insert}(NPK, \mathsf{end}_2(A, S))$$

Notice that the gray steps prevent unauthenticated key registration because keys can only be registered if inserted into begin_2 by an honest agent. If we *did*

---

[1] We require also well-formedness of the $\star$-projected protocols. This is violated, for instance, if a protocol contains a rule where only one outgoing message is labeled $\star$ and this message contains variables. However, given that the concrete protocol is already well-formed, this is easy to fix automatically, transparent to the user.

not ensure such authenticated key-registration then the intruder would be able to register arbitrary keys in $\mathcal{P}^\star_{ks,2}$. This would lead to an attack on secrecy in the protocol $\mathcal{P}_{ks,1} \parallel \mathcal{P}^\star_{ks,2}$.

One may wonder why there is no similar specification for secrecy, i.e., that $\mathsf{inv}(NPK)$ is secret for every key NPK that is being inserted into valid. In fact, below we will declare all private keys to be secret by default. Thus, unless explicitly declassified, they are (implicitly) required to be secret.

5.2   Shared Terms

Before giving the compositionality conditions we first formally define what terms can be shared: Every term t that occurs in multiple component protocols must be either a *basic public term* (meaning that the intruder can derive t without prior knowledge, i.e., $\emptyset \vdash t$) or a *shared secret*. If the intruder learns a shared secret (that has not been explicitly declassified) then it is considered a violation of secrecy in *all* component protocols. For instance, agent names are usually basic public terms whereas private keys are secrets. In fact, we will have that *all* shared terms (except basic public terms) are by default secrets—even public keys—before they are declassified.

Let *Sec* be a set of ground terms, representing the initially shared secrets of the protocols. Note that the set of shared secrets *Sec* is not a fixed predefined set of terms, but rather just a parameter to our compositionality condition. We require that all shared terms of the protocols are either in *Sec* or basic public terms. To precisely define this requirement, we first define the *ground sub-message patterns (GSMP)* of a set of terms M as $GSMP(M) \equiv \{t \in SMP(M) \mid fv(t) = \emptyset\}$. This definition is extended to constraints $\mathcal{A}$ as the set $GSMP(\mathcal{A}) \equiv GSMP(trms(\mathcal{A}) \cup setops(\mathcal{A}))$, and similarly for protocols. To make matters smooth, we also require that $Sec \cup \{t \mid \emptyset \vdash t\}$ is closed under subterms (which is trivially the case for the basic public terms).

Example 3. We will typically study the ground subterms of each individual protocol in parallel with the abstraction of the other. For the example, the set $GSMP(\mathcal{P}_{ks,1} \parallel \mathcal{P}^\star_{ks,2})$ is the closure under subterms of the following set:

$$\{\mathsf{attack}_1, (pk, \mathsf{ring}(a)), (pk, \mathsf{valid}(a, s)), (pk, \mathsf{revoked}(a, s)), (pk, \mathsf{begin}_i(a, s)),$$
$$(pk, \mathsf{end}_i(a, s)), \mathsf{sign}(\mathsf{inv}(pk), \mathsf{pair}(a, npk)) \mid i \in \{1, 2\}, pk, npk, a, s \in \mathcal{C},$$
$$\Gamma(\{pk, npk\}) = \{\mathsf{PubKey}\}, \Gamma(\{a, s\}) = \{\mathsf{Agent}\}\}$$

and $GSMP(\mathcal{P}^\star_{ks,1} \parallel \mathcal{P}_{ks,2})$ is the closure under subterms of the following set:

$$\{\mathsf{attack}_2, (pk, \mathsf{valid}(a, s)), (pk, \mathsf{seen}(a, s)), (pk, \mathsf{begin}_i(a, s)), (pk, \mathsf{end}_i(a, s)),$$
$$(pk, \mathsf{pubkeys}(s)), \mathsf{inv}(pk), \mathsf{crypt}(pk, \mathsf{update}(a, s, npk, \mathsf{pw}(a, s))) \mid i \in \{1, 2\},$$
$$pk, npk, a, s \in \mathcal{C}, \Gamma(\{pk, npk\}) = \{\mathsf{PubKey}\}, \Gamma(\{a, s\}) = \{\mathsf{Agent}\}\}$$

For composition we will require that two protocols are disjoint in their ground sub-message patterns except for basic public terms and shared secrets:

Definition 4 (GSMP disjointedness). *Given two sets of terms M_1 and M_2, and a ground set of terms Sec (the shared secrets), we say that M_1 and M_2 are Sec-GSMP disjoint iff $GSMP(M_1) \cap GSMP(M_2) \subseteq Sec \cup \{t \mid \emptyset \vdash t\}$. This is extended to constraints and protocols as expected.*

5.3 Declassification and Leaking

Up until now the set of shared secrets has been static. We now remove this restriction by introducing a notion of declassification that will allow shared secrets to become public during protocol execution. For instance, in protocol $\mathcal{P}_{ks,1}$ we give revoked private keys of the form $\mathsf{inv}(PK)$ to the intruder by transmitting them over the network: $\mathsf{send}(\mathsf{inv}(PK))$. The transmitted key $\mathsf{inv}(PK)$ should no longer be secret after transmission and so we call such steps *declassification*. Since declassification involves shared secrets we require that they are declassified for all component protocols together. Thus we label them with $\star$.

For any constraint $\mathcal{A}$ with model $\mathcal{I}$ we can now formally define the set of secrets that has been declassified in $\mathcal{A}$ under $\mathcal{I}$:

Definition 5 (Declassification). *Let $\mathcal{A}$ be a labeled constraint and $\mathcal{I}$ a model of $\mathcal{A}$. Then $declassified(\mathcal{A}, \mathcal{I}) \equiv \mathcal{I}(\{t \mid \star: \mathsf{receive}(t) \text{ occurs in } \mathcal{A}\})$ is the set of declassified secrets of $\mathcal{A}$ under $\mathcal{I}$.*

Given a protocol $\mathcal{P}$, a reachable constraint $\mathcal{A}$ (i.e., $0 \Rightarrow_{\mathcal{P}}^{\bullet\star} \mathcal{A}$), and a model $\mathcal{I}$ of $\mathcal{A}$, then $\mathcal{I}(\mathcal{A})$ represents a concrete protocol run and the set $declassified(\mathcal{A}, \mathcal{I})$ represents the messages that have been declassified by honest agents during the protocol run. Note that in this definition we have reversed the direction of the declassification transmission, because the send and $\mathsf{receive}$ steps of reachable constraints are duals of the transaction rules they originated from.

Declassification also allows us to share terms that have shared secrets as subterms but which are not themselves meant to be secret. For instance, public key certificates have as subterm the private key of the signing authority, and such certificates can be shared between protocols by modeling them as shared secrets that are declassified when first published.

Finally, if the intruder learns a secret that has not been declassified then it counts as an attack. We say that protocol $\mathcal{P}$ *leaks* a secret s if there is a reachable satisfiable constraint $\mathcal{A}$ where the intruder learns s before it is declassified:

Definition 6 (Leakage). *Let Sec be a set of secrets and $\mathcal{I}$ be a model of the labeled constraint $\mathcal{A}$. $\mathcal{A}$ leaks a secret from Sec under $\mathcal{I}$ iff there exists $s \in Sec \setminus declassified(\mathcal{A}, \mathcal{I})$ such that $\mathcal{I} \models \mathcal{A}|_1.\mathsf{send}(s)$ or $\mathcal{I} \models \mathcal{A}|_2.\mathsf{send}(s)$.*

Our notion of leakage requires that one of the components in isolation leaks a secret. This is important for our compositionality result later—we will require protocols not to leak in isolation (which can be verified on the protocols in isolation) for the composition to work. Note also that the set $declassified(\mathcal{A}, \mathcal{I})$ is unchanged during projection of $\mathcal{A}$, and so it suffices to pick the leaked s from the set $Sec \setminus declassified(\mathcal{A}, \mathcal{I})$ instead of $Sec \setminus declassified(\mathcal{A}|_i, \mathcal{I})$.

Example 4. The terms occurring in the GSMP intersection of the two keyserver protocols are (a) public keys pk, (b) private keys of the form inv(pk), (c) agent names, and (d) operations on the shared set families valid, $begin_i$, and end_i. Agent names are basic public terms in our example, i.e., $\emptyset \vdash$ a for all constants a of type Agent. The public keys are initially secret, but we immediately declassify them whenever they are generated. To satisfy GSMP disjointedness of $\mathcal{P}_{ks,1} \parallel \mathcal{P}^\star_{ks,2}$ and $\mathcal{P}^\star_{ks,1} \parallel \mathcal{P}_{ks,2}$ it thus suffices to choose the following set as the set of shared secrets (where the sec_f are special secret constants used in the encoding of the private function symbol f):

$$Sec = \{pk, \mathsf{inv}(pk), (pk, f(a, s)), f(a, s), \mathsf{sec_{inv}}, \mathsf{sec}_f \mid \Gamma(\{a, s\}) = \{\mathsf{Agent}\},$$
$$\Gamma(pk) = \mathsf{PubKey}, f \in \{\mathsf{valid}, \mathsf{begin_1}, \mathsf{end_1}, \mathsf{begin_2}, \mathsf{end_2}\}, pk, a, s \in \mathcal{C}\}$$

Note that we want the set symbols like valid to be private. This is because terms like valid(A, S) occurs in both component protocols and so we have to prevent the intruder from constructing them.

5.4 Parallel Compositionality for Constraints

With these concepts defined we can list the requirements on constraints that are necessary to apply our result on the constraint level:

Definition 7 (Parallel composability). *Let $\mathcal{A}$ be a constraint and let Sec be a ground set of terms. Then $(\mathcal{A}, Sec)$ is* parallel composable *iff*

1. *$\mathcal{A}|_1$ and $\mathcal{A}|_2$ are Sec-GSMP disjoint,*
2. *for all terms t the step $\star$: $\mathsf{send}(t)$ does not occur in $\mathcal{A}$,*
3. *for all $s \in Sec$ and $s' \sqsubseteq s$, either $\emptyset \vdash s'$ or $s' \in Sec$,*
4. *for all $\ell : (t, s), \ell' : (t', s') \in labeledsetops(\mathcal{A})$, if (t, s) and (t', s') are unifiable then $\ell = \ell'$,*
5. *$\mathcal{A}$ is type-flaw resistant and $\mathcal{A}, \mathcal{A}|_1, \mathcal{A}|_2$, and $\mathcal{A}|_\star$ are all well-formed,*

where $labeledsetops(\mathcal{A}) \equiv \{\ell : (t, s) \mid \ell : \mathsf{insert}(t, s)$ or $\ell : \mathsf{delete}(t, s)$ or $\ell : t \doteq s$ or $\ell : (\forall \bar{x}.\ t \not\doteq s)$ occurs in $\mathcal{A}\}$. (This definition is also extended to protocols.)

The first requirement is at the core of our compositionality result and states that the protocols can only share basic public terms and shared secrets. The second requirement ensures that $\star$ steps are only used for declassification, checks, and stateful steps. The third condition is our only requirement on the shared terms; it ensures that the set $Sec \cup \{t \mid \emptyset \vdash t\}$ is closed under subterms. The fourth condition is our requirement on stateful protocols; it implies that shared sets must be labeled with a $\star$. Finally, the last condition is needed to apply the typing result and it is orthogonal to the other conditions; it is indeed only necessary so that we can apply Theorem 1 and restrict ourselves to well-typed attacks. Typing results with different requirements could potentially be used instead. Note that we require well-formedness of *all* projections of $\mathcal{A}$. This is because we usually consider constraints reachable in composed and augmented protocols, and we need well-formedness to apply the typing result to these constraints.

With these requirements defined we can state our main result on constraints:

Theorem 2. *If $(\mathcal{A}, Sec)$ is parallel composable and $\mathcal{I} \models \mathcal{A}$ then there exists a well-typed interpretation $\mathcal{I}_\tau$ such that either $\mathcal{I}_\tau \models \mathcal{A}|_1$ and $\mathcal{I}_\tau \models \mathcal{A}|_2$ or some prefix $\mathcal{A}'$ of $\mathcal{A}$ leaks a secret from Sec under $\mathcal{I}_\tau$.*

That is, we can obtain a well-typed model of projections $\mathcal{A}|_1$ and $\mathcal{A}|_2$ for satisfiable parallel composable constraints $\mathcal{A}$—or one of the projections has leaked a secret. In other words, if we can verify that a parallel composable constraint $\mathcal{A}$ does not have any well-typed model of both projections, and no prefix of $\mathcal{A}$ leaks a secret under any well-typed model, then it is unsatisfiable.

5.5   Parallel Compositionality for Protocols

Until now our parallel compositionality result has been stated on the level of constraints. As a final step we now explain how we can use Theorem 2 to prove a parallel compositionality result for protocols.

First, we define the *traces* of a protocol $\mathcal{P}$ as the set of reachable constraints: $traces(\mathcal{P}) \equiv \{\mathcal{A} \mid 0 \Rightarrow_{\mathcal{P}}^{\bullet \star} \mathcal{A}\}$. We then define a compositionality requirement on protocols that ensures that all traces are parallel composable:

Definition 8 (Parallel composability, for protocols). *Let $\mathcal{P}_1 \parallel \mathcal{P}_2$ be a composed protocol and let Sec be a ground set of terms. Then $(\mathcal{P}_1 \parallel \mathcal{P}_2, Sec)$ is parallel composable iff*

1. *$\mathcal{P}_1 \parallel \mathcal{P}_2^\star$ and $\mathcal{P}_1^\star \parallel \mathcal{P}_2$ are Sec-GSMP disjoint,*
2. *for all terms t the step $\star$: receive(t) does not occur in $\mathcal{P}_1 \parallel \mathcal{P}_2$,*
3. *for all $s \in Sec$ and $s' \sqsubseteq s$, either $\emptyset \vdash s'$ or $s' \in Sec$,*
4. *for all $\ell: (t, s), \ell': (t', s') \in labeledsetops(\mathcal{P}_1 \parallel \mathcal{P}_2)$, if (t, s) and (t', s') are unifiable then $\ell = \ell'$,*
5. *$\mathcal{P}_1 \parallel \mathcal{P}_2$ is type-flaw resistant and $\mathcal{P}_1, \mathcal{P}_2, \mathcal{P}_1^\star$, and $\mathcal{P}_2^\star$ are all well-formed.*

For protocols we need to require that their composition is type-flaw resistant. It is not sufficient to simply require it for the component protocols in isolation; unifiable messages from different protocols might break type-flaw resistance otherwise. Note also that type-flaw resistance of a protocol $\mathcal{P}$ implies that the traces of $\mathcal{P}$ are type-flaw resistant, because $SMP(\mathcal{A}) \subseteq SMP(\mathcal{P})$ for any $\mathcal{A} \in traces(\mathcal{P})$ and because the traces consists of the duals of the transaction strands occurring in the protocol; likewise for GSMP disjointedness. Thus if $(\mathcal{P}_1 \parallel \mathcal{P}_2, Sec)$ is parallel composable then $(\mathcal{A}, Sec)$ is parallel composable for any $\mathcal{A} \in traces(\mathcal{P}_1 \parallel \mathcal{P}_2)$.

Example 5. Continuing Example 4 we now show that $\mathcal{P}_{ks,1} \parallel \mathcal{P}_{ks,2}$ is parallel composable, i.e., that it satisfies the conditions of Definition 8. We have previously shown type-flaw resistance and well-formedness for a similar keyserver protocol [17] and so we focus on the remaining four conditions here. GSMP disjointedness of the composed keyserver protocols was explained in Example 4. Hence the first condition of Definition 8 is satisfied. Conditions two and three are satisfied since $\mathcal{P}_{ks,1} \parallel \mathcal{P}_{ks,2}$ does not contain any steps of the form

$\star$: receive(t) and since any subterm of a term from *Sec* (as defined in the previous example) is either in *Sec* or an agent name (a basic public term). Note that *labeledsetops*($\mathcal{P}_{ks,1} \parallel \mathcal{P}_{ks,2}$) consists of instances of labeled terms from the following set: $\{1\colon (PK_0, \mathsf{ring}(A_0)), 1\colon (PK_1, \mathsf{revoked}(A_1, S_1)), 2\colon (PK_2, \mathsf{seen}(A_2, S_2)),$ $\star\colon (PK_3, \mathsf{valid}(A_3, S_3)), \star\colon (PK_4^i, \mathsf{begin}_i(A_4^i, S_4^i)), \star\colon (PK_5^i, \mathsf{end}_i(A_5^i, S_5^i)) \mid i \in \{1, 2\}\}$. For all pairs $\ell\colon (t, s)$, $\ell'\colon (t', s')$ in this set we have that $\ell = \ell'$ if (t, s) and (t', s') are unifiable. Hence condition 4 is satisfied.

As a consequence of Theorem 2 we have that any protocol $\mathcal{P}_1$ can be safely composed with another protocol $\mathcal{P}_2$ provided that $\mathcal{P}_1 \parallel \mathcal{P}_2^\star$ is secure and that $\mathcal{P}_1^\star \parallel \mathcal{P}_2$ does not leak a secret:

Theorem 3. *If $(\mathcal{P}_1 \parallel \mathcal{P}_2, Sec)$ is parallel composable, $\mathcal{P}_1 \parallel \mathcal{P}_2^\star$ is well-typed secure in isolation, and $\mathcal{P}_1^\star \parallel \mathcal{P}_2$ does not leak a secret under any well-typed model, then all goals of $\mathcal{P}_1$ hold in $\mathcal{P}_1 \parallel \mathcal{P}_2$ (even in the untyped model).*

Note that the only requirement on protocol $\mathcal{P}_2$ is that it does not leak any secrets (before declassifying), but we do not require that $\mathcal{P}_2$ is completely secure. This means, if we have a secure protocol $\mathcal{P}_1$, that the goals of $\mathcal{P}_1$ continue to hold in any composition with another protocol $\mathcal{P}_2$ that satisfies the composability conditions and does not leak secrets, even if $\mathcal{P}_2$ has some attacks. This is in particular interesting if we run a protocol $\mathcal{P}_1$ in composition with a large number of other protocols that are too complex to verify in all detail.

Finally, the composition of parallel composable and secure protocols is secure:

Corollary 1. *If $(\mathcal{P}_1 \parallel \mathcal{P}_2, Sec)$ is parallel composable and $\mathcal{P}_1 \parallel \mathcal{P}_2^\star$ and $\mathcal{P}_1^\star \parallel \mathcal{P}_2$ are both secure in isolation then the composition $\mathcal{P}_1 \parallel \mathcal{P}_2$ is also secure (even in the untyped model).*

5.6   Sequential Composition

Until now we have focused entirely on parallel composition where protocols are run "side-by-side". Another type of protocol composition is sequential composition where protocols are run in sequence, e.g. most recently [6] for PKIs. Thanks to the generality of our result, we can cover such sequential compositions as a parallel composition with sets dedicated to the hand-over between the protocols. Let us take a key-exchange protocols like TLS as an example, where the handshake protocol establishes a pair of shared keys between a client A and a server S, and then subsequently, the transport protocol uses these keys to encrypt communication between A and S. We illustrate how the last transition of the handshake and the first transition of the transport protocol look for A where t_1 and t_2 are terms representing the two shared keys established in the handshake (and there are similar rules for S):

$$\forall A \in \mathsf{Hon}, S \in \mathsf{Ser}.$$
$$1\colon \cdots$$
$$\star\colon \mathsf{insert}((t_1, t_2), \mathsf{keys}(A, S))$$

$$\forall A \in \mathsf{Hon}, S \in \mathsf{Ser}.$$
$$\star\colon (K_1, K_2) \mathbin{\dot{\in}} \mathsf{keys}(A, S).$$
$$\star\colon \mathsf{delete}((K_1, K_2), \mathsf{keys}(A, S)).$$
$$2\colon \cdots$$

Note that, like in the keyserver example, the set keys(A, S) does not represent a means of communication between two participants, but rather a buffer or glue between two protocols: one protocol is producing keys, the other protocol is consuming them. Of course, one needs to require here that the first protocol only inserts authenticated and secret keys into the set, which is similar to the assume-guarantee reasoning we have illustrated for our keyserver example.

In fact, our result allows for a generalization of existing sequential composition results: while all results like [6] and the similar vertical result [11] are specialized to a particular set of data to be transferred from one protocol to another, our result does not prescribe a particular setup, but allows for any exchange of data through shared sets. This only requires one to specify sufficient assumptions on the shared-set operations for the assume-guarantee reasoning, but one does no longer need to establish a new composition theorem for each new form of sequential composition. In fact, the composition does not even need to be strictly sequential, e.g. if the first protocol establishes keys for the second protocol, one may well have that additionally the second protocol can also establish new keys for subsequent sessions.

6   Conclusion and Related Work

Our composition theorem for parallel composition is the newest in a sequence of parallel composition results that are each pushing the boundaries of the class of protocols that can be composed [1–3, 7–9, 12–14]. The first results simply require completely disjoint encryptions; subsequent results allowed the sharing of long-term keys, provided that wherever the common keys are used, the content messages of the different protocols are distinguished, for instance by tagging. Other aspects are which primitives are supported as well as what forms of negative conditions, e.g. to support as goals the full geometric fragment.

Our result lifts the common requirement that the component protocols only share a fixed set of long-term public and private constants. Our result allows for stateful protocols that maintain databases (such as a key server) and the databases may even be shared between these protocols. This includes the possibility to declassify long-term secrets, e.g., to verify that a protocol is even secure if the intruder learns all old private keys. Both databases, shared databases, and declassification are considerable generalizations over the existing results.

Like [1] our result links the parallel compositionality result with a typing result such as the result of [17], i.e., essentially requiring that all messages of different meaning have a distinguishable form. Under this requirement it is sound to restrict the intruder model to using only well-typed messages which greatly simplifies many related problems. While one may argue that such a typing result is not strictly necessary for composition, we believe it is good practice and also fits well with disjointness requirements of parallel composition. Moreover, many existing protocols already satisfy our typing requirement, since, unlike tagging schemes, this does not require a modification of a protocol as long as there is some way to distinguish messages of different meaning.

There are other types of compositionality results for sequential and vertical composition, where the protocols under composition do build upon each other, e.g., one protocol establishes a key that is then subsequently used by another protocol [2,6,8,10,11,19]. This requires that one protocol satisfies certain properties (e.g. that the key exchange is authenticated and secret) for the other protocol to rely on. Our composition result allows for such sequential composition through shared databases: a key exchange protocol may enter keys into a shared set, and the other protocol consumes these keys. Thus our concept of sharing sets generalizes the interactions between otherwise independent protocols, and one only needs to think about the interface (e.g., only authenticated, fresh, secret keys can be entered into the database; they can only be used once). Moreover, we believe that sets are also a nice way to talk about this interaction.

There are several interesting aspects of compositionality that our result does not cover, for instance, [7] discusses the requirements for composing password-based protocols, and [3] investigates conditions under which privacy properties can be preserved under protocol composition.

So far, compositionality results are solely "paper-and-pencil" proofs. The proof arguments are often quite subtle, e.g., given an attack where the intruder learned a nonce from one protocol and uses it in another protocol, one has to prove that the attack does not rely on this, but would similarly work for distinct nonces. It is not uncommon that parts of such proofs are a bit sketchy with the danger of overlooking some subtle problems as for instance described in [16]. For this reason, we have formalized the compositionality result—on the level of ordinary constraints—in the proof assistant Isabelle/HOL [20], extending the formalization of [16,17], giving the extremely high correctness guarantee of machine-checked proofs. To our knowledge, this work is the first such formalization of a compositionality result in a proof assistant, with the notable exception of a study in Isabelle/HOL of compositional reasoning on concrete protocols [5].

Finally, all the works discussed so far are based on a black-box model of cryptography. There are several cryptographic frameworks for composition, most notably universal composability, reactive simulatability [4], and [18]. Considering the real cryptography makes compositional reasoning several orders of magnitude harder than abstract cryptography models. It is an intriguing question whether stateful protocol composition can be lifted to the full cryptographic level.

Acknowledgments. This work was supported by the Sapere-Aude project "Composec: Secure Composition of Distributed Systems", grant 4184-00334B of the Danish Council for Independent Research. We thank Luca Viganò for helpful comments and discussions.

References

1. Almousa, O., Mödersheim, S., Modesti, P., Viganò, L.: Typing and compositionality for security protocols: a generalization to the geometric fragment. In: Pernul, G., Ryan, P.Y.A., Weippl, E. (eds.) ESORICS 2015. LNCS, vol. 9327, pp. 209–229. Springer, Cham (2015). https://doi.org/10.1007/978-3-319-24177-7_11
2. Andova, S., Cremers, C.J.F., Gjøsteen, K., Mauw, S., Mjølsnes, S.F., Radomirović, S.: A framework for compositional verification of security protocols. Inf. Comput. **206**(2–4), 425–459 (2008)

3. Arapinis, M., Cheval, V., Delaune, S.: Composing security protocols: from confidentiality to privacy. In: Focardi, R., Myers, A. (eds.) POST 2015. LNCS, vol. 9036, pp. 324–343. Springer, Heidelberg (2015). https://doi.org/10.1007/978-3-662-46666-7_17

4. Backes, M., Pfitzmann, B., Waidner, M.: The reactive simulatability (RSIM) framework for asynchronous systems. Inf. Comput. **205**(12), 1685–1720 (2007)

5. Butin, D.F.: Inductive analysis of security protocols in Isabelle/HOL with applications to electronic voting. Ph.D. thesis, Dublin City University, November 2012

6. Cheval, V., Cortier, V., Warinschi, B.: Secure composition of PKIs with public key protocols. In: CSF, pp. 144–158, August 2017. https://doi.org/10.1109/CSF.2017.28

7. Chevalier, C., Delaune, S., Kremer, S., Ryan, M.D.: Composition of password-based protocols. Formal Methods Syst. Des. **43**(3), 369–413 (2013). https://doi.org/10.1007/s10703-013-0184-6

8. Ciobâcă, Ş., Cortier, V.: Protocol composition for arbitrary primitives. In: CSF, pp. 322–336. IEEE (2010)

9. Cortier, V., Delaune, S.: Safely composing security protocols. Formal Methods Syst. Des. **34**(1), 1–36 (2009). https://doi.org/10.1007/s10703-008-0059-4

10. Escobar, S., Meadows, C., Meseguer, J., Santiago, S.: Sequential protocol composition in Maude-NPA. In: Gritzalis, D., Preneel, B., Theoharidou, M. (eds.) ESORICS 2010. LNCS, vol. 6345, pp. 303–318. Springer, Heidelberg (2010). https://doi.org/10.1007/978-3-642-15497-3_19

11. Groß, T., Mödersheim, S.: Vertical protocol composition. In: CSF, pp. 235–250 (2011). https://doi.org/10.1109/CSF.2011.23

12. Guttman, J.D.: Cryptographic protocol composition via the authentication tests. In: de Alfaro, L. (ed.) FoSSaCS 2009. LNCS, vol. 5504, pp. 303–317. Springer, Heidelberg (2009). https://doi.org/10.1007/978-3-642-00596-1_22

13. Guttman, J.D., Thayer, F.J.: Protocol independence through disjoint encryption. In: CSFW, pp. 24–34. IEEE (2000)

14. Heintze, N., Tygart, J.D.: A model for secure protocols and their compositions. In: Security and Privacy, pp. 2–13, May 1994. https://doi.org/10.1109/RISP.1994.296596

15. Hess, A.V., Mödersheim, S.A., Brucker, A.D.: Stateful protocol composition (extended version). Technical report, DTU Compute (2018). Technical report-2018-03. https://people.compute.dtu.dk/samo/

16. Hess, A.V., Mödersheim, S.: Formalizing and proving a typing result for security protocols in Isabelle/HOL. In: CSF (2017)

17. Hess, A.V., Mödersheim, S.: A typing result for stateful protocols. In: CSF (2018)

18. Küsters, R., Tuengerthal, M.: Composition theorems without pre-established session identifiers. In: CCS, pp. 41–50. ACM, New York (2011). https://doi.org/10.1145/2046707.2046715

19. Mödersheim, S., Viganò, L.: Secure pseudonymous channels. In: Backes, M., Ning, P. (eds.) ESORICS 2009. LNCS, vol. 5789, pp. 337–354. Springer, Heidelberg (2009). https://doi.org/10.1007/978-3-642-04444-1_21

20. Nipkow, T., Paulson, L.C., Wenzel, M.: Isabelle/HOL - A Proof Assistant for Higher-Order Logic. LNCS, vol. 2283. Springer, Heidelberg (2002). https://doi.org/10.1007/3-540-45949-9

Privacy (I)

Towards Understanding Privacy Implications of Adware and Potentially Unwanted Programs

Tobias Urban[1,2]([✉]), Dennis Tatang[2], Thorsten Holz[2], and Norbert Pohlmann[1]

[1] Institute for Internet-Security, Gelsenkirchen, Germany
urban@internet-sicherheit.de
[2] Ruhr-University Bochum, Bochum, Germany

Abstract. Web advertisements are the primary financial source for many online services, but also for adversaries. Successful ad campaigns rely on good online profiles of their potential customers. The financial potentials of displaying ads have led to the rise of malicious software that injects or replaces ads on websites, in particular, so-called *adware*. This development leads to continuously further optimized and customized advertising. For these customization's, various tracking methods are used. However, only little work has gone into privacy issues emerging from adware.

In this paper, we investigate the tracking capabilities and related privacy implications of adware and potentially unwanted programs (PUPs). Therefore, we developed a framework that allows us to analyze any network communication of the Firefox browser on the application level to circumvent encryption like TLS. We use this framework to dynamically analyze the communication streams of over 16,000 adware or potentially unwanted programs samples that tamper with the users' browser session. Our results indicate that roughly 37% of the requests issued by the analyzed samples contain private information and are accordingly able to track users. Additionally, we analyze which tracking techniques and services are used by attackers.

Keywords: Adware · Potentially unwanted programs · Privacy

1 Introduction

Nowadays, browsers almost substitute application programs for particular tasks such as e-mail. They allow users to socially interact with others, work on projects, share ideas, or access a broad variety of multimedia content. The amount of private and critical data that browsers mediate continues to increase every year. Naturally, this leads to new risks in the scope of the browsers ecosystem (e.g., banking fraud, user tracking, spam, etc.) since it becomes an attractive target for adversaries. New threats are potentially unwanted programs (PUPs), adware, and malicious browser extensions which tamper with the user's browser session.

© Springer Nature Switzerland AG 2018
J. Lopez et al. (Eds.): ESORICS 2018, LNCS 11098, pp. 449–469, 2018.
https://doi.org/10.1007/978-3-319-99073-6_22

Injecting and replacing ads, as well as redirecting search queries, are popular ways of attackers to make profit.

Gathering, analyzing, and predicting user behavior using private information (e.g., clickstream data) has become a considerable spread phenomenon on the Internet [1]. It is well-known that tracking users and building user profiles is part of the business model of websites and other applications (e.g., mobile applications) [2–8]. However, privacy implications of malware are not well explored yet. In this work, we research privacy leakage by adware and PUPs—to the best of our knowledge, we are the first ones to report such implications on a larger scale.

As these topics are somehow related, technical differences and disparities in the motivation why users are being tracked exist. On the technical side, in contrast to websites and browser extensions, adware and PUPs are not installed with the users' consent or their knowledge, and therefore they do not know that they are being tracked. If it comes to tracking capabilities, websites and extensions are limited to the browser while adware and PUPs have richer access to the users' device and can thereby access more sensitive information (e.g., passwords). Especially malicious programs can track every step of a user by injecting tracking tools into every website a user visits. Thus, these programs can quickly create a comprehensive profile of a particular user which contains highly sensitive data and this is of potentially great value to ad companies.

However, on the motivational side, websites track users to monitor the users' behavior on their sites to improve their services (e.g., suggesting videos the users might like). Extensions might leak private information to third parties, or the extensions server, due to the service they offer (e.g., an extension that checks if a user visits a malicious URL might naturally send the URL to a third party). On the contrary, malware exfiltrates personal data in a purely malicious manner. As scamming money in classical Internet frauds (e.g., credit-card fraud) gets harder and harder, attackers search for new ways to maximize their monetizing efforts (e.g., ransomware or ad injection). Another, not well-explored way, to do that is to exfiltrate private data to build personalized online profiles e.g., the users' clickstreams which can be sold to third parties [9].

In this work, we show the scope of this unnoticed privacy breaches that emerge from adware and PUPs. We found that adware and PUPs heavily focus on the users' clickstream data which can give great detail about the users' personal life. Roughly 27% of all analyzed adware and around 30% of the PUP samples steal the full visited URLs of their victims. Furthermore, we show that data exfiltration is a central component of the malicious activities of adware and PUPs. Our results show that Asian tracking services are popular data sinks for the exfiltrated data. Given the high prevalence of adware and PUPs [10], this data exfiltration is a considerable threat to our modern society.

To sum up, we make the following contributions:

- We introduce a framework that allows us to capture traffic of software that tampers with the browser session on the application level (see Sect. 4) when visiting a predefined set of websites (see Sect. 4.2).

- We provide a detailed analysis of the negative privacy impact emerging from adware and PUPs. Our results show that more than 45% of all analyzed adware and PUPs samples exfiltrate personal data or track users (see Sect. 4.3). To the best of our knowledge, we are the first to report on data leakage and profiling by adware and PUPs on a large scale.
- Finally, we identified (1) the services used to track users, (2) the websites most commonly tracked, (3) and data that is predominantly exfiltrated by adware or PUPs (see Sect. 5.1).

2   Background

In this section, we explain the terms *adware*, *potentially unwanted programs*, and browser extensions. Further, we give a brief overview of the adware ecosystem and describe several tracking mechanisms.

2.1   Adware, Potentially Unwanted Programs, and Browser Extensions

In this work, we analyze two different types of software, namely adware and potentially unwanted programs (PUPs). We further analyze browser extensions to assess our results and to make them more comparable to other related work (e.g., [2,11–13]). In the following, we explain these types of software and discuss how we understand them in the scope of this work:

1. **Adware** is (malicious) software that generates revenue by displaying ads to users (e.g., by injecting or replacing ads on websites). Aside from the ad injection, adware often redirects search requests to advertising websites or collects private data of the users (e.g., clickstream data). Commonly, adware is considered to be malicious if the collection of data or ad-injection happens without adequately notifying the user and if it is installed like other malware (e.g., drive-by-downloads).
2. Potentially unwanted programs (**PUPs**), is a type of software that users might perceive undesirable, as it is installed along with software the user intends to install. The PUPs are bundled with popular benign software and are distributed by so-called pay-per-install services (PPI). PPI services get paid for installations of software (the installer bundle) on target hosts. PUPs could be software with any capability, malicious or benign. However, in the wild, this kind of software often shows similar behavior as adware [10] (e.g., ad-injection or user-tracking).
3. **Browser extensions** are programs that extend the functionality of a web browser (e.g., block advertisements). Extensions have generous access to many functions provided by the browser.

In this work, we examine the negative privacy implications of adware and PUPs and compare these findings to extension downloaded from the Firefox

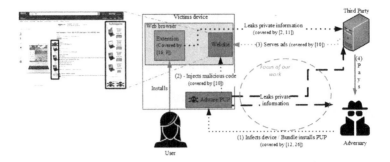

Fig. 1. Overview of the adware ecosystem. The adversary infects the victim's device with malicious software which insert ads into a visited website. After displaying the ads, or a click on the ad by the user, the adversary gets paid typically by a an ad network.

Add-On repository [14]. In the past, adware or PUPs could come in form of an extension but due to policy changes of Firefox one can only install extensions present in their repository. This is probably why none of the analyzed samples successfully installed an extension. We focus on the negative privacy impact of adware and PUPs but also give hints regarding the "ad injection" and "search query redirection" capabilities of the analyzed samples (see Sect. 5).

As just defined, adware and PUPs have similar capabilities, and therefore it is reasonable to analyze both and compare them to each other. In order to make our results more comparable to previous work, we additionally analyzed browser extensions which are well explored regarding their (malicious) behavior. Of course, adware has more access to the operating system and could, therefore, come along with many other malicious capabilities than browser extensions. Therefore, we analyze the outbound network traffic that is not emerging from the browser ("second channel") to examine privacy breaches on that channel, too.

2.2   Adware Ecosystem

The focus of this work lies in the analysis of privacy implications of adware and PUPs. The adware ecosystem is presented in Fig. 1: (1) The user's system is infected with software (i.e., adware, PUPs, or extensions) that tampers with the browser session. (2) The extensions, PUPs, and adware inject their (malicious) objects (e.g., JavaScript code, or images) into the visited website. These objects might be used to load some content from a third party (e.g., ads), or might exfiltrate private information about the user.

Many parts of the ecosystems are already well explored (dotted lines). In this work, we analyze the privacy implications of adware an PUPs for users (dashed lines). To the best of our knowledge, there has been no research analyzing this part systematically on a large scale.

The main monetization technique of adware (as the name hints) is injecting ads into websites and getting paid based on the payment model of the ad-network (e.g., pay-per-view) (3). Nevertheless, authors of adware, PUPs, or malicious extensions might also sell private data they exfiltrate from their victims [15] (4).

2.3   Tracking Mechanisms

Tracking mechanisms can be subdivided into *stateful* and *stateless* tracking methods. Stateful tracking identifies users through a unique identifier chosen by the tracker. On the contrary, stateless tracking tries to determine users through properties of the users' device or browser (e.g., installed fonts or drivers).

Two exemplary *stateful* tracking techniques are explained in the following:

- A *web beacon* (sometimes called *tracking pixel* or *web bug*) is often not larger than 1×1 pixel and usually a transparent graphic image, which is placed on a website for monitoring the user behavior [16]. It is often used with cookies as an additional tracking mechanism. Software that tampers with the user's browser session, like browser extensions, can insert such web beacons on every visited website.
- `Third party cookies` are a popular way to track users across different servers. In contrast to first-party cookies, which are set by the currently visited website, third party cookies are set, e.g., by content loaded from the third party by the visited website. However, third-party cookies are set for the same reason than standard first-party cookies so that a visited website can identify a user later on.

Two examples of *stateless* tracking are browser and canvas fingerprints:

- `Browser fingerprinting` enables website providers to recognize and identify a user's system by unique properties of each browser. Eckersley demonstrates that a combination of browser and device features can almost uniquely identify most users on the web [17]. Web-based browser fingerprinting is, therefore, a conventional technique that has been investigated by several other researchers [17–20]. This technique can further be abused for customization of displayed products, e.g., recently Hupperich et al. showed that the location plays a role in the price offered for hotel bookings [21].
- `Canvas fingerprinting` is possible by abusing the HTML canvas element, that was introduced in HTML5, to draw graphics onto websites. Mowery and Shacham demonstrate that it is feasible to use for user tracking [7].

3   Related Work

Adware and Malicious Add-Ons. Jagpal et al. [22] present WEBEVAL, a system that identifies malicious extensions for the Google Chrome web browser. The authors identify different types of malicious extensions. The two most common types are Facebook session hijackers and ad-injectors (adware). Similar to our work, they perform a dynamic analysis of each extension and log how it interacts with the browser and operating system. Jagpal et al. do that by performing everyday tasks like querying search engines, visiting social media, and browsing favorite news sites. Aside from their dynamic approach they also conduct a static code analysis to decide if an extension is malicious or not.

HULK [11] is another framework that is used to identify malicious browser extensions. Hulk employs so-called *HoneyPages* and a technique called "event handler fuzzing". HoneyPages are empty HTML pages. If an extension queries for a tag on a website (e.g., `getElementById ("foo")`) this tag is automatically inserted into the HoneyPage. Thus, the extension assumes the element is present on the website and interacts with it. Using *event handler fuzzing*, `Hulk` pretends to visit all websites on the Alexa Top 1M [23] but just presents a HoneyPage to the extension.

Thomas et al. [12] combine HULK and WEBEVAL to measure the effect of malicious extensions on the websites google.com, amazon.com, and walmart.com. They report that 5% of the daily unique IP addresses visiting `google.com` are infected with malware that injects ads into websites.

ORIGINTRACER [8] is a tool developed by Arshad et al., which allows tracking the provenance of web content injected into websites by web extensions. They evaluate the usability and performance of the introduced tool and show that such a tool is of great value for users to identify content that was injected into websites by third parties.

Neither HULK, WEBEVAL nor ORIGINTRACER target privacy implications but focus on identifying malicious browser extensions. We measured and analyzed the negative privacy impact for users that are infected by adware or PUPs.

Analysis About Fingerprinting on the Web. In a large-scale study, Acar et al. examine three advanced web tracking mechanisms (canvas fingerprinting, evercookies, and cookie syncing) [3]. According to their study, 5% of the top 100k websites use canvas fingerprints to identify users.

In 2010, Ashkan et al. conducted a study on the use of Flash cookies [24]. 50% of the websites in their set (Alexa top 100 sites [23]) use this kind of cookie mostly without disclosing this in their privacy policies. Note that since May 2011, all EU countries adopted a directive which says amongst others that websites have to display a "warning" to users if they use cookies [25].

FPDETECTIVE, a framework to analyze and detect web-based fingerprints, is introduced by Acar et al. [26]. They used their framework to crawl the most popular websites and analyze if the JavaScript code that is transmitted is used to create fingerprints. In their work, the authors show that fingerprinting is a growing problem and significantly more attractive than previous work suggested.

Englehardt and Narayanan [5] present the most recent study on online tracking. They introduce the open-source measurement tool OPENWPM, which they used to crawl and analyze the top one million websites on the internet. They measure several stateful and stateless tracking techniques and discover some methods that have not been noticed in the wild before (e.g., audio fingerprinting).

The introduced work measures the tracking capabilities and other privacy implications of modern websites. In this work, we analyze the exfiltration of private data and user tracking by malware, i.e., adware and PUPs.

Prevalence of Potentially Unwanted Programs. The prevalence and distribution of PUPs are examined by Kotzias et al. [10]. By analyzing AV telemetry, Kotzias et al. show that around 54% of 3.9 million analyzed hosts have PUPs installed. Furthermore, they found that the top PUP publisher ranks 15 among all software publisher (benign or not). They analyze the PUP-malware relationship and conclude that PUP and malware distribution is independent from another.

The pay-per-install (PPI) ecosystem is analyzed by Thomas et al. [27]. The authors show that PPIs sell access to the users' systems for prices ranging from 0.10\$ to 1.50\$ per installation. Furthermore, they show that PPI services take a considerable part in distributing PUPs. Based on Google Safe Browsing telemetry, they show that PUPs are downloaded three times more often than classical malware. Both works show the massive prevalence of PUPs but do not investigate the influence this type of software has on the users' privacy.

Privacy Implications of Browser Extensions. The privacy diffusion enabled by browser extensions is examined by Starov and Nikiforakis [2]. They dynamically analyze the privacy leakage of extensions available for the Google Chrome browser. They find that a non-negligible amount (6.3%) of the top 10,000 extensions leak privacy-sensitive data. To counter the leakage, they design BROWSINGFOG a tool to conceal the user's actual interest on the web. The tool pretends to visit different websites on the internet ("fog") which makes it arguably harder to distinguish between intended and non-intended page visits.

The most recent work in this field of research is written by Weissbacher et al. [13]. The authors present a prototype implementation called EX-RAY that can identify the privacy-violating behavior of browser extensions. In their work, they use an unsupervised learning approach to identify those extensions. The proposed experimental setup is comparable to our setup but only captures traffic on the network level. Thus, they cannot access and analyze the data, if they are transferred over a TLS secured channel.

The work of Starov and Nikiforakis is to some extent comparable to our work but, due to the nature of their analysis framework, does not cover tracking capabilities of extensions and does not look for exfiltrated metadata (e.g., user-agents or passwords). In [2] the software is analyzed that might need some personal information to successfully run their service (e.g., to identify malicious URLs). In contrast, we focus on malware that exfiltrates data in a purely malicious manner which foreshadows that there is a clear distinction between these two types of software. On a technical level we extend the findings of [2] by (1) identifying all exfiltrated data, (2) showing that there is a significant difference in type and amount of exfiltrated data, (3) identify websites to which visits are primary tracked, (4) analyzing the tracking behavior of malware, (5) determining the tracking services used by different malware families, and (6) identifying the used tracking techniques.

4   Approach

In this section, we introduce our framework, describe its working principles, inform about our analyzed data set, and give an overview of the investigated samples. Note that in contrast to most related work, due to the application-level monitoring, our system can even inspect HTTPS traffic, can find private data in encoded and deflated content, and allows a stateful analysis.

4.1   Framework

We developed a framework (see Fig. 2) that allows us to (1) perform a *stateful* analysis of each sample, (2) *capture*, if needed *decrypt, decode* and *analyze* HTTP(s) communication on application level, and further (3) collect and analyze all network traffic not emerging from the browser.

The general workflow of a single analysis run goes as follows. The analysis slave pulls and installs an adware sample, PUP sample or extension from the server (1). Afterward, the slave visits a predefined set of websites (2a) and logs the resulting communication. To do so, we developed a browser extension that captures all network traffic on the application level. Since we save the traffic on the application level, we can inspect all requests and responses before or after they are encrypted or decrypted, by the TLS layer. After visiting a website, we wait for 30 seconds so it can finish loading and the analyzed software has time to inject content into the site. Additionally, we record all traffic on network level that is originated from aside the browser (2b). We cannot decrypt the traffic apart from the browser. Thus in our analysis, we are limited to the unencrypted traffic. At the end of the analysis run, the plain HTTP(s) traffic and the further communication is sent to the server for review. Before the analysis we—if needed and possible—inflate (e.g., `gzip`) and decode (e.g., `BASE64`) all data (see also Sect. 4.3).

In this work, we perform a *stateful* analysis which means that the used browser has properties that a mock browser or a default state would typically not show (e.g., a browsing history or cookies). If one wants to analyze the tracking capabilities of the software, it is inevitable to perform a *stateful* analysis because resetting the state of the browser during the investigation of a sample might disable some mechanisms that are used for tracking (e.g., cookies). The clean installation state of our slaves—that is recovered after each restart—has a browsing history, several cookies set, passwords in the browser's password vault, and other properties that are usually set when using a browser. Note that most prior work performs a stateless analysis of ad-injectors or browser extensions [11,12,26]. Only OPENWPM performs a stateful analysis [5].

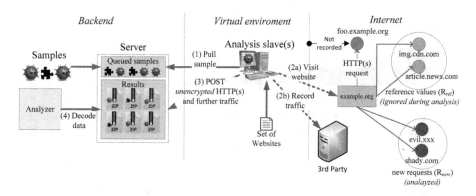

Fig. 2. Overview of our developed framework for the dynamic traffic analysis of adware, PUPs and browser extensions.

To conduct a representative analysis, we need to learn the regular communication of a website to distinguish between requests regularly issued by the site and requests issued by an object injected by the adware, PUP, or extension. We collect the non-malicious regular communication of a website for our analysis by visiting all sites with an analysis slave— but without installed sample or browser extension.

Since websites tend to load dynamic content from various and often changing sources, each slave collects new reference values after analyzing two samples. All collected reverence values are combined to one reference set R_{ref}. In our analysis, we consider requests that target domains (TLD+1) that are not part of R_{ref} for a given site. We call that set R_{new} Example (see also the right side of Fig. 2): Let's assume that R_{ref} for `example.org` contains requests to `cdn.com` and `news.com`. However, if an infected client visits `example.com` the websites issues requests to `evil.xxx`, and `shady.com`. In our study, we only consider requests `evil.xxx`, and `shady.com` because they are not in R_{new}.

4.2   Dataset

We used the global Alexa Top 100 [23] (as of 01/15/2017) as the basis for our set of websites which are visited by the analysis slaves. We restricted our analysis to unique hostnames from this list (e.g., we only analyze `google.com` even if `google.co.uk` is on the list as well) because we assume that the communication would be similar.

After filtering the sets consists of 57 domains. We added five popular e-commerce domains (e.g., `bestbuy.com`) because we expect the adware or PUPs to be more active on e-commerce websites, which turned out to be true for PUPs but not necessarily for adware (see Sect. 5. For each of those domains, we chose two subsites either randomly by visiting the domain and selecting two links, or if possible by selecting the most popular subsites for this site (e.g., products).

Fig. 3. Distribution, on a logarithmic scale, of the analyzed malware sample families. One adware family (`Dealply`) is dominant in our set while the rest is more or less balanced - which allows us to generalize our results.

A more detailed overview of the set can be found in Appendix A. In total, the analysis of each sample takes around 70 min (including booting, infection, visiting the 128 websites, waiting 30 s, etc.). Previous work either visited a broad set of websites once to conduct their analysis (e.g., [5]), used some mock pages to analyze the injected content (e.g., [11]), or did not disclose how many sites they visit (e.g., [22]).

For our analysis, we used 8,536 distinct adware samples (referred to as S_{AD}) and 8,109 distinct PUP samples (S_{PUP}) (different regarding SHA256 hashes). The samples in $S_{AD} \cup S_{PUP}$ come from 484 different malware families (AV labels). Less than 12% of the samples belong to the most common adware family (`DealPly`), and 5% belong to the most common PUP family (`InstallCore`). The full distribution—on a logarithmic scale—of malware families is displayed in Fig. 3. The distribution of samples across malware families shows that the data set is balanced and allows to generalize our results.

We used samples that were submitted to VirusTotal [28] between 01/01/2017 and 12/20/2017. VirusTotal shut down their API in August and ever since then provides a data set for researchers on Google drive that is updated monthly. The used samples are either identified to be a potentially unwanted program (PUP) or adware by the anti-malware engines used by VirusTotal. We used samples with these labels because we expect that those samples will primarily exfiltrate private data and inject content into websites. To better assess our findings regarding adware and PUPs and to make our work more comparable with previous work, we analyzed the top 5,500 Firefox extensions (S_{ext}) available in the Firefox add-on repository [14]. According to the number of users, we took from the add-on repository, the top 5,500 extension cover 97.2% off all Firefox extension installations. Previous work focused on Chrome extensions, and therefore our analysis also complements these results.

4.3   Analysis

In the following, we focus on analyzing the communication of adware and PUPs. More specifically, we analyze the used tracking services, exfiltrated information, and tracked websites. Additionally, we compare these findings to privacy leakage of the browser extensions we analyzed and with results of previous work.

A website can implement a Content Security Policy (CSP) as a defense mechanism to mitigate certain types of attacks like cross-site scripting or data injection attacks. During our analysis, we found that only 17 subsites use CSPs.

Exfiltrated Personal Information. In this work, we consider information to be private if it holds: (1) data that can be used to identify the client (e.g., IP-addresses), (2) can be used to create a user profile (e.g., visited URLs), or (3) contain sensitive data stored on the computer (e.g., passwords). We consider a website to be a tracker (or tracking service) if it gathers data that can be used to identify users or create profiles about them.

We identified the exfiltrated data by analyzing the transferred cookie, or data sent via the HTTP body. Individual headers can be used to gather personal information about the user (e.g., the user agent or user's preferred language), but these headers are commonly set by default. Hence, we cannot measure if the analyzed sample utilizes these fields. Before analyzing the fields we, if possible, deflate (e.g., `gzip/deflate`) and decode (e.g., `BSAE64`) them. If possible, we repeat this process in case fields are encoded or inflated multiple times, as observed by Starov et al. [2] (e.g., `base64_enc(base64_enc(url_enc(<data>)))`).

After the inflating and decoding, we perform a keyword matching to determine whether a request is used to leak private information. We identified the keywords by manual inspection of several requests issued by the different analyzed samples. We used 13 keyword categories that on the one hand are commonly used to identify or track users (e.g., screen resolution or installed fonts) and on the other hand information that is specific for our analysis setup (e.g., IP addresses or passwords). Some categories are identified by multiple keywords others just by one (e.g., the password is equal for all machines all the time while the user agent varies from sample to sample). We found 15,462 keywords in the analyzed requests. A manual inspection of a sample of the requests we identified a small (less than ten requests) to be false negatives (e.g., a keyword in a seemingly random string - *AR5 **WIN7SP1** UFB2RI3*). A list of the most relevant keywords (based on their occurrence) is given in Table 2. Furthermore, we check if script code that is sent to the client within the response might be used to track users. If possible, we implemented several metrics provided in [5, 26] to identify JavaScript that is used to track users.

To summarize, we consider a request to have negative privacy implication if and only if (1) it is part of R_{new}, and (2) it is used for tracking or contains private information.

5 Results

In this section, we provide an overview of the results of our analysis. Throughout this section, if not stated otherwise, we only consider requests used to track users or leak personal data to third parties.

Table 1. Websites that were actively tracked by the analyzed samples (Alexa Ranks as off 11/30/2017).

Adware				PUPs				Extensions			
%-Sam.	Website	Cat.	Rank	%-Sam.	Website	Cat.	Rank	%-Sam.	Website	Cat.	Rank
15.94	tmall.com	shopping	14	17.02	tmall.com	shopping	14	19.74	tmall.com	shopping	14
6.54	msn.com	misc	49	6.65	cnn.com	news	106	10.05	instagram.com	image	17
5.40	cnn.com	news	106	6.07	asos.com	shopping	360	9.40	youtube.com	video	2
5.28	youtube.com	video	2	5.96	ebay.com	shopping	38	7.11	microsoft.com	shopping	50
4.93	asos.com	shopping	360	5.90	target.com	shopping	283	6.13	cnn.com	news	106

In total, we analyzed 16,645 malicious software samples (8,536 adware samples and 8,109 PUPs) and 5,500 Firefox extensions. We analyzed about 850GB (compressed JSON data) of generated adware/PUP traffic. 45% of the adware samples, 40% of the PUP samples, and 45% of the Firefox extensions inject content into a website that issued requests to domains not present in R_{ref}. Our results, if not stated otherwise, only take these samples into account.

We found that the adware and PUP samples issued 21,429 requests to domains not present in our reference dataset, an increase of 10%. 61 of the adware samples changed the home page of the browser, and 221 changed the browser's standard search engine or redirected search queries. In contrast, only 6 PUPs changed the home page, but still, 180 replaced the default search engine. Due to Firefox policies, Firefox extensions cannot change these attributes.

5.1   Privacy Aspects

In this subsection, we present the results of the analysis of the HTTP(s) traffic emerging from the browser. Remember that our framework allows to (1) analyze all traffic in plain text—no matter if HTTPs was used or not—and (2) tries to deflate and decode all data before the analysis (e.g., HTTP GET parameters).

Tracked Websites. Table 1 displays the top websites to which visits were actively tracked by the analyzed samples. We consider a website to be tracked if the analyzed sample injects content that can be used for tracking (e.g., a web beacon), or if an observed outgoing request contains any personal information. In our set of websites, each site is tracked by at least 1.5% of the adware and PUP samples. These samples circumvent the CSPs used by websites.

It is notable that the extensions and adware focus on popular websites (e.g., Youtube or Instagram) from different categories while PUPs predominantly focuses on shopping sites. This indicates that PUPs try to understand what a user plans to buy while adware is gathering information that gives a broader overview of the users habits since they track more general websites as well as shopping sites. Accordingly, this allows providing targeted ads for individual persons, making these kinds of information valuable for ad-companies. Overall, way fewer extensions exfiltrate personal information (31.64%) compared to adware and PUPs (46.41%).

Our results show that user tracking is a significant part of the malicious behavior of adware and PUPs. Almost 40% of the request issued by the adware samples, and 35% of the requests issued by PUPs contain personal information or may be used to track users (e.g., they include the visited URL: *shady.com/?url=google.com%2Fiphone%2B6*). In contrast, only 28% of the requests are used by the extensions for those purposes.

Leaked Personal Information. To measure the privacy impact, we first identify the transferred personal information triggered by the tested samples. We analyze the transferred cookie, and data sent in the HTTP body requests. Furthermore, we inspect if a response contains JavaScript that is used for stateless tracking or if the answer includes a web beacon.

As described in Sect. 4.3, after deflating and decoding, we perform a keyword matching to determine whether a request leaks personal information usable for tracking mechanisms or not. Table 2 shows the results of that matching.

Figure 4 displays the third parties receiving the personal information. Note, if a request contains multiple keywords, we count the request numerous times.

In general, compared to PUPs, extensions and adware focus on meta information (e.g., language, time, IP address, etc.). The visited domain is exfiltrated by all analyzed software types alike (32%) while PUPs and adware predominately exfiltrate the full request URL (domain and GET parameters). However, one can argue that some extensions transfer this information as part of their service (e.g., an extension that checks if the users visit a malicious website will naturally send the current URL to a third party). In contrast, adware or PUPs leak personal data in a malicious manner or because the used ad services requires the current URL. In either way, the user's privacy is undermined unnoticed and without the user's consent. Table 2 shows that PUPs and adware, in contrast to extensions, focuses on the user's clickstream (i.e., browsing history). This is a more significant threat to the user privacy due to the detailed information leaked users' personal life (e.g., habits).

We can *not* identify any privacy-related information in about 6.9% of the requests issued by adware and PUPs (e.g., `cdn.gigya.com/JS/gigya.js?apiKey=3_GL3L[...]`) and 56% of the requests did *not* contain any data we analyzed (e.g., `code.jquery.com/jquery-2.2.4.min.js`).

To the best of our knowledge, there has not been any report on privacy breaches of adware and PUPs. Our measurements show that a significant part, more than ⅓, of the adware's and PUPs communication leaks personal information of users or tracks them. If one takes into account that the majority of the leaked data is the user's browsing history (Domain and URL in Table 2) this kind of leakage is way more severe than the extension leaks.

Starov and Nikiforakis observed that several Chrome extensions, 6.3% of the top 10k, 'unintentionally' leak the HTTP referrer header to third parties (e.g., by embedding objects on every website) [2]. We observed a comparable leakage by 6.55% of the analyzed Firefox extensions and by 6.91% of the analyzed adware.

Table 2. Most commonly leaked personal information

Information	Adware			PUP			Extensions		
	%-S.	Median	Max	%-S.	Median	Max	%-S.	Median	Max
IP address	0.92	3	3	0.69	2	3	0.85	6	30
Operating sys.	5.49	2	5	5.54	2	5	6.21	2	30
User-Agent	5.41	2	2	4.77	2	3	5.35	14	60
Desktop res.	7.35	3	20	6.32	2	7	7.19	2	9
Domain	32.16	2	27	35.12	2	26	32.77	2	126
Full URL	27.18	2	13	29.52	2	10	15.56	2	66
Referrer leak	6.91	0	19	3.31	3	23	6.55	0	20

We did not further investigate this unintentional leakage because the header provides only little utility for the adversary and there are several other ways for her to access this information (e.g., by merely reading the visited URL) and furthermore we cannot measure if the header is utilized. Naturally, the third party receiving the referrer header could use this information. Thus, this kind of leakage still poses a threat to the user's privacy.

Tracking Services. Figure 4 displays the tracking services used by the different malware families. To increase readability, we only listed services used at least seven times by any family and the top 16 malware families individually and combined all other families to *Others*. `Agent`, `Dealply`, the most common adware families in our dataset, and `InstallCore`, the most common PUP family in our dataset, are using a broad variety of tracking services One can see that `TaboTabo` and `MMStat` are overall the most common services used to track users. `taobao.com` is operated by `Zhejiang Taobao Network Ltd.`, while `mmstat.com` is operated by `Alibaba Co., Ltd.` Both two big Chinese players in the Internet landscape. The third most common observed tracker, `GoogleVideo`, is a content delivery network—which is also a known tracker—used to host video or sound files. An overall overview of the most commonly used tracking services and the personal data used by these services is given in Appendix B.

Along with the findings that ad-injection targets users in South Asia, and South East Asia [12] our results indicate that adware and PUPs use services based in Asia. The usage of these services is understandable because access to big American tracking services (e.g., Facebook or Google) is not possible since they are blocked in China [29].

Tracking Techniques. Table 3 presents the tracking techniques utilized by the analyzed samples—only requests are listed that are used for a specific tracking technique. Previous work shows that stateless tracking is becoming more common on popular websites [5]. However, the analyzed adware samples and PUPs do not utilize stateless tracking techniques. This behavior is comprehensible since

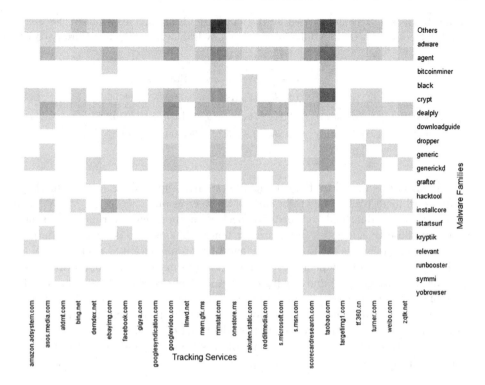

Fig. 4. Top tracking services used by the analyzed adware (A) and PUP (P) families.

the samples can manipulate every website the user visits and therefore can inject a stateful tracking object into each site. Thus, they do not have to rely on more complex and error-prone stateless tracking techniques.

Our analysis shows that web beacons are the most common tracking method among all analyzed samples (adware, PUPs and browser extensions). This result is reasonable since they are easy to implement and are not as easy to block as third-party cookies. It is notable that extensions do not as often use web beacons but utilize 3rd party cookies more commonly.

The results indicate that user tracking is less critical to adware and PUP authors than exfiltrating personal data. But one can argue that exfiltrating the visited URL or domain is also a form of tracking. Requests that contain personal information but do not follow a specific tracking scheme are not considered (e.g., A request contains personal information and loads a picture bigger than a typical web beacon is not counted). The vast majority (around 88%) of requests that impact the users' privacy leak personal information.

Non-browser Emitted Communication. The analysis in this section includes all malware and PUP samples even if they did not insert any object into a website. Similar to the analysis of the traffic emitted by the browser, we used the communication of R_{ref} as reference values for non-malicious communication

Table 3. Tracking techniques used by the analyzed adware and extensions. The vast majority tracks the users in a different way (e.g., by leaking the URL to a third party).

		Cookies	Web beacon	Stateless	Data leakage
Adware	(%-Sam.)	0.03 %	17.36 %	0.02 %	88.55 %
PUPs	(%-Sam.)	0.02 %	16.93 %	1.07 %	87.42 %
Extensions	(%-Sam.)	4.47 %	9.83 %	0.09 %	89.32 %

(e.g., connections issued by the operating system). The analysis in this chapter *excludes* all local traffic and traffic on the browser level.

We used our identified keywords to check if any personal information is sent to any of these IP addresses (malicious or non-malicious). To do that we match the identified keywords against the payload of each unencrypted packet.

Less than 0.5% of the packets contain meta information (e.g., operation system, or used language), and no packet included clickstream data. The small amount of exfiltrated data shows that adware and PUPs do not leak unencrypted personal information on network level which makes this kind of leakage hard to detect. Due to the low amount of identified exfiltrated data, we did not further investigate this communication, but this analysis could be part of future work on this topic.

6   Discussion

In the following, we discuss ethical considerations and limitations of our work.

6.1   Ethical Considerations

Running live malware samples always comes with some ethical issues. On the one hand, one wants to understand how malware works in a realistic environment but on the other hand, running malware might result in harming individuals not involved in the analysis process (e.g., via credit card fraud). Since we run malware that generates revenue by displaying ads and stealing private information we eventually created some income for the malware authors during our analysis. We implemented measures to decrease the potential harm a sample can cause (e.g., by limiting the upload bandwidth to minimize their participation in a possible DDoS attack).

6.2   Limitations

Our developed framework allows the dynamic analysis of software that tampers with the users' browser session. However, it comes, like most dynamic approaches, with some limitations. Using a predefined set of websites leaves the risk that the analyzed software does not get active on the visited websites (e.g., banking-malware might only get active on specific subsites of a particular banking site). However, previous work has shown that the top-ranked pages trigger a lot of malware samples and extensions [2,11,12,26]. Also, some samples might only inject content into websites only if certain search words appear, as shown in [12]. Since we use a predefined set of websites and therefore predefined keywords, we will not see injections related to other keywords.

Currently, our analysis slaves do not interact with the websites in a way a real user might (e.g., scrolling, or clicking on links). Some malware samples might only trigger if an event occurs, if the user interacts with a website we missed this kind of behaviour.

Since we are using a virtual environment to execute the malware, some samples might recognize that they are being analyzed. We took several measures to hide that the malware is executed on a virtual machine (e.g., changing CPU information and some registry keys). However, a malware sample might still detect that it is being analyzed and show a different behavior.

7   Conclusion

Our results show that not only websites and browser extensions but also—on a massive scale—adware and PUPs negatively impact the user's privacy. We analyzed over 16,000 adware and PUP samples towards their privacy implications to the user. Our results illustrate that these kinds of software excessively leak private data (e.g., IP addresses or clickstream data). More than 37% of all requests issued by malware or PUPs is used for one of these two purposes. Adware and PUPs mainly focus on the user's clickstream which holds sensitive personal information and may give great detail of the user's life ranging from e.g., habits, personal preferences to political views. Thus, adware is a not negligible threat to the user's privacy especially because the leakage happens without consent or knowledge of the user. Regarding the tracking behavior PUPs and adware are quite similar and, since they heavily focus on the users' clickstream, pose a far worse threat to the users' privacy than extensions do.

We could show that while there are—regarding the privacy influence— similarities between extensions and adware/PUPs there are also apparent differences. Adware and PUPs mainly focus on the users' clickstream and can, therefore, create comprehensive profiles of users' which are valuable to different companies (e.g., ad-networks). Furthermore, our results show that adware and PUPs do not adopt state of the art tracking techniques.

Acknowledgment. This work was partially supported by the Ministry of Culture and Science of the German State of North Rhine-Westphalia (MKW grant 005-1703-0021 "MEwM") and partially supported by the German Federal Ministry of Education and Research (BMBF grants 16KIS0395 "secUnity" and 01IS14009B "BD-Sec"). We would like to thank the anonymous reviewers for their valuable feedback.

A   Set of Websites

The websites used in our analysis are listed in Table 4. We used the Alexa top 100 as the basis for the set. The set of the websites is described in detail in Sect. 4.2.

The set consists of ten search engines, 20 social media sites, 11 online-shops, 5 domains hosting adult content, and 16 domains that do not fit in any of these categories (e.g., `github.com` or `cnn.com`). 34 of the domains are hosted in the United States of America, 14 are hosted in the People's Republic of China, four in the Russian Federation, three in the Kingdom of the Netherlands, two in the Republic of Ireland, and five sites are hosted in different countries in Asia (ROK, SVR, JPN, HKG, and TWN).

Table 4. Set of websites used in our analysis.

search.rakuten.co.jp	instagram.com	coccocqc.com
movie.youku.com	search.naver.com	forums.craigslist.org
www.baidu.com	everysinglewordspoken.tumblr.com	www.ebay.com
health.china.com.cn	foodwishes.blogspot.com	coccoc.com
www.flipkart.com	edition.cnn.com	news.xinhuanet.com
www.zalando.de	www.google.com	hyperboleandahalf.blogspot.com
channel.pixnet.net	www.youtube.com	history.gmw.cn
vk.com	www.bing.com	sd.360.cn
marketplace.asos.com	stock.sohu.com	2kindsofpeople.tumblr.com
imgur.com	github.com	www.xvideos.com
zy.youku.com	xhamster.com	www.pixnet.net
military.china.com.cn	news.gmw.cn	www.alibaba.com
finance.qq.com	en.bongacams.com	world.taobao.com
mall.360.com	stackoverflow.com	www.microsoftstore.com
www.reddit.com	www.asos.com	bbs.tianya.cn
www.twitch.tv	www.so.com	www.apple.com
world.tmall.com	en.wikipedia.org	news.mail.ru
www.quora.com	www.aliexpress.com	news.youth.cn
ok.ru	news.naver.com	www.xinhuanet.com
www.groupon.com	www.sogou.com	auto.mail.ru
www.pornhub.com	www.facebook.com	twitter.com
yandex.ru	cbachina.sports.sohu.com	www.msn.com
www.linkedin.com	www.amazon.com	de.pinterest.com
newyork.craigslist.org	intl.target.com	www.imdb.com
ent.qq.com	www.hao123.com	www.microsoft.com
www.walmart.com	v.youth.cn	

B   Tracking Services

Table 5 displays the most common services to which privacy-related information are leaked or which provide tracking tools (e.g., web beacons). Only one service gathers additional information about the client's system aside from the domain. All, but one, tracking services are operated by "big players" based in China. The analyzed extensions tend to use tracking services operated by American companies (e.g., Google or Facebook). Our results show that the services used by Firefox extensions are comparable to Google Chrome extensions [2].

In total only 151 different trackers were used. 60 trackers are used by just three or fewer samples. Adware and PUP authors tend to rely on existing infrastructure rather than setting up their own. Among the observed tracking services, there is no indication for any preferred service. The top 20 services are used on average by 7.48% (±0.78%) of the adware and PUP samples. This result indicates that the used services do not differentiate among each other regarding the utility of the adware or PUP.

Table 5. Tracking services used by the analyzed adware, leaked information, and the most common communication path

Service	%-S.	Information	Company
taobao.com	10.04	URL, time, language, os.	Taobao Network
mmstat.com	8.47	URL, time, language, os, browser, screen res.	Alibaba
sogoucdn.com	8.36	domain	Sogou Info. Service
ebaystatic.com	8.28	domain	eBay
ykimg.com	8.23	domain	Nexperian Holding

References

1. Bucklin, R.E., Sismeiro, C.: A model of web site browsing behavior estimated on clickstream data. J. Mark. Res. **40**(3), 249–267 (2003)
2. Starov, O., Nikiforakis, N.: Extended tracking powers: measuring the privacy diffusion enabled by browser extensions. In: Proceedings of the 26th International Conference on World Wide Web, WWW 2017, pp. 1481–1490. International World Wide Web Conferences Steering Committee, Republic and Canton of Geneva (2017)
3. Acar, G., Eubank, C., Englehardt, S., Juarez, M., Narayanan, A., Diaz, C.: The web never forgets: persistent tracking mechanisms in the wild. In: Proceedings of the 2014 ACM SIGSAC Conference on Computer and Communications Security, CCS 2014, pp. 674–689. ACM, New York (2014)
4. Boda, K., Földes, Á.M., Gulyás, G.G., Imre, S.: User tracking on the web via cross-browser fingerprinting. In: Laud, P. (ed.) NordSec 2011. LNCS, vol. 7161, pp. 31–46. Springer, Heidelberg (2012). https://doi.org/10.1007/978-3-642-29615-4_4
5. Englehardt, S., Narayanan, A.: Online tracking: a 1-million-site measurement and analysis. In: Proceedings of the 2016 ACM SIGSAC Conference on Computer and Communications Security, CCS 2016, pp. 1388–1401. ACM, New York (2016)

6. Olejnik, Ł., Acar, G., Castelluccia, C., Diaz, C.: The leaking battery. In: Garcia-Alfaro, J., Navarro-Arribas, G., Aldini, A., Martinelli, F., Suri, N. (eds.) DPM/QASA -2015. LNCS, vol. 9481, pp. 254–263. Springer, Cham (2016). https://doi.org/10.1007/978-3-319-29883-2_18

7. Mowery, K., Shacham, H.: Pixel perfect: fingerprinting canvas in HTML5. In: Fredriksonn, M. (ed.) Proceedings of the Web 2.0 Security and Privacy Workshop (W2SP), pp. 1–12. IEEE Computer Society, New York, May 2012

8. Arshad, S., Kharraz, A., Robertson, W.: Identifying extension-based ad injection via fine-grained web content provenance. In: Monrose, F., Dacier, M., Blanc, G., Garcia-Alfaro, J. (eds.) RAID 2016. LNCS, vol. 9854, pp. 415–436. Springer, Cham (2016). https://doi.org/10.1007/978-3-319-45719-2_19

9. LLC, WS: WOT API—WOT (Web of Trust) (2017). https://www.mywot.com/en/api. Accessed 31 Oct 2017

10. Kotzias, P., Bilge, L., Caballero, J.: Measuring PUP prevalence and PUP distribution through pay-per-install services. In: 25th USENIX Security Symposium (USENIX Security 16), pp. 739–756. USENIX Association, Austin (2016)

11. Kapravelos, A., Grier, C., Chachra, N., Kruegel, C., Vigna, G., Paxson, V.: Hulk: eliciting malicious behavior in browser extensions. In: Proceedings of the 23rd USENIX Conference on Security Symposium, SEC 2014, pp. 641–654. USENIX Association, Berkeley (2014)

12. Thomas, K., et al.: Ad injection at scale: assessing deceptive advertisement modifications. In: Proceedings of the 2015 IEEE Symposium on Security and Privacy, SP 2015, pp. 151–167. IEEE Computer Society, Washington (2015)

13. Weissbacher, M., Mariconti, E., Suarez-Tangil, G., Stringhini, G., Robertson, W., Kirda, E.: Ex-Ray: detection of history-leaking browser extensions. In: Proceedings of the 33rd Annual Computer Security Applications Conference, pp. 1–13. ACM, New York (2017)

14. Mozilla Foundation: Add-ons for Firefox (2017). https://addons.mozilla.org/. Accessed 05 July 2017

15. Bonderud, D.: WOT privacy breach: trust tanks as browser add-on caught selling user data (2017). https://securityintelligence.com/news/wot-privacy-breach-trust-tanks-as-browser-add-on-caught-selling-user-data. Accessed 31 Oct 2017

16. Smith, R.M.: The web bug faq. Nov **11**, 4 (1999)

17. Eckersley, P.: How unique is your web browser? In: Atallah, M.J., Hopper, N.J. (eds.) PETS 2010. LNCS, vol. 6205, pp. 1–18. Springer, Heidelberg (2010). https://doi.org/10.1007/978-3-642-14527-8_1

18. Hupperich, T., Maiorca, D., Kührer, M., Holz, T., Giacinto, G.: On the robustness of mobile device fingerprinting: can mobile users escape modern web-tracking mechanisms? In: Proceedings of the 31st Annual Computer Security Applications Conference, ACSAC 2015, pp. 191–200. ACM, New York (2015)

19. Kurtz, A., Gascon, H., Becker, T., Rieck, K., Freiling, F.C.: Fingerprinting mobile devices using personalized configurations. Proc. Priv. Enhanc. Technol. (PoPETs) **2016**(1), 4–19 (2016)

20. Nikiforakis, N., Kapravelos, A., Joosen, W., Kruegel, C., Piessens, F., Vigna, G.: Cookieless monster: exploring the ecosystem of web-based device fingerprinting. In: Proceedings of the 2013 IEEE Symposium on Security and Privacy, SP 2013, pp. 541–555. IEEE Computer Society, Washington (2013)

21. Hupperich, T., Tatang, D., Wilkop, N., Holz, T.: An empirical study on online price differentiation. In: Proceedings of the Eighth ACM Conference on Data and Application Security and Privacy, CODASPY 2018, pp. 76–83. ACM, New York (2018)

22. Jagpal, N., et al.: Trends and lessons from three years fighting malicious extensions. In: Proceedings of the 24th USENIX Conference on Security Symposium, SEC 2015, pp. 579–593. USENIX Association, Berkeley (2015)
23. Alexa Internet: Top 500 global sites (2017). http://www.alexa.com/topsites
24. Soltani, A., Canty, S., Mayo, Q., Thomas, L., Hoofnagle, C.J.: Flash cookies and privacy. In: AAAI Spring Symposium: Intelligent Information Privacy Management, pp. 1–6. Association for the Advancement of Artificial Intelligence, Palo Alto (2010)
25. European Parliament: The Council: Directive 2009/136/ec (2009)
26. Acar, G., et al.: FPDetective: dusting the web for fingerprinters. In: Proceedings of the 2013 ACM SIGSAC Conference on Computer and Communications Security, CCS 2013, pp. 1129–1140. ACM, New York (2013)
27. Thomas, K., et al.: Investigating commercial pay-per-install and the distribution of unwanted software. In: 25th USENIX Security Symposium (USENIX Security 16), pp. 721–739. USENIX Association, Austin (2016)
28. VirusTotal: Free online virus, malware and url scanner (2017). https://virustotal.com/. Accessed 24 July 2017
29. GreatFire: Blocked sites in China - bringing transparency to the great firewall of China (2017). https://en.greatfire.org/search/blocked

Anonymous Single-Sign-On
for n Designated Services
with Traceability

Jinguang Han, Liqun Chen, Steve Schneider, Helen Treharne,
and Stephan Wesemeyer$^{(\boxtimes)}$

Department of Computer Science, University of Surrey,
Guildford, Surrey GU2 7XH, UK
s.wesemeyer@surrey.ac.uk

Abstract. Anonymous Single-Sign-On authentication schemes have been proposed to allow users to access a service protected by a verifier without revealing their identity. This has become more important with the introduction of strong privacy regulations. In this paper we describe a new approach whereby anonymous authentication to different verifiers is achieved via authorisation tags and pseudonyms. The particular innovation of our scheme is that authentication can occur only between a user and its designated verifier for a service, and the verification cannot be performed by any other verifier. The benefit of this authentication approach is that it prevents information leakage of a user's service access information, even if the verifiers for these services collude. Our scheme also supports a trusted third party who is authorised to de-anonymise the user and reveal her whole service access information if required. Furthermore, our scheme is lightweight because it does not rely on attribute or policy-based signature schemes to enable access to multiple services. The scheme's security model is given together with a security proof, an implementation and a performance evaluation.

Keywords: Anonymous Single-Sign-On · Security · Privacy
Anonymity

1 Introduction

Single-Sign-On (SSO) systems are a user-friendly way of allowing users access to multiple services without requiring them to have different usernames or passwords for each service. SSO solutions (e.g. OpenID 2.0 [35] by the OpenID foundation or Massachusetts Institute of Technology (MIT)'s Kerberos [33]) are designed to make the users' identities and possibly additional personal identifiable information (PII) available to the verifiers of the services which they wish to access. However, for some services, a verifier may not require the user's identity (nor any associated PII), just that the user is authorised to access the desired service. Moreover, the introduction of more stringent obligations with regards to

© Springer Nature Switzerland AG 2018
J. Lopez et al. (Eds.): ESORICS 2018, LNCS 11098, pp. 470–490, 2018.
https://doi.org/10.1007/978-3-319-99073-6_23

the handling of PII in various jurisdictions (e.g. GDPR in Europe [20]), requires service providers to minimise the use of PII.

Anonymous Single-Sign-On schemes [19,26,29,38] exist which can protect a user's identity, but may not do so for all entities within a scheme. Moreover, a user's service request can be verified by all verifiers of a system and not just the one it is intended for, which may pose a potential privacy risk to both the user and that verifier. Our proposed scheme addresses these issues and provides the following features: (1) only one authentication ticket is issued to a user, even if she wants to access multiple distinct services; (2) a user can obtain a ticket from a ticket issuer anonymously without releasing anything about her personal identifiable information — in particular, the ticket issuer cannot determine whether two ticket requests are for the same user or two different users; (3) a designated verifier can determine whether a user is authorised to access its service but cannot link different service requests made by the same user nor collude with other verifiers to link a user's service requests; (4) designated verifiers can detect and prevent a user making multiple authentication requests using the same authentication tag ("double spend") but cannot de-anonymise the user as a result; (5) tickets cannot be forged; and (6) given a user's ticket, a central verifier is authorised to recover a user's identity as well as the identities of the verifiers for the requested services in the user's ticket.

Our contributions are: a novel anonymous single-sign-on scheme providing the above features; its associated security model and security definitions; a corresponding formal proof of its security as well as an empirical performance analysis based on a Java-based implementation of our scheme.

1.1   Related Work

We now look at previous research which is most closely related to our scheme in the areas of: (i) Anonymous Single-Sign-On protocols, (ii) anonymous authentication schemes, (iii) multi-coupon schemes and (iv) designated verifiers signature schemes.

Anonymous Single-Sign-On Schemes

One of the anonymous Single-Sign-On system was proposed by Elmufti *et al.* [19] for the Global System for Mobile communication (GSM). In their system, a user generates a different one-time identity each time they would like to access a service and, having authenticated the user, a trusted third party will then authenticate this one-time identity to the service provider. Consequently, the user is anonymous to the service provider but, unlike in our scheme, not the trusted third party who authenticated the one-time identity.

In 2010, Han *et al.* [26] proposed a novel dynamic SSO system which uses a digital signature to guarantee both the unforgeability and the public verification of a user's credential. In order to protect the user's privacy, their scheme uses broadcast encryption which means that only the designated service providers can check the validity of the user's credential. Moreover, zero-knowledge proofs are used to show that the user is the owner of those valid credentials to prevent impersonation attacks. However, again unlike our scheme, the user is still known to the trusted third party which issued the credentials.

Wang *et al.* [38], on the other hand, propose an anonymous SSO based on group signatures [3]. In order to access a service, the user generates a different signature-based pseudonyms from her credentials and sends the signature to the service provider. If the signature is valid, the service provider grants the user access to the service to the user; otherwise, the service request is denied. The real identities of users can be identified by using the opening technique in [3]. While the user remains anonymous, their scheme (unlike ours) does not, however, provide designated verifiers, i.e. all verifiers can validate a user's request.

Lastly, Lee [29] proposed an efficient anonymous SSO based on Chebyshev Chaotic Maps. In this scheme, an issuer, the "smart card processing center", issues secret keys to users and service providers when they join in the system and to access a service, a user and service provider establish a session key with their respective secret keys. If the session key is generated correctly, the service request is granted; otherwise, it is denied. However, unlike our scheme, each service provider knows the identity of the user accessing their service.

While in [29,38], a user can access any service in the system by using her credentials, in our scheme, a user can only access the services which she selects when obtaining a ticket but can do so while remaining completely anonymous to both issuer and service provider.

Anonymous Authentication Schemes

With respect to anonymous authentication solutions, we consider schemes whose primary feature is to support multiple anonymous authentication. As in our scheme, anonymous authentication enables users to convince verifiers that they are authorised users without releasing their exact identities.

Teranishi *et al.* [37] proposed a k-times anonymous authentication (k-TAA) scheme where the verifiers determine the number of anonymous authentication that can be performed. The k-TAA scheme provides the following two features: (1) no party can identify users who have been authenticated within k times; (2) any party can trace users who have been authenticated more than k times. The verifier generates k tags and for each authentication, a user selects a fresh tag. Nguyen *et al.* [34] proposed a similar dynamic k-TAA scheme to restrict access to services not only the number of times but also other factors such as expiry date.

Camenisch *et al.* [9] proposed a periodic k-TAA scheme which enables users to authenticate themselves to the verifiers no more than k times in a given time period but supports reuse of the k times authentication once the period is up. In this scheme, the issuer decides the number of anonymous authentication request a user can make in a given time period. When a user makes an anonymous authentication request, he proves to a verifier that he has obtained a valid CL signature [11] from the issuer.

Note, however, that our scheme also prevents a verifier from establishing whether a user has used any of the other services thereby also guaranteeing verifier anonymity.

Furthermore, in all of these k-TAA schemes [9,34,37], authentication is not bound to a particular verifier, whereas in our scheme authentication tags are bound to specific verifiers. Moreover, k-TAA schemes allow verifiers to determine a user's identity who has authenticated more than k times while in our scheme multiple authentications to a single verifier is considered "double spending" which a verifier can detect but which does not lead to the de-anonymisation of a user. However, to prevent users from potentially abusing the system, our scheme allows for a central verifier who, given a user's ticket, can extract from it both the user's and verifiers' public keys using the authentication tags contained within it and thus establish the identities of both the user and her associated verifiers.

Lastly, Camenisch *et al.* in [13] and the IBM identity mixer description of its features in [27] define a scheme that has similar properties to ours including that of a central verifier (called "inspector") trusted to reveal a user's identity. The scheme is based on users obtaining a list of certified attributes from an issuer and the users using a subset of their attributes to authenticate to verifiers. The distinguishing difference between their scheme and ours is that their verification of anonymous credentials is not bound to a designated verifier whereas our is.

Multi-coupon Schemes

There is some degree of similarity between our scheme and a number of multi-coupon schemes. Armknecht *et al.* [1] proposed a multi-coupon scheme for federated environments where multiple vendors exist. In [1], a user can redeem multiple coupons anonymously with different vendors in an arbitrary order. To prevent double-spending of a coupon, a central database is required to record the transaction of each multi-coupon. The main difference to our scheme is that each coupon can be redeemed against any service provider while our authentication tags can only be validated by its designated verifier. Moreover, our "double-spend" detection is done by the verifier and does not require a central database.

Similarly, the schemes propose by Liu *et al.* [31] which provides strong user privacy and where a user can use an e-coupon anonymously no more than k times before his identity can be recovered. However, the user's coupons can be redeemed against any service rather than a designated verifier as our scheme provides.

Designated Verifiers

Jakobsson in [28] introduced the concept of a designated verifier which means that in a proof we ascertain that nobody but this verifier can be convinced by that proof while the authors in [21] present an anonymous attribute-based scheme using designated-verifiers. In their work they focus on identifying multiple designated verifiers. This is achieved through using the verifier's private key in the verification so that no other third party can validate the designated verifier signature. We adopt the high level concept of a designated verifier in our approach, i.e. given a valid authentication tag for service A, only service A's verifier can establish its validity. As this property is conceptually similar to the designated signatures described in [21,28], our verifiers are called designated verifiers. However, this is where the similarity ends with Jakobsson's designated verifiers. Notably, in [28], a verifier cannot convince others that the signature is from the signer because the verifier can generate the signature by himself. In our scheme, everyone can check that the authentication tags are signatures generated by the ticket issuer.

In summary, while a number of previous authentication schemes address the anonymity of the user and multiple authentications, the novelty of our work is that we ensure no information leakage across verifiers, since authentication can only occur between a user and its designated verifier while also providing a central verifier who can de-anonymise the user and reveal the identity of the verifiers in case of a misbehaving user. To the best of our knowledge, our anonymous Single-Sign-On scheme using designated verifiers is the first which has been formally presented in term of definitions, security models and proven to be secure under various cryptographic complexity assumptions together with an empirical performance evaluation.

1.2 Paper Organisation

This paper is organised as follows: Sect. 2 provides a high-level overview of the scheme and its claimed security properties; Sect. 3 outlines the applicable security model; Sect. 4 introduces the cryptographic building blocks and notation used throughout this paper; Sect. 5 describes the formal construction of our while Sect. 6 presents the theorems for its security proof; Sect. 7 provides a performance evaluation of our scheme; and Sect. 8 concludes the paper with directions for future work. The full version of this paper in [25] contains detailed formal definitions, security models and proofs of the scheme.

2 Scheme Overview and Security Properties

Entities in Our Proposed Scheme

Before providing a high-level overview of our anonymous single-sign-on scheme, we first introduce the various entities in the scheme as shown in Fig. 1, and define their purpose and roles: the **Central Authority ($\mathcal{CA}$)** is a trusted third party responsible for establishing the cryptographic keys and parameters used in the scheme and issues credentials to the other entities in the scheme; a **User ($\mathcal{U}$)** is someone who wishes to access some distinct services anonymously; the **Ticket Issuer ($\mathcal{I}$)** issues tickets to registered, yet anonymous users for the requested services; a **Designated Verifier ($\mathcal{V}$)** is a verifier for a specific service that a user might want to access; the **Central Verifier ($\mathcal{CV}$)** is another trusted third party which is allowed to retrieve the identities of the user, $\mathcal{U}$, and the verifiers, $\mathcal{V}$s, from the authentication tags present in a user's ticket, T_U; an **Authentication Tag (Tag_V)** is both tied to a user, $\mathcal{U}$, and a designated verifier, $\mathcal{V}$ and is used to prove to the designated verifier that the user is a valid user and allowed to

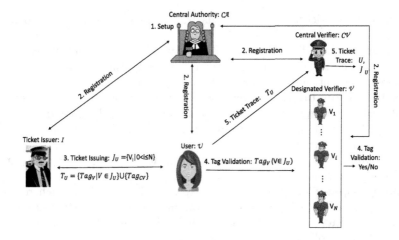

Fig. 1. Interaction of the various entities in our scheme

access the associated service; a **Ticket** (T_U) contains the authentication tags for the services a user, $\mathcal{U}$, has requested.

Overview of Proposed Scheme

Figure 1 illustrates at a high-level how our scheme works. For its detailed formal construction, please refer to Sect. 5. Conceptually, our scheme operates as follows: **Registration:** The issuer, verifiers, central verifier and users all register with the CA. **Ticket Issuing:** A user decides which services (and thus which verifiers) she wants to access and requests an appropriate ticket from the issuer. **Tag Validation:** To access a service, the user presents the appropriate authentication tag to the service. The validity period and any other restrictions of the tag can be captured in the free text part of the tag or be a default set by the verifier. If a user's tag is valid then the user is logged in to the service. Note that, unlike some other Single-Sign-On systems, the issuer does not need to be on-line for the tag validation to succeed. **"Double-Spend" detection:** If the user present the same tag twice then the verifier can warn the user that she is already logged in and that she should resume the already existing session or offer to terminate the previous session and start with a fresh one. **Ticket trace:** If a user is seen to abuse the service (e.g. violate the terms and conditions), the central verifier might be called upon to de-anonymise the user and determine any other services she has used.

Security Properties in Our Proposed Scheme

Having defined the different entities and described how they interact, we now list the security properties of our scheme:

– **User Anonymity:** In our scheme, users use pseudonyms whenever they interact with the issuer or a verifier. As such, the issuer cannot link a user across different ticket requests. Similarly, a user's identity is also hidden from a designated verifier.

– **Authentication Tag Unlinkability:** Apart from the central verifier and the issuer, no set of colluding verifiers can establish whether two or more different authentication tags came from the same anonymous user.
– **Verifier Anonymity:** The verifier's identify is protected from other users and verifiers, i.e. given an authentication tag, only the designated verifier can validate it and no other verifier (apart from the central verifier and the issuer) can determine for whom it is.
– **Designated Verifiability:** Given an authentication tag, Tag_V for verifier, $\mathcal{V}$, only $\mathcal{V}$ can validate it.
– **"Double-spend" detection:** Any verifier, $\mathcal{V}$, can detect when a user attempts to re-use an authentication tag but cannot de-anonymise the user.
– **Unforgeability:** Neither tickets nor individual authentication tags can be forged by any colluding users or verifiers.
– **Traceability:** There exists a trusted third party, a central verifier, who can, given a user's ticket, T_U, retrieve the user's and the verifiers' public keys (and hence their respective identities) from the authentication tags contained within T_U.

In the next section, we provide the security models in which these properties hold while Sect. 6 contains the associated theorems which are used to prove those models.

3   Security Model Overview

We now present a high-level overview of the security models which are used to prove the security of our scheme. The models are defined by the following games executed between a challenger and an adversary. Detailed formal security models as well as their proofs are presented in the full version of this paper [25] which also demonstrates the correctness of our scheme.

Unlinkability Game

This game covers the security properties of user anonymity, authentication tag unlinkability, verifier anonymity, designated verifiability and "double spend" detection. In this game verifiers and other users can collude but cannot profile a user's whole service information. In other words, no party can link different tags to the same user and determine a verifier's identity included in an authentication tag (thus proving verifier anonymity) except for the designated verifier, the ticket issuer or the central verifier. Moreover, for each authentication tag, the adversary can query its validity once, which in the context of this game addresses the properties of designated verifiability and "double spending".

Unforgeability Game

This game focuses on proving the unforgeability property of our scheme. Users, verifiers and the central verifier can collude but cannot forge a ticket on behalf of the ticket issuer.

Table 1. Syntax summary

Syntax	Explanations	Syntax	Explanations
1^ℓ	A security parameter	V_i	The i-th ticket verifier
$\mathcal{CA}$	Central authority	J_U	The service set of $\mathcal{U}$ consisting of the
$\mathcal{I}$	Ticket issuer		identities of ticket verifiers & ID_{CV}
$\mathcal{V}$	Ticket verifier	PP	Public parameters
$\mathcal{U}$	User	Ps_U	A set of pseudonyms of $\mathcal{U}$
$\mathcal{CV}$	Central verifier	Ps_V	The pseudonym generated for $\mathcal{V}$
ID_I	The identity of $\mathcal{I}$	Tag_V	An authentication tag for $\mathcal{V}$
ID_V	The identity of $\mathcal{V}$	Tag_{CV}	An authentication tag for $\mathcal{CV}$
ID_U	The identity of $\mathcal{U}$	T_U	A ticket issued to $\mathcal{U}$
ID_{CV}	The identity of $\mathcal{CV}$	$|X|$	The cardinality of the set X
$\epsilon(\ell)$	A negligible function in ℓ	$x \xleftarrow{R} X$	x is randomly selected from the set X
σ_I	The credential of $\mathcal{I}$	$A(x) \rightarrow y$	y is computed by running the
σ_V	The credential of $\mathcal{V}$		algorithm $A(\cdot)$ with input x
σ_U	The credential of $\mathcal{U}$	$\mathcal{KG}(1^\ell)$	A secret-public key pair generation
σ_{CV}	The credential of $\mathcal{CV}$		algorithm
MSK	Master Secret Key	$\mathcal{BG}(1^\ell)$	A bilinear group generation algorithm
H_1, H_2	Cryptographic hash functions	p, q	Prime numbers

Traceability Game

This game focuses on the traceability property of our scheme. It shows that even if users, verifiers and the central verifier collude, they cannot generate a ticket which is linked to a user who has never obtained a ticket or a user who is not the real owner of the ticket.

4 Preliminaries

In this section, we introduce the cryptographic building blocks used by our scheme including bilinear groups, the BBS+ signature scheme, zero knowledge proofs and various complexity assumptions needed to ensure its security. The mathematical notation and symbols used throughout this paper are summarised in Table 1.

4.1 Bilinear Groups and Pairings

In our scheme, bilinear groups are used to support the BBS+ signature scheme (defined in Sect. 4.2 below).

Let $\mathbb{G}_1$, $\mathbb{G}_2$ and $\mathbb{G}_\tau$ be three cyclic groups with prime order p. A pairing is defined to be a bilinear, non-degenerative and computable map $e : \mathbb{G}_1 \times \mathbb{G}_2 \rightarrow$

$\mathbb{G}_\tau$[7]. Given a security parameter, 1^ℓ, we define $\mathcal{BG}(1^\ell) \to (e, p, \mathbb{G}_1, \mathbb{G}_2, \mathbb{G}_\tau)$ to be a bilinear group generation algorithm. Note that Galbraith, Paterson and Smart [22] classified parings into three basic types and our scheme is based on the Type-III pairing where the elements on $\mathbb{G}_1$ are short (≈ 160 bits). This was chosen because for all $g \in \mathbb{G}_1$ and $\mathfrak{g} \in \mathbb{G}_2$, there exists an polynomial-time efficient algorithm to compute $e(g, \mathfrak{g}) \in \mathbb{G}_\tau$ resulting in a more efficient algorithm.

4.2   BBS+ Signature

Based on the group signature scheme [6], Au, Susilo and Mu [2] proposed the BBS+ signature. This signature scheme works as follows:

- Setup: Let $\mathcal{BG}(1^\ell) \to (e, p, \mathbb{G}_1, \mathbb{G}_2, \mathbb{G}_\tau)$, h be a generator of $\mathbb{G}_1$ and $g, g_0, g_1, \cdots,$ g_n be generators of $\mathbb{G}_2$.
- KeyGen: The signer selects $x \xleftarrow{R} \mathbb{Z}_p$ and computes $Y = h^x$. The secret-public key pair is (x, Y).
- Signing: To sign a block message $(m_1, m_2, \cdots, m_n) \in \mathbb{Z}_p^n$, the signer selects $w, e \xleftarrow{R} \mathbb{Z}_p$, and computes $\sigma = (g_0 g^w \prod_{i=1}^n g_i^{m_i})^{\frac{1}{x+e}}$. This signature on $(m_1, m_2, \cdots, m_n)$ is (w, e, σ).
- Verification: Given a signature (w, e, σ) and $(m_1, m_2, \cdots, m_n)$, the verifier checks $e(Y h^e, \sigma) \stackrel{?}{=} e(h, g_0 g^w \prod_{i=1}^n g_i^{m_i})$. If so, the signature is valid; otherwise, it is invalid.

Au, Susilo and Mu [2] reduced the security of the above signature to the q-SDH assumption (see Definition 2 below) in Type-II paring. Recently, Camenisch, Drijvers and Lehmann [8] reduced its security to the JOC-version-q-SDH assumption (see Definition 3 below) for Type-III pairing.

4.3   Zero-Knowledge Proof

In our scheme, zero-knowledge proof of knowledge protocols are used to prove knowledge and statements about various discrete logarithms including: (1) proof of knowledge of a discrete logarithm modulo a prime number [36]; (2) proof of knowledge of equality of representation [15]; (3) proof of knowledge of a commitment related to the product of two other commitments [12]. We follow the definition introduced by Camenish and Stadler in [14] which was formalised by Camenish, Kiayias and Yung in [10]. By PoK:$\{(\alpha, \beta, \gamma) : \Upsilon = g^\alpha h^\beta \wedge \tilde{\Upsilon} = \tilde{g}^\alpha \tilde{h}^\gamma\}$, proof on knowledge of integers α β and γ such that $\Upsilon = g^\alpha h^\beta$ and $\tilde{\Upsilon} = \tilde{g}^\alpha \tilde{h}^\beta$ hold on the groups $\mathbb{G} = \langle g \rangle = \langle h \rangle$ and $\tilde{\mathbb{G}} = \langle \tilde{g} \rangle = \langle \tilde{h} \rangle$, respectively. The convention is that the letters in the parenthesis (α, β, γ) represent the knowledge which is being proven by using the other values to which the verifier can have access.

4.4 Complexity Assumptions

The security of our scheme relies on a number of complexity assumptions defined in this subsection.

Definition 1 (Discrete Logarithm (DL) Assumption [24]). *Let $\mathbb{G}$ be a cyclic group with prime order p and g be a generator of $\mathbb{G}$. Given $Y \in \mathbb{G}$, we say that the discrete logarithm (DL) assumption holds on $\mathbb{G}$ if for all adversary can output a number $x \in \mathbb{Z}_p$ such that $Y = g^x$ with a negligible advantage, namely*

$$Adv_{\mathcal{A}}^{DL} = \Pr\left[Y = g^x | \mathcal{A}(p, g, \mathbb{G}, Y) \to x\right] \le \epsilon(\ell).$$

The *DL* assumption is used in the proof of the traceability property of our scheme.

Definition 2 (*q*-Strong Diffie-Hellman (*q*-SDH) Assumption [4]). *Let $\mathcal{BG}(1^\ell) \to (e, p, \mathbb{G}_1, \mathbb{G}_2, \mathbb{G}_\tau)$. Suppose that g and $\mathfrak{g}$ are generators of $\mathbb{G}_1$ and $\mathbb{G}_2$, respectively. Given a $(q + 2)$-tuple $(g, g^x, g^{x^2}, \cdots, g^{x^q}, \mathfrak{g}) \in \mathbb{G}_1^{q+1} \times \mathbb{G}_2$, we say that q-strong Diffie-Hellman assumption holds on $(e, p, \mathbb{G}_1, \mathbb{G}_2, \mathbb{G}_\tau)$ if for all probabilistic polynomial-time (PPT) adversary $\mathcal{A}$ can output $(c, g^{\frac{1}{x+c}}) \in \mathbb{Z}_p \times \mathbb{G}_1$ with a negligible advantage, namely $Adv_{\mathcal{A}}^{q-SDH} = \Pr[\mathcal{A}(\mathfrak{g}, g, g^x, g^{x^2}, \cdots, g^{x^q}) \to (c, g^{\frac{1}{x+c}})] \le \epsilon(\ell)$, where $c \in \mathbb{Z}_p - \{-x\}$.*

Definition 3 ((JOC Version) *q*-Strong Diffie-Hellman (JOC-*q*-SDH) Assumption [5]). *Let $\mathcal{BG}(1^\ell) \to (e, p, \mathbb{G}_1, \mathbb{G}_2, \mathbb{G}_\tau)$. Given a $(q + 3)$-tuple $(g, g^x, \cdots, g^{x^q}, \mathfrak{g}, \mathfrak{g}^x) \in \mathbb{G}_1^{q+1} \times \mathbb{G}_2^2$, we say that the JOC- q-strong Diffie-Hellman assumption holds on the bilinear group $(e, p, \mathbb{G}_1, \mathbb{G}_2, \mathbb{G}_\tau)$ if for all probabilistic polynomial-time (PPT) adversaries $\mathcal{A}$ can output $(c, g^{\frac{1}{x+c}}) \in \mathbb{Z}_p \times \mathbb{G}_1$ with a negligible advantage, namely $Adv_{\mathcal{A}}^{JOC-q-SDH} = \Pr\left[(c, g^{\frac{1}{x+c}}) \leftarrow \mathcal{A}(g, g^x, \cdots, g^{x^q}, \mathfrak{g}, \mathfrak{g}^x)\right] < \epsilon(\ell)$, where $c \in \mathbb{Z}_p - \{-x\}$.*

The security of the BBS+ signature used in our scheme relies on both the (*q*-SDH) and JOC-*q*-SDH) assumptions.

Definition 4 (Decisional Diffie-Hellman (DDH) Assumption [18]). *Let $\mathcal{BG}(1^\ell) \to (e, p, \mathbb{G}_1, \mathbb{G}_2, \mathbb{G}_\tau)$. Give a 3-tuple $(\xi, \xi^\alpha, \xi^\beta, T) \in \mathbb{G}_1^3$, we say that the decisional Deffie-Hellman assumption holds on $(e, p, \mathbb{G}_1, \mathbb{G}_2, \mathbb{G}_\tau)$ if for all probabilistic polynomial-time (PPT) adversaries $\mathcal{A}$ can distinguish $T = \xi^{\alpha\beta}$ or $T = M$ with negligible advantage, namely $Adv_{\mathcal{A}}^{DDH} = |\Pr[\mathcal{A}(\xi, \xi^\alpha, \xi^\beta, T = \xi^{\alpha\beta}) = 1] - \Pr[\mathcal{A}(\xi, \xi^\alpha, \xi^\beta, T = M) = 1]| < \epsilon(\ell)$ where $M \xleftarrow{R} \mathbb{G}_1$.*

Note that the DDH assumption is believed to be hard in both $\mathbb{G}_1$ and $\mathbb{G}_2$ for the Type-III pairing [23] used in our scheme which means that we actually makes use of the following stronger complexity assumption.

Definition 5 (Symmetric External Diffie-Hellman (SXDH) Assumption [23]). *Let $\mathcal{BG}(1^\ell) \to (e, p, \mathbb{G}_1, \mathbb{G}_2, \mathbb{G}_\tau)$. We say that the symmetric external Diffie-Hellman assumption holds on $(e, p, \mathbb{G}_1, \mathbb{G}_2, \mathbb{G}_\tau)$ if the decisional Diffie-Hellman (DDH) assumption holds on both $\mathbb{G}_1$ and $\mathbb{G}_2$.*

5   Scheme Construction

In this section, we present a more detailed description of the interactions (cf. Fig. 1) between the entities of our scheme. These interactions are: (i) System Set-up, (ii) Registration, (iii) Ticket Issuing, (iv) Tag Verification and (v) Ticket Tracing. Moreover, we provide details of the mathematical operations involved in these interactions. Formal definitions of the algorithms presented in this section can be found in the full version of this paper [25].

5.1   System Set-Up

Figure 2 shows the details of the system initialisation in which the central authority $\mathcal{CA}$ generates a master secret key, MSK, and the required public parameters, PP. **Note:** Once the system has been set up, all communication between the different entities in our scheme is assumed to be over secure, encrypted channels which can be established by the various entities using standard Public Key Infrastructure. This ensures that our scheme is not susceptible to simple Man-In-The-Middle attacks.

System Set-up: $\mathcal{CA}$ runs $\mathcal{BG}(1^{\ell}) \rightarrow (e, p, \mathbb{G}_1, \mathbb{G}_2, \mathbb{G}_\tau)$ with $e : \mathbb{G}_1 \times \mathbb{G}_2 \rightarrow \mathbb{G}_\tau$. Let $g, h, \xi, \tilde{h}$ be generators of the group $\mathbb{G}_1$ and $\mathfrak{g}$ be generators of $\mathbb{G}_2$. Suppose that $H_1 : \{0,1\}^* \rightarrow \mathbb{Z}_p$ and $H_2 : \{0,1\}^* \rightarrow \mathbb{Z}_p$ are two cryptographic hash functions. $\mathcal{CA}$ selects $x_a \overset{R}{\leftarrow} \mathbb{Z}_p$ and computes $Y_A = \mathfrak{g}^{x_a}$. The master secret key is $MSK = x_a$ and the public parameters are $PP = (e, p, \mathbb{G}_1, \mathbb{G}_2, \mathbb{G}_\tau, g, h, \xi, \tilde{h}, \mathfrak{g}, Y_A, H_1, H_2)$.

Fig. 2. System set-up algorithm

5.2   Registration

Figure 3 depicts the registration processes. When registering with the $\mathcal{CA}$, $\mathcal{I}$, $\mathcal{V}$, $\mathcal{U}$ and $\mathcal{CV}$ use the PP and generate their own secret-public key pairs. They then send their identities and associated public keys to $\mathcal{CA}$ which, after receiving a registration request from an entity, uses MSK to generate the corresponding credential for them. Note that only the ticket issuer has two public keys, Y_I and $\tilde{Y}_I$. The first one is used to sign the tickets while the second one is used to validate the ticket.

5.3   Ticket Issuing

During the ticket issuing process (shown in Fig. 4), the user $\mathcal{U}$ defines J_U to be the set containing the identities of the ticket verifiers whose services she wants to access as well as the identity of the central verifier. In order to request a ticket from $\mathcal{I}$, $\mathcal{U}$ creates pseudonyms, (P_V, Q_V), for each $ID_V \in J_U$ by using her secret key to protect the anonymity of the verifiers. She also produces a proof of knowledge of her credentials and submits this proof together with the set J_U and

---

Ticket-Issuer-Registration

Ticket Issuer: $\mathcal{I}$ Central Authority: $\mathcal{CA}$

Selects $x_i \xleftarrow{R} \mathbb{Z}_p$, and computes
$Y_I = \xi^{x_i}$ and $\tilde{Y}_I = \mathfrak{g}^{x_i}$.
The secret-public key pair is

$(x_i, Y_I, \tilde{Y}_I)$. $\xrightarrow{ID_I, Y_I, \tilde{Y}_I}$ Selects $e_i, r_i \xleftarrow{R} \mathbb{Z}_p$ and

Verifies: $e(\sigma_I, Y_A \mathfrak{g}^{e_i}) \overset{?}{=} e(gh^{r_i}Y_I, \mathfrak{g})$. $\xleftarrow{\sigma_I, r_i, e_i}$ computes $\sigma_I = (gh^{r_i}Y_I)^{\frac{1}{x_a + e_i}}$.

Keeps the credential as   Stores $(ID_I, Y_I, \tilde{Y}_I, (r_i, e_i, \sigma_I))$.
$Cred_I = (e_i, r_i, \sigma_I)$.

Ticket-Verifier-Registration

Ticket-Verifier: $\mathcal{V}$ Central Authority: $\mathcal{CA}$

Selects $x_v \xleftarrow{R} \mathbb{Z}_p$ and computes
$Y_V = \xi^{x_v}$.

The secret-public key pair is (x_v, Y_V). $\xrightarrow{ID_V, Y_V}$ Selects $\lambda_v, r_v \xleftarrow{R} \mathbb{Z}_p$ and

Verifies: $e(\sigma_V, Y_A \mathfrak{g}^{e_v}) \overset{?}{=} e(gh^{r_v}Y_V, \mathfrak{g})$. $\xleftarrow{\sigma_V, r_v, \lambda_v}$ computes $\sigma_V = (gh^{r_v}Y_V)^{\frac{1}{x_a + \lambda_v}}$.

Keep the credential as   Stores $(ID_V, Y_V, (r_v, \lambda_v, \sigma_V))$.
$Cred_V = (\lambda_v, r_v, \sigma_V)$.

User-Registration

User: $\mathcal{U}$ Central Authority: $\mathcal{CA}$

Selects $x_u \xleftarrow{R} \mathbb{Z}_p$, and computes
$Y_U = \xi^{x_u}$.

This secret-public key pair is (x_u, Y_U). $\xrightarrow{ID_U, Y_U}$ Select $e_u, r_u \xleftarrow{R} \mathbb{Z}_p$ and

Verifies: $e(\sigma_U, Y_A \mathfrak{g}^{e_u}) \overset{?}{=} e(gh^{r_u}Y_U, \mathfrak{g})$. $\xleftarrow{\sigma_U, e_u, r_u}$ computes $\sigma_U = (gh^{r_u}Y_U)^{\frac{1}{x_a + e_u}}$.

Keep the credential as   Stores $(ID_U, Y_U, (r_u, e_u \sigma_U))$.
$Cred_U = (e_u, r_u, \sigma_U)$.

Central-Verifier-Registration

Central Verifier: $\mathcal{CV}$ Central Authority: $\mathcal{CA}$

Selects $x_{cv} \xleftarrow{R} \mathbb{Z}_p$, and computes
$Y_{CV} = \xi^{x_{cv}}$

The secret-public key pair is (x_{cv}, Y_{CV}). $\xrightarrow{ID_{CV}, Y_{CV}}$ Select $\lambda_{cv}, r_{cv} \xleftarrow{R} \mathbb{Z}_p$ and
                 computes

Verifies: $e(\sigma_{cv}, Y_A \mathfrak{g}^{\lambda_{cv}}) \overset{?}{=} e(gh^{r_{cv}}Y_{CV}, \mathfrak{g})$. $\xleftarrow{\sigma_{CV}, \lambda_{cv}, r_{cv}}$ $\sigma_{CV} = (gh^{r_{cv}}Y_{CV})^{\frac{1}{x_a + \lambda_{cv}}}$.

Keep the credential as   Stores $(ID_{CV}, Y_{CV}, (r_{cv},$
$Cred_{CV} = (\lambda_{cv}, r_{cv}, \sigma_{CV})$. $\lambda_{cv}, \sigma_{CV}))$.

Fig. 3. Registration algorithm

the pseudonyms to $\mathcal{I}$ to convince him that she is a registered user and created the pseudonyms. Once $\mathcal{I}$ has received this information and verified the proof of knowledge, he generates an authentication tag Tag_V for each $ID_V \in J_U$ as well

---

Ticket-Issuing

Let J_U is $\mathcal{U}$'s list of the identities of verifiers which $\mathcal{U}$ wants to access as well as ID_{CV}

User: $\mathcal{U}$	Ticket Issuer: $\mathcal{I}$

Computes $B_U = gh^{r_u}Y_U$

Select $v_1, v_2, z_u \xleftarrow{R} \mathbb{Z}_p$ and
computes $v_3 = \frac{1}{v_1}$, $\bar{\sigma}_U = \sigma_U^{v_1}$,
$v = r_u - v_2 v_3$, $\tilde{B}_U = B_U^{v_1} h^{-v_2}$,
$\tilde{\sigma}_U = \bar{\sigma}_U^{-e_u} B_U^{v_1} (= \bar{\sigma}_U^{x_a})$, $(z_v = H_1(z_u\|ID_V)$, $P_V = Y_U Y_P^{z_v}$,
$Q_V = \xi^{z_v})_{ID_V \in J_U}$

Computes the proof $\prod_U^1$:

PoK$\{(x_u, r_u, e_u, \sigma_U, v_1, v_2, v_3, v,$
$(z_v)_{ID_V \in J_U}) : \frac{\tilde{\sigma}_U}{\tilde{B}_U} = \bar{\sigma}_U^{-e_u} h^{v_2}$
$\wedge \ g^{-1} = \tilde{B}_U^{-v_3} \xi^{x_u} h^v \wedge (P_V =$
$\xi^{x_u} Y_P^{z_v} \wedge Q_V = \xi^{z_v})_{V \in J_U}\}$
Let $\Delta = (((P_V, Q_V)_{ID_V \in J_U}),$
$\bar{\sigma}_U, \tilde{\sigma}_U, \tilde{B}_U, J_U, \prod_U^1)$

$\xrightarrow{\Delta}$ Verifies $\prod_U^1$ and $e(\bar{\sigma}_U, Y) \overset{?}{=} e(\tilde{\sigma}_U, \mathfrak{g})$.
Selects $t_u \xleftarrow{R} \mathbb{Z}_p$ and computes $C_U = \xi^{t_u}$
For $ID_V \in J_U$, selects $d_v, w_v, e_v \xleftarrow{R} \mathbb{Z}_p$
and computes $D_V = H_2(C_U\|ID_V)$,
$E_V = \xi^{d_v}$, $F_V = Y_V^{d_v}$, $K_V = Y_V Y_P^{d_v}$,
$s_v = H_1(P_V\|Q_V\|E_V\|F_V\|K_V\|Text^a)$
and $Z_V = (gh^{w_v}\tilde{h}^{s_v})^{\frac{1}{x_i+e_v}}$
Let $Tag_V = (P_V, Q_V, E_V, F_V, K_V, Text,$
$\qquad\qquad s_v, w_v, e_v, Z_V)$
For the central verifier ID_{CV}, selects
$w_{cv}, e_{cv} \xleftarrow{R} \mathbb{Z}_p$ and computes
$s_{cv} = H_1(s_1\|s_2\|\cdots\|s_{|J_U|})$ and
$Z_{CV} = (gh^{w_{cv}}\tilde{h}^{s_{cv}})^{\frac{1}{x_i+e_{cv}}}$

a) For $ID_V \in J_U$, verify

$D_V \overset{?}{=} H_2(C_U\|ID_V)$,
$s_v \overset{?}{=} H_1(P_V\|Q_V\|E_V\|F_V\|K_V\|Text)$
and $e(Z_V, \tilde{Y}_I \mathfrak{g}^{e_v}) \overset{?}{=} e(gh^{w_v}\tilde{h}^{s_v}, \mathfrak{g})$.
b) Verify $s_{cv} \overset{?}{=} H_1(s_1\|s_2\|\cdots\|s_{|J_U|})$
and $e(Z_{CV}, \tilde{Y}_I \mathfrak{g}^{e_{cv}}) \overset{?}{=} e(gh^{w_{cv}}\tilde{h}^{s_{cv}}, \mathfrak{g})$
c) Keep (z_u, C_U) secret

$\xleftarrow[C_U]{T_U}$ The ticket is:

$T_U = \{(D_V, Tag_V)|V \in J_U\} \cup \{s_{cv}, w_{cv},$
$e_{cv}, Z_{CV}\}$ where s_v and s_{cv} are the
serial numbers of Tag_V and T_U,
respectively.

---

^{a} $Text$ consists of the system version information and all other information which can be used by verifiers to validate the tag, e.g. valid period, tag type, *etc.*

Fig. 4. Ticket issuing algorithm

as an overall Tag_{CV} for $\mathcal{CV}$ in case the ticket needs to be traced. Note that these tags are constructed using the public keys of the respective verifiers and thus can only be validated by the corresponding $\mathcal{V}$ or the central verifier, $\mathcal{CV}$. The ticket is formed from these individual tags. Note that each tag and the overall ticket are signed by the issuer using his private key while the integrity of the tags and the overall ticket is assured using hashes of their respective content. The ticket is sent back to $\mathcal{U}$ who verifies the integrity of each tag and the overall ticket using the supplied hash values as well as that each tag and the overall ticket have been signed by the issuer.

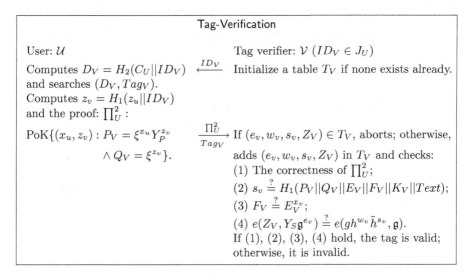

Fig. 5. Tag Verification algorithm

5.4   Tag Verification

The tag verification process is shown in Fig. 5. When the user $\mathcal{U}$ wants to access a service, the ticket verifier $\mathcal{V}$ send his identity information to the user which $\mathcal{U}$ uses to look up the corresponding tag, Tag_V. In order to access the service, $\mathcal{U}$ must submit a proof of knowledge of her secret key alongside the relevant authentication tag Tag_V to prevent users from sharing authentication tags. $\mathcal{V}$ checks his table of previously received tags to ensure that the tag has not already been used previously (double-spend detection), before verifying the user's proof of knowledge in Step 1. Step 2 checks the integrity of the tag using a hash function while Step 4 verifies that it has been issued by the ticket issuer, $\mathcal{I}$. Step 3 can only be verified by $\mathcal{V}$ as it requires the private key of the verifier. Only if $\mathcal{V}$ can complete all steps successfully, is the user granted access.

5.5   Ticket Tracing

Lastly, in the case that a user $\mathcal{U}$'s whole service information J_U needs to be traced, the central verifier, $\mathcal{CV}$, sends its identity to $\mathcal{U}$ who is then required to submit the information, Π_U^2, Tag_{CV}, (which is the same information as that of the Tag Verification algorithm) as well as her overall ticket. Note that, provided a

---

Ticket-Trace

User: $\mathcal{U}$ Central Verifier: $\mathcal{CV}$

Computes $D_V = H_2(C_U||ID_{CV})$ $\xleftarrow{ID_{CV}}$

and searches (D_V, Tag_{CV}).

Computes $z_v = H_1(z_u||ID_{CV})$

and the proof: $\prod_U^2$:

$\text{PoK}\{(x_u, z_v) : P_V = \xi^{x_u} Y_{CV}^{z_v}$ $\xrightarrow[Tag_{CV}]{\prod_U^2, T_U}$ Firstly, verify Tag_{CV} is contained in T_U;

$\wedge\, Q_V = \xi^{z_v}\}.$ abort if this check fails

Secondly, verify that the tag is valid by:

(1) The correctness of $\prod_U^2$;

(2) $s_v \stackrel{?}{=} H_1(P_V||Q_V||E_V||F_V||K_V||Text)$;

(3) $F_V \stackrel{?}{=} E_V^{x_v}$;

(4) $e(Z_V, Y_S\mathfrak{g}^{e_v}) \stackrel{?}{=} e(gh^{w_v}\tilde{h}^{s_v}, \mathfrak{g})$.

If (1), (2), (3), (4) hold, the tag is valid;

otherwise abort as it is invalid.

Finally, de-anonymise the user and

her services by:

(5) Let $\Omega_U = \{\}$. For each Tag_V in T_U

  (i) Compute: $Y_U = \frac{P_V}{Q_V^{x_p}}$ and $Y_V = \frac{K_V}{E_V^{x_p}}$.

  (ii) Look up the ID_V of Y_V. Check:

    (iia) $s_v \stackrel{?}{=} H_1(P_V||Q_V||E_V||K_V||Text)$;

    (iib) $e(Z_V, Y_S\mathfrak{g}^{w_v}) \stackrel{?}{=} e(gh^{w_v}\tilde{h}^{s_v}, \mathfrak{g})$;

    (iii) If (5i) and (5ii) hold, set $\Omega_U = \Omega_U \cup \{ID_V\}$; otherwise abort.

    (iv) verify Y_U remains the same for all tags.

(6) $s_{cv} \stackrel{?}{=} H_1(s_1||s_2||\cdots||s_{|\Omega_U|})$;

(7) $e(Z_{CV}, \tilde{Y}_S\mathfrak{g}^{w_{cv}}) \stackrel{?}{=} e(gh^{w_{cv}}\tilde{h}^{s_{cv}}, \mathfrak{g})$.

Provided (5), (6), (7) can be computed,

$\mathcal{CV}$ can determine that the service

information of $\mathcal{U}$ with public key Y_U is:

$J_U = \Omega_U$; otherwise, the trace has failed.

Fig. 6. Ticket trace algorithm

single tag is known, the whole ticket information could also be obtained directly from the issuer, $\mathcal{I}$, in case the user is not co-operating.

On receipt of this information, the central verifier first validates that the submitted tag Tag_{CV} passes the standard verification process (see Sect. 5.4) as the central verifier's ID_{CV} is always included in J_U. As discussed previously, this steps ensures that $\mathcal{U}$ is a valid user and that the tag belongs to her. Once this steps has passed, the central verifier can then validate the integrity of the ticket and that the previously presented authentication tag is indeed part of the ticket which establishes that the ticket does indeed belong to the user who presented it. Using his private key, the central verifier can now compute the user $\mathcal{U}$'s public key as well as the public keys of all the verifiers contained within the authentication tags and thus determine the user's identity and her service information J_U.

6 Security Analysis

In this section we present the theorems which establish the security of our scheme. Their proofs can be found in the full version of this paper [25].

Theorem 1 (Unlinkability). *An anonymous Single-Sign-On for n designated services with traceability scheme in Figs. 2, 3, 4, 5 and 6 is $(\rho_1, \rho_2, \rho_3, \epsilon'(\ell))$-* **selectively unlinkable** *if the DDH assumption holds on the bilinear group $(e, p, \mathbb{G}_1, \mathbb{G}_2, \mathbb{G}_\tau)$ with the advantage at most $\epsilon(\ell)$, and H_1, H_2 are secure cryptographic hash functions, where ϱ_1 is the total number of verifiers selected by $\mathcal{A}$ to query tickets, ϱ_2 is the number of ticket validation queries, ϱ_3 is the number of ticket trace queries, $\epsilon(\ell) = \frac{\epsilon'(\ell)}{2}$.*

Theorem 2 (Unforgeability). *An anonymous Single-Sign-On for n designated services with traceability scheme in Figs. 2, 3, 4, 5 and 6 is $(\varrho, \epsilon'(\ell))$-* **unforgeable** *if the JOC-version-q-SDH assumption holds on the bilinear group $(e, p, \mathbb{G}_1, \mathbb{G}_2, \mathbb{G}_\tau)$ with the advantage at most $\epsilon(\ell)$, and H_1, H_2 are secure cryptographic hash functions, where ϱ is the total number of verifiers selected by $\mathcal{A}$ to query tickets, $\varrho \leq q$, $\epsilon(\ell) = (\frac{p-q}{p} + \frac{1}{p} + \frac{p-1}{p^3})\epsilon'(\ell)$.*

Theorem 3 (Traceability). *An anonymous Single-Sign-On for n designated services with traceability scheme in Figs. 2, 3, 4, 5 and 6 is $(\rho, \epsilon(\ell))$-* **traceable** *if the q-SDH assumption holds on the bilinear group $(e, p, \mathbb{G}_1, \mathbb{G}_2, \mathbb{G}_\tau)$ with the advantage at most $\epsilon_1(\ell)$, the DL assumption holds on the group $\mathbb{G}_1$ with the advantage at most $\epsilon_2(\ell)$, and H_1, H_2 are secure cryptographic hash functions, where $\epsilon(\ell) = max\left\{\frac{\epsilon_1(\ell)}{2}(\frac{p-q}{p} + \frac{1}{p} + \frac{p-1}{p^3}), \frac{\epsilon_2(\ell)}{2}\right\}$, ϱ is the total number of ticket issuing queries made by $\mathcal{A}$ and $\varrho < q$.*

7 Benchmarking Results

In order to evaluate the performance of our scheme, it has been implemented in Java using a benchmarking framework [17] to extract the computational timings of the algorithms. The benchmark was executed on a Dell Inspiron Latitude E5270 laptop with an Intel Core i7-6600U CPU, 1TB SSD and 16 GB of RAM running Fedora 27. Our implementation makes use of bilinear maps using elliptic curves as well as other cryptographic primitives. The implementation of the scheme relies on the JPBC library [16] for the bilinear maps and uses the cryptographic functions provided by bouncycastle [30]. Note that the Java based implementation of the JPBC API [16] was used throughout.

Table 2. Benchmark results (in ms)

Protocol phase	Entity	$r = 160$ bits	$r = 320$ bits
System Initialisation - Central Authority ($\mathcal{CA}$)			
Initialise the system	CA	1398	3385
Registration - Issuer ($\mathcal{I}$)			
Generate I credentials	CA	12	45
Verify I credentials	I	641	979
Registration - User ($\mathcal{U}$)			
Generate user credentials	CA	12	20
Verify user credentials	User	301	498
Registration - Central Verifier ($\mathcal{CV}$)			
Generate CV credentials	CA	9	23
Verify CV credentials	CV	269	497
Registration - Verifier ($\mathcal{V}$)			
Generate V credentials	CA	10	23
Verify V credentials	V	290	623
Tag Verification - Verifier ($\mathcal{V}$)			
Retrieve Tag_V & generate Π_U^2	User	13	34
Verify Π_U^2 & Tag_V	V	225	575

Issuing phase					
Protocol phase	Entity	V = #verifiers			
		2	3	2	3
Generate Π_U^1 & ticket request	User	93	101	280	309
Verify Π_U^1, generate ticket	Issuer	481	515	916	1044
Verify ticket	User	764	960	1960	2567
Ticket Tracing - Central Verifier ($\mathcal{CV}$)					
Retrieve ticket T_U & Tag_{CV}; generate Π_U^2	User	8	9	33	37
Verify Π_U^2, Tag_{CV}; trace T_U	CV	983	1146	2575	3182

7.1 Timings

Table 2 shows the results of the computational time spent in the various phases of our proposed scheme which required more complex computations (i.e. some form of verification using bilinear maps or generation of zero knowledge proofs). The bilinear map used in the protocol implementations was a Type F elliptic curve provided by the JPBC library where G is the group of points of the elliptic curve and $|G| = p$ is its prime order whose binary representation requires r-bits. We chose to benchmark primes p with $r = 160$ bits and $r = 320$ bits using 2 or 3 verifiers per ticket. The number of verifiers only impacts on the issuing and ticket tracing phases while the size of r impacts on all phases. The generation of credentials by the $\mathcal{CA}$ for the issuer, user and the (central) verifiers during the registration phase of the protocol is on average around 12 ms for $r = 160$ bits and 30 ms for $r = 320$ bits while the verification of those credentials by the various parties takes about 300 ms and 650 ms for 160 bits and 320 bits respectively. It can be seen from Table 2 that the current implementation of the our scheme is reasonably fast for elliptic curves when $r = 160$ (e.g. $\approx$1.5 s and $\approx$250 ms for ticket issuing and verification respectively) and still acceptable for $r = 320$ bits ($\approx$4 s and $\approx$600 ms for the same steps). Moreover, it should be possible to improve the performance of the code considerably by pre-computing static values off-line where possible and switching from the current Java-based version to using a Java-wrapper to the C-based implementation of the pbc libraries [32], instead.

8 Conclusion and Future Work

Previous Anonymous Single-Sign-On schemes usually protect the user's identity from other verifiers but not always the issuer nor the verifier to whom the user needs to authenticate. However, previously, the identity of these verifiers has not been considered extensively and neither has the need to ensure that only a designated verifier can validate a given access request. In this paper we proposed an Anonymous Single-Sign-On scheme which enables users and verifiers to remain anonymous throughout while protecting the system from misbehaving users through a central verifier who can, if required, trace the identities of a user and her associated verifiers. Moreover, we provided a formal security model and proofs for the security properties of our scheme as well as an implementation demonstrating the feasibility of deployment.

In our scheme, a user can currently only authenticate to a verifier once as there is only one authentication tag for each verifier in a user's ticket. If the user needs to authenticate herself to a verifier, $\mathcal{V}$, multiple times, she must request additional tickets with the required authentication tag for $\mathcal{V}$ from the issuer. Our scheme could alternatively be amended to allow multiple authentication tags per verifier in each ticket. In this case the scheme's security model and proofs would need to be amended to support this.

Anonymous Single-Sign-On was the main motivational use case for our scheme, but there are other scenarios to which the could be applied, e.g. the purchase of tickets for tourist attractions, where being able to issue a ticket through an Android implementation would be appropriate. Initial results however demonstrate that the timings on an Android client are significantly slower, for example ticket validation can take $\approx$200 times longer than on the laptop. Future work will focus on improving the scheme's performance further (especially on the Android platform) by moving from a pure Java-based implementation to a C-based version as well as performing pre-computations of static values required by proofs of knowledge where possible. Lastly, extending our scheme with an option for users to enable the controlled release of personal information to a given verifier, e.g. by letting a user control which verifier is allowed to de-anonymise her authentication tag, is another area of future research.

Acknowledgement. This work has been supported by the EPSRC Project DICE: "Data to Improve the Customer Experience", EP/N028295/1. The authors would also like to thank the anonymous reviewers and Dr François Dupressoir for their valuable feedback and comments.

References

1. Armknecht, F., Löhr, H., Manulis, M., Sadeghi, A.-R., et al.: Secure multi-coupons for federated environments: privacy-preserving and customer-friendly. In: Chen, L., Mu, Y., Susilo, W. (eds.) ISPEC 2008. LNCS, vol. 4991, pp. 29–44. Springer, Heidelberg (2008). https://doi.org/10.1007/978-3-540-79104-1_3
2. Au, M.H., Susilo, W., Mu, Y.: Constant-size dynamic k-TAA. In: De Prisco, R., Yung, M. (eds.) SCN 2006. LNCS, vol. 4116, pp. 111–125. Springer, Heidelberg (2006). https://doi.org/10.1007/11832072_8
3. Bellare, M., Micciancio, D., Warinschi, B.: Foundations of group signatures: formal definitions, simplified requirements, and a construction based on general assumptions. In: Biham, E. (ed.) EUROCRYPT 2003. LNCS, vol. 2656, pp. 614–629. Springer, Heidelberg (2003). https://doi.org/10.1007/3-540-39200-9_38
4. Boneh, D., Boyen, X.: Short signatures without random oracles. In: Cachin, C., Camenisch, J.L. (eds.) EUROCRYPT 2004. LNCS, vol. 3027, pp. 56–73. Springer, Heidelberg (2004). https://doi.org/10.1007/978-3-540-24676-3_4
5. Boneh, D., Boyen, X.: Short signatures without random oracles and the SDH assumption in bilinear groups. J. Cryptol. **21**(2), 149–177 (2008)
6. Boneh, D., Boyen, X., Shacham, H.: Short group signatures. In: Franklin, M. (ed.) CRYPTO 2004. LNCS, vol. 3152, pp. 41–55. Springer, Heidelberg (2004). https://doi.org/10.1007/978-3-540-28628-8_3
7. Boneh, D., Franklin, M.: Identity-based encryption from the Weil pairing. In: Kilian, J. (ed.) CRYPTO 2001. LNCS, vol. 2139, pp. 213–229. Springer, Heidelberg (2001). https://doi.org/10.1007/3-540-44647-8_13
8. Camenisch, J., Drijvers, M., Lehmann, A.: Anonymous attestation using the strong Diffie Hellman assumption revisited. In: Franz, M., Papadimitratos, P. (eds.) Trust 2016. LNCS, vol. 9824, pp. 1–20. Springer, Cham (2016). https://doi.org/10.1007/978-3-319-45572-3_1
9. Camenisch, J., Hohenberger, S., Kohlweiss, M., Lysyanskaya, A., Meyerovich, M.: How to win the clonewars: efficient periodic n-times anonymous authentication. In: ACM CCS 2006, pp. 201–210. ACM (2006)
10. Camenisch, J., Kiayias, A., Yung, M.: On the portability of generalized Schnorr proofs. In: Joux, A. (ed.) EUROCRYPT 2009. LNCS, vol. 5479, pp. 425–442. Springer, Heidelberg (2009). https://doi.org/10.1007/978-3-642-01001-9_25
11. Camenisch, J., Lysyanskaya, A.: A signature scheme with efficient protocols. In: Cimato, S., Persiano, G., Galdi, C. (eds.) SCN 2002. LNCS, vol. 2576, pp. 268–289. Springer, Heidelberg (2003). https://doi.org/10.1007/3-540-36413-7_20
12. Camenisch, J., Michels, M.: Proving in zero-knowledge that a number is the product of two safe primes. In: Stern, J. (ed.) EUROCRYPT 1999. LNCS, vol. 1592, pp. 107–122. Springer, Heidelberg (1999). https://doi.org/10.1007/3-540-48910-X_8
13. Camenisch, J., Mödersheim, S., Sommer, D.: A formal model of identity mixer. In: Kowalewski, S., Roveri, M. (eds.) FMICS 2010. LNCS, vol. 6371, pp. 198–214. Springer, Heidelberg (2010). https://doi.org/10.1007/978-3-642-15898-8_13

14. Camenisch, J., Stadler, M.: Efficient group signature schemes for large groups (extended abstract). In: Kaliski, B.S. (ed.) CRYPTO 1997. LNCS, vol. 1294, pp. 410–424. Springer, Heidelberg (1997). https://doi.org/10.1007/BFb0052252

15. Chaum, D., Pedersen, T.P.: Wallet databases with observers. In: Brickell, E.F. (ed.) CRYPTO 1992. LNCS, vol. 740, pp. 89–105. Springer, Heidelberg (1993). https://doi.org/10.1007/3-540-48071-4_7

16. De Caro, A., Iovino, V.: JPBC: Java pairing based cryptography. In: ISCC 2011, pp. 850–855. IEEE (2011)

17. DICE Project: Benchmark E-ticketing Systems (BETS) (2017). https://github. com/swesemeyer/BenchmarkingETicketingSystems

18. Diffie, W., Hellman, M.: New directions in cryptography. IEEE Inf. Theory Soc. **22**(6), 644–654 (1976)

19. Elmufti, K., Weerasinghe, D., Rajarajan, M., Rakocevic, V.: Anonymous authentication for mobile single sign-on to protect user privacy. Int. J. Mob. Commun. **6**(6), 760–769 (2008)

20. European Commission and European Council: Regulation (EU) 2016/679: General Data Protection Regulation (2016). https://eur-lex.europa.eu/legal-content/EN/ TXT/PDF/?uri=CELEX:32016R0679&from=EN

21. Fan, C.I., Wu, C.N., Chen, W.K., Sun, W.Z.: Attribute-based strong designated-verifier signature scheme. J. Syst. Softw. **85**(4), 944–959 (2012)

22. Galbraith, S.D., Paterson, K.G., Smart, N.P.: Pairings for cryptographers. Discret. Appl. Math. **156**(16), 3113–3121 (2008)

23. Ghadafi, E., Smart, N.P., Warinschi, B.: Groth–Sahai proofs revisited. In: Nguyen, P.Q., Pointcheval, D. (eds.) PKC 2010. LNCS, vol. 6056, pp. 177–192. Springer, Heidelberg (2010). https://doi.org/10.1007/978-3-642-13013-7_11

24. Gordon, D.M.: Discrete logarithms in GF(P) using the number field sieve. SIAM J. Discret. Math. **6**(1), 124–138 (1993)

25. Han, J., Chen, L., Schneider, S., Treharne, H., Wesemeyer, S.: Anonymous Single-Sign-On for n services with traceability (2018). https://arxiv.org/abs/1804.07201

26. Han, J., Mu, Y., Susilo, W., Yan, J.: A generic construction of dynamic single sign-on with strong security. In: Jajodia, S., Zhou, J. (eds.) SecureComm 2010. LNICSSITE, vol. 50, pp. 181–198. Springer, Heidelberg (2010). https://doi.org/ 10.1007/978-3-642-16161-2_11

27. IBM Research Zürich: Identity mixer (2018). https://www.zurich.ibm.com/ identity_mixer/

28. Jakobsson, M., Sako, K., Impagliazzo, R.: Designated verifier proofs and their applications. In: Maurer, U. (ed.) EUROCRYPT 1996. LNCS, vol. 1070, pp. 143–154. Springer, Heidelberg (1996). https://doi.org/10.1007/3-540-68339-9_13

29. Lee, T.F.: Provably secure anonymous single-sign-on authentication mechanisms using extended chebyshev chaotic maps for distributed computer networks. IEEE Syst. J. **12**(2), 1499–1505 (2015)

30. Legion of the Bouncy Castle Inc: Bouncy Castle Crypto APIs. https://www. bouncycastle.org/

31. Liu, W., Mu, Y., Yang, G., Yu, Y.: Efficient e-coupon systems with strong user privacy. Telecommun. Syst. **64**(4), 695–708 (2017)

32. Lynn, B.: The pairing-based cryptography (PBC) library (2010). https://crypto. stanford.edu/pbc/

33. MIT Kerberos: Kerberos: The network authentication protocol (2017). https:// web.mit.edu/kerberos/

34. Nguyen, L., Safavi-Naini, R.: Dynamic k-times anonymous authentication. In: Ioannidis, J., Keromytis, A., Yung, M. (eds.) ACNS 2005. LNCS, vol. 3531, pp. 318–333. Springer, Heidelberg (2005). https://doi.org/10.1007/11496137_22
35. Recordon, D., Reed, D.: OpenID 2.0: a platform for user-centric identity management. In: DIM 2006, pp. 11–16. ACM (2006)
36. Schnor, C.P.: Efficient signature generation by smart cards. J. Cryptol. **4**(3), 161–174 (1991)
37. Teranishi, I., Furukawa, J., Sako, K.: k-times anonymous authentication (extended abstract). In: Lee, P.J. (ed.) ASIACRYPT 2004. LNCS, vol. 3329, pp. 308–322. Springer, Heidelberg (2004). https://doi.org/10.1007/978-3-540-30539-2_22
38. Wang, J., Wang, G., Susilo, W.: Anonymous single sign-on schemes transformed from group signatures. In: INCoS 2013, pp. 560–567. IEEE (2013)

Efficiently Deciding Equivalence
for Standard Primitives and Phases

Véronique Cortier[1], Antoine Dallon[1,2,3(✉)], and Stéphanie Delaune[3]

[1] LORIA, CNRS, Nancy, France
dallon@lsv.fr
[2] LSV, CNRS and ENS Paris-Saclay, Cachan, France
[3] Univ Rennes, CNRS, IRISA, Rennes, France

Abstract. Privacy properties like anonymity or untraceability are now well identified, desirable goals of many security protocols. Such properties are typically stated as equivalence properties. However, automatically checking equivalence of protocols often yields efficiency issues.

We propose an efficient algorithm, based on graph planning and SAT-solving. It can decide equivalence for a bounded number of sessions, for protocols with standard cryptographic primitives and phases (often necessary to specify privacy properties), provided protocols are well-typed, that is encrypted messages cannot be confused. The resulting implementation, SAT-Equiv, demonstrates a significant speed-up w.r.t. other existing tools that decide equivalence, covering typically more than 100 sessions. Combined with a previous result, SAT-Equiv can now be used to prove security, for some protocols, for an unbounded number of sessions.

1 Introduction

Security protocols are notoriously difficult to design. A common good practice is to formally analyse protocols using symbolic techniques, in order to spot flaws possibly before their deployment (e.g. TLS 1.3 [4,20], an avionic protocol [5]). These symbolic techniques are mature for reachability properties like confidentiality or authentication. More recently, this approach has been extended to privacy properties, such as vote secrecy, anonymity, untraceability, or unlinkability. These properties are expressed through equivalences. For example, in the case of biometric passports, an attacker should not be able to distinguish whether she is in contact with Alice's passport or Bob's passport.

Recently, a new tool, SAT-Equiv [16], has been proposed to decide such equivalence properties for security protocols, for a bounded number of sessions.

The research leading to these results has received funding from the European Research Council under the European Union's horizon 2020 research and innovation program (ERC grant agreement $n°$ 714955-POPSTAR and $n°$ 645865-SPOOC), as well as from the French National Research Agency (ANR) under the project TECAP, and the DGA.

© Springer Nature Switzerland AG 2018
J. Lopez et al. (Eds.): ESORICS 2018, LNCS 11098, pp. 491–511, 2018.
https://doi.org/10.1007/978-3-319-99073-6_24

It is based on a standard model-checking approach, namely graph planning [7,23] and SAT-solving. Intuitively, protocols executions are over-approximated as a graph planning problem, which allows to consider several possible interleavings in parallel, allowing the analysis of dozen of sessions of a protocol in a few seconds. However, this result is limited to a very small set of primitives, namely symmetric encryption and concatenation.

Our Contributions. Building upon this novel approach, we enrich SAT-Equiv in order to cover protocols using asymmetric primitives and/or phases. As for the original SAT-Equiv, we assume a non confusion property: encrypted messages should not be confused, a condition automatically checked by our tool and which can be enforced e.g. through appropriate labelling.

First, we extend SAT-Equiv to cover all standard primitives: symmetric and asymmetric encryption, signatures, and hashes. Since graph planning is a bounded model-checking technique, SAT-Equiv relies on a small model property, that bounds the size of messages. More precisely, [12] guarantees that if there is an attack, then there is a well-typed attack, where messages follow a fix format. This result has been recently extended to standard primitives [14]. The straightforward extension of SAT-Equiv to standard primitives however yields severe efficiency issues. Indeed, unlike the symmetric encryption case, checking whether two sequences of messages are equivalent (i.e. in static equivalence) may require complex tests where the attacker *construct* messages (that is, hash or asymmetrically encrypt messages). We therefore provide a precise characterisation of the set of tests that need to be considered when checking for static equivalence. This characterisation is of independent interest and could be used in other contexts. We also extend SAT-Equiv to consider protocols with phases, which are useful to model game-based properties.

Our extension of SAT-Equiv now provably terminates. In [16], termination can be guaranteed by checking that any state of the planning graph is indeed reachable, which requires to query a SAT-solver at each step. While this provides termination in theory, this yields a non practical algorithm and has not been implemented. Instead, we exhibit a bound on the maximal length of the smallest attack (bounding the attacker steps as well). It is therefore sufficient to stop the construction of the graph planning once this bound has been reached, enforcing termination for free (no computation overhead).

Finally, we have considerably revisited and improved the original implementation of SAT-Equiv. This significant speedup now allows for security proofs for an unbounded number of sessions. Indeed, [13] shows decidability of equivalence, for an unbounded number of sessions, for protocols with an acyclic dependency graph. The notion of dependency graph is introduced in [13] and intuitively captures how the input/output actions of the protocol may use messages from other steps of the protocol. As a corollary, [13] induces a bound on the number of sessions that needs to be considered for an attack, which depends on the size and structure of the graph. This bound can be rather large (50 to 100 sessions, even on small examples) but SAT-Equiv is now able to reach such bounds.

These novelties are implemented in an extension of SAT-Equiv and compared with the other tools of the literature, namely Spec [25], Akiss [8] and the very recent DeepSec [11] tool. Our experiments show that SAT-Equiv is much faster on all the examples, allowing to reach typically more than 100 sessions. As an application, we consider two protocols, Denning-Sacco and Needham-Schroeder symmetric keys, shown to have acyclic dependency graphs in [13]. Considering the necessary number of sessions as induced by [13], we establish trace equivalence for these two protocols, for an unbounded number of sessions.

Due to lack of space, the reader is referred to the companion technical report [17] for the missing proofs and additional details.

Related Work. There are two main families of tools to analyse equivalence properties on security protocols. Some tools prove equivalence for an arbitrary number of sessions, that is, no matter how often a protocol is used. The main tools in this category are ProVerif [6], Tamarin [24], Maude-NPA [22], Type-Eq [18]. Maude-NPA often suffers from termination issues when used for equivalence properties. Type-Eq [18,19] is a sound (but incomplete) type-checker for equivalence properties that has good performance. It requires that protocols have a similar structure. ProVerif and Tamarin work well in practice. They actually prove a stronger notion of equivalence, diff-equivalence, that also requires that the two considered protocols have a very similar structure. Moreover, equivalence properties are undecidable in general for an unbounded number of sessions. Therefore, ProVerif may not terminate and Tamarin may need some user guidance.

A second approach consists in *deciding* equivalence, for a bounded number of sessions. Spec [25] is one of the first tool that decides equivalence of security protocols but it does not scale well when the number of sessions grows (it can typically handle up to three sessions for small protocols). DeepSec [11] is a very recent tool that builds upon Akiss [8] and Apte [9]. All these tools analyse symbolic executions and typically have to consider all possible interleavings between the roles of the protocol, which often raises efficiency issues.

2   Model

Protocols are modeled through a process algebra, in the spirit of the applied-pi calculus [1]. We consider here a model similar to the ones used *e.g.* in [14,16].

2.1   Term Algebra

As usual, messages are modeled by terms. Private data are represented through an infinite set $\mathcal{N}$ of *names* used to model *e.g.* keys or nonces. We consider an infinite set $\mathcal{C}_0$ of constants to represent public data such as agent names or attacker's nonces or keys. We consider also two sets of *variables* $\mathcal{X}$ and $\mathcal{W}$. Variables in $\mathcal{X}$ model arbitrary data expected by the protocol, while variables in $\mathcal{W}$ are used to store messages learnt by the attacker. A *data* is either a constant, a variable, or a name. Cryptograhic primitives are represented by function symbols. We consider the *signature* Σ parameterised by $n \geq 2$:

- $\Sigma_c = \{\mathsf{senc},\ \mathsf{aenc},\ \mathsf{hash},\ \mathsf{pub},\ \mathsf{sign},\ \mathsf{vk},\ \mathsf{ok}\} \cup \{\langle\ \rangle_k \mid 2 \leq k \leq n\}$;
- $\Sigma_d = \{\mathsf{sdec},\ \mathsf{adec},\ \mathsf{getmsg}\} \cup \{\mathsf{proj}_j^k \mid 2 \leq k \leq n \text{ and } 1 \leq j \leq k\}$; and
- $\Sigma = \Sigma_c \cup \Sigma_d \cup \{\mathsf{check}\}$.

The symbols senc, aenc, sdec, and adec of arity 2 are used to model resp. symmetric and asymmetric encryption. We also consider signature sign and hash function hash. Concatenation of messages is modeled through tuple operators together with their projection functions. For example, $\langle m_1, m_2, m_3 \rangle_3$ represents the concatenation of the three messages m_1, m_2, and m_3. It is syntactically different from the nested pairs $\langle m_1, \langle m_2, m_3 \rangle_2 \rangle_2$. These two representations correspond to different implementation choices. We distinguish between *constructors* in Σ_c and *destructors* in Σ_d. The symbol check of arity 2, which corresponds to the verification of a signature, is neither a destructor nor a constructor. The set of terms built from a signature $\mathcal{F}$ and a set of data D is denoted $\mathcal{T}(\Sigma, D)$. Given a term u, we denote $St(u)$ the set of its *subterms*, $vars(u)$ the set of its *variables*, and $\mathsf{root}(u)$ its root symbol. A term is *ground* if it contains no variable. The application of a substitution σ to a term u is written $u\sigma$. We denote $dom(\sigma)$ its *domain* and $img(\sigma)$ its *image*. Two terms u_1 and u_2 are *unifiable* when there exists a substitution σ such that $u_1\sigma = u_2\sigma$.

We consider two *sorts*: atom and bitstring. The sort atom represents atomic data like nonces or keys while bitstring models arbitrary messages. Names in $\mathcal{N}$ and constants in $\mathcal{C}_0$ have sort atom. Any $f \in \Sigma_c$ comes with its sorted arity:

$\langle\ \rangle_k : \mathsf{bitstring} \times \cdots \times \mathsf{bitstring} \to \mathsf{bitstring}$	$\mathsf{ok} : \qquad\quad \to \mathsf{bitstring}$
$\mathsf{senc} : \mathsf{bitstring} \times \mathsf{atom} \to \mathsf{bitstring}$	$\mathsf{pub} : \mathsf{atom} \to \mathsf{bitstring}$
$\mathsf{aenc} : \mathsf{bitstring} \times \mathsf{bitstring} \to \mathsf{bitstring}$	$\mathsf{vk} : \quad \mathsf{atom} \to \mathsf{bitstring}$
$\mathsf{sign} : \mathsf{bitstring} \times \mathsf{atom} \to \mathsf{bitstring}$	$\mathsf{hash} : \mathsf{bitstring} \to \mathsf{bitstring}$

Given $D \subseteq \mathcal{C}_0 \uplus \mathcal{X}$, the set $\mathcal{T}_0(\Sigma_c, D)$ is the set of terms t in $\mathcal{T}(\Sigma_c, D)$ such that *(i)* for any term $\mathsf{pub}(u)$ (resp. $\mathsf{vk}(u)$) in $St(t)$, u is of sort atom; *(ii)* for any $\mathsf{aenc}(u, v) \in St(t)$, $v = \mathsf{pub}(v')$ for some v'. Terms in $\mathcal{T}_0(\Sigma_c, \mathcal{N} \uplus \mathcal{C}_0)$ are called *messages*. Intuitively, messages are terms with atomic keys.

The properties of the cryptographic primitives are reflected through the following convergent rewriting rules.

$$\mathsf{sdec}(\mathsf{senc}(x, y), y) \to x \qquad \mathsf{adec}(\mathsf{aenc}(x, \mathsf{pub}(y)), y) \to x$$
$$\mathsf{getmsg}(\mathsf{sign}(x, y)) \to x \qquad \mathsf{check}(\mathsf{sign}(x, y), \mathsf{vk}(y)) \to \mathsf{ok}$$
$$\mathsf{proj}_j^k(\langle x_1, \ldots, x_k \rangle_k) \to x_j \qquad \text{with } 2 \leq k \leq n \text{ and } 1 \leq j \leq k$$

A term u can be rewritten into v if there is a position p in u, and a rewriting rule $g(t_1, \ldots, t_n) \to t$ such that $u|_p = g(t_1, \ldots, t_n)\theta$ for some substitution θ, and $v = u[t\theta]_p$, i.e. u in which the subterm at position p has been replaced by $t\theta$. Moreover, we assume that $t_1\theta, \ldots, t_n\theta$ as well as $t\theta$ are messages, in particular they do not contain destructor symbols. As usual, we denote $\to^*$ the reflexive-transitive closure of $\to$, and $u{\downarrow}$ the *normal form* of a term u.

An attacker builds her own messages by applying public function symbols to terms she already knows and which are available through variables in $\mathcal{W}$. Formally, a computation done by the attacker is a *recipe*, *i.e.* a term in $\mathcal{T}(\Sigma, \mathcal{W} \uplus \mathcal{C}_0)$.

2.2   Process Algebra

We consider processes that may receive and send messages. We assume that each process communicates on a dedicated public channel. In practice, IP addresses and sessions identifiers are typically used to desambiguate which message is addressed to whom and for which session. Of course, these channels may be freely manipulated by the attacker. Since we consider equivalence properties, distinct (public) channels provide more abilities for the adversary to distinguish between protocols. Formally, given a set $\mathcal{C}h$ of channels, we consider the fragment of simple processes without replication built on basic processes as defined *e.g.* in [10].

Definition 1. *A basic processes is defined as follows:*

$$P, Q := 0 \mid \text{in}(c, u_1).P \mid \text{out}(c, u_2).P \mid i{:}P$$

with $u_1, u_2 \in \mathcal{T}_0(\Sigma_c, \mathcal{C}_0 \uplus \mathcal{N} \uplus \mathcal{X})$, $c \in \mathcal{C}h$, and increasing phase numbers. A simple process *is a multiset of basic processes on pairwise distinct channels. A* protocol *is a simple process such that all its variables are in the scope of an input.*

The process 0 does nothing and we often omit it. The process "$\text{in}(c, u_1).P$" expects a message m of the form u_1 on channel c and then behaves like $P\sigma$ where σ is a substitution such that $m = u_1\sigma$. Note that checking whether a received message has the expected form is done through pattern-matching instead of explicit tests. The process "$\text{out}(c, u_2).P$" emits u_2 on c, and then behaves like P. Our calculus also has a phase instruction, in the spirit of [6], denoted $i{:}P$. This instruction is useful to model security requirements, for example in case the attacker interacts with the protocol before being given some secret.

Example 1. As an illustrative example, we consider a simplified version of the Denning-Sacco protocol which is a key distribution protocol relying on asymmetric encryption and signature. Informally, the protocol is as follows.

$$A \rightarrow B : \text{aenc}(\text{sign}(\langle A, B, K_{ab}\rangle, \text{prv}(A)), \text{pub}(B))$$

The agents A and B aim at authenticating each other and establishing a fresh session key K_{ab}. We model this protocol in our formalism through the simple process $\mathcal{P}_{\text{DS}} = \{P_A; P_B\}$ where $P_A = \text{out}(c_A, \text{aenc}(\text{sign}(\langle a, b, k_{ab}\rangle_3, sk_a), \text{pub}(sk_b))).0$ and $P_B = \text{in}(c_B, \text{aenc}(\text{sign}(\langle a, b, x\rangle_3, sk_a), \text{pub}(sk_b))).0$ where sk_a, sk_b, and k_{ab} are names, a and b are constants, and x is a variable.

The operational semantics of a process is defined using a relation over configurations. A *configuration* is a tuple $(\mathcal{P}; \phi; \sigma; i)$ with $i \in \mathbb{N}$ and such that:

- $\mathcal{P}$ is a multiset of processes (not necessarily ground);
- $\phi = \{w_1 \triangleright m_1, \ldots, w_n \triangleright m_n\}$ is a *frame*, i.e. a substitution where $w_1, \ldots, w_n$ are variables in $\mathcal{W}$, and $m_1, \ldots, m_n$ are messages;
- σ is a substitution such that $fv(\mathcal{P}) \subseteq dom(\sigma)$, and $img(\sigma)$ are messages.

IN $(i{:}\text{in}(c,u).P \cup \mathcal{P}; \phi; \sigma; i) \xrightarrow{\text{in}(c,R)} (i{:}P \cup \mathcal{P}; \phi; \sigma \uplus \sigma_0; i)$ where R is a recipe
     such that $R\phi\!\downarrow$ is a message, and $R\phi\!\downarrow = (u\sigma)\sigma_0$ for σ_0 with $dom(\sigma_0) = vars(u\sigma)$.

OUT $(i{:}\text{out}(c,u).P \cup \mathcal{P}; \phi; \sigma; i) \xrightarrow{\text{out}(c,w)} (i{:}P \cup \mathcal{P}; \phi \cup \{w \triangleright u\sigma\}; \sigma; i)$
                    with w a fresh variable from $\mathcal{W}$, and $u\sigma$ is a message.

MOVE $(\mathcal{P}; \phi; \sigma; i) \xrightarrow{\text{phase } i'} (\mathcal{P}; \phi; \sigma; i')$ with $i' > i$.

PHASE $(i'{:}i''{:}P \cup \mathcal{P}; \phi; \sigma; i) \xrightarrow{\tau} (i''{:}P \cup \mathcal{P}; \phi; \sigma; i)$

Fig. 1. Semantics for processes

A configuration is said to be *initial* when $\sigma = \emptyset$. Intuitively, $\mathcal{P}$ represents the processes that still remain to be executed; ϕ represents the sequence of messages that have been learnt so far by the attacker, and σ stores the value of the variables that have already been instantiated. We write P instead of $0{:}P$ and $P \uplus \mathcal{P}$ instead of $\{P\} \uplus \mathcal{P}$. Given a protocol $\mathcal{P}$, we also often write $\mathcal{P}$ instead of $(\mathcal{P}; \emptyset; \emptyset; 0)$. The operational semantics is induced by the relation $\xrightarrow{\alpha}$ over configurations defined in Fig. 1. For example, the IN rule defines how messages can be input on a (public) channel: the adversary may send any message, provided she can construct it through a recipe R applied on her previous knowledge ϕ. Note that only messages can be received (and sent). The relation $\xrightarrow{\text{tr}}$ between configurations (where tr is a possibly empty sequence of actions) is defined in the usual way. Given a configuration $\mathcal{K}$, we write:

$$\text{trace}(\mathcal{K}) = \{(\text{tr}, \phi) \mid \mathcal{K} \xrightarrow{\text{tr}} (\mathcal{P}'; \phi; \sigma; i) \text{ for some configuration } (\mathcal{P}'; \phi; \sigma; i)\}.$$

Example 2. Continuing Example 1, let $\mathcal{K}_{\text{DS}} = (\{P_A; P_B; P_{B'}\}; \phi_0; \emptyset; 0)$ where $P_{B'}$ models an additional session of the role B obtained by simply renaming c_B and x with c'_B and x'. The frame $\phi_0 = \{w_a \triangleright \text{vk}(sk_a), w_b \triangleright \text{pub}(sk_b)\}$ models the fact that the attacker initially knows the public key of b and the verification key of a. We consider a simple scenario without dishonest participant. The trace $\text{tr}_0 = \text{out}(c_A, w_1).\text{in}(c_B, w_1).\text{in}(c'_B, w_1)$ is executable from $\mathcal{K}_{\text{DS}}$, and yields $\phi = \phi_0 \uplus \{w_1 \triangleright \text{aenc}(\text{sign}(\langle \text{a}, \text{b}, k_{ab}\rangle_3, sk_a), \text{pub}(sk_b))\}$, i.e. $(\text{tr}_0, \phi) \in \text{trace}(\mathcal{K}_{\text{DS}})$.

2.3   Type-Compliance

We present here our main assumption on protocols. Intuitively, we assume that ciphertexts cannot be confused, and we rely for this on a notion of typing system.

Definition 2. *A typing system is a pair* $(\mathcal{T}_{\text{init}}, \delta)$ *where* $\mathcal{T}_{\text{init}}$ *is a set of elements called* initial types, *and* δ *is a function mapping data in* $\mathcal{C}_0 \uplus \mathcal{N} \uplus \mathcal{X}$ *to types* τ:

$$\tau, \tau_1, \tau_2 = \tau_0 \mid \text{f}(\tau_1, \ldots, \tau_n) \text{ with } \text{f} \in \Sigma_c \text{ and } \tau_0 \in \mathcal{T}_{\text{init}}$$

Then, δ *is extended to constructor terms as follows:*

$$\delta(\text{f}(t_1, \ldots, t_n)) = \text{f}(\delta(t_1), \ldots, \delta(t_n)) \text{ with } \text{f} \in \Sigma_c.$$

A configuration is type-compliant if two unifiable encrypted subterms have the same type. We write $ESt(t)$ for the set of *encrypted subterms* of t, i.e. $ESt(t) = \{u \in St(t) \mid u \text{ is of the form } f(u_1, \ldots, u_n) \text{ and } f \neq \langle \ \rangle_i\}$.

Definition 3. *An initial configuration $\mathcal{K}$ is type-compliant w.r.t. a typing system $(\mathcal{T}_{\text{init}}, \delta)$ if for every $t, t' \in ESt(\mathcal{K})$ we have that t and t' unifiable implies that $\delta(t) = \delta(t')$.*

Example 3. Continuing our running example, we consider the typing system generated from $\mathcal{T}_{\text{DS}} = \{\tau_a, \tau_b, \tau_k, \tau_{sk}\}$ of initial types, and the function δ_{DS} that associates the expected type to each constant/name ($\delta_{\text{DS}}(a) = \tau_a$, $\delta_{\text{DS}}(k_{ab}) = \tau_k$, etc.), and such that $\delta_{\text{DS}}(x) = \delta_{\text{DS}}(x') = \tau_k$. We have that $\mathcal{K}_{\text{DS}}$ is type-compliant w.r.t. $(\mathcal{T}_{\text{DS}}, \delta_{\text{DS}})$: unifiable encrypted subterms occurring in the configuration have the same type since $\delta_{\text{DS}}(x) = \delta_{\text{DS}}(x') = \delta_{\text{DS}}(k_{ab})$.

Type-compliant protocols have the property that, when looking for attacks, it is sufficient to consider well-typed execution: $\mathcal{K} \xrightarrow{\text{tr}} (\mathcal{P}; \phi; \sigma; i)$ is *well-typed* w.r.t. a typing system $(\mathcal{T}_{\text{init}}, \delta)$, if σ is a well-typed substitution, i.e. every variable of its domain has the same type as its image.

2.4 Trace Equivalence

Many privacy properties such as vote-privacy or untraceability are expressed as trace equivalence [2,21]. Intuitively, two configurations are trace equivalent if an attacker cannot tell with which of the two configurations she is interacting. We first introduce a notion of equivalence (actually, inclusion) between frames.

Definition 4. *Two frames ϕ_1 and ϕ_2 are in static inclusion, written $\phi_1 \sqsubseteq_s \phi_2$, when $dom(\phi_1) = dom(\phi_2)$, and:*

- *for any recipe R, we have that $R\phi_1\downarrow$ is a message implies that $R\phi_2\downarrow$ is a message;*
- *for any recipes R, R' such that $R\phi_1\downarrow$, $R'\phi_1\downarrow$ are messages, we have that: $R\phi_1\downarrow = R'\phi_1\downarrow$ implies $R\phi_2\downarrow = R'\phi_2\downarrow$.*

Intuitively, ϕ_1 is included in ϕ_2 if any recipe producing a message in ϕ_1 also produces a message in ϕ_2 and if any equality satisfied in ϕ_1 is also satisfied in ϕ_2.

Example 4. We consider $\phi_1 = \phi \uplus \{w_2 \triangleright \text{senc}(m_1, k_{ab}), w_2' \triangleright \text{senc}(m_1, k_{ab})\}$, and $\phi_2 = \phi \uplus \{w_2 \triangleright \text{senc}(m_2, k), w_2' \triangleright \text{senc}(m_2, k')\}$ where $m_1, m_2 \in \mathcal{C}_0$. We have that $w_2\phi_1\downarrow = w_2'\phi_1\downarrow$ whereas this equality does not hold in ϕ_2. Hence $\phi_1 \not\sqsubseteq_s \phi_2$.

Trace inclusion is the active counterpart of static inclusion. Two configurations are in trace inclusion if, however the attacker behaves, the resulting sequences of messages observed by the attacker are in static inclusion.

Definition 5. *Let $\mathcal{K}$ and $\mathcal{K}'$ be two configurations. We have that $\mathcal{K} \sqsubseteq_t \mathcal{K}'$, if for every $(\text{tr}, \phi) \in \text{trace}(\mathcal{K})$, there exists $(\text{tr}, \phi') \in \text{trace}(\mathcal{K}')$ such that $\phi \sqsubseteq_s \phi'$.*

We easily derive a notion of trace equivalence: two configurations $\mathcal{K}$ and $\mathcal{K}'$ are trace equivalence, denoted $\mathcal{K} \approx_t \mathcal{K}'$, if $\mathcal{K} \sqsubseteq_t \mathcal{K}'$ and $\mathcal{K}' \sqsubseteq_t \mathcal{K}$. This notion of trace equivalence slightly differs from the one used in e.g. [12] but they actually coincide on the class of protocols we consider in this paper [8].

Example 5. To model secrecy of the key k_{ab}, we define *strong secrecy* of k_{ab} by requiring that k_{ab} is indistinguishable from a fresh value. Formally, we consider P_B^1 (resp. $P_{B'}^1$) obtained by replacing the process 0 with $1{:}\mathsf{out}(c_B, \mathsf{senc}(\mathsf{m}_1, x))$ (resp. $1{:}\mathsf{out}(c_B', \mathsf{senc}(\mathsf{m}_1, x')))$. On the other side of the equivalence, we consider P_B^2 and $P_{B'}^2$ obtained by replacing the process 0 with $1{:}\mathsf{out}(c_B, \mathsf{senc}(\mathsf{m}_2, k))$ (resp. $1{:}\mathsf{out}(c_B', \mathsf{senc}(\mathsf{m}_2, k')))$ with fresh names k and k'.

$$\mathcal{K}_{\mathsf{DS}}^1 = (\{P_A; P_B^1; P_{B'}^1\}; \phi_0) \text{ and } \mathcal{K}_{\mathsf{DS}}^2 = (\{P_A; P_B^2; P_{B'}^2\}; \phi_0).$$

Then, we can show that $\mathcal{K}_{\mathsf{DS}}^1 \not\sqsubseteq_t \mathcal{K}_{\mathsf{DS}}^2$ since k_{ab} is not strongly secret. An attacker can replay the message sent by A due to lack of freshness. This is exemplified by the trace $\mathsf{tr}_0.\mathsf{out}(c_B, \mathsf{w}_2).\mathsf{out}(c_B', \mathsf{w}_2')$ and the test given in Example 4.

3   From Static Inclusion to Planning

The overall objective of this paper is to provide a practical algorithm for deciding trace inclusion (and thus trace equivalence) relying on graph planning and SAT solving. We start here by explaining how to build a planning problem from two frames such that the planning problem has a solution if, and only if, the two corresponding frames are not in static inclusion.

3.1   Planning Problems

We first recall the definition of a planning problem, slightly simplified from [15]. Intuitively, a planning system defines a transition system from sets of facts to sets of facts. New facts may be produced and some old facts may be deleted.

Definition 6. *A planning system is tuple $\langle \mathcal{F}act, \mathcal{I}nit, \mathcal{R}ule \rangle$ where $\mathcal{F}act$ is a set of ground formulas called facts, $\mathcal{I}nit_0 \subseteq \mathcal{F}act$ is a set of facts representing the initial state, and $\mathcal{R}ule$ is a set of rules of the form $\mathsf{Pre} \rightarrow \mathsf{Add}; \mathsf{Del}$ where $\mathsf{Pre}, \mathsf{Add}, \mathsf{Del}$ are finite sets of facts such that $\mathsf{Add} \cap \mathsf{Del} = \emptyset$, $\mathsf{Del} \subseteq \mathsf{Pre}$. We write $\mathsf{Pre} \rightarrow \mathsf{Add}$ when $\mathsf{Del} = \emptyset$.*

Given a rule $r \in \mathcal{R}ule$ of the form $\mathsf{Pre} \rightarrow \mathsf{Add}; \mathsf{Del}$, we denote $\mathsf{Pre}(r) = \mathsf{Pre}$, $\mathsf{Add}(r) = \mathsf{Add}$, and $\mathsf{Del}(r) = \mathsf{Del}$. If $S \subseteq \mathcal{F}act$ are such that $\mathsf{Pre}(r) \subseteq S$, then we say that the rule is *applicable* in S, denoted $S \xrightarrow{r} S'$, and the state $S' = (S \smallsetminus \mathsf{Del}) \cup \mathsf{Add}$ is the state resulting from the application of r to S. We allow some rules to be applied in parallel when no facts are deleted. Given $S \subseteq \mathcal{F}act$, and a set of rules $\{r_1, \ldots, r_k\}$ such that $\mathsf{Del}(r_i) = \emptyset$ and $\mathsf{Pre}(r_i) \subseteq S$ for any $i \in \{1, \ldots, k\}$, $\{r_1, \ldots, r_k\}$ is *applicable* in S, denoted $S \xrightarrow{\{r_1, \ldots, r_k\}} S'$, and the state $S' = \bigcup_{i=1}^{k} \mathsf{Add}(r_i) \cup S$ is the state resulting from the application of $\{r_1, \ldots, r_k\}$ to S.

A *planning path* from $S_0 \subseteq \mathcal{F}act$ to $S_n \subseteq \mathcal{F}act$ is a sequence $r_1, \ldots, r_n$ made of rules or sets of rules in $\mathcal{R}ule$ such that $S_0 \xrightarrow{r_1} S_1 \xrightarrow{r_2} \ldots S_{n-1} \xrightarrow{r_n} S_n$ for some states $S_1, \ldots, S_{n-1} \subseteq \mathcal{F}act$. A *planning problem* for a system $\Theta = \langle \mathcal{F}act, \mathcal{I}nit, \mathcal{R}ule \rangle$ is a pair $\Pi = \langle \Theta, S_f \rangle$ where $S_f \subseteq \mathcal{F}$ represents the target facts. A solution to $\Pi = \langle \Theta, S_f \rangle$, called a *plan*, is a planning path from $\mathcal{I}nit$ to a state S_n such that $S_f \subseteq S_n$.

A transition $S \xrightarrow{\{r_1, \ldots, r_k\}} S'$ can be mimicked by $S \xrightarrow{r_1} S_1 \xrightarrow{r_2} \ldots \xrightarrow{r_k} S'$, thus the possibility of applying set of rules in a single step does not change the set of reachable states from a given state S. However, this allows us to consider plans of smaller length and will be useful later on to derive a tight bound and ensure the termination of our algorithm.

In this section, we explain the translation of static inclusion into a planning problem. We consider an (infinite) set $\mathcal{F}act_0$ of facts that represent the attacker's knowledge, i.e. formulas of the form $\text{att}(u_P, u_Q)$ where u_P and u_Q are messages, plus a special symbol bad. Intuitively, $\text{att}(u_P, u_Q)$ means that the attacker knows u_P in the "left" frame, while she knows u_Q in the "right" one.

3.2   Attacker Analysis Rules

Following [16], we first describe the planning rules that correspond to the analysis part of the attacker behaviours. We start by describing a set of abstract rules $\mathsf{R}_{\mathsf{Ana}}$ that will be instantiated later on, yielding a (concrete) planning system.

$$\text{att}(\langle x_1, \ldots, x_k \rangle_k, \langle y_1, \ldots, y_k \rangle_k) \to \text{att}(x_i, y_i) \text{ with } i \leq k$$
$$\text{att}(\text{senc}(x_1, x_2), \text{senc}(y_1, y_2)), \text{att}(x_2, y_2) \to \text{att}(x_1, y_1)$$
$$\text{att}(\text{aenc}(x_1, \text{pub}(x_2)), \text{aenc}(y_1, \text{pub}(y_2))), \text{att}(x_2, y_2) \to \text{att}(x_1, y_1)$$
$$\text{att}(\text{sign}(x_1, x_2), \text{sign}(y_1, y_2)) \to \text{att}(x_1, y_1)$$

These rules correspond to the attacker's ability to project, decrypt, and retrieve messages from their signature. There is no Del since the attacker never forgets. Given a rule $r \in \mathsf{R}_{\mathsf{Ana}}$, we explain how to compute its concretization denoted $\mathsf{Concrete}(r)$. Formally, we have that $\mathsf{Concrete}(r) = \mathsf{Concrete}^+(r) \cup \mathsf{Concrete}^-(r)$.

$\mathsf{Concrete}^+(r)$. The positive concretizations of r consist of instantiating r such that the resulting terms are messages. More formally, we have:

$$\mathsf{Concrete}^+(r) = \{r\sigma \mid \sigma \text{ substitution such that } r\sigma \text{ only involve messages.}\}$$

$\mathsf{Concrete}^-(r)$. We say that a sequence of ground facts $\text{att}(u_1, v_1), \ldots, \text{att}(u_k, v_k)$ left-unifies with a sequence $\text{att}(u'_1, v'_1), \ldots, \text{att}(u'_k, v'_k)$ if there exists σ such that $u'_1\sigma = u_1, \ldots, u'_k\sigma = u_k$ (and symmetrically for right-unification). Given an abstract attacker rule $r = \mathsf{Pre} \to \mathsf{Add}$, we define $\mathsf{Concrete}^-(r)$ as the set containing $f_1, \ldots, f_k \to \mathsf{bad}$ for any sequence of facts $f_1, \ldots, f_k \in \mathcal{F}act_0$ such that $f_1, \ldots, f_k$ left-unifies with Pre, whereas $f_1, \ldots, f_k$ does not right-unify with Pre.

Example 6. The negative concretizations of the abstract rule corresponding to asymmetric decryption are all the concrete rules of the form

$$\mathsf{att}(\mathsf{aenc}(u_1,\mathsf{pub}(u_2)),v),\ \mathsf{att}(u_2,v') \to \mathsf{bad}$$

where u_1, u_2, v, v', $\mathsf{aenc}(u_1,\mathsf{pub}(u_2))$ are messages, whereas $\mathsf{adec}(v,v')\!\downarrow$ is not.

3.3   Static Inclusion

According to Definition 4, to break static inclusion, an attacker may build new terms (using both analysis and synthesis rules) but also check for equalities and computation failures. To encode static inclusion using planning in an efficient way, we need to strictly control the terms that an attacker has to synthesize.

We say that R is *destructor-only* if $R \in \mathcal{T}(\Sigma_{\mathsf{d}}, \mathcal{C}_0 \cup \mathcal{W})$. It is *simple* if there exists destructor-only recipes $R_1, \ldots, R_k$, and a context C made of constructors such that $R = C[R_1, \ldots, R_k]$.

Definition 7. *Let ϕ, ψ be such that $dom(\phi) = dom(\psi)$. We write $\phi \sqsubseteq_s^{\mathsf{simple}} \psi$ if:*

1. *For each destructor-only recipe R such that $R\phi\!\downarrow$ is a (resp. atomic) message, $R\psi\!\downarrow$ is a (resp. atomic) message.*
2. *For each simple recipe R and destructor-only recipe R' such that $R\phi\!\downarrow, R'\phi\!\downarrow$ are messages and $R\phi\!\downarrow = R'\phi\!\downarrow$, we have that $R\psi\!\downarrow = R'\psi\!\downarrow$.*
3. *For each destructor-only recipes R, R', if $R\phi\!\downarrow = \mathsf{sign}(t,s)$, and $R'\phi\!\downarrow = \mathsf{vk}(s)$ for some term t and atom s, then $R\psi\!\downarrow = \mathsf{sign}(t',s')$, and $R'\psi\!\downarrow = \mathsf{vk}(s')$ for some term t' and atom s'.*
4. *For each destructor-only recipe R, such that $R\phi\!\downarrow = \mathsf{pub}(s)$ for some atom s, $R\psi\!\downarrow = \mathsf{pub}(s')$ for some atom s'.*

We write $\phi \sqsubseteq_s^{\mathsf{simple}^+} \psi$ when the test described at item 2 is only performed when (i) either R is destructor-only; (ii) or $\mathsf{root}(R) \notin \{\mathsf{senc}\} \cup \{\langle\ \rangle_k \mid 2 \le k \le n\}$, and $\mathsf{root}(R') \ne \mathsf{adec}$.

This notion of static inclusion is equivalent to the original one.

Lemma 1. *Let ϕ and ψ be two frames having the same domain. We have that:*

$$\phi \sqsubseteq_s \psi \iff \phi \sqsubseteq_s^{\mathsf{simple}} \psi \iff \phi \sqsubseteq_s^{\mathsf{simple}^+} \psi.$$

From this new characterisation of static inclusion $\sqsubseteq_s^{\mathsf{simple}}$, we derive the planning rules that capture all the cases of failures with those in $\mathsf{Concrete}^-(\mathcal{R}_{\mathsf{Ana}})$.

$\mathcal{R}_{\mathsf{fail}}^{\mathsf{atom}} = \{\mathsf{att}(u,v) \to \mathsf{bad} \mid u$ is an atom but v is not$\}$

$\mathcal{R}_{\mathsf{fail}}^{\mathsf{pub}} = \{\mathsf{att}(\mathsf{pub}(u),v) \to \mathsf{bad} \mid v$ is not of the form $\mathsf{pub}(v')\}$

$\mathcal{R}_{\mathsf{fail}}^{\mathsf{check}} = \left\{ \begin{array}{l} \mathsf{att}(\mathsf{sign}(u_1,u_2),v_1) \\ \mathsf{att}(\mathsf{vk}(u_2),v_2) \end{array} \to \mathsf{bad} \mid \mathsf{check}(v_1,v_2)\!\downarrow$ is not a message$\right\}$

$\mathcal{R}_{\mathsf{fail}}^{\mathsf{test}} = \left\{ \begin{array}{l} \mathsf{att}(u_1,v_1), \ldots, \mathsf{att}(u_k,v_k) \\ \mathsf{att}(C[u_1, \ldots, u_k], v) \end{array} \to \mathsf{bad} \mid \begin{array}{l} C \text{ is a constructor context,} \\ C[u_1, \ldots, u_k] \in St(\phi) \cup \mathcal{C}_0 \\ v \ne C[v_1, \ldots, v_k]. \end{array} \right\}$

Actually, not all subterms of $St(\phi)$ need to be considered. Therefore, we consider an optimised version that captures only the terms that may not be reconstructed from their subterms. Formally, $St_{\text{opti}}(t)$ is defined as follows.

- $St_{\text{opti}}(\langle t_1, t_2 \rangle) = St_{\text{opti}}(t_1) \cup St_{\text{opti}}(t_2)$;
- $St_{\text{opti}}(\text{senc}(t_1, t_2)) = St_{\text{opti}}(t_1)$;
- $St_{\text{opti}}(\text{aenc}(t_1, t_2)) = \{\text{aenc}(t_1, t_2)\} \cup (St_{\text{opti}}(t_1) \smallsetminus \{t_1\})$
- $St_{\text{opti}}(\text{sign}(t_1, t_2)) = \{\text{sign}(t_1, t_2)\} \cup St_{\text{opti}}(t_1)$;
- $St_{\text{opti}}(\mathsf{f}(t)) = \{\mathsf{f}(t)\}$ with $\mathsf{f} \in \{\text{hash}, \text{pub}, \text{vk}\}$.

Thanks to the fact that $\sqsubseteq_s^{\text{simple}^+}$ is equivalent to static inclusion, we may only consider simple recipes which evaluation yields a term in $St_{\text{opti}}(\phi)$.

Lemma 2. *Let ϕ be a frame, $R = C[R_1, \ldots, R_k]$ be a simple recipe such that $\text{root}(R) \notin \{\text{senc}\} \cup \{\langle\ \rangle_k \mid 2 \leq k \leq n\}$, and R' be a destructor-only recipe such that $\text{root}(R') \neq \text{adec}$. Assume that $R\phi{\downarrow}$ and $R'\phi{\downarrow}$ are both messages such that $R\phi{\downarrow} = R'\phi{\downarrow}$. We have that either C is the empty context, or $R\phi{\downarrow} \in St_{\text{opti}}(\phi) \cup \mathcal{C}_0$.*

Therefore, $\mathcal{R}_{\text{fail}}^{\text{test}}$ can be replaced by the following (smaller) set of rules:

$$\mathcal{R}_{\text{fail}}^{\text{test}_1} = \{\text{att}(u_1, v_1), \text{att}(u_1, v_2) \rightarrow \text{bad} \mid v_1 \neq v_2\}$$

$$\mathcal{R}_{\text{fail}}^{\text{test}_2} = \{\text{att}(u_1, v_1), \ldots, \text{att}(u_k, v_k), \text{att}(C[u_1, \ldots, u_k], v) \rightarrow \text{bad} \mid C \text{ is a non-empty}$$
$$\text{constructor context}, C[u_1, \ldots, u_k] \in St_{\text{opti}}(\phi) \cup \mathcal{C}_0, \text{ and } v \neq C[v_1, \ldots, v_k].\}$$

Let ϕ and ψ be two frames with $dom(\phi) = dom(\psi)$ and built using constants from $\mathcal{C} \subseteq \mathcal{C}_0$. The set of facts associated to ϕ and ψ is defined as follows:

$$\text{Fact}_\mathcal{C}(\phi, \psi) = \{\text{att}(\mathsf{a}, \mathsf{a}) \mid \mathsf{a} \in \mathcal{C}\} \cup \{\text{att}(\mathsf{w}\phi, \mathsf{w}\psi) \mid \mathsf{w} \in dom(\phi)\}$$

Two frames are in static inclusion if, and only if, the corresponding planning system has no solution. Actually, when the frames are not in static inclusion, we provide a bound on the length of the (minimal) plan witnessing this fact.

Proposition 1. *Let ϕ and ψ be two frames with $dom(\phi) = dom(\psi)$, and $\Theta = \langle \mathcal{F}act_0, \text{Fact}_{\mathcal{C}_0}(\phi, \psi), \mathcal{R} \rangle$ where*

$$\mathcal{R} = \text{Concrete}(\mathsf{R}_{\text{Ana}}) \cup \mathcal{R}_{\text{fail}}^{\text{test}_1} \cup \mathcal{R}_{\text{fail}}^{\text{test}_2} \cup \mathcal{R}_{\text{fail}}^{\text{atom}} \cup \mathcal{R}_{\text{fail}}^{\text{check}} \cup \mathcal{R}_{\text{fail}}^{\text{pub}}.$$

Let $\Pi = \langle \Theta, \{\text{bad}\} \rangle$. We have that $\phi \not\sqsubseteq_s \psi$ if, and only if, Π has a solution of length at most $(N + 1) \times \text{depth}(\phi) + 1$ where N is the number of names n occurring in ϕ at a key position, i.e. such that n (resp. $\text{pub}(n)$) occurs in key position of an encryption in ϕ.

Intuitively, once all needed keys are derived, the minimal plan witnessing non-inclusion contains at most $\text{depth}(\phi)$ rules where $\text{depth}(\phi)$ is the maximal depth of a term occurring ϕ. Then we may need $\text{depth}(\phi)$ rule to derive each deducible key, hence the bound.

4   From Trace Inclusion to Planning

We are now ready for the active case. Given two configurations, we show how to build a planning problem such that the planning problem has a solution if, and only if, the two corresponding configurations are not in trace inclusion.

In several places of this section, we will consider three special constants, namely $c_0^\star$ and $c_1^\star$ of sort atom, and $c_+^\star$ of sort bitstring. These three constants have a special type, denoted $\tau_\star$.

4.1   Abstract Protocol Rules

We first define the abstract rules describing the protocol behaviour. We denote $\mathcal{C}_\mathcal{P}$ (resp. $\mathcal{C}_\mathcal{Q}$) the constants from $\mathcal{C}_0$ occurring in $\mathcal{P}$ (resp. $\mathcal{Q}$), and we consider $\mathcal{C}^\star = (\mathcal{C}_\mathcal{P} \cup \mathcal{C}_\mathcal{Q}) \uplus \{c_0^\star, c_1^\star, c_+^\star\}$. For simplicity we assume that variables of $\mathcal{P}$ and $\mathcal{Q}$ are disjoint. In addition to the facts of the form $\mathsf{att}(u, v)$ used to represent attacker's knowledge, we also consider:

- facts of the form $\mathsf{Phase}(i)$ with $i \in \mathbb{N}$ to represent phases; and
- facts of the form $\mathsf{St}(P, Q) = \mathsf{state}_{P,Q}^c(id_P, id_Q)$ where P, Q are two basic processes on channel c, and id_P (resp. id_Q) is the identity substitution of domain $fv(P)$ (resp. $fv(Q)$).

Therefore, in this section, we consider the infinite set of facts $\mathcal{F}act_0$ that consists of all the ground facts of this form, plus the special symbol bad.

To deal with phases, we mimic the PHASE rule by considering basic processes in normal form w.r.t. the rule $i{:}j{:}P \rightarrow j{:}P$. Then, the transformation $\mathsf{Rule}(P; Q)$ from basic processes (in normal form) to abstract planning rules is defined by $\mathsf{Rule}(P; Q) = \emptyset$ when $P = i{:}0$, and otherwise:

1. Case output: i.e. if $P = i{:}\mathsf{out}(c, u).P'$.
   - $\{\mathsf{St}(P, Q), \mathsf{Phase}(i) \rightarrow \mathsf{att}(u, v), \mathsf{St}(P', Q'); \ \mathsf{St}(P, Q)\} \cup \mathsf{Rule}(i{:}P'; i{:}Q')$
        when if $Q = i{:}\mathsf{out}(c, v).Q'$
   - $\{\mathsf{St}(P, Q), \mathsf{Phase}(i) \rightarrow \mathsf{att}(u, c_0^\star), \mathsf{bad}\}$ otherwise.
2. Case input: i.e. $P = i{:}\mathsf{in}(c, u).P'$.
   - $\{\mathsf{St}(P, Q), \mathsf{att}(u, v), \mathsf{Phase}(i) \rightarrow \mathsf{St}(P', Q'); \ \mathsf{St}(P, Q)\} \cup \mathsf{Rule}(i{:}P'; i{:}Q')$
        when $Q = i{:}\mathsf{in}(c, v).Q'$
   - $\{\mathsf{St}(P, Q), \mathsf{att}(u, x), \mathsf{Phase}(i) \rightarrow \mathsf{bad}\}$ otherwise (with x fresh).

Intuitively, abstract rules simply try to mimic each step of P by a similar step in Q. Clearly, if Q cannot follow P, the two processes are not in trace equivalence, which is modelled here by the bad state. Note that, in case $P = i{:}\mathsf{out}(c, u).P'$ whereas Q is not ready to perform an output, bad will be triggered only if the sent term is indeed a message. This transformation is then extended to protocols in a natural way considering in addition planning rule to model phase changes. We consider $\mathcal{P} = \{P_1, \ldots, P_n\}$ and $\mathcal{Q} = \{Q_1, \ldots, Q_n\}$, and we assume w.l.o.g. that P_i and Q_i are basic processes on channel c_i. We define:

- $\mathsf{Rule}(\mathcal{P}, \mathcal{Q}) = \mathsf{Rule}(P_1, Q_1) \cup \ldots \cup \mathsf{Rule}(P_n, Q_n)$.
- $\mathcal{R}^{\mathsf{phase}} = \{\mathsf{Phase}(i) \rightarrow \mathsf{Phase}(i + 1); \mathsf{Phase}(i) \mid i \in \mathbb{N}\}$.

4.2   Concrete Protocol Rules

To derive concrete rules from the abstract ones, we could instantiate them with arbitrary terms. However, this would not allow us to derive a decision procedure. Moreover, we would like our algorithm to have good performance. To achieve this, we first show that only three constants need to be considered (and no nonces), in addition to those explicitly mentioned in the protocol.

Given a protocol $\mathcal{P}$ that is type-compliant w.r.t. to a typing system $(\mathcal{T}_\mathcal{P}, \delta_\mathcal{P})$ (and such that $\tau_\star$ does not occur in $\delta_\mathcal{P}(\mathcal{P})$), an execution $\mathcal{P} \xrightarrow{\text{tr}} (\mathcal{P}'; \phi'; \sigma'; i')$ is *quasi-well-typed* if $\delta_\mathcal{P}(x\sigma') \preceq \delta_\mathcal{P}(x)$ for every variable $x \in dom(\sigma')$ where $\preceq$ is the smallest relation on types defined as follows:

- $\tau_\star \preceq \tau$ and $\tau \preceq \tau$ for any type τ (initial or not);
- $f(\tau_1, \ldots, \tau_k) \preceq f(\tau_1', \ldots, \tau_k')$ when $\tau_1 \preceq \tau_1', \ldots, \tau_k \preceq \tau_k'$, and $f \in \Sigma_c$.

The attacker needs at most the constants $c_0^\star, c_1^\star, c_+^\star$ to mount an attack.

Theorem 1. *Let $\mathcal{K}_\mathcal{P}$ be an initial configuration type-compliant w.r.t. $(\mathcal{T}_\mathcal{P}, \delta_\mathcal{P})$ and $\mathcal{K}_\mathcal{Q}$ be another initial $\mathcal{C}_0$-configuration. We have that $\mathcal{K}_\mathcal{P} \not\sqsubseteq_t \mathcal{K}_\mathcal{Q}$ if, and only if, there exists a witness $(\text{tr}, \phi) \in \text{trace}(\mathcal{K}_\mathcal{P})$ of this non-inclusion which only involves constants from $\mathcal{C}^\star$, simple recipes, and with a quasi-well-typed underlying execution.*

The existence of a quasi well-typed witness comes from [14] with some extra work to guarantee that we can consider simple recipes. The reduction to three constants extends the previous reduction [16] to asymmetric primitives.

Flattening. In terms of efficiency, one key step of our algorithm is to avoid composition rules from the attacker. For static inclusion, we only consider specific contexts, hence very specific synthesis rules, guided by the form of the underlying frames. For the active case, we transform protocol rules in order to pre-compute all necessary composition steps. This flattening step was already used in *e.g.* [3, 16], and is quite intuitive.

Example 7. Consider our Denning Sacco protocol presented in Example 1. Agent B expects a message of the form $u = \{\text{sign}(\langle a, b, x \rangle_3, sk_a)\}_{\text{pub}(sk_b)}$. Either the attacker obtains a message m of the expected form, or the attacker obtains several components of it and forges the whole message. For example, it is sufficient for him to obtain m_1 of the form $u_1 = \text{sign}(\langle a, b, x \rangle_3, sk_a)$ and m_2 of the form $u_2 = \text{pk}(sk_b)$. Therefore, in addition to the (informal) protocol rule $u \to \ldots$, we also consider the rule $u_1, u_2 \to \ldots$. Similarly, we also need to consider the rules $a, b, x, sk_a, \text{pk}(sk_b) \to \ldots$ and $a, b, x, sk_a, sk_b \to \ldots$.

More generally, given an abstract protocol rule r, we now define $\text{Flat}(r)$ the set of rules obtained by performing flattening on each fact. To decompose a term, we follow its structure, and the structure of a variable is given by its type. Moreover, when the other side of the process is not able to follow the decomposition, this leads us to a failure rule.

Definition 8. *Given a term* $u \in \mathcal{T}_0(\Sigma_c, \mathcal{C}_0 \uplus \mathcal{N} \uplus \mathcal{X})$, *we say that* u *is decomposable when either* $u \in \mathcal{X}$ *and* $\delta_\mathcal{P}(u)$ *is not an initial type; or* $u \notin \mathcal{C}_0 \uplus \mathcal{N} \uplus \mathcal{X}$.

A variable of non initial type is decomposable since it may be instantiated by a non atomic term which, in turns, may have been obtained by composition. Given $\mathsf{att}(u,v)$ with u decomposable, and let $\mathsf{f} \in \Sigma_c$ be such that $\delta_\mathcal{P}(u) = \mathsf{f}(\tau_1, \ldots, \tau_k)$, $\mathsf{split}(\mathsf{att}(u,v)) = (\mathsf{f}; \{\mathsf{att}(x_1, y_1), \ldots, \mathsf{att}(x_k, y_k)\}; \sigma_\mathcal{P}; \sigma_\mathcal{Q})$ where

- $x_1, \ldots, x_k$ are fresh variables of type $\tau_1, \ldots, \tau_k$, $\sigma_\mathcal{P} = mgu(u, \mathsf{f}(x_1, \ldots, x_k))$;
- $y_1, \ldots, y_k$ are fresh variables, $\sigma_\mathcal{Q} = mgu(v, \mathsf{f}(y_1, \ldots, y_k))$.

Note that $\sigma_\mathcal{P}$ exists and is necessarily a quasi-well-typed substitution. By convention, we assume that $mgu(u, u') = \bot$ when u and u' are not unifiable.

Let r be an abstract rule of the form $\mathsf{Pre} \to \mathsf{Add}; \mathsf{Del}$ with $f = \mathsf{att}(u,v) \in \mathsf{Pre}$ such that u is decomposable and $\mathsf{split}(f) = (\mathsf{f}, S, \sigma_\mathcal{P}, \sigma_\mathcal{Q})$. The decomposition of r w.r.t. f, denoted $\mathsf{decom}(r, f)$, is defined as follows:

1. $\big((\mathsf{Pre} \smallsetminus f) \cup S \to \mathsf{bad}\big)\sigma_\mathcal{P}$ in case $\sigma_\mathcal{Q} = \bot$;
2. $\big((\mathsf{Pre} \smallsetminus f) \cup S \to \mathsf{Add}; \mathsf{Del}\big)(\sigma_\mathcal{P} \uplus \sigma_\mathcal{Q})$ otherwise.

Then, decomposition is applied recursively on each rule.

$$\mathsf{Flat}(r) = \{r\} \cup \mathsf{Flat}(\{\mathsf{decom}(r, f) | f = \mathsf{att}(u, v) \in \mathsf{Pre}(r) \text{ with } u \text{ decomposable}\})$$

Concretization. Given an abstract rule r, we denote $vars_{\mathsf{left}}(r)$ the variables occurring on the left (first parameter) of a predicate occurring in r, i.e.

$$vars_{\mathsf{left}}(\mathsf{att}(u, v)) = vars(u); \text{ and } vars_{\mathsf{left}}(\mathsf{state}^c_{P,Q}(\sigma_P, \sigma_Q)) = vars(img(\sigma_P)).$$

Given a substitution σ grounding for r, the application of σ on an abstract state is the concrete state obtained by simply composing the substitutions, i.e.

$$st^c_{P,Q}(\sigma_P, \sigma_Q)\sigma = st^c_{P,Q}(\sigma \circ \sigma_P, \sigma \circ \sigma_Q).$$

Given an abstract protocol rule r, its concretizations $\mathsf{Concrete}(r)$ simply consist in all its positive and negative concretizations. The positive concretizations are all its instantiations that are quasi-well-typed w.r.t. the left side of the rule.

$$\mathsf{Concrete}^+(r) = \{r\sigma \mid \sigma \text{ substitution such that } r\sigma \text{ only involves messages}$$
$$\text{with constants in } \mathcal{C}^\star \text{ and} \delta_\mathcal{P}(x\sigma) \preceq \delta_\mathcal{P}(x) \text{ for any } x \in vars_{\mathsf{left}}(r)\}$$

Similarly to the static case, we need to make sure that we can detect when P and Q are *not* in trace inclusion, and we therefore consider some additional rules. Given an abstract protocol rule $r = \mathsf{Pre} \to \mathsf{Add}; \mathsf{Del}$, $\mathsf{Concrete}^-(r)$ is the set of planning rules that contains: $f_1, \ldots, f_k \to \mathsf{bad}$ for any sequence of facts $f_1, \ldots, f_k$ such that $f_1, \ldots, f_k$ left-unify with Pre with substitution σ_L and $u \in \mathcal{T}_0(\Sigma_c, \mathcal{N} \cup \mathcal{C}^\star)$ for any $\mathsf{att}(u, v) \in \mathsf{Add}\sigma_L$, and such that one of the following conditions holds:

- $f_1, \ldots, f_k$ does not right-unify with Pre;
- $f_1, \ldots, f_k$ right-unify with Pre with substitution σ_R but $v \notin \mathcal{T}_0(\Sigma_c, \mathcal{N} \cup \mathcal{C}^\star)$ for some $\mathsf{att}(u, v) \in \mathsf{Add}\sigma_R$.

Main Result. Our main technical result states that our encoding is sound and complete: two protocols are in trace inclusion if, and only if, the corresponding planning system has a solution. Moreover, when a witness of non-inclusion exists, we are able to bound the length of the resulting plan. Below, $\mathsf{nb_{in}}(\mathcal{P})$ (resp. $\mathsf{nb_{out}}(\mathcal{P})$) denotes the number of inputs (resp. outputs) occurring in $\mathcal{P}$ whereas $\mathsf{max_{phase}}(\mathcal{P})$ is the maximal integer occurring in a phase instruction in $\mathcal{P}$.

Theorem 2. *Let $\mathcal{P}$ a protocol type-compliant w.r.t. $(\mathcal{T}_\mathcal{P}, \delta_\mathcal{P})$, and $\mathcal{Q}$ be another protocol. We consider the following set $\mathcal{R}$ of concrete rules:*

$$\mathsf{Concrete}(\mathsf{R_{Ana}} \cup \mathsf{Flat}(\mathsf{Rule}(\mathcal{P}, \mathcal{Q}))) \cup \mathcal{R}^{\mathsf{phase}} \cup \mathcal{R}^{\mathsf{test}_1}_{\mathsf{fail}} \cup \mathcal{R}^{\mathsf{test}_2}_{\mathsf{fail}} \cup \mathcal{R}^{\mathsf{atom}}_{\mathsf{fail}} \cup \mathcal{R}^{\mathsf{check}}_{\mathsf{fail}} \cup \mathcal{R}^{\mathsf{pub}}_{\mathsf{fail}}$$

Let $\Theta = \langle \mathcal{F}act_0, \mathsf{Fact}_{C^*}(\mathcal{P}, \mathcal{Q}), \mathcal{R} \rangle$ and $\Pi = \langle \Theta, \{\mathsf{bad}\} \rangle$. We have that $\mathcal{P} \not\sqsubseteq_t \mathcal{Q}$ if, and only if, Π has a solution of length

$$1 + \mathsf{nb_{in}}(\mathcal{P}) + \mathsf{nb_{out}}(\mathcal{P}) + \mathsf{max_{phase}}(\mathcal{P}) + \mathsf{depth}(\delta_\mathcal{P}(\mathcal{P})) \times [1 + \mathsf{nb_{in}}(\mathcal{P}) + N]$$

where N is the number of names occurring in $\mathcal{P}$ having a key type, i.e. such that $\delta_\mathcal{P}(n)$ (resp. $\mathsf{pub}(\delta_\mathcal{P}(n))$) occurs in key position of an encryption in $\delta_\mathcal{P}(\mathcal{P})$.

Proof (Sketch). It is rather easy to establish that a solution to the planning problem defines a witness of non trace inclusion. Conversely, thanks to Theorem 1, if $\mathcal{P} \not\sqsubseteq_t \mathcal{Q}$, then there exists a quasi well-typed witness of non trace inclusion, that uses at most three constants (besides the constants of $\mathcal{P}$ and $\mathcal{Q}$). This witness guides the definition of a plan of Π. Establishing a not too coarse bound on its length requires some care. It relies on the flattening of the protocol and the fact that the plan can mimic the computation of several messages in parallel.   □

5   Algorithm

Similarly to the algorithm presented in [16], we decide trace inclusion by applying graph planning and SAT-solving techniques to the planning problem that encodes trace inclusion (thanks to Theorem 2). Given a protocol $\mathcal{P}$, type-compliant w.r.t. $(\mathcal{T}_\mathcal{P}, \delta_\mathcal{P})$, and a protocol $\mathcal{Q}$, our algorithm proceeds as follows.

1. It first computes the corresponding abstract rules, namely $\mathsf{Flat}(\mathsf{Rule}(\mathcal{P}; \mathcal{Q})) \cup \mathsf{R_{Ana}}$ and the initial state $\mathsf{Fact}(\mathcal{P}, \mathcal{Q})$.
2. It then applies a planning graph algorithm, a standard technique to solve planning problems (see e.g. [7]). The only difference is that, for efficiency reasons, we do not construct the planning problem Π *a priori* but instead, we compute it "on the fly", while building the associated planning graph. This planning graph over-approximates the possible solutions by executing several actions in parallel, even if they may be incompatible. Some incompatibilities are recorded and propagated through so-called mutex. The planning graph is deemed to capture all possible plans. More precisely, the planning graph built until depth k captures all possible plans of length at most k.

3. In case no fact bad has been reached while building the planning graph, we can immediately conclude that $\mathcal{P} \sqsubseteq_t \mathcal{Q}$. Otherwise, since the planning graph over-approximates the possible executions, we need to check that bad is truly reachable. This is done by encoding each path leading to bad as a SAT formula. We then call the SAT solver mini-SAT to decide its satisfiability. In case bad is indeed reachable, mini-SAT provides a solution that is translated back to a witness of non-inclusion. To improve termination, we check accessibility of a state containing bad as soon as it appears in the graph, even if the construction of the graph is not completed yet.

Termination. The algorithm defined above may not terminate. The planning graph contains facts of the form $\mathsf{att}(u, v)$ where u must be (quasi) well-typed. There is therefore only a finite number of such u. However, the planning graph construction may introduce several facts of the form $\mathsf{att}(u, v_1), \ldots, \mathsf{att}(u, v_k)$, where the v_i get arbitrarily large. We exhibit some (contrived) examples where the algorithm does not terminate (see Appendix A). [16] suggests that termination could be enforced by checking at each step (thanks to the SAT-solver) that each node of the planning graph is indeed reachable. This would however not be practical. Instead, we can enforce termination thanks to the bound provided in Theorem 2 that also bounds the maximal depth of the planning graph that needs to be considered. Indeed, it is sufficient to simply stop the construction of the planning graph as soon as the bound is reached. The interest of this approach is that we guarantee termination at no cost (computing the bound is immediate). In practice, the planning graph is typically much smaller than this bound.

SAT-Equiv. We have implemented our new algorithm in the tool SAT-Equiv, extending it to protocols with phases and all the standard cryptographic primitives and guaranteeing termination. Moreover, we significantly improve its efficiency by rewriting parts of the codes and modifying the data structure.

6   Experiments

In this section, we analyse several protocols of the literature and compare the results obtained using different tools. We ran our experiments a single Intel 3.1 GHz Xeon. We limit the memory to 128 Go (MO stands for memory out) and the execution time to 24 h (TO stands for time out).

For all the considered protocols, we analyse strong secrecy of the exchanged key or nonce, as for Example 5, except for the passport protocol (PA), for which we prove anonymity as in [2]. We progressively increase the number of sessions in order to consider *a semi complete scenario*, where Alice's role is instantiated by honest a talking to honest b or dishonest c and Bob's role is instantiated by b talking to a or c. This typically corresponds to 7 sessions in the case of a symmetric key protocol (with 3 roles).

	Spec	Akiss	Deepsec	CSF'17	Sat-Eq	
Denning-Sacco	7	10	35	98	> 210	(4h)
Needham-Schroeder sym	6	6	21	21	94*	(20h30)
Wide Mouth Frog	7	12	28	84	> 210	(6min)
Yahalom-Paulson	6	6	12	7	> 28	(7h)
Passive Authentication	6	8	46	–	> 400	(98s)
Active Authentication	6	8	50	–	> 400	(78s)
Needham-Schroeder-Lowe	4	6	16	–	> 64	(11min)
Denning-Sacco signature	8	8	18	–	> 64	(100s)

Fig. 2. Comparison of SAT-Equiv with the other tools. We indicate the number of sessions for which the tool fails (time out, memory out, or other issues). When we did not reach the limit of the tool, we write $>k$ to indicate that the tool can analyse more than k sessions, and we indicate the analysis time for k. *See Sect. 6.2

6.1 Comparison with the Other Tools

Our experiments show a significant speed-up w.r.t. the original version of SAT-Equiv [16]. Our new is 100 faster in average, allowing to analyse about twice more sessions, as exemplified in Fig. 2. We compare SAT-Equiv with other tools of the literature that decide equivalence for a bounded number of sessions, namely Spec [25], Akiss [8] and Deepsec [11]. We did not include APTE in our study [9] as it is now subsumed by Deepsec. For each protocol, we progressively increased the number of sessions until we reached a time out. The overall results of our experiments are summarized in Fig. 2. They show a significant speed-up even w.r.t. the very recent Deepsec tool. Note however that Deepsec covers more protocols (with else branches, or not type compliant), except if they include phases. Deepsec can also be parallelized thus the analysis time can be divided by the number of available cores. The detailed results for the Denning-Sacco protocol are below.

Denning-Sacco	Spec	Akiss	Deepsec	CSF'17	SAT-Equiv	
3	12 s	0.08 s	<0.01 s	0.3 s	0.07 s	42
6	5 h	9 s	<0.01 s	1 s	0.1 s	64
7	MO	75 s	<0.01 s	2 s	0.2 s	74
10		MO	0.01 s	4 s	0.3 s	114
21			18 s	60 s	1.3 s	216
35			TO	9 min	6 s	344
84				13 h	164 s	792
98				TO	6 min	920
210					4 h 20	1942

The 2nd column for SAT-Equiv indicates the theoretical bound on the length of the planning graph, as given by Theorem 2. This illustrates that this bound remains reasonable although our tool actually terminates before reaching it.

6.2 Towards an Unbounded Number of Sessions

Although equivalence is undecidable in general for an unbounded number of sessions, [13] exhibits a decidability result, for type-compliant protocols that have an *acyclic* dependency graph. Intuitively, the dependency graph captures how a message expected as input may be built (and therefore may depend) from messages sent as output of the protocol. Decidability is proven by showing that a (minimal) attack trace may be mapped to this dependency graph. Looking at the dependency graphs of the Denning-Sacco and the Needham-Schroeder symmetric key protocols, we deduce that it is sufficient to analyse respectively 42 and 94 sessions. Thanks to the efficiency of SAT-Equiv, we can easily analyse 42 sessions of Denning-Sacco (in 10 s). We can therefore deduce from [13] that the protocol remains secure even if the considered sessions are arbitrarily replicated. The case of the Needham-Schroeder protocol requires a bit more work as 94 sessions is slightly out of reach of SAT-Equiv. However, we noticed that, according to [13], we do not need to analyse 94 full sessions. Instead, some of them may be truncated (a minimal attack will use only the first step for example). Since SAT-Equiv can prove equivalence of these refined 94 sessions (in 20h30min), we can again deduce from [13] that the protocol remains secure even if the considered sessions are arbitrarily replicated.

As future work, we plan to optimize the bound on sessions induced by [13] and automatically generate the desired scenario, in order to extend SAT-Equiv to proofs of equivalence for an unbounded number of sessions.

A   Examples of Non Termination

We exhibit two examples on which the original SAT-Equiv algorithm does not terminate. Given a channel c, consider $P(c)$ and $Q(c)$ defined as follows.

$$P(c) := \mathsf{in}(c, \langle x, \mathsf{a} \rangle).\mathsf{out}(c, \langle x, \mathsf{a} \rangle)$$
$$Q(c) := \mathsf{in}(c, \langle x, \mathsf{a} \rangle).\mathsf{out}(c, \langle \langle x, x \rangle, \mathsf{a} \rangle)$$

where a is a public constant and x a variable. We consider $\mathcal{K}_P = \{P(c_1); P(c_2)\}$ and $\mathcal{K}_Q = \{Q(c_1); Q(c_2)\}$ for some public channel names c_1, c_2. Starting with $\mathsf{att}(\mathsf{b}, \mathsf{b})$ (with b a public constant in the initial knowledge of the attacker), the following facts will be successively added when computing the planning graph:

$\mathsf{att}(\langle \mathsf{b}, \mathsf{a} \rangle, \langle \mathsf{b}, \mathsf{a} \rangle), \ \mathsf{att}(\langle \mathsf{b}, \mathsf{a} \rangle, \langle \langle \mathsf{b}, \mathsf{b} \rangle, \mathsf{a} \rangle), \ \mathsf{att}(\langle \mathsf{b}, \mathsf{a} \rangle, \langle \langle \langle \mathsf{b}, \mathsf{b} \rangle, \langle \mathsf{b}, \mathsf{b} \rangle \rangle, \mathsf{a} \rangle), \ldots$

Actually, $\mathsf{att}(\langle \mathsf{b}, \mathsf{a} \rangle, \langle \langle \mathsf{b}, \mathsf{b} \rangle, \mathsf{a} \rangle)$ can be added in two different ways: either considering the output on c_1, or the one on c_2. Therefore this fact will not be put in mutex with the other ones. In particular, the fact $\mathsf{att}(\langle \mathsf{b}, \mathsf{a} \rangle, \langle \langle \mathsf{b}, \mathsf{b} \rangle, \mathsf{a} \rangle)$

and the state fact indicating that the process on channel c_1 has not yet started are not in mutex, and can be used to trigger the planning rules leading to $\mathsf{att}(\langle \mathsf{b}, \mathsf{a} \rangle, \langle \langle \langle \mathsf{b}, \mathsf{b} \rangle, \langle \mathsf{b}, \mathsf{b} \rangle \rangle, \mathsf{a} \rangle)$. Since the term computed on the Q's side grows at each step, this computation is endless.

Here, $\mathcal{K}_P$ is not trace included in $\mathcal{K}_Q$: an attacker can distinguish between b and $\langle \mathsf{b}, \mathsf{b} \rangle$. So, as soon as a message is outputted, the resulting frames are not in static inclusion. Therefore, termination can be retrieved by enforcing SAT-Equiv to stop the exploration of the planning graph as soon as an attack is found.

We can turn this example into a more complex one on which the original SAT-Equiv will not terminate even if we decide to stop the exploration of the planning graph as soon as an attack is found. Consider the processes $P_0(c)$, $P_1(c)$ and $Q_1(c)$ given below. We assume that k is name representing a symmetric secret key, whereas $\mathsf{a}, \mathsf{b}, \mathsf{c}$ are public constants.

$$P_0(c) = \mathsf{in}(c, x).\mathsf{out}(c, \mathsf{senc}(x, k))$$
$$P_1(c) = \mathsf{in}(c, \langle \mathsf{senc}(\mathsf{a}, k), \mathsf{senc}(\mathsf{b}, k), \mathsf{senc}(\mathsf{c}, k) \rangle_3).P(c)$$
$$Q_1(c) = \mathsf{in}(c, \langle \mathsf{senc}(\mathsf{a}, k), \mathsf{senc}(\mathsf{b}, k), \mathsf{senc}(\mathsf{c}, k) \rangle_3).Q(c)$$

We consider the configurations $\mathcal{K}'_P = \{P_0(c_0); P_0(c_1); P_1(c_2); P_1(c_3)\}$ and $\mathcal{K}'_Q = \{P_0(c_0); P_0(c_1); Q_1(c_2); Q_1(c_3)\}$ where c_0, c_1, c_2, c_3 are public channel names. Processes P_0 on channels c_0 and c_1 are used as oracles. Roughly, we can get two ciphertexts among the three ciphertexts: $\mathsf{senc}(\mathsf{a}, k)$, $\mathsf{senc}(\mathsf{b}, k)$, and $\mathsf{senc}(\mathsf{c}, k)$. It is however not possible to get the three of them. Noticing this, it is then easy to see that $\mathcal{K}_P$ and $\mathcal{K}_Q$ are trace included.

However, as in the previous example, the planning graph is not precise enough to detect that it is not possible to obtain these three ciphertexts. Once the inputs on channel c_2 and c_3 are executed, we reach a situation similar to the one discussed in the previous example. Each time bad will be added into the planning graph, our SAT encoding will tell us that this state is not truly reachable (but only exists in the over-approximation). Thus, we will continue to explore the planning graph for ever since no attack will be found (the protocols are trace-equivalent).

References

1. Abadi, M., Fournet, C.: Mobile values, new names, and secure communication. In: Proceedings of 28th ACM Symposium on Principles of Programming Languages, POPL 2001, pp. 104–115. ACM (2001)
2. Arapinis, M., Chothia, T., Ritter, E., Ryan, M.: Analysing unlinkability and anonymity using the applied pi calculus. In: Proceedings of 23rd Computer Security Foundations Symposium (CSF 2010), pp. 107–121. IEEE Computer Society Press (2010)
3. Armando, A., Compagna, L.: Sat-based model-checking for security protocols analysis. Int. J. Inf. Secur. **7**, 3–32 (2008)
4. Bhargavan, K., Blanchet, B., Kobeissi, N.: Verified models and reference implementations for the TLS 1.3 standard candidate. In: Proceedings of 38th IEEE Symposium on Security and Privacy (S&P 2017). IEEE Computer Society Press (2017)

5. Blanchet, B.: Symbolic and computational mechanized verification of the ARINC823 avionic protocols. In: Proceedings of 30th IEEE Computer Security Foundations Symposium (CSF 2017), pp. 68–82. IEEE Computer Society Press (2017)
6. Blanchet, B., Abadi, M., Fournet, C.: Automated verification of selected equivalences for security protocols. J. Logic Algebr. Program. **75**(1), 3–51 (2008)
7. Blum, A., Furst, M.: Fast planning through planning graph analysis. Artif. Intell. **90**, 281–300 (1997)
8. Chadha, R., Ciobâcă, Ș., Kremer, S.: Automated verification of equivalence properties of cryptographic protocols. In: Seidl, H. (ed.) ESOP 2012. LNCS, vol. 7211, pp. 108–127. Springer, Heidelberg (2012). https://doi.org/10.1007/978-3-642-28869-2_6
9. Cheval, V.: APTE: an algorithm for proving trace equivalence. In: Ábrahám, E., Havelund, K. (eds.) TACAS 2014. LNCS, vol. 8413, pp. 587–592. Springer, Heidelberg (2014). https://doi.org/10.1007/978-3-642-54862-8_50
10. Cheval, V., Cortier, V., Delaune, S.: Deciding equivalence-based properties using constraint solving. Theoret. Comput. Sci. **492**, 1–39 (2013)
11. Cheval, V., Kremer, S., Rakotonirina, I.: DEEPSEC: deciding equivalence properties in security protocols - theory and practice. In: Proceedings of 39th IEEE Symposium on Security and Privacy (S&P 2018), pp. 525–542. IEEE Computer Society Press (2018)
12. Chrétien, R., Cortier, V., Delaune, S.: Typing messages for free in security protocols: the case of equivalence properties. In: Baldan, P., Gorla, D. (eds.) CONCUR 2014. LNCS, vol. 8704, pp. 372–386. Springer, Heidelberg (2014). https://doi.org/10.1007/978-3-662-44584-6_26
13. Chrétien, R., Cortier, V., Delaune, S.: Decidability of trace equivalence for protocols with nonces. In: Proceedings of the 28th IEEE Computer Security Foundations Symposium (CSF 2015). IEEE Computer Society Press (2015)
14. Chrétien, R., Cortier, V., Dallon, A., Delaune, S.: Typing messages for free in security protocols. Technical report (2018)
15. Compagna, L.: SAT-based model-checking of security protocols. Ph.D. thesis, Università degli Studi di Genova and the University of Edinburgh (joint programme), September 2005
16. Cortier, V., Dallon, A., Delaune, S.: SAT-equiv: an efficient tool for equivalence properties. In: Proceedings of the 30th IEEE Computer Security Foundations Symposium (CSF 2017). IEEE Computer Society Press, August 2017
17. Cortier, V., Dallon, A., Delaune, S.: Efficiently deciding equivalence for standard primitives and phases. Research report, June 2018. https://hal.archives-ouvertes.fr/hal-01819366
18. Cortier, V., Grimm, N., Lallemand, J., Maffei, M.: A type system for privacy properties. In: Proceedings of 24th ACM Conference on Computer and Communications Security (CCS 2017), pp. 409–423. ACM (2017)
19. Cortier, V., Grimm, N., Lallemand, J., Maffei, M.: Equivalence properties by typing in cryptographic branching protocols. In: Bauer, L., Küsters, R. (eds.) POST 2018. LNCS, vol. 10804, pp. 160–187. Springer, Cham (2018). https://doi.org/10.1007/978-3-319-89722-6_7
20. Cremers, C., Horvat, M., Hoyland, J., Scott, S., van der Merwe, T.: A comprehensive symbolic analysis of TLS 1.3. In: Proceedings of 24th ACM Conference on Computer and Communications Security (CCS 2017), pp. 1773–1788. ACM (2017)
21. Delaune, S., Kremer, S., Ryan, M.: Verifying privacy-type properties of electronic voting protocols. J. Comput. Secur. **4**, 435–487 (2008)

22. Escobar, S., Meadows, C., Meseguer, J.: A rewriting-based inference system for the NRL protocol analyzer and its meta-logical properties. Theoret. Comput. Sci. **367**(1–2), 162–202 (2006)
23. Kautz, H., Selman, B.: Planning as satisfiability. In: Proceedings 10th European Conference on Artificial Intelligence (ECAI 1992), pp. 359–363 (1992)
24. Meier, S., Schmidt, B., Cremers, C., Basin, D.: The TAMARIN prover for the symbolic analysis of security protocols. In: Sharygina, N., Veith, H. (eds.) CAV 2013. LNCS, vol. 8044, pp. 696–701. Springer, Heidelberg (2013). https://doi.org/10.1007/978-3-642-39799-8_48
25. Tiu, A., Dawson, J.: Automating open bisimulation checking for the spi calculus. In: Proceedings of 23rd IEEE Computer Security Foundations Symposium (CSF 2010), pp. 307–321. IEEE Computer Society Press (2010)

DigesTor: Comparing Passive Traffic Analysis Attacks on Tor

Katharina Kohls[1($\boxtimes$)] and Christina Pöpper[2]

[1] Ruhr-University Bochum, Bochum, Germany
`katharina.kohls@rub.de`
[2] New York University Abu Dhabi, Abu Dhabi, United Arab Emirates
`christina.poepper@nyu.edu`

Abstract. The Tor anonymity network represents a rewarding target for de-anonymization attacks, in particular by large organizations and governments. Tor is vulnerable to confirmation attacks, in which powerful adversaries compromise user anonymity by correlating transmissions between entry and exit nodes. As the experimental evaluation of such attacks is challenging, a fair comparison of passive traffic analysis techniques is hardly possible. In this work, we provide a first comparative evaluation of confirmation attacks and assess their impact on the real world. For this purpose, we release *DigesTor*, an analysis framework that delivers a foundation for comparability to support future research in this context. The framework runs a virtual private Tor network to generate traffic for representative scenarios, on which arbitrary attacks can be evaluated. Our results show the effects of recent and novel attack techniques and we demonstrate the capabilities of *DigesTor* using the example of mixing as a countermeasure against traffic analysis attacks.

Keywords: Tor · Traffic analysis · Confirmation attack · Mixing

1 Introduction

With more than 2 million daily users [29] and 7000 active relays, Tor [28] is the most prominent example of an anonymity system that took the step from a scientific concept into the real world. Tor protects user privacy on the Internet by separating the origin of a connection from the requested services using onion-encrypted circuits. This mechanism cannot differentiate between benign use cases like censorship circumvention and malicious or illegal activities, but it protects the identities of both groups equally. While legal authorities are motivated in revealing identities to prosecute criminal behavior, censoring authorities can apply the same techniques to identify the origin of unwanted contents or links and thereby maintain control over the dissemination of information.

The existence of successful de-anonymization attacks against Tor is tremendously impactful because of its broad use. As a consequence, many classes of attacks have been introduced that attempt to reveal sensitive information about

© Springer Nature Switzerland AG 2018
J. Lopez et al. (Eds.): ESORICS 2018, LNCS 11098, pp. 512–530, 2018.
https://doi.org/10.1007/978-3-319-99073-6_25

entities in the network [1,8,19]. These academic approaches are an essential building block for improving Tor, by more clearly defining the threat model it must address. At the same time, we may wonder if documented research attacks fully encapsulate the threat model experienced by Tor in practice. Scientific attacks *can* pose a serious threat and affect millions of users, but are driven by a focus on novelty rather than realism. This leads to a fundamental challenge of estimating an attack's real-world impact.

Our focus in this work is on passive traffic analysis attacks. These attacks are a current concern to the Tor community, in which user anonymity is compromised by an adversary correlating transmissions at the entry and exit of the circuit [20, 26]. Recent work [1,2,14,16] has demonstrated that an autonomous system (AS)-level adversary can successfully conduct confirmation attacks, correlating the characteristics of transmitted data to identify connections within the network.

The weakness to correlation is aggravated by routing attacks and nation-state adversaries with capabilities to surveil substantial fractions of the network. Border Gateway Protocol (BGP) attacks like RAPTOR [27] can increase the efficacy of confirmation attacks by directing traffic through an adversarial AS. This allows adversaries to have a near-total view of the network, a threat model not addressed by Tor. Mitigating traffic confirmation attacks, in particular against a *global adversary*, remains an open research problem [30].

Tor threat research is lacking comparable evaluation methodologies. Instead, analyses have been very divergent, ranging from theoretical models on the basis of statistical assumptions [3,4], to approximate simulation systems [11], to experiments on the live Tor network [32,33]. Theoretical models provide upper and lower bounds, but are limited by the assumptions made. Simulated systems can incorporate more real-world characteristics and often analyze network characteristics at a realistic scale, but only approximate certain parameters like the dynamics of an underlying network. The complexity of real-world network conditions makes it impossible to define holistic models that cover all potential cases, a fact that only allows for an estimation of effects on theoretical models and simulations. In contrast, experiments on the live Tor system demonstrate realistic conditions. However, especially in the context of traffic analysis attacks, work on the live network puts users at risk and is ethically discouraged [31].

Beyond the individual strengths of each of these methods, their *diversity* has led to a fundamental drawback: it is difficult to compare different attacks or understand their combined impact. This lack of comparability hinders the ability to understand existing attack vectors and progress defensive research in response.

We introduce *DigesTor* to address this fundamental shortcoming. *DigesTor* is an evaluation framework that guarantees comparability for recent, current, and future passive traffic analysis attacks, combining the strengths of simulated and real-world evaluation. The framework runs a virtual private Tor network to generate traffic for representative scenarios on which arbitrary attacks can be evaluated. The network uses virtual machines with individual CPU cores for each node and transmissions of realistic traffic through the actual network stack.

Intermediate links simulate realistic network conditions using traffic shaping with parameters from empirical measurements in the live Tor network. This experimental setup increases realism over artificial traffic generation in simulated environments [11], can provide realistic link models, and satisfies the ethical guidelines for Tor research.

DigesTor includes a suite of state-of-the-art attack techniques that we evaluate using our framework. As a starting point for future work, this analysis provides a first performance comparison of existing attacks for their deanonymization capabilities. Also, we demonstrate *DigesTor* by evaluating the use of delays as a potential countermeasure. The results of our attacks are summarized on https://digestor.selfip.org to demonstrate the features of our framework.

In short, our major contributions are:

- We release *DigesTor*, a comprehensive evaluation framework for passive traffic analysis attacks on Tor. This framework provides a basis to enable a fair comparison of existing and future attacks, is made publicly available, and includes an extensive corpus of transmission traces.
- We demonstrate the usefulness of *DigesTor* to evaluate the performance of state-of-the-art attack techniques. This leads to a first empirical overview of attack performance for different exemplary use cases and is a starting point for the development of future techniques.
- We use *DigesTor* to analyze low-latency mixing as a potential countermeasure to passive traffic analysis attacks. Results show that mixing, in fact, can counter confirmation attacks at a limited performance overhead only.

2   Traffic Analysis in Tor

Tor is a circuit-based transmission system that selects paths over network relays to form circuits. Usually, a circuit consists of one entry node, one middle node, and one exit node. Through successive layers of encryption to each relay, Tor separates the source of data from its destination, offering anonymity. We survey the attacks known to exist against Tor as follows and discuss two empirical adversary models.

2.1   Traffic Analysis Attacks

Tor defends against a set of known attack vectors, for instance, by ensuring unlinkable byte patterns through layered onion encryption. However, Tor ensures low-latency transmissions that trade performance for vulnerability against traffic analysis attacks. We introduce different classes of such attacks as follows.

In general, traffic analysis attacks exploit side channel information of encrypted transmissions through the network. This allows an adversary to monitor activities in the underlying network and reveal related connections. We distinguish the attack type, if an attack is (A/P) active (●) or passive (○), adversary model (Adv.) (◐: partial adversary, ●: global adversary), the evaluation setup (●: evaluated in live Tor, ◐: reduced private network model, ○: theoretical model), the consideration of background noise (●: real noise, ◐: empirical noise, ○: statistical noise), and the consideration of different application types (App.) (●: yes, ○: no). Furthermore, we document whether a traffic metadata feature was used and define an attack metric (`Corr`: Correlation, `MI`: Mutual Information, `Enc`: Encoding, `Cell`: Cell Manipulation, `Blend`: Blending, `Stat`: Statistical Analysis) (Table 1).

Table 1. Overview of end-to-end confirmation attack classes. In the Traffic Analysis Framework, we focus on passive attacks and flow comparison attacks.

Attack	Ref.	A/P	Adv.	Setup	Noise	App.	Feature	Metric
Flow comp.	[15, 26]	○	●	◐	◐	○	iat	Corr
	[14, 35]	○	●	◐	◐	○	iat	MI
IXP samples	[21]	○	◐	●	●	●	iat	Stat
Disclosure	[3, 4, 13, 18]	○	●	○	○	○	-	Stat
Watermarking	[1, 7, 8, 32]	●	◐	●	●	●	iat	Corr
Coding	[16, 17, 24, 34]	●	◐	●	●	○	-	Enc
Protocol	[6, 9]	●	◐	●	●	○	-	Cell
n-1	[5, 23, 25]	●	●	○	○	○	-	Blend

Passive Flow Comparison. A passive adversary monitors traffic at strategic points in the network and tries to detect related streams to de-anonymize users. This is accomplished through similarity/distance metrics that reveal relations between traffic measured at the source (client) and destination (server) of a connection. For this comparison, features like the timing between arriving packets [14, 26] are derived from unencrypted packet headers or transmission dynamics.

Further Attack Classes. In the literature we find further classes of passive attacks, e. g., disclosure attacks [4] or IXP (Internet exchange point) sampling [21] use statistical methods to compute the probability of two streams being related. An active adversary extends the scope of passive attacks by interference with the traffic stream, e. g., for injecting watermarks [1] or specific codes [16] that help to distinguish individual streams.

Even though the above attack landscape is motivated by the shared goal of learning sensitive information about anonymity systems and their users, we see a high diversity in their evaluation approaches. One example for this are statistical attacks, where we face evaluation results either from the live network [21] or a fully theoretical setup [4]. *DigesTor* overcomes this diversity by providing a consistent evaluation framework for passive flow comparison attacks. In particular, the use of *DigesTor* enables us to analyze the *technical* limitations of existing attacks. Furthermore, we introduce two empirical adversary models as follows.

2.2 Empirical Adversary

Besides their technical limitations, the success of traffic analysis attacks further depends on the adversarial network coverage, i. e., the probability of monitoring the *correct* Tor relays increases with higher coverage [27]. In a worst-case scenario, a global adversary has access to all traffic in the network. While this is a highly restrictive assumption and not considered in Tor's original attacker model, recent empirical studies reveal the potential threat of colluding and nation-state adversaries that achieve a significant coverage of the network. We derive two empirical attacker models from this:

1. *Partial Passive Attacker:* Approximately 40% of Tor circuits are vulnerable to confirmation attacks by a single malicious AS [22]. This threat represents the view of an "average" adversary—or the impact of compromising an individual AS at the core of the Internet.
2. *Strong Partial Passive Attacker*: When ASes are considered on the state level, an adversarial nation could potentially compel multiple ASes within its governance to collude in correlation. Such an adversary could observe as many as 85% of circuits [27].

However, for our experiments (see Sect. 5), we consider the *global passive* adversary as the upper bound. This encompasses weaker models, where a decreased network coverage limits the success probability of an attack (see Sect. 4.4).

3 *DigesTor* Framework

DigesTor is an open source analysis framework that provides comparability for the evaluation of passive traffic analysis attacks. We provide a high-level overview and introduce its evaluation set in the following.

3.1 System Components

DigesTor provides two core features: a Traffic Analysis Framework and a Virtual Private Tor Network. The *Traffic Analysis Framework* applies a set of attack techniques from related work to traces of our experimental network and outputs a performance assessment regarding the success of existing confirmation attacks. The framework covers five comparison metrics, which estimate the similarity or distance between observations in the network, i. e., pairs of client and server traces.

The *Virtual Private Tor Network* is used to generate network traffic that corresponds to typical use case scenarios. The traces are the monitored traffic streams an adversary would gather in a confirmation attack and are thus used as an input to generic passive end-to-end confirmation attacks. We use a virtualized private network for two main reasons. First, isolating the setup protects users of the live Tor network and ensures we do not violate the existing ethical guidelines for Tor research [31]. Second, the technical characteristics of a virtual setup provide significant advantages compared to a simulated setup. Using virtual machines for all nodes in the network, we utilize the actual protocol stack and transmit realistic application data. To improve the realism of our private network, we use empirical link models to imitate transmission delays monitored in the live Tor network.

3.2 Traffic Analysis Framework

In the following, we detail the traffic analysis component of *DigesTor*. Recent work suggests two types of metrics for flow comparison attacks. Correlation-based [15, 26] attacks compute the similarity in monitored traffic and identify relations between streams using the inter-arrival times, i. e., time periods between packets. Mutual information [14, 35] is a measure of the dependence of two streams and estimates similarity based on the entropy of observed pairs. Again, inter-arrival times are mentioned as a traffic feature for this type of attack.

From the current state of passive end-to-end confirmation attacks, we adopt the Pearson correlation coefficient (P) and Mutual Information (MI). We extend this by the Root-Mean-Square Error (RMSE) as a measure of distance between two observations, and a scalar comparison (SC) of features, in which we compare the sum of a metadata vector. Moreover, we sample an optional preprocessing step with the combination of the principal component analysis and Pearson correlation (PCA-P).

Eventually, we measure the success of an attack through the number of correctly guessed client/server connections, defined as *success rate*, and compare its improvement over random guessing, defined as ΔRG. The success rate describes the relative number of correct guesses in a setup, whereas the ΔRG indicates the strength of an attack. Furthermore, we use the area under the curve (AUC) for CDFs (cumulative distribution function) that summarize the results for combinations of multiple scenario setups. The AUC is a measure of the robustness of a successful attack, i. e., a smaller AUC indicates *higher* success rates.

3.3 Helpers

Besides the core components of *DigesTor*, we utilize a parser for transforming raw traces of network traffic to aggregated metadata vectors. More precisely, we extract a set of five features f_i: (f_1 = cnt) packet counts, (f_2 = iat) inter-arrival-timing, (f_3 = len) packet length, (f_4 = ttl) time to live, and (f_5 = wis) TCP window size. This metadata can be read from the header information of a TCP/IP packet (len, ttl, wis) or derived from packet occurrences (cnt, iat).

Using a window-based aggregation [15, 26], an average of all packets falling into one window is collected, e. g., for a measurement of 10 s and a window length of 0.1 s, we aggregate data in 100 equidistant windows. This results in time vectors of metadata information $(f_{i,1}, f_{i,2}, \cdots, f_{i,n})$ with features f_i over n time windows.

This feature set is parsed for each connection and filtered in the downlink direction (data flow from server to client). The feature set is non-exhaustive but extends the standard features in the literature (packet counts, inter-arrival times) with three more characteristics (packet length, window size, time to live) whose relevance will be part of the experimental analysis in Sect. 5.

4   Experimental Setup

In our experiments, we perform a comparative performance evaluation of attack metrics and demonstrate *DigesTor* by analyzing mixing as a potential counter-measure against traffic analysis attacks. We introduce the experimental setup, define the analyzed use case scenarios, and discuss the influence of Tor's network infrastructure as follows.

4.1   Technical Specification

Our experimental network (cf. Fig. 1) is defined by the different node types, i.e., clients, servers, and Tor relays, and by the topology that connects them.

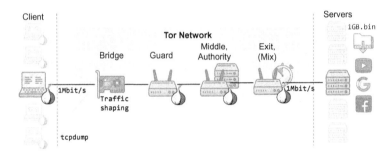

Fig. 1. Clients connect to servers through circuits of three relays. The bridge applies empirical traffic shaping for each client connection individually. Servers provide random binary files for downloads or proxy web requests [10].

Nodes. Entities in the network are configured to serve as (i) clients that make requests through Tor, (ii) servers that provide requested data, and (iii) relay nodes that build the private Tor network. Each client connects to a predefined server and follows a use case scenario which includes either download requests via the *cURL* library or website browsing using the browser automation framework *Selenium* and a headless browser (developed as part of *Mozilla Firefox*). Requests are made through the SOCKS5 proxy at port 9050. They are synchronized via NTP for all clients, i.e., experiments start and end at the same time. The server nodes provide file downloads over HTTP at port 80 and reverse proxy requests to a set of Alexa Top 50 websites at port 80 and 443. We use three relay nodes of which one is configured as guard, one as middle and authority, and one as exit relay. The relay, authority, and client nodes run Tor version 0.2.9.8.

Network. We use an empirical link model for the downlink connection of all clients. The link model adds per-packet delays drawn from measurements of arbitrary circuits in the live Tor network, which are individually assigned for each connection. This traffic shaping is accomplished by a bridge interface, where each client connection samples from an individual delay distribution. For the network topology either a directed setup, using 1:1 connections between n clients and n servers, or a grouped setup, using n:2 connections between n clients and two servers, is used. The number of relays is fixed to three.

Hardware. The VMs run in a cloud space hosted in one central location, each node is assigned a distinct CPU core. The full setup can utilize up to 63 cores, 132 GB of RAM, and 504 GB of disk space. We capture the traffic of all client and server nodes using `tcpdump`. Raw network traces are gathered on one central file server for further processing outside the Tor network environment and therefore do not interfere with the performance of network nodes.

4.2 Scenarios

We test individual *topologies* of 2 to 30 clients to 2 to 30 servers in a *Directed* and of 2 to 30 clients to two servers in a *Grouped* setup. Furthermore, we distinguish three individual *application* models:

- **Static download.** The user requests a file from the server via *cURL* and permanently loads it during the entire duration of the measurement.
- **Random download.** Each user requests a file from the server via *cURL*, whereas on/off periods for the downloads are randomized for the entire duration of the measurement. Off periods are uniformly distributed between 2 s to 10 s, on periods are uniformly distributed between 2 s to 5 s.
- **Browsing.** From the Alexa Top 50 web pages, each client requests a random set of sites using a scripted headless browser. Between site requests, clients wait for a random period with a uniform distribution between 2 s to 5 s before the next request is sent.

We emphasize that the randomization of on/off periods can influence the results, as a higher variance in the duration of off periods helps to distinguish individual transmissions. Consequently, our results can only represent the parameter choices made above. We discuss the definition of more sophisticated use case scenarios in Sect. 6.

4.3 Comparison of Attack Metrics

In the following, we apply the Traffic Analysis Framework (combinations of features `cnt,iat,len,ttl,wis` and metrics `P,MI,RMSE,SC,PCA-P`) to all combinations (directed, grouped; static, random, browsing) and an increasing number of clients $n = 2$ to 30; each experiment is repeated for five random repetitions. We compute the general attack success (AS: how many connections were guessed correctly?), the improvement over random guessing (ΔRG: how much better was the attack compared to an uneducated guess?), and the area under the curve (AUC: how convincing and robust was a result?) of the cumulative distribution function (CDF) of results.

4.4 Tor Network Infrastructure

While our experimental setup covers the *technical* comparison of attack metrics and traffic features, we are further interested how Tor's network infrastructure influences the *organizational* aspects of an attack. Therefore, we discuss the scalability of our setup and the relay selection process as a preliminary step to the performance comparison in Sect. 5.

Scalability. In the setups we demonstrate, clients run at a maximum rate of 1 Mbit/s. For the described *Grouped* and *Directed* scenarios, this translates into a throughput of 30 Mbit/s passing through each of the relays. This scale places these relays within the top 10% of active Tor relays by bandwidth. Experiments with fewer active clients would approximate the traffic of less active relays, with approximately $\frac{2}{3}$ of relays transmitting at least 4 Mbit/s of traffic, the level of traffic we simulate in our smallest experiments. We do not model the number of active connections experienced by Tor relays. While we can expect a total of 500000 active clients at any given point [12], it is less clear how those clients are distributed across relays and bridges. However, the median relay will have less than 50 active clients regardless of the distribution. With up to 30 parallel connections our network setup achieves a similar relay workload.

Relay Popularity. Tor's network infrastructure is skewed towards the countries where we find the most Tor supporters, e.g., Germany (19.4%), the US (18.7%), and France (14.2%) maintain more than half of the entire network. Furthermore, higher bandwidth relays are preferred in the circuit buildup procedure. An attacker can benefit from these characteristics and focus on frequently used nodes, e.g., it is possible to cover 75% of all *selected* exit relays by monitoring approximately 26% of nodes (cf. Fig. 2). This situation supports the empirical adversary models (Sect. 2) and is incorporated by the attack setup of *DigesTor*.

5   Evaluation

We use the above experimental setup of *DigesTor* for a first comparative analysis to (i) derive the best performing metric and feature combinations for each setup, compare the characteristics of different (ii) topologies and application types, and (iii) analyze mixing as one possible countermeasure against traffic confirmation. Finally, we (iv) give an overview of the takeaway messages of our evaluation.

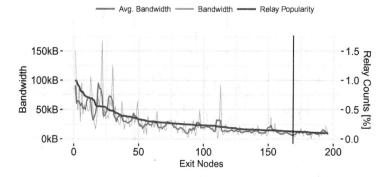

Fig. 2. Distribution of exit relay popularity and respective advertised bandwidth, measured for a total of 100,000 Tor standard circuits.

5.1 Metrics and Features

As initial research question, we address the performance comparison of attack metrics and metadata features. Beginning with the overall *global* performance, we get a first impression of the impact of confirmation attacks in generic scenarios. We continue with an analysis of *individual* combinations of metrics and features for all scenarios.

Global Performance. In our first evaluation step, we identify the overall best-performing metrics and features for a combination of all scenario setups. Figure 3 summarizes the attack success, i. e., the relative number of successful connection identifications, for all traces in the *DigesTor* corpus. Each box represents the full performance range of a metric/feature, whereas we focus on the comparison median (horizontal bar) results. We see that Mutual information (MI) provides the best overall result (median = 0.48) in a global comparison. This result summarizes the attack success for all combinations of MI with the given traffic features and applies for all scenarios introduced in Sect. 4.2. In the comparison of metadata features the time to live field (ttl) performs best (median = 0.44).

Individual Performance. Figure 4 highlights the performance of all individual combinations of metrics and features. Darker tiles in the heat map indicate a higher attack success at a specific experimental setup. Table 2 summarizes these results and provides an overview of the best performing metric and feature combinations for individual setups. We see that (MI,iat) performs best in a global comparison, i. e., it is the most robust combination while performing 23% better than random guessing. Overall, iat is the most reliable metadata feature for most scenarios, whereas we see varying metrics for individual setups.

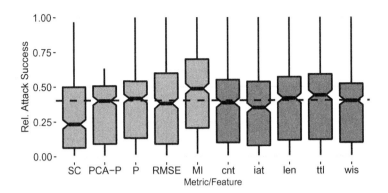

Fig. 3. Comparison of attack success for individual metrics (red) and features (blue) for all topologies and applications combined. Results show the median (horizontal bar in box) aggregated for 2 clients to 30 clients in comparison to the average success of random guessing (dashed line). (Color figure online)

Table 2. Best performing metric and feature combinations. Results show the improvement over random guessing (Δ RG), global performance (AUC), and average success rate (AS) through all experiments.

Scenario	Metric	Feature	Δ RG	AUC	AS
Directed	P	ttl	35%	0.72	0.49
Grouped	MI	iat	22%	0.50	0.55
Random	RMSE	cnt	52%	0.48	0.80
Static	MI	iat	16%	0.65	0.46
Browsing	SC	iat	7.4%	0.70	0.34
Global	MI	iat	23%	0.61	0.52

What Metric and Feature Combination Performs Best? Without any prior knowledge of the use case and number of concurrent transmissions, MI/ttl outperform an average random guessing attack. As soon as it is possible to adjust to a certain scenario, the targeted combination of a metric and feature helps to increase the improvement over random guessing.

5.2   Scenarios

Different topologies have two characteristics that influence the success of an attack. First, grouped setups, where n clients connect to only 2 individual servers, induce more noise through concurrent transmissions for traffic that is captured at the server. Such noise complicates the application of comparison metrics and destroys connection-individual parameters. One example for this is the attack success for a *random* download in the directed (cf. Fig. 4(c)) and grouped (cf. Fig. 4(d)) topology. We see that it is possible to distinguish connections even for high user numbers in the directed setup (ΔRG = 35%), whereas we lose too much information in the grouped experiments (ΔRG = 22%). Second, the number of

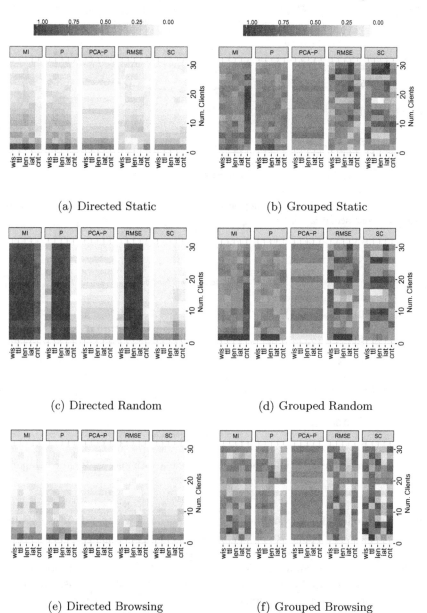

Fig. 4. Average performance of all metrics and features for both topologies and all application types. The heatmap indicates the relative attack success, ranging from 0, no success, lighter to 1, high success, darker.

candidates for guessing a connection is limited to two serves in the grouped setup. Consequently, we experience more stable results for grouped topologies (AUC = 0.5) than in directed setups (AUC = 0.72) with overall more connection candidates (Figs. 5 and 6).

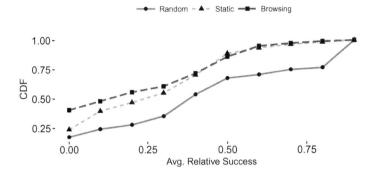

Fig. 5. Cumulative distribution function of average attack success for the comparison of three use case scenarios.

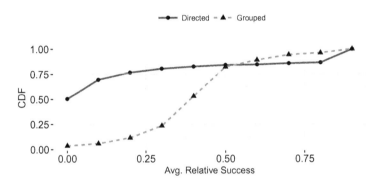

Fig. 6. Cumulative distribution function of average attack success for the comparison of directed and grouped network topologies.

What Scenarios Favor Attacks? Guessing on fewer candidates (grouped topology) makes it easier to achieve positive success rates for an attack. At the same time, it becomes harder to distinguish individual traffic characteristics through simple comparison metrics. Our results show that random downloads, where a high amount of data is sent in individual patterns, provide the best improvement over an uneducated guess. In combination with a setup that reduces noise of concurrent transmissions, this leads to a successful attack even for higher user numbers. The same does not apply to user-individual browsing, where traffic patterns are unique but the amount of data sent is insufficient for distinguishing connections reliably.

5.3   Countermeasures

We can counter traffic analysis by perturbing traffic features during the transmission process. One example for this is mixing [35], where intended delays for packets change the timing relations of a connection. As such countermeasures can decrease a system's performance, we analyze mixing concerning its protection capabilities and performance impairments.

Implementation. We implement a mix within the Tor code and deploy it in the exit relay of our experimental setup. The mix delays TLS records within Tor before they are emitted for further transmission; it uses a defined delay duration (time held back) and rate (relative amount affected). TLS records are, within a Tor relay, closest to the transport layer on which an adversary monitors connections. We, therefore, expect a maximum effect on traffic analysis attacks. In the following, we give an example for different mix delays (time added to sending of TLS records) and mix rates (a portion of records affected by mixing). The mix does not provide any differentiation of TLS records from different connections, e.g., mixing is applied to a fraction of *all* records in the relay.

Results. At a static mix rate of 20% (directed network topology, static download application), we achieve an AUC in the range of 0.9 to 0.95 for delay durations between 10 ms to 1 ms, which represents at least 20% improvement over the unmixed attack success (AUC = 0.72). At the same time, we see that varying mix rates do not influence the attack success significantly (Fig. 7).

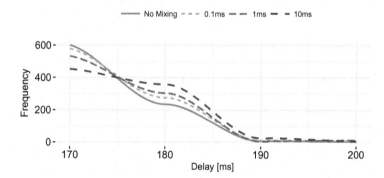

Fig. 7. Distribution of end-to-end delays measured in our experimental setup. Results show slightly increasing round trip time for mixed setups, where we tested a static mixing rate of 20% and increasing mix delays.

Moreover, we analyze the end-to-end delays for increasing mix delays at a fixed rate of 20%. Results show slightly increased delays for mixed connections, while the performance impairments are still in an acceptable range. **Does Mixing Counter Attacks?** Our results support the concept of mixing, whereas the delays can only protect a subset of metadata features. The achieved obfuscation is sufficient for casual scenarios at an acceptable performance overhead, but at this price cannot guarantee *perfect* traffic analysis resistance.

5.4   Overview of Results

We summarize the results of our experimental evaluation as follows.

1. **Metrics and Features Combined.** For all topologies and applications we found a metric and feature combination that outperformed random guessing (Table 2). These combinations do *not* focus on a single traffic feature, hence, an isolated obfuscation of metadata features cannot protect against traffic analysis in general.
2. **Topologies and Applications.** Even though we found topologies and applications that hinder an attack, the attack framework outperformed random guessing attacks by 26.48% on average (individual scenarios) and 23% in generic scenarios.
3. **Affordable Countermeasures.** We use the comparative evaluation of *DigesTor* to demonstrate low-latency mixing as a countermeasure to traffic analysis attacks. Such effects can be achieved at minimal additional delays of 1 ms, which renders this solution an actual option for the live system.

6   Discussion

After demonstrating the experimental benefits of our traffic analysis framework, we now introduce how *DigesTor* can be used to support future research and what limitations the system faces at the moment. Furthermore, we discuss the ethical guidelines for this work and the potential of mixing as a countermeasure.

6.1   Goals of *DigesTor*

The goal of our evaluation framework is to accelerate the deployment of new defenses. To achieve this, we must provide a set of conditions which appropriately represent Tor's infrastructure, but also operate at sufficient scale to approximate the parameters of the real network.

How to Use *DigesTor*? The results of this work provide a first comparative overview of attack metrics and metadata features. Our work supports future research as follows.

- **Trace Corpus.** Our trace corpus represents standard topologies and application types and can be used to evaluate generic passive attacks without harming users of the live network. Furthermore, this once more supports the comparability of results.
- **Attacks.** The traffic analysis framework already provides a representative set of metrics and can be extended further by new attack metrics and metadata features. This allows comparing new approaches with the success of existing work.
- **Defenses.** Following the example of mixing as a countermeasure, future defensive research can use the performance comparison to assess the effects of novel countermeasures.

Limitations. For the use case scenarios, we approximate real user behavior by simple models, e. g., through randomized web requests to a restricted set of sites or random download patterns. This does not represent the user behavior that defines the traffic patterns in a real-world scenario. In end-to-end confirmation attacks, a matching between client and server traces is the primary interest. Adding user models to the experimental setup in a future revision of *DigesTor* helps to create more realistic scenarios, but is not crucial for the technical evaluation of attacks.

6.2 Ethics

In compliance with the Tor Ethical Research Guidelines [31], we designed this work in a way that does not harm users of the live network. We emphasize that especially the experimental evaluation of traffic analysis attacks can cause damage to real-world users and should always be conducted in a controlled environment. In turn, this applies to the analysis of countermeasure implementations whose security yet has to be proven.

6.3 Mix Countermeasure

Our TLS mix concept is implemented at exit nodes and can support a slow rollout over the existing network. Mixing of TLS records means there cannot be mixed and unmixed connections at the same time in one relay, reducing the unmixed bandwidth for the sake of increased security. However, not all nodes in the network must provide mixing, as a small fraction is sufficient to introduce uncertainty for an adversary across many active circuits. Along with the dynamic adaption of mix parameters, this makes the mix concept flexible: instead of using fixed setups, mix parameters can be coupled with monitoring the current network status and load.

7 Conclusion

DigesTor is an appeal to comparability in security research on Tor. The attack landscape of current research offers various classes of offensive work that *might or might not* pose a threat to the live Tor network. With *DigesTor* we share two core features: We generated a first traffic analysis corpus of this kind that we share to support the comparability of future research. The second core feature is the Traffic Analysis Framework, which applies a set of recent attack techniques for comparative performance analysis. To demonstrate the benefits of *DigesTor*, we analyze mixing as a potential countermeasure against passive traffic analysis attacks. Our results indicate that mixing, in fact, hinders the success of otherwise successful confirmation attacks.

Acknowledgments. This work was supported in part by Intel (ICRI-CARS) and the German Research Foundation (DFG) Research Training Group GRK 1817/1. We would like to thank Maximilian Golla for his support with the experimental setup.

References

1. Biryukov, A., Pustogarov, I., Weinmann, R.-P.: Trawling for Tor hidden services: detection, measurement, deanonymization. In: Symposium on Security and Privacy, pp. 80–94. IEEE (2013)
2. Chakravarty, S., Barbera, M.V., Portokalidis, G., Polychronakis, M., Keromytis, A.D.: On the effectiveness of traffic analysis against anonymity networks using flow records. In: Faloutsos, M., Kuzmanovic, A. (eds.) PAM 2014. LNCS, vol. 8362, pp. 247–257. Springer, Cham (2014). https://doi.org/10.1007/978-3-319-04918-2_24
3. Danezis, G.: Statistical disclosure attacks. In: Gritzalis, D., De Capitani di Vimercati, S., Samarati, P., Katsikas, S. (eds.) SEC 2003. ITIFIP, vol. 122, pp. 421–426. Springer, Boston, MA (2003). https://doi.org/10.1007/978-0-387-35691-4_40
4. Danezis, G., Diaz, C., Troncoso, C.: Two-sided statistical disclosure attack. In: Borisov, N., Golle, P. (eds.) PET 2007. LNCS, vol. 4776, pp. 30–44. Springer, Heidelberg (2007). https://doi.org/10.1007/978-3-540-75551-7_3
5. Diaz, C., Preneel, B.: Taxonomy of mixes and dummy traffic. In: Deswarte, Y., Cuppens, F., Jajodia, S., Wang, L. (eds.) SEC 2004. IIFIP, vol. 148, pp. 217–232. Springer, Boston, MA (2004). https://doi.org/10.1007/1-4020-8145-6_18
6. Fu, X., Ling, Z., Luo, J., Yu, W., Jia, W., Zhao, W.: One cell is enough to break Tor's anonymity. In: Proceedings of Black Hat Technical Security Conference, pp. 578–589 (2009)
7. Houmansadr, A., Borisov, N.: SWIRL: a scalable watermark to detect correlated network flows. In: NDSS (2011)
8. Houmansadr, A., Borisov, N.: The need for flow fingerprints to link correlated network flows. In: De Cristofaro, E., Wright, M. (eds.) PETS 2013. LNCS, vol. 7981, pp. 205–224. Springer, Heidelberg (2013). https://doi.org/10.1007/978-3-642-39077-7_11
9. Houmansadr, A., Brubaker, C., Shmatikov, V.: The parrot is dead: observing unobservable network communications. In: Symposium on Security and Privacy, pp. 65–79. IEEE (2013)
10. icons8. Figure Icons. https://icons8.com. Accessed 23 Apr 2018
11. Jansen, R., Hopper, N.: Shadow: running Tor in a box for accurate and efficient experimentation. In: Symposium on Network and Distributed System Security, ser. NDSS 2012. Internet Society, San Diego, February 2012
12. Jansen, R., Johnson, A.: Safely measuring Tor. In: Conference on Computer and Communications Security, pp. 1553–1567. ACM (2016)
13. Kedogan, D., Agrawal, D., Penz, S.: Limits of anonymity in open environments. In: Petitcolas, F.A.P. (ed.) IH 2002. LNCS, vol. 2578, pp. 53–69. Springer, Heidelberg (2003). https://doi.org/10.1007/3-540-36415-3_4
14. Kwon, A., AlSabah, M., Lazar, D., Dacier, M., Devadas, S.: Circuit fingerprinting attacks: passive deanonymization of tor hidden services. In: USENIX Security Symposium (2015)
15. Levine, B.N., Reiter, M.K., Wang, C., Wright, M.: Timing attacks in low-latency mix systems. In: Juels, A. (ed.) FC 2004. LNCS, vol. 3110, pp. 251–265. Springer, Heidelberg (2004). https://doi.org/10.1007/978-3-540-27809-2_25

16. Ling, Z., Fu, X., Jia, W., Yu, W., Xuan, D., Luo, J.: Novel packet size-based covert channel attacks against anonymizer. IEEE Trans. Comput. **62**(12), 2411–2426 (2013)

17. Ling, Z., Luo, J., Yu, W., Fu, X., Xuan, D., Jia, W.: A new cell counter based attack against Tor. In: Conference on Computer and Communications Security, pp. 578–589. ACM (2009)

18. Mathewson, N., Dingledine, R.: Practical traffic analysis: extending and resisting statistical disclosure. In: Martin, D., Serjantov, A. (eds.) PET 2004. LNCS, vol. 3424, pp. 17–34. Springer, Heidelberg (2005). https://doi.org/10.1007/11423409_2

19. Mittal, P., Khurshid, A., Juen, J., Caesar, M., Borisov, N.: Stealthy traffic analysis of low-latency anonymous communication using throughput fingerprinting. In: Conference on Computer and Communications Security, ser. CCS 2011, pp. 215–226. ACM, Chicago, October 2011

20. Murdoch, S.J., Danezis, G.: Low-cost traffic analysis of Tor. In: Symposium on Security and Privacy, ser. SP 2005, pp. 183–195. IEEE, Oakland, May 2005

21. Murdoch, S.J., Zieliński, P.: Sampled traffic analysis by internet-exchange-level adversaries. In: Borisov, N., Golle, P. (eds.) PET 2007. LNCS, vol. 4776, pp. 167–183. Springer, Heidelberg (2007). https://doi.org/10.1007/978-3-540-75551-7_11

22. Nithyanand, R., Starov, O., Zair, A., Gill, P., Schapira, M.: Measuring and mitigating as-level adversaries against Tor. In: Symposium on Network and Distributed System Security, ser. NDSS 2016. Internet Society, San Diego, February 2016

23. O'Connor, L.: On blending attacks for mixes with memory. In: Barni, M., Herrera-Joancomartí, J., Katzenbeisser, S., Pérez-González, F. (eds.) IH 2005. LNCS, vol. 3727, pp. 39–52. Springer, Heidelberg (2005). https://doi.org/10.1007/11558859_4

24. Sengar, H., Ren, Z., Wang, H., Wijesekera, D., Jajodia, S.: Tracking Skype VoIP calls over the internet. in International Conference on Computer Communications, pp. 1–5. IEEE (2010)

25. Serjantov, A., Dingledine, R., Syverson, P.: From a trickle to a flood: active attacks on several mix types. In: Petitcolas, F.A.P. (ed.) IH 2002. LNCS, vol. 2578, pp. 36–52. Springer, Heidelberg (2003). https://doi.org/10.1007/3-540-36415-3_3

26. Shmatikov, V., Wang, M.-H.: Timing analysis in low-latency mix networks: attacks and defenses. In: Gollmann, D., Meier, J., Sabelfeld, A. (eds.) ESORICS 2006. LNCS, vol. 4189, pp. 18–33. Springer, Heidelberg (2006). https://doi.org/10.1007/11863908_2

27. Sun, Y., et al.: RAPTOR: routing attacks on privacy in Tor. In: USENIX Security Symposium, ser. USENIX 2016, pp. 271–286. USENIX, Washington, D.C., August 2015

28. The Tor Project. The Onion Router. https://www.torproject.org. Accessed 23 Apr 2018

29. The Tor Project. Tor Metrics. https://metrics.torproject.org. Accessed 23 Apr 2018

30. The Tor Project. Tor Security Advisory: "Relay Early" Traffic Confirmation Attack, July 2014. https://blog.torproject.org/blog/tor-security-advisory-relay-early-traffic-confirmation-attack. Accessed 23 Apr 2018

31. The Tor Project. Ethical Tor Research: Guidelines, November 2015. https://blog.torproject.org/blog/ethical-tor-research-guidelines. Accessed 23 Apr 2018

32. Wang, X., Chen, S., Jajodia, S.: Network flow watermarking attack on low-latency anonymous communication systems. In: Symposium on Security and Privacy, pp. 116–130. IEEE (2007)

33. Wang, X., Reeves, D.S.: Robust correlation of encrypted attack traffic through stepping stones by manipulation of interpacket delays. In: Conference on Computer and Communications Security. ACM, pp. 20–29 (2003)

34. Yu, W., Fu, X., Graham, S., Xuan, D., Zhao, W.: DSSS-based flow marking technique for invisible traceback. In: Symposium on Security and Privacy. IEEE, pp. 18–32 (2007)

35. Zhu, Y., Fu, X., Graham, B., Bettati, R., Zhao, W.: On flow correlation attacks and countermeasures in mix networks. In: Martin, D., Serjantov, A. (eds.) PET 2004. LNCS, vol. 3424, pp. 207–225. Springer, Heidelberg (2005). https://doi.org/10.1007/11423409_13

CPS and IoT Security

Deriving a Cost-Effective Digital Twin of an ICS to Facilitate Security Evaluation

Ron Bitton[1], Tomer Gluck[1], Orly Stan[1], Masaki Inokuchi[2], Yoshinobu Ohta[2], Yoshiyuki Yamada[2], Tomohiko Yagyu[2], Yuval Elovici[1], and Asaf Shabtai[1(✉)]

[1] Department of Software and Information Systems Engineering,
Ben-Gurion University of the Negev, Beersheba, Israel
shabtaia@bgu.ac.il
[2] Security Research Laboratories, NEC Corporation, Minato, Japan

Abstract. Industrial control systems (ICSs), and particularly supervisory control and data acquisition (SCADA) systems, are used in many critical infrastructures and are inherently insecure, making them desirable targets for attackers. ICS networks differ from typical enterprise networks in their characteristics and goals; therefore, security assessment methods that are common in enterprise networks (e.g., penetration testing) cannot be directly applied in ICSs. Thus, security experts recommend using an isolated environment that mimics the real one for assessing the security of ICSs. While the use of such environments solves the main challenge in ICS security analysis, it poses another one: the trade-off between budget and fidelity. In this paper we suggest a method for creating a digital twin that is network-specific, cost-efficient, highly reliable, and security test-oriented. The proposed method consists of two modules: a problem builder that takes facts about the system under test and converts them into a rules set that reflects the system's topology and digital twin implementation constraints; and a solver that takes these inputs and uses 0–1 non-linear programming to find an optimal solution (i.e., a digital twin specification), which satisfies all of the constraints. We demonstrate the application of our method on a simple use case of a simplified ICS network.

Keywords: Industrial control systems
Supervisory control and data acquisition · Penetration test
Non linear integer programming

1 Introduction

Supervisory control and data acquisition (SCADA) is user to refer to a range of industrial control systems (ICSs) which assist in overseeing complex industrial processes. SCADA systems are used in a long list of industrial applications and processes in facilities including electricity generation plants, chemical plants, manufacturing plants, water and sewage treatment facilities, and industries such

© Springer Nature Switzerland AG 2018
J. Lopez et al. (Eds.): ESORICS 2018, LNCS 11098, pp. 533–554, 2018.
https://doi.org/10.1007/978-3-319-99073-6_26

as the transportation industry. SCADA systems have gained increasing popularity, and industries have become heavily dependent on these systems for collecting data from industrial processes in order to control and monitor their operations to ensure that they are functioning properly. A failure in a SCADA system or one of its elements may result in a failure of the industrial process being controlled. In some cases those systems are life critical, and thus a successful attack on them can jeopardize thousands of people's lives [12,18]. Because of this, the foremost design considerations of such systems have always included a high level of reliability and availability. In general, modern SCADA systems are comprised of a communication infrastructure and the following major elements:

The programmable logical controller (PLC) is one of the main components of the SCADA system. Field devices, e.g., sensors and controllers, send signals and status updates to the PLC and receive operational commands from the PLC, usually without the direct involvement of a human operator. The PLC is also responsible for reflecting the field device state to remote devices (e.g., HMI).

The engineering workstation (EWS) is a computer workstation used to update the PLC software and program the PLC logic.

The human machine interface (HMI) is a computer workstation that makes the industrial process controlled by a SCADA system accessible to a human operator. The operator can monitor processes (e.g., the HMI may display the current water level at an automated reservoir) and send commands to the field devices through an HMI (e.g., stopping the operation of a pump).

Sensors are used in order to reflect the state of an industrial element (e.g., wind speed in a wind tunnel) or the environment (e.g., air temperature). The information from sensors is used by the PLC to control the industrial elements.

Communication infrastructure includes switches, cables, wireless receivers, etc. Contemporary SCADA systems are able to use Ethernet and TCP/IP infrastructure in order to achieve connectivity; legacy SCADA systems rely on older technologies and communication protocols. SCADA components communicate by utilizing standard SCADA protocols, such as DNP3 and IEC 61850, or proprietary vendor-specific protocols, such as S7 and variants of Modbus.

Additional components such as **controllers and actuators**, **databases** which store historical information (i.e., Historian), and **security elements** such as Firewall and one-way traffic devices can also be found in a typical SCADA system.

SCADA systems, especially legacy SCADA systems, are inherently insecure. Initially they were designed and built using specialized and proprietary protocols, implemented by old software and hardware which were rarely patched [11]. Security measures such as anti-viruses and encryption are usually not considered in ICSs. These security measures are not capable of identifying and defending against ICS-specific attacks (e.g., attacks against SCADA protocols such as Modbus) and might harm the availability of the system, which is one of its most important requirements [7,14].

The use of SCADA systems in critical infrastructures makes them desirable targets for attackers. Attacks on such systems have been increasing in recent years. As demonstrated by the Stuxnet worm, and more recently by the TRITON malware, a successful SCADA attack can have serious impact on a nation's economy, safety, and stability. For this reason, continuous security evaluation of ICSs is crucial for mitigating cyber-attacks.

Penetration testing (pen-testing) [1] is a commonly used security measure. The goal of pen-testing is to detect weaknesses in the network such as hosts running vulnerable software, misconfiguration of network components or security countermeasures, usage of default passwords for login services, etc.

The security evaluation of an ICS is quite different from the security evaluation of a typical enterprise network. Typical pen-testing activity focuses on an enterprise's IT environment, especially IT components that can be exploited via the Internet. These kinds of tests usually represent a small part of a typical security evaluation of an ICS [1]. Pen-testing for ICSs mainly focuses on the industrial components (e.g., Historian, HMI, PLC, and sensors) which communicate over dedicated industrial protocols (e.g., Modbus, DNP3). These components and protocols were originally developed for serial communication based on the assumption that ICSs are isolated from the IT environment (and thus not connected to the Internet); therefore, security properties such as authentication and encryption are usually not implemented in these protocols. Currently, industrial protocols are commonly transmitted over TCP/IP; in addition, many ICSs are connected to the Internet, thus making them easy targets for attackers.

The fact that SCADA systems are implemented in critical infrastructures also makes it difficult to evaluate their security. A typical pen-testing activity (for a non-industrial environment) is usually executed within the enterprise network, however this cannot be done in the case of an ICS. Pen-testing activities involve intrusive actions such as port scanning (e.g., using Nmap) and vulnerability assessment (e.g., using OpenVAS or a Zeus scanner), which may crash industrial components and therefore cannot be directly executed in operational industrial environments. Given this, security experts have suggested the construction of a dedicated testbed for evaluating the security of an ICS [5,7,9].

A testbed is an isolated environment which contains a generic implementation of the architecture of the system under test and allows safe execution of penetration tests. The creation of a testbed requires significant investment of funds and effort. Therefore, an efficient testbed should be able to mimic a variety of ICS setups [5]. For this reason, most testbeds are not designed to represent a specific ICS environment, but are more generic so as to be able to address the needs of multiple facilities in the same industry. Keeping the testbed generic can compromise the fidelity (i.e., the requirement that a testbed should represent the system under inspection as accurately as possible) [17].

In this paper, we introduce a new automated method for inferring the specification of a *digital twin* that is designed to facilitate the security evaluation of a specific industrial environment. In contrast to testbeds, which are generic, a digital twin is a replica of a specific ICS; i.e., a model that consists of all of the components from the original industrial environment. Each replicated component can either be implemented as a digital clone (e.g., by using simulation or virtualization software), or alternatively can be physically installed in the twin model. The components that are implemented within the digital twin, as well as the level of implementation of each component, defines the specific security tests that can be conducted on the digital twin (e.g., a digital twin without the HMI implemented does not support the execution of security tests on the HMI). The primary benefit of using a digital twin, as opposed to a testbed, is that it reliably represents the real industrial environment. In other words, the results of a pen-test conducted on the digital twin genuinely reflect the expected results of conducting the same test in the real environment.

One of the most challenging tasks in the process of creating a digital twin is determining the implementation level (specification) of its components. The implementation level of the components in the digital twin directly affects the overall cost of establishing the digital twin as well as the degree to which it reflects the industrial environment (fidelity). For example, a twin model that is completely identical to the real industrial environment (i.e., a physical clone) has the highest fidelity (as it allows the execution of all possible tests), but implementing such a model is extremely expensive. We present a method for deriving the specification of a cost-effective digital twin that is specifically designed to facilitate the security evaluation of a specific industrial environment. The proposed method models the problem of deriving the digital twin for a specific industrial environment as an optimization problem. The optimization problem attempts to maximize the impact of the digital twin under strict budget constraints (i.e., allowing the execution of the most important penetration tests for improving the security of the industrial environment).

The contributions of this paper are as follows:

– We introduce the concept of creating a cost-effective digital twin that is specifically designed to facilitate the security evaluation of a specific industrial environment.
– We propose a method that is based on a constrained optimization problem, specifically, 0–1 non-linear programming, for deriving the configuration of the digital twin model of a specific industrial environment.
– We demonstrate the application of our proposed method on a simplified thermal power plant architecture.

2   Related Work

In order to conduct penetration testing on ICS networks, the use of a testbed has been proposed. A testbed is an isolated environment that simulates the operation of some real system.

According to a recent survey conducted by Qassim *et al.* [15] testbed implementation approaches can be categorized as follows:

Physical implementation: refers to a physical clone of the components. This approach reflects the industrial environment at the highest degree. However, physical implementation of all of the components of a specific factory is in most cases, not feasible because of the high costs of such implementation. As a result, the majority of physical testbeds are more generic, aimed at being able to address the needs of multiple facilities in the same industry, rather than specific facilities.

Virtualization/emulation software: eliminates the software's dependency on the hardware. Virtualization/emulation software enables the establishment of large-scale testbeds, while requiring less hardware, thereby reducing the implementation costs. This approach enables the testing of software components and protocols, but it does not enable the testing of hardware components. In addition, by eliminating software and hardware dependencies, some of the penetration tests may not provide the expected results as tests performed in the real environment.

Software simulation: designed to simulate the inputs, outputs, and behavior of real components (e.g., temperature sensor). This approach can provide large-scale implementation at a low cost, however, it provides very low fidelity. Therefore, the main usage of simulation software is to enable the testing of other components (e.g., to feed a virtual or physical component with simulated inputs/outputs).

To avoid the high costs (as described above), as well as the maintenance involved in a physical replication testbed, many researchers chose to implement their testbed using the simulation, virtualization, or hybrid approaches.

Genge et al. [4] and Lemay et al. [8] presented testbeds for assessing the security of ICS networks. Both works suggested the combination of emulated and simulated components in order to reduce implementation costs. Lemay et al. [8] provided the following methodology for component implementation: the components that are relevant to the test objectives should be emulated; components that directly interface with the emulated components should be implemented as closely as possible to real life; the remaining components can be implemented at any level, and can even be simulated.

Unlike Genge et al. [4] and Lemay et al. [8], Gao et al. [3] and Green et al. [5] suggested the integration of physical devices in their testbeds.

Alves et al. [2] also addressed the discrepancies between different implementation levels. They established physical and virtual gas pipeline testbeds and showed that the testbeds behave differently under a denial of service attack, and behave similarly under a man-in-the-middle attack.

A digital twin is a concept from the product life-cycle management (PLM) domain introduced by Grieves et al. [6]. It is a virtual representation of a specific physical product. The idea behind this concept is that the digital twin should be linked to the physical product throughout the product's life-cycle and constantly mirror it. By doing so, the digital twin enables the prediction of the future behavior and performance of the real product.

Unlike the previously mentioned works that suggested general testbed architectures, we propose an *adaptive* method for deriving the configuration of a cost-effective digital twin for a specific industrial environment. The cost-effective digital twin defines the implementation level of the different industrial components (physical implementation, virtualization/emulation software, and simulation software) to allow the evaluation of the desired security tests.

3   Cost-Effective Digital Twin for ICS

In this section, we present an adaptive method for deriving a digital twin specification for a given ICS, under strict budget constraints. The proposed method maximizes, within the budgetary limitations, the impact of the digital twin. The impact of a digital twin is evaluated by the number and types of security penetration tests that it supports. On one hand, each test has its own *benefit* i.e., security-wise, one test might be more important than another. On the other hand, each test has its own cost. The cost of a test is determined by the costs of the participating components (i.e., the direct cost of implementing them in the digital twin), as well as the test's execution costs (e.g., security expert's time/salary). Note that a component might be required for multiple security tests.

Similar to the creation of testbeds, we consider three types of implementation levels for each element: *physical, virtualization/emulation*, and *software simulation*. The output of the proposed method specifies the digital twin configuration, i.e., which components of the ICS should be implemented and at which implementation level.

Our proposed method models the problem of deriving a cost-effective digital twin as a 0–1 non-linear programming problem. Such problems optimizes a non-linear target function (e.g., the overall benefit of the tests supported by the digital twin), while being subjected to multiple related constraints (e.g., budget limits).

3.1   Notations

In order to formally describe the problem and the method's inputs, we define the following notations.

General ICS Environment Information. The set of possible ICS components is denoted by

$$C = \{c_1, \ldots, c_{n_C}\}.$$

For example, $C = \{PLC, EWS, Historian, PC, \ldots\}$.
We also define the following subsets of C:

- $N \subset C$ - ICS component communicating over IP
- $M \subset N$ - ICS components running modern operating systems (e.g., desktops, Web servers, HMI, EWS, Historian)
- $NC \subset N$ - Network components (e.g., router, switch, and firewall)
- $F \subset C$ - Field devices (e.g., generator and boiler)

- $D \subset N$ - ICS components which are part of the direct control layer (e.g., RTU and PLC)
- $S \subset M$ - ICS components which are part of the supervision layer (e.g., HMI, EWS, and Historian)

General Test Specification. The set of all possible tests is denoted by

$$T = \{t_1 \ldots t_{n_T}\}$$

A list of possible tests for the penetration testing of electric utilities based on the NESCOR methodology [16] is presented in Appendix C.

We denote the execution of test t_i on component c_j by $t_i(c_j)$. For each test $t_i \in T$ we specify three types of prerequisites in order to be able to execute t_i on c_j: device implementation requirements (DIR), environment implementation requirements (EIR), and prerequisite test (PT).

- $DIR(t_i, c_j)$, $t_i \in T \wedge c_j \in C$ - denotes the minimal implementation level of a tested component c_j, which enables the execution of test t_i in the digital twin. For example, disassembling an embedded device (test $t_{4.1.1}$ in Appendix C) cannot be performed on either an emulated or simulated device, thus a physical implementation of the component in the digital twin is essential for executing this test. The formal representation of this requirement is as follows (p stands for *physical*):

$$DIR(t_{4.1.1}, f \in F) = f^p$$

- $EIR(t_i, c_j)$, $t_i \in T \wedge c_j \in C$ - denotes the minimal implementation level of components that communicate with c_j and are required for executing t_i. For example, in order to perform functional analysis (test $t_{4.2.1}$ in Appendix C) on $d \in D$, such as a PLC, one must emulate the components that communicate with the PLC from the direct control group, such as other PLCs (denoted by D_d), and from the supervisory control group, such as HMI (denoted by S_d). In addition, there is a need to simulate field devices that communicate with the PLC (denoted by F_d). The formal representation of these requirements is as follows (e stands for *emulation*, and s stands for *simulation*):

$$EIR(t_{4.1.1}, d \in D) = \{D_d^e, S_d^e, F_d^s\}$$

- $PT(t_i, c_j)$, $t_i \in T \wedge c_j \in C$ - represents the dependencies between tests; for example,

$$PT(t_{4.2.5}, f \in F) = \{t_{4.2.3}, t_{4.2.2}, t_{4.2.1}\}$$

indicates that tests $t_{4.2.3}$, $t_{4.2.2}$, $t_{4.2.1}$ should be executed first in order to execute test $t_{4.2.5}$ on f.

Using these three types of requirements, we define the set of test dependencies (TD) for executing test $t_i \in T$ on a component $c_j \in C$, as follows:

$$TD(t_i, c_j) = <DIR(t_i, c_j), EIR(t_i, c_j), PT(t_i, c_j)>$$

- **Example I: Device disassembly.** In order to enable the disassembling of a field device $f \in F$ ($t_{4.2.1}$), the digital twin model must physically implement f. Thus, the test dependencies for device disassembly of field devices $f \in F$ are as follows:

$$TD(t_{4.2.1}, f \in F) = <f^p, \emptyset, \emptyset>$$

- **Example II: Endpoint fuzzing.** Endpoint fuzzing ($t_{4.2.5}$) is a pen-testing activity that could be executed on an emulated or physical device. However, it is not possible to perform fuzzing without understanding the tested interface and without capturing and analyzing the communication with the interface. For these reasons, capture analysis ($t_{4.2.3}$), communication capture ($t_{4.2.2}$), and interface functional analysis ($t_{4.2.1}$) are prerequisite tests for endpoint fuzzing. In addition, in order to perform this test the digital twin must also emulate the direct control devices which communicate with the tested device. Thus, the test dependencies for fuzzing a field device $f \in F$ are as follows:

$$TD(t_{4.2.5}, f \in F) = <f^e, \{D_f^e\}, \{t_{4.2.3}, t_{4.2.2}, t_{4.2.1}\}>$$

Specific ICS Environment Information. The specific ICS environment (for which we would like to derive the digital twin definition) is denoted as follows:

- $E = \{e_1, \ldots, e_{n_E}\}$ - the set of elements in a specific ICS environment, e.g., e_i is a specific PLC in the ICS.
- $Communication = \{<e_i, e_j> \mid e_i, e_j \in E\}$ - the set of links between elements in the specific ICS environment, as was observed in the ICS's network, e.g., $<e_i, e_j>$ indicates that a communication was observed between element e_i and element e_j.
- $Topology = <E, Communication>$ - the topology of the specific ICS, which consists of the set of elements (E) and their communication links ($Communication$).
- $I = \{p, v, s\}$ - the set of possible implementation levels of an element in E where p stands for physical replica, v for virtualization, and s for simulation.
- $role : E \rightarrow C$ - a function that maps an element in the specific ICS environment to its type, e.g., $role(e_1) = PLC$ indicates that element e_1 is an instance of a PLC in the ICS.

In addition, we define the specific environment dependencies (ED) as follows:

$$ED(t_i, e_j), t_i \in T \wedge e_j \in E$$

Unlike the test dependencies (TD), the environment dependencies (ED) are derived for a specific ICS environment, e.g., the following expression: $ED(t_m, e_n) = \{e_2^v, e_4^s, e_5^s\}$ indicates that in order to execute test t_m on the specific element e_n, the digital twin must contain the following: a virtual (or higher) implementation of element e_2 and at least a simulation of elements e_4, and e_5.

According to the proposed method the main prerequisite for deriving the digital twin is the topology of the specific ICS environment. Typical ICS environments are extremely complex and may change over time; thus, acquiring the environment information is not a trivial task. There are several tools and methods that can be used to collect the required information, including the ICS blueprints which usually contain the architecture design of the specific ICS environment, as well as passive monitoring tools such as the GRASSMARLIN that are able to extract information from the live (or recorded) network traffic (including IP addresses, operating system of components, vendors, and component types).

Costs, Benefits and Budget

- $cost : E \times I \rightarrow \mathbb{R}$ - a function that maps a specific implementation of an element to its cost, e.g., $cost(e, p) = 650$ indicates that a physical implementation of element e in the digital twin costs \$650.
- $benefit : T \times E \rightarrow \mathbb{R}$ - a function that defines the benefit of executing a test on an element, e.g., by setting the $benefit(t, e)$ to b, the asset owner indicates that the benefit of executing test t on element e is b; where, a high b value will increase the probability that this test will be supported by the digital twin model (by setting the $benefit(t, e)$ to ∞, the asset owner can force the algorithm to derive a digital twin which support this test). The benefit of a test is assigned according to the importance of the test (the significance of the expected findings) and the element being tested.
- $Budget \in \mathbb{R}$ - the overall budget assigned to create the digital twin.

3.2 Proposed Method

The proposed method consists of the following three main modules (see Fig. 2 in Appendix E):

The **Data Processor** is responsible for integrating the general test dependencies (i.e., TD) and the topology of a specific industrial environment (i.e., $Topology$), in order to derive the list of environment dependencies (i.e., ED) of the specific industrial environment.

The **Problem Builder** is responsible for translating the information provided for the specific industrial environment (e.g., budget and test dependencies) to a non-linear maximization problem.

The **Solver** solves the non-linear maximization problem in order to derive the specification of the cost-effective digital twin.

The input to the proposed method includes the following:

ICS Architecture: the specification of the architecture of the industrial environment for which the digital twin is created. The specification includes: system topology

($Topology$) i.e., a description of the elements in the system (E) and their communication patterns ($Communication$); the role of each element ($role(e)$);

the cost for each possible implementation of the elements $(cost(e, i))$; and the benefit of executing tests on elements $(benefit(t, e))$.

Budget: ($Budget$) the overall budget allocated for the creation of the digital twin.

Test Specification: includes the set of possible tests $T = \{t_1 \ldots t_{n_T}\}$ and the set of test dependencies $TD(t_i, c_j), t_i \in T \wedge c_j \in C$.

3.3 Data Processor

The Data Processor derives the set of environment dependencies (ED) by analyzing the following inputs: (1) a general specification of test dependencies (TD); (2) the specific topology of the industrial environment under test $(Topology = <E, Communication>)$; and (3) an element in the environment $(e \in E)$. This is done according to the process presented in Algorithm 1.

Given the inputs, the Data Processor initially adds the appropriate device implementation requirement (DIR) to the environment dependencies (lines 10–12). Then, for each environment implementation requirement $r \in EIR$ it adds the elements in the ICS that communicate with e and are of the type specified in r (lines 13–16). Finally, it recursively adds the environment dependencies of the prerequisite tests (lines 19–21). The output of the procedure are the environment dependencies for executing t on e, which are specific for the particular ICS architecture.

3.4 Problem Builder

The Problem Builder represents the digital twin inference problem as a 0–1 non-linear programming problem. The non-linear integer programming problem focuses on the optimization of a non-linear target function, while satisfying a set of non-linear constraints (that are represented as algebraic equations) [10]. The non-linear integer problem is formally defined as follows:

$$\min / \max f(x)$$
$$s.t \; g_i(x) \leq b_i, i = 1, \ldots, m \quad h_i(x) = y_i, j = 1, \ldots, k$$
$$x \in X, X \subset \mathbb{Z}^n \text{ and } X \text{ is a finite set}$$

where $f(x)$ is the target function that we wish to maximize (or minimize), and the constraints are represented by $g_i(x)$ and $h_i(x)$.

A 0–1 non-linear programming problem is a special case of the non-linear integer programming problem, in which x can either be 0 or 1. In this section, we describe how we define the target function ($f(x)$) and the constraints ($g_i(x)$), in order to represent the digital twin specification inference problem as a 0–1 non-linear programming problem.

The specification of a given digital twin model is defined by the variables of the 0–1 non-linear programming problem, which are denoted as follows:

$$X = <x_1^s, x_1^e, x_1^p, \ldots, x_{n_E}^s, x_{n_E}^e, x_{n_E}^p>. \tag{1}$$

Algorithm 1. Data Processor

1: **Inputs:**
2:     $\{TD(t,c)|t \in T \wedge c \in C\}$
3:     $Topology \leftarrow <E, Communication>$
4:     $e \in E$
5: **Precondition:**
6:     $role(e) \in C$
7: **Initialize:**
8:     $ED \leftarrow \emptyset$
9: **function** PROCESSDATA$(TD(t,c), e , Communication)$
10:     $DIR \leftarrow GetDeviceImplementationRequirement(TD(t,c))$
11:     $i \leftarrow GetImplementationLevel(DIR)$
12:     $ED \leftarrow ED \cup e^i$
13:     $EIR \leftarrow GetEnvironmentImplementationRequirement(TD(t,c))$
14:     **for each** $r \in EIR$ **do**
15:         $i \leftarrow GetImplementationLevel(r)$
16:         $C \leftarrow GetIndustrialControlSubGroup(r)$
17:         **for each** $<j,k> \in Communication|j = e \wedge role(k) \in C$ **do**
18:             $ED \leftarrow ED \cup k^i$
19:     $PT \leftarrow GetPrerequisiteTests(TD(t,c))$
20:     **for each** $t^* \in PT$ **do**
21:         $ED \leftarrow ED \cup Process(TD(t^*,c), e, Communication)$
22:     **return** ED

Each variable indicates whether a specific element e is implemented as i within the digital twin as defined by Eq. 2.

$$X = \{x_e^i \mid i \in I, \ e \in E\} \tag{2}$$

These variables can be equal to 0 (zero) or 1 (one), and thus the first set of constraints is:

$$x_e^i \in \{0,1\} \tag{3}$$

where $x_e^i = 1$ indicates that element e is implemented in the digital twin as i, and $x_e^i = 0$ indicates that element e is not implemented in the digital twin as i.

Equation 4 presents the *implementation constraint*, which ensures that an element e is implemented as either *simulated*, *virtualized*, *physical*, or not implemented at all. The number of implementation constraints is equal to the number of elements in the given ICS (i.e., n_E).

$$x_e^p + x_e^v + x_e^s \leq 1 \tag{4}$$

In order to ensure that the overall cost of the digital twin implementation does not exceed the allocated budget, we define the *cost constraint* presented in Eq. 5.

$$\sum_{x_e^i \in X} cost(x_e^i) \leq Budget \tag{5}$$

Each assignment for X defines a possible configuration of the digital twin, where a valid assignment satisfies all of the defined constraints.

Given the above constraints, the target function (defined in Eq. 6) is designed to maximize the impact of the digital twin model.

$$\max \left(\sum_{e \in E, t \in T} benefit(t, e) \cdot \prod_{e_j^i \in ED(t,e)} x_{e_j}^i \right) \tag{6}$$

where the impact of a given digital twin model (defined by the assignment X) is defined as the sum of all of the benefit values for the tests in T that can be executed on X. As can be seen, the benefit value is added only if all of the dependencies of a test are satisfied.

3.5 Solver

A 0–1 non-linear programming problem is NP-hard [13]. In small environments the solution for this problem can be determined by applying a brute force approach, i.e., for each possible assignment for X, first check whether it satisfies all of the constraints; if all of the constraints are satisfied, compute the value of the target function, and finally, select a valid assignment that provides the maximal value.

The time that it will take for the brute force approach to provide the optimal result is significant as it grows exponentially by the number of components. Given n components, and m security tests, and three implementation levels (real, emulated, simulated), the time complexity for the brute force algorithm is as follows:

$$O(3^n \cdot nm \cdot n) \tag{7}$$

where, 3^n represents all of the possible implementation of a components, nm represents the maximum tests per component, and n is the calculation of the cost per implementation state. The exponential time complexity makes the brute force algorithm unsuitable for large ICS environments (more than 20 components). For example, executing the brute force approach on the simple ICS environment presented in Appendix E in Fig. 3, which consisted of 14 components, takes three minutes when using a standard personal computer. In future work, we plan to develop and evaluate different heuristics which are on average sub-exponential (but may not provide the best setup for the digital twin.)

4   Demonstration

In this section, we demonstrate the application of the proposed method on a simplified ICS environment of a thermal power station with one boiler and two generators.

4.1   Description of the Tested ICS Environment

The simplified environment (illustrated in Appendix E, Fig. 3) consists of an enterprise network, a supervision layer, a direct control layer, and field devices.

The enterprise network contains an IT client and an IT server, which are connected to the supervision layer through a firewall that filters improper packets. The supervision layer consist of the following components which monitor and control the direct control components:

- **Historian.** Responsible for logging all events occurring during the process. To do so, the historian periodically queries the PLCs for their states (via Modbus/TCP in the case of PLC-1, or S7comm in the case of PLC-2).
- **Human machine interface (HMI).** Provides a human-friendly interface for interacting with the field devices. In order to report the field devices' states and alarms to the operator, the HMI periodically queries the PLCs, as the Historian does (via Modbus/TCP in the case of PLC-1, or S7comm in the case of PLC-2). Moreover, the HMI enables the operator to remotely change field devices' parameters.
- **Engineering Work Station (EWS).** Enables the operator to change the PLCs' configurations and logic. The EWS has all of the required programming and configuration software installed. It communicates with the PLCs and HMI through the S7comm protocol when such updates occur.

The supervision layer's components are connected to the direct control devices through a switch. The direct control components include:

- **Two Siemens S7-300 PLCs.** These components directly control the field devices. PLC-1 controls both the boiler (BLR) and one of the generators (GEN-1). It can turn the boiler's heater on or off, change the generator's rotation speed, and start or stop its operation. PLC-2 controls only GEN-2 and can perform the two latter actions as well. The PLCs are connected to the supervision layer via the switch (SW-2), and communicate with each other via the S7comm protocol.
- **Remote Terminal Unit (RTU).** This component is connected directly to the PLCs and enables the operator to manually change the field devices' parameters and present their current states and alarms.

The field devices include the components that physically perform the process. This simplified environment contains two generators (GEN-1 and GEN-2) and one boiler (BLR).

4.2   Security Test Specifications

For the demonstration, we followed the pen-testing methodology presented by the National Electric Sector Cybersecurity Organization Resource (NESCOR) [16]. This methodology provides guidelines for executing penetration tests on smart grid systems. Although the NESCOR methodology is specifically designed for smart grid systems such as advanced metering infrastructure (AMI), wide-area monitoring, protection and control (WAMPAC), and home area network (HAN), it provides an extensive list of pen-testing activities that can be applied on other types of ICSs.

The various testing activities presented in their methodology are classified into four categories: *embedded device penetration tasks*, which address the physical attack vector against field devices; *network communication penetration tasks*, which address the exploitation of devices through network protocol manipulation; *server application penetration tasks*, which address testing applications that are running on the control servers; and, *server operating system penetration tasks*, which address testing of the operating system of the control servers.

Execution of the pen-tests presented in the NESCOR methodology on a digital twin in which not all of the components are physically implemented is not trivial, because, as described in Sect. 3.2, the execution of some activities in a digital twin may depend on a specific set of requirements (denoted by DIR, EIR, and PT).

We thoroughly analyzed more than 80 penetration tests presented in the NESCOR methodology and defined the three types of requirements for each test. The complete set of tests and requirements is summarized in Appendix C. For our demonstration we select the following five tests: Device Disassembly (4.1.1), Interface Functional Analysis (4.2.1) Communication Capture (5.2.1), Fuzzing (5.2.4), Application Fingerprinting (7.1.1), and Application Functional Analysis (7.1.2).

4.3   Implementation Cost Description

In the proposed method we considered three types of implementation levels: *physical*, *virtual*, and *simulation*.

Obviously, not all of the components can be implemented by all type of implementations, and some physical devices may not have an emulated/virtual version. In addition, the pricing of different implementation levels is not the same for different vendors. For example, a physical SIEMENS PLC can cost from hundreds of dollars to thousands with an average cost of about $2500 for the S7300 models[1]; a license for S7-Plcsim software, which can be used for emulating a SIEMENS PLC or HMI costs $700[2]; and using third party tools to simulate a PLC can be less expensive (e.g., *awlsim*[3] is free of charge, with costs just for the setup time).

For simplicity, in our demonstration we assumed that a physical implementation of a device would have the highest cost and a simulation-based implementation the lowest. Specifically, as presented in Appendix B, a physical implementation is ten times more expensive than virtualization, which is three times more expensive than simulation. In addition, an equal benefit for all tests i.e., $benefit(t, e) = 1 \ \forall t \in T \wedge e \in E$ was assumed. It should be mentioned that these assumptions do not affect the construction of the problem or its solution by using 0–1 non-linear methods; therefore we believe that these assumptions are plausible.

---

[1] http://www.isgautomation.com/siemens-simatic-s7-300-plc-6es7.html.

[2] https://www.steinerelectric.com/p/siemens-simatic-s7-s7-plcsim-v5-4-floating-lic/429647.

[3] https://github.com/mbuesch/awlsim.

4.4   Results

The creation of the cost-effective digital twin model for the specific ICS environment starts with processing the generic test specification (TD) and the specific topology inputs $(Topology = <E, Communication>)$. This is done by applying the data processing algorithm presented in Algorithm 1 on each combination of element $e \in E$ and test $t \in T$. The output of this algorithm produces 42 different tests (presented in Appendix D), each of which includes a set of environment dependencies (ED). The environment dependencies are specific to the ICS environment described in Sect. A.

Next, given the specific budgetary limitations, we apply the Problem Builder module and create the 0–1 non-linear programming problem (A formal representation of the problem is presented in Appendix A). We implemented a naive brute force algorithm to find the optimal configuration for a given budgetary limitation.

We conducted an experiment in which we derived the configuration of a digital twin model for different budgetary limitation values, while considering all of the tests presented in Appendix D (a total of 42 tests).

The results of this experiment are presented in Fig. 1. As expected, the higher the available budget the higher the impact of the digital twin.

In this figure, it can also be seen that when $Budget = \$3700$, all of the elements are implemented as virtual devices; in this case, the digital twin model supports 36 tests of the 42 possible tests. The remaining tests require physical implementation of various elements; in order to support all of the tests, the budget required is \$23500 (while the total cost of the industrial system is \$40000).

The results show a logarithmic increase of the benefit (impact) with the increase in the available budget.

5   Conclusions and Future Work

We present a method for deriving the specification of a digital twin for an ICS for the purpose of security analysis. The resulting specification is a cost-effective representation of the ICS under test that provides the high fidelity required for executing a given set of security tests. The method is designed as a three step process. First, the Data Processor derives the ICS's environment dependencies from its topology and the tests' dependencies. Then, the Problem Builder uses the ICS's architecture, tests' dependencies, and budgetary limitations to create a 0–1 non-linear programming problem representation. Finally, the Solver applies a search algorithm to find the best solution for the problem, i.e., finds the digital twin specification with the highest impact and an affordable cost (i.e., its implementation cost does not exceed the specified budget). To demonstrate the application of the proposed method, we used a simplified structure of a thermal power station and the NESCOR pen-testing methodology to define the tests and their requirements.

In future work we plan to evaluate the method on more realistic environments from a diverse range of industries and propose a heuristic algorithm for finding a

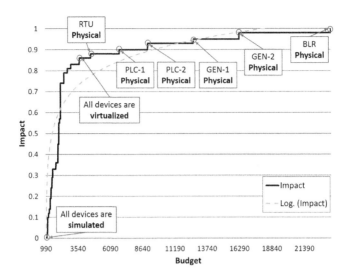

Fig. 1. The trade-off between the budget and the impact of the digital twin computed for the simple thermal power station.

near-optimal solution (digital twin setup) with sub-exponential time complexity. In addition, we plan to extend the solution to support different pricing strategies for the various implementations, such as software bundles with contribution margin-based pricing. We also plan to (1) add new types of constraints, e.g., constraints that take the physical space available within the digital twin that will be implemented (e.g., a small room or an open space) into account; (2) consider implementations of multiple elements as virtual or simulations on the same machine; and (3) handle identical setups in an industrial environment (e.g., if two similar production lines are implemented, there is no need to test both of them). Finally, a general knowledge base of possible tests and their test dependencies should be researched and established.

A   Formal Representation

1. $C = \{PC, Server, Switch, Firewall, EWS, HMI,$
   $Historian, PLC, RTU, Generator, Boiler\}$
2. $N = \{PC, Server, Historian, HMI, EWS, PLC\}$
3. $M = \{PC, Server, Historian, HMI, EWS\}$
4. $NC = \{Switch, Firewall\}$
5. $F = \{Generator, Boiler\}$
6. $D = \{PLC, RTU\}$
7. $S = \{EWS, HMI, Historian\}$
8. $E = \{IT - Client, IT - Server, SW - 1, FW - 1, EWS - PC, HMI - PC, SW - 2, Hist - PC, PLC - 1, PLC - 2, RTU - 1, GEN - 1, GEN - 2, BLR\}$

9. $Communication = \{<IT - Client, IT - Server>,$
$<IT - Server, IT - Client>, <Hist - PC, PLC - 1>,$
$<Hist - PC, PLC - 2>, <HMI - PC, PLC - 1>,$
$<HMI - PC, PLC - 2>, <EWS - PC, HMI - PC>,$
$<EWS - PC, PLC - 1>, <EWS - PC, PLC - 2>,$
$<PLC-1, GEN-1>, <PLC-1, BLR>, <PLC-2, GEN-2>, <RTU-1,$
$PLC - 1>, <RTU - 1, PLC - 2>\}$

10. $T = \{4.1.1, 4.2.1, 5.2.1, 5.2.4, 7.1.1, 7.1.2\}.$

11. $role(e) = \begin{cases} PC, & e = IT - Client \\ Server, & e = IT - Server \\ Switch, & e \in \{SW - 1, SW - 2\} \\ Firewall, & e = FW - 1 \\ EWS, & e = EWS - PC \\ HMI, & e = HMI - PC \\ Historian, & e = Hist - PC \\ PLC, & e \in \{PLC - 1, PLC - 2\} \\ RTU, & e = RTU - 1 \\ Generator, & e \in \{GEN - 1, GEN - 2\} \\ Boiler, & e = BLR \end{cases}$

12. The *cost* function is defined in Appendix B.

B   Implementation Costs of the ICS Components (USD)

	p	v	s
$IT - Client$	1000	100	30
$IT - Server$	4000	100	30
$SW - 1$	3000	300	90
$SW - 2$	3000	300	90
$FW - 1$	4000	400	120
$EWS - PC$	1000	100	30
$HMI - PC$	1000	100	30
$Hist - PC$	1000	100	30
$PLC - 1$	2500	250	75
$PLC - 2$	2500	250	75
$RTU - 1$	1000	100	30
$GEN - 1$	4000	400	120
$GEN - 2$	4000	400	120
BLR	8000	800	120

C   Specification of Penetration Testing Activities Based on NESCOR Methodology

Category	Subcategory	ID	Name	T	DIR	EIR	PT
Embedded Device	Electronic Component	4.1.1	Device Disassembly	$f \in F$	f^p	{}	
		4.1.2	Circuit Analysis	$f \in F$	f^p	{}	4.1.1
		4.1.3	Datasheet Analysis	$f \in F$	f^s	{}	4.1.2
		4.1.4	Dumping Embedded Data	$f \in F$	f^p	{}	4.1.3
		4.1.5	Bus Snooping	$f \in F$	f^p	{}	4.1.3
		4.1.6	String Analysis	$f \in F$	f^p	{}	4.1.4,4.1.5
		4.1.7	Entropy Analysis	$f \in F$	f^p	{}	4.1.4,4.1.5
		4.1.8	Systematic Key Search	$f \in F$	f^p	{}	4.1.4,4.1.5
		4.1.9	Data Decoding	$f \in F$	f^p	{}	4.1.6,4.1.7,4.1.8
		4.1.10	Embedded Hardware Exploitation	$f \in F$	f^p	{}	4.1.9
		4.1.1	Device Disassembly	$d \in D$	d^p	{}	
		4.1.2	Circuit Analysis	$d \in D$	d^p	{}	4.1.1
		4.1.3	Datasheet Analysis	$d \in D$	d^s	{}	4.1.2
		4.1.4	Dumping Embedded Data	$d \in D$	d^p	{}	4.1.3
		4.1.5	Bus Snooping	$d \in D$	d^p	{}	4.1.3
		4.1.6	String Analysis	$d \in D$	d^p	{}	4.1.4,4.1.5
		4.1.7	Entropy Analysis	$d \in D$	d^p	{}	4.1.4,4.1.5
		4.1.8	Systematic Key Search	$d \in D$	d^p	{}	4.1.4,4.1.5
		4.1.9	Data Decoding	$d \in D$	d^p	{}	4.1.6,4.1.7,4.1.8
		4.1.10	Embedded Hardware Exploitation	$d \in D$	d^p	{}	4.1.9
	Technician Interface	4.2.1	Interface Functional Analysis	$f \in F$	f^e	$\{D^e\}$	
		4.2.2	Communication Capture	$f \in F$	f^e	$\{D^e\}$	4.2.1
		4.2.3	Capture Analysis	$f \in F$	f^e	$\{D^e\}$	4.2.2
		4.2.4	Endpoint Impersonation	$f \in F$	f^e	$\{D^e\}$	4.2.3
		4.2.5	Endpoint Fuzzing	$f \in F$	f^e	$\{D^e\}$	4.2.3
		4.2.6	Exploitation	$f \in F$	f^e	$\{D^e\}$	4.2.4,4.2.5
		4.2.1	Interface Functional Analysis	$d \in D$	d^e	$\{D^e, F^s, S^e\}$	
		4.2.2	Communication Capture	$d \in D$	d^e	$\{D^e, F^s, S^e\}$	4.2.1
		4.2.3	Capture Analysis	$d \in D$	d^e	$\{D^e, F^s\}$	4.2.2
		4.2.4	Endpoint Impersonation	$d \in D$	d^e	$\{D^e, F^s, S^e\}$	4.2.3
		4.2.5	Endpoint Fuzzing	$d \in D$	d^e	$\{D^e, F^s, S^e\}$	4.2.3
		4.2.6	Exploitation	$d \in D$	d^e	$\{D^e, F^s, S^e\}$	4.2.4,4.2.5

(*continued*)

(*continued*)

Category	Subcategory	ID	Name	T	DIR	EIR	PT
	Firmware Binary	4.3.1	Disassembly	$f \in F$	f^p	{}	
		4.3.2	Code Analysis	$f \in F$	f^p	{}	4.3.1
		4.3.3	Exploitation	$f \in F$	f^p	{}	4.3.2
		4.3.1	Disassembly	$d \in D$	d^p	{}	
		4.3.2	Code Analysis	$d \in D$	d^p	{}	4.3.1
		4.3.3	Exploitation	$d \in D$	d^p	{}	4.3.2
Network	Protocol Analysis	5.2.1	Communication Capture	$n \in N$	n^e	$\{N^e\}$	
		5.2.2	Cryptographic Analysis	$n \in N$	n^e	$\{N^e\}$	5.2.1
		5.2.3	Unknown Protocol Decoding	$n \in N$	n^e	$\{N^e\}$	5.2.2
		5.2.4	Fuzzing	$n \in N$	n^e	$\{N^e\}$	5.2.1
		5.2.5	Exploitation	$n \in N$	n^e	$\{N^e\}$	5.2.4
Server OS	Information Gathering	6.1.1	DNS Interrogation	$m \in M$	m^e	{}	
		6.1.2	Port Scanning	$m \in M$	m^e	{}	
		6.1.3	Service Fingerprinting	$m \in M$	m^e	{}	6.1.2
		6.1.4	SNMP Enumeration	$m \in M$	m^e	{}	6.1.3
		6.1.5	Packet Sniffing	$m \in M$	m^e	$\{M^e, D^e\}$	6.1.4
		6.1.2	Port Scanning	$n \in NC$	n^e	{}	
		6.1.3	Service Fingerprinting	$n \in NC$	n^e	{}	6.1.2
		6.1.5	Packet Sniffing	$n \in NC$	n^e	{}	6.1.4
	Vulnerability Analysis	6.2.1	Unauthenticated Vulnerability Scanning	$m \in M$	m^e	{}	6.1.4
		6.2.2	Authenticated Vulnerability Scanning	$m \in M$	m^e	{}	6.1.4
		6.2.3	Vulnerability Validation	$m \in M$	m^e	{}	6.2.1,6.2.2
		6.2.4	Packet Capture Analysis	$m \in M$	m^e	$\{M^e, D^e\}$	6.1.5
		6.2.1	Unauthenticated Vulnerability Scanning	$n \in NC$	n^e	{}	6.1.4
		6.2.2	Authenticated Vulnerability Scanning	$n \in NC$	n^e	{}	6.1.4
		6.2.3	Vulnerability Validation	$n \in NC$	n^e	{}	6.2.1,6.2.2
		6.2.4	Packet Capture Analysis	$n \in NC$	n^e	{}	6.1.5
	Exploitation	6.3.1	Identify Attack Avenues	$m \in M$	m^e	$\{M^e, D^e\}$	6.1,6.2
		6.3.2	Vulnerability Exploitation	$m \in M$	m^e	$\{M^e, D^e\}$	6.3.1
		6.3.3	Post Exploitation	$m \in M$	m^e	$\{M^e, D^e\}$	6.3.2
		6.3.1	Identify Attack Avenues	$n \in NC$	n^e	{}	6.1,6.2
		6.3.2	Vulnerability Exploitation	$n \in NC$	n^e	{}	6.3.1
		6.3.3	Post Exploitation	$n \in NC$	n^e	{}	6.3.2
Server Applications	Application Mapping	7.1.1	Application Fingerprinting	$m \in M$	m^e	{}	
		7.1.2	Functional Analysis	$m \in M$	m^e	$\{M^e, D^s\}$	7.1.1
		7.1.3	Process Flow Modeling	$m \in M$	m^e	$\{M^e, D^s\}$	7.1.2
		7.1.4	Request/Resource Mapping	$m \in M$	m^e	$\{M^e, D^s\}$	7.1.3
	Application Discovery	7.2.1	Default Configuration Testing	$m \in M$	m^e	{}	
		7.2.2	Authentication Testing	$m \in M$	m^e	$\{M^e, D^s\}$	
		7.2.3	Session Management Testing	$m \in M$	m^e	$\{M^e, D^s\}$	7.2.2
		7.2.4	Authorization Testing	$m \in M$	m^e	$\{M^e, D^s\}$	7.2.3
		7.2.5	Business Logic Testing	$m \in M$	m^e	$\{M^e, D^s\}$	
		7.2.6	Code Injection Testing	$m \in M$	m^e	$\{M^e, D^s\}$	
		7.2.7	Denial of Service Testing	$m \in M$	m^e	$\{M^e, D^s\}$	
		7.2.8	Client-Side Code Testing	$m \in M$	m^e	$\{M^e, D^s\}$	
	Application Exploitation	7.3.1	Identify Attack Avenues	$m \in M$	m^e	$\{M^e, D^s\}$	7.1,7.2
		7.3.2	Vulnerability Exploitation	$m \in M$	m^e	$\{M^e, D^s\}$	7.3.2
		7.3.3	Post Exploitation	$m \in M$	m^e	$\{M^e, D^s\}$	7.3.3

D   Environment Dependencies

ID	Test	Element	The list of environment dependencies
1	5.2.1	IT-client	$\{IT - client^e, IT - server^e, SW - 1^e\}$
2	5.2.4	IT-client	$\{IT - client^e, IT - server^e, SW - 1^e\}$
3	7.1.1	IT-client	$\{IT - client^e\}$
4	7.1.2	IT-client	$\{IT - client^e, IT - server^e\}$
5	5.2.1	IT-server	$\{IT - server^e, IT - client^e, SW - 1^e\}$
6	5.2.4	IT-server	$\{IT - server^e, IT - client^e, SW - 1^e\}$
7	7.1.1	IT-server	$\{IT - server^e\}$
8	7.1.2	IT-server	$\{IT - server^e, IT - client^e\}$
9	5.2.1	SW-1	$\{SW - 1^e, IT - server^e, IT - client^e, SW - 2^e, FW - 1^e\}$
10	5.2.4	SW-1	$\{SW - 1^e, IT - server^e, IT - client^e, SW - 2^e, FW - 1^e\}$
11	5.2.1	SW-2	$\{SW - 2^e, SW - 1^e, FW - 1^e, HMI - PC^e, EWS - PC^e, PLC - 1^e, PLC - 2^e\}$
12	5.2.4	SW-2	$\{SW - 2^e, SW - 1^e, FW - 1^e, HMI - PC^e, EWS - PC^e, PLC - 1^e, PLC - 2^e\}$
13	5.2.1	EWS-PC	$\{EWS - PC^e, PLC - 1^e, PLC - 2^e, SW - 2^e\}$
14	5.2.4	EWS-PC	$\{EWS - PC^e, PLC - 1^e, PLC - 2^e, SW - 2^e\}$
15	7.1.1	EWS-PC	$\{EWS - PC^e\}$
16	7.1.2	EWS-PC	$\{EWS - PC^e, PLC - 1^s, PLC - 2^s\}$
17	5.2.1	HMI-PC	$\{HMI - PC^e, PLC - 1^e, PLC - 2^e, SW - 2^e\}$
18	5.2.4	HMI-PC	$\{HMI - PC^e, PLC - 1^e, PLC - 2^e, SW - 2^e\}$
19	7.1.1	HMI-PC	$\{HMI - PC^e\}$
20	7.1.2	HMI-PC	$\{HMI - PC^e, PLC - 1^s, PLC - 2^s\}$
21	5.2.1	Hist-PC	$\{Hist - PC^e, PLC - 1^e, PLC - 2^e, SW - 2^e\}$
22	5.2.4	Hist-PC	$\{Hist - PC^e, PLC - 1^e, PLC - 2^e, SW - 2^e\}$
23	7.1.1	Hist-PC	$\{Hist - PC^e\}$
24	7.1.2	Hist-PC	$\{Hist - PC^e, PLC - 1^s, PLC - 2^s\}$
25	4.1.1	PLC-1	$\{PLC - 1^p\}$
26	4.2.1	PLC-1	$\{PLC - 1^e, RTU - 1^e, BLR^s, GEN - 1^s, HMI - PC^e, EWS - PC^e, Hist - PC^e\}$
27	5.2.1	PLC-1	$\{PLC - 1^e, RTU - 1^e, HMI - PC^e, EWS - PC^e, Hist - PC^e, SW - 2^e\}$
28	5.2.4	PLC-1	$\{PLC - 1^e, RTU - 1^e, HMI - PC^e, EWS - PC^e, Hist - PC^e, SW - 2^e\}$
29	4.1.1	PLC-2	$\{PLC - 2^p\}$
30	4.2.1	PLC-2	$\{PLC - 2^e, RTU - 1^e, GEN - 2^s, HMI - PC^e, EWS - PC^e, Hist - PC^e\}$
31	5.2.1	PLC-2	$\{PLC - 2^e, RTU - 1^e, HMI - PC^e, EWS - PC^e, Hist - PC^e, SW - 2^e\}$
32	5.2.4	PLC-2	$\{PLC - 2^e, RTU - 1^e, HMI - PC^e, EWS - PC^e, Hist - PC^e, SW - 2^e\}$
33	4.1.1	RTU-1	$\{RTU - 1^p\}$
34	4.2.1	RTU-1	$\{RTU - 1^e, PLC - 1^e, PLC - 2^e\}$
35	5.2.1	RTU-1	$\{RTU - 1^e, PLC - 1^e, PLC - 2^e\}$
36	5.2.4	RTU-1	$\{RTU - 1^e, PLC - 1^e, PLC - 2^e\}$
37	4.1.1	GEN-1	$\{GEN - 1^p\}$
38	4.2.1	GEN-1	$\{GEN - 1^e, PLC - 1^e\}$
39	4.1.1	GEN-2	$\{GEN - 2^p\}$
40	4.2.1	GEN-2	$\{GEN - 2^e, PLC - 2^e\}$
41	4.1.1	BLR	$\{BLR^p\}$
42	4.2.1	BLR	$\{BLR^e, PLC - 1^e\}$

E   Illustrations

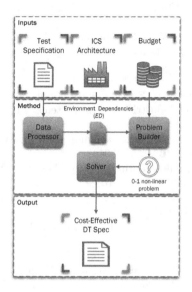

Fig. 2. An illustration of the proposed method.

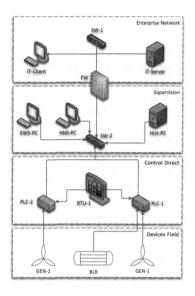

Fig. 3. Simple thermal power station environment.

References

1. Cyber security assessment of industrial control systems - a good practice guide. Technical report, Centre for the Protection of National Infrastructure, April 2011
2. Alves, T., Das, R., Morris, T.: Virtualization of industrial control system testbeds for cybersecurity, pp. 10–14. ACM
3. Gao, H., Peng, Y., Dai, Z., Wang, T., Jia, K.: The design of ICS testbed based on emulation, physical, and simulation (EPS-ICS testbed). In: 2013 Ninth International Conference on Intelligent Information Hiding and Multimedia Signal Processing, pp. 420–423. IEEE (2013)
4. Genge, B., Siaterlis, C., Fovino, I.N., Masera, M.: A cyber-physical experimentation environment for the security analysis of networked industrial control systems. Comput. Electr. Eng. **38**(5), 1146–1161 (2012)
5. Green, B., Lee, A., Antrobus, R., Roedig, U., Hutchison, D., Rashid, A.: Pains, gains and PLCs: ten lessons from building an industrial control systems testbed for security research. In: 10th USENIX Workshop on Cyber Security Experimentation and Test (CSET 2017). USENIX Association, Vancouver (2017)
6. Grieves, M., Vickers, J.: Digital twin: mitigating unpredictable, undesirable emergent behavior in complex systems. In: Kahlen, F.-J., Flumerfelt, S., Alves, A. (eds.) Transdisciplinary Perspectives on Complex Systems, pp. 85–113. Springer, Cham (2017). https://doi.org/10.1007/978-3-319-38756-7_4

7. Holm, H., Karresand, M., Vidström, A., Westring, E.: A Survey of Industrial Control System Testbeds. Springer, Cham (2015)
8. Lemay, A., Fernandez, J., Knight, S.: An isolated virtual cluster for SCADA network security research. In: Proceedings of the 1st International Symposium for ICS & SCADA Cyber Security Research, p. 88 (2013)
9. Leszczyna, R., Egozcue, E., Tarrafeta, L., Villar, V.F., Estremera, R., Alonso, J.: Protecting industrial control systems-recommendations for Europe and member states. Technical report (2011)
10. Li, D., Sun, X.: Nonlinear Integer Programming, vol. 84. Springer, Cham (2006)
11. McLaughlin, S., Konstantinou, C., Wang, X., Davi, L., Sadeghi, A.-R., Maniatakos, M., Karri, R.: The cybersecurity landscape in industrial control systems. Proc. IEEE **104**(5), 1039–1057 (2016)
12. Mitchell, R., Chen, I.-R.: A survey of intrusion detection techniques for cyber-physical systems. ACM Comput. Surv. (CSUR) **46**(4), 55 (2014)
13. Murray, W., Ng, K.-M.: An algorithm for nonlinear optimization problems with binary variables. Comput. Optim. Appl. **47**(2), 257–288 (2010)
14. Nazir, S., Patel, S., Patel, D.: Assessing and augmenting SCADA cyber security: a survey of techniques. Comput. Secur. **70**, 436–454 (2017)
15. Qassim, Q., et al.: A survey of SCADA testbed implementation approaches. Indian J. Sci. Technol. **10**, 26 (2017)
16. Searle, J.: NESCOR guide to penetration testing for electric utilities. Technical report, National Electric Sector Cybersecurity Organization Resource (NESCOR)
17. Siaterlis, C., Genge, B.: Cyber-physical testbeds. Commun. ACM **57**(6), 64–73 (2014)
18. Stouffer, K., Falco, J., Scarfone, K.: Guide to industrial control systems (ICS) security. NIST Spec. Publ. **800**(82), 16 (2011)

Tracking Advanced Persistent Threats in Critical Infrastructures Through Opinion Dynamics

Juan E. Rubio[1]([✉]), Rodrigo Roman[1], Cristina Alcaraz[1], and Yan Zhang[2]

[1] Department of Computer Science, University of Malaga,
Campus de Teatinos s/n, 29071 Malaga, Spain
{rubio,roman,alcaraz}@lcc.uma.es
[2] Department of Informatics, University of Oslo, Oslo, Norway
yanzhang@ieee.org

Abstract. Advanced persistent threats pose a serious issue for modern industrial environments, due to their targeted and complex attack vectors that are difficult to detect. This is especially severe in critical infrastructures that are accelerating the integration of IT technologies. It is then essential to further develop effective monitoring and response systems that ensure the continuity of business to face the arising set of cyber-security threats. In this paper, we study the practical applicability of a novel technique based on opinion dynamics, that permits to trace the attack throughout all its stages along the network by correlating different anomalies measured over time, thereby taking the persistence of threats and the criticality of resources into consideration. The resulting information is of essential importance to monitor the overall health of the control system and correspondingly deploy accurate response procedures.

Keywords: Advanced persistent threat · Detection · Traceability
Opinion dynamics

1 Introduction

Traditional SCADA (Supervisory Control and Data Acquisition) systems that manage the main production cycle of most of the industries have been working in an isolated fashion during years. In turn, the current scenario shows an evolution towards a model in which the organization externalizes some services by interconnecting their resources to Internet networks. The counterpart of this modernization is the appearance of new cyber-security threats and an increase of vulnerabilities in the industrial sector, as some reports show [1].

Many of these attack vectors are leveraged in APTs (Advanced Persistent threats). This is a type of sophisticated attack perpetrated against a particular organization, where the perpetrator has significant experience and resources to penetrate the victim network without being noticed for a prolonged period

© Springer Nature Switzerland AG 2018
J. Lopez et al. (Eds.): ESORICS 2018, LNCS 11098, pp. 555–574, 2018.
https://doi.org/10.1007/978-3-319-99073-6_27

of time [2]. Mechanisms such as firewalls, Intrusion Detection Systems (IDS), antivirus, etc. represent a first solution to the wide range of cyber-security threats faced by an industrial control system in presence of an APT. However, there is still a latent need to find advanced mechanisms that are capable of firstly detecting and then tracing one of this threats from a holistic perspective, during its entire life-cycle.

In this context, graph theory can be leveraged to apply distributed algorithms. Such algorithms can correlate various anomalies measured over the network that are potentially consequence of these attacks, while being able to locate the most affected areas within the topology. More specifically, we take the proposed scheme in [3] as a basis for our extended solution. This previous work proposed the use of opinion dynamics as a multi-agent collaborative algorithm, focusing only on the detection of topological changes over a graph-defined network. In this article, we show the feasibility of using the core of this approach to actually include realistic sources of anomaly and successfully trace the movement of an APT within a defined network architecture, which helps to deploy tailored response techniques. In order to achieve this, we review the literature of the most reported cases of APTs with the aim to realistically represent their stages and the sort of anomalies detected in each step of their kill chain. Finally, the effectiveness of the solution is theoretically demonstrated and shown in a test-case. We can summarize our contributions as:

– Modeling of an APT and its attack actions considering the persistence and criticality of resources.
– Adaptation and implementation of a distributed algorithm to detect realistic anomalies affecting the network nodes.
– Creation of indicators to inform about the threat evolution and the network health status.

The remainder of this paper is organized as follows: Sect. 2 outlines the proposed architecture and introduces the concept of opinion dynamics. In Sect. 3 the literature is reviewed to extract information about the APT modus operandi. Based on this extracted model, an algorithm that can detect and trace the presence of APT is simulated in Sect. 4. Then, the approach is experimentally analyzed using Matlab in Sect. 5. Finally, the conclusions drawn are presented in Sect. 6.

2   Preliminaries

In this section, we lay the theoretical base that permits, on the one hand, the formal representation of actual APT attacks over a defined network, and the execution of the detection technique, on the other.

2.1   Proposed Network Architecture

As discussed in the Introduction, most industrial ecosystems are nowadays adopting cutting-edge technologies onto their production chain and monitoring systems. The counterpart of the modernization of industrial technologies (which we will refer to as 'operational technologies' or OT) and its integration of IT ('information technology') in this context comes with the appearance of new cyber-security threats. Some of them are inherited from the IT paradigm and some other arise from the growing integration between IT and OT. We are talking about attack vectors such as denial of service, presence of malware in the control teams, exploitation of vulnerabilities in communication protocols, phishing and social engineering, etc. that will be further described in Sect. 3.1. For this reason, since there are several reported APTs that attempt to compromise resources belonging to both the IT and OT parts of the industrial network, it makes sense that the whole industrial topology can be split into these different sections: IT and OT, which will be interconnected by firewalls.

The formalization of the proposed network architecture is explained in the following. Let $G(V, E)$ be a graph that represents the entire network topology, that contains devices and communication links that transmit information and control commands between them. This network is composed by the IT and OT sections, which are respectively represented with subgraphs $G(V_{IT}, E_{IT})$ and $G(V_{OT}, E_{OT})$. These sections are joined by a set of firewalls placed in between (V_{FW} henceforth), so that $V = V_{IT} \cup V_{OT} \cup V_{FW}$. In order to understand how these network sections are merged, we firstly must introduce a graph theory concept related structural controllability [4] and power dominance [5]. The aim is to select the set of those nodes within the network that have the maximum dominance, which are called the *driver nodes* (denoted by N_D). As introduced in [5] and extended in [6], let us assume the following two observation rules over a given network $G(V, E)$:

OR1. *A driver node n_d in $\mathbf{D_N}$ observes itself and all its neighbors*: this is, the rest of nodes that share a communication link with n_d. This conforms the DOMINATING SET (DS) of G, and implies that every node not in $\mathbf{D_N}$ is adjacent to at least one member of $\mathbf{D_N}$.

OR2. *If a driver node n_d in $\mathbf{D_N}$ of degree $d \geq 2$ is adjacent to $d - 1$ observed driver nodes, then the remaining un-observed vertex becomes observed as well.* This also implies that **OR1** $\subseteq$ **OR2** given that the subset of nodes that comply with **OR1** becomes part of the set of nodes that complies with **OR2**, conforming the POWER DOMINATING SET (PDS). It means that every edge in E is adjacent to at least one node of $\mathbf{D_N}$.

An example of the election of these driver nodes is depicted in Fig. 1. More specifically, the PDS will be used in the OT section of the industrial topology to represent the set of devices that are connected to the firewalls that also connect to the IT nodes, thereby merging both sections. The reason for such election is that in an operational environment multiple kinds of devices coexist. However, apart from sensors and actuators, PLCs and HMIs, only SCADA systems and high-level servers are actually connected to external networks (i.e., the IT section or Internet). Therefore, these are the nodes that hierarchically have more connectivity (so they will be linked to the firewall nodes), which is equivalent to the controllability concept introduced before. As for the IT section, since most

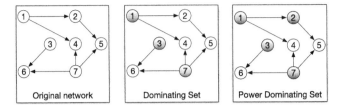

Fig. 1. Observation rules for the election of the most dominating nodes

of the devices range from ERP to customer-end systems (and whose computational capabilities are not as restricted as OT devices), we assume all nodes are connected to the firewalls and thereby can access the operational area.

However, concerning the network topology of the IT and OT section, we must note that each of these subnetworks is built with a different network distribution. On the one hand, $G(V_{OT}, E_{OT})$ follows a specific network construction centered on power-law distributions of type $y \propto x^{-\alpha}$, which is extensively used to model the topological hierarchy of a electric power grid and their monitoring systems [7]. These networks commonly contain substations, which are nodes with high degree (i.e., the number of edges incident on the node) connected to nodes with lower degree, like sensors and actuators. In turn, the IT section (given by $G(V_{IT}, E_{IT})$) is modeled according to a small-world network distribution, that represents the conventional topology of TCP/IP networks [8].

Once we have established the architecture for the network, we are in position to not only simulate attacks over the topology, but also deploying the detection system based on opinion dynamics, which is the main contribution of our work.

2.2 Opinion Dynamics

In this section, we present the fundamentals behind the distributed detection technique from a theoretical point of view. In order to better understand what this solution measures and how it provides a valuable insight for further monitoring and response procedures, we must attend to how an APT behaves. As introduced in the first section, one of these threats comprises several stages over which the attacker manages to compromise certain devices over the victim network until he/she reaches an interest point. It is then when the intruder usually chooses to either disrupt the productive process or exfiltrate information to the attacker headquarters, as described further in Sect. 3.1.

This chain of individual attack actions commonly takes quite a long time to perpetrate the network resources; over this evolution, it would be of paramount interest to extract two main pieces of information:

1. The portion of the network that is subject of attack at any time, being possible to distinguish what set of devices are experiencing the same degree of anomaly, which can be produced by an attack. This is essential for applying effective response techniques and potentially isolate the attack, while the rest

of the areas can keep functioning as in normal conditions, hence ensuring the continuity of the production by this way.
2. The traceability of events occurred to the network, with respect to the evolution of the intrusion throughout the network since the very first moment it broke into it. In this sense, when it comes to APTs, we must also take the persistence of attacks into special consideration at all times, since an advanced threat can go unnoticed during months and suddenly perform a new attack. In terms of the detection technique, this implies that it is also necessary to keep track of old subtle anomalies noticed in the network, to serve as feedback to the technique and correlate their relevance with current detected anomalies, that altogether may be part of a more ambitious threat. As it is technically described in Sect. 4, this weight given to anomalies experienced on the network in the past devalues over time depending on the criticality of the victim devices and the type of anomaly detected.

These objectives are accomplished by the means of a distributed cooperative algorithm called based on Opinion Dynamics [9], since it models the actual opinion formation among the individuals of a society: each of these individuals (denoted as agents in the following) does not simply share or disregard the opinion of the rest of agents, but he/she takes them into account to a certain extent in order to form his own opinion. From this moment on, what the opinion dynamics process does is to take an average over the opinions that can be repeated over and over again. This eventually leads to formed consensus of opinions belonging to different agents closer to each other. Correspondingly, it is equivalent to obtaining a fragmentation of the different opinions within the society, which can be applied to intrusion detection by representing the opinion according to the level of anomaly that each agent (representing a device of the network) experiences.

In the following, we formalize the intrinsics of this multi-agent algorithm, which constitutes a light modification of the approach proposed in [9] and an extension of the work presented in [3]. Let A be the set of agents of the system such that $A = \{a_1, a_2, \ldots, a_n\}$. Here, $x_i(t)$ represents the individual opinion of each a_i at time t (ranging from zero to one), where t refers to the iteration of the algorithm. On the other hand, the weight given to the opinion of any other agent j is denoted by w_{ij}, where $\sum_{k=1}^{n} w_{ik} = 1$ (therefore, agent i also takes its own opinion into account). Finally, the formation of the opinion for agent i in the next iteration $t + 1$ is described as follows:

$$x_i(t + 1) = w_{i1}x_1(t) + w_{i2}x_2(t) + \ldots + w_{in}x_n(t)$$

Consequently, every agent adjusts its opinion in period $t + 1$ by taking a weighted average of the opinions of the rest of agents. When t tends to infinity, consensus of opinions are formed (so finally there are just a few opinions shared by clusters of agents), which can also be represented visually. Conversely, what we want to accomplish in our particular scenario is to use these opinions as a way to represent a detected anomaly by a given agent that is installed within the network, so that similar values (provoked by the same threats) converge the most critically affected areas from a high-level perspective (and the severity of such attacks) can be ultimately located.

One aspect that needs to be clarified is the assignment of weight among agents: for simplicity, for a given agent, we assume that the weight value assign to its neighbors is uniformly divided into those agents whose opinion is very close to its one (we establish a epsilon value of 0.2 of deviation between both values). This models the fact that agents close to each other with the same degree of anomaly are likely to be detecting the same threat in their surroundings.

In order to successfully apply this concept of a multi-agent algorithm to the context of anomaly detection in an industrial setting, there are various questions that need to be further addressed: (i) who can play the role of agents within the industrial network, considering that there should be as many logical agents as nodes within the network ($|V|$ in our case); (ii) how each anomaly can be represented as an opinion held by an agent, and how to retrieve such anomaly values; and (iii) how the attacks affect the persistence and the anomaly detection, depending on their severity and the criticality of the victim nodes, which influences the persistence and the application of the opinion dynamics. These questions will be reviewed and answered in Sect. 3 through the analysis of real-word APTs and existing defense mechanisms and architectures.

3   Attack and Defense Models

3.1   Review of Existing APTs, APT Stages, and Defenses

For the specification of the opinion dynamics algorithm, we need to provide an accurate representation of APT attacks in the context of our network model. Therefore, here we will first review the most important APT threats and groups that have specifically targeted industrial control systems. For the interested reader, a more detailed review of these APTs – including exploited vulnerabilities, software modules, etc. – is available at [10].

Stuxnet (2009). Stuxnet was one of the APTs that popularized this concept and brought it to the limelight. Developed by a state agent, the main goal of this worm was to hinder the enrichment of uranium in the Iranian nuclear facility of Natanz [11]. It is believed that its primary infection vector, which was used to infiltrate the facility, was USB flash drives. Once the malware was installed in the 'patient zero' computer, it also used other mechanisms (network shares, infected project files) to spread through the internal network, searching for the computers that directly controlled the uranium enriching centrifuges. Finally, the malware modified the code that controlled the centrifuges in order to silently destroy them.

DragonFly group (2013–2014, 2015-). Active since 2010, this particular APT actor has always focused on cyberespionage. On 2013, it started several campaigns against energy suppliers [12]. In its first wave of attacks, the main goal was to discover and map the existence of OPC (Open Platform Communications) SCADA servers located in the attacked network. For this purpose, after the initial infection, the malware queried the network in search of OPC servers using specific OPC DCOM (Distributed Component Object Model) calls. On the other hand, its second wave of attacks followed a more conservative approach: it retrieved information mostly by extracting documents and screenshots from the infected computers.

BlackEnergy (2015–2016). The BlackEnergy malware, created by an APT actor known as Sandworm, was used to attack the energy infrastructure of Ukraine in December 2015 [13]. After the initial infection, the first goal of the malware was to replicate to as much computers as possible through Windows Admin Shares (e.g. through PsExec and remote file execution). The second goal of the malware was to set up various connections to external command&control networks. Using these networks, malicious operators were able to activate various components (KillDisk, circuit breaker manipulator) that caused havoc in electricity distribution companies.

ExPetr (2017). ExPetr was a wiper disguised as ransomware, which targeted local administrations and various industrial companies in Russia and Ukraine [14]. It used two primary infection vectors: a modified version of the EternalBlue exploit used by WannaCry, and an trojanized version of the MEDoc tax accounting software. Once 'patient zero' was infected, this malware used both the EternalBlue exploit and the BlackEnergy propagation mechanisms to propagate over the local network. Immediately afterwards, the fake ransomware component of the malware would be activated.

Another element that is essential for the formalization of the behaviour of APTs in our network model is the definition of the different attack stages (i.e. intrusion kill chains) that are performed by APTs. These attack stages – whose order can be changed depending on the specific APT – have been extensively studied and described by various academic and industrial researchers [15–17], and can be summarized in the following steps:

- **Reconnaissance.** Adversaries gather information about the targeted industrial network, and create an attacking plan.
- **Delivery.** After choosing a set of vulnerable computers ('patient zero') at the targeted industrial network, adversaries deliver the malware to those computers, either directly (e.g. through email or vulnerable services) or indirectly (e.g. contaminating websites with malware).
- **Compromise.** At this stage, the malware is executed in the target machine, and takes control of it. This stage involves several steps, such as *privilege escalation*, maintaining *persistence*, and executing *defense evasion techniques*.
- **Command and Control.** Once the malware controls 'patient zero', it opens a communication channel with the remote attacker, which will be used to send commands, extract information, etc.

- **Lateral Movement.** The concept of lateral movement encompasses the different steps that the malware takes in order to control other computers located in the targeted network. Lateral movement includes *internal reconnaissance, compromise* of additional systems, and *collection of sensitive information.*
- **Execution.** The malware finally performs the attack against the targeted industrial network. Attacks range from *exfiltration* (extraction of sensitive data) to *destruction* of resources.

Finally, in order to define our defense model, and to provide an answer to the questions raised in the previous section, it is necessary to provide a brief overview on the actual state of the art of the existing defense mechanisms against the attack stages defined above. This information is extracted from more detailed reviews that are already available in the literature, such as [18]. Here, we will only highlight the most important aspects that will influence over the defense model of our network and the different detection probabilities:

- *Detection coverage.* As of 2018, there are multiple intrusion detection and prevention mechanisms, both commercial and academic, that are able to analyze the state of all elements and communication systems in industrial networks, including the field devices.
- *Central correlator systems.* There are several commercial platforms, such as [19], whose goal is to provide support for event correlation. These platforms can retrieve events and alerts from various domains (e.g. IT, OT networks) and from various sources (e.g. SIEM systems, vulnerability scanners) in a distributed way.
- *Beyond attack signatures.* There exist several solutions that are able to indicate the potential existence of anomalous situations, even if the attack signatures are unknown. Examples include not only diverse statistics (e.g. traffic volume, network connections, protocols used), but also machine learning mechanisms, specification-based systems, and industrial honeypots.
- *Network features.* In comparison to the IT infrastructure, OT networks exhibit a more consistent behaviour. This feature is actually used by certain detection mechanisms to more accurately pinpoint the existence of anomalies.

3.2   Representation of APT Attacks and Detection Probabilities

After reviewing the behaviour of industrial APTs and the state of the intrusion detection mechanisms, we can define a realistic attack and defense model for our network architecture, thereby addressing the questions raised in Sect. 2.2. Our *attack model* is simple: we assume that, given a certain goal (exfiltration and/or destruction), adversaries are able to successfully perform an APT attack against the network architecture defined in Sect. 2.1 using any set of the attack stages defined in Sect. 3.1. As for the *defense model*, and given the actual state of the art in the area, we assume that all the elements of the network are covered by anomaly detection mechanisms, whose outputs can be retrieved by correlation systems similar to the ones described in [18].

By assuming the existence of a correlation system, it is possible to centralize the computation of the opinion dynamics algorithm in a more computationally powerful node (that gathers all the opinions and perform the correlation). As a consequence, the agents described in Sect. 2.2 can now be instantiated as logical agents, whose inputs will be retrieved from the different outputs of the anomaly detection mechanisms. From those inputs, every agent can now derive a certain opinion $x_i(t)$, or detection probability (i.e. the probability that an attack is taking place) for a given interval of time. These opinions are in turn influenced by the amount of alerts and their criticality. For example, a combination of anomalous statistics will slightly raise the opinion of an agent, and the existence of a confirmed attack (e.g. through the detection of an attack signature) will maximize that opinion. Compared to traditional detection mechanisms, the effectiveness of this approach resides in the ability to correlate anomalies throughout the network and hence trace the location of attacks, also considering their severity and persistence.

Taking into account the attacker model, we can now provide a formal representation of the intrusion kill chain of APT attacks. Let *attackStages* be a *set of potential attack stages* that an APT can perform against the industrial control network $G(V, E)$ as defined in Sect. 2.1, such that *attackStages* = $\{attack\ stage_1, attack\ stage_2, \ldots, attack\ stage_n\}$. This set comprises the following elements:

- *initialIntrusion*$_{(IT,OT,FW)}$. The initial access that affects a node n_0 (known as 'patient zero') of the IT network, OT network, and firewall, respectively.
- *compromise.* The adversary takes control of a certain node n_i, obtaining higher privileges, maintaining persistence, and executing defense evasion techniques. Moreover, this stage also includes the internal reconnaissance of the direct neighbourhood of n_i, $neighbours(n_i)$.
- *targetedLateralMovement*$_{(IT,OT,FW)}$. From a certain node n_i, the adversary chooses a FW, IT, or OT node n_j from the set $neighbours(n_i)$, and executes a lateral movement towards that node. Note that, in this model, the concept of lateral movement only encompasses the delivery of malware towards the target node.
- *controlLateralMovement.* From a certain node n_i, the adversary chooses the node n_j from the set $neighbours(n_i)$ with the highest betweeness (i.e. the node with significant influence over the network), and executes a lateral movement towards that node.
- *randomLateralMovement.* From a certain node n_i, the adversary chooses a random node n_j from the set $neighbours(n_i)$, and executes a lateral movement towards that node.
- *spreadLateralMovement.* From a certain node n_i, the adversary executes a lateral movement towards all nodes from the set $neighbours(n_i)$.
- *exfiltration.* From a certain node n_i, the adversary establishes a connection to an external command&control network, and extracts information using that connection.

- **destruction.** The adversary either destroys the node n_i, or manipulates the physical equipment (e.g. uranium enriching centrifuges) controlled by node n_i.
- **idle.** In this phase, no operation is performed.

Once the set *attackStages* is defined, it is possible to represent APT attacks that target our particular network model $G(V, E)$. In particular, for every APT *APT*, there can be an ordered set *attackSet_APT*, comprised by one or more elements of the *attackStages* set, that represent the APT chain of attack actions. As an example, the attack set of Stuxnet can be represented as follows:

$$attackSet_{Stuxnet} = \{initialIntrusion_{IT}, compromise, exfiltration,$$
$$targetedLatMove_{FW}, compromise, targetedLatMove_{OT},$$
$$\ldots, targetedLatMove_{OT}, idle, \ldots, destruction\}$$

These particular instances are defined taking into consideration the overall goal of every APT. For example, in the case of the Stuxnet malware, its goal is to find a particular node $n_{OT'} \in V_{OT}$ that manages an uranium enriching centrifuge. Therefore, after infecting patient zero $n_{IT^0} \in V_{IT}$, it seeks the location of a firewall node $n_{FW} \in V_{FW}$ that connects the $G(V_{IT}, E_{IT})$ and $G(V_{OT}, E_{OT})$ regions. Afterwards, it moves inside the $G(V_{OT}, E_{OT})$ region until it finds node $n_{OT'}$. Finally, after waiting for some time, the malware executes its payload, manipulating the centrifuge.

Regarding how the different attack stages influence over the application of the opinion dynamics and the calculation of the detection probabilities, we need to consider that certain attack stages will generate more security alerts. This, in turn, will increase the probability of detecting that particular attack stage. Therefore, we need to consider the existence of different classes of detection probabilities. Here, we define Θ as an *ordered set of detection probabilities of size d*, where $\Theta = \{\theta_1, \ldots, \theta_d\}$ and $\theta_i = [0, 1]$, such that $\forall \theta_i, \theta_i > \theta_{i+1}$.

Table 1. Map of *attackStages* to Θ

$initialIntrusion(n_0)$	θ_3
$compromise(n_i \rightarrow neighbours(n_i))$	$\theta_2 \rightarrow \theta_5$
$*LateralMovement_{IT,FW}(n_i \rightarrow n_j)$	$\theta_5 \rightarrow \theta_4$
$*LateralMovement_{OT}(n_i \rightarrow n_j)$	$\theta_5 \rightarrow \theta_3$
$spreadLateralMovement(n_i \rightarrow neighbours(n_i))$	$\theta_5 \rightarrow \theta_4$
$exfiltration(n_i)$	θ_4
$destruction(n_i)$	θ_1

Once Θ is defined, we can create a model that maps every element of the set *attackStages* to the elements of Θ. Such model, where $d = 5$ and $\Theta = \{\theta_1, \theta_2, \theta_3, \theta_4, \theta_5\}$, is described in Table 1. We explain the rationale behind this mapping in Appendix B.

4   Detection of APTs

After formally representing the attack stages, plus their relation to the detection probabilities, we can now use the proposed detection probabilities as inputs to the opinion dynamics algorithm, and hence simulate its response in an industrial architecture when it faces a particular instance of APT.

Algorithm 1 describes the life cycle of an APT composed by a set of attack actions against a given network. Each of these attacks generates an anomaly that is detected by the corresponding agents (and possibly by their neighbors), increasing their opinion in a value defined by the previously introduced Θ. After this, as commented in earlier sections, we also introduce a attenuation value on the opinion that represents the effect of old attacks in order to reduce their influence when computing the current opinion. This "decay" value, applied in the UPDATEOPINIONSWITHDECAY function, depends on the attack stages suffered in the past by the agent and the criticality of its monitored device: the more devastating the alert generated is (during the detection phase), the longer its effect will take to disappear. Consequently, we define Φ as an ordered set of decay values, where $\Phi = \{\phi_1, \ldots, \phi_d\}$ and $\phi_i = [0, 1]$, such that $\forall \phi_i, \phi_i < \phi_{i+1}$. Therefore, for all $i \in d$, ϕ_i is inversely proportional to the θ_i value, and both are applied to the detected anomaly value after each stage. This procedure, explained in Algorithm 2, is a way to account for the persistence when computing the opinion dynamics. It is important to note that both the respective anomaly and decay addition or reduction implies a normalization of the opinion value, from 0 to 1.

Once the x vector of opinions is updated with the new attack action (with θ) and attenuated due to old stages (through Φ), the opinion dynamics algorithm is executed to identify the affected areas of nodes and the level of severity of these attacks. However, although this gives insight of the location of threats (as it is visualized in the experimentation section), it would be also necessary to obtain an overall value of the network health from the opinion dynamics processing. Therefore, we have created the so-called delta indicator, which represents a global anomaly value and is computed in the COMPUTEDELTA function. This value is calculated with the weighted average of opinions by the amount of agents that hold the same detected abnormality, as described in Algorithm 3. However, since this aggregated value is dependent on the number of agents to calculate the average, in practice we can compute it over different sections of the network (i.e., IT or OT), thereby increasing its granularity. Using these values, we can quickly know the overall anomaly degree of every portion of the network.

Note that all these algorithms and the approach itself are validated from a theoretical point of view in Appendix A.

5   Experimental Simulations and Discussion

In the following, we present a test case for illustrating how we can apply the opinion dynamics-based technique while representing an APT against a given

---

Algorithm 1. APT life cycle - anomaly calculation

---

output: δ representing the delta value
local: Graph $G(V, E)$ representing the network, where $V = V_{IT} \cup V_{OT} \cup V_{FW}$
input: $attackSet \leftarrow attackStage_{APT_x}$, representing the APT chain of attack actions

$x \leftarrow zeros(|V|)$ (initial opinion vector)
$\{performedAttacks \leftarrow \oslash\}$
$\{attack \leftarrow firstattackfromattackSet\}$
while $attackSet \neq \oslash$ do
   if $attack == initialIntrusion_{(IT,OT,FW)}$ then
      $attackedNode \leftarrow random\ v \in V_{(IT,OT,FW)}$
      $x(attackedNode) \leftarrow x(attackedNode) + \theta_3$
   else if $attack == compromise$ then
      $x(attackedNode) \leftarrow x(attackedNode) + \theta_2$
      for neighbour in neighbours(attackedNode) do
         $x(attackedNode) \leftarrow x(attackedNode) + \theta_5$
      end for
   else if $type(attack) == LateralMovement$ then
      $previousAttackedNode \leftarrow attackedNode$
      $attackedNode \leftarrow$ SELECTNEXTNODE$(G, attackedNode)$
      $x(previousAttackedNode) \leftarrow x(previousAttackedNode) + \theta_5$
      $x(attackedNode) \leftarrow x(attackedNode) + \theta_{3,4}$
   else if $attack == exfiltration$ then
      $x(attackedNode) \leftarrow x(attackedNode) + \theta_4$
   else if $attack == destruction$ then
      $x(attackedNode) \leftarrow x(attackedNode) + \theta_1$
   else if $attack == idle$ then
      No attack performed
   end if

   $x \leftarrow$ UPDATEOPINIONSWITHDECAY$(x, performedAttacks)$
   $performedAttacks \leftarrow performedAttacks \cup attack$
   $mergedOpinions \leftarrow$ COMPUTEOPINIONDYNAMICS(x)
   $\delta \leftarrow$ COMPUTEDELTA$(mergedOpinions)$
   $attackSet \leftarrow attackSet \setminus attack$
end while

Algorithm 2. Decay of anomaly values over time depending on the attack action

---

function UPDATEOPINIONSWITHDECAY$(x, performedAttacks)$
   for attack in performedAttacks do
      $affectedNode \leftarrow$ GETAFFECTEDNODE$(attack)$
      if $attack == initialIntrusion_{IT,OT,FW}$ then
         $x(affectedNode) \leftarrow x(affectedNode) - \phi_3$
      else if $attack == compromise$ then
         $x(affectedNode) \leftarrow x(affectedNode) - \phi_2$
         for neighbour in NEIGHBOURS(affectedNode) do
            $x(affectedNode) \leftarrow x(affectedNode) - \phi_5$
         end for
      else if $type(attack) == LateralMovement$ then
         $origin \leftarrow$ GETORIGINOFMOVEMENT$(attack)$
         $x(origin) \leftarrow x(origin) - \phi_5$
         $x(affectedNode) \leftarrow x(affectedNode) - \phi_{3,4}$
      else if $attack == exfiltration$ then
         $x(affectedNode) \leftarrow x(affectedNode) - \phi_4$
      else if $attack == destruction$ then
         $x(affectedNode) \leftarrow x(affectedNode) - \phi_1$
      end if
   end for
   return x
end function

Algorithm 3. Computation of delta value

```
function ComputeDelta(mergedOpinions)
    opinionClusters ← UniqueValues(mergedOpinions)
    frequencyVector ← zeros(|opinionClusters|)
    for i:=1 to size(opinionClusters) step 1 do
        frequencyVector(i) ← CountOccurrencesOfOpinion(opinionClusters(i), mergedOpinions)
    end for
    δ ← 0
    for j:=1 to size(opinionClusters) step 1 do
        δ ← δ + frequencyVector(j) * uniqueValues(j)
    end for
    δ ← δ/size(mergedOpinions)
    return δ
end function
```

IT/OT industrial topology, as described in the paper. For this test case, we have implemented the network topology and Algorithms 1, 2 and 3 in Matlab.

Let us assume that we have a topology composed by three OT nodes and three IT nodes connected by a firewall, as explained in Sect. 2.1. According to Sect. 3.2, Stuxnet comprises a set of nine different attack actions that will be perpetrated against the proposed network, where each node counts on an individual agent to monitor its anomalies. If we execute the opinion dynamics algorithm after each stage, we can analyze the different clusters of anomalies detected by sets of agents. Following the model presented in Sect. 3.2, we have assigned values for each θ and ϕ according to the ordered set of probabilities in Table 2, considering a realistic scenario. We have also introduced a deviation of 0.1 to values in θ to simulate a low level of noise or probability of detecting the corresponding anomaly after each attack stage. Figure 2 visually represents the resulting values in each agent after the four most representative stages, where (1) the attacker compromises the IT node and exfiltrates information, (2) compromises the firewall and then (3) moves to the last OT of the network and remains idle, right before the destruction of this node is performed (4). Four different idle operations are performed in this point, with a total of twelve attack actions. Numbers by the name of nodes represent the value of anomaly (opinions) that each agents holds.

Table 2. Detection probability and decay values used in the Stuxnet test case

i	1	2	3	4	5
θ_i	0.9	0.7	0.5	0.3	0.1
ϕ_i	0.01	0.025	0.05	0.075	0.1

As we can also see in Fig. 2, the attacker traverses the whole network according to the Stuxnet behavior (where the current attacked node appears rounded), while the agents and its neighbors are able to detect the anomalies that consequently take place (the more red the node is, the greater the detected anomaly

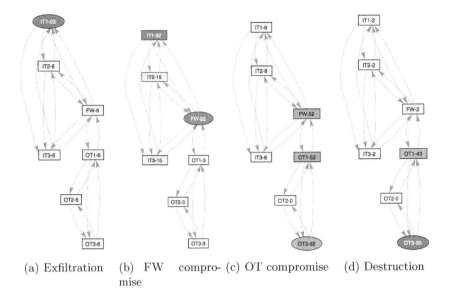

(a) Exfiltration   (b) FW compro- (c) OT compromise   (d) Destruction
                        mise

Fig. 2. Network topology used in the test case (Color figure online)

is). At the same time, we see how attenuation of anomalies also occurs, especially visible when the attacker leaves a node. In this example, the first IT node compromised is the number 1 while the final one is the OT number 3; the former is gradually attenuating its value as the attack evolves, according to the behavior explained in Sect. 4.

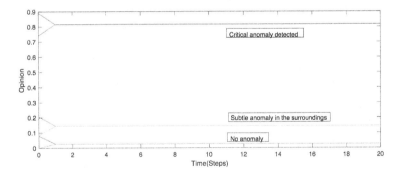

Fig. 3. Opinion dynamics after the second stage

This ability to identify where the threat is active within the network is enabled by opinion dynamics. If we have a look at its value in form of a plot in some point, we obtain the graph in Fig. 3. This corresponds to the execution of the algorithm (with 20 inner iterations) after the second stage depicted in Fig. 2, where the FW is compromised after attacking the first IT nodes. As we can rapidly see in the resulting graph, there are two agents (the a_{FW} and the a_{IT} node) that successfully detect the same level of critical abnormality in their area; this is also detected by some of their neighbors mildly, which is represented with the central consensus. Apart from these, the rest of nodes only detect a negligible value of anomaly.

By this means, we can statically identify where the threat is located and which severity it experiences. However, as commented in Sect. 2.2, it would be also necessary to trace all the events of the APT and highlight the most affected nodes it has traversed. In this sense, if we represent the succession of opinions agreed by agents over time for the Stuxnet attack described previously, we easily have such information, which is represented with Fig. 4.

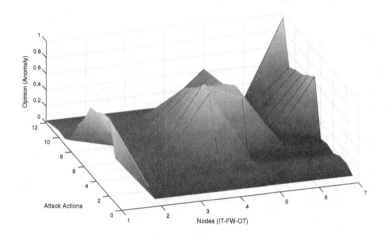

Fig. 4. Evolution of the opinions over time to trace the APT stages

As we can see there, the opinion profile for all agents evolves over the set of APT attack actions, showing a more pronounced value in the IT section in earlier stages and the OT in latter phases of the Stuxnet APT, as the attack aims to ultimately compromise a PLC by firstly intruding the network through a IT node. A similar effect is seen when we study the change in the delta value, which can be calculated either in the whole network or on any of its subnetworks (i.e., IT or OT). Figure 5 shows the progression of this indicator in each case, which also shows us how IT delta decreases over time and its value in OT increases according to the chain of attacks. In general, the value acquires the highest value when the last OT node is compromised, since the network has suffered most of the attacks in the previous stages. Beyond that point, delta decreases (due to the idle operations) and then it finally increases with the destruction of the node.

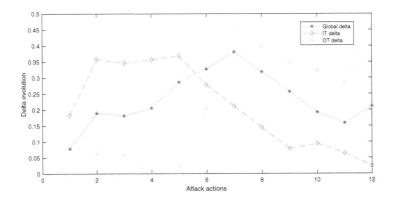

Fig. 5. Evolution of delta opinions over the network for the Stuxnet attack

6   Conclusions

APTs nowadays represent a dramatic source of economic losses and reputation damage for the industry, which obligates researchers, managers and operators to make a great effort to analyze them to trace their behavior and anticipate their effect. It then becomes mandatory to explore new ways of detecting and tracing anomalies beyond traditional detection techniques. In this paper, we have described the feasible application of an already available theoretical approach based on a distributed collaborative algorithm (opinion dynamics). We review the literature to gather the set of attack vectors that these threats leverage with the aim of representing the anomalies and show the effectiveness of the algorithm in a realistic setting, which also considers the influence of persistence over time. As a result, we have valuable information about the status of the network at all times. This design constitutes the middle step towards a future implementation in a real testbed that is currently being under development, which also takes into account additional sources of detection and accurate indicators.

Acknowledgments. This work has been partially supported by the research project SADCIP (RTC-2016-4847-8), financed by the Ministerio de Economía y Competitividad, and DISS-IIoT, financed by the University of Malaga (UMA) trough the "I Plan Propio de Investigación y Transferencia" of UMA. Likewise, the work of the first author has been partially financed by the Spanish Ministry of Education under the FPU program (FPU15/03213). The authors also thank J. Rodriguez (NICS Lab.) for his valuable comments, support, ideas, and incredible help. You rock.

A   Correctness Proof: Consensus-Based Detection and Traceability

This section presents the correctness proof of the consensus-based detection and traceability problem for APTs. This problem is solved when the following conditions are met:

1. The attacker is able to find an IT/OT device in the system and attack it.
2. The detection system is able to trace the threat, thanks in part to the consensus (detection and traceability).
3. The system is able to properly finish in a finite time (termination).
4. The algorithm is capable of terminating and providing advanced detection at any moment (validity).

The first requirement is satisfied because we assume that the attacker is capable (i) declaring the chain of attacks in advance, such as scanning, lateral movement, exfiltration or destruction (see Sect. 3.2), and (ii) identifying kinds of devices (e.g. IT/OT nodes and firewalls) by their functionalities. The modus operandi of the attacker is systematic except when the attacker needs to make a specific lateral movement, either through the selection of a new random neighbor node within the network or the selection of the neighbor with the highest betweeness. To comply with the predefined attack patterns, the attacker first needs to identify the first target node, which generally belongs to IT network – evidently, this characteristic depends on the type of attacker (insider or outsider) and their skills. If the attacker is an outsider, her goal is to find a $v_{IT_i} \in V_{IT}$ in order to penetrate by itself within the system, and to advance until reaching those nodes serving as firewalls such that $v_{FW_i} \in V_{FW}$. Once a v_{FW_i} is finally reached, the attacker tries to gain access in the operative network to compromise the most critical devices, i.e. $v_{OT_i} \in V_{OT}$. If the attacker is an outsider, the compromises relies, in this case, on the pre-established APT threat chain; i.e. on $attackSet$.

The second requirement is also found due to the software prevention agents, $a_i \in A$, integrated as part of v_{IT_i}, v_{FW_i} and v_{OT_i} of $G(V, E)$. These agents present capacities to detect anomalies and trace the intrusive presence by means of opinion dynamic parameters, the values of the which are attenuated according to time and aggressiveness of the threat (the decay factor). This attenuation, dependent on Φ_i, does not means to completely forget an incident in past. But rather, in remembering the most significant aftermaths of the previous attacks in order to show the advance of the threat in real time, and therefore its traceability.

Through induction we demonstrate the third requirement, corresponding to termination of the approach. To do this, we specify the initial and final conditions together with the base case. Namely:

Precondition: by assumptions, we assume that the attacker is an advanced expert with skills to reach the IT-OT communication channels belonging to $G(V, E)$. However, this capacity depends on the set $attackSet$ defined in Algorithm 1, which defines threat chain such that $attackSet \neq \oslash$.

Postcondition: (i) the attacker reaches the network $G(V, E)$ and compromises at least a node in V such that $attackSet = \oslash$ after the loop in Algorithm 1. And (ii) the system successful detects the threat such that $\delta > 0$ and marks the traceability according to the real consensus state of $G(V, E)$, registered in the array vector x.

Case 1: $attackSet \neq \oslash$, but $\mid attackSet \mid = 1$. In this case, the attacker needs to launch the unique attack defined in $attackSet$. As mentioned, if the attack does not imply a lateral movement, the success of the threat is concentrated on just one node in V, since the following iteration of the loop implies that $attackSet \leftarrow attackSet \setminus attack$, and therefore $attackSet = \oslash$. To the contrary, if the attack entails a lateral movement, then the attacker has to select a new neighbor node, either from a random or target point of view.

Any attack in V means an impact on the attacked node with a significant influence in its opinion dynamic (i.e. $x(attackednode)$). If, in addition, the decay factor is activated, the system weakens, but does not delete, the aggressiveness of the threat to stress the current trace of threat over the time. This computation is possible through Φ_i in Algorithm 2. Once x is updated, the system computes the δ value taking into account the weighted average of the opinion dynamics of the entire system (see Algorithm 3).

Induction: if we assume that we are in step k ($k \geq 1$) of the loop where $attackSet \neq \oslash$, then **Case 1** is going to be considered each time. When $k = |attackSet|$, the system computes **Case 1** and ends the detection algorithm with $\delta > 0$ since $attackSet = \oslash$, showing the traceability of the threat through x and complying with the postcondition.

Finally, the latter requirement is also satisfied since the algorithm finalizes and detects the threat through opinion dynamic (either individual or collective) and shows the traceability of the threat over the time.

B   The Mapping of the *attackStages* to Θ

We have presented in Sect. 3.2 a model that maps every element of the set *attackStages* to the elements of $\Theta = \{\theta_1, \theta_2, \theta_3, \theta_4, \theta_5\}$. For this mapping, we have taken into consideration the defense mechanisms analyzed in Sect. 3.1. In particular, the rationale behind this mapping is as follows:

- We assign θ_1 only to the *destruction* stage, because any major disruption in the functionality of a device (e.g. unavailable resources, device turned off) will trigger multiple high priority alerts. Note that, as explained in our defense model, we assume that all field devices are also covered by detection mechanisms, thus any attack (e.g. the Stuxnet final payload) against these sensitive devices can be easily detected.
- θ_2 is only assigned to the element at the left side of the *compromise* stage $(n_i \rightarrow neighbours(n_i))$. The reason is simple: the act of compromising and taking control of n_i will not only trigger various host alerts, but also multiple network alerts due to the various discovery queries targeting all $neighbours(n_i)$. The correlation of all these events will draw attention to the state of n_i.
- For θ_4, we consider the security alerts caused by combination of a single anomalous connection to a node plus the delivery of malware to that node. As such, this θ covers all the elements at the right side of the *lateralMovement* stages. Note, however, that in some particular cases (like the *initialIntrusion* stage and the $*LateralMovement_{OT}$ stages), additional anomalies will be

detected: a potentially anomalous external connection, and a certain instability in the otherwise stable OT communication environment, respectively. Therefore, the θ assigned to the elements of those stages will be θ_3.

- Finally, θ_5 is assigned to those stages where the nodes produce or receive anomalous traffic (e.g. a connection that deviates from what is considered as normal traffic). Again, in situations where a connection with the outside world is made (e.g. *exfiltration* stage), as the possibility of anomalous traffic will increase, the θ will be increase as well.

References

1. Cazorla, L., Alcaraz, C., Lopez, J.: Cyber stealth attacks in critical information infrastructures. IEEE Syst. J. **12**(2), 1778–1792 (2018)
2. Singh, S., Sharma, P.K., Moon, S.Y., Moon, D., Park, J.H.: A comprehensive study on apt attacks countermeasures for future networks communications: challenges solutions. J. Supercomput. 1–32 (2016). https://doi.org/10.1007/s11227-016-1850-4
3. Rubio, J.E., Alcaraz, C., Lopez, J.: Preventing advanced persistent threats in complex control networks. In: Foley, S.N., Gollmann, D., Snekkenes, E. (eds.) ESORICS 2017. LNCS, vol. 10493, pp. 402–418. Springer, Cham (2017). https://doi.org/10.1007/978-3-319-66399-9_22
4. Lin, C.-T.: Structural controllability. IEEE Trans. Autom. Control **19**(3), 201–208 (1974)
5. Haynes, T.W., Hedetniemi, S.M., Hedetniemi, S.T., Henning, M.A.: Domination in graphs applied to electric power networks. SIAM J. Discret. Math. **15**(4), 519–529 (2002)
6. Kneis, J., Mölle, D., Richter, S., Rossmanith, P.: Parameterized power domination complexity. Inf. Process. Lett. **98**(4), 145–149 (2006)
7. Pagani, G.A., Aiello, M.: The power grid as a complex network: a survey. Phys. A: Stat. Mech. Appl. **392**(11), 2688–2700 (2013)
8. Watts, D.J., Strogatz, S.H.: Collective dynamics of 'small-world' networks. Nature **393**(6684), 440 (1998)
9. Hegselmann, R., Krause, U., et al.: Opinion dynamics and bounded confidence models, analysis, and simulation. J. Artif. Soc. Soc. Simul. **5**(3), 1–33 (2002)
10. Lemay, A., Calvet, J., Menet, F., Fernandez, J.M.: Survey of publicly available reports on advanced persistent threat actors. Comput. Secur. **72**, 26–59 (2018)
11. Falliere, N., Murchu, L.O., Chien, E.: W32.stuxnet dossier, version 1.4, February 2011. https://www.symantec.com. Accessed Apr 2018
12. Symantec Security Response Attack Investigation Team. Dragonfly: Western energy sector targeted by sophisticated attack group (2017). https://www.symantec.com. Accessed Apr 2018
13. SANS Industrial Control Systems. Analysis of the cyber attack on the Ukrainian power grid (2016). https://ics.sans.org. Accessed Apr 2018
14. Cherepanov, A.: Telebots are back - supply-chain attacks against Ukraine (2017). https://www.welivesecurity.com. Accessed Apr 2018
15. MITRE Corporation. MITRE ATT&CK (2018). https://attack.mitre.org. Accessed Apr 2018

16. Chen, P., Desmet, L., Huygens, C.: A study on advanced persistent threats. In: De Decker, B., Zúquete, A. (eds.) CMS 2014. LNCS, vol. 8735, pp. 63–72. Springer, Heidelberg (2014). https://doi.org/10.1007/978-3-662-44885-4_5

17. Hutchins, E.M., Cloppert, M.J., Amin, R.M.: Intelligence-driven computer network defense informed by analysis of adversary campaigns and intrusion kill chains. Lead. Issues Inf. Warf. Secur. Res. **1**(1), 80 (2011)

18. Rubio, J.E., Alcaraz, C., Roman, R., Lopez, J.: Analysis of intrusion detection systems in industrial ecosystems. In: 14th International Conference on Security and Cryptography, pp. 116–128 (2017)

19. S2Grupo. Emas SOM - Monitoring System for Industrial Environments (2018). https://s2grupo.es/es/emas-ics/. Accessed Apr 2018

Hide Your Hackable Smart Home from Remote Attacks: The Multipath Onion IoT Gateways

Lei Yang[1], Chris Seasholtz[2], Bo Luo[2], and Fengjun Li[2(✉)]

[1] Amazon LLC., Seattle, WA, USA
ynglei@amazon.com
[2] The University of Kansas, Lawrence, KS, USA
{seasholtz,bluo,fli}@ku.edu

Abstract. The rapid expansion of IoT-enabled home automation is accompanied by substantial security and privacy risks. A large number of real-world security incidents exploiting various device vulnerabilities have been revealed. The *Onion IoT gateways* have been proposed to provide strong security protection for potentially vulnerable IoT devices by hiding them behind IoT gateways running the Tor hidden services, in which the gateways can only be accessed by authorized users with the *.onion* addresses of the gateways and correct credentials. However, the limited bandwidth of Tor makes this approach very impractical and unscalable. To tackle this issue, we present two novel designs of *multipath Onion IoT gateway* and *split channel Onion IoT gateway*. The first design implements a customized multipath routing protocol in Tor to construct a multi-circuit anonymous tunnel between the user and the Onion gateway to support applications that require low latency and high bandwidth. The second scheme splits command and data channels so that small-sized command packets are transmitted through the more secure channel over the Tor hidden service, while the less secure data channel over the public network is used for outbound very-high-bandwidth data traffic. Experiment results show that the proposed approaches significantly improve the performance of Onion IoT gateways, so that they can be practically adopted to securely transmit low-latency and high-bandwidth data, such as HD video streams from home surveillance cameras. We also prove the security guarantees of the proposed mechanism through security analysis.

Keywords: IoT security · Smart homes · Tor hidden service

1 Introduction

By connecting billions of smart devices to the Internet, the Internet-of-Things leads to a pervasive deployment of intelligence into our daily life with innovative applications. In a recent estimation, approximately 8.4 billion IoT devices are connected to the Internet worldwide in 2017 – a 31% increase from 2016. By

© Springer Nature Switzerland AG 2018
J. Lopez et al. (Eds.): ESORICS 2018, LNCS 11098, pp. 575–594, 2018.
https://doi.org/10.1007/978-3-319-99073-6_28

2020, the number of connected device will reach 20.4 billion, resulting in a global market of $2 trillion [22]. One of the fastest growing IoT fields is smart home systems, sometimes referred as *home automation*, in which smart appliances such as baby monitors, security cameras, smoke alarms, smart locks, smart lights, and smart switches/plugs are connected to the home network and remotely controllable through the Internet. Beyond convenience, the smart home technology also provides tangible benefits such as safety and energy-efficiency.

While we are witnessing a rapid expansion of IoT-enabled home automation, the increasing use of the networked IoT devices is accompanied by substantial security and privacy risks [29,31,35], which in some cases could lead to chilling safety consequences since the smart devices in home automation are monitoring our personal activities at home. For example, burglars can hack into our surveillance system [13] or analyze our electricity consumption [43] to observe our life pattern, and get into our homes with the help of our smart locks [18]. To make things worse, the compromised devices can be turned into bots to launch a DDoS attack. For example, the Mirai botnet compromising millions of cameras and digital video recorders took down the Dyn DNS servers in 2016 and caused a massive Internet outage as well as up to $110 million economic loss [17].

As security and privacy has become a most important consideration in the design and implementation of the smart home technology, various security solutions have been proposed to secure light-weight IoT communication protocols (e.g., DTLS [27,32] for RPL [38], 6LoWPAN [33] and CoAP [34]), enhance authentication [28,30] and access control [25,26,36], attest operational status of remote devices and detect intrusions, etc. However, over the recent years, a large number of real-world attack incidents have been revealed by academia, security firms and individual researchers, which have exploited various types of vulnerabilities in consumer IoT devices and applications involving the use of surveillance cameras [4,13] and baby cameras [1], smart locks and garage openers [18], smart appliances [2,9], thermostats [3], plugs and light bulbs [29], etc.

A root cause of these vulnerabilities is that the manufacturers have been lax in adopting appropriate or even basic security measures. For example, the D-LINK DCS2132L Internet cameras require no credential to access the management interface [4,35], and the WeMo devices allow mobile Apps to access them through an unencrypted SOAP API [31]. The lack of security protection is due to several reasons. First, it is difficult to extend conventional security schemes to IoT devices that are usually resource-constrained. Moreover, implementing security measures on IoT devices especially on the low-end ones requires skills and resources, and thus increases design and development costs. Finally, manufacturers are under business pressures to hit the market so that security is not their priority.

Consider the large number of heterogeneous IoT devices, manufacturers' general lack of incentives to adopt appropriate security practices, and the slow progress in IoT security standardization/regulation, it is difficult, if not completely impossible, to develop security solutions for each individual device, nor to force each device vendor to ensure a flawless implementation or adopt adequate security protections. Recognizing the fact that security vulnerabilities always exist in IoT devices, the question we pose is *in what strategy the chance of adversaries attacking vulnerable devices can be reduced and where this protection should be deployed?*

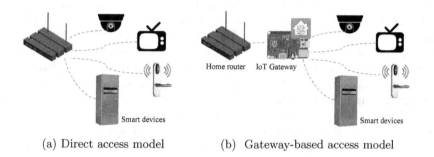

(a) Direct access model   (b) Gateway-based access model

Fig. 1. Home automation operational models

This naturally leads to an isolation-based approach that uses a dedicated IoT gateway to separate the private network, in which the IoT devices are deployed, from the public network, and secure the perimeter of the private network at the gateway. As shown in Fig. 1b, the IoT gateway coordinates the connected home automation devices and isolates them from direct access from the public Internet. Open-source platforms such as *Home Assistant* [5] and *open Home Automation Bus* (openHAB) [8] are introduced to support the interconnection of devices in different types and from different manufacturers. In this work, we developed our secure IoT gateways on the Home Assistant platform, but our design can be easily extended to other platforms. Since all devices are managed and controlled through the gateway, individual devices no longer offer interfaces for remote control and thus are not directly exposed to remote adversaries. However, the gateway, which may have its own security vulnerabilities, becomes the new target of interest to the adversaries, and also the single point of failure.

One approach to secure the IoT gateway is to connect it to a back-end cloud server that relays all the commands from the cloud so that it can utilize the existing security mechanisms provided by the cloud. Samsung's SmartThings [11], Apple's HomeKit and Google's Brillo are several examples. However, the cloud-based approach needs to store IoT data on the cloud and thus yields a serious privacy issue if the cloud service provider is not fully trusted to view our private IoT data. In fact, users have expressed serious security and privacy concerns due to data breaches and various types of data abuses [20].

Therefore, we propose to integrate the Tor hidden service onto the potentially vulnerable IoT gateway so that it is protected from being directly exposed to remote adversaries. This is because in most network attacks, a critical step is to identify vulnerable, Internet-facing nodes through reconnaissance. By hiding the gateway behind the Tor network, the adversaries, without knowing the gateway's *.onion* address, cannot directly scan or access the gateway. In this way, the Tor hidden service acts as an additional security buffer between the smart home applications and the adversaries. This idea was first introduced by Nathan Freitas from the Tor Project in [21], which described a straightforward approach of obtaining an *.onion* address for the IoT gateway and running the Tor hidden service directly on it. However, in practice, this approach suffer from a well-known performance problem of the Tor network, in which Tor users often experience very high delays [41,42]. The poor performance of the IoT gateway running the Tor hidden service affects any IoT applications with realtime requirements. Moreover, to prevent congestion, Tor actively throttles high-bandwidth applications. Consequently, IoT gateways with high-bandwidth services such as video streaming will be blocked.

To tackle the performance problem, we propose two novel and practical designs of multi-path Onion IoT gateways, namely *IoT gateway over multipath Tor hidden services*, and *IoT gateway over split channels*. Both designs provide strong security protection by hiding the IoT devices behind the gateway running the Tor hidden services. In the first solution, we extended the multipath routing protocol *mTor* [42] and customized it to construct an end-to-end tunnel consisting of multiple Tor circuits between the user and the proposed Onion IoT gateway. By applying a self-adaptive scheduling scheme, the tunnel transfers data over multiple circuits efficiently and thus achieves a good throughput to support IoT applications that require low network latency. Since the traffic is routed through the anonymous tunnel, this scheme provides a same security protection as the original Tor-based approach. Therefore, it fits the user who requires strong security protection and a reasonable performance.

We further improved the performance of the Onion gateway in our second design by using split channels for command and data transmission. In particular, the IoT gateway running the Tor hidden service maintains two separate channels: the command channel handles requests and responses, which are tiny messages, through the hidden service ports over the Tor network, and the data channel is only used to send high-bandwidth traffic to remote users over the public network. By separating the command and data channels, we provide a good security protection by hiding the security-sensitive command interface behind Tor, while avoiding injecting high-bandwidth traffic into the Tor network.

The main contributions of this work are as follows:

- We present a general security solution to safeguard IoT devices with potential security vulnerabilities by hiding them behind the specially designed IoT gateways running the Tor hidden services.
- We propose two novel designs of Onion IoT gateways to provide strong security protection by integrating the Tor hidden services on the IoT gateway with optimized performance to support high-bandwidth and low-latency IoT applications.
- To our best knowledge, the proposed Onion IoT gateway design is the first practical solution to integrate Tor hidden service with secure IoT gateways.

The rest of this paper is organized as follows. We first introduce the preliminaries in Sect. 2, and then present our IoT gateway designs, namely *multipath Onion IoT gateway* and *split channel Onion IoT gateway*, in Sects. 3 and 4, respectively. We evaluate the performance of the proposed designs through experiments in Sect. 5 and analyze their security in Sect. 6. Finally, we discuss the related work in Sect. 7 and conclude this work in Sect. 8.

2   Preliminaries

2.1   One Instance of Smart Home Gateway: Home Assistant

Home Assistant (HA) is an open-source home automation platform running on Python 3, which is able to automatically discover, monitor, control and automate various consumer IoT devices [5]. It can run on major operating systems (e.g., Linux, Windows, OS X) and hardware modules ranging from PCs to microcontrollers such as Raspberry Pi. Home Assistant offers a web interface and allows users to remotely access it through web browsers or mobile applications.

We choose Home Assistant as our implementation platform for several reasons. First, HA is an open-source platform supporting the major brands of IoT devices, and thus is widely used in home automation application development. It also has good community supports. Moreover, Freitas implemented the Tor-based gateway on HA [21], so it is fair to compare his scheme with ours on the same platform. It worths noting that our designs do not rely on the HA platform. In particular, the first design using the customized multipath Tor routing protocol is platform-independent, and the second design can be easily implemented in other platforms with a small effort.

2.2   Tor and Tor Hidden Service

The Tor network [19] is an overlay network consisting of Onion Routers (ORs) contributed by volunteers to support anonymous communication over the Internet. To do so, the client's proxy, known as the Onion Proxy (OP), randomly selects three routers to establish a Tor circuit to the destination. It then encrypts the data in layers, packs them into 512-byte cells and sends data cells through the circuit. Each router along the circuit peels off one layer of encryption and forwards the cell to the next router until it reaches the last relay (known as "exit"), which further forwards the data to the original destination. Each hop only knows who has sent the data (predecessor) and to whom it is relaying (successor) due to the layered encryption.

Tor hidden services use rendezvous points (RPs) to allow service operators to offer TCP-based services, such as web or instant messaging servers, without revealing their real IP addresses. Service operators can enable it by setting up Tor as the proxy for their services. Figure 2 illustrates the basic components of Tor hidden services: (1) The hidden server (HS) randomly selects several routers as its introduction points (IPs) and builds onion circuits to them. (2)

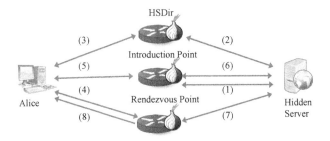

Fig. 2. Tor hidden services architecture

HS uploads its service descriptor to the hidden service directory (HSDir), where the descriptor along with HS's public key and the set of IPs is signed by HS's private key. Now, HS is ready to accept connections from clients. (3) To connect to the hidden service, a client (e.g., Alice) contacts HSDir to retrieve the service descriptor of HS using its onion address, which Alice learns out of band. (4) With the set of IPs and HS's public key from the service descriptor, Alice randomly selects a router as her RP, gives it a rendezvous cookie (RC) which is a one-time secret, and builds a circuit to it. (5) Alice sends an introduce message to one of the IPs and (6) asks it to forward the message to HS, which contains the rendezvous cookie, RP address and the first part of a Diffie-Hellman (DH) handshake encrypted by HS's public key. (7) After decrypting the introduce message, HS establishes a new circuit to Alice's RP and sends a rendezvous cell to it, containing RC and the second part of DH handshake. (8) RP relays the rendezvous cell to Alice. (9) After verifying RC and generating the end-to-end session key, Alice and HS start communicating through RP, which relays data cells between the two circuits without change.

In our design, the IoT gateway built on the Home Assistant platform is running Tor hidden services, so it can only be accessed by its .onion address with an optional authentication token shared between authorized users. By applying multiple-hop onion routing and the end-to-end encryption, Tor hidden services provide strong protection to traffic flows and the location of the hidden server. This prevents the remote adversaries from knowing the IP address of the IoT gateway by probing or scanning the network, or even the existence of the IoT gateways, and thus reduces the risks of remote exploitation.

Flow Control. Tor uses a two-layer window-based end-to-end flow control scheme to guarantee a steady flow between two ends. Since multiple streams multiplex a circuit, the outer layer performs a circuit-level control which restricts the number of cells transmitted over a circuit for all streams. The inner layer enforces a stream-level control for individual streams. At both ends of a circuit, two OPs (one for sender and one for receiver) control the speed of data cells entering and leaving the circuit by keeping track of the circuit and stream windows. By default, a circuit window starts with 1000 cells and a stream window is initialized to 500 cells. When a data cell is sent, both windows decrease by one. When a stream window becomes empty, the sender stops sending from this stream; when a circuit window reaches zero, the sender stops sending from all streams on this circuit. Windows are increased when the corresponding acknowledgment cell known as SENDME is received. For every 100 cells received on a circuit, the receiver sends a circuit SENDME to inform the sender to forward another 100 cells from this circuit. For every 50 cells received from a stream in this circuit, the receiver sends a stream SENDME to request another 50 cells from this stream.

The Performance Problem of Tor. There are about 7,000 onion routers in the Tor network, among which the majority is low-bandwidth relays. So, the donated bandwidth resource is relatively scarce comparing to the large user scale (i.e., almost 2.5 million users per day). Besides, due to the current path selection scheme, many users tend to select relays from a very small set of high-bandwidth relays when constructing the circuits, which causes frequent congestions on these relays. When congestion happens, a congested relay in a 3-hop circuit will greatly degrade the performance of the entire circuit. Hence, the problem becomes worse in hidden services, in which the circuit connecting the user to the hidden server contains six relays. In [21], Freitas proposed to directly deploy Home Assistant over the Tor hidden service, therefore, this scheme inevitably suffers the same performance problem stated above.

3 IoT Gateway over Multipath Tor Hidden Services

To overcome the performance problem of the current deployment of Tor for IoT gateway, we extend the mTor approach in [42], and customize it into an end-to-end multipath routing scheme to support Tor hidden services, namely mTorHS.

As illustrated in Fig. 3, mTorHS constructs an anonymous *tunnel* consisting of m circuits, where m is a client-specified parameter. While the capacity of each circuit is dynamic over time, our proposed mTorHS scheme can adaptively distribute traffic onto m circuits in proportion to their dynamic capacities, and thus avoid the communication being blocked by a congested circuit and achieve an optimal overall performance. mTorHS is transparent to the Tor network, that is, no modification needs to be made on regular Tor relays. Only the two Tor Onion Proxies (OPs) on the user side (for users who choose to use mTorHS) and the hidden server side (i.e., Tor OP for Home Assistant) need to be updated. In particular, new functions are added for associating multiple circuits to a client stream, adding sequence number to data cell, reordering out-of-sequence cells, and scheduling cells across multiple circuits. Next, we will elaborate the process of tunnel construction and data transmission. For the ease of presentation, we denote user's Onion Proxy as OP or Alice interchangeably, and call hidden server's OP as HS in the following sections.

3.1 Tunnel Construction

In our scheme, the server establishes hidden service and client retrieves service descriptors in the same way as the conventional Tor hidden service (i.e., *step 3–6* in Sect. 2.2). Our modification starts from *step 4*.

Tunnel Initialization. Different from the current scheme which randomly selects one router as the rendezvous point (RP), the user Alice chooses m routers and constructs m circuits of 3 hops, each ending at a distinct router. Then, Alice gives m different rendezvous cookies (RC) to the RPs, which will be used to link the joining circuits established from the hidden server. We denote the first established circuit as the *primary circuit* and the other $m - 1$ circuits as the *auxiliary circuits*. Once m circuits are established, Alice does the same thing as *steps 5–6* in Sect. 2.2. In particular, Alice sends an introduce1 message to an introduction point, which will forward it to the hidden server with an introduce2 message. The message contains the rendezvous cookie, RP address and the first part of a DH handshake for the primary circuit. We add two new fields to this message, namely, *is_multipath* and *tunnel_width*, which indicate the request is to build a multipath tunnel with tunnel width m. After receiving the introduce2 message, HS checks if *is_multipath* is set. If so, HS generates a unique 32-bit tunnel identifier (TID); otherwise, HS follows the original Tor protocol. HS establishes a new circuit to the RP of the primary circuit and sends Alice a rendezvous1 cell containing RC, the second part of DH handshake, and TID. RP relays the content of the rendezvous1 cell to Alice with a rendezvous2 cell. Once Alice receives it and successfully verifies RC, she extracts TID and generates the end-to-end session key. A 6-hop circuit is established between Alice and HS. Now, Alice and HS can communicate with each other through the primary circuit. It is worth noting that while two 3-hop anonymous circuits (between client and RP and between server and RP) join at the RP conceptually, we re-design the entire circuit construction protocol to enable end-to-end encryption between the client and the server so that no intermediate router can observe the clear traffic in Tor.

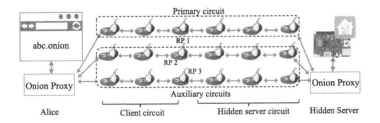

Fig. 3. An example of mTorHS architecture where $m = 3$.

With TID, Alice adds the remaining auxiliary circuits to the tunnel by sending $m - 1$ next_rp_m[1] messages to HS along the primary circuit. The format of

---

[1] To distinguish from the commands in current Tor, all the newly added commands in mTorHS have a suffix m.

each next_rp_m message is similar to the introduce1 message, which contains TID and RP's address used in auxiliary circuits. In response to the next_rp_m message, HS builds a new circuit connecting to the corresponding RP, and acknowledges each successful joining with a rendezvous1 to that RP. HS associates all circuits with the same TID to form a tunnel for Alice. After Alice receives all m rendezvous2 cells including 1 cell from the primary circuits and $m-1$ cells from the auxiliary circuits, a multipath tunnel is successfully constructed.

Tunnel Management. Atop circuit management of Tor, mTorHS introduces additional tunnel management to oversee circuits in the tunnel. mTorHS manages the multipath tunnel dynamically according to the congestion status of member circuits over time. If OP detects that the transmission on a member circuit becomes very slow, OP will construct a new circuit to replace it (will be elaborated in the next subsection). The slow circuit closing scheme provides OP the ability of responding to real-time network dynamics, and prevents a slow circuit from becoming a bottleneck of the entire tunnel. In particular, OP can add new auxiliary circuits or tear down any existing circuit at any time. In particular, a new auxiliary circuit can be added by sending a next_rp_m command to inform HS of the new RP address. To tear down a circuit, OP informs HS to drop it using a drop_m message. After receiving drop_m cell, HS immediately stops sending on this circuit and responds to OP using a dropped_m message with the number of cells that have already been sent on this circuit (denoted as n_s). Once OP receives n_s cells on this circuit, it terminates the circuit.

3.2   Data Transmission

When Alice's data stream arrives at OP via SOCKS, OP spawns the client stream (denoted as the *parent* stream) to m subflows and appends them to the tunnel by associating each subflow with a circuit. Each subflow has its own stream window and inherits a common stream ID from the parent. Next, OP sends a relay_begin cell through a random member circuit to start the access.

Scheduling and Data Cell Allocation. Conceptually, data cells can be forwarded through any member circuit in the tunnel. However, if the number of allocated cells on a particular circuit exceeds its capacity, it will become congested. Since the overall performance of a tunnel is bounded by the slowest circuit, two endpoints of a tunnel need to cooperate to schedule cells across multiple circuits based on the capacities of individual circuits. A naive approach for cell allocation is to probe the capacity of each circuit after it is initiated and schedule traffic according to the probed capacity.

However, the method is problematic in practice. First, it will introduce a large amount of probing traffic to the Tor network. Moreover, the capacity of each circuit may change dramatically after probing. Therefore, the static scheduling scheme cannot adapt to network dynamics so that it is ineffective. In [14], Alsabah et al. presented an opportunistic probing approach to estimate the round-trip-time (RTT) of a circuit based on Tor's circuit-level congestion control scheme. The RTT-based approach is reactive to network dynamics, but

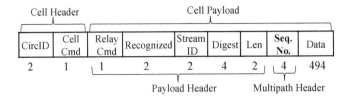

Fig. 4. *m*TorHS cell format: a new filed, *sequence number* marked in red, is added as the multipath header, representing the sequence number of sent-out cells. (Color figure online)

it is still not very accurate because the congestion feedbacks are received infrequently [15]. We argue that RTT-based approach may not be a good choice in cross-layer scheduling, which is also recognized in multipath TCP design [16].

In *m*TorHS, we adopt a "pulling" scheduling scheme – instead of pushing data cells to circuits by a scheduler, we let each subflow actively pull data from a shared send buffer, whenever its stream window becomes nonempty. Initially, each subflow has a stream window of 500 cells. As described in Sect. 2.2, the stream window decreases by one when sending a cell out and increases by 50 when receiving a stream-level SENDME. Consequently, a subflow stops sending cells when its stream window size drops to zero and resumes when it receives a SENDME. When the circuit to which a subflow is appended becomes congested, cells will be moving much slower towards the receiver, resulting in delayed stream-level SENDMEs and long waiting at the sender end. Whereas, subflows on fast circuits will send out data cells fast and steadily. In this way, the "pulling" scheduling is subflow self-adaptive without accurate explicit circuit RTT measurements. When multiple subflows have a nonzero stream window, we adopt a FIFO (first-in-first-out) queue to schedule them.

Slow Circuit Detection. Another challenge in *m*TorHS design is the detection of slow circuits. To avoid a congested circuit becoming the bottleneck of the entire tunnel, OP will replace slow circuits with new ones. We adopt a distance-based outlier detection approach to determine whether a circuit is congested based on a sliding window of 50 cells. In particular, we measure the time of receiving every 50 cells and find the lower and upper quartiles (Q_1 and Q_3) of ten most recent records to calculate the interquartile range (IQR) where $IQR = Q_3 - Q_1$. If a new measurement falls out of the range of $(0, Q_3 + 1.5IQD]$, it is considered as an outlier indicating the circuit is experiencing a congestion. To increase detection reliability, OP considers a circuit as congested if at least three consecutive outliers occur. Once detected, OP and HS will collaborate to tear down the congested circuit and replace it with a new one. This can be done through the tunnel management discussed above.

Data Re-ordering. Combining the self-adaptive "pulling" scheduling and active congestion detection schemes, *m*TorHS is able to adapt to network dynamics, which potentially prevents slow circuits from degrading the overall performance of multipath tunnel. However, due to dynamic scheduling, data cells may arrive at the receiver out of order. To solve this issue, we have to modify the format of Tor data cell to incorporate a 32-bit sequence number in the multipath data packets. As shown in Fig. 4, the first four bytes of data payload is reserved for this purpose. Moreover, we add a new *relay_subdata_m* command to indicate a data cell is multipath data. When OP receives a multipath data cell from a subflow, it first checks if the sequence number is expected. An expected cell is immediately forwarded to the application stream, while an out-of-order cell is stored in a buffer and ordered according to its sequence numbers.

3.3 Discussions

By applying congestion detection, users of multipath hidden services can route traffic through multiple circuits (some may be lightly occupied), and thus improve the overall performance. Such a congestion avoidance scheme also benefits single-path users, since mTorHS stops using the congested paths to give bandwidth to others' traffic. To further balance the usage on high-bandwidth relays between multipath users and general users, we can force multipath users to use the low-bandwidth relays to establish their tunnel and still achieving an acceptable performance, since most Tor relays are low-bandwidth and they are under-utilized in the current Tor [42]. We can bundle these idle, low-bandwidth relays to effectively serve the multipath users without hurting general users. In terms of security, this solution, namely IoT gateway over multipath Tor hidden services, transmits all traffic, including incoming and outgoing traffic, on gateway through Tor network, so the IP address of gateway is still hidden from the public Internet and thus the adversary cannot scan and attack the gateway.

mTorHS improves the network utilization by employing low-bandwidth relays. However, it will not increase the overall bandwidth of Tor network. If millions of users access their gateways via Tor, especially for bulk traffic like watching camera videos, the huge demand on bandwidth may exceed the capacity of Tor. Therefore, IoT gateway over mTorHS is best for users who have very strong security requirement but only need an acceptable performance. For the majority users who want to achieve a better balance between security and performance, we propose an alternative solution, namely *IoT gateway with split command and data channels*, which will be presented in next section.

4 IoT Gateway with Split Command and Data Channels

Tor provides very strong security protection but limited bandwidth, while the public Internet has the opposite – high bandwidth but weak security protection. To combine the advantages, we propose a novel scheme, namely *IoT gateway with split command and data channels*, which leverages the security of Tor and the good performance of the public Internet. More specifically, the IoT gateway only accepts incoming traffic from the Tor channel, while responding to the remote client with encrypted (data) traffic through the Internet channel.

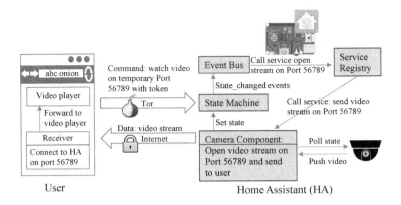

Fig. 5. An example of IoT gateway with split command and data channels: user sends request to watch camera video on port 56789 through the Tor channel, while Home Assistant temporarily opens port 56789 to deliver encrypted video through Internet.

With this scheme, the IoT gateway can still defend against vulnerability scanning by refusing to respond to any request coming from the Internet, such as ICMP ping, telnet, or HTTP request. The adversary obtains nothing by scanning the gateway with IP address. Besides, since the onion address of hidden service is only known by the user himself, the adversary cannot scan the gateway through Tor. Therefore, the security of the IoT gateway is still well protected. From the efficiency perspective, the incoming command traffic to the IoT gateway is usually transient and very small, so transmitting the commands through Tor will not introduce much overhead to Tor. In response to the command coming from the Tor channel, the gateway sends out bulk traffic, such as camera videos, to the user through the Internet channel. Since the video stream is transfered through the public Internet, we need to ensure strong encryption and mutual authentication between the user and the IoT gateway.

An overview of the protocol is shown in Fig. 5. Next, we deliberate this protocol with an example in which a user remotely requests video stream from a camera behind the IoT gateway.

Step 1: Connection Initialization Through Tor. The user connects to the IoT gateway, such as Home Assistant, using its onion address (e.g., abc.onion). At the client side, the user selects a device (e.g., a camera) and specifies a random high TCP port p_d for the data stream. Meanwhile, a 256-bit random token r_A, a 1024-bit random number x and its corresponding g^x (for Diffie-Hellman) will be generated. The random token r_A will be used for the later mutual authentication, and g^x will be used to generate the session key. Then, user submits this configuration to IoT gateway (e.g., Home Assistant) through Tor.

Step 2: Service Initialization at IoT Gateway. In a conventional IoT gateway, data will be disseminated to the user through the same channel as the incoming request. For example, video from the camera will be sent back to the user on the web interface, transmitted through Tor, if the request comes from Tor HS. In our scheme, we redesign the interfaces of the data-intensive devices, such as the Camera Component, so that the data stream is re-directed to a temporary port specified by the user, and transmitted to the user through the public Internet channel. To do so, we add a new functionality to the Camera Component and register this service (i.e., camera through Internet) to the Service Registry. Since this new service is implemented at the component level, it can work with different types of cameras seamlessly.

When Home Assistant receives user's request from the Tor channel, it generates a 256-bit random token r_{HS}, a 1024-bit random number y and its corresponding Diffie-Hellman number g^y. HA uses the received g^x and y to generate the session key g^{xy} and responds to user with the random token r_{HS} through the Tor channel. Meanwhile, HA opens port p_d, which is specified by the user, and waits for the connection for data dissemination, e.g., video streaming.

Step 3: Initialization of Data Channel Through Internet. After user receives the token r_{HS} and the second half of Diffie-Hellman handshake g^y through Tor, he will generate the session key g^{xy}, and send a request containing r_{HS} to Home Assistant through the data channel, which is encrypted with g^{xy}.

Step 4: Data Dissemination Through Internet. Once user's request for video stream arrives at port p_d through the Internet channel, Home Assistant decrypts it with the session key and verifies the token r_{HS}. If the authentication succeeds, Home Assistant sends r_A followed by the subsequent data to the user. The communication is encrypted with the session key. Meanwhile, HA discards requests that fail the authentication. Finally, when the user receives the reply, he decrypts it to get r_A to verify the server. If the authentication succeeds, he will accept the subsequent data stream. Otherwise, the connection will be closed.

5   Experiment and Performance Evaluation

To demonstrate the performance improvement of our proposed schemes, we implement all three Tor-based IoT gateway approaches, and perform experiments on the live Tor network. In particular, we compare network throughput for video streaming in the following settings: (1) the original Home Assistant without Tor hidden services (denoted by *HA-No-Tor*), (2) HA with single-path Tor hidden services (*HA-sTorHS*), (3) HA with multipath Tor hidden services (*HA-mTorHS*) and (4) HA with split command and data channel (*HA-Split*).

Setup. We deployed Home Assistant on a dedicated Raspberry Pi 2 [10] to simulate the proposed IoT gateway, which connects to a VStarCam IP camera [12]. The video stream is fed into Home Assistant via FFmpeg. The Raspberry Pi 2 is equipped with a 700 MHz ARM A6 microprocessor and 512 MB of RAM. The client accesses Home Assistant through a laptop with 2.5 GHz Intel i5 CPU, 8 GB RAM and OSX.

Experiments. To compute the throughput, we measure the overall time for the client to receive a 10 MB streaming data from Home Assistant. For *HA-Split*, we modify Home Assistant using Python 3 on the backend and Polymer on the frontend. For *HA-mTorHS*, we change the source code of Tor-v0.2.9.10. Note that all changes are made to the client's proxy and hidden server's proxy, so no change is needed on the Tor network. We compare two different multipath settings where the tunnel width m is set to 2 and 4, respectively. To eliminate the difference caused by circuits' capacities, we let the *HA-4TorHS* scheme to use the default path selection algorithm to choose relays for 4 circuits and record the used relays. Then, we let the *HA-2TorHS* scheme randomly choose 2 out of 4 circuits, while *HA-sTorHS* randomly chooses 1 from the 4 circuits. Each experiment is repeated 60 times over different time of a day, and the average transmission time for each approach is recorded.

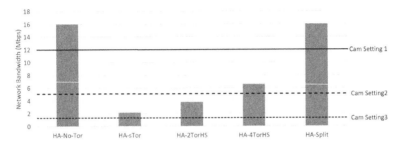

Fig. 6. Average network throughput provided by various approaches, compared with throughput needs of household IoT devices: Setting 1: two full HD (1280 × 1080) surveillance cameras, 30 fps, H.264 high quality compression; Setting 2: two HD 720p (1280 × 720) cameras, 30 fps, H.264 high quality compression; Setting 3: two HD 720p cameras, 15 fps, H.264 medium quality compression.

Results. Figure 6 compares the performance of different schemes. The Y-axis is the throughput measured from transmitting 10 MB video from the IoT camera. We can see that the baseline approach (HA-sTor) that directly integrates Tor hidden services into Home Assistant achieves the worst performance, which is almost 7 times slower than the direct access to HA through the public Internet (HA-No-Tor).

Figure 6 also shows that the proposed multipath Tor hidden services can improve the performance significantly. In particular, the *HA-2TorHS* scheme adopting two multipath circuits is 1.7 times faster than *HA-sTorHS*, while *HA-4TorHS* is 3 times faster. In fact, *HA-4TorHS* is fast enough for a typical home surveillance setting with two HD 720p (1280 × 720) cameras capturing at 30 fps with H.264 high quality compression.

Lastly, *HA-Split* can achieve the same performance as accessing Home Assistant without using Tor with a comparably weaker security guarantee. More specifically, it provides the same security guarantee for the command channel and the same anti-scanning feature for the IoT devices and HA. In summary, both *HA-mTorHS* (with $m > 3$) and *HA-Split* schemes can achieve an acceptable performance with enhanced security as we expect. We recommend users with larger throughput requirement to adopt the *HA-Split* scheme, which also avoids overloading the Tor network with a large amount of IoT data. While for users with higher security requirements, we recommend using the *HA-mTorHS* scheme, which hide both the IoT devices and the client behind Tor hidden service with a strong anonymity protection.

As we have discussed, a single Tor path can (and often) get congested. mTorHS with slow circuit detection and congestion control overcomes this problem. To demonstrate this, we conduct another experiment – a 6-hop path between the client and the hidden server is established using very fast relays measured by Tor, i.e., 3 relays used by client are 2391A, 92CFD and 3E13E, while 3 relay used by client are A7047, 96DAF and 8C23B. They are respectively Top $1\%, 5\%, 14\%, 30\%, 11\%$ and 20% fastest relays among all Tor routers at the time of experiment (July 12, 2017). Unfortunately, the real throughput of this path consisting of very fast relays was lower than average: it takes 55 s to transmit the 10 MB video file. This poor performance is usually due to congestion on at least one of relays in the path [37]. Then, for *HA-2TorHS*, we keep the first path as is, and add another path with congestion control. The performance is improved to 16 s for transmitting a 10 MB file, since most traffic can be routed through the second path, which may also alleviate the congestion on the first path. For *HA-4TorHS*, we add 2 more paths with congestion control, and the performance is further improved to 10 s.

6   Security Analysis

In this section, we analyze the security of two proposed schemes in terms of authentication, encryption and anti-scanning.

Authentication. Home Assistant provides optional password-based authentication, but it is not required. Besides, such an authentication approach has several known weaknesses such as weak passwords, which is a commonly observed in many use cases. Moreover, password-based authentication is particularly vulnerable if adversaries are allowed unlimited attempts when guessing the password. As a result, the embedded authentication of Home Assistant is not reliable.

To tackle this problem, our proposed schemes offer two additional layers of authentication provided by Tor hidden services. First, adversaries cannot access Home Assistant over hidden services without knowing the onion address of the device behind the gateway. Since the onion address generated by Tor is an 80-bit number in base32, it is not easy for adversaries to predict the one used by a target. In addition, even if the adversary obtains the onion address by chance, Tor hidden services also require users to have a 132-bit authentication cookie in base64 to access the hidden server. It is very difficult for adversaries to guess the correct combination of onion address and authentication cookie. Therefore, our schemes, by integrating Tor hidden services with the gateway, can provide a reliable authentication service to secure the IoT gateway.

Encryption. Home Assistant does not use HTTPS by default, so it is very insecure when accessing from remote. To address this problem, users are often suggested to set up additional link encryption using Let's Encrypt [7] for example. However, this requires a tedious process to configure the setup, especially for users who has little knowledge about networking and security. In practice, this usually discourages users from adopting secure configurations. On the contrary, our schemes are atop Tor hidden services, which have built-in onion encryption and end-to-end encryption. With a very simple configuration process during installation, we can set up the IoT gateway running over Tor hidden service. After that, all traffic that goes through Tor is well protected without any user involvement.

In the *HA-mTorHS* scheme, since all communication is over Tor, the data confidentiality completely relies on Tor's strong cryptography technologies. In the *HA-Separation* scheme, we use Tor channel for command and Internet channel for data. All commands are protected by Tor as discussed before, while data is also encrypted by an AES session key, which is negotiated through the command channel between user-end application and Home Assistant over hidden service.

Anti-scanning. Anti-scanning approach is an effective solution for cyberattacks against smart homes. The current Home Assistant running on the default port 8123 will respond to adversary's scanning on this port, so the adversary can find vulnerabilities and exploit them. In our *HA-mTorHS* scheme, all the access to Home Assistant must pass through the hidden services. Without knowing the onion address and the authentication cookie, adversary does not know the existence of Home Assistant, and thus cannot probe and access it. In our *HA-Separation* scheme, authentication and key negotiation are conducted through the command channel over Tor, so those vulnerability scanning techniques will not work any more. For data channel, it is still resistant to scanning when the port is temporarily open to the public Internet for data transmission due to two reasons: (1) On the data channel Home Assistant only responds to the connection request that contains the nonce encrypted by session key, which is sent to the user through Tor. Any other traffic will be dropped, so the scanning without the correct nonce will receive no response; (2) Since the port on Home Assistant is a random port and only temporarily open during data transmission, the adversary even may not have enough window of time to detect a open port via massive scanning, let alone a successful attack.

7   Related Work

Extensive research has been conducted to enhance the security of individual devices. For authentication, Liao et al. [28] propose a secure ECC-based RFID authentication scheme to realize the mutual authentication between devices.

Wu et al. [39] further improve the security by proposing lightweight private mutual authentication and private service discovery. For encryption, traditional cryptography can be applied to secure IoT. Dinu et al. introduce a benchmark framework to evaluate how well lightweight block ciphers, such as AES, RC5, Simon and Speck, etc., are suited to IoT devices. For communication, a bunch of dedicated protocols such as CoAP [34], RPL [38], and 6LoWPAN [33] and their variants have been proposed, which are not only lightweight for IoT devices but also security-oriented.

Another direction of approach that aims to achieve both security and efficiency is cloud-assisted IoT security designs. Since resource-constrained IoT devices usually cannot afford costly cryptographic techniques and large data storage, many schemes propose to solve this problem by leveraging the connected cloud, which provides powerful computation and storage capacity [23,24,40,44]. For example, [17,29] focus on cloud-assisted healthcare IoT, which mainly use the storage resources of the cloud. In [17], they proposed a scheme to add watermark into the collected data of a patient to avoid the privacy leakage on the cloud, while Yang et al. proposed a scheme that allows health service providers such as doctors to access and verify the encrypted medical records stored on the cloud by using a searchable encryption with forward privacy support [29]. In contrast, [28] utilizes the computation resources of the cloud to implement a data publishing scheme adopting attribute-based encryption, while [24] proposes a data access control scheme for constrained IoT devices and cloud computing based on hierarchical attribute-based encryption. The above solutions mainly focus on securing individual IoT devices, while IoT gives us a way to manage and secure a bunch of heterogeneous devices. For example, Intel IoT gateway can support comprehensive device protection with integrated McAfee, including secure boot, application integrity monitor, encrypted storage and more [6].

This work is also related to Tor routing optimization. Several multipath Tor schemes have been proposed to balance security and performance in Tor routing [14,41,42]. AlSabah et al. [14] first explored how to use multipath routing to improve Tor's performance, and Yang et al. [42] further analyzed the relay usage and proposed to use low-bandwidth relays to construct multiple circuits to improve performance and increase network utilization. Yang et al. [41] proposed a partial multipath routing scheme for Tor hidden services to enhance the resistance to traffic analysis. The tunnel is only built between the rendezvous point and the hidden server. They improve the anonymity based on the insight that traffic pattern are distorted by flow splitting and flow merging operations and by the multiple routes with different network dynamics. In contrast, with the goal of improving the performance, our proposed multipath Tor hidden services for IoT gateway adopts an end-to-end multipath structure, which leverages the end-to-end traffic management to work with network dynamics. Another notable difference is that our multipath scheme is transparent to Tor network, namely, no modifications are required on existing Tor routers except user proxy who is using multipath Tor, and thus, our scheme can be seamlessly adopted, while all other three schemes require new Tor routers to support their designs.

8   Conclusion

Security and privacy are critical issues in the adoption of IoT devices. IoT onion gateways provide strong security protection, but they suffer from the performance bottleneck caused by the limited bandwidth of Tor. To tackle this issue, we present a *multipath Onion IoT gateway*, which transmits IoT data stream through an anonymous tunnel with multiple Tor circuits with congestion control. We also present a *split channel Onion gateway*, which splits the command and data channels, to utilize the less-secure public Internet to route encrypted data streams. We have demonstrated the effectiveness, efficiency, and security guarantees of the proposed approach through experiments and security analysis.

Acknowledgment. This work is sponsored in part by the National Security Agency (NSA) Science of Security Initiative and the US National Science Foundation under NSF CNS-1422206 and DGE-1565570.

References

1. 9 baby monitors wide open to hacks that expose users' most private moments. https://arstechnica.com/security/2015/09/9-baby-monitors-wide-open-to-hacks-that-expose-users-most-private-moments/
2. Hack Samsung Fridge. https://www.pentestpartners.com/security-blog/hacking-defcon-23s-iot-village-samsung-fridge/
3. Hackers Make the First-Ever Ransomware for Smart Thermostats. https://motherboard.vice.com/en_us/article/aekj9j/internet-of-things-ransomware-smart-thermostat
4. Hacking 14 IoT Devices. https://www.iotvillage.org/slides_DC23/IoT11-slides.pdf
5. Home Assistant. https://home-assistant.io/
6. Intel IoT Gateway. https://www.intel.com/content/www/us/en/internet-of-things/gateway-solutions.html
7. Let's Encrypt. https://letsencrypt.org/
8. Openhab. https://www.openhab.org/
9. Ransomware Ruins Holiday By Hijacking Family's LG Smart TV on Christmas Day. https://www.yahoo.com/tech/ransomware-ruins-holiday-hijacking-familys-201136667.html
10. Raspberry Pi. https://www.raspberrypi.org/
11. Smartthings. http://www.samsung.com/us/smart-home/smartthings/hubs/f-hub-us-2-f-hub-us-2/
12. VStarCam Eye4. http://www.eye4.so/
13. Trendnet cameras - i always feel like somebody's watching me (2012). http://console-cowboys.blogspot.com/2012/01/trendnet-cameras-i-always-feel-like.html
14. AlSabah, M., Bauer, K., Elahi, T., Goldberg, I.: The path less travelled: overcoming Tor's bottlenecks with traffic splitting. In: De Cristofaro, E., Wright, M. (eds.) PETS 2013. LNCS, vol. 7981, pp. 143–163. Springer, Heidelberg (2013). https://doi.org/10.1007/978-3-642-39077-7_8
15. AlSabah, M., et al.: DefenestraTor: throwing out windows in Tor. In: Fischer-Hübner, S., Hopper, N. (eds.) PETS 2011. LNCS, vol. 6794, pp. 134–154. Springer, Heidelberg (2011). https://doi.org/10.1007/978-3-642-22263-4_8

16. Barré, S., Paasch, C., Bonaventure, O.: MultiPath TCP: from theory to practice. In: Domingo-Pascual, J., Manzoni, P., Palazzo, S., Pont, A., Scoglio, C. (eds.) NETWORKING 2011. LNCS, vol. 6640, pp. 444–457. Springer, Heidelberg (2011). https://doi.org/10.1007/978-3-642-20757-0_35

17. Burke, S.: Massive cyberattack turned ordinary devices into weapons (2016). http://money.cnn.com/2016/10/22/technology/cyberattack-dyn-ddos/index.html

18. Coldewey, D.: Smart locks yield to simple hacker tricks (2016). https://techcrunch. com/2016/08/08/smart-locks-yield-to-simple-hacker-tricks/

19. Dingledine, R., Mathewson, N., Syverson, P.: Tor: the second-generation onion router. In: Proceedings of the 13th USENIX Security Symposium, August 2004

20. Fernandes, E., Jung, J., Prakash, A.: Security analysis of emerging smart home applications. In: Proceedings of the 37th IEEE Symposium on Security and Privacy (2016)

21. Freitas, N.: Internet of onion things (2016). https://blog.torproject.org/blog/ quick-simple-guide-tor-and-internet-things-so-far

22. Gartner Inc.: Gartner IoT forecast (2017). http://www.gartner.com/newsroom/ id/3598917

23. Hossain, M.S., Muhammad, G.: Cloud-assisted industrial internet of things (IIoT)-enabled framework for health monitoring. Comput. Netw. **101**, 192–202 (2016)

24. Huang, Q., Wang, L., Yang, Y.: DECENT: secure and fine-grained data access control with policy updating for constrained IoT devices. World Wide Web **21**(1), 151–167 (2018)

25. Jia, Y.J., et al.: ContexIoT: towards providing contextual integrity to appified IoT platforms. In: Proceedings of The Network and Distributed System Security Symposium, vol. 2017 (2017)

26. Kim, J.E., Boulos, G., Yackovich, J., Barth, T., Beckel, C., Mosse, D.: Seamless integration of heterogeneous devices and access control in smart homes. In: 2012 8th International Conference on Intelligent Environments (IE), pp. 206–213. IEEE (2012)

27. Kothmayr, T., Schmitt, C., Hu, W., Brünig, M., Carle, G.: DTLS based security and two-way authentication for the internet of things. Ad Hoc Netw. **11**(8), 2710–2723 (2013)

28. Liao, Y.P., Hsiao, C.M.: A secure ECC-based RFID authentication scheme integrated with ID-verifier transfer protocol. Ad Hoc Netw. **18**, 133–146 (2014)

29. Ling, Z., Luo, J., Xu, Y., Gao, C., Wu, K., Fu, X.: Security vulnerabilities of internet of things: a case study of the smart plug system. IEEE Internet Things J. **4**(6), 1899–1909 (2017)

30. Ning, H., Liu, H., Yang, L.T.: Aggregated-proof based hierarchical authentication scheme for the internet of things. IEEE Trans. Parallel Distrib. Syst. **26**(3), 657–667 (2015)

31. Notra, S., Siddiqi, M., Gharakheili, H.H., Sivaraman, V., Boreli, R.: An experimental study of security and privacy risks with emerging household appliances. In: 2014 IEEE Conference on Communications and Network Security (CNS), pp. 79–84. IEEE (2014)

32. Raza, S., Shafagh, H., Hewage, K., Hummen, R., Voigt, T.: Lithe: lightweight secure CoAP for the internet of things. IEEE Sens. J. **13**(10), 3711–3720 (2013)

33. Shelby, Z., Bormann, C.: 6LoWPAN: The Wireless Embedded Internet, vol. 43. Wiley, Hoboken (2011)

34. Shelby, Z., Hartke, K., Bormann, C.: The constrained application protocol (CoAP) (2014)

35. Sivaraman, V., Chan, D., Earl, D., Boreli, R.: Smart-phones attacking smart-homes. In: Proceedings of the 9th ACM Conference on Security and Privacy in Wireless and Mobile Networks, pp. 195–200. ACM (2016)

36. Sivaraman, V., Gharakheili, H.H., Vishwanath, A., Boreli, R., Mehani, O.: Network-level security and privacy control for smart-home IoT devices. In: 2015 IEEE 11th International Conference on Wireless and Mobile Computing, Networking and Communications (WiMob), pp. 163–167. IEEE (2015)

37. Wang, T., Bauer, K., Forero, C., Goldberg, I.: Congestion-aware path selection for Tor. In: Keromytis, A.D. (ed.) FC 2012. LNCS, vol. 7397, pp. 98–113. Springer, Heidelberg (2012). https://doi.org/10.1007/978-3-642-32946-3_9

38. Winter, T.: RPL: IPv6 routing protocol for low-power and lossy networks (2012)

39. Wu, D.J., Taly, A., Shankar, A., Boneh, D.: Privacy, discovery, and authentication for the internet of things. In: Askoxylakis, I., Ioannidis, S., Katsikas, S., Meadows, C. (eds.) ESORICS 2016. LNCS, vol. 9879, pp. 301–319. Springer, Cham (2016). https://doi.org/10.1007/978-3-319-45741-3_16

40. Yang, L., Humayed, A., Li, F.: A multi-cloud based privacy-preserving data publishing scheme for the internet of things. In: Proceedings of the 32nd Annual Conference on Computer Security Applications, pp. 30–39. ACM (2016)

41. Yang, L., Li, F.: Enhancing traffic analysis resistance for tor hidden services with multipath routing. In: 2015 IEEE Conference on Communications and Network Security (CNS), pp. 745–746. IEEE (2015)

42. Yang, L., Li, F.: mTor: a multipath tor routing beyond bandwidth throttling. In: 2015 IEEE Conference on Communications and Network Security (CNS), pp. 479–487. IEEE (2015)

43. Yang, L., Xue, H., Li, F.: Privacy-preserving data sharing in smart grid systems. In: 2014 IEEE International Conference on Smart Grid Communications (SmartGridComm), pp. 878–883. IEEE (2014)

44. Yang, L., Zheng, Q., Fan, X.: RSPP: a reliable, searchable and privacy-preserving e-healthcare system for cloud-assisted body area networks. In: INFOCOM. IEEE (2017)

SCIoT: A Secure and sCalable End-to-End Management Framework for IoT Devices

Moreno Ambrosin[1]([⊠]) [ID], Mauro Conti[3][ID], Ahmad Ibrahim[2],
Ahmad-Reza Sadeghi[2], and Matthias Schunter[1]

[1] Intel Labs, Hillsboro, OR, USA
`moreno.ambrosin@intel.com`, `matthias.schunter@intel.com`
[2] TU Darmstadt, Darmstadt, Germany
{`ahmad.ibrahim`,`ahmad.sadeghi`}`@trust.tu-darmstadt.de`
[3] University of Padova, Padova, Italy
`conti@math.unipd.it`

Abstract. The Internet of Things (IoT) is connecting billions of smart devices. One of the emerging challenges in the IoT scenario is how to efficiently and securely manage large deployments of devices. This includes sending commands, monitoring status and execution results, updating devices firmware, and interactively resolving problems.

In this paper we propose SCIoT, a Secure and sCalable framework for IoT management. SCIoT guarantees low complexity in terms of communication, storage and computation on both managed devices and the management entity. SCIoT enables secure management of large deployments with a single low-power management device, by leveraging trees of common untrusted intermediate infrastructures. SCIoT brings three technical contributions: (1) a domain-independent management specification by means of extended finite state machines, which specifies states and desired transitions to describe the whole management process; (2) a protocol for securely and efficiently distributing applicable transitions of the automaton corresponding to commands; and (3) a protocol for securely aggregating status responses from the managed nodes using a tree of untrusted nodes. We show feasibility and efficiency of SCIoT by both a proof-of-concept implementation of the client agent on Riot-OS – an operating system for the IoT, and a large scale evaluation, using realistic assumptions. Our thorough evaluation highlights the efficiency of our command distribution protocol, as well as the small (logarithmic) runtime and overhead of data collection.

This research was co-funded by the German Science Foundation, as part of project S2 within CRC 1119 CROSSING, HWSec, the Intel Collaborative Research Institute for Collaborative Autonomous & Resilient Systems (ICRI-CARS), the EU TagItSmart! Project (agreement H2020-ICT30-2015-688061), and by the Intel grant "Scalable IoT Management and Key security aspects in 5G systems".

© Springer Nature Switzerland AG 2018
J. Lopez et al. (Eds.): ESORICS 2018, LNCS 11098, pp. 595–617, 2018.
https://doi.org/10.1007/978-3-319-99073-6_29

1   Introduction

The increasing demand of connectivity and services that rely on distributed sensing and control is populating the world with billions of interconnected devices. Cisco [2] forecasts that 50 billion of such devices will exist in 2020. This phenomenon is commonly called the Internet of Things (IoT). IoT devices are utilized in many different domains, ranging from small-size ecosystems, such as smart homes, to very large scale deployments for automation or distributed sensing. Examples of large IoT deployments are the experimentation facility at Santander city [27], which currently counts more than 2000 interconnected devices, and, at a much larger scale, smart metering systems, which only in the US count over 65 million devices [17].

IoT devices have constrained resources and limited (usually intermittent) connectivity. They are usually connected to edge (or gateway) devices, which provide services such as protocol translation, access to intermediate connectivity infrastructures, and data caching and aggregation at the edge of the network; these features are particularly useful in large scale deployments [12,20,22,33].

In many deployments, an efficient and effective management of IoT devices is fundamental [29]. Device management comprises critical tasks, such as distribution of commands and software updates, or device monitoring. Management processes are typically planned and controlled by systems administrators. In this paper, we consider a scenario in which a system administrator, which may have limited computational resources, needs to manage a large population of IoT devices.[1] We consider a management process comprising two main tasks: (1) broadcasting a subset of commands to targeted devices (accompanied by additional corresponding data, such as command parameters or a firmware update package); and (2) collecting statistics on the outcome of commands execution. As an example, the system administrator of a large deployment may want to know the percentage of devices that are in a correct (known) state, after a collective software update has been executed. Management operations are performed over an intermediate aggregation and cache-capable network, which is untrusted for providing data integrity or authenticity.

In the above scenario, secure and efficient management turns out to be particularly challenging: On the one hand, while solutions and standards for secure and lightweight IoT device management already exist (e.g., the work in [29], or the Lightweight Machine to Machine protocol from the Open Mobile Alliance – OMA LWM2M [25]), they are designed for *individual* device management. Therefore, unless all intermediate aggregation nodes are trusted, their cost scales linearly with the number of devices to be managed. On the other hand, existing approaches for efficient aggregate statistics collection over an aggregation tree impose a linear verification overhead on the management entity [16,34].

Contribution. This paper presents SCIoT, a framework for IoT device management that targets large deployments. SCIoT considers a layered and realistic

---

[1] Industrial trends envision using low-power devices, e.g., a smartphone, for managing a large number of devices.

architecture, and on top of it defines a set of protocols for scalable and secure IoT device management. In particular, this paper brings the following contributions:

- A simple domain-independent management process abstraction by means of a finite state machine, that we call Management Finite State Machine (M-FSM). M-FSM allows to express potentially complex management tasks using a concise and high-level representation.
- The design of a simple, fully-cacheable, and end-to-end secure protocol for commands distribution, based on the management representation provided by M-FSM. Our protocol can sit on top of any pull-based message-response protocols. It leverages in-network caching to speed-up commands distribution. SCIoT's commands distribution protocol allows clients to "manage themselves", i.e., only selectively download the specific subset of information needed to take the next management action (e.g., a specific software update).
- The design of a protocol for scalable monitoring of large deployments. We devise an aggregation protocol based on the protocol from [16] that leverages an *untrusted* tree-based aggregation infrastructure to aggregate inbound status information, while maintaining a constant verification overhead at both device and management side, and a logarithmic traffic. Our protocol ensures that even if millions of nodes report back to a central management node, traffic and required computation at the server remains manageable.
- We implemented and tested a client device agent for Riot-OS – an operating system for resource-constrained devices – and ran a thorough experimental evaluation of our protocols via simulation (similar to [7,8]); our evaluation demonstrates the scalability of SCIoT, and its low overhead at the management side.

2 Background and Primitives

2.1 Multi-signature

A multi-signature scheme allows a set of users to compute a signature on the same message m so that individual signatures can be aggregated into a single compact multi-signature. The multi-signature can be verified in constant time by means of a unique aggregate public key. Signature verification succeeds if *all* the computed signatures are included into the multi-signature. In this paper, we consider the multi-signature scheme in [10], built using bilinear pairings [11].

Consider three multiplicative groups $\mathbb{G}_1$, $\mathbb{G}_2$ and $\mathbb{G}_T$ of prime order p, and an efficiently computable bilinear map $e : \mathbb{G}_1 \times \mathbb{G}_2 \to \mathbb{G}_T$ s.t., $e(g_1, g_2)^{xy} = g_t^{xy}$, where g_1, g_2, g_T are generators for $\mathbb{G}_1$, $\mathbb{G}_2$ and $\mathbb{G}_T$, respectively, and $x, y \in \mathbb{Z}_p$. Let $H : \{0,1\}^* \to \mathbb{G}_1$ be a hash function that maps a bitstring of arbitrary size into an element of $\mathbb{G}_1$. A multi-signature scheme is defined as follows:

Key Generation. Each signer i generates a random secret key $x_i \in \mathbb{Z}_p$, and computes its public key as $pk_i \leftarrow g_2^{x_i}$. Public keys can be aggregated into an aggregate public key $Y \leftarrow \prod_{i=1}^{n} pk_i$, where n is the number of signers.

Multisignature Generation. A signer i produces a signature σ_i on a message m as $\sigma_i \leftarrow H(m)^{x_i}$; all σ_i-s can be combined into a multi-signature $\Sigma \leftarrow \prod_{i=1}^{n} \sigma_i$, where n is the number of signers.

Multisignature Verification. Given the aggregate public key Y, the multi-signature Σ can be verified by checking whether $e(\Sigma, g_2) = e(H(m), Y)$.

This multi-signature scheme is provably secure against existential forgery under chosen message attacks in any Gap Diffie-Hellman (GDH) group [10].

2.2   Secure In-Network Aggregation

In-network aggregation allows reducing the communication overhead when performing queries and collecting statistics from nodes in large networks. In this paper, we devise a hierarchical in-network aggregation scheme with constant verification overhead. Our scheme is based on the solution from [16] and satisfies the requirement of SCIoT.

Our in-network aggregation scheme is organized in two main phases: (i) a query dissemination and response collection phase, and (ii) a result verification phase.

Collection Phase. In this phase a central querying entity (i.e., the manager in SCIoT) broadcasts a query to all nodes in the network along an aggregation tree. Then, starting at leaves, nodes recursively aggregate responses coming from their child nodes and forward the result to their parent nodes. Each node also commits to its aggregation by computing and forwarding a hash over all the responses it aggregates. The computed hash also include hashes that come from child nodes. Finally, the final aggregate response and commitment are reported back to the querying entity.

Verification Phase. In this phase the querying entity broadcasts the received aggregate response and commitment, asking nodes to check whether their contribution has been integrated correctly in that response. Each individual device verifies their correct contribution to the final response and creates an acknowledgment message and sends it the querying entity. Acknowledgment messages are authenticated using the multi-signature scheme we introduced above, which allows their secure aggregation with constant communication and verification overhead.

3   SCIoT Architecture Design

3.1   System Model

We define the system model in Fig. 1, where a manager $\mathcal{M}$, is in charge of carrying out the management of (some or all the devices in) a network G. More

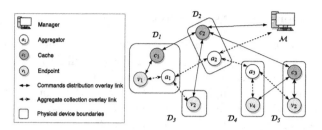

Fig. 1. System model as a network of devices; each device acts as at least one of the following entities: endpoint (v_j), aggregator (a_l), and cache (c_u).

precisely, we consider a network of interconnected physical devices $\mathcal{D}_i \in G$ (each pictured as a dotted rectangle in Fig. 1), where each can act as one or more of the following logical entities: *endpoint* (v_j), *aggregator* (a_l), or *cache* (c_u). A endpoint v_j is the endpoint entity of the management process; v_j receives and executes commands from $\mathcal{M}$ and, upon request, provides $\mathcal{M}$ with statistical information regarding its current status. Aggregators and caches are relay entities (i.e., edge or gateway devices) that have different roles: a_l is capable of aggregating statistics collected from endpoints, while c_u caches commands distributed by $\mathcal{M}$. As a consequence, they play a role in distinct parts of the management process, i.e., c_u helps speeding up one-to-many commands distribution, while a_l has the purpose of reducing both network and $\mathcal{M}$-side computation overhead when collecting statistics from v_j.

Entities in the system are organized into two logical tree structures:[2] a *distribution tree* where inner nodes are caching entities and leaf nodes are managed entities (solid lines in Fig. 1), and an analogous *aggregation tree* that has aggregating entities as inner nodes, and managed entities are leaves (dashed lines in Fig. 1). Note that, in this model a failing inner node can be simply replaced by its parent in the tree. The connection interfaces between nodes are purely logical, i.e., they do not necessarily have a one-to-one mapping with a single physical communication interface. A clear example is v_1 in Fig. 1: interactions with both c_1 and a_1 are performed internally to the physical device $\mathcal{D}_1$. Similarly, v_4 communicates with a_3 through an internal interface, while it communicates with c_3 (which is located in $\mathcal{D}_5$) through a network link.

This representation is sufficiently generic to represent different scenarios and use cases, from Wireless Sensor Networks (WSNs), where all the devices in the network act as all the three entities, to infrastructured settings, where IoT devices act as endpoint entities, while gateways represent either caches, or aggregators, or both. Note that, the definition of our management scheme is independent from the caching strategy adopted by caching entities. However, the capacity of caches together with the adopted caching policy, play an important role in improving the performance of the system. Nevertheless, this usually depends on the deployment scenario, and the capabilities of devices. Thus, we consider this to be out-of-scope.

---

[2] See [8] for how aggregation trees are constructed and maintained.

3.2   Requirements and Assumptions

Scalability and Security Requirements. We aim at providing a highly scalable solution for management systems, which enables handling a large number of devices, through a resource constrained manager. Our goal is to reduce both computation and storage complexity for $\mathcal{M}$, while at the same time maintain a low communication and computation overhead on a_l, c_u and v_j. More precisely, we identify the following set of properties that defines a scalable and secure management system:

1. *Outbound efficiency.* The management system should guarantee an efficient broadcast distribution of management commands to endpoints.
2. *Commands freshness.* The system should provide mechanisms to allow endpoints to assess whether a received command is still valid.
3. *Inbound efficiency.* $\mathcal{M}$ should efficiently collect aggregate statistics of endpoints (e.g., the number of endpoints in a certain state).
4. *Outbound security.* It should be guaranteed that only legitimate management commands coming from the manager are executed on endpoints.
5. *Inbound security.* The integrity of the statistics collected from endpoints should be ensured.

Security Model. We assume $\mathcal{M}$ is trusted, i.e., it honestly follows the management process and protocols. We also assume that $\mathcal{M}$ issues authorized management commands for distribution. We do not trust all the intermediate entities that are responsible for aggregation and caching, i.e., a_l, and c_u. All these entities can be under full control of the adversary. As for v_j, we assume these entities are trusted in executing management commands and providing statistical information. We assume all devices that contain a v_j to have the necessary security hardware that protect v_j from compromise (e.g., TrustLite [24]). Finally, we consider a stealthy adversary that aim at manipulating the management and collection process without being detected. Thus, we consider Denial of Service (DoS) attacks that aim at undermining the availability of these services to be out-of-scope.

Attacker Goals. The goals of the adversary controlling c_u are to: (i) Tamper with commands sent by $\mathcal{M}$; and (ii) Impersonate $\mathcal{M}$ issuing commands to v_j. Analogously, an adversary controlling one or more aggregating entities a_l, has the following goals: (a) Tampering with the statistics collected from one or more devices; and (b) Impersonating a device sending fake statistics to $\mathcal{M}$.

3.3   FSM Abstract Specification of Management Objectives

An important component of SCIoT is the abstraction we use to decouple domain-specific management requirements from the actual realization of the management process. Such abstraction allows to define a management-independent communication protocol between endpoints and $\mathcal{M}$, which is both simple and highly scalable. The main intuition behind this abstraction is to allow $\mathcal{M}$ to carry out the whole management process by simply serving, upon devices' request, a set of static (and therefore cacheable) contents. These contents are efficiently delivered to the endpoints by leveraging the intermediate caching entities c_u.

We represent our management process specification by means of an extended finite state machine, that we call Management Finite State Machine (M-FSM). M-FSM represents, in its minimal form (i.e., sub-M-FSM), a single command execution. Sub-M-FSM comprises (see Fig. 2):

- At least three *states* a device can assume: (1) a *starting* state, representing a device waiting for a command to execute; (2) an *attempted execution* state, representing the device after the execution of the command; and (3) at least one *termination* state (e.g., a system failure). Each state is uniquely identified by an ID SID.
- At least two *transitions*: (1) one transition from the starting state to the attempted execution state. This transition is labeled by an `execute` event and a corresponding `COMMAND` action (i.e., a command to execute); and (2) at least one transition ending to a terminal state. Actions are executed by the function `Execute`, and may write into global variables. In particular, the `COMMAND` writes its outcome (i.e., the return code of the command) in the `out` variable. Outgoing transitions from the attempted execution state are labeled with a `switch` event, parametrized on the value of the `out` variable, and an `OTHER_ACTION` to execute. These transitions can "point" to either a terminal state, or the starting state of another sub-M-FSM.

Figure 2 provides a graphical representation of a sub-M-FSM, where ovals represent states, and arrows represent state transitions. Events and corresponding actions are placed on top of each transition and separated by "|". Boolean guards, based on which transition is chosen, are indicated within squared brackets. The sub-M-FSM in Fig. 2 represents a single command execution (or may represent a loop, in case the sub-M-FSM has a transition from the executing to the starting state). More complex execution processes can be obtained combining several sub-M-FSMs, to represent the execution of consecutive commands where the execution of a subsequent command depends on the successful execution of the previous one. This is done by adding an outgoing transition (based on the outcome of the command) from the attempted execution state to the starting state of another sub-M-FSM.

M-FSM Composability and Overhead. It is worth noticing that, as the M-FSM is a composition of single sub-M-FSMs, each representing a command execution, in a management process the M-FSM can be arbitrarily incremented with additional M-FSMs *over time*. This property is particularly useful in the management scenario, as it allows to model management processes that cannot be completely defined statically, such as subsequent firmware/software update releases. As a consequence, from an endpoint perspective, at a generic point in time t_i the entire management process can be represented only as the *current* command to execute. This guarantees an almost *constant* overhead at the endpoint.

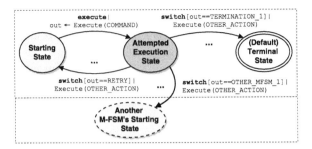

Fig. 2. Basic sub-M-FSM. A device in "Starting" state executes the only transition to the attempted execution state, performing an action Execute. Depending on the outcome (e.g., return code) out of Execute, the device might follow one of the outgoing transitions: to the starting state, to a termination state, or to (the starting state of) another sub-M-FSM.

Use Case Example (Device Firmware Update M-FSM). An interesting use case M-FSM is the (simplified) device firmware update process shown in Fig. 3. A single device update process is composed of an update installation phase, and a recovery attempt phase. These two phases are represented by analogous sub-M-FSMs. The update process starts from a "Not Updated" state (S1); the execute transition (and the consequent execution via Execute of UPDATE) brings the device into an "Update Attempted" state (S2). The function Execute writes its outcome (e.g., an integer code) into the global variable out. Based on out, the device follows a specific switch transition, and executes the NULL action (i.e., no action is executed). In case of FATAL_ERROR, the process moves to a terminal "System Failure" state (S3). If, instead, the update process terminates successfully (i.e., out == SUCCESS), the device jumps to the starting state of the next sub-M-FSM in the process specification.[3] Finally, if the update process encountered a recoverable error (SIMPLE_ERROR), it switches to a recovery phase, jumping to the initial state "Erroneous State" of the Recovery Phase sub-M-FSM. In such phase, the device tries to recover the previous software state by executing a RECOVERY action with the function execute, jumping to a "Recovery Attempted" state. The outcome of execute is written into out2, which is used to switch to an end state (representing a fatal unrecoverable error), or to the previous "Not Updated" state.

Note that, in order to avoid an infinite number of attempts, the action RECOVERY maintains a counter, recording the number of attempts made by the device; if this number is greater than a threshold, execute will return a FATAL_ERROR (this is not shown in Fig. 3 for simplicity). Furthermore, while shown in Fig. 3 as a transition to a different state S7, in practice, in order to avoid state explosion [32], S2 switch transition may simply return to S1, which represents a "Not Updated" state, but with a different SID.

---

[3] New "Not Updated" state, which will have a different SID w.r.t. the previous analogous state.

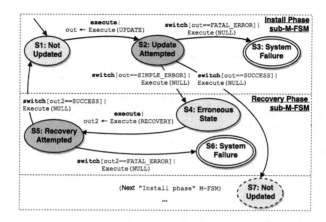

Fig. 3. Example: firmware update management.

4   SCIoT Protocols

4.1   A Scalable Self-management Protocol

The first main component of SCIoT is a simple and scalable protocol to distribute management commands from $\mathcal{M}$ to endpoints v_j. Commands distribution is based on an M-FSM specification (e.g., firmware update M-FSM in Sect. 3.3). Based on abstraction provided by the M-FSM, we designed a secure pull-based message-response protocol which allows: (1) domain-independent device management; (2) efficient cacheable distribution of management commands, suitable for caching networks or content delivery networks; and (3) minimal storage requirement on endpoints.

In order to simplify the exposition, in what follows we detail our self-management protocol between a single endpoint v_j, and $\mathcal{M}$.

The main idea behind our protocol is the following. Each endpoint v_j "moves" inside the M-FSM maintaining information about its current state only, while pulling the next available transition from $\mathcal{M}$. More precisely, v_j pulls either: (a) An `execute` event, and corresponding `COMMAND` action, from a starting state; or (b) A `switch` event and corresponding `OTHER_ACTION` action from an attempted execution state. v_j queries $\mathcal{M}$ issuing a *request message* (*req*) that is forwarded through intermediate c_u entities. $\mathcal{M}$ then responds with a *response messages* (*resp*). Note that, caching entities may cache response messages, before serving them back to the querier, to better serve "bursty" requests and reduce latency. This is particularly important when devices request large payloads, such as firmware updates [6]. This communication model is supported by existing application level protocols (such as CoAP [14], which implements a message-response protocol on top of UDP), as well as by recently proposed information-centric protocols (such as Named-Data Networking [23]).

Protocol Description. As shown in Fig. 4, from a state SID, v_j queries $\mathcal{M}$ for the next available transition (and event-action pair). More precisely, v_j sends a

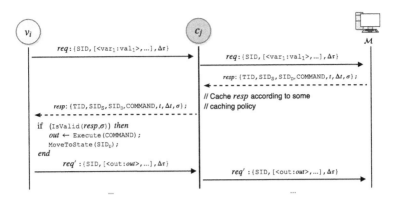

Fig. 4. Self-management protocol using μTesla. Here, we assume v_i already has a commitment (i.e., a key it trusts) corresponding to time interval $\tau - 2$.

req message, which contains v_j's current state ID SID, and a list of key-value pairs $[< var_1 : val_1 >, ...]$ indicating M-FSM variables, and their current value. These parameters are used by $\mathcal{M}$, or by caching entities, to select the matching response packet to return to v_j. Note that, the way SID and the key-value pairs are included as parameters of v_j's request depends on the adopted underlying transport protocol.

The response supplied by $\mathcal{M}$ contains the next event and action to execute (using the function Execute). Once the command in action is executed, v_j jumps to the next attempted execution state, and issues a new request message *req'*. The endpoint then obtains a new event and action to execute and move to the next M-FSM state, which can be either terminal or starting state – MoveToState.

In case of large command payloads, e.g., a new firmware, the action specifies only a "pointer", e.g., a hash of the payload, to use for (potentially cached) payload retrieval. v_j then downloads the payload in an additional step. Note that, as caching entities may directly respond to *req* with a cached response, we added a timestamp parameter t and a validity interval Δt to each (signed) response returned to v_j. In this way, endpoints can determine whether a received transition (or command payload) is "fresh", i.e., not expired according to t and Δt. In order to guarantee availability, intermediate caching entities must ensure that devices are able to detect whether a content is fresh or not, and should provide mechanisms to "force" requests to be served directly from the source.[4]

Protocol Security. SCIoT works in conjunction with several security layers suitable for large scale broadcast distribution. In particular, in SCIoT $\mathcal{M}$ may either

---

[4] This feature is transport specific: In content-centric protocols such as Named-Data Networking (NDN) [23], content freshness is controlled by flags contained inside headers, i.e., via data packet's **Freshness** and interest's **MustBeFresh** header fields. In CoAP [14], however, this is not possible. Response packets carry a **Max-Age** option indicating that the response is to be considered not fresh after its age is greater than the specified number of seconds.

use digital signatures, or μTesla authenticated broadcast protocol [26] to authenticate management commands. Using μTesla, SCIoT's management automation protocol guarantees public verifiability for resource-constrained devices (i.e., devices able to compute only basic cryptographic operations, such as hash functions and Message Authentication Codes – MACs), while preserving the cacheability of the distributed data.

Depending on the authentication mechanism in use, responses generated by $\mathcal{M}$ are sent along with either a digital signature, or a MAC. In the case of digital signatures, $\mathcal{M}$ signs each response with its secret key $sk_\mathcal{M}$ and endpoints verify it using $\mathcal{M}$'s public key $pk_\mathcal{M}$. On the other hand, while using μTesla $\mathcal{M}$ attaches a MAC to each response, computed using a symmetric key k_τ that is valid only within a certain time interval τ. At time $\tau + d$, k_τ is disclosed, i.e., broadcasted in a special packet. Endpoints can then verify the MAC on the buffered response packets received during time interval τ [26]. In detail, v_j downloads the next transition packet from $\mathcal{M}$ at time τ, and stores it in a local cache. v_j verifies the message at time $\tau + d$, i.e., after receiving the broadcasted key k_τ. This process is shown in Fig. 4. In order to build a cryptographically verifiable key series, $\mathcal{M}$ makes use of one way hash chains, i.e., the key used at time τ is obtained as the hash of the key that will be used at time $\tau + 1$ [26]. Note that, different applications may require different key disclosure time intervals. For this reason, $\mathcal{M}$ keeps several *key sequences*, generated from different hash chains and have different key disclosure time intervals. Upon receiving a request *req*, $\mathcal{M}$ computes the MAC on each response using different keys. The key sequence to be used is specified in *req*.

While the digital signature is permanently cacheable, MACs have an expiration period, which corresponds to the key disclosure time. Endpoints are free to choose between requesting a response with a digital signature or a MAC. In other words, endpoints can autonomously determine the best trade-off between computation overhead and the delay in the reception of the data. Devices choose between different options based on a set of factors, including their computational power, remaining energy, and the time limits specified by the application. Moreover, endpoints can choose between MACs with different "delays" (i.e., key disclosure interval $\Delta\tau$) based on their degree of synchronization. This provides a trade-off between security level and response delay. The number of MACs and the time interval for each hash chain are design parameters that may depend on the properties of the network (e.g., bandwidth or size), and on the requirements for different applications.

4.2 Scalable Device Monitoring and Assessment

The protocol described in Sect. 4.1 alone enables managed entities to execute available commands, perform state transitions, and conduct error recovery as specified by the management finite-state automaton. However, it does not allow the management layer to learn to what extent the management strategy has been successful. A simple example is that $\mathcal{M}$ would not learn if a given firmware update always leads to failures. More generally, $\mathcal{M}$ needs to collect and maintain statistics, such as the percentage of endpoints that are in a certain state in the update process shown in Sect. 3.3.

Naïve Approach. A naïve approach for device state assessment would be by requesting the required information from each device individually; $\mathcal{M}$ could broadcast a challenge, and collect the individual responses from endpoints. This approach, however, is hard to scale, as it would result in $\mathcal{O}(|G|)$ traffic and verification complexity.

In-Network Aggregation. A more scalable way to collect the global network state is relying on in-network aggregation. Each device reports its state to its upstream aggregating node. This, in turn, computes the aggregate sum of each value coming from its children and forwards it to its parent aggregating node in the internal tree structure, and so on. Using authenticated channels, $\mathcal{M}$ can efficiently verify the authenticity of the received aggregate counts. This simple approach has been adopted in several solutions, such as in [8]. However, a major important drawback of simple aggregation is the absence of end-to-end integrity in presence of malicious aggregating entities, i.e., in-network aggregation requires fully trusted aggregators [7].

Secure In-Network Aggregation. Our approach for collecting statistics on endpoints over untrusted aggregators is based on the hierarchical secure in-network aggregation scheme presented in Sect. 2. It allows: (1) using in-network aggregation to compute an aggregate value, and (2) integrity verification by $\mathcal{M}$ in *constant time*. Recall that aggregation in SCIoT is performed by logical aggregating entities, which (similarly to [7,8]) can form an overlay aggregation tree rooted at $\mathcal{M}$, where aggregating entities a_l are inner nodes, and v_j are leaves. Finally, aggregating nodes are also untrusted for authenticity of aggregation. The overall protocol runs as follows:

- The manager $\mathcal{M}$ broadcasts the state it is interested in collecting statistics for (either signed with $\mathcal{M}$'s secret key, or using an authenticated broadcasts protocol, such as the one described in Sect. 4.1).
- Each endpoint v_j responds with 1 if it is currently in that state, and with 0 otherwise.
- Intermediate aggregators sum the received values, and forward the computed value up to $\mathcal{M}$.
- After collecting the aggregate value computed on phase (i), $\mathcal{M}$ broadcasts the final aggregate result authenticated in the same manner as above.
- Based on the commitments (see Sect. 2), endpoints can verify that their contribution has been added to the aggregate value. If this is the case, each endpoint v_i produces a multi-signature σ_i on a pre-established "OK" message using its secret key sk_i. Otherwise (in case the verification fails), it sends a negative acknowledgment (NACK) to its gateway aggregator.
- Aggregators combine all the signatures (along the formed overlay aggregation tree) according to the multi-signature scheme described in Sect. 2, and finally deliver a single aggregate signature Σ to $\mathcal{M}$.
- $\mathcal{M}$ can verify the signature using the pre-computed aggregate public key Y.

Note that, in the case in which the verification fails, $\mathcal{M}$ can conclude that an error happened, i.e., the contribution of a node was lost, or that some aggregator maliciously modified either the aggregate value, or the signature.

Inspecting Individual Devices. The protocol discussed in the previous sections, count the devices in each given state. However, in some cases, inspection of a given small number of devices may be desirable. In order to enable device inspection, the manager can issue a call-back command to all endpoints in a given state. This command triggers the devices to "call home", report their ID, and then be available for further debugging. To enable this, an endpoint can be "probed" by $\mathcal{M}$, and respond with the identifier of its current status in a signed response message. Note that, unless debugging is constrained to few devices, this might quickly create a bottleneck on the whole system, especially in the case in which $\mathcal{M}$ needs to collect several periodical statistics from the devices.

5   Prototype Implementation

We implemented SCIoT's client agent as a module for Riot-OS [9, 21] (i.e., targeting IETF Class 1 and 2 devices [13]). This module implements both SCIoT's commands distribution protocol, and responds to device assessment requests from $\mathcal{M}$. $\mathcal{M}$ implementation is fairly simple, as it consists in a simple server application that exposes basic APIs (later discussed in this section), and periodically queries devices; for this reason, it will not be discussed in this section.

Riot-OS [9, 21] is an operating systems suitable for resource constrained environments. It implements a micro-kernel architecture, and allows applications to include only the minimum modules necessary for their execution. Furthermore, Riot-OS does not differentiate between processes and threads. Each application runs on its own thread of execution, but can freely create other threads (the limit in number is given by the available memory). Our client implementation module exposes a concise set of APIs, and can be easily utilized by applications to automate management tasks.

Our implementation uses CoAP [14] for both M-FSM management, and to deliver statistics collection queries from $\mathcal{M}$ to endpoints.

The device agent runs on its own thread of execution (see Fig. 5), and interacts with a simple CoAP server. An application that needs to carry out a management process should wait for transitions (i.e., commands) coming from the agent via Riot-OS IPC (Inter-Process Communication), and react accordingly, i.e., execute a command with a specific ID. The device "talks" to a server via a minimal set of CoAP REST APIs. The server runs either at the manager, or on an edge node, which may act as a proxy and translate CoAP requests into HTTP [18]. The client device requests transitions by issuing a CoAP request

$$\texttt{coap} : //[\texttt{SERVER\_IP}]/\texttt{sid?sid} = \texttt{SID}\&\ldots,$$

where SERVER_IP is either the IP address of $\mathcal{M}$, or of the 1st-hop aggregating node, and $\texttt{sid} = \texttt{SID}$ is the only mandatory parameter of the query. Similarly,

the agent running on the device accepts CoAP assessment requests for a state
ID SID, of the form:

$$\text{coap} : //[\text{BROADCAST\_IP}]/\text{assess}/?\text{nonce} = \text{N}\&\text{sid} = \text{SID}.$$

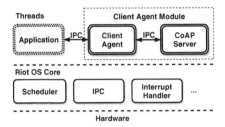

Fig. 5. Client agent module for Riot-OS.

6   Performance Evaluation

In this section, we present an evaluation of our solution, based on our implementation presented in Sect. 5, and on an emulated, yet realistic setting. Our
considered setting consists of low-end devices compatible in capabilities with M3
Open Node devices from the IoT-Lab/SensLAB testbed [3]. These devices are
featured with an ARM Cortex M3, 32-bits microcontroller running at 72 MHz,
64 Kbyte of RAM, and a 2.4 GHz IEEE 802.15.4 capable transceiver [4]. Moreover, we consider $\mathcal{M}$ to be a low-cost medium-power device, compatible with a
Raspberry Pi Mod B, i.e., equipped with a 700 MHz CPU, 512 Mbyte of RAM,
and 2 Gbyte of storage.

We implemented the multi-signature scheme we introduced in Sect. 4.2, based
on the embedded system library in [31]; we used the mbedTLS library [1] for the
remaining cryptographic operations: SHA-1 based HMAC (Hmac_1), and ECDSA.
We evaluated the approaches we presented in Sect. 4 at large scale using network
simulation.

6.1   Storage Overhead

Aggregating nodes, a_l, do not need to store any information. Caching entities
have a storage overhead which depends on the size of their cache, and the data
currently contained in it. An endpoint v_i keeps in its persistent storage: (i) $\mathcal{M}$'s
public key $pk_\mathcal{M}$ (32 byte in case of public key), or the commitment for the
whole key chain (20 byte in case of μTesla [26]); (ii) the current state of the
M-FSM, which comprises the ID SID_j (2 byte); (iii) $\mathcal{D}_i$'s public and private
multi-signature keys (256 byte and 32 byte, respectively). The overall storage
requirement of each device is 322 byte, if public key is used, and 310 byte if
μTesla is used. Low-end devices targeted by SCIoT have at least 1024 bytes of
secondary memory [7], and thus SCIoT will use 31.4% of it when the public key
is used, and 30.3% otherwise.

6.2   Communication Overhead

We now provide an estimate of the bytes transmitted between an endpoint v_j, and $\mathcal{M}$. In general the use of μTesla generates an overhead of one key release (approx 30 byte [26]) per time interval τ of each time series. Note that, we focus only on the overhead introduced by SCIoT protocols, and thus, we do not include the overhead generated by the underlying protocol stack.[5]

Commands Distribution. When requesting a transition, $\mathcal{D}_i$ produces a request indicating the ID SID of its current state, and, if using μTesla, the parameter $\Delta\tau$, indicating the time series $\mathcal{D}_i$ is using. This generates at most as little as 6 bytes. $\mathcal{M}$ sends out a packet comprising a transition (TID, SID_S, SID_D, and a command), a timestamp t, a validity interval Δt, and an authenticator (i.e., a digital signature or a MAC). Referring to our implementation in Sect. 5, and considering 4 bytes for both t and Δt, the overall communication overhead of command distribution protocol is between 80 and 334 byte, when using digital signatures, and between 37 and 291 byte, when using μTesla.

Device Assessment. In the first phase of this scheme each device sends a 26 byte *label*. The amount of bytes generated by the second part of the protocol is logarithmic in the size of the network. More precisely, the overhead of this protocol varies based on the height of the aggregation tree, and the number of leaf endpoint nodes. This overhead is mainly due to the *off-path*[6] information required by the scheme to allow each device to verify whether its contribution has been added to the aggregate value. The off-path values are locally cached by each aggregating node during the data collection, and re-distributed by the network in the second step of the scheme. Each label has a size of 26 byte. Thus, let h be the height of the tree formed by aggregating nodes (only), and l the number of leaves (i.e., endpoints) connected to the last layer of the aggregating tree; the total communication overhead on each endpoint, in terms of received data, is $26 \times (h+l)$ byte. As an example, consider a binary tree, and let $l = 2^4 = 16$, and $n = 2^{10}$; in this case, $h = 14$, and thus, the average amount of bytes received by each endpoint will be 780 byte. Finally, the acknowledgment sent by each endpoint (and aggregated by aggregators) consists of 84 byte (a 20 byte nonce, and a 64 byte multi-signature).

6.3   Runtime

We estimate the runtime of both the command distribution protocol (Sect. 4.1), and the statistics collection protocol (Sect. 4.2). Execution time is mainly dominated by cryptographic operations, and data transmission. Table 1 shows the time overhead introduced by the adopted cryptographic operations on two types of devices: M3 device (low- end) from IoT-LAB, and Raspberry Pi Mod B (higher-end).

---

[5] Typically, the stack comprises CoAP, 6LowPAN, IPv6 and 802.15.4. Additional overhead is introduced by protocol headers, plus possible segmentation or fragmentation.

[6] For each node, off-path information are the commitments of every child nodes of each node that is on its path to the manager.

Table 1. Cryptographic overhead

Function	Time (ms)	
	M3 IoT-LAB (Endpoint)	Raspberry Pi Mod B (Aggregator)
$H(m) \in \mathbb{G}_1$[a]	360.319	89.168
g_1^x, $g_1 \in \mathbb{G}_1$	494.619	124.604
$g_1 \times g_1'$, $g_1, g_1 \in \mathbb{G}_1$	23.615	8.459
$e : \mathbb{G}_1 \times \mathbb{G}_2 \to \mathbb{G}_T$	$-$[b]	1.736
Hash_1[c]	0.102	0.031
Hmac_1[c]	0.408	0.124
ECDSA Verify[c]	1181.140	$-$[b]

[a]Computed on a 20 bytes nonce
[b]Not performed by the device during the protocol
[c]Computed on 64 bytes

In addition to real world implementation and testing, we evaluated scalability of SCIoT based on a large scale simulation using the OMNeT++ discrete event simulator [5]. We considered two different settings: (I) An infrastructured setting where low-end devices, acting as endpoints, are directly connected to higher-end nodes, which form a layer of aggregators and caches; and (II) an ad-hoc setting comprising low-end devices acting as both endpoints, aggregators and caches. We simulated the execution of the various protocol operations by adding respective delays. Furthermore, we configured the communication rate for links among low-end devices, and between them and high-end devices, to 75 Kbps, i.e., the effective measured data rate for ZigBee, a common communication protocol for IoT devices [30]. We set links among high-end devices (comprising manager), with a bandwidth of 10 Mbps.

Setting (I) has a variable number of low-end nodes (i.e., endpoints), between 2^6 and $2^{20} = 1,048,5761$; the layer of aggregators and caches is internally organized as a binary tree, e.g., as an overlay. We set the size of this intermediate layer to be proportional to the number of low-end devices, i.e., the number of endpoints per aggregator/cache is constant. We indicate with r the ratio between the number of high-end nodes acting as aggregators/caches, and low-end devices. For simplicity, we assume the tree configuration is static, and pre-determined; as an example, this may be the case of an infrastructure supporting data collection in a smart city scenario.

Setting (II) comprises a variable number of low-end devices that embody all the three entities, between 2^6 and $2^{20} = 1,048,5761$. Similarly, we assume low-end devices can form a binary tree, rooted at the manager.

Commands Distribution. We configured setting (I) with $r = 32$. Caches use a First-In-First-Out (FIFO) policy. Endpoints (i.e., low-end devices) request a transition from $\mathcal{M}$, starting at a random time between 0 and 1 s, and can either verify a digital ECDSA signature on the received response, or use μTesla; in the latter case, the endpoint waits for the subsequent key disclosure interval $\tau + d$ (in our setting, we considered $\Delta\tau \in \{0.5, 1\}$ s, and $d \in \{1, 2\}$ s) to fetch the necessary information and verify the response from $\mathcal{M}$. Similar to [6], we compared direct fetching, and cache-aided fetching of transitions (the latter is enabled by SCIoT); we measured the average time it takes for an endpoint low-end device to fetch a transitions from $\mathcal{M}$. Results are shown in Fig. 6. As expected the distributed caching of responses helps speed up the response fetching for a given request: The download time grows logarithmically in the size of the device population. Moreover, with the considered parameters, μTesla with $d = 1$ shows a reduced overhead than using digital signatures; this, however, comes at the price of a more complex and expensive key management, and stricter constraints (e.g., each device must be loosely synchronized with $\mathcal{M}$) [26].

This simple experiment shows the scalability of our protocol, which indeed maximizes the cacheability of each response issued by $\mathcal{M}$. These results are in line with previous evaluation, such as the one in [6], where the experiments where conducted on top of a Named-Data Networking (NDN) network [23], but on smaller scale.

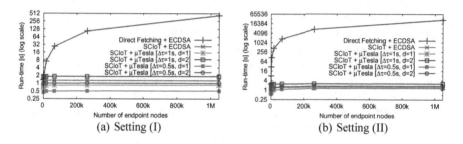

Fig. 6. Commands fetching in SCIoT.

Device Assessment. We compared our in-network aggregation scheme to the work from [16]. We evaluated these protocols in the same settings, settings (I) and (II), used in the evaluation of the commands distribution protocol. In Setting (I) the ratio between the number of endpoints and aggregators is constant. Results are shown in Fig. 7. In general, we observe that the runtime introduced by the protocol in [16] grows linearly in the number of endpoints, while the runtime of our scheme grows logarithmically with the number of endpoints. The most expensive part of the protocol in [16] is the verification of the acknowledgments received by $\mathcal{M}$, which consists of computing linear number of HMACs (i.e., n). Instead, our scheme that is adopted by SCIoT, introduces a *constant* overhead for such verification.

The runtime of both [16] and our aggregation scheme depends also on the depth of the aggregation tree, which in our settings depends on the ratio between the number of endpoints r and aggregator nodes; in our setting, the runtime is higher when $r = 32$, compared to $r = 16$. This is due to the required off-path information that the network must provide to endpoints, and the derived computation for verifying the inclusion of each endpoint. As previously mentioned in Sect. 6.2, this is proportional to both the height of aggregation tree, and r.

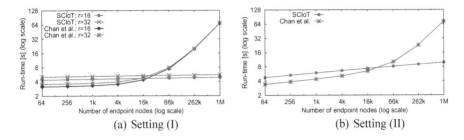

(a) Setting (I)   (b) Setting (II)

Fig. 7. Device assessment overhead. Axes are in logarithmic scale.

For small-medium scale settings, the scheme from [16] is more efficient than our scheme, requiring less than 4 s to complete the assessment. Indeed, computing a multi-signature costs more than computing a Hmac for low-end devices. However, in case of very large settings the runtime of the scheme from [16] quickly grows, requiring a non-negligible overhead on $\mathcal{M}$. On the other hand, the use of multi-signatures presents a much more manageable overall overhead. As an example, considering $r = 16$ in our evaluation setting, when number of endpoints is $32,768$ the use of multi-signatures shows an improvement in system's scalability: The runtime grows slowly compared to the scheme from [16], taking 4.7 s to run an assessment (compared to 5.4 s of [16]). This suggests the possibility of using an hybrid approach tailored to the specific setting, where $\mathcal{M}$ can select the protocol to use depending on the number of endpoints.

7   Security Consideration

We now briefly discuss the security of our management system, w.r.t. our requirements. We consider a probabilistic polynomial time (PPT) adversary $\mathcal{A}$, whose target is twofold: (1) inject fake commands, i.e., transitions, inside the network of devices, with the aim to interfere with the management process (i.e., with the protocol in Sect. 4.1) and thus fooling *benign* endpoints into performing different actions than the ones specified by the M-FSM; (2) manipulate the aggregate state collected by $\mathcal{M}$ (i.e., interfere with the protocol in Sect. 4.2), and make $\mathcal{M}$ accept such manipulated value, that does not reflect the values reported by endpoints. In order to perform the attack, $\mathcal{A}$ can compromise one or more aggregators or caching entities, i.e., a_l or c_u, or act as a man-in-the-middle. Furthermore, $\mathcal{A}$ can also compromise a limited number of endpoints v_j. However, we assume that the number of compromised endpoints is too small to influence the collected statistics.

We formalize goals (1) and (2) as two security experiments: $\mathbf{Exp}_1$, between $\mathcal{A}$ and a benign endpoint v_j, and $\mathbf{Exp}_2$, between $\mathcal{A}$, and v_j and $\mathcal{M}$, respectively. In $\mathbf{Exp}_1$, after a polynomial number of steps by $\mathcal{A}$, in terms of the security parameters ℓ_{Sign}, ℓ_{Hash}, and ℓ_{MAC}, v_j outputs $o_1 = 1$ if it accepts the received transition, or $o_1 = 0$ otherwise. Similarly, in $\mathbf{Exp}_2$ after a polynomial number of steps by $\mathcal{A}$ in terms of ℓ_{Sign} or ℓ_{Hash} and ℓ_{MAC}, and ℓ_N, $\mathcal{M}$ outputs $o_2 = 1$, if it accepts the manipulated aggregate value, or $o_2 = 0$ otherwise.

Definition 1 (Secure management service). *A management service is secure if* $Pr[o_1 = 1 | \mathbf{Exp}_1(1^\ell) = o_1]$ *is negligible in* $\ell = f(\ell_{\mathsf{Sign}}, \ell_{\mathsf{Hash}}, \ell_{MAC})$, *and* $Pr[o_2 = 1 | \mathbf{Exp}_2(1^\ell) = o_2]$ *is negligible in* $\ell' = f'(\ell_{\mathsf{Sign}}, \ell_N, \ell_{\mathsf{Hash}}, \ell_{MAC})$; *the functions f and f' are polynomial in all the parameters specified.*

Theorem 1 (Management service security). *Our management service is secure, according to Definition 1, if both the adopted multi-signature scheme and the public key signatures are unforgeable, and μTesla is secure.*

Proof (Proof (Sketch)). We now provide an intuition of our statement regarding the security of our scheme.

(1) $Pr[o_1 = 1 | \mathbf{Exp}_1(1^\ell) = o_1]$: v_j outputs $o_1 = 1$ iff $\mathsf{IsValid}(resp) = true$, that is, if the verification of the digital signature, or MAC in case of using μTesla, σ taken over $\{\mathrm{TID}, \ldots, t, \Delta t\}$ is valid. In order to carry out this attack, $\mathcal{A}$ can create a new response with a signature σ' attributed to $\mathcal{M}$. If $\mathcal{M}$ uses public key signatures, e.g., using RSA, $\mathcal{A}$ should be able to forge σ. However, using an unforgeable public key signature scheme, the success probability for $\mathcal{A}$ is negligible in ℓ_{Sign}.

In case of using μTesla, authenticity and integrity of the received transition is guaranteed by a MAC. In this scenario, however, besides trying to forge the MAC σ (which has negligible success probability in ℓ_{MAC}), $\mathcal{A}$ may also try to use an older key $k_{\tau'}$ belonging to a time interval $\tau' < \tau$, where τ is the current time interval, to compute the MAC on the response, for the time interval τ. Recall that, a key sequence is created from a reverse hash chain, in a way such that: $k_{\tau-1} \leftarrow \mathsf{Hash}(k_\tau)$; thus, for the properties of hash algorithms, the probability of $k_{\tau-1} = k_\tau$ is negligible in ℓ_{Hash}.

(2) $Pr[o_2 = 1 | \mathbf{Exp}_2 1^\ell) = o_2]$: $\mathcal{A}$ can perform the following attacks on the assessment protocol: (a) attack part (i) of the device assessment protocol by modifying the value sent by $\mathcal{M}$ to v_j; (b) attack part (ii) of the protocol by creating a valid acknowledgment of v_j, using an old signature σ_{old} from a previous interaction; or (c) attack part (ii) of the protocol by creating a fake acknowledgment with a multi-signature σ that attributes to v_j.

In order to perform the attack (a), $\mathcal{A}$ should be able to either forge a signature generated by $\mathcal{M}$, or to violate the security of μTesla; this is unfeasible for $\mathcal{A}$, similar to (1). Finally, strategies (b) and (c) are unfeasible for a PPT attacker like $\mathcal{A}$, due to the security of the multi-signature scheme against existential forgery attacks.

8   Related Work

Device Management. The Lightweight Machine to Machine protocol (LWM2M) [25], proposed by the Open Mobile Alliance (OMA), is a protocol designed for secure device management. Unfortunately, while certainly a valid solution, the protocol is intended for management of individual devices, and therefore not suitable in our scenario. In general, previous work in the literature either focus on network management for IoT devices [28], or consider scenarios where devices can be managed individually [29]. We consider all the above works to be complementary to ours; they can be used, for example, to perform one time bootstrap operation, topology maintenance, or individual device inspection. In [6] Ambrosin et al. proposed a protocol for efficient and secure delivery of confidential software updates to devices, by leveraging untrusted inner cache enabled networks. The authors provided the description of their solution over a Named-Data Networking (NDN) based inner network. However, different from our work, the authors did not provide an efficient protocol to collect device statistics. Burke et al. [15] presented a secure NDN-based security architecture for instrumented environments, such as building automation systems, and in particular for one of its sub-domains, i.e., lighting control. Their proposed solution provides privacy and authenticity for both command and acknowledgment messages, but unfortunately does not provide multicast features, i.e., for management of multiple devices, the management entity must issue multiple individual commands.

Secure Data Aggregation. There is a rich literature dealing with secure in-network data aggregation, especially in the context of Sensor Networks (SN), and Wireless Sensor Networks (WSN). These approaches are typically executed on top of an aggregation tree, and allow to combine the contribution of each node in a secure way, i.e., in a way that is *verifiable* by the collector node. In other words, the collector can verify that the aggregate result has not been tampered by inner aggregator nodes, and that all nodes contributed[7] to the computed aggregate value. Secure aggregation protocols usually focus on limiting communication and computation overhead for end nodes, and in the network, but pay less attention to the overhead at the verifier, which is assumed to be powerful enough to perform a (usually linear) number of cryptographic operations to verify the aggregate result. However, in our scenario, i.e., in case of large scale network managed by a low/medium power entity, the complexity at the management entity should be reduced as much as possible. In the following, we discuss only some related protocols. In [16], Chan et al. propose a secure data aggregation scheme for SN and WSN. Overall, the algorithm incurs in $\mathcal{O}(\Delta \log^2 n)$ node congestion, where node congestion is the worst case communication load on each sensor node. Frikken et al. [19] further reduces the node congestion of [16] to $\mathcal{O}(\Delta \log n)$, proposing a new commitment structure. Unfortunately, both schemes impose a linear verification overhead on the collector node, which

---

[7] This does not apply to every in-network data aggregation scheme.

needs to compute the XOR of all MACs created by end nodes. A different approach is considered by Yang et al. in SDAP [34]. SDAP is a non-exact mechanism which reduces the complexity of the verification while adding an (albeit small) overhead on the data collector.

9 Conclusions

In this paper we present the design of SCIoT, a framework for scalable and secure IoT device management. SCIoT represents the management process using an abstract finite state machine, thus decoupling it from its specific domain. Based on this representation, we design a protocol that allows devices to efficiently retrieve control messages, such as commands or firmware updates, from the management control entity. Another important feature provided by SCIoT is the ability for the control entity to monitor the status of the managed devices (e.g., number of devices that are in a given state). This is done by efficiently collecting device state information. Messages carrying device statistics are securely aggregated by an inner aggregation network, to minimize communication and computation complexity. Our evaluation shows the benefits of our approach in terms of improved scalability and manageable overhead.

References

1. ARM® mbedTLS cryptographic library (2016). https://tls.mbed.org/
2. Cisco Forecast on Internet of Things (2016). https://newsroom.cisco.com/feature-content?type=webcontent&articleId=1208342
3. IoT-LAB: a very large scale open testbed (2016). https://www.iot-lab.info/
4. IoT-LAB M3 Open Node (2016). https://www.iot-lab.info/hardware/m3/
5. Omnet++ Discrete Event Simulator (2016). https://omnetpp.org/
6. Ambrosin, M., Busold, C., Conti, M., Sadeghi, A.-R., Schunter, M.: Updaticator: updating billions of devices by an efficient, scalable and secure software update distribution over untrusted cache-enabled networks. In: Kutyłowski, M., Vaidya, J. (eds.) ESORICS 2014. LNCS, vol. 8712, pp. 76–93. Springer, Cham (2014). https://doi.org/10.1007/978-3-319-11203-9_5
7. Ambrosin, M., Conti, M., Ibrahim, A., Neven, G., Sadeghi, A.R., Schunter, M.: SANA: secure and scalable aggregate network attestation. In: CCS 2016, pp. 731–742 (2016)
8. Asokan, N., et al.: SEDA: scalable embedded device attestation. In: CCS 2015, pp. 964–975 (2015)
9. Baccelli, E., Hahm, O., Gunes, M., Wahlisch, M., Schmidt, T.C.: RIOT OS: towards an OS for the internet of things. In: INFOCOM WKSHPS 2013, pp. 79–80 (2013)
10. Boldyreva, A.: Threshold signatures, multisignatures and blind signatures based on the Gap-Diffie-Hellman-group signature scheme. In: Desmedt, Y.G. (ed.) PKC 2003. LNCS, vol. 2567, pp. 31–46. Springer, Heidelberg (2003). https://doi.org/10.1007/3-540-36288-6_3
11. Boneh, D., Gentry, C., Lynn, B., Shacham, H.: Aggregate and verifiably encrypted signatures from bilinear maps. In: Biham, E. (ed.) EUROCRYPT 2003. LNCS, vol. 2656, pp. 416–432. Springer, Heidelberg (2003). https://doi.org/10.1007/3-540-39200-9_26

12. Bonomi, F., Milito, R., Zhu, J., Addepalli, S.: Fog computing and its role in the internet of things. In: MCC 2012, pp. 13–16 (2012)
13. Bormann, C., Ersue, M., Keranen, A.: Terminology for constrained-node networks. Technical report, iETF RFC-7228, May 2014
14. Bormann, C., Shelby, Z.: Block-wise transfers in the constrained application protocol (CoAP). Technical report, iETF RFC-7959, August 2016
15. Burke, J., Gasti, P., Nathan, N., Tsudik, G.: Securing instrumented environments over content-centric networking: the case of lighting control and NDN. In: INFO-COM WKSHPS 2013, pp. 394–398 (2013)
16. Chan, H., Perrig, A., Song, D.: Secure hierarchical in-network aggregation in sensor networks. In: CCS 2006, pp. 278–287 (2006)
17. Cooper, A.: Electric company smart meter deployments: foundation for a smart grid. Technical report, October 2016
18. Dijk, E., Rahman, A., Fossati, T., Loreto, S., Castellani, A.: Internet-draft: guidelines for HTTP-CoAP mapping implementations. Technical report, iETF-draft, November 2016
19. Frikken, K.B., Dougherty IV, J.A.: An efficient integrity-preserving scheme for hierarchical sensor aggregation. In: WiSec 2008, pp. 68–76 (2008)
20. Garcia Lopez, P., et al.: Edge-centric computing: vision and challenges. ACM SIG-COMM Comput. Commun. Rev. 45(5), 37–42 (2015)
21. Hahm, O., Baccelli, E., Petersen, H., Tsiftes, N.: Operating systems for low-end devices in the internet of things: a survey. IEEE Internet Things J. 3(5), 720–734 (2016)
22. Hong, K., Lillethun, D., Ramachandran, U., Ottenwälder, B., Koldehofe, B.: Mobile fog: a programming model for large-scale applications on the internet of things. In: MCC 2013, pp. 15–20 (2013)
23. Jacobson, V., Smetters, D.K., Thornton, J.D., Plass, M.F., Briggs, N.H., Braynard, R.L.: Networking named content. In: CoNEXT 2009, pp. 1–12 (2009)
24. Koeberl, P., Schulz, S., Sadeghi, A.R., Varadharajan, V.: TrustLite: a security architecture for tiny embedded devices. In: European Conference on Computer Systems (2014)
25. Open Mobile Alliance: Lightweight Machine to Machine Technical Specification, v 1.0. Technical report, April 2016
26. Perrig, A., Szewczyk, R., Tygar, J.D., Wen, V., Culler, D.E.: SPINS: security protocols for sensor networks. Wirel. Netw. 8(5), 521–534 (2002)
27. Sanchez, L., et al.: SmartSantander: IoT experimentation over a smart city testbed. Comput. Netw. 61, 217–238 (2014)
28. Sehgal, A., Perelman, V., Kuryla, S., Schonwalder, J.: Management of resource constrained devices in the internet of things. IEEE Commun. Mag. 50(12), 144–149 (2012)
29. Sheng, Z., Mahapatra, C., Zhu, C., Leung, V.C.: Recent advances in industrial wireless sensor networks toward efficient management in IoT. IEEE Access 3, 622–637 (2015)
30. Spanogiannopoulos, G., Vlajic, N., Stevanovic, D.: A simulation-based performance analysis of various multipath routing techniques in ZigBee sensor networks. In: Zheng, J., Mao, S., Midkiff, S.F., Zhu, H. (eds.) ADHOCNETS 2009. LNICST, vol. 28, pp. 300–315. Springer, Heidelberg (2010). https://doi.org/10.1007/978-3-642-11723-7_20
31. Unterluggauer, T., Wenger, E.: Efficient pairings and ECC for embedded systems. In: Batina, L., Robshaw, M. (eds.) CHES 2014. LNCS, vol. 8731, pp. 298–315. Springer, Heidelberg (2014). https://doi.org/10.1007/978-3-662-44709-3_17

32. Valmari, A.: The state explosion problem. In: Reisig, W., Rozenberg, G. (eds.) ACPN 1996. LNCS, vol. 1491, pp. 429–528. Springer, Heidelberg (1998). https://doi.org/10.1007/3-540-65306-6_21
33. Vögler, M., Schleicher, J.M., Inzinger, C., Dustdar, S.: A scalable framework for provisioning large-scale iot deployments. ACM Trans. Internet Technol. **16**(2), 11 (2016)
34. Yang, Y., Wang, X., Zhu, S., Cao, G.: SDAP: a secure hop-by-hop data aggregation protocol for sensor networks. ACM Trans. Inf. Syst. Secur. **11**(4), 18:1–18:43 (2008)

Author Index

Printed in the United States
By Bookmasters